Annals of the Labouring Poor

Social Change and Agrarian England, 1660–1900

Cambridge Studies in Population, Economy and
Society in Past Time 2

Series Editors:

PETER LASLETT, ROGER SCHOFIELD and
E. A. WRIGLEY

ESRC Cambridge Group for the History of Population and
Social Structure

and DANIEL SCOTT SMITH

University of Illinois at Chicago

Recent work in social, economic and demographic history has revealed much that was previously obscure about societal stability and change in the past. It has also suggested that crossing the conventional boundaries between these branches of history can be very rewarding.

This series will exemplify the value of interdisciplinary work of this kind, and will include books on topics such as family, kinship and neighbourhood; welfare provision and social control; work and leisure; migration; urban growth; and legal structures and procedures, as well as more familiar matters. It will demonstrate that, for example, anthropology and economics have become as close intellectual neighbours to history as have political philosophy or biography.

Annals of the Labouring Poor

Social Change and Agrarian England, 1660–1900

K. D. M. SNELL

Lecturer in the Department of Economics and Related Studies,
University of York

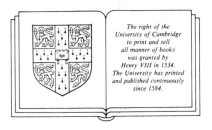

The right of the
University of Cambridge
to print and sell
all manner of books
was granted by
Henry VIII in 1534.
The University has printed
and published continuously
since 1584.

CAMBRIDGE UNIVERSITY PRESS

Cambridge

London   New York   New Rochelle

Melbourne   Sydney

Published by the Press Syndicate of the University of Cambridge
The Pitt Building, Trumpington Street, Cambridge CB2 1RP
32 East 57th Street, New York, NY 10022, USA
10 Stamford Road, Oakleigh, Melbourne 3166, Australia

First published 1985
First paperback edition 1987

Printed in Great Britain at The Bath Press, Avon

Library of Congress catalogue card number: 84–21351

British Library Cataloguing in Publication Data

Snell, K. D. M.
Annals of the labouring poor. – (Cambridge
studies in population, economy and society in
past time)
1. Rural poor – England – History
2. England – Rural conditions
I. Title
305.5′63 HN385

ISBN 0 521 24548 6 hardcovers
ISBN 0 521 33558 2 paperback

To my parents,
Malcolm and Mary Snell

Of all history, that of our own country is of the most importance; because, for want of a thorough knowledge of what has been, we are, in many cases, at a loss to account for what is, and still more at a loss, to be able to show what ought to be.

William Cobbett, *Advice to Young Men* (1830)

What might have been and what has been
Point to one end, which is always present.
Footfalls echo in the memory
Down the passage which we did not take
Towards the door we never opened . . .
    Other echoes
Inhabit the garden. Shall we follow?
Quick, said the bird, find them, find them . . .

T. S. Eliot, 'Burnt Norton', *Four Quartets* (1944)

Contents

Preface

I have many acknowledgements which can only briefly be made here. I am grateful for a Cambridge History Faculty S.S.R.C. Studentship, held at Trinity Hall, and to King's College for electing me to a Research Fellowship. I am particularly grateful to Tony Wrigley for supervising my early research, and for his advice and continued support during this period. John Barrell considerably extended my original interests, and I am happy to acknowledge his constant encouragement, impressive erudition, and advice on matters of literary style. Peter Laslett too has been a source of enthusiasm and stimulating conversation. I am most grateful to Michael Anderson for his very detailed and rigorous comments. And the encouragement and assistance of Janet Coleman, Paul Ryan, Dinah Parums, and Roger Schofield has also meant much to me.

There are many others to whom I am indebted in various ways, and I have space only to list their names and express my gratitude. They have included: Liz Bellamy, Mary Bouquet, Elizabeth Capelle, Jane Caplan, Raj Chandavarkar, Greg Claeys, Donald Coleman, Ed Cooney, Stephen Davies, Natalie Davis, Michael Flinn, Harriet Guest, Venetia Hauk, Eric Hobsbawm, Caroline Humphrey, Joanna Innes, Peter King, Ann Kussmaul, Joe Melling, Jane Millar, Jim Oeppen, Roy Porter, Mike Ryder, Reinhard Sieder, Peter Solar, George Souza, Gareth Stedman Jones, Barry Supple, David Thomson, Steve Tolliday, Michael Walker, Richard Wall, Tom Williamson, Keith Wrightson, and Jonathan Zeitlin.

My thanks also go to the Twenty-Seven Foundation for providing funds towards the publication costs of this book, to the Archivists and staff of the thirty-two Record Offices in which I have worked, to the faculties and students of universities where parts of the book were given as seminar papers, to Mrs J. Ashman and Mrs S. Barry for their accurate typing, and to Linda Randall for her excellent subediting. Finally, I am most grateful to the students I have taught for their lively and stimulating interest in the subject.

Introduction

This book will reconsider and try to broaden debate on changes in the quality of life in the eighteenth and nineteenth centuries. It covers English and Welsh counties south of Yorkshire, Derbyshire, Stafford-shire, Shropshire, and Radnor, and deals with the agricultural and artisan sectors and London. A subsequent and comparative book is planned on the north, and I will not deal with that region here. This initial specialisation on the south is felt to be justified by the particular experiences of the region, which separate it in so many respects from the north. Contemporaries recognised a growing split after about 1770 between the 'North and South' – epitomised in the title of Gaskell's novel. By the mid-nineteenth century the economic divides between the poorly paid, 'de-industrialised' south and the high wage, industrial north were clearly recognised, as for example in James Caird's distinction of high and low wage sectors. Indeed, the high and low wage regions of the early eighteenth century had become entirely reversed. And in contemporary characterisations of the labour force too, the impoverished and stolidly comic figure of 'Hodge' in the agrarian south came to have little in common with his unionised and assertive northern counterparts. I want here to outline and assess the southern changes which contributed to this contrast.

The standard of living in the industrial north has received most attention from historians, and it is unfortunate that there have been so few long-term studies covering social change and the quality of life in the agricultural and artisan south. I hope that these chapters will help to remedy this, and treat the preconditions and effects of industrialisation in an adequately encompassing manner; for the regional specialisations and interdependencies which one connects with the Industrial Revolution make it essential to examine the social consequences of economic growth in the economy as a whole. I have

1

not conceived the problem of living standards as one to be concerned simply with the immediate regional effects of the factory system, nor as one to be tackled only by an appraisal of real wages. The view has been taken that this problem should encompass the whole period from the early eighteenth century to the later nineteenth, assessing the effects of long-term changes associated with, as well as the consequences of, industrialisation; and that it should cover a broader spectrum of social changes than those immediate ones which, because they merge into the confines of our own moral awareness, have usually been taken as the problem's defining features. The debate is here treated broadly as applying to social changes (some of which do not readily admit to value judgement) which were associated with a greater sophistication of the economy, of which the growth of industrial output from the late eighteenth century was both a consequence and a catalyst.

The book has a further and connected intention. It combines research of a quantitative nature with work more strictly on attitudinal changes. The topics treated here are used to assess the quality of life; but they are adapted also to raise questions on how economic and structural changes influenced social attitudes, and to make regional and socially specific comparisons – to help answer the need, expressed by Michael Anderson, for a 'reorientation in research methods . . . with a greater stress on how attitudinal change is to be measured and on systematic comparison between different social and regional contexts'.[1] This will be particularly the case in discussion of sexual divisions of labour and the family – subjects of obvious importance for the quality of life, but which also lend themselves to a broader understanding of attitudinal changes. To this end, and more generally, I hope throughout to avoid dependence only on either quantitative or literary evidence, and to aim for a fusion of both types of documentation, in the interests of mutual reinforcement and validation.

Debate on the changing quality of life during this period has probably been more polemical and vituperative than any other aspect of British historiography. The literature produced by 'pessimists' and 'optimists' is well known, and I do not intend this introduction to be a bibliographical essay. But a few observations are in order, to clarify the position taken here. The division of historians into optimist and pessimist schools has been regrettable in the sense that so much will always depend on the region studied. This book is on the south, and its arguments are mainly pessimistic. This is unavoidable and entirely

[1] M. Anderson, *Approaches to the History of the Western Family, 1500–1914* (1980), p. 63.

appropriate. But a subsequent volume on the rural and artisan north will argue more optimistic views, and there is no incompatibility in so doing. The relative real wage movements alone of the north and south suggest the need for flexible arguments which take account of regional diversity, and we shall see marked differences even within the south. The attempt to arrive at an overall categoric judgement is probably best rejected as unrealistic if not historically insensitive, because of the inadequacy of real wages alone for an assessment of this issue, and the crudity of quantitative proxies for considering the 'quality of life' – and because of the scanty regional wage data currently available. After all, essentially there has been only the wage data provided by Bowley and Wood, Phelps-Brown and Hopkins, Neale and Tucker to help us consider the crucial transition period from the late eighteenth century, and no amount of weighting and econometric manipulation can compensate for this exceptionally limited regional and occupational coverage.[2] Even when much more detailed data becomes available, arguments for regionally diverse changes, which relate discussion of the standard of living to other questions, would be preferable to the encamped deadlock which currently exists.

And there is of course another reason for that deadlock. The methodology adopted by different scholars has been various, and has not invited much discussion, let alone agreement. There are two possible approaches which can be taken here, and most scholars have moved uncertainly or unconsciously somewhere between them. The problem concerns the choice of criteria to assess the 'standard of living'. The ahistorical option is for a historian or economist to take modern criteria or priorities, and superimpose them onto the eighteenth and nineteenth centuries. What is meant by, and important in, one's 'standard of living' today? Many economists would define the term as Gross National Product at constant prices, taking account of the way it is distributed, and the way it is split between investment, private consumption, government expenditure, and so on. More specifically, some financial institutions assess the matter in terms of television sets, cars and deep-freezes per household.[3] In fact, priorities often seem to be male real wages, public health, employment, housing, education, indications of consumption and financial status, and the like, perhaps in that order, though of course with much

---

[2] For a bibliography on the standard of living debate, see M. W. Flinn, 'Trends in real wages, 1750–1850', *Economic History Review*, XXVII (1974), 412–13; and footnotes in chapter 1, below.

[3] See, for example, the *Lloyds Bank Economic Bulletin*.

personal and class variation. Now it is an easy matter (and the usual practice) to adopt such criteria and impose them on the past, and omissions (particularly over employment) are excused by the inadequacy of historical documentation. This approach of course has a built-in bias towards optimism and self-justification.

Alternatively, the view may be taken that, qua historian, one is dealing with the changing quality of life as experienced by people in the past (mainly from a lowly social background), and that a more appropriate way to do this is to comprehend and adopt the priorities of the contemporary labouring poor, by which they themselves assessed the social and economic changes which affected them. The matter now becomes more complicated, demanding a more sensitive historical understanding. For while some eighteenth- and early nineteenth-century concerns overlap with ours today, many have become quite remote to us. We shall consider these in more detail shortly, for this approach will be the one taken in this book. But these concerns would include considerations such as the integrity of the 'family economy', certain sexual divisions of labour and opportunities for female work, the preservation of yearly hiring, continued access to the land, with the possibility of keeping livestock, the safeguarding of traditional seven-year apprenticeships, ready access to poor relief in one's 'own' parish, a particular quality of social relationships, and so on. Of course, real wages, paid employment, mortality rates, or literacy were also important, but arguably less so than they subsequently became. For example, large segments of the agricultural or artisan labour force in the mid-eighteenth century were yearly hired on a 'live-in' basis, or served lengthy 'live-in' apprenticeships, and their work was rewarded by about 80 per cent payment in kind, making real wages a less important consideration. Such workers were in effect guaranteed 'full employment' throughout the year. Their priorities were very different to ours today, with more attention paid, for example, to the quality of social relations in the household where they resided. Despite this, the 'standard of living debate' has been conducted almost entirely by considering real wage trends.[4] In part,

---

[4] E. P. Thompson was a notable exception; Hobsbawm too has used a wider range of indicators: E. P. Thompson, *The Making of the English Working Class* (1963), ch. 10; E. J. Hobsbawm, 'The British standard of living, 1790–1850', *Economic History Review*, X (1957), also in his *Labouring Men* (1964); and his 'The standard of living debate: a postscript', in *Labouring Men*. See also S. Pollard, 'Investment, consumption and the Industrial Revolution', *Econ. Hist. Rev.*, XI (1958); N. Gash, 'Rural unemployment, 1815–1834', *Econ. Hist. Rev.*, VI (1935). But the bulk of the literature deals primarily with real wage trends; and the recent tendency (particularly among econometricians) to construct an overall 'national' picture from available wage data strongly perpetuates this.

the first chapter of this book will do the same, but such an approach by itself has always been an inadequate one, and the subsequent chapters will concentrate less on it.

The way the usual emphasis on real wages imputes needs to the labouring poor, assuming a greatly limited range of requirements and priorities, is paralleled in an interesting way by the nineteenth-century stereotypes of 'Hodge'. The complaint made by Holdenby against the contemporary stereotyping caused by social ignorance and class isolation seems appropriate here:

It seemed to me that the countryman was getting more isolated and becoming more and more of a silent and negligible unit . . . how often do we hear the complaint, 'I can't get at these country chaps at all . . .', yet we find appalling cases of ignorance among those who have opportunity for finding out. I was talking to a 'gentleman farmer' who owned his own land and had farmed it twelve years – and put in his two days a week with the hounds during the season. 'I hear you're one of these social reformers', he began: 'why don't you go and talk to some of the practical men, and see what they've got to say to you? All that chaps want is more wages, and a minimum wage'll ruin half the farmers in the country' – 'Wages aren't everything', I interposed; 'the countryman wants a great many other things'. 'Yes, beer – I suppose', broke in my friend. 'Wages and beer are the only things I've found a countryman keen on, and I've worked with 'em pretty often'. This was as far as my friend had got after twelve years' farming on his own land. No wonder countrymen are reserved . . . they have also a reserve born of poverty, of being under-valued, of being alienated from the land, or being mere lodgers upon it.[5]

The historiographical equivalent today is readily found. Here is one example: 'The British working-man has always shown more direct interest in wage levels than he has in other ingredients in living standards like public health, housing, education, and social insurance, and historians of living standards would do well to follow his lead.'[6] Even here, the other possibilities mentioned, like 'social insurance', are modern priorities, arguably rather distant from the major concerns of the eighteenth-century poor. And by Holdenby's time, as Richard Jefferies argued, wages had become more important than hitherto, and yet still Holdenby stressed that the discontents of the poor were not to be relieved simply by higher wages.[7]

So let us delve further into this question of needs, using the clue provided by Holdenby. Ignorance of the rural labourer in the nineteenth century was general, even among the best known authors

---

[5] C. Holdenby, *The Folk of the Furrow* (1913), pp. 11–12.
[6] Flinn, 'Trends in real wages', 395.
[7] R. Jefferies, *The Hills and the Vale* (1909, Oxford, 1980 edn), pp. 251–2, 255. Similar points on a shift of priorities towards wages during the nineteenth century have been made by E. J. Hobsbawm & G. Rudé, *Captain Swing* (1969, 1973 edn), e.g., p. 17.

on rural society. Insofar as such insensitivity is particularly apparent in concentration only on real wage trends, let us explore the stereotype of 'Hodge' and his needs. For this stereotype is also in many respects the revealing end-product of changes analysed in this book: a crudely insensitive caricature, but one the more significant for having been largely unchallenged by contemporaries, and one indicative of the unprecedentedly low social standing in which rural labour had come to be held by 1850.

Among nineteenth-century authors, very few made the effort to discard stereotypes of 'Hodge' when discussing the labouring poor. George Sturt was one of them – estranged and troubled by what he called 'an ill-defined but chronic anxiety' among his villagers:

If one could get down to understand village life! I have reached that initiatory stage in which one is convinced of ignorance. . . . It were as easy to write of the Chinese.

From speculating how the world looks to [labouring men], I have come to discern that there are two quite diverse modes of studying them. One – an 'objective' method – views them with biologist eyes, as though they were animals whose ways were to be observed wholly from the outside . . . The 'subjective' method on the other hand would seek in the labourer himself and his emotional life the chief formative influence . . . What are his hopes and ambitions? What his ideas of momentary happiness, or of life-long success? Upon what does he pride himself? . . . These are some of the directions along which the 'subjective' student of labour would push his investigation. I say would, because in fact it is hardly ever done, and perhaps hardly ever can be done. Certain novelists – Hardy, Phillpotts – pretend to do it, yet with a great air of having found the solution of the question in their own imagination rather than in facts . . . And the reason for all this failure, as I think it, is the want of those intimacies, which alone can reveal . . . the character of the labourer's mind, and the activities that go on there. No-one knows the labourer.[8]

We shall consider Hardy in detail later. The problem worried many others. 'These people know no ideal' wrote Richard Jefferies, 'It seems impossible to reach them, because there is no chord that will respond.'[9] Here is the correspondent for the *Morning Chronicle* speaking of the rural labourer:

When you accost him, if he is not insolent – which he seldom is – he is timid and shrinking, his whole manner showing that he feels himself at a distance from you greater than should separate any two classes of men. He is often doubtful when you address, and suspicious when you question him; he is

---

[8] G. Sturt, *Change in the Village* (1912), pp. x, 40; and his *The Journals of George Sturt, 1890–1927* (Cambridge, 1967), 2 vols., vol. 2, pp. 540–1.

[9] R. Jefferies, *Hodge and His Masters* 2 vols. (1880), vol. 2, p. 253.

seemingly oppressed with the interview whilst it lasts, and obviously relieved when it is over.[10]

Holdenby too complained of the 'mysterious barrier of "Ay, ay", "may be", "likely enough", with which the labourer hedges himself in'.[11] Or at a more chilling level, one recalls Wordsworth's description – 'like a caterpillar sheathed in ice'.

But the difficulties of social understanding were infrequently stated, and Sturt's 'objective' method usually sufficed as description. Here is one of many such descriptions by Richard Jefferies:

> A sturdy ploughboy ... sits down outside the shed on a broken and rusty iron wheel. ... He is utterly indifferent ... he makes no inquiry about this or that, and shows no desire to understand ... Something in this attitude – in the immobility, the almost animal repose of limb; something in the expression of his features, the self-contained oblivion, so to say, suggests an Oriental absence of aspiration ... He munches his crust; and when he has done, carefully, and with vast deliberation, replaces his heavy shoe.[12]

Graham wrote to the same effect of 'Hodge, his awkward gait and ungainly manners, his slow wit and drawled out patois ... objects of laughter and mockery.' If labourers 'had shelter, a crust of bread, and some kind of clothing, they were as happy as, and no happier than, their horses'.[13] To others they were recognisable 'by their smocks, tattered hats and utter simplicity'. Hodge was 'that familiar oddity in smock and tattered hat ... that patient, silent and dispirited being'.[14] 'A physical scandal, a moral enigma, an intellectual cataleptic', commented one journalist.[15] Sydney Smith's description was even harsher: 'a ploughman marries a ploughwoman because she is plump; generally uses her ill; thinks his children an encumbrance; very often flogs them; and, for sentiment, has nothing more nearly

[10] *Morning Chronicle*, 1 Dec. 1849. Or see 'Orme Agnus' (John C. Higginbotham), *Jan Oxber* (Boston, 1902), pp. 17–18: 'Open as the peasant's life is, he shuts himself up as a sensitive plant before the stranger ... skilled investigators ... can tell he wears a smock-frock, and has a sun-tanned face, but that is all they know of him.'

[11] Holdenby, *Folk of the Furrow*, p. 7.

[12] Jefferies, *Hodge and His Masters*, p. 78. Or, to similar effect, see G. Eliot, *Felix Holt* (1866, Harmondsworth, 1975 edn), p. 76: 'The shepherd with a slow and slouching walk, timed by the walk of grazing beasts, moved aside, as if unwillingly, throwing out a monosyllabic hint to his cattle; his glance, accustomed to rest on things very near the earth, seemed to lift itself with difficulty to the coachman. Mail or stage coach for him belonged to that mysterious distant system of things called "Gover'ment", which, whatever it might be, was no business of his, any more than the most out-lying nebula or the coal-sacks of the southern hemisphere: his solar system was the parish; the master's temper and the casualties of lambing-time were his region of storms.'

[13] P. A. Graham, *The Rural Exodus* (1892), p. 25.

[14] See E. W. Martin, *The Secret People: English Village Life after 1750* (1954), pp. 26, 145.

[15] *Morning Chronicle*, 18 Jan. 1850.

approaching to it than the idea of broiled bacon and mashed potatoes'.[16] The agricultural labourer was 'perverse, stupid and illiterate', wrote Bishop Watson. As Cobbett complained, the labouring poor had come to be 'spoken of by everyone possessing the power to oppress them . . . in just the same manner in which we speak of the animals which compose the stock upon a farm. This is not the manner in which the forefathers of us, the common people, were treated.' As he wrote elsewhere:

There has come into the heads of these people [the Country Gentlemen], I cannot very well tell how, a notion, that it is proper to consider the Labouring Classes as a *distinct cast*. They are called, now-a-days, by these gentlemen, *'The Peasantry'*. This is a new term as applied to Englishmen. It is a French word, which, in its literal sense, means *Country Folks*. But, in the sense, in which it is used in France and Flanders and Germany, it means, not only country people, or country folks, but also a *distinct and degraded class of persons*, who have no pretensions whatever to look upon themselves, in any sense, as belonging to the same *society*, or *community*, as the *Gentry*; but who ought always to be *'kept in their proper place'*. And it has become, of late, the fashion to consider the Labouring Classes in England in the same light, and to speak of them and treat them accordingly, which never was the case in any former age [his italics].[17]

The term 'peasantry' was to be one of the words used, often derogatively, throughout the nineteenth century to describe the rural working population; a paradoxical term when one considers that the period saw the virtual extinction of rights to land among the rural poor. Some authors saw this as one key to the change in attitude. 'The elements of bitter class war', wrote Sturt,

frequently mark the attitude of middle-class people towards the labouring class. It seems to be forgotten that the men are English. One hears of them spoken of as an alien and objectionable race, worth nothing but to be made to work . . . By becoming wage earners solely, the villagers have fallen into the disfavour of the middle-classes, most of whom have no other desire than to keep them in a sufficient state of servility to be useful. . . . The animus of which I am speaking is almost a commonplace. In truth, I have heard it expressed dozens of times, in dozens of ways . . . that the English labouring classes are a lower order of beings, who must be treated accordingly.[18]

There were many reasons for this animus and stereotyping, which will become clearer, perhaps, in the course of these chapters. They included the tendency of rural society to become isolated from a more sophisticated urban culture, and the growing view of agriculture after

---

[16] Cited in B. Inglis, *Poverty and the Industrial Revolution* (1971, 1972 edn), p. 288.
[17] W. Cobbett, *Political Register*, LXXVIII, 710; and G. D. H. & M. Cole (eds.), *The Opinions of William Cobbett* (1944), p. 217.
[18] Sturt, *Change in the Village*, p. 109.

the mid-eighteenth century as an alternative investment for capital, with labour seen strictly for its productive potential. But George Crewe's explanations in *A Word for the Poor* are especially noteworthy. Speaking of the rising poor rates and immiseration after the Napoleonic Wars, he wrote:

I did anticipate that a very unjust and unfavourable opinion of the character, habits, and practices of the Agricultural Poor would be created at their expense . . . I do say that, in many instances . . . [authors] were not practically and personally acquainted with the minutiae of the subject as regarded the Poor themselves. – We had the experience of the Petty Sessions; of the Vestries; but we had not the experience of those who had studied the necessities or the claims of poverty, in its humble dwelling. For want of this, Necessity was called Improvidence; Despair was deemed Recklessness; the Broken-hearted and worn-out were called Idle and Importunate; and the struggle of the Destitute to keep life and soul together was characterized living upon the Poor Rates – no allowance made for Ignorance – none for Neglect. The cry was against 'Demoralized, degraded Pauperism', – the result, as was asserted, of the Poor Laws, and the vices of poverty. But how, you may ask, came the public to adopt so groundless a statement of facts, so wanting in material points? For two reasons; first – Because the study of poverty amongst the poor is, even in a charitable country, not a general practice; and second – Because the outcry had been raised, not for the protection of the poor, but for the protection of the rich.[19]

My concern here is less to explain the widely used and unfavourable stereotypes of Hodge, than to arrive at a fuller understanding of what the poor considered most important in their 'standard of living'. The social insensitivity of so many nineteenth-century commentators makes this hard to assess; but it may still be shown that neither real wages, nor simply 'animal' requirements of food and shelter, are appropriate criteria by themselves to consider this question. To define a broader and more realistic range of priorities, we must examine the records left by the poor themselves: autobiographies and diaries, emigrants' letters, letters from paupers to poor law officials requesting non-resident relief, anonymous letters (as against enclosure, or threshing machinery), petitions from mothers to foundling homes, or autobiographical statements in settlement examinations. Space is lacking here for a detailed discussion of the priorities revealed in this material, which are partly discussed in the context of later chapters. But some summary can be made by way of introduction. Let us take evidence simply from one source.

The letters of rural emigrants from the south of England contain the

[19] Sir G. Crewe, *A Word for the Poor, and against the Present Poor Law* (Derby, 1843), pp. 6–7.

most useful information.[20] For they often made detailed comparison of conditions in America, Canada, or Australia with those the emigrant had lately abandoned, with a view to attracting or (much less commonly) dissuading further emigration from relatives. The priorities of the writer were made clear, and may be taken to correspond closely with those of the relatives and friends to whom he wrote. Now, such letters certainly contain occasional comments on wages, and more often on prices and the availability of food. But these were subsidiary concerns, which, if they appeared at all, usually emerged towards the end of the letter. Less than one letter in ten mentioned wages at all, although they all covered a range of other features, assessing them against the situation in England. One is struck initially by the intense family feelings and concern of the letters (written in the most affectionate and endearing of terms), and then by other points of comparison: particularly to do with the availability of land (and the possibility of owning and stocking one's own farm, owning one's cottage, or of hunting game without hindrance); the favourable relations of master and man, with frequent mention of 'living-in' arrangements; and the availability of employment for oneself and women in the family.

The tightness of family ties should first be stressed, for it indicates how important family matters were in the emigrants' assessment of the quality of life. Despite the views of some historians on the absence of affection among the labouring poor (of which more elsewhere), letter after letter was written in terms such as these:

Dear wife and my dear children this comes with my kind love to you hoping to find you all well as it leaves me at present thanks be to God for it dear wife ... dear wife if please god should spare your life to come to me ... dear wife give my kind love to my mother and my brothers and sisters and i hope they will send me word how thay all be ... from your loving husband antill death ...

---

[20] All subsequent citations are taken from the letters printed in Anon., 'Wiltshire emigrants', *Quarterly Review*, XLVI (1832), 349–90; Poor Law Report, XXXVII (1834), pp. 155–60; *ibid.*, XXVIII (1834), pp. 207–10, 379–82; Anon., 'The impolicy of emigrating to America', *Annals of Agriculture*, XXVI (1796), pp. 184–8; R. H. Horne, 'Pictures of life in Australia' and C. Dickens & C. Chisholm (eds.), 'A bundle of emigrant letters', *Household Words*, I (1850), 19–24; O. MacDonagh (ed.), *Emigration in the Victorian Age* (Farnborough, Hants, 1973), pp. 138–42, 413–29; S.C. on Emigration, V (1826–7), pp. 94, 128–31; S. F. Surtees (ed.) *Emigrants' Letters from Settlers in Canada and South Australia collected in the Parish of Banham, Norfolk* (1852). For further letters like these, see: C. Barclay (ed.), *Letters from the Dorking Emigrants who Went to Upper Canada in the Spring of 1832* (1833); J. Mathieson (ed.), *Counsel for Emigrants ... with Original Letters from Canada and the United States* (Aberdeen, 1835); *Letters from Sussex Emigrants* (1833, 1837 edn); S.C. on Emigration, IV (1826), pp. 184–6; Anon., *Emigration and the Condition of the Labouring Poor* (Colchester, 1832).

This letter included the phrase 'dear wife' ten times. Or here is another example:

My Dear and most beloved Wife this is the 7th letters I have written and sincerely hope this may find you and my dear children in good health . . . I am realy very anxious about you particularly as I hear such bad accounts from home you are in my thoughts day and night Oh that I could see you here . . . My dear wife do keep up your spirits . . . give my love to my dear children. Oh that the day may not be far distant when my happiness may be more Complete by seeing them and you . . . I think my dear I have stated facts wich ought to cheer you up and you must consider that the sun has been clouded from us a long time but thank God that cloud I hope is being removed and our sunny day are yet to come.

Or to take another letter:

Give my love to all your family and particularly to Mary . . . and send me word wether John got better and give my love to all your Family and tell I am well and to . . . all the Girles and tell I am well Dear Brother . . . Dr. Brother I should be happy to come back to see you and all old Friends . . . Brother Stichbon Gives Love to you and often says he wishes you were here with us and William gives his love to you and he is sober and steadey as he always was and . . . Give my love to Mrs. Bayly and all her Family and tell the Girls that Mary often talks about them and she would like to see them . . . Give my love to Mrs. Charly and to all her Family . . . and give my love to all my old friends and send me word wether Sam Campany is living . . . Give our best love to Mr. and Mrs. Marchant . . . Dear Brother Henrry got tom and betty now and they of talke about you and says he very much wish his poor unkil was here . . . his Wife and Child is well and better off than they would be at home . . . I long to hear from you and send me word where you live and who you live with and Rite to me as soon as you can . . . and send me word whether Thomas Bailey and Sophia got marred yet member me to Edward Frend and tell him we heard he was Mother sick . . .

– and so on, in letter after letter. Perhaps absence made the heart grow fonder, but when all allowance is made for that the letters still show how important were family ties and relationships. The affection found in the letters could also readily be demonstrated from auto-biographies and diaries.[21] It was clear that the quality of family life was a (if not the) major priority among the rural labouring and artisan classes, and particular attention will be paid to it in these chapters. 'If I never see you no more on earth, I hope I shall in heaven. May the Lord bless you all, my little dears.'

There was also frequent concern expressed in emigrants' letters about the possibilities for women's work. Here are just three examples:

[21] See D. Vincent, 'Love and death and the nineteenth-century working class', *Social History*, V (1980).

Tell the Yong Girls not to stop in England but to come here they want servants and they think nothing of 20 or 30 guineas a year and the Mrs. dont dare to be Cross to them for there are but very few here but now I expect you will think I tell you lies but its the truth indeed.

My mothers says . . . here she can Earn more in one day than you can in a week.

Give my love to all the Gails and tell them thay bee better of hear then at home.

After the family, almost every letter voiced another major concern – land. This was a priority widely noticed by contemporaries like Arthur Young, and the letters bear constant witness to it.[22] Here are some examples:

There is no difficulty of a man's geting land here . . . many will let a man have land with a few acres improvement and a house on it without any deposit . . . I think God my wife and I never found ourselves so comfortable in England as we do here, we have a good comfortable house to live in, and a good cow for our use, and a plenty of firing . . .

We have got grants of land . . . if the Lord give strength we are going to bild ourselves Cottageas its for our own and for our Children after us and we shold never have had that in England.

I am going to work on my own farm of 50 acres, which I bought at £55, and I have 5 years to pay it in. I have bought me a cow and 5 pigs . . . if I had stayed at Corsley I never should have had nothing . . . I seem now to want to tell this, that, and the other story, about men who came here without a single shilling, but have now good farms of their own.

We three brothers have bought 200 acres of land at 12s. 6d. per acre.

Here you can raise every thing of your own that you want to make use of in your family.

The desire for some land and livestock was an almost overwhelming concern, and I will deal with changes in England which affected access to land as an important part of the standard of living. And in connection with this, the letters constantly stress the availability of game, with no restrictions on obtaining it.

Brother Dennis say I have a farm of my own, pretty well stocked; I can work when I like and play when I have a mind to; I can take my gun and go a shooting, as well as any of the farmer's sons; and we can go a fishing when we please, and when we are hunting we don't have no need to be afraid of the gamekeeper. I tell you my dear brothers that if you was here you would be better off then you are now.

[22] For statements by Arthur Young stressing this, see in particular his *An Inquiry into the Propriety of Applying Wastes to the Better Maintenance and Support of the Poor* (Bury St Edmunds, 1801), pp. 22–5.

(And one notes here the meaning of the phrase 'better off'.) Another writer wrote of how 'I am at liberty to shoot turkeys, quail, pigeon, and all kinds of game which I have in my backwood.' Indeed, this point could become symbolic of the escape to a better life which emigration had entailed:

[We] shoot anywhere, and there are a great many Cockatoo white ones and black ones with red tails and black ones with tails and the butiful parretes and Golden peegent very pretty ones much prettyer ones than England can afford – I cant say whether we are above you or below you but the Sun get up wear the sun go down in England and the Cookho sing anights and the NightGail a days.

Finally, attention was commonly drawn to differences in the quality of social relations by emigrants, and it is clear that for them this was an important priority. Many letters started with this consideration:

Dear friends, We were very happy and comfortable, and I have plenty of employment for this winter season. I am chiefly threshing for which I get the 10th bushel of all kind of grain and our board; it is the custom of the country to be boarded and lodged, let you work at what you will; and tradesmen the same; and Master and Mistress and all the family sit all at 1 table, and if there is not room at the table for the whole family to sit down, their children sit by till workmen were served; there is no distinction between the workman and his master, they would as soon shake hands with a workman as they would with a gentleman.

It is not here as in England if you dont liket you may leaveet et is here pray do stop i will raise your wages.

Dear Brother, we have no overseers to tred us under foot.

Or another writer spoke of America as the place where 'all could be their own masters, and where there was no fear of the overseer'.

These then were some of the major concerns expressed when emigrants compared their standard of living with that they had lately left behind, which was still being endured by their relatives. Such concerns could be extensively documented from other personal records of the labouring poor. Wages were mentioned as well in the letters, but little more than occasionally. Constancy of employment was a much more commonly found concern, and I shall pay particular attention to this. 'Here is plenty of work. *Thank God we are here*' (his italics), wrote William Snelgrove from Canada in 1830, and repeated the phrase a few lines later. Many letters stressed the availability of winter employment. 'Dear fathar and mothar and brother and all inquiring frends,' began 'Bill', 'i make myself verry happy and comfortebell and have found a very good home aver sines i have been in the country and planty of work . . . and I got a winters work a wood coting . . . I would sunner be hear than in the old contrey.' Bill's relatives lived in a parish near Chichester, and one can imagine them crowded round, eagerly reading on. But for all his enthusiasm, the letter had to be finished by a fellow woodcutter, explaining how Bill met with an accident hoisting 'a log of timber, the strap broke and caught poor Bill under the log and broke is neck in too, and he never spoke a word'. But Bill aside, the *Quarterly Review* rightly commented on 'the expressions scattered through these letters of joy and thankfulness to God . . . for so great a change in their condition . . . allusions to the sufferings from which they have escaped, but which are still endured by their friends and fellow-labourers at home'. It is the changing quality of life in southern England and Wales which prompted these comparisons that I intend to assess in the chapters that follow; and my assessment will be based on the priorities of the labouring poor themselves.

1

Agricultural seasonal unemployment, the standard of living, and women's work, 1690–1860

I

It is common for historians working on changes in the standard of living and real wage trends to acknowledge the importance and the intractibility of the problem of changing levels of unemployment.[1] Questions relating to the extent, regionality, and changes over time of yearly or seasonal unemployment have almost invariably been seen as unanswerable. M. W. Flinn, for example, reconsidering the problems of real wages for the standard of living debate, has argued to this effect:

What matters from the point of view of the assessment of secular trends in the standard of living is secular trends in the short-run variation of levels of unemployment . . . Changes in the levels of unemployment and under-employment are probably doomed to remain among the imponderables of

I am grateful to Tony Wrigley, in particular, Natalie Davis, and Peter Laslett for their comments. This chapter is an extended version based on additional research of an article published in the *Economic History Review* (1981), and I would like to thank Barry Supple for his helpful editorial advice.

[1] For a bibliography of literature dealing with the debate on living standards, see M. W. Flinn, 'Trends in real wages, 1750–1850', *Econ. Hist. Rev.*, XXVII (1974), 412–13. See also T. R. Gourvish, 'Flinn and real wage trends in Britain, 1750–1850: a comment', *Econ. Hist. Rev.*, XXIX (1976); M. W. Flinn, 'Real wage trends in Britain, 1750–1850: a reply', *Econ. Hist. Rev.*, XXIX (1976); G. N. von Tunzelmann, 'Trends in real wages, 1750–1850, revisited', *Econ. Hist. Rev.*, XXXII (1979); N. F. R. Crafts, 'National income estimates and the British standard of living debate: a reappraisal of 1801–1831', *Explorations in Economic History*, XVII (1980); E. H. Phelps-Brown & S. V. Hopkins, *A Perspective of Wages and Prices* (1981); and for an overview of the work of P. H. Lindert & J. G. Williamson, see their 'English workers' living standards during the Industrial Revolution: a new look', *Econ. Hist. Rev.*, XXXVI (1983). On unemployment in the pre-industrial period, see D. C. Coleman, 'Labour in the English economy of the seventeenth century', *Econ. Hist. Rev.*, VIII (1956). On the problem of agricultural unemployment in the early nineteenth century, see in particular N. Gash, 'Rural unemployment, 1815–1834', *Econ. Hist. Rev.*, VI (1935); E. L. Jones, 'The

this problem ... There were, of course, in this period, some groups among the working classes whose employment, and even wage-rates, fluctuated according to a fairly regular annual pattern. Given that this pattern remained fixed, the earnings of these groups would move in sympathy with wage-rates of those in permanent employment. It is possible, however, that one consequence of the not inconsiderable changes in the nature and pattern of employment over the whole period 1750–1850 was some disruption to the patterns of employment-distribution of the seasonally or irregularly employed. At the present time it is doubtful whether it would be possible to generalize with any confidence about any trends in this aspect of seasonal movements.[2]

I want to present evidence here which enables us to do precisely that, and to consider long-term changes in male and female seasonal distributions of unemployment in agriculture, predominantly in the southern and eastern counties of England, although some attention will also be paid to wider regional variations in these patterns. This issue will be closely related to trends in male and female agricultural wages, both to provide supportive and explanatory evidence for

agricultural labour market in England, 1793–1872', *Econ. Hist. Rev.*, XVII (1964); G. E. Fussell & M. Compton, 'Agricultural adjustments after the Napoleonic Wars', *Econ. Hist.*, IV (1939); A. Digby, 'The labour market and the continuity of social policy after 1834: the case of the eastern counties', *Econ. Hist. Rev.*, XXVIII (1975); M. W. Flinn, 'The Poor Employment Act of 1817', *Econ. Hist. Rev.*, XIV (1961); D. C. Barnett, 'Allotments and the problem of rural poverty, 1780–1840', in E. L. Jones & G. E. Mingay (eds.), *Land, Labour and Population in the Industrial Revolution* (1967); E. J. T. Collins, 'Harvest technology and labour supply in Britain, 1790–1870', *Econ. Hist. Rev.*, XXII (1969), and his 'Migrant labour in British Agriculture in the nineteenth century', *Econ. Hist. Rev.*, XXIX (1976); M. Blaug, 'The myth of the old poor law and the making of the new', *Journal of Economic History*, XXIII (1963), and his 'The Poor Law Report re-examined', *Jnl of Econ. Hist.*, XXIV (1964); D. A. Baugh, 'The cost of poor relief in south-east England, 1790–1834', *Econ. Hist. Rev.*, XXVIII (1975); D. N. McCloskey, 'New perspectives on the Old Poor Law', *Explorations in Economic History*, X (1972–3); J. R. Poynter, *Society and Pauperism: Ideas on Poor Relief, 1795–1834* (1969); M. E. Rose, 'The allowance system under the New Poor Law', *Econ. Hist. Rev.*, XIX (1966); F. G. Emmison, 'Relief of the poor at Eaton Socon, Bedfordshire, 1706–1834', *Beds Hist. Rec. Soc.*, XV (1933); A. Digby, 'The rural poor law', in D. Fraser (ed.), *The New Poor Law in the Nineteenth Century* (1976); A. J. Peacock, *Bread or Blood; a Study of the Agrarian Riots in East Anglia in 1816* (1965). For two excellent discussions of the rural standard of living, see: D. R. Mills, 'The quality of life in Melbourn, Cambridgeshire, in the period 1800–1850', *International Review of Social History*, XXIII (1978); and T. L. Richardson, 'Agricultural labourers' standard of living in Kent, 1790–1840', in D. J. Oddy & D. Miller (eds.), *The Making of the British Diet* (1976). For the relation of unemployment to the introduction of the threshing machine, see: S. Macdonald, 'The progress of the early threshing machine', *Agricultural History Review*, XXIII (1975); N. E. Fox, 'The spread of the threshing machine in central southern England', *Agric. Hist. Rev.*, XXVI (1978); S. Macdonald, 'Further progress with the early threshing machine: a rejoinder', *Agric. Hist. Rev.*, XXVI (1978); E. J. T. Collins, 'The diffusion of the threshing machine in Britain, 1790–1880', *Tools and Tillage*, II (1972). And, of course, see E. J. Hobsbawm & G. Rudé, *Captain Swing* (1969, 1973 edn).

[2] Flinn, 'Trends in real wages', 410–11.

long-term changes in the seasonal distribution of unemployment, and to draw out some implications which these changes may carry for an assessment of trends in familial income. In discussing these issues, I will develop an argument on the changing roles of men and women in the agricultural work force between 1690 and 1860, and point to its significance for the 'standard of living debate', for the study of the history of women, and of the family. I hope in doing this to contribute an answer to those questions which concern the causal connections between economic and attitudinal changes – in this case by re-assessing the importance of nineteenth-century attitudes to femininity in bringing about a diminution of female work in agriculture.

II

To consider these issues I shall use rural settlement examinations which, under the Settlement Act of 1662,[3] were intended to enquire into the parish of settlement of applicants for poor relief, or of those felt to be a potential burden on the poor rates. This source allows the analysis of seasonal distribution of unemployment as it provides the exact date at which the examinant for relief came to require parochial aid. In the course of the examination as to settlement, other details (for example sex, marital status, and occupation) were given which allow very specific geographical, occupational, and sexual location of the patterns of seasonal unemployment. The application for relief, followed by the examination to find where the applicant was eligible for it, provide the indication of unemployment – roughly the same indication, in fact, as is used today. It is complicated only by the 1795 settlement legislation,[4] which laid down that removal could take place only when a person became chargeable to the parish, and so ended the powers given under the 1662 Settlement Act for removal when a person was thought 'likely' to become chargeable. For our purposes, before 1795 examinations could be conducted on newly arrived parish inhabitants, on inhabitants felt likely to become chargeable, and of course on those who had just become chargeable, as after 1795. This legislative change, however, does not appear to call into question the utility of this source before 1795 – newly arrived examinants would have experienced recent unemployment possibly

[3] 13 & 14 Car II c. 12. And see 1 Jac II c. 17; 3 Wm & Mary c. 11; 8 & 9 Wm III c. 30; 12 Anne c. 18; 9 Geo I c. 7; 3 Geo II c. 29.

[4] 35 Geo III c. 101. Some groups earlier could not be removed until chargeable, such as holders of settlement certificates, soldiers, sailors, and their families, and friendly society members. See 8 & 9 Wm III c. 30; 24 Geo III c. 6; 33 Geo III c. 54.

in their old parish, and certainly over the past week, or however long it had taken them to journey from their old parish to the new, and would probably still be unemployed in their new parish (given the rapidity of local authorities' action against those felt to be a potential encumbrance on the rates). Such action would not be taken if they had moved to take up already arranged employment. The perception of local overseers and constables, in closely tied rural communities, of who might soon become a burden on the parish, mediated by the disincentive to examine posed by the very high fees charged for an examination by the parish clerk,[5] is probably a good second best to the exact date of chargeability. And the examination immediately following chargeability, very common before 1795, gives the precise seasonal date we require. In short, the 1795 Act does not appear to mark a significant discontinuity of policy for the purposes of using the examinations an an indicator for long-term patterns of seasonal unemployment, and the material extracted from them would support this, showing no break for example in the clear-cut male patterns before and after 1795.

It should be noted that this source can tell us nothing about the relative size of the male and female work force in different periods, or of the total numbers seasonally unemployed. These problems, particularly for the eighteenth century, will probably remain largely beyond the reach of historians. We shall be discussing here only long-term changes in the seasonal distribution, or patterns, of unemployment, and considering the probable implications of these changes. The method adopted has been to take the surviving examinations in different parishes (for both married and unmarried labour), and to plot the percentage of these which occurred in each calendar month. (The figures have been adjusted to eliminate the effects of irregularity in the number of days in each month.) This has been done for Cambridgeshire, Bedfordshire, Huntingdonshire, Norfolk, Suffolk, Essex, Hertfordshire, Northamptonshire, Buckinghamshire and Berkshire in Figures 1.1 and 1.2 – that is, for those counties which, when analysed in isolation from each other, very clearly showed the male pattern of seasonal unemployment which I shall associate with regions where grain growing predominates. I have excluded urban parishes, although have included some obvious cases of farm-servants and agricultural labourers out of work and examined

---

[5] This fee could be between 3s. and 7s. for one examination in the late eighteenth century, and would be considerably more for extra copies made and removal orders drawn up, with notices of pending removal sent. The removal itself would usually cost over £8 and if attended by legal expenses would go well over £20. Such a sum would maintain a single pauper continuously for about three years.

in towns where hiring fairs were held. Most rural parishes in Cambridgeshire, Bedfordshire, Huntingdonshire, Suffolk, and Hertfordshire are represented, and many rural parishes in the other counties. Examinations resulting from illness, old age, familial desertion, and bastardy have been excluded. The two figures have been subdivided into five chronological categories, between 1690 and 1860, which are intended to demonstrate the seasonal pattern before the rising wheat prices of the second half of the eighteenth century, during that rise, during the Napoleonic Wars, after the war until the New Poor Law, and after the New Poor Law.[6] ·

Figure 1.1 gives the male long-term changes, and represents the grain-growing pattern of seasonal unemployment, with high employment during the harvest and high winter unemployment. Comparable agricultural distributions for the region are of course found today. The extent to which grain growing was supplemented by livestock can be seen in the slight rise of unemployment occurring just after the calving and dairying season, that is, for the months of April and May before 1793. In the western pastoral region we will consider later, this was often the point of highest employment insecurity during the year, and the hiring fair commonly took place in

---

[6] The counties represented in these figures indicate a reasonable continuity of their proportional contribution over the five periods, and the explanation for the figures does not appear to be bound up with a temporal change in their geographical incidence. Discontinuities of emphasis were small, and the agricultural specialisation of these counties was sufficiently homogeneous to make these insignificant. All these counties very clearly indicate the male grain-growing pattern when analysed separately, and the descriptions of women's work presented in the 1834 Poor Law Report were very similar for each county.

The removal orders which went with examinations sometimes give occupations, and such cases are incorporated here, alongside a relatively small number of orders for people examined in heavily agricultural parishes. The order was intended to follow the examination through the post (to the parish to which removal was to take place) by two weeks, but was commonly drawn up by the clerk (and even sent) on the same day. Any slight time lag becomes insignificant when using a three month moving average. Orders usually lack the occupational specificity of examinations, although this problem can largely be obviated by careful choice of agricultural parishes, leaving aside centres of cottage industry. The information given by parish in the 1801 census on numbers engaged in agriculture and handicraft manufacturing is a helpful guide for this. A very large majority of rural examinants commonly worked in agricultural occupations. The advantages of orders are their consistent precision on chargeability, marital status, family size, and ages of children. The addition here makes no significant difference to the distributions from examinations, and usefully supplements them; no cases of removal for which the examination survives are included. Further figures were also calculated using a much larger number of rural removal orders only, and this produced similar distributions and changes to those presented here.

These figures should not be used to generalise further on the changing sex ratios of applicants for relief over time, as additional sex-specific research provided a stronger numerical basis for some of the distributions.

May (as in the north-west) when the agricultural year was felt to have ended. In the east the hiring fair was in Michaelmas (29 September), coinciding with the immediate post-harvest period. Figure 1.1 is remarkable for the continuous pattern of male seasonal unemployment which it presents, for the disappearance of any such later spring unemployment by 1793, with the periods 1793–1814 and after showing no signs of it, and for the more acute pattern of the early nineteenth century.

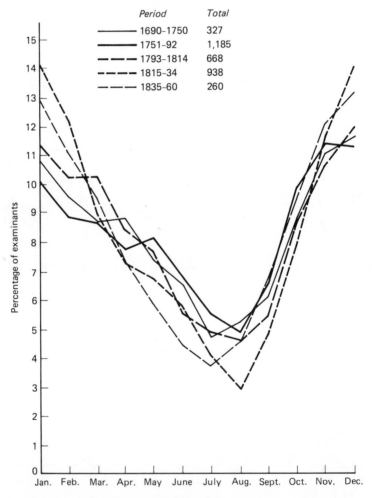

Period	Total
1690–1750	327
1751–92	1,185
1793–1814	668
1815–34	938
1835–60	260

Figure 1.1 *Male seasonal distribution of unemployment, 1690–1860*
Camb, Beds, Hunts, Norf, Suff, Ess, Herts, Berks, Bucks & N'hants (3 month moving average)

If one turns to Figure 1.2, it will be apparent that women experienced much more drastic changes in their seasonal distribution of unemployment. From 1690 to 1750 the pattern for women in these counties was almost exactly that which we find for men in the earlier period. In 1751–92, however, there was a marked change in the females' pattern, which indicates that their role was being transferred to the spring activities away from the harvest, at the same time as men appeared to be moving to a greater relative involvement in the

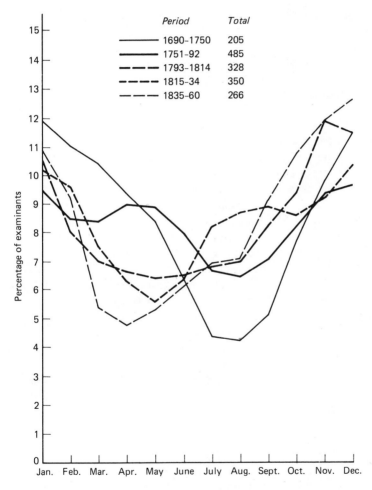

Figure 1.2 *Female seasonal distribution of unemployment, 1690–1860*
Camb, Beds, Hunts, Norf, Suff, Ess, Herts, Berks, Bucks & N'hants (3 month moving average)

harvest. The periods of highest employment security for women (1751–92) had become equally the spring and the harvest, in contrast to the earlier tendency, which they had shared with men, for them to retain their jobs most readily in harvest time. By 1793–1814 the female pattern had proceeded further in the same direction, although the change was probably delayed by the temporary shortage of male labour during the war, ensuring relatively equal female involvement in both the spring and the harvest. By this period men showed less apparent involvement in March and April. By 1815–34 women were even more unlikely to maintain their employment during the harvest, and they appear to be least likely to become unemployed in the spring. Men experienced more acute winter unemployment than in the earlier periods. The female pattern of 1835–60 was the reverse of the pattern for 1690–1750, and the shift towards greater employment security during the spring than in the harvest had come to its completion. The male pattern continued much as it was in 1690–1750, but with less noticeable unemployment after the spring activities, in which women would now seem to be much more heavily concentrated. After spring, women became increasingly vulnerable to unemployment until December. So from an environment with a relatively high degree of sexually shared labour, in which gender differences appear to have been almost a matter of indifference to employers, we have moved to a situation indicating an unprecedentedly marked sexual specialisation of work. Women had come to be most secure from unemployment during a period of the year characterised in the east by relatively slight labour costs and by a low demand for labour.[7] The change was long-term, and its origin can certainly be dated from a period before 1793 – almost certainly between 1750 and 1790. This description of change affecting female work and the sexual division of labour, with its implications of a decline in annual female participation rates and potential earning capacity, can be well supported by long-term trends in male and female money wages, and by early nineteenth-century literary evidence for the region. We will turn now to evidence on wages to support this argument, and to develop an explanation of it.

---

[7] The monthly wage payments made by farmers in the east were, of course, in direct inverse correlation to the male seasonal unemployment patterns of Figure 1.1. See, for example, W. Marshall, *Review and Abstract of the County Reports to the Board of Agriculture. Vol. III: The Eastern Department* (1811, York, 1818 edn), p. 256; Rev. C. D. Brereton, *A Practical Inquiry into the Number, Means of Employment and Wages of Agricultural Labourers* (Norwich, 1824), p. 74, giving the monthly wage expenditure for a large Norfolk farm between 1805 and 1824.

III

The evidence is provided in Figures 1.3, 1.4, 1.5, 1.6, 1.7, 1.8 and 1.9. This is derived again from settlement examinations, from rural parishes in southern and eastern counties. It refers to unmarried men and women, hired by the year, and can be taken to reflect the yearly wages paid at hiring fairs in these counties to agricultural 'farm-servants' and domestic servants.[8] The wages are predominantly agricultural, with a greater emphasis on domestic servants for London and Middlesex. Because of the high degree of movement between purely agricultural employment and employment in small market-town and village occupations, and because the same hiring fairs served the purposes of both these categories of employment, no attempt has been made to distinguish between them. This would probably be an unrealistic task, given the combining of occupations by many employers, and this close interaction of agricultural and market-town or village employment. It was common for a 'farm-servant' to be employed for a year by a publican, or in a similar village or market-town context, and then move back to agriculture, and the wages of the hirings (taking place at the same hiring fair) appear to have been much the same. For our present purposes they have been combined to form general series for yearly hirings within the agricultural sector and in London.

Details of past yearly hirings were given in settlement examinations in connection with gaining a settlement by hiring for a year. The account was from the examinant's memory of the hiring, and there does not appear to have been any motive for him or her to under- or over-state the wages earned. Examinants must have been aware that accounts of the hiring by which a settlement was gained would, whenever possible, be checked by the parish officers with the former employer. The accounts given may be more reliable than the details of wages given by farmers to early nineteenth-century Select Committees, or to agricultural investigators, where the social prestige of the farmer would have been affected by his statement, and where the farmer chosen may in any case have been atypical. For our purposes, the details of the wages contained in the examinations (and they are

---

[8] The wages are for full fifty-two week hirings. Wages for other variants of service (fifty-one weeks, nine months, provision of 'board' wages, etc.) are not included. Such variants on the full yearly hiring are discussed in chapter 2. I have also included yearly wages from other sources besides examinations, such as diaries, farm accounts, pamphlets on agriculture and the poor law, and the like. The wage rates from other sources generally match closely those in the examinations, which comprise most of the citings aggregated here.

frequently given in very full detail, with accounts of deductions for
days absent, of money given 'in earnest', or rises during or after the
year) allow the wages of unmarried persons to be located exactly
temporally and regionally, and some general long-term patterns of
change between 1662 and 1834 to be seen. (The New Poor Law ended
hiring as a head of settlement, although some wages are available in
the first few years after it, perhaps through the failure of parish clerks
to realise this.) They have some advantages over other wage material,
most notably because the problem of unemployment, which affects
any consideration of agricultural weekly wage rates, was absent;
because they were available every year during this period (rather than
only in 1767–70, 1795, 1824, and 1833, as for Bowley's data); and
because full details were given alongside other particulars as, for
example, the nature of employment, the length and conditions of
hiring, or the sex and marital status of the examinant.[9] But because
the series presented here are for yearly hirings of unmarried people,
inclusive of board and lodging, they have some disadvantages
compared to labourers' wage rates. It seems likely that short-term
trends in the latter, however, were closely paralleled by trends in
wages paid for yearly hirings, and for the purpose of generalising
about agricultural wages for married people this assumption has been
made. One must be aware, however, that the balance of yearly
hirings, and hirings for a shorter time, began to change after 1780,[10]
and that generalisations from these wage series about the long-term
movement of weekly real wages must be made more tentatively. But
the short-term changes (that is for periods of up to about twenty
years) in wages of both types of hiring probably followed each other
closely.[11] And it is unlikely that the types of work of the weekly and
yearly hired were sufficiently dissimilar to render the sexual wage
differentials of the latter unrepresentative of the long-term sexual
differentials for the weekly hired labourers.

[9] For the importance of trends in yearly wages, particularly in relation to questions of
the location of the home market, and the determinants of marriage, see J. Hajnal,
'European marriage patterns in perspective', D. V. Glass & D. E. C. Eversley (eds.),
Population in History (1965).

[10] See chapter 2.

[11] The correspondent for the rural districts in the *Morning Chronicle* in 1849 gave a view,
which supports this, that yearly wages, arranged at the hiring fair, were closely
related to weekly wage rates: 'The servants hired at this fair are generally such as are
boarded and lodged on the farm, but the wages offered them were a good indication
of what was likely to be the rate in vogue, so far as the ordinary farm labourer was
concerned.' *Morning Chronicle*, 27 Oct. 1849. It is difficult to gauge how representative of weekly wage movements the annual wage trends were, particularly after the
1780s. From then there was a growing tendency to hire for shorter periods –
necessitated, in the context of escalating poor rates, by the desire to avoid the

While some general conclusions do emerge from these series, we must also note that most examinations did not go into details of wages, and that the numbers of citings of wages presented here, while almost representing the complete availability of examinations for these counties, are at times nevertheless small. In this regard they have much in common with other series covering the eighteenth and early nineteenth centuries, as compiled by Bowley or Gilboy,

settlements created by yearly hiring, and to ease the increasing parochial dependency of the married, who were, of course, more expensive to maintain on the rates than the single. Yearly hiring also became unsuited to the intensive, but short-term labour requirements of cereal-producing regions, which we noted in regard to Figure 1.1. The system had also probably been more compatible with the family life-cycle demand for labour of small farms and owner-occupiers in an earlier period. On the one hand, it could be held that as a consequence of the factors undercutting the viability of the yearly hiring system, yearly wage rates fell more than did weekly. On the other, it could be argued with equal weight that the categories of labour remaining hired by the year were increasingly those which were indispensable to the farmer, and who had traditionally received higher wages (e.g., carters, shepherds, and so on), and that, in consequence, these yearly figures underrepresent the actual weekly real wage decline. I do not consider Bowley's figures for weekly wage trends to be that adequate fully to resolve this problem. But we can note that my figures tend to represent rural wages as being at the same or a marginally higher level by the 1830s as they had been around 1760 (e.g., Figure 1.3). If we turn to Bowley, we find to support this that Berkshire, Buckinghamshire, Cambridgeshire, Essex, Suffolk, and Norfolk all had wages as late as 1850 which were within 6d. of their 1767–70 level (A. L. Bowley, 'Statistics of wages in the United Kingdom during the last hundred years', pt I, 'Agricultural wages', *Jnl of the Royal Statistical Society*, LXI (1898), 704. Further weekly wage data which I have collected could also be introduced here to make the same point.

There was also no doubt among contemporaries that weekly real wages fell in the southern (and many Midland) counties. For example, see: D. Davies, *The Case of the Labourers in Husbandry* (1795), e.g., pp. 25ff, 56–7, 68–74, 87ff, 124–5, 156ff; S.C. on Agricultural Labourers' Wages, VI (1824), p. 22; S.G. & E.O.A. Checkland (eds.), *The Poor Law Report of 1834* (1974), p. 284; Marshall, *Review and Abstract*, p. 304; *Annals of Agriculture*, XXV (1795), 609 (communication from Rev. J. Howlett, claiming that real wages had been falling since 1756); G. Dyer, *The Complaints of the Poor People of England* (1792), p. 100; W. Frend, *Peace and Union recommended to the associated Bodies of Republicans and Anti-Republicans* (Cambridge, 1793), pp. 47–9; A. Smith, *The Wealth of Nations* (1776, Harmondsworth, 1977 edn), p. 177: 'The high price of provisions during these ten years past has not in many parts of the kingdom been accompanied with any sensible rise in the money price of labour'; C. Vancouver, *General View of the Agriculture of the County of Devon* (1808, 1969 edn), p. 362: 'The price of labour has certainly not kept pace with the depreciation in the value of money within the last 20 years'; G. D. H. & M. Cole (eds.), *The Opinions of William Cobbett* (1944), pp. 86, 181; G. Glover, 'Observations on the state of pauperism', *The Pamphleteer*, X (1817), 389; T. P. MacQueen, *Thoughts and Suggestions on the Present Condition of the Country* (1830), p. 9; R. Pashley, *Pauperism and the Poor Laws* (1852), pp. 254ff; T. Postans, *Letter to Sir Thomas Baring on Causes which have produced the Present State of the Agricultural Labouring Poor* (1831), p. 8; Rev. J. Howlett, *An Examination of Mr. Pitt's Speech in the House of Commons, Feb. 12, 1796* (1796); Arthur Young (Board of Agriculture), *General Report on Enclosures* (1808), p. 19; J. Wedge, *General View of the Agriculture of the County of Warwick* (1794), p. 24. The list could be considerably extended, and there were virtually no contrary opinions. Bread purchases probably

which were frequently based on smaller numbers of cases.[12] They are less open to the charge of being very irregularly located in time, which might be made of some of Bowley's figures, particularly for agriculture. His figures were based on discontinuous, and often polemical, evidence, as provided by Arthur Young (1767–70), Sir Frederick Eden (1795), the Report of the Commission on Paying Labourers' Wages out of the Poor Rates (1824), and the Poor Law Report of 1834. This evidence provided Bowley with his 'pivot years', for which he had evidence, and the trends between them were then 'interpolated' in an unclarified manner. Nevertheless, the trends for the eastern counties considered here are in agreement with the impression given by Bowley's figures for this region, which pointed to very low agricultural weekly wage rates in the early nineteenth century. It should be stressed that we are dealing with a group of counties in the south-east which were notoriously badly paid, and that their wage trends should not be taken as generally typical of other areas, particularly in the north.

It might also be claimed that the figures represent going rates of yearly payment prevalent at the regional hiring fairs in different periods, and in this sense have a regularity and representativeness which would be conspicuously lacking for hirings arranged for a shorter period on a more individual basis, away from the institutional context of the statute fairs. The wages varied more by age than by regionality within the compass of individual fairs, and some examinations indeed gave lengthy past details of wages, including those obtained when the examinant was in his or her teens. Such early wages have generally been excluded, to help remove the problem of variation through age-specific earnings. It was of course only the last yearly hiring which conferred settlement, and this would normally take place shortly before marriage, after which 'farm-servants' in this

constituted about 44 per cent of total family expenditure in the 1760s, but this had risen to about 60 per cent by 1790. See R. N. Salaman, *The History and Social Influence of the Potato* (Cambridge, 1949), p. 497. The point has also been well made that the bread scale was much reduced in the early nineteenth century, implying falling real familial income. See Blaug, 'Myth of the old poor law', in Flinn & Smout, *Essays in Social History*, pp. 131–3; J. L. & B. Hammond, *The Village Labourer* (1911, 1978 edn), pp. 129–31, 173; Hobsbawm & Rudé, *Captain Swing*, p. 31. The downward trend of agricultural real wages for the east after about 1790 is also well supported by Mills, 'Quality of life in Melbourn, Cambridgeshire', and Richardson, 'Agricultural labourers' standard of living in Kent'.

[12] See in particular Bowley, 'The statistics of wages', pt 1, 'Agricultural wages', 702–22; A. L. Bowley, 'The statistics of wages in the United Kingdom during the last hundred years', pt IV, 'Agricultural wages – concluded. Earnings and general averages', *Jnl Roy. Stat. Soc.*, LXII (1899), 555–70; E. W. Gilboy, *Wages in Eighteenth-Century England* (Cambridge, Mass., 1934).

region normally became 'labourers' and moved outside this system of hiring. In consequence, most examinations were concerned only with the last hiring, and the figures may be taken to indicate the mean 'adult' wage of farm-servants, usually aged in their early twenties. Information in the examinations indicated a mean marriage age for men and women of twenty-six and twenty-four respectively, which remained reasonably constant over time. The 'adult' wage was reached by about the age of nineteen and remained steady thereafter, and it seems unlikely that any possible changes in the marriage age could have influenced the trends presented. Nevertheless, despite these supportive comments, it must be noted that these wage series are in some instances based on small numbers, and should be handled tentatively. They are presented as bearing directly on the regions and labour force which concern us, being largely derived from the same settlement documents on which the seasonal unemployment data is based, and as providing the most satisfactory evidence available.[13]

[13] 1741–5 has been chosen as a base for these series as price fluctuations for these five years appear to balance each other out, and produce a mean which is neither exceptionally high nor low. It is at the start of the general upswing of food prices, and so also a convenient point from which to consider the effects of that price rise.

The figures have been calculated by taking five year means of the data available for each group of counties, and then producing a three point moving average of these five year means to give an effect which would be similar to a fifteen year moving average of the data. (The five year means of the wage data are given in an Appendix.) This was felt to be appropriate as some hirings can only be located to within about three years of their actual date. This was also done to the Phelps-Brown price index. The latter was chosen as it is one of the few price indices which spans the requisite period, rather than through any particular suitability which it was felt to have for the wage data. The London bread price series, which also extends over the entire period, was also tried, and produced a trend which was almost exactly interchangeable with that of the Phelps-Brown index. This was felt to justify the use of the latter here. We can also recall M. W. Flinn's argument for the 'quite remarkable degree of agreement' of price indices in this connection (Flinn, 'Trends in real wages', 402). Indeed, I calculate a multiple correlation coefficient between the Exeter, Eton, and Winchester price series of 0.9927 (1700–1820). It has been suggested that prior to the mid-eighteenth century greater regional price variations existed, and that these appear to have levelled off in the course of the eighteenth century. See A. H. John, 'The course of agricultural change, 1660–1760', in L. S. Pressnell (ed.), *Studies in the Industrial Revolution* (1960), pp. 125–56; C. W. J. Granger & C. M. Elliott, 'Wheat prices and markets in the eighteenth century', *Econ. Hist. Rev.*, XX (1967). But the yearly fluctuations of prices, at any rate, were very similar by region in 1700–50: the multiple correlation coefficient between the Exeter, Eton, and Winchester price series was still very high, at 0.9797.

The high price years of 1795–6, 1800–1, and 1812–13 have been included in the formulation of the Phelps-Brown index presented. It was appreciated that such inclusion would have the effect of accentuating the appearance of falling real wages after about 1790, and so the index was also recalculated by omitting these years, and substituting instead a mean of the two years immediately before and after each of the three very high price periods. This produced a trend the peak of which was only

It is necessary to make a few further introductory points on these wage series. The hirings and their details recorded in the examinations were past biographical events of those examined, and so the wages paid cannot be held to be atypical as a consequence of the immediate circumstances of the examinant on examination. In addition, rural poverty in this period had a particular life-cycle, with family men aged about thirty-four with three or more children as yet economically unproductive, and the aged being particularly prone to dependence on the poor rates. Many also came under examination because of illness, familial desertion, or the death of a spouse. While such cases have been eliminated in the consideration of seasonal unemployment, their accounts of past wages are included here. The marked seasonality of eastern agricultural employment also made it very likely that agricultural workers would be examined at some point in their lives. In addition, estimates of relief dependency were very high, particularly in the late eighteenth and early nineteenth centuries, varying between a quarter and a half of village populations requiring assistance.[14] And in the numerous cases where a labour rate

ten points down from the original index including the high price years, and gave an intersection of the male wage index with the price index which was only about five years later for Figure 1.3. In view of these very minor differences, which certainly will not affect the general argument, the six high price years were incorporated. It would in any case have been a 'rather dubious procedure' to have omitted them.

[14] I would agree with C. R. Oldham, who pointed out that experience of the poor law must have been almost universal for labourers in Oxfordshire. See his 'Oxfordshire poor law papers', *Econ. Hist. Rev.*, V (1934–5), 94. There are reasons for believing that some counties to the east were even more highly pauperised than Oxfordshire. On the high levels of rural poverty or poor law dependency, giving estimates of between 25 and 51 per cent, see: Hobsbawm & Rudé, *Captain Swing*, pp. 50–3; J. D. Chambers, 'Enclosure and labour supply in the Industrial Revolution', in D. V. Glass & D. E. C. Eversley (eds.), *Population in History* (1965) pp. 321–2, n. 45; J. M. Martin, 'Marriage and economic stress in the Felden of Warwickshire in the eighteenth century', *Population Studies*, XXXI (1977), 528; G. Edwards, *From Crow-Scaring to Westminster* (1922), p. 16; Emmison, 'Relief of the poor at Eaton Socon', 1–9, 48–50, 54–5, and n. 136; W. Hasbach, *The History of the English Agricultural Labourer* (1908), pp. 188–90; A. H. John (ed.), *Enclosure and Population* (Farnborough, 1973), intro., p. 3; R. Williams, *The Country and the City* (St Albans, 1973), p. 185; Mills, 'Quality of life in Melbourn, Cambridgeshire', 383ff; R. Jefferies, *The Hills and the Vale* (1909, Oxford, 1980 edn), p. 159; C. S. Orwin & B. I. Felton, 'A century of wages and earnings in agriculture', *Jnl Roy. Agric. Soc.*, XCII (1931), 242ff. The S.C. on Agricultural Labourers' Wages, VI (1824), pp. 3, 34, reported that it was 'impossible' to avoid parish assistance. A labourer is 'identified altogether with the rates'. And see William Cobbett, *Advice to Young Men* (1830, Oxford, 1980 edn), pp. 320ff, on the unfortunate and unpredictable nature of pauperism, affecting ex-ratepayers, ex-overseers of the poor, and so on: 'How many thousands of industrious and virtuous men have, within these few years, been brought down from a state of competence to that of pauperism!' It is also worth noting that total poor relief (1815–20) was slightly over 3 per cent of the national income of England and Wales – a figure as high as the percentage of national income spent on unemployment relief

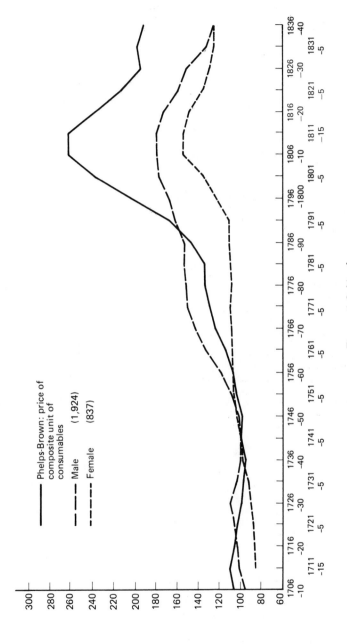

Figure 1.3 *Yearly wages*
Camb, Beds, Hunts, N'hants, Surr, Kent, Ess, Herts, Norf, Suff, Bucks, Berks, Oxon & Hants (1741–5 = 100)

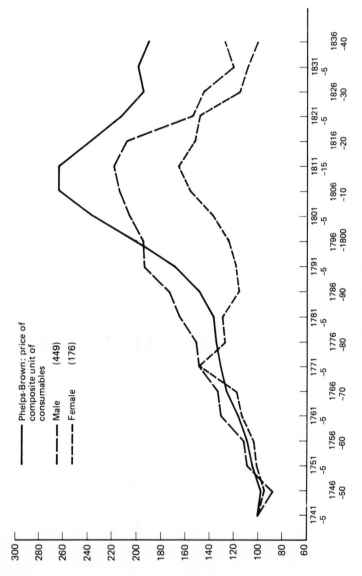

Figure 1.4 *Yearly wages*
Suff (1741–5 = 100)

Phelps-Brown: price of
composite unit of
consumables

Male   (449)

Female   (176)

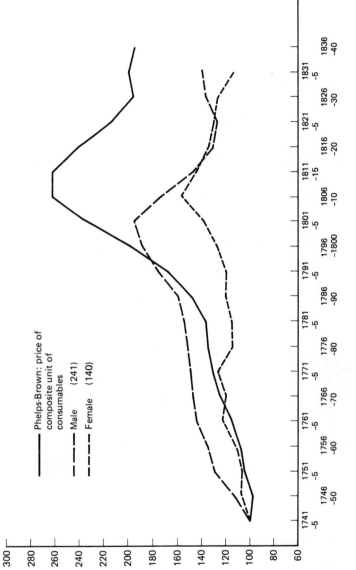

Figure 1.5 *Yearly wages*
Norf (1741–5 = 100)

Phelps-Brown: price of
composite unit of
consumables

Male   (241)

Female (140)

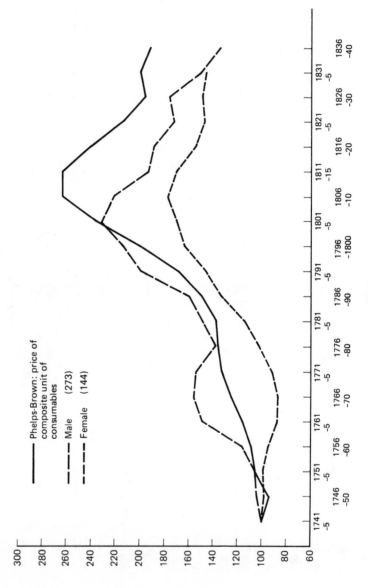

Figure 1.6 *Yearly wages*
Camb, Beds, Hunts & N'hants (1741–5 = 100)

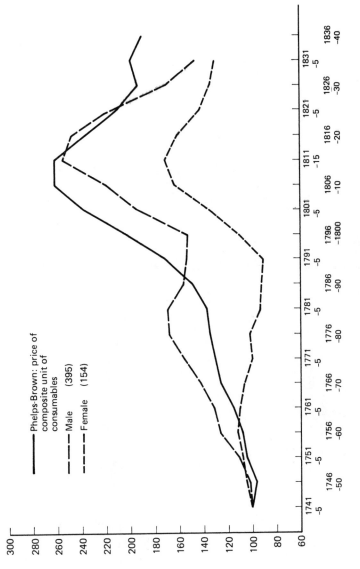

Figure 1.7 *Yearly wages*
Surr, Kent, Ess & Herts (1741–5 = 100)

Phelps-Brown: price of
composite unit of
consumables

Male   (395)
Female   (154)

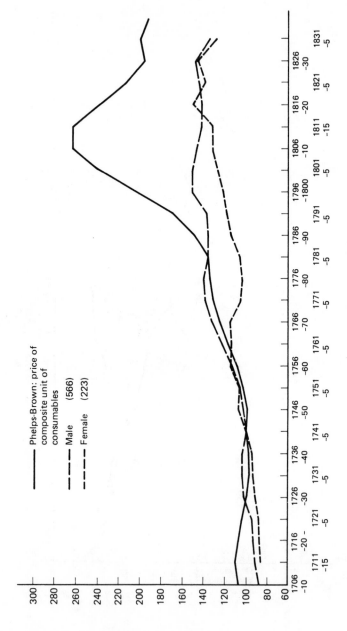

Figure 1.8 *Yearly wages*
Bucks, Berks, Oxon & Hants (1741–5 = 100)

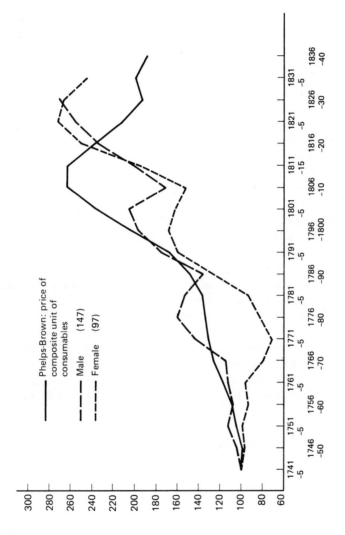

Figure 1.9 *Yearly wages*
London & Msx (1741–5 = 100)

Phelps-Brown: price of
composite unit of
consumables

- - - Male (147)
- - - Female (97)

or roundsman system was used, it was possible for 'unemployment' among the labour force to become total, with free labour having to become pauperised to find employment.

Furthermore, as we shall see elsewhere, there were many apprenticed artisans examined as to settlement, particularly in urban parishes, who (as for those claiming settlement by renting more than £10 per annum) were in a higher social and economic category than the agricultural labour covered here. And examinants would either sign or make their mark at the end of examinations, making it possible to compare illiteracy rates for examinants with occupationally specific material uncovered by Schofield from parish marriage registers. He found that male illiteracy for servants and labourers (1754–1844) varied between 59 and 66 per cent.[15] During the same period, male illiteracy in examinations, for a sample of two thousand for this occupational group, was 63 per cent. (For male examinants regardless of occupation it varied by county between 40 and 58 per cent. Bedfordshire had the highest illiteracy – also found by Schofield.[16]) It is therefore most unlikely that we are dealing with an unrepresentative sample of the (increasingly homogeneous) agricultural labouring class – those referred to by contemporaries as the 'labouring poor'.

Nor, one should note, is it likely that the localised mobility of examinants makes the settlement data in any way unrepresentative of yearly wages (or of the seasonal unemployment patterns of agricultural labour). Such mobility was a general characteristic of farm-servants, and the high turnover of village populations is now well documented. In addition, a significant proportion of examinations were purely intra-parochial affairs, concerned to check eligibility to relief upon chargeability, and these would not be followed by removal. This proportion settled in their parish of examination varied

in the 1930s. Of course, the figure of 3 per cent conceals large regional differences, and the much more acute problems of the south. See K. N. Raj, 'Towards the eradication of poverty – an European precedent', in K. S. Krishnaswamy *et al.* (eds.), *Society and Change. Essays in Honour of S. Chaudhuri* (Oxford, 1977), p. 63.

[15] R. S. Schofield, 'Dimensions of illiteracy, 1750–1850', *Explorations in Econ. Hist.*, X (1973), 450.

[16] *Ibid.*, 447. See also Hobsbawn & Rudé, *Captain Swing*, p. 42, on high illiteracy in Bedfordshire. D. Jones, 'Thomas Campbell Foster and the rural labourer: incendiarism in East Anglia in the 1840's', *Social History*, I (1976), 7, reports male illiteracy of 74.5 per cent for labourers in four Suffolk parishes (1837–51). Female farm-servant/ex-farm-servant illiteracy from examinations was 73.3 per cent. The only comparable figure is that given by Jones, *ibid.*, 7, of 78.5 per cent illiteracy among rural labourers' wives. (Illiteracy figures from examinations are of course subject to the usual precautionary remarks on the usefulness of a signature as a test of literacy.)

according to such factors as the size of parish population or administrative efficiency, and normally ranged from between 20–55 per cent, most commonly around 30 per cent. Many examinants who were to be removed had of course been long resident parochially before becoming chargeable. In short, it seems that the immediate conditions which produced an examination do not render this source unreasonably atypical of the standard hiring fair wages in different periods for the unmarried class of 'farm-servants'.

For the purposes of the argument here this introduction can suffice, as I will be mainly concerned with only one feature of these wage statistics – the long-term relative movements of male and female wages, and in particular with the marked tendency for male and female wages to move in inverse correlation at some point between 1750 and 1800 in all the groups of counties covered. In Figure 1.6, for Cambridgeshire, Bedfordshire, Huntingdonshire, and Northamptonshire, the period was 1755 to 1780. In Figure 1.7, for a group of counties immediately circling London, it was 1755 to 1800. In London and Middlesex (Figure 1.9) we can see this between 1765 and 1790. In Norfolk (Figure 1.5) it was after 1765. In Suffolk (Figure 1.4) it was between 1770 and 1800. In Buckinghamshire, Berkshire, Oxfordshire and Hampshire (Figure 1.8) a similar movement occurred after 1760. The same tendency can be seen in the large overall grouping of counties featured in Figure 1.3, between 1755 and 1795, although here, as one would expect, it is less chronologically specific than in the other figures.[17] From the 1790s male and female wages moved more closely in unison, responding to the price rises of the Napoleonic Wars. The inverse correlation was largely a pre-1800 phenomenon, but one that was clearly marked. In virtually all these eastern counties, female real wages were falling from about 1760, which is from when I am dating the changes in female work during the agricultural year.

Some further points might also be noted. Male real wages rose, notably in the thirty years after 1740, and then stabilised. But this gain was lost in the Napoleonic Wars. There was little recovery after 1815, when real wages frequently continued to fall, in the context of agricultural depression, disbanding of the forces, high poor rates, intensified structural unemployment, and widespread, largely unprecedented, agrarian unrest in the east. This general trend can be seen in Figure 1.3. Figure 1.7 for the circle of counties around London,

---

[17] The use of some counties in this figure not covered by Figures 1.1 and 1.2 could be dropped for the purposes of consistency, but this would have no significant effect on the male and female trends as presented.

shows a decline in male real wages from 1780, a recovery between 1811 and 1825, but then another decline. A long-term fall is clearly apparent in Norfolk and Suffolk, strikingly so in Buckinghamshire, Berkshire, Oxfordshire, and Hampshire, and there appears to have been little recovery in Cambridgeshire, Bedfordshire, Huntingdonshire, or Northamptonshire. The London and Middlesex wages (Figure 1.9) can be supplemented with the urban wages of St Clement Danes, Middlesex (Figure 1.10). They give the most optimistic picture with their tendency to rise after 1820, but even here there was a decline between 1795 and 1820. These London and Middlesex series are also remarkable for the manner in which female wages kept up with male wages, after (in Figure 1.9) the inverse movement of 1765 to 1790. There is much evidence on the awareness of single women of their possibilities in London, particularly in domestic service, and the series would seem to support this.[18] Furthermore, London and Middlesex money wages were far higher than those of the surrounding counties, which is, of course, a difference well known from other wage series. The counties immediately surrounding London had the next highest money wages, with Norfolk and Suffolk's structural unemployment, high poor rates, and depressed rural industries producing the lowest money wages in the early nineteenth century of all south-eastern counties examined, which is what Bowley's figures would lead us to expect.[19] The major point to stress in regard to these eastern wage series, however, is the tendency (especially outside London and Middlesex) of female real wages to fall continuously from about 1760; but for there then to be a period when male money wages continued to rise, and male real wages either to rise or to remain steady (in inverse correlation to the female trend), until about thirty years later, when they too underwent what appears to be a long-term decline. We shall return to this for its implications for real familial income at a later point. For the present I shall be concerned to explain the post-1750 sexual division of labour, which these wage series appear nicely to substantiate.

---

[18] See, for example, D. C. Coleman, *Courtaulds, an Economic and Social History*, vol. 1 (Oxford, 1969), pp. 96–101, 236–44; A. Young, *A Farmer's Letters to the People of England* (1767), pp. 353–4. ('Young men and women in the country fix their eye on London as the last stage of their hope ... The number of young women that fly there is incredible.')

[19] Bowley, 'Statistics of wages', pt I, 'Agricultural Wages' (1898), 704–7, and 711–22. See also E. H. Hunt, *Regional Wage Variations in Britain, 1850–1914* (Oxford, 1973), pp. 62–4; Coleman, *Courtaulds*, vol. 1, pp. 244–5; and D. C. Coleman, 'Growth and decay during the Industrial Revolution: the case of East Anglia', *Scandinavian Econ. Hist. Rev.*, X (1962).

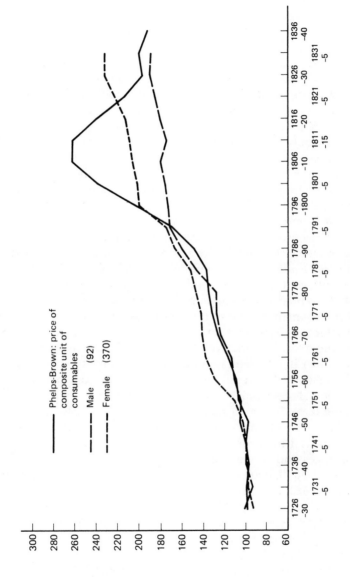

Figure 1.10 *Yearly wages*
St Clement Danes, Msx (1741–5 = 100)

IV

In doing this, let us turn to the very different pattern of female wages in the more pastoral west, as seen in Figures 1.11, 1.12, 1.13, and 1.14. In this area there was no downward movement of female real wages. Indeed, the period of the Napoleonic Wars and after was generally associated with buoyant or rising female real wages, in a way certainly not found in the east. This was probably related to growing specialisation of these western counties in pastoral farming, and its consequent enhancement of the role of the female farm-servant. In contrast, the east continued a transition in the later eighteenth century to greater concentration on grain production – a trend probably begun in the late seventeenth century, and facilitated by the new husbandry techniques. A consequence of this may have been a diminution of the importance of female labour, as reflected in their wage trends. This strengthening of arable husbandry in the south-east, and its effects on the farming of the heavy Midland clays, has now been well documented particularly for the period before the later eighteenth century. It seems probable that the continued up-ward movement of wheat prices was conducive to further extension of the arable acreage on the light soils of the south-east until the early nineteenth century. Recent study of changing agricultural technology has also pointed to this specialisation and employment of men, and it may help explain the very different female real wage movements of the eastern and western counties.[20] These differences may be based on a simple formula: that livestock and dairy farming were associated with a fuller deployment of female labour, in contrast to the growing predominance of men in grain production. This may help explain the rise of female real wages in the western counties, as compared with the long-term decline of their real wages in the east.

Similarly, this formula may provide a reason why male and female wages moved in inverse correlation in the east before 1800. Rising grain prices and production in the south-east enhanced the import-ance of male labour, and reduced pastoral farming, which was perhaps traditionally more closely associated with the farm labour of women. Female real wages fell in consequence, particularly during those periods when male money wages were rising, with agricultural prosperity being closely tied up with rising cereal production and prices. By about 1800, when the inverse correlation in the east no longer holds, the regional specialisation of agriculture had probably

[20] See Collins, 'Harvest technology'; and M. Roberts, 'Sickles and scythes: women's work and men's work at harvest time', *History Workshop*, VII (1979).

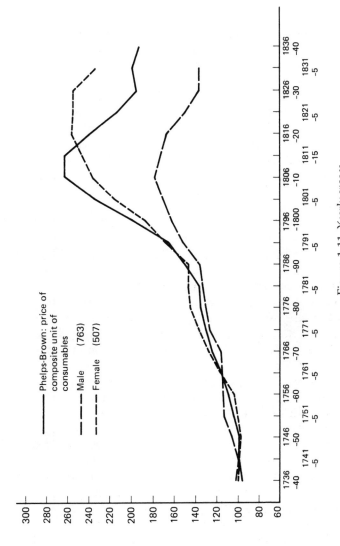

Figure 1.11 *Yearly wages*

Mon, Heref, Worcs, Salop, Glos, Brecons, Glam, Som, Wilts, Devon & Dorset (1741–5 = 100)

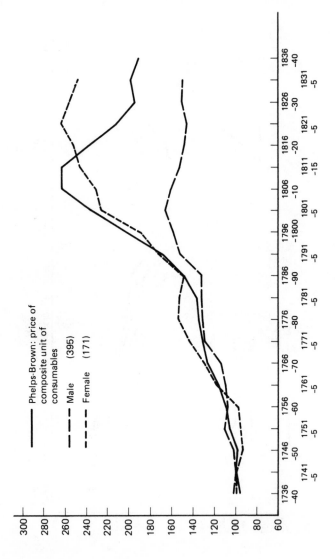

Figure 1.12 *Yearly wages*
Devon & Dorset (1741–5 = 100)

Phelps-Brown: price of
composite unit of
consumables

Male   (395)

Female   (171)

42

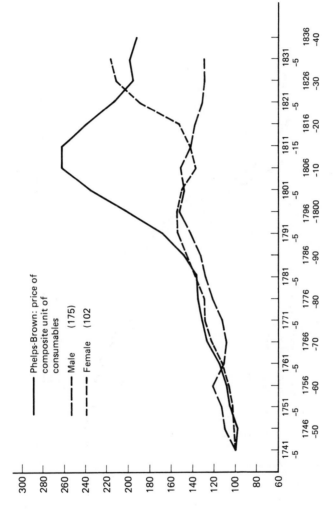

Figure 1.13 *Yearly wages*
Wilts & Som (1741–5 = 100)

Phelps-Brown: price of
composite unit of
consumables

Male   (175)

Female   (102

43

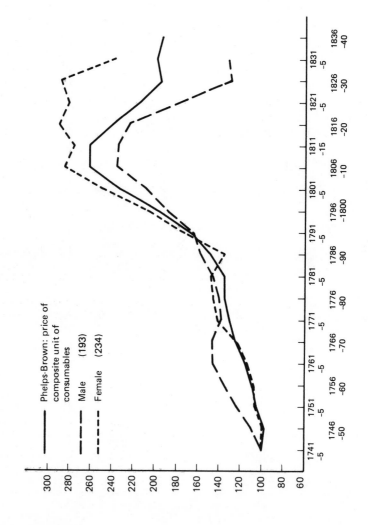

Figure 1.14 *Yearly wages*
Mon, Heref, Worcs, Salop, Glam, Brecons & Glos (1741–5 = 100)

44

reached a limit, and developed no further. Indeed, there may have been some movement back to pasture, stemming from falling grain prices after 1813,[21] although the strength of eastern farmers' loyalties to grain production by then may have hindered such a development on a wide scale. It is my contention here that the periods of inverse correlation of male and female wages saw the most rapid specialisation in cereal production. As the corn output of the south-east continued to expand after the mid-eighteenth century, in the context of growing structural unemployment, so female agricultural labour became less in demand, and their money wages fell relative to men. The growing sexual specialisation of labour further depressed female wages, at a time when the involvement of women in the region's increasingly heavy grain production was declining in favour of their participation in the increasingly insignificant dairy and calving season, in spring weeding, and in early summer haymaking. The seasonality of their employment had become more obviously aligned with forms of pastoral agriculture now more firmly associated with the Midlands and areas to the west. As the eighteenth century progressed, this simple formula – of female involvement in pastoral activities and of men in the harvest – became more applicable.[22]

---

[21] See Fussell & Compton, 'Agricultural adjustments', 202; M. Turner, *English Parliamentary Enclosure* (Folkestone, Kent, 1980), p. 93. But see also A. R. Wilkes, 'Adjustments in arable farming after the Napoleonic Wars', *Agric. Hist. Rev.*, XXVIII (1980).

[22] It was, of course, true that there were enclaves of pastoral farming in the east – most notably in the east Suffolk parishes lying in the area within Coddenham, Hacheston, Cookly, Metfield, Thrandeston, Wyverstone, Stonham – and my Suffolk material is heavily representative (perhaps significantly so) of the more strictly arable parishes lying outside this area. The division of cereal and pastoral farming, made only with reference to the eastern and western counties covered here, is necessarily crude; local exceptions can readily be made to it, and it serves the purpose only of general explanation. It is felt to be justified through being indicated strongly in the contrasts of the eastern 'cereal' pattern of seasonal unemployment (with its sharp 'V' shape – Figure 1.1), and the much flatter pattern of the western counties, with more noticeable insecurity of employment during May (Figure 1.16). The very marked constancy of these patterns within separate eastern and western counties in the eighteenth and nineteenth centuries, and the use of the division by J. Caird (*English Agriculture in 1850–1* (1851)) was held to justify the division of farming as used. This division is also very clearly apparent in the regional seasonality of marriages, peaking in October–November in the south-east (outside Sussex, or north-west Norfolk before the innovations there), and in May–June in the western counties taken here – after the south-eastern Michaelmas hiring fairs, and those of May in the west. Such marriage seasonality provides a rough indication of regional agricultural specialisation by positing high frequency of marriage immediately following payment of yearly wages to 'farm-servants', and, in other words, by pointing to the dominant hiring period of yearly labour in each region. It provides only a general picture of agricultural specialisation, of course, as there could still be much variation of agriculture in regions having either May or Michaelmas hiring fairs; and there

This account can be substantiated further by considering male and female wages in the Midland counties of Leicestershire, Nottinghamshire, and Rutland (Figure 1.15), and the counties of Buckinghamshire, Berkshire, Oxfordshire, and Hampshire (Figure 1.8). For most of these counties were significantly enclosed during the first phase of parliamentary enclosure, before 1790, when there was generally an intensification of pasture and livestock rearing, and reduction of arable farming, most particularly in Leicestershire, Nottinghamshire, and Rutland.[23] Given the changes in the west, one might therefore expect female wages here to keep up with male more than occurred to the south and east. The figures (notably Figure 1.15) show this to have been the case. There were comparatively slight inverse movements of male and female wages after about 1760, with again a tendency for female real wages to fall rather earlier than male. But over the long-term male and female wage trends were quite similar, with the eastern disparities less in evidence. Real wages fell in the later eighteenth century in both groups of counties, but most markedly in the more southern counties.[24]

We can briefly supplement the western wage data with seasonal distributions of unemployment for some border counties with Wales (Figure 1.16). The figure also gives the pastoral pattern for men and women together, which is similar to that found in these counties taken separately, although some indicate greater insecurity of employment around May.[25] The seasonally regular distribution of unemployment may be taken as a standard pattern for most of the region (with its common May hiring fairs), in the way that the eastern pattern is representative of the general seasonality of the south-eastern counties dealt with here. Preliminary research suggests that this western seasonality of employment would be that frequently found in the rural north-west and extreme north, and it helps to explain why yearly hiring survived longer in the west and north than in the east. Both the male and female patterns indicate that employment was spread comparatively evenly over the year. There are

were obvious religious factors affecting the seasonality of marriage. See E. A. Wrigley & R. S. Schofield, *The Population History of England, 1541–1871* (1981), pp. 302–4. The research of Ann Kussmaul on changes in regional marriage seasonality should significantly advance our understanding of shifts in agricultural specialisation. And see also D. B. Grigg, 'An index of regional change in English farming', *Trans. Inst. Brit. Geog.*, XXXVI (1965).

[23] For discussion of cropping changes in these counties, see chapter 4.

[24] Similar changes occurred in the seasonal distributions of female unemployment for the south Midlands as for the east. See chapter 4.

[25] Examinations for Monmouthshire have been supplemented by removal orders for heavily agricultural parishes, which provide very similar distributions.

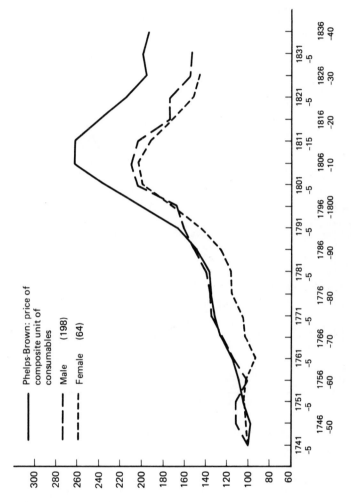

Figure 1.15 *Yearly wages*
Leics, Notts & Rut (1741–5 = 100)

suggestions of a distinct sexual division of labour in this period (men
are clearly more involved in the harvest), but it was one which (given
a relatively constant level of female activity during the year) seems to
be mutually complementary, and probably had favourable implications for familial income.[26]

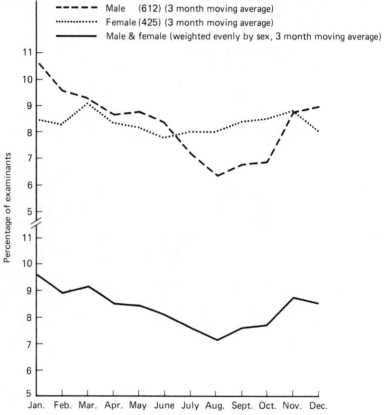

Figure 1.16 *Seasonal distribution of unemployment, 1780–1834*
Mon, Heref, Worcs, Salop & Glos

[26] The relation of these two eastern and western patterns to the regionality of
nineteenth-century agricultural unrest will be immediately apparent. There was
very little unrest in the western counties covered here, while the eastern counties,
and regions within them, which were most affected by the 'Bread or Blood' riots in
1816 and by 'Swing' unrest, were notably those with the most acute seasonality of
unemployment (Hobsbawm & Rudé, *Captain Swing*, p. 158). I will deal with this
issue, and with the relation of these patterns to the situation of cottage industry,
more extensively elsewhere.

For discussion of seasonal distributions in the south-west and Midlands, see
chapters 4 and 8. I will discuss distributions for northern and other Midland counties
in a later publication.

This comparison of east and west raises the possibility that female specialisation in livestock, dairying, and haymaking, while adversely affecting women in the east, may have been more favourable for them in the west, and so raises problems concerning the emergence, or perpetuation, of sexual attitudes. Without detracting from the importance and complications of this issue, we can simply note such problems here. For example, did the west see livestock and dairying increasingly become the preoccupation of men, as they became more markedly the area's dominant agricultural feature? The assumptions underpinning some feminist historiography might carry this implication, by seeing long-held attitudes of male dominance as being imposed on the changing economic structure of the area. Yet the rising female money wages of the west would question such a theoretical framework. Even by the early nineteenth century, the period immediately after the spring calving and dairying season in the west was not noticeably one of security for male employment, which was rather located most evidently during the harvest. The female work allocation seems to have been more closely aligned with the seasonality of pastoral specialisations, and perhaps the absence of a tight harvest time schedule made these better suited to women.

V

The contention that the eastern specialisation in grain was accompanied by a greater emphasis on male harvest labour can also be shown with reference to changing agricultural harvest technology in the east. The rising grain prices, and the changing or intensified economic rationalisation of the agricultural sector which accompanied them, brought a desire from tenant farmers to quicken the harvest and so catch the pre-harvest peak of prices. This was, of course, to be one of the motives behind the introduction of the threshing machine. It was also achieved by changes in hand-tool technology. It has been argued by E. J. T. Collins that the widespread supplanting of the sickle by the bagging hook and scythe, on a national level, occurred mainly after 1790. However, it also appears that for the southern region the innovations of heavier hand-tool technology can be dated before this. As Collins says:

The status quo was first threatened in the mid eighteenth century at about which time the practice of 'bagging' with the heavy hook began to replace hand reaping in the London area, Devon, and the English Marcher counties ... Yet by 1790 the impact of these innovations was confined to just a few districts of southern Britain. The corn scythe, which had become established in southern England in the medieval period, had by this late stage failed to penetrate much beyond the Humber.[27]

It seems clear that there was much regional variation in the adoption of heavier tools, with some southern areas experiencing their introduction from the mid-eighteenth century. We might expect that the south-eastern areas most strongly manifesting the grain-growing pattern of seasonal unemployment were those in which such changes took place relatively early. Given the sharp fluctuations of grain prices during the year, peaking immediately before the harvest, it was economically rational for the regions most dependent on grain to lead the way. In this connection, we can draw upon Michael Roberts' interesting discussion of harvest technology. With the surplus grain production of the early eighteenth century, concern with wastage became (he argued) less important, and the scythe was extended from its traditional use for barley, oats, peas, and beans to the harvesting of wheat and rye. Women never used the scythe, and so: 'as the male-dominated corn scythe became more popular the value of men's wages was enhanced and women had to start looking elsewhere for well-paid employment'.[28] This statement is exactly reflected in the figures for the changing sexual division of labour from the mid-eighteenth century, and is further substantiated by the inverse correlations of male and female wages. The chronology of the hand-tool innovations, and the regional specialisations of farming which underlay it, continues to be debated. But it seems likely that such innovations were an important cause of the changing sexual division of labour after about 1750, being accompanied by greater demand for male harvesters. But these factors must also be supplemented as explanations by the effects of male vulnerability to unemployment (an enabling factor for, and consequence of, cereal specialisation), which also excluded female competition; and perhaps

---

[27] Collins, 'Harvest technology', 456–7.

[28] Roberts, 'Sickles and scythes', 19. And see A. Young, *The Farmer's Kalendar; Containing the Business Necessary to be Performed on Various Kinds of Farms during Every Month of the Year* (1771, 1778 edn), pp. 231–9, for a detailed assessment of the contemporary debate on the advantages of mowing over reaping wheat – 'a subject that has been much discussed within a few years, and with great warmth'. In an earlier period, the harvest had been gathered in a few days, by very large numbers of male and female workers, rather than by a smaller group of skilled male scythe users, taking a couple of weeks. See for example, G. E. Evans, *The Farm and the Village* (1969), pp. 64–5, quoting Sir John Cullum and Langland; Brereton, *Practical Inquiry*, pp. 46–7. See also K. Thomas, 'Work and leisure in pre-industrial society', *Past and Present*, XXIX (1964), 52–3, on English bye-laws from the thirteenth century requiring *all* villagers (regardless of sex) to work in the harvest. This was re-enacted by the Statute of Artificers.

also by the employing motivations of farmers concerned with rising familial dependence on the poor rates. I shall return to these points later.

VI

As I am using a previously untested source, it seems appropriate now to consider what literary evidence there is to support the argument for an intensified sexual specialisation of agricultural work after the mid-eighteenth century; and to develop the suggestion that this specialisation brought with it a declining participation of women within the agricultural work force. The large pamphlet literature on eighteenth- and nineteenth-century poor relief, the Annals of Agriculture, and the County Surveys in the early nineteenth century are generally unhelpful, although all these sources frequently mention female unemployment. The major evidence presented in the unfortunately rather late Poor Law Report of 1834, in the subsequent Poor Law Reports, and in the 1843, 1867–8, and 1868–9 Reports on the Employment of Women and Children in Agriculture provide numerous indications of the increasingly insignificant role of female agricultural labour in this region. But the evidence usually fails to provide any background to the change, which could help identify its origins and causes. Hence historians have concerned themselves with the tail-end of the process, and have missed both its regional variations and long-term character.[29]

Nevertheless, if one approaches these reports with the views advanced earlier in mind, a great deal emerges which suggests that change in the sexual division of labour, and indeed, in the extent of female participation, had already taken place to a large degree, and that it cannot in consequence be seen as initially stemming from particular Victorian moral sentiments regarding the 'proper' roles of

[29] For the usual views on this question, see for example: I. Pinchbeck, *Women Workers and the Industrial Revolution, 1750–1850* (1930); G. E. Mingay, *Rural Life in Victorian England* (Glasgow, 1979), pp. 73, 217–18; E. Hostettler, 'Gourlay Steell and the sexual division of labour', *History Workshop*, IV (1977), 95–101; J. Kitteringham, 'Country work girls in nineteenth-century England', in R. Samuel (ed.), *Village Life and Labour* (1975), pp. 127–33; P. Horn, *Labouring Life in the Victorian Countryside* (Bristol, 1976), pp. 117, 125; J. D. Chambers & G. E. Mingay, *The Agricultural Revolution, 1750–1880* (1966, 1978 edn), p. 189. I suspect that the problem has been complicated by the immediate effects of the New Poor Law, which probably led to some resurgence of female and child labour to supplement falling familial income, resulting from the measures of 1834, but this should not obscure the long-term character of the change. On this immediate effect of the New Poor Law see, for example, Hasbach, *English Agricultural Labourer*, pp. 223–6; Pinchbeck, *Women Workers*, pp. 54–8, 67; Orwin & Felton, 'A century of wages', 241.

women. The strength of these by the 1860s cannot be doubted, and they are well represented in these reports. But they reflected the relative absence of female labour in this region by then, rather than being significantly instrumental in its decline.[30] As Thomas Lawrence of Childry (Berkshire), a labourer aged eighty-two, told the 1868–9 Commission: 'The women don't work so much as they used to, they don't employ them . . . my master employed as many as the whole parish does now, and so the farms ain't kept so clean now. The young men that are out of work won't go elsewhere to look for it.'[31] Two implications emerge from this statement: that even in Lawrence's younger days women were mainly engaged in 'cleaning' land for corn and then in weeding it (during the spring), and that male unemployment was a major factor excluding female labour. We shall return to this latter theme shortly.

What is striking about the earlier evidence of the 1843 Select Committee is the limited role women had when compared to the early eighteenth century, or the seventeenth century, when their work was very similar in its seasonality to that of men, and the differential between male and female wages was much less notable. There is abundant supportive evidence for a very wide range of female participation in agricultural tasks before 1750 in the south-east, when their work extended to reaping, loading and spreading dung, ploughing, threshing, thatching, following the harrow, sheep shearing, and even working as shepherdesses.[32] In other regions

---

[30] Here, for example, is an opinion cited by George Culley to the 1868–9 Commission:
   Farm labour is the certain ruin of the female character; they become bold, impudent, scandal-mongers, hardened against religion, careless of their homes and children, most untidy, given to drink, coarse-minded, debased, depravers of any virtuous girls who work with them, having no pride in their home or their children, and few home feelings. Their children are ragged and quite untaught, and a dirty home often drives the husband to the public house.
   Report on the Employment of Children, Young Persons, and Women in Agriculture, XIII (1868–9), p. 158.

[31] *Ibid.*, p. 619.

[32] See, for example, n. 28 above, and A. Clark, *Working Life of Women in the Seventeenth Century* (1919), pp. 57, 66–7, 73, 87; Pinchbeck, *Women Workers*, pp. 16–18, 55; Roberts, 'Sickles and scythes', 7, 17–20; C. Middleton, 'The sexual division of labour in feudal England', *New Left Review*, CXIII–CXIV (1979), 153, 160–1: 'arrangements were generally flexible and sexually non-exclusive, and there is evidence of women being engaged in most male tasks – such as reaping, binding, mowing, carrying corn, shearing sheep, thatching, and breaking stones for road maintenance . . . Women were hired to carry out virtually the whole gamut of agricultural routines . . . women's role in the reserve labour force of feudalism differed hardly at all from that of men – a strong indication that the housewife role was but weakly developed in the poorest strata'; P. Laslett, *The World We Have Lost* (1973), pp. 115–16 (quoting John Locke); J. Barrell, *The Dark Side of the Landscape* (Cambridge, 1980), pp. 50–1; J. Turner, *The Politics of Landscape* (Oxford, 1979), p. 177; E. Richards, 'Women in the

similar work continued more noticeably into the nineteenth century (particularly in parts of the north, where the 'bondage' system was practised), but there is almost nothing in the 1843 Report to suggest such a range of female participation for this district. In the area around Bury St Edmunds, for example, our earlier description of female work by this period is reinforced by being told that they work mainly in March, April, and May, at stone-picking, weeding and dropping corn, and in gleaning after the harvest in August. 'In other months they are generally unemployed.' They were not even employed significantly in haymaking in late May in this area.[33] Around Hadleigh 'out-door labour for women is confined to a little weeding of corn in spring; occasional labour in the hay-time; gleaning at harvest; and for children and young women, dropping wheat about Michaelmas'.[34] At Lavenham: 'Women are not much employed on the land on the whole, not more than four months in the year.'[35] And around Hunston it was 'the want of employment, and I may almost say complete idleness, during a great part of the year (particularly with women and girls), that increases the bastardy list, among other evils'.[36]

British economy since about 1700: an interpretation', *History*, LIX (1974), 337–57; Sir A. Fitzherbert, *Book of Husbandry* (1534), ed. by W. W. Skeat (1882), pp. 97–8; James Thomson, *The Seasons* (1744), Autumn, lines 151ff; B. H. Putnam, 'Northamptonshire wage assessments of 1560 and 1667', *Econ. Hist. Rev.*, I (1927), 133. And more generally, see also P. Laslett, 'Les Rôles des femmes dans l'histoire de la famille occidentale', in E. Sullerot (ed.), *Le Fait féminin* (Paris, 1977), pp. 447–65; E. Boserup, *Women's Role in Economic Development* (1970); J. W. Scott & L. A. Tilly, 'Women's work and the family in nineteenth-century Europe', *Comparative Studies in Society and History*, XVII (1975); A. Macfarlane, *The Origins of English Individualism* (Oxford, 1978), pp. 78–82, 91, 131–5; and especially B. Ankarloo, 'Agriculture and women's work: direction of change in the west, 1700–1900', *Jnl of Family History*, IV (1979), 114–15, 119: in Sweden 'the direction of change was towards a more pronounced preference for males in the agrarian labor force . . . Advanced areas . . . were moving in the direction of excluding women from the labor force as early as the end of the eighteenth century.' See also the interesting discussion by Hunt, *Regional Wage Variations*, pp. 121–3, where he argues that women worked most where male wages were highest. (Chapter 6 below covers similar long-term changes affecting the apprenticed trades.)

[33] Report on the Employment of Women and Children in Agriculture, XII (1843), p. 247.

[34] *Ibid.*, p. 247.

[35] *Ibid.*, p. 244.

[36] *Ibid.*, p. 234. If this is so, the argument may be of relevance to the problems of the eighteenth-century rise of illegitimacy, and changes in nuptiality and female marriage age, stressed by Wrigley & Schofield, *Population History of England*. One would expect the diminution of female employment to necessitate a younger female marriage age, and reduce both their ability and inclination to delay marriage. It seems probable that this occurred. See in particular M. Anderson, 'Marriage patterns in Victorian Britain: an analysis based on registration district data for England and Wales', *Jnl of Family History*, I (1976). He stresses the low proportion unmarried in East Anglia and the East Midlands in 1861; the effect of female

If we turn to the most valuable, and earliest, systematic evidence open to us – the answers to questions 11, 12, and 13 of the Poor Law Commission of 1832–4, on the extent of female agricultural labour, the same conclusion is strongly borne out. In Great Shelford in Cambridgeshire, for example, it was the case that 'We have no employment for women and children but haymaking and weeding'.[37] In Caddington (Bedfordshire) 'the women and children are rarely, if ever, employed in field labour'.[38] And 'Women are scarcely ever employed in agriculture', in Lidlington, also in Bedfordshire.[39] At Gestingthorpe (Essex) 'We have no employment for women.'[40] It was said of Kelveden (Essex) that 'The parish being entirely agricultural, and the number of labourers more than equal to the demand (about five Men, besides Boys, to the 100 acres) there is little employment for Women and Children.'[41] Once again, structural unemployment seemed to contribute to the diminution of female agricultural work. In Great Waltham, there was 'Scarcely any [employment for women or children]; a few are occasionally employed in picking stones off the land.'[42] At Thorpe le Soken, there was 'very little [female employment]. At particular seasons, as Spring and Autumn, some employment is afforded for Women and Children on the land.'[43] Or at Bassingbourne (Cambridgeshire) there was 'A little, only for a short time, in the Spring, in field work.'[44] As for the role of women in the harvest by this date, it was usually limited to the very short-term work of gleaning. This was so, for example, in Wisbech St Mary (Cambridgeshire): 'in Harvest a few are able to reap, but the major

employment in service as a major factor delaying marriage, where such employment persisted; and the influence of the sex ratio on marriage chances, such that where women considerably outnumbered men (i.e., 'less agricultural areas', because of female rural out-migration) they were marrying on average eighteen months later, and nearly twice as many would ultimately remain spinsters than in areas (such as East Anglia and the East Midlands) where this sex ratio was reversed. It can therefore be suggested that rural out-migration (because of the changes documented in this chapter) produced a rural sex ratio conducive to higher female marriage chances, leading to relatively early marriage and a high proportion of women marrying, with obvious consequences for fertility. This effect of female unemployment on marriage (via out-migration and the sex ratio) was compounded by the necessity of early marriage for women when they had so little ability to delay. Anderson comments that: 'as female employment increases, non-marriage and late marriage increases' (p. 69).

When one considers the growing attention being focussed by English demographers on the determinants of marriage, and the near universality of yearly hiring as a life-cycle stage before marriage in the early eighteenth-century agricultural sector, the importance of changes in this hiring system will be apparent. For further discussion of marriage age and nuptiality, see in particular chapters 2, 4, and 7 below.

[37] Poor Law Report, XXX (1834), p. 64. [38] *Ibid.*, p. 3. [39] *Ibid.*, p. 5.
[40] *Ibid.*, p. 175. [41] *Ibid.*, p. 180. [42] *Ibid.*, p. 188. [43] *Ibid.*, p. 190. [44] *Ibid.*, p. 49.

part who are not confined with a large family go gleaning'.[45] In Holy Trinity (Isle of Ely) it was said that 'Women's time in harvest is generally employed in gleaning.'[46] There were many other statements to this effect throughout the counties which concern us. Examples include Clavering, in Essex ('Not any except harvest gleaning'),[47] Standen Massey, in Essex ('But little, except stone and twitch picking, haymaking, and gleaning in harvest time'),[48] Witham, in Essex ('They glean corn after the harvest, but they do nothing in it'),[49] Welwyn, in Hertfordshire ('The women of Hertfordshire seldom work at corn harvest'),[50] and All Saints, in Suffolk ('Women and Children are not much employed, either in Summer or Winter, or in Harvest, except gleaning').[51]

An analysis of all the parishes returning answers to the Poor Law Commission (in the counties covered by my seasonal unemployment figures) provides a wider picture of the agricultural events mentioned most frequently as involving female participation. The female occupation most commonly reported was that of spring weeding, essentially of corn, with ninety-eight parishes mentioning this. It was clearly the main factor making for the high security of female spring employment found in the nineteenth-century patterns of Figure 1.2. Haymaking was noted by seventy-three parishes, gleaning by fifty-eight parishes, stone-picking by forty-three parishes, 'the harvest' (which could of course mean gleaning only) by thirty-three parishes, reaping by nineteen parishes, wheat planting (in October) by fifteen parishes, and the pulling and topping of turnips by seven parishes.[52]

[45] *Ibid.*, p. 72.   [46] *Ibid.*, p. 67.   [47] *Ibid.*, p. 171.   [48] *Ibid.*, p. 188.
[49] *Ibid.*, p. 190.   [50] *Ibid.*, p. 226.   [51] *Ibid.*, p. 447.
[52] The association of women with the root crop is unexpectedly slight, but this was nevertheless an additional aspect of their spring work. The gang system in particular grew up in the mid-1820s because of demand for labour essentially for turnip husbandry and the spring weeding of corn in newly drained and enclosed Fen parishes, and in closed parishes. That the system developed at all was, we should note, partly attributable to the acute female and child unemployment of the surrounding parishes. The relatively slight appearance of female labour in connection with turnip husbandry in the 1834 Report may be associated with the very regional incidence of the gang system at this time – limited to the immediate parishes around Castle Acre, and a few other Fen parishes. The system had expanded into parts of surrounding counties where similar conditions obtained by the time of the reports of the 1860s, but the controversy it aroused appears to have been significantly disproportionate to its extent, particularly in the 1830s and 1840s. It was reported in the 1843 Report, for example, that: 'I am rejoiced to find my own county, Suffolk, free from such unhappy proceedings as those around Castle Acre. I had never heard of it, nor can I find any one in this neighbourhood that has; and I feel assured that Norfolk landowners and farmers, as a body, are not aware of it' (p. 226). And we should note also the young age of gang labour: 'There are but few grown-up women, and those of the worst characters, who join the gangs' (*ibid.*, p. 279). Outside the gang parishes the employment of women in turnip husbandry

Bean-setting was mentioned by four, 'burning' by four, and all other agricultural tasks by only two or less parishes.

David Davies, in the *Case of the Labourers in Husbandry* (1795) – among the most famous contemporary publications on rural poverty, and probably the most reliable – argued that the two most needed remedial measures were an increase of wages to counteract falling real wages, and a revival of employment for women. Previously, he argued, there had been many opportunities for women and children to work, 'whereas now, few of *these* are constantly employed ... so that almost the whole burden of providing for their families rests upon the *men*' (his italics). The result had been a fall in familial income, and 'the consequence is universally felt in the increased number of the dependent poor'. The measures, he continued, 'which appear most necessary to be immediately adopted, are the two following; viz. that of *raising wages*, and that of *providing employment for women and girls*. These two measures should go together' (his italics).[53]

Thus, as Figure 1.2 suggested, female labour in the east by the 1830s had become heavily limited to the spring work of weeding corn, and to haymaking, with a subsidiary involvement in the harvest as gatherers and tyers, and particularly as gleaners. There is little evidence in government reports which would lead us to question the long-term pattern and timing of change outlined earlier from the settlement material, and much also to support the contention, made with reference to female wages, that the concentration of women on a few specific tasks was accompanied by a tendency for them to be excluded from a traditionally fuller and more sexually equal participation in agriculture. This development was a Victorian phenomenon only in the sense that the Victorian period saw the completion of the process. It cannot be held to have been primarily a product of Victorian morality and middle-class assumptions regarding the roles of women. It is indeed more tempting to see the economic rationality

---

does not seem to have been that marked, and typical parochial comments on female employment at this were: 'There is very little turniping here' (*ibid.*, p. 252), or 'not much done in this district' (*ibid.*, pp. 227–8).

[53] Davies, *Case of the Labourers*, pp. 65–7, 69–74, 87ff, 124–5, 156ff. Significantly, he also stressed the need for fuller employment to be provided during the winter. Many poor law measures, such as the roundsman system or labour rate, were aimed only to help male labourers, and either assumed female unemployment or restricted it further. (Parish lists made up of labour to be employed would be of men.) And such measures certainly accentuated sexual disparities of income. See, for example, the Labour Rate Act, 2 & 3 Will. IV c. 96; Brereton, *Practical Inquiry*, pp. 75–90; Rose, 'The allowance system under the New Poor Law', 619–21.

of this sexual differentiation as lying behind these attitudes and morality.[54]

VII

Some concluding remarks can now be made on the long-term changes I have outlined. The implications of the eastern patterns of seasonal unemployment for the standard of living debate lie in the increased acuteness of the male pattern in 1815–34, though we may note that their general pattern continued much the same over the whole period.[55] The acuteness of this early nineteenth-century pat-

[54] One correspondent to the Society for Bettering the Condition of the Poor (III, 1806, pp. 75–7), complained of the lack of female agricultural employment, of women becoming 'a burthen upon the father of the family, and in many cases upon the parish', and continued: 'The wife is no longer able to contribute her share towards the weekly expenses ... In a kind of despondency she sits down, unable to contribute anything to the general fund of the family, and conscious of rendering no other service to her husband, except that of the mere care of his family.'

The occupational censuses are, of course, too late to document these changes being argued for, but the earliest (1841) fully supports them. Women in the eastern counties included in Figures 1.1 and 1.2 constituted only 2.9 per cent of the total agricultural labour force of those counties (they would be only 2.2 per cent if one discounted Cambridgeshire and Berkshire). In Bedfordshire they were as low as 0.6 per cent by this date. This is, we should note, *despite* the fact that the occupational census was taken in the months of March and April, which we noted as having the highest employment security for women in the east during the year. In the western counties of Monmouthshire, Herefordshire, Worcestershire, Wiltshire, and Gloucestershire, by contrast, women constituted 9.1 per cent of the total agricultural labour force in 1841, supporting the suggestion that such a region saw greater continuity and involvement of women in agriculture than the east. We should also note that the census months coincided with the period of greatest female *insecurity* of employment in the west, and that the regional disparity of female participation has been minimised to the maximum possible extent by the choice of months in which the census was taken. Such greater involvement also seems possible for the south-west, as in Dorset and Devon in the late eighteenth and early nineteenth centuries male and female patterns of unemployment were almost identical, in a way certainly not found in the east (see chapter 8). And literary evidence is available for this region in the early nineteenth century suggesting a much wider range of female work than existed in the later nineteenth century, when female work had become more strictly limited to dairying activities (chapter 8).

While these regional differences certainly existed, they should not be over-stressed, as women in England as a whole only made up 3.9 per cent of the agricultural labour force in 1841 (4.6 per cent if one excludes the eastern counties treated here); suggesting that the argument for significant diminution of female labour having already taken place by the early nineteenth century has a wider applicability than just to the eastern counties, although it seems that in this region it had been earliest and most extreme. Comparable research under way on the north and Midlands will soon permit the pattern of rural change elsewhere to be outlined in detail.

[55] The growing seasonal acuteness of unemployment can also be shown by using overseers' accounts. See chapters 2 and 4.

tern questions the capacity of enclosure and the new, improved, agricultural practices to provide greater and more regular employment throughout the year for the growing male labour force, particularly in seasons previously characterised by high employment insecurity.[56] Because of a tendency under the New Poor Law for there to be a greater reluctance to apply for relief, the pattern after 1835 is not readily comparable to those which preceded it. The greater availability of piecework in the nineteenth century may have lessened the problem of winter unemployment, or prevented any further intensification of it. Alternatively, such piecework may have represented a more calculating use of labour, and may have replaced more permanent forms of employment. The pattern for the later nineteenth century may appear less extreme only because of the changes in poor law administration of 1834, and the well documented hostile attitudes of the poor to those changes.[57]

That the nineteenth-century male patterns were not more acute was partly a result of the eighteenth-century fall-off of female employment, which I have suggested accompanied the sexual specialisation of agricultural work. Had women continued with their pre-industrial agricultural involvement, male employment would probably have become even more seasonally precarious. In assessing implications for *familial* income (a more important consideration for the 'standard of living' than male wage trends alone), one should see the male

---

[56] For the influential contrary view, see Chambers, 'Enclosure and labour supply'. For the effects of enclosure, see chapter 4.

[57] A. Digby, *Pauper Palaces* (1978), ch. 12; U. Henriques, 'How cruel was the Victorian poor law?', *Hist. Jnl.* XI (1968); and chapter 3 below. See also Collins, 'Diffusion of the threshing machine', 28, on changes in winter unemployment after 1835. He suggests that this probably diminished, using the point that employers now had greater motivation to employ in the winter because of the high costs of maintaining families in the workhouse; one of the arguments made at the time in defence of the New Poor Law. Without developing the point, one should recall, however, that there was some continuity of out-relief (mainly to the married) after 1835, partly for this reason, which may have made such employing motivations unnecessary; that statements to this effect were made by defenders of the New Poor Law in a period of intense controversy, and that many contrary opinions could be juxtaposed against them; and that the extreme animosity of the poor to the new law makes relief figures after 1835 a dubious comparative index of actual improvement or deterioration in winter provision of employment. And if the law did indeed force tenant farmers to employ surplus labour during the winter on a significant scale, its widespread popularity among them might in retrospect seem rather odd. The view that the law had increased winter employment in this way was put to Rev. Huxtable by the 1847 S.C. on Settlement and Poor Removal (XI, p. 561). He was then asked: 'Does that accord with your experience?' He replied: 'No, certainly not.' Nevertheless, between about 1850 and the later 1870s, at any rate, it seems almost certain that employment provision improved; and there may also have been improvement in the later 1830s, although I doubt that this was a direct effect of the law.

pattern in relation to the deterioration of employment possibilities for women which accompanied and helped determine it.[58] When one considers in conjunction with this the falling male real wages of the period after about 1780, through to the New Poor Law (and arguably thereafter, as an effect of that law),[59] and the even more extreme long-term depression of female real wages from about 1760, the effects on familial income seem clear – effects compounded of course by the rising demographic dependency ratio: the fertility changes of the period produced much larger family sizes. Female labour was not diverted elsewhere in the east. Against the widespread decline of cottage industry in the region after the Napoleonic Wars,[60] and the reduced role of women in many apprenticed trades, and in family-based artisan production,[61] one can mainly set work in the straw-plait industry in parts of Bedfordshire, Buckinghamshire, and Hertford-shire, and in the silk mills of some Essex parishes. Domestic service, especially in London, for the unmarried only, and some other more poorly paid London occupations (such as dressmaking and millinery, or 'slop-shop' tailoring), were other female economic options open by the early nineteenth century.[62] And demand for domestic servants in

[58] It is almost certain that changes in single women's employment and wages also affected married women – single and married women's work in agriculture was very similar, as descriptions in the government reports make clear.

[59] See chapter 3.

[60] Pinchbeck, *Women Workers*, pp. 210–39. Of course, William Cobbett had his own forthright views on the loss of cottage-industrial employment: 'One of the great misfortunes of England at this day is, that the land has had taken away from it those employments for its women and children which were so necessary to the well-being of the agricultural labourer. The spinning, the carding, the reeling, the knitting; these have been all taken away . . . But let the landholder mark how the change has operated to produce his ruin. He must have the labouring MAN and the labouring BOY; but, alas! he cannot have these, without having the man's wife and the boy's mother, and little sisters and brothers. Even Nature herself says, that he shall have the wife and little children, or that he shall not have the man and the boy. But the Lords of the Loom, the crabbed-voiced, hard-favoured, hard-hearted, puffed-up, insolent, savage and bloody wretches of the North have, assisted by a blind and greedy Government, taken all the employment away from the agricultural women and children.' See his *Cottage Economy* (1822, Oxford, 1979 edn), pp. 180–1.

[61] See chapter 6.

[62] Prostitution was another. London, the main destination for female out-migrants from these eastern counties, had 80,000 to 120,000 'prostitutes' by the mid-nineteenth century. R. Pearsall, *The Worm in the Bud: The World of Victorian Sexuality* (1972), p. 313. William Cobbett complained in 1830 of the rise of illegitimacy and of growing numbers of prostitutes in southern country villages. See his *Advice to Young Men*, p. 226. The Victorian prostitution problem is of course a major issue in its own right, and I have not the space to discuss it here. But its historiography might usefully take more account of changes in women's work. See S. Marcus, *The Other Victorians* (1966); F. Henriques, *The Immoral Tradition: Prostitution and Society* (1965); Pearsall, *Worm in the Bud*; B. Harrison, 'Underneath the Victorians', *Victorian Studies*,

the early nineteenth century probably helped hold up female wages then. But these south-eastern counties, besides paying notoriously low agricultural wages, lacked the developing sectors providing alternative female employment and the steady or rising female real wages which characterised other regions in the west or north.

A wide range of factors was responsible for the extremity of the early nineteenth-century pattern of male unemployment, and for the fall in real wages, which came in marked contrast to the trends for male real wages in the period between 1740 and about 1780. Such factors would certainly include the eastern specialisation in grain, demographic pressure and its associated structural unemployment, the agricultural depression caused by falling prices after 1813, and perhaps a failure of farming profits to rise commensurate with rents after enclosure. And as we shall see elsewhere, enclosure was a major factor in parishes enclosed by act. Real wages may also have been hit by a possible shift back to pasture when prices fell in the early nineteenth century. While it is not clear how extensive such a reversion was, it would certainly have reduced general demand for a labour force by now over-abundant even for the intensive, but short-term, requirements of cereal production. This pessimistic picture of the early nineteenth-century south-eastern agricultural sector could be amply supported by evidence from parliamentary or newspaper enquiries; by the evidence of Speenhamland and the wide range, and short-term variability, of alternative poor relief measures;[63] by the changing depiction of the agricultural labourer in the poetry and painting of the eighteenth and early nineteenth centuries;[64] by the rising poor rates of the later eighteenth century, and their very high level during the high price years, after the Napoleonic Wars, and in the later 1820s; by changes in hiring

X (1967); J. R. & D. J. Walkowitz, '"We are not beasts of the field": prostitution and the poor in Plymouth and Southampton under the Contagious Diseases Act', in M. Hartman & L. W. Banner (eds.), *Clio's Consciousness Raised* (New York, 1974); F. Finnegan, *Poverty and Prostitution: A Study of Victorian Prostitution in York* (Cambridge, 1979). And see the following contemporary accounts: M. Ryan, *Prostitution in London with a Comparative View of that of Paris and New York* (1839); W. Tait, *An Enquiry into the Extent, Causes, and Consequences of Prostitution in Edinburgh* (Edinburgh, 1840); R. Wardlaw, *Lectures on Female Prostitution: its nature, extent, effects, guilt, causes, and remedy* (Glasgow, 1842); W. Logan, *An Exposure, from Personal Observation, of Female Prostitution in London, Leeds and Rochdale, and especially in the City of Glasgow* (Glasgow, 1843); J. B. Talbot, *The Miseries of Prostitution* (1844); W. Acton, *Prostitution considered in its Moral, Social and Sanitary Aspects, in London and other large Cities* (1857); T. C. Newby, *Our Plague Spot* (1859); W. Logan, *The Great Social Evil* (1871).

[63] See for example, Poynter, *Society and Pauperism*; Emmison, 'Relief of the poor at Eaton Socon'; E. M. Hampson, *The Treatment of Poverty in Cambridgeshire, 1597–1834* (Cambridge, 1934).

[64] See the inspired argument of Barrell, *Dark Side of the Landscape*.

practices, and the growing difficulty in gaining settlements as employers increasingly hired for periods a few days under the full year;[65] by the causes and consequences of the decline of apprenticeship in the south-east, outside London, after 1750;[66] and by the well documented evidence of continual agrarian unrest from 1795 through to 'Swing', and thereafter. All were witnesses to the problem of unemployment.[67] Lack of employment provision may, in the period after 1850, have been the major factor behind outward mobility from the land,[68] but an almost opposite situation may have obtained in the early nineteenth century, when lack of agricultural capital, a reluctance of rents to fall commensurate with prices, and structural unemployment produced widespread periodical reliance on a still highly localised settlement and poor relief system, which tended to hinder outward mobility in the east. This set up a depressing circularity of cause and effect which was broken only with the mid-century revival of agricultural profitability.[69]

As was suggested earlier, the sexual specialisation of work in the east is only partly to be explained as a consequence of the region's expansion of grain production, bringing a more extensive use, by employers, of male harvest labour and heavier technology. Male vulnerability to periodical unemployment, an associated feature of cereal production, may also have produced measures, originating from within the labour force, to reduce female competition.[70] We have noted literary indications which suggest this, and while the scythe may have been a major excluding factor in relation to the harvest, male structural unemployment probably led to pressure against women working in other tasks, such as ploughing, dung-spreading,

---

[65] See chapter 2.

[66] See chapter 5.

[67] And see Peacock, *Bread or Blood*; Hobsbawm & Rudé, *Captain Swing*; J. P. D. Dunbabin, *Rural Discontent in Nineteenth-Century Britain* (1974). For supportive discussion of the standard of living in this area, see: Mills, 'Quality of life in Melbourn, Cambridgeshire'; and Richardson, 'Agricultural labourers' standard of living in Kent'.

[68] J. Saville, *Rural Depopulation in England and Wales, 1851–1951*, (1957).

[69] For an interesting contrary argument to this last statement, see J. P. Huzel, 'The demographic impact of the Old Poor Law: more reflexions on Malthus', *Econ. Hist. Rev.*, XXXIII (1980). Huzel argues, for rural parishes in Kent, that high poor rates were positively correlated with out-migration. It is possible, however, that he has picked the county where one would most expect such a finding – given the immediate proximity of the south London labour market, and the well established links between this and Kent, via the migration routes through north Kent. For a discussion of this, and the way it affected wages in south London and Kent, see E. J. Hobsbawm, 'The nineteenth-century London labour market', in R. Glass (ed.), *London: Aspects of Change*, ed. by the Centre of Urban Studies (1964).

[70] For similar developments in the artisan trades, see chapter 6.

or threshing. Such unemployment was increasingly in evidence after 1760, as the well documented rising parish poor rates would suggest. Employers may have cooperated in this, and may have been inclined to limit employment to men to guard against familial dependence on the poor rates. No doubt an effect of the resulting decline of female participation was to soften the potential vulnerability of men to unemployment and to the experience of falling real wages, but it did so at the expense of real familial income.[71]

One must also consider the possibility that a decline of a pre-industrial 'family economy' may have contributed to the changes analysed – by which term I mean the synonymity of home and work place for husband and wife. In the early eighteenth century, access to the commons, a greater prevalence of owner-occupiers and small tenants, and less dependence on weekly wage labour away from the home place, may have laid the groundwork for a more equal sexual division of labour than that which became increasingly apparent after 1760. The argument for the east has, indeed, suggested that the model of the 'pre-industrial family economy', with more equally shared sex roles, may have been a real feature of the period from 1690 to the mid-eighteenth century. While the early eighteenth century certainly already had a significant agricultural proletariat, it was probably the case that the decline then of both small tenants and owner-occupiers reduced the potential for a wide participation of women within the family economy.[72] Such a development may also have brought a re-assessment of the roles of women within the wage-dependent labour force. Certainly such a decline of a 'family economy' form of production made men more vulnerable to the effects of unemployment; and in this sense the decline, with its associated separation of male place of work and home place, may have limited the possibilities for fuller female participation at the same time as its closely related effect on employment security produced pressures against female competition from the male labour force itself. But at this point it seems premature to develop more fully

[71] This argument concentrates on the probable significance of sexual divisions of labour, and male and female wage trends, for real familial income. The issue has another equally important but more problematical dimension in relation to the standard of living: the qualitative assessment of how these changes affecting familial relations, and earlier forms of production based more on the family unit, were subjectively experienced by the poor themselves. This can await later discussion.

[72] In this respect, the diminution of female agricultural participation could be dated back to the mid- or late seventeenth century, rather than only to the mid-eighteenth century. There is a wide historiography on these landownership changes, but see the bibliography in G. E. Mingay, *Enclosure and the Small Farmer in the Age of the Industrial Revolution* (1968); and chapter 4 below.

this line of explanation, and its significance for the history of the family. Insofar as the seasonal unemployment figures relate mostly to partially or wholly wage-dependent labour, rather than to families of owner-occupiers, it would have to be demonstrated that female work in the family economy created a social acceptance of similar work roles for more wage-dependent women, before an argument for a relatively shared sexual division of labour being based on the family economy could become fully convincing. This may depend on an assessment of the degree to which owner-occupier families were partially dependent on wage labour, and such an assessment is not currently accessible. Neither are we yet in a position to be entirely certain that a larger degree of sexually shared labour was a common characteristic of the 'pre-industrial' period. While a greater predominance of family-economy production earlier would suggest this, it may also have been to some extent an associated feature of population stagnation.[73] Earlier periods, as, for example, the late sixteenth and early seventeenth centuries, may have witnessed limited changes in the sexual division of labour parallel to those discussed here, because of demographic influences on the labour market.

The divergence of the female pattern of seasonal unemployment away from that of men after the mid-eighteenth century, to a concentration of work during a less labour-intensive period of the year, with low labour costs, and the associated long-term decline of female wages, implies a fall-off from their earlier participation rates, and a decline of their annual earning capacity. This seems well supported by early nineteenth-century literary evidence for the region. It is also likely that these changes brought an associated decline of women as a percentage of the total labour force, although one can only deduce this from the evidence provided, which cannot directly confront this more intangible problem. The definition of a 'female agricultural work force' in a period and region so characterised by seasonal fluctuations in labour demand is in any case problematic; and it may be unrealistic to pose the discussion in these terms, and of greater value to limit generalisation to the more certain effects on familial income of the changes analysed. We might, however, recall Eric Richards' argument in this context that: 'in the pre-industrial framework women were absorbed in a broad range of activity which was subsequently narrowed by the structural changes associated with the Industrial Revolution'.[74] The progressive domina-

---

[73] For strong suggestions that we are dealing with change from the 'pre-industrial' pattern, see all the references in n. 32 above.
[74] See his excellent discussion, 'Women in the British economy', 347.

tion of the economy by men, which he stressed, seems reinforced by the eastern evidence, although it is doubtful if this was so marked in the pastoral west. The availability of relatively highly paid agricultural and alternative female employment in many areas of the north, coupled with the much greater continuity of northern agricultural employment practices (in particular, the 'bondage system', and yearly hiring[75]), and the relative absence of structural and acute seasonal unemployment, make it likely that these regions witnessed more prolonged and fuller female economic participation and greater buoyancy of real familial income than in the south and east.[76]

One might take this point further and emphasise the regional variety of male and female wage trends, patterns of unemployment, and differences in the sexual division of labour. Such diversity could be demonstrated more extensively by incorporating material for northern or south-western regions lying outside the groups of counties I have considered. Even if one takes only the southern agricultural sector, seasonal distributions of male unemployment existed (for example, in Sussex, or in parts of the south-west) which are unlike the dominant patterns contrasted here. And this is to say nothing of the different and varying patterns of unemployment experienced by men and women in the apprenticed trades in the south-east, or of how the decline of apprenticeship affected these. The same diversity is clearly apparent in rural and other wage trends. To a limited extent this has been shown by a few excellent regional studies of the standard of living. But it would be dubious to suppose

[75] See for example, Dunbabin, *Rural Discontent*, chs. 6 and 11.

[76] Compare the interesting discussion by T. M. Devine, 'Social stability and agrarian change in the eastern lowlands of Scotland, 1810–1840', *Social History*, III (1978), 335: 'The social effects of agrarian change in a mixed-farming region were almost the reverse of those in a specialist cereal zone.' A similar point is constantly made by W. Cobbett, *Rural Rides* (1830, Harmondsworth, 1967 edn), pp. 81, 206, 215, 258: 'Invariably have I observed . . . the more purely a corn country, the more miserable the labourers.'

We may note, with reference to the related question of the location and continuity of the home market, that this material points to unexpected buoyancy of male and female demand in the south-eastern agricultural sector before about 1770 (most apparent in the rising male real wages after 1740, and in the evidence of fuller female participation and relatively low sexual wage differentials before the later eighteenth century); but for there then to have been a collapse of that demand in the south-east outside London (although not of female demand in the west), suggesting that the continued course of industrialisation was increasingly dependent upon exports, and the northern and middle-class market. I hope soon to develop this further, partly on the basis of more regionally disparate wage material also covering the north, and in more class-specific detail. For the role of female demand, see N. McKendrick, 'Home demand and economic growth: a new view of the role of women and children in the Industrial Revolution', in his (ed.) *Historical Perspectives. Studies in English Thought and Society in Honour of J. H. Plumb* (1974). And on the important role of farm-servant spending on marriage, see Hajnal, 'European marriage patterns', 132.

that the wage data currently available for the eighteenth and nineteenth centuries (which lack *any* indicators of unemployment), is anything other than highly localised and sparse, and barely hints at the regional diversity which existed. That diversity becomes all the more complex when one takes into account the regionality and changes of seasonal unemployment and the sexual division of labour, with their implications for familial income. It may be the case that attempts to generalise discussion of the standard of living, or of the extent and continuity of the home market, are as yet premature, and that the immediate aim of research should be to delineate much more sharply the regional differences and changes of the period. When this is more adequately achieved it is possible that the resulting appreciation of a wide variety of regional and occupational experience may reduce the importance of drawing conclusions at a national level; and one hopes then for a much more accurate and specific understanding of the local economic, demographic, and social processes involved, of their interrelation with cultural attitudes, and for a sensitive understanding of how they affected the labouring classes.

The problems of structural unemployment and cereal specialisation in the east have pointed my discussion primarily to the inadequacy of demand for labour. The surplus population (especially female) of the region has made a consideration of labour supply relatively unimportant. However, the significance of the changes in female employment may also bear directly on the question of provision of labour for cottage industry (as indeed may the two regional employment seasonalities I have contrasted). In the eastern counties covered here one thinks particularly of lace and straw-plait. The way the agricultural changes affecting women provided a labour force for such activities will be readily apparent, and it may also be the case that the attractiveness of such industries in the mid- and late eighteenth century contributed to the agricultural division of labour. But one can only stress the short-term significance of this in the east, given the decline of most cottage industries after 1815. The decline of female spinning in particular, probably most marked after 1800, and much commented on in early nineteenth-century government reports for the region, may have aggravated female unemployment and depressed familial income. The importance of these changes for the provision of domestic servants may be especially noted, and I would have no quarrel with the characterisation of nineteenth-century domestic service (in the south-east) as a form of 'disguised underemployment'.[77]

<hr>

[77] Richards, 'Women in the British economy', 348.

Finally, a main theme of this chapter can be re-emphasised: the historical determinants of women's economic and domestic roles would appear to be located primarily in seemingly autonomous changes in the structure of the economy, rather than in shifts of social attitudes. Moral sentiments antagonistic to female labour in the nineteenth century may have reinforced the pattern of change described here, and contributed to the process begun in the mid-eighteenth century. But insofar as they cannot readily be dated from before 1800, at the very earliest, their significance seems heavily undercut by the evidence that the major sexual division of labour began at least fifty years before such 'middle-class' attitudes towards the roles of women can have had influence. Insofar as economic change and its accompanying motivations alone probably began that process in the south-east, there is a need to re-evaluate the origins and effects of Victorian attitudes to femininity. This would reveal with greater clarity their causal dependency on, and compatibility with, changes in the economic structure, particularly in relation to the factors acting on male employment, and would attempt a fuller understanding of their origins in the poorly documented and elusive eighteenth-century background. Such an exercise would also contribute to a fuller and more instructive understanding of the formation and relativity of social attitudes to concrete, but changing, social and economic environments.

2

Social relations – the decline of service

I

> That good old fame the farmers earned of yore,
> That made as equals, not as slaves, the poor,
> That good old fame did in two sparks expire –
> A shooting coxcomb and a hunting squire;
> And their old mansions that were dignified
> With things far better than the pomp of pride;
> At whose oak table, that was plainly spread,
> Each guest was welcomed and the poor were fed,
> Where master, son, and serving-man and clown
> Without distinction daily sat them down,
> Where the bright rows of pewter by the wall
> Served all the pomp of kitchen or of hall –
> These all have vanished like a dream of good;
> And the slim things that rise where once they stood
> Are built by those whose clownish taste aspires
> To hate their farms and ape the country squires.[1]

The labouring Northamptonshire poet John Clare wrote 'The Parish: A Satire' between 1820 and 1824, and was only one among many poets and writers who lamented the end of an older social order in such terms. Crabbe, Cobbett, Goldsmith, Elliott, John Robinson, Robert Bloomfield, Thomas Batchelor, William Holloway, and others could be quoted to similar effect. Probably there was nostalgia in Clare's description, but we need to respect the mood in which he wrote:

This poem was begun & finished under the pressure of heavy distress with embittered feeling under a state of anxiety & oppression almost amounting to slavery – when the prosperity of one class was founded on the adversity and distress of the other – The haughty demand by the master to his labourer was

---

[1] John Clare, *John Clare, Selected Poems*, ed. by J. W. & A. Tibble (1979), p. 140.

work for the little I chuse to alow you & go to the parish for the rest – or starve – to decline working under such advantages was next to offending a magistrate & no oppertunity was lost in marking the insult by some unqualified oppression.[2]

I want in this and the next chapter to turn to the social reality behind such statements, and consider reasons for the deterioration of social relations in southern agriculture. The matter is crucial for an understanding of living standards. To the poor themselves, as to the poets of labouring status, it was of paramount importance alongside considerations directly related to their material standard of life. And the two matters were closely inter-connected, making the issue of social relations one of obvious relevance. The conditions of material comfort were of course closely determined by the relations of employment. The changing details of social relationships (defined here as those of employment or training, of farmer to farm-servant or labourer) are equally worthy of attention both for their qualitative importance to the poor themselves, and because they help us to understand the changing conditions of employment and wage payment.

In the literature of the period, the sentiments expressed by Clare were frequently focussed on the decline of farm service, which was felt to have aggravated social relations. According to various authors it contributed to conditions of intensified unemployment and falling real wages; a falling marriage age and wayward sexual behaviour; growing crime; vagrancy; an alienation of master and employed and a segregation of class interest and cultures; rising pauperism and poor rates; Speenhamland; or the agrarian unrest of the early nineteenth century culminating in 'Swing' and later incendiarism. In fact, there were few agrarian changes in the early nineteenth century which an imaginative contemporary did not adduce (sometimes in a far-fetched manner) to the decline of service.

Most noticeably, this decline gave rise to descriptions of an earlier social proximity under 'living-in' hiring. Contemporary descriptions shared Clare's sense of loss, although sometimes they lacked his intensity of feeling. Another author who made frequent, and indignant, statements on this was William Cobbett. As in most accounts, his descriptions of the 'living-in' system stressed the common elements of a shared table with members of the farmer's family eating alongside farm-servants, and the high standard of living enjoyed by the latter as a consequence. There would seem to be little 'class'

---

[2] *Ibid.*, p. 140. I have used the version cited from the original manuscript, in R. Sales, *English Literature in History, 1780–1830. Pastoral and Politics* (1983), p. 100.

antagonism inherent in this arrangement, and one is drawn to Bloomfield's language of 'rank to rank . . . as man to man'[3] when reading Cobbett:

Everything about this farmhouse was formerly the scene of *plain manners* and *plentiful living.* Oak clothes-chests, oak bed-steads, oak chests of drawers, and oak tables to eat on, long, strong, and well supplied with joint stools. Some of the things were hundreds of years old. But all appeared to be in a state of decay and nearly of *disuse.* There appeared to have been hardly any *family* in that house, where formerly there were, in all probability, from ten to fifteen men, boys and maids: and, which was the worse of all, there was a *parlour!* Aye, and a *carpet* and *bell-pull* too! . . . and there was the mahogany table, and the fine chairs, and the fine glass . . . And, there were the decanters, the glasses, the 'dinner-set' of crockery ware, and all just in the true stock-jobber style . . . This Squire Charington's father used, I dare say, to sit at the head of the oak table with his men, say grace to them, and cut up the meat and the pudding. He might take a cup of *strong beer* to himself, when they had none; but, that was pretty nearly all the difference in their manner of living. So that *all* lived well. But, the 'Squire had many *wine-decanters* and *wine-glasses* and a *'dinner-set',* and a *breakfast-set',* and *'desert knives';* and these evidently imply carryings on and a consumption that must of necessity have robbed the long oak table if it had remained fully tenanted. That long table could not share in the work of the decanters and the dinner set. Therefore, it became almost untenanted; the labourers retreated to hovels, called cottages; and, instead of board and lodging, they got money; so little of it as to enable the employer to drink wine; but, then, that he might not reduce them to *quite starvation,* they were enabled to come to him, in the *king's name,* and demand food as *paupers* [his italics].[4]

In this account, the change seems fundamental in its effect on social relationships. But despite its obvious importance to contemporaries, historians have surprisingly neglected farm service, and little is known of its decline.[5] I want here to present a more precise chronology for the latter, and consider the causes, before assessing its effect on social relations.

Discussion of this decline became widespread from the 1820s. It was vague over when and why, but can be found extensively in pamphlets and parliamentary reports on agriculture, the poor laws, settlement, vagrancy, and crime. As with Cobbett, accounts usually

---

[3] R. Bloomfield, *The Farmer's Boy* (1800, Lavenham 1971 edn), p. 88.
[4] W. Cobbett, *Rural Rides* (1830, Harmondsworth, 1975 edn), p. 228.
[5] The exception to this has been A. Kussmaul, *Servants in Husbandry in Early Modern England* (Cambridge, 1981). Further related discussion can be found in P. Laslett, *Family Life and Illicit Love in Earlier Generations* (Cambridge, 1977), chs. 1 & 2; R. S. Schofield, 'Age-specific mobility in an eighteenth-century rural English parish', *Annales de démographic historique* (1970); P. Laslett & R. Wall (eds), *Household and Family in Past Time* (Cambridge, 1972), chs. 1, 4, & 5. The subject has received very scanty discussion in major publications covering rural history by Hasbach, the Hammonds, Slater, E. P. Thompson, or Chambers and Mingay.

involved simple accusations of social pretension and refinery in the
farmer class – for example, the mimicry of urban fashion and
consumption. Most contemporaries were content to explain it in such
terms, and point their finger at the farmer's wife. 'I think farmers'
wives of the present day are not what they were,' confided John
Ellman, as he broke the news to the 1828 Select Committee on
Criminal Commitments and Convictions, 'there is an objection made
by them to taking servants into the house.'[6] And this sentiment was
frequently repeated elsewhere. Others went rather further, and
mentioned the desire to avoid settlements gained by yearly hiring.
The Rev. John Cox, of Fairsted in Essex, examined by an 1847 Select
Committee, thought

that farmers, now-a-days, are too much of gentlemen, and the ladies too
smart to live, as formerly, with the farm labourers . . . that system has gone,
and never can be revived again . . . I would never hire a servant for a year,
because I should be bound to employ the man . . . It might be advantageous
to the man; but there is no such thing as hiring a yearly servant, I believe,
now in husbandry, at least not in my district . . . I am not aware of any
agricultural labourer being hired by the year, because we can get plenty of
labourers by the week, there is no necessity for us to do so . . . People began
to see that by hiring by the year they created settlements in their parishes,
and they did not do it long.[7]

And asked whether labourers were aware of their employers' motives
in employing them, he replied significantly: 'I do not know how they
reason at all.'[8]

Similarly, E. C. Tufnell, Assistant Poor Law Commissioner, believed yearly hiring ceased 'in great measure' before 1834.[9] Or an 1828
Select Committee, concerned with the deterioration of agricultural
social relations, advocated the abolition of hiring as a 'head' of
settlement 'to revive the almost forgotten, but excellent practice, of
domesticating the Agricultural Labourer in the establishment of his
employer, and therefore improve the moral feelings, industrious
habits, and real comforts of the Poorer Classes'.[10] At about the same
time, a Cambridgeshire magistrate commented:

The custom of hiring yearly servants is not so common as it was, as it is not
wished to give settlements; they do it in a way to avoid that, by hiring for a
period less than a year; generally speaking, the farmers can do that and board
them cheaper than they can get weekly servants, and they prefer doing it.[11]

[6] S.C. on Criminal Commitments and Convictions, VI (1828), pp. 53–4. Or see W.
Marshall, *Review of the Reports to the Board of Agriculture from the Southern and Peninsular
Departments of England* (York, 1817), p. 131.
[7] S.C. on Settlement and Poor Removal, XI (1847), p. 495.   [8] *Ibid.*, p. 497.
[9] *Ibid.*, p. 362.   [10] S.C. on the Law of Parochial Settlements, IV (1828), p. 1.
[11] S.C. on Criminal Commitments and Convictions, VI (1826–7), p. 20.

And the Rev. G. Glover in 1817 wrote to the same effect:

Formerly the hind went to yearly service during the best part of his youth and the first vigour of his age, made his settlements upon different parishes, none of them being uneasy as to where he might ultimately fix himself by marriage . . . But it is now the great object of the farmer to avoid admitting a male servant into his house. No man will hire either labourer or servant for a year from another parish.[12]

'Are farming servants less frequently lodged in farmers' houses than before?' a witness from Cambridgeshire was asked in 1826–7, and his reply was more reliable than most:

They have been less generally so than they used to be twenty years ago, within the last few years; but they are generally lodged in houses in large farms. . . . The house-keepers, the ploughmen and shepherds, are generally hired for a longer period; those who thresh and do the out-door piece work are for shorter periods.[13]

Interestingly, he noted in association with this change that there had been 'very great' unemployment for the last five or six years.

II

These accounts suggest that the custom was unusual or had ended by the 1830s in the south, although, as we shall see, they were overdrawn, and there could be much regional variation of survival, with greater persistence in parts of the west and north. Even in the south-east, large numbers of yearly hirings can be found up to 1834 and after in settlement examinations, and census data also suggests this, of which more below. Nor does literary evidence indicate when decline started, or provide a complete explanation for it. It is possible, however, to improve on these short impressionistic accounts by considering the work experience of men and women examined under the settlement laws in the south-east, quantifying their accounts so as to point to the chronology, regionality, and extent of change. Under the settlement laws, one 'head' of settlement was hiring for a complete year when unmarried.[14] As a settlement was the precondition to receiving relief, it was both essential for the poor to obtain and prove their legal settlements, and for parish officials to ensure that an applicant for relief was legally entitled to it in that parish. The conditions of hiring and past employment were particular subjects of enquiry, as they were the most common way for a settlement to be

---

[12] Rev. G. Glover, 'Observations on the state of pauperism', *The Pamphleteer*, X (1817). 392.   [13] S.C. on Criminal Commitments and Convictions, VI (1826–7), p. 23.
[14] See 3 Wm & Mary c. 11.

gained. A hiring that was interrupted, or for less than a year, or for which the agreed wages were not paid, or to a master with a settlement certificate, did not confer settlement. For this reason, examinations provide detailed information on the length and conditions of hiring, occasionally with supportive evidence to test the veracity of testimony, surviving alongside the examination. At best, the date, place, length and age specificity of hiring, agreed wages and time of payment, name of employer, whether board and lodging were included, and other related subjects were noted by the parish clerk. The basic information required remained the same from the 1691 Act of Settlement to the New Poor Law. The New Poor Law abolished yearly hiring as a head of settlement, and less can be said after 1834; although the law was not immediately applied in some areas, and information on hiring occasionally conferred settlement in the later 1830s, and is contained in some later nineteenth-century examinations, but not by then for the purposes of settlement.

Let me first stress the significance to the poor of settlement. They treated proof of a claim on 'their' parish much as a family heirloom.[15] Settlement certificates acknowledging settlement (or apprenticeship indentures) were passed from father to son; receipts of rent paid in excess of £10 per annum were produced decades later in evidence. Details of old removal cases affecting the family were told during examinations. Their knowledge of the law sometimes rivalled that of lawyers consulted in parochial settlement disputes. This knowledge came from experience of the law, and from awareness that in a period of seasonal unemployment, or with a large family, or in old age, they would become subject to it. Adam Smith expressed this when he wrote: 'There is scarce a poor man in England of forty years of age, I will venture to say, who has not in some part of his life felt himself most cruelly oppressed by this ill-contrived law of settlements.'[16]

No doubt they had the experience of the law he suggested; but his statement was polemical (he wanted the settlement laws repealed), and misleading. For he missed an important aspect of the labouring man's view of settlement: the law was seen as his guarantee of parish relief during a period of poverty, and this compensated for any imposition on freedom of movement. If it restricted his mobility it still provided a framework of economic security, a system of compulsory paternalism on which he (unlike his French, Irish, German, American, or Scottish counterparts) could depend regardless of his geographical position. When the law came under review in the nineteenth

---

[15] See for example W. E. Tate, *The Parish Chest* (Cambridge, 1946), pp. 201–2.
[16] A. Smith, *The Wealth of Nations* (1776, Harmondsworth, 1977 edn), p. 245.

century this was one of its defenders' arguments – that abolition would cause unrest, that the poor depended on the law and found security from it. 'There was a time', wrote Pashley in his *Pauperism and the Poor Laws* (1851), 'when judges used to ... consider [a settlement] not in its real light of a great restriction on natural liberty, but as a peculiar privilege of the poor.'[17] Whatever its 'real light', the poor continued to see the law as their peculiar privilege long after judges and parliamentarians began to interpret it differently. More can be said on their views below, but let us initially draw attention to them, as expressed for example in the 1765 East Anglian riots, against the introduction of large workhouses catering for Incorporations of parishes. Their commitment to relief only in their 'own' respective parishes led them to maintain that they would 'fight for their liberties'. 'If the King was to send 1,000 soldiers it would give them no concern, for they could raise 10,000 and did not fear defeating the soldiers.' 'God would not suffer it to rain' until these union work-houses were destroyed.[18]

With this attitude towards settlement and relief it was crucial that gaining a settlement be accessible. Failure to settle oneself could mean a lengthy and humiliating excursion on the contractor's cart to a (perhaps unvisited) area where one's father or grandfather had been settled. (Some urban areas, notably London, were increasingly dis-inclined even to remove, and the pauper was left entirely to his or her own devices, with not even a claim for removal on the parish of residence.) Hiring for the year, for most of those too poor to rent for £10 per annum, or pay an apprenticeship premium, was virtually the only method to gain one's own settlement. In the early eighteenth century this had been common practice for the unmarried. Leaving home at about fourteen they moved from one yearly hiring to another, via the annual hiring fair. On marriage, the man would move from being a 'yearly servant' to a 'labourer', hired generally by the week or day, and no longer boarded and lodged by the employer. Instead of being paid after the yearly hiring he would receive weekly wages. It had been possible to gain many settlements before mar-riage, moving yearly from one hiring to another, with the last settlement supplanting those previously gained. But the decline of service made settlement far more difficult to gain, distorted the

---

[17] R. Pashley, *Pauperism and the Poor Laws* (1852), pp. 267–9.
[18] Quoted in M. D. George, *England in Transition* (1931, Harmondsworth, 1965 edn), pp. 98–9, 137. (As she says, 'A settlement was a form of insurance.') See also A. J Peacock, *Bread or Blood; a Study of the Agrarian Riots in East Anglia in 1816* (1965), p. 32, on the 1765 determination to be relieved in their own parishes.

distinction between 'yearly servant' and 'labourer', and marked a fundamental re-assessment of the relations of employment.

The hiring of single people by the year became less common and the unmarried man or woman came to share the work experience of the married day 'labourer'. Hiring became shorter – there was a move

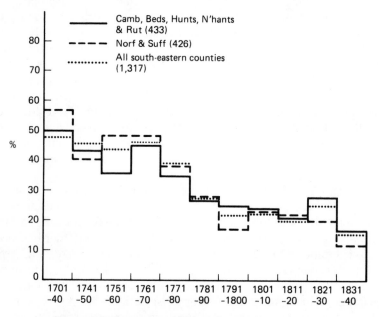

Figure 2.1 *Percentage of hirings for two or more years*
South-eastern counties

to hiring the unmarried by the week, month, or three or six month period, and the number of years spent by a 'farm-servant' with his or her employer, when still hired by the year, declined markedly. Figures 2.1 and 2.2 indicate change in the length of time spent in years with one's employer, for south-eastern counties. In the early eighteenth century nearly 50 per cent of yearly hirings continued for two or more years. In some counties, notably Surrey, Kent, London, and Middlesex, the figure was much higher, possibly pointing to a shortage of yearly servants during this period of rapid London expansion. But by the 1830s the position was quite different, with only about 15 per cent of yearly hirings lasting for two or more years with the same employer. The trend was universal for these counties, with most rapid change after about 1780, a transitional point to which one returns as repeatedly here as when discussing real wages, or apprenticeship.[19]

Figure 2.3 gives the percentage distribution of hirings by duration, between 1701 and 1840. Let us look first at the proportion of hirings for weekly or monthly periods, or for three to six months. The most

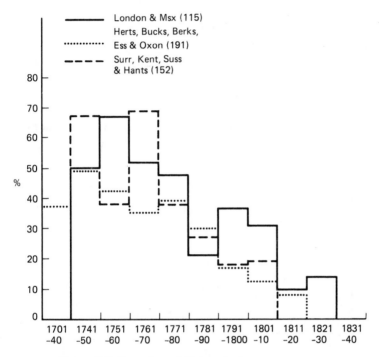

Figure 2.2 *Percentage of hirings for two or more years*
South-eastern counties

marked upswings came in 1781–1810, and particularly the two decades after 1820. The practice of yearly hiring was persistently giving way to shorter hirings. The figure also shows the proportion of hirings for only fifty-one weeks. As is clear, the adoption of such hirings came later, particularly from the 1820s, and was a deliberate measure to avoid settlements. In some areas the hiring agreement specified only fifty-one weeks; in others the employer conveniently found cause to terminate the hiring a few days short of the year. This practice was particularly resented by the poor, having agreed to the

[19] I have presented the figures for males here. Patterns for women are less reliably located, as information on the exact lengths of female hirings was given less often.

hiring in the belief that the parish would be a secure one to 'belong' to
– only to be dismissed at the end of the year with no settlement to
show for their year's service. Almost invariably wages were deducted

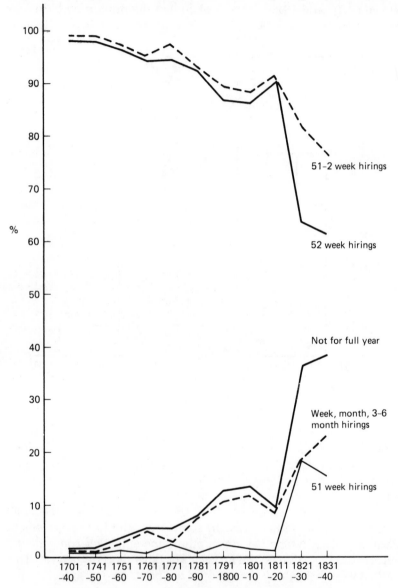

Figure 2.3 *Percentage distribution of male hirings by duration*
South-eastern counties (1,272 hirings)

from the agreed annual rate for the few days short of the year, on a scale in excess of what would be earned during those days. Edward Fudge was dismissed one day less than the full year in Salop in 1782 after a quarrel, as he had 'broken a pair of traces at plough'. When he was examined thirty-nine years later in June 1821 in Cheltenham he had still failed to gain a settlement.[20] Ann Preece served a few days less than a year in Herefordshire in the early eighteenth century. 'Her master said that she should not stay any longer there, for it would not be safe for the parish for her to continue there, this examinant said she would stay her year, he said she should not, her mistress paid her full wages, without deductions.'[21] Thomas Dent, hired in Great Waldingfield (Suffolk) in 1825, found himself in a similar situation.

Mr. Bartlett within about a month previously to the present old Michaelmas Day [1826] told Examinant that the Gentlemen (meaning the principal parishioners) had been talking to him about him and that he could not think of keeping him any longer because if he did he would belong to the parish. And he discharged him from service deducting five shillings from the year's wages for the time. Examinant was unwilling to take the money and wished to have stopt his year out but his master said he must go away.[22]

Here was another case from early nineteenth-century Berkshire:

About three weeks before Michaelmas the Bailiff told him he was ordered to discharge him because he had slip out some nights since he had been in the service, (which was never objected to before), and when he objected to leaving before his time was out it was told him that they had a meeting at Church, and it was agreed to put him and the carter away, because they should not belong to the Parish of Shaw.[23]

Another alternative with the same effect was not to hire until about three days after Michaelmas. This was common in Kent, and examples of it can be found elsewhere.[24]

Of course, this led to growing difficulty in gaining settlements among the poor, which involved them in considerable inconvenience and distress, particularly when unemployed, or with a large family, in old age or when ill; and this was adversely to affect the quality of social relations. One result of the decline, producing this effect, is seen in Figure 2.4, showing the lengthening time between examination and the last yearly hiring, looking backwards from the date of

---

[20] I. Gray (ed.), *Cheltenham Settlement Examinations, 1815–1826* (Bristol & Glos Arch. Soc., 1968), no. 381.
[21] Hereford & Worcs C.R.O., L. 51/124–243.
[22] West Suffolk C.R.O., Acc. 2564/1–63.
[23] Berkshire C.R.O., D/P. 34/13/3. Or see D/P. 20/13, for cases of fifty-one week hirings, from as early as 1753. To find them this early was very rare.
[24] Poor Law Report, XXXIII (1834), p. 245.

examination. As one would expect from Figure 2.3, this period grew considerably in the two groups of counties taken here: from about four years, to between nine and twelve. Just as with the decline of apprenticeship, the changes in the western counties lag those of the south-east by twenty or more years, being less extreme because

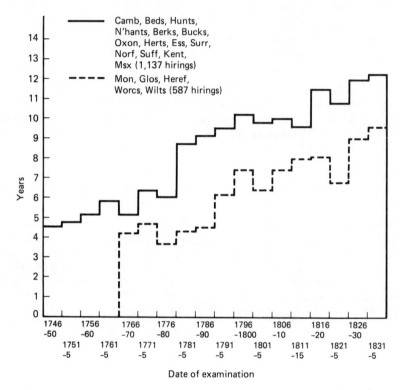

Figure 2.4 *Average years from last yearly hiring to examination (males)*
South-eastern & western counties

smaller pastoral farms were more compatible with service. In the south-east, change accelerated once again from the 1780s, stabilised during the war, but then renewed the late eighteenth-century trend.

The long-term effect of these changes can be seen in Figure 2.5, which shows the growing proportion of examinants who had failed to gain a settlement in their own right, and so who took that of their father or grandfather. Where the paternal settlement was unclear, the birth place was commonly taken instead, and so cases of the latter are included here (excluding bastards, who also took settlement from

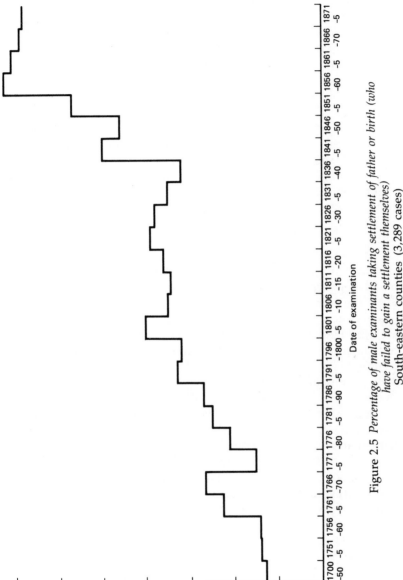

Figure 2.5 *Percentage of male examinants taking settlement of father or birth (who have failed to gain a settlement themselves)*
South-eastern counties (3,289 cases)

birth place).[25] Such cases were equally indicative of failure to gain one's own settlement. The figure is striking, and can be discussed more fully in connection with the family.[26] Once again, there were changes after about 1770. There was some stabilisation from 1800, to be shattered by the abolition of yearly hiring as a head of settlement in 1834. As the generation who had gained their settlements by yearly hiring died out thereafter, so the proportion who had failed to gain a settlement in their own right grew considerably, underlining the importance of this head of settlement. By 1856–60, the earlier generation had largely died – and there was restabilisation at the point at which as many as 70 per cent of examinants had failed to gain a settlement themselves. Settlement became for them a question of inheritance, which increasingly they took from their grandfather rather than father.

Details of the 'family' settlement were now carefully preserved, repeated to children from an early age. By the mid-nineteenth century many settlements were being claimed on the basis of hirings back under the old poor law, often fifty or so years before. The irremovability legislation of 1846 and 1861 helped avoid some of the hardship which followed this development; but 'irremovability' was never the same as 'settlement', did not confer the latter, and was legally distinct from it.[27] The settlement laws remained firmly operative throughout, directly removing large numbers, and indirectly influencing the lives of countless more. It could be argued, ironic though this may seem, that they had become by the early nineteenth century more of a distressing inconvenience than they had ever been a century before. For many people vulnerable to unemployment, residence in the parish of their historically remote settlement became highly advisable, if not a necessity; particularly if it was one of the many parishes which generally refused payment of non-resident relief, as Chadwick ordered after 1834.[28]

This was a factor conducive to inter-generational continuity which had hardly obtained in the early eighteenth century, when the vast majority of examinants gained many settlements for themselves in

[25] There were relatively few such cases (of unclear paternal settlement, producing settlement as taken from birth place), and their inclusion does not affect the figures.

[26] See chapter 7.

[27] 9 & 10 Vic. c. 66; 24 & 25 Vic. c. 66. See also 10 & 11 Vic. c. 110. (The 1861 Act changed the 1846 five year irremovability stipulation to three years.) These acts themselves were liable to a range of abuses, and furthered urban–rural and 'open'–'close' parish conflicts.

[28] For further discussion of the New Poor Law's curtailment of non-resident relief, see chapter 3.

their places of work, the last always supplanting the others. The trend was even more acute than in Figure 2.5, as the age structure of examinants rose after 1834, with the extreme ill-feeling against the New Poor Law raising the age structure of relief applicants. (The elderly had the least alternative, and were most in need of relief.) By contrast, of the 12 to 14 per cent of examinants who had yet to gain their own settlements in and before the mid-eighteenth century, most were young and would do so in due course. Figure 2.5 raises many other questions: on the operation of the poor law; on long-term patterns of labour mobility; on the structure of communities over time (and associated questions, such as the transmission of political belief); and is important in relation to the history and inter-generational stability of the family – of which more elsewhere.[29] All these figures strongly corroborate each other, pointing to a similar chronology in the south-east, and suggest some of the wider ramifications which the decline had.

There is similar evidence for counties in the south-west (not included in these figures) on a comparable decline of yearly hiring, although its exact chronology has not been uncovered. Practices of hiring for eleven months, and sometimes for half a year, were common in Dorset or Wiltshire by the 1820s, and to a lesser degree, in Somerset, Devon, and Cornwall. Shorter variants on a full yearly hiring became more noticeable after about 1780. Taking the south as a whole, the decline started around 1750 (later in the west), accelerated during the 1780s, was temporarily halted during the Napoleonic Wars, and recommenced thereafter.

A variety of practices existed within the system of service, which became more evident during its decline. 'The institution of farm service' has occasionally been seen by historians as historically invariable, giving way abruptly over time (or during a person's life) to day or weekly labour, albeit with separate chronologies in differing regions.[30] But as is partly apparent from Figure 2.3, there was variety in this system, particularly in its later years. It was not simply a uniform yearly contract, but also encompassed those for fifty-one weeks; for three, six, nine or eleven months; those where the actual hiring was for a year but was split into monthly periods to avoid settlements, and so on. In this regard, service shaded more imper-

---

[29] See chapter 7.
[30] See Kussmaul, *Servants in Husbandry*, pp. 31ff, 93, 133–4. Service is compared to a 'small brained animal' which became extinct, its 'habitat occupied by coeval species better suited to the environment'. Or see her 'Servants in husbandry in early-modern England' (unpub. Ph.D. thesis, Univ. of Toronto, 1978), pp. 52, 56, 194, 209.

ceptibly into forms of weekly or day labour than is usually acknowledged, and could in practice be very flexible – whether to avoid settlements, or to comply with regional agricultural specialisations.

Just as with the decline of traditional apprenticeship, there were also differing arrangements for boarding farm-servants, and board wages were sometimes paid rather than having them in the farmhouse, or in nearby accommodation on farm premises. 'A custom is coming in around Waterden', wrote Arthur Young in 1770,

> of allowing board-wages to farm servants, instead of the old way of feeding in the house . . . This is one material cause of an increased neglect of the Sabbath, and looseness of morals; they are free from the master's eye, sleep where and with whom they please, and are rarely seen at church. A most pernicious practice, which will by-and-bye be felt most severely in its consequences by the farmers.[31]

Pernicious or not (but presumably with servants still 'sleeping with whom they pleased' – that thrilling phrase for family modernisation theorists), this arrangement was being used in Bedfordshire seventy years later. 'They give them board wages, to board themselves', reported T. W. Overman, without adding moral commentary.[32] Another option, as summarised in 1868–9 for Oxfordshire, was to hire 'with usually a Michaelmas fee or mutual understanding which amounts to a yearly hiring, in so far as they are regularly employed throughout the year though at weekly wages, so that the farmer is not compelled to support them in case of sickness.'[33] (Such a weekly wage was 1s. more than for ordinary day men, because of the Sunday labour of farm-servants.) Similar practices existed in Berkshire in the 1860s – when many (perhaps a third) of adult farm labourers were yearly hired, although they would be paid weekly, especially if married.[34] Shepherds, foggers, under carters and carters, or cattlemen in particular would be yearly hired. I am speaking here of the south – further variants existed in the north, as for example the

---

[31] A. Young, *General View of the Agriculture of the County of Norfolk* (1804), p. 484.

[32] S.C. on Poor Law Amendment Act, XVIII (1837–8), pt II, p. 535.

[33] Report on the Employment of Children, Young Persons, and Women in Agriculture, XIII (1868–9), pp. 150–1; or see 593–4, 601–2, for further variants. (See also Report on the Employment of Women and Children in Agriculture, XVII (1867–8), pp. 185, 687.) It had previously fallen to employers to look after the farm-servant if he or she became ill during service. See R. Burn, *The Justice of the Peace and Parish Officer* (1755, 1797 edn), vol. 4, p. 41. They had tried many expedients to escape this obligation, which involved them in obvious economic loss, and which could put their own family at risk – for example, in cases of smallpox.

[34] Report on the Employment of Children, Young Persons, and Women in Agriculture, XIII (1868–9), p. 151.

'bondage' system.[35] One readily finds examples of these (and other) arrangements in settlement examinations. Such diversity became more evident after about 1750, partly to accommodate regional agricultural specialisations. The decline of farm service involved the growth of such variants, as well as a move to strictly day labour. Rather than seeing only two options open to employers ('farm service' as opposed to day labour), one should stress the adaptability of the system in the changing circumstances after 1750.

Just as there could be much flexibility of service arrangements, so increasingly the applicability of the system to the unmarried began to break down. In earlier centuries a terminological distinction had been drawn between the unmarried 'servant' and the married 'labourer', although this should not be insisted on too rigidly.[36] Perhaps even in the seventeenth century the distinction was not entirely clear-cut; but from the mid-eighteenth century one becomes more aware of unmarried people working at day labour. Rather than going to service from their early 'teens and working in that way to marriage, many went to day labour at perhaps ten years of age, worked for some years while remaining resident at home – then went into service until they married. Some single people never went into service at all, and worked at day labour like a married person. The marital distinction between 'servant' and 'labourer' was becoming looser.

Connected with this, and a symptom of the decline of service, was an increasing confusion over the older terminology of 'servant' and 'labourer'. By the early nineteenth century the distinction was often unfamiliar to those who came in contact with the country. Descriptions applied to examinants in the early nineteenth century frequently muddle the terms, referring to an unmarried man as a 'labourer', or calling married men 'farm-servants'. Examples of this before the 1780s were rare, but it became more common thereafter. Thomas Godfrey, examined at Mendlesham (Suffolk) in January 1800, had been a 'labourer' until 1796 'and then he married'.[37] The term

---

[35] On the bondage system, see J. P. D. Dunbabin, *Rural Discontent in Nineteenth-Century Britain* (1974), pp. 130–73; *Morning Chronicle*, 5 and 9 Jan. 1850.

[36] For rather inflexible insistence on this distinction, see: Kussmaul, *Servants in Husbandry*, e.g., pp. 31ff, 93, 133–4. Or see Laslett, *Family Life and Illicit Love*, pp. 61–2. Laslett complains of terminological confusion over these terms among historians, and perhaps the similar early nineteenth-century confusion helps explain this. Nevertheless, E. P. Thompson was unusually muddled when he wrote that 'Many cereal farmers' (in the eighteenth century) 'continued the custom of selling cheap grain to their own labourers. But this applied only to regular, annually-hired labourers.' 'The moral economy of the English crowd in the eighteenth century', *Past and Present*, L (1971), 119.

[37] East Suffolk C.R.O., FB/159/G3. 80–158.

'labourer' was defined in 1838 by James Turner of Ampthill as follows: 'When we say labourers, we mean men, and those whom they call boys, all those who go to work for the farmers . . . I mean those of 15, or 16 or 17 years of age; if they went to work for the farmers, we called them labourers.' 'Those labourers would, a number of them, have families? – Yes.' One of the 'children' he discusses 'is 20', 'and I put him down in my table of labourers as a labourer . . . he pays his mother so much a week'.[38] E. C. Tufnell, Assistant Poor Law Commissioner for the south of England, muddled 'servants' and 'labourers' as though he saw no difference, although the Select Committee insisted that there was a distinction.

Are you not aware that it was formerly the custom, say 50 or 60 years ago, for the ploughman, the shepherd, and the carter, to live in the house as servants of the farmer? – Yes. And that . . . that practice was discontinued? – Yes . . . I do not think that the practice of keeping labourers (sic) in houses has been restored.[39]

Another witness to a parliamentary select committee in 1868–9 talked of the custom of hiring living-in servants by the year in Oxfordshire, but of paying weekly wages, and referred to such a person as 'a domestic labourer, if I may so call him'.[40] And a distinction now being used was that of 'boys' and 'men', familiar to readers of later nineteenth-century rural literature. They are considered 'boys' in Ampthill – 'till they get married'.[41]

III

So the decline of service took different forms, progressively splintering an older uniformity – its details in the south-east are now clear. To some commentators it seemed nearly complete by the 1820s, although they tended to overstate its extent. Settlement records bear witness to large numbers still hiring for the full fifty-two weeks during the 1820s and 1830s. And in 1831 the agricultural labour force in the southern counties discussed here still comprised between 15 and 38 per cent 'farm-servants'.[42] Contemporaries singled out two causes in particular for the decline: the social pretensions of the

[38] S.C. on the Poor Law Amendment Act, XVIII (1837–8), pt II, pp. 104–5, 186–7.
[39] S.C. on Settlement and Poor Removal, XI (1847), pp. 362–3.
[40] Report on the Employment of Children, Young Persons, and Women in Agriculture, XIII (1868–9), pp. 593–4.
[41] See F. Thompson, *Lark Rise to Candleford* (1939, Harmondsworth, 1976 edn), p. 69; S.C. on the Poor Law Amendment Act, XVIII (1837–8), pt II, pp. 104–5, 186–7.
[42] For the south, these percentages are likely to be overestimates. See Kussmaul, *Servants in Husbandry*, pp. 126, 171–2.

farmer class, and their desire to avoid settlements. But we should consider the causes in fuller detail, and not rely only on such opinion.

Mention should first be made of findings based on changes in marriage seasonality, analysed by Kussmaul from parish register data collected by the Cambridge Group.[43] Marriage for farm-servants frequently occurred shortly after their last yearly hiring, with the annual wages they received then (alongside previous savings) allowing them to marry and form a separate household. In a predominantly rural area such as the south-east, with Michaelmas hiring fairs ending and starting the agricultural year for farm-servants, there was a peak in marriage seasonality immediately after Michaelmas, in October. (Elsewhere the peak followed different dates for the hiring fair, such as May and June in western pastoral areas.) Changes in the proportion of marriages during the year which were in October provide a guide to the determinate role exercised by service, and can serve as a rough indicator of its extent over time. As Kussmaul has shown, in a group of fifty-six predominantly agricultural parishes in the south-east, there was a rise after 1650 in the prevalence of October marriages, to a peak around 1725–45. Thereafter, findings closely follow Figure 2.3: there was a fall from 1750, which was slightly reversed during the Napoleonic Wars, to develop more sharply thereafter.[44] There are some hazards in the use of this method such as the problems of under-registration, the changing observance of Lent as it affected marriage seasonality, shifts of mixed farming emphases between pastoral and arable, affecting hiring seasonality, or the growth of cottage industries. Such extraneous factors also influenced marriage seasonality. Nevertheless, the close similarity of such findings with the changes presented here, from a totally different source dealing directly with evidence of hirings, suggests confidence in the marriage seasonality method.

Insofar as this method seems vindicated after 1750, its results for an earlier period should similarly be worthy of attention, suggesting more long-term changes affecting service. In this earlier period, the proportion of total marriages which were in October declined after 1550 to a low point around 1650, with the upturn from then to about 1745. (The decline after 1550 parallels, rather less steeply, that after 1750.) Two striking features of these long-term cycles were the way in which periods of inflation, after 1550 and 1750, saw diminishing emphasis on service, and the way in which the peak around 1740 of October marriages coincided with price changes favouring pastoral products over grain. Low or zero population growth after 1650, grain

---

[43] *Ibid.*, ch. 6, esp. p. 98.   [44] *Ibid.*, p. 98.

price stabilisation or even deflation, culminating in the low prices of 1725–45, and corresponding shifts to agricultural techniques requiring greater emphasis on livestock seem to have been associated with more extensive use of servants.

One should then initially stress how hiring changes were based on a 'rational' assessment of loss and gain, even in the sixteenth century. In a period of low grain prices (1725–45) it was economically most rational for farmers to pay in kind rather than money. About 80 per cent of the wages of 'farm-servants' were paid in kind. (Probably the same, or a higher proportion, of the wages of 'labourers' were paid in money. This varied by region.) Harvest abundance, after all, was a major factor behind falling prices and agricultural depression in the early eighteenth century. Payment in kind to a labour force more heavily comprising farm-servants was an answer to the lack of credit and ready money associated with depression and low prices, and an obvious option with good harvests. It also had a similar effect to the large grain exports of the early eighteenth century: holding prices higher by withholding grain from the domestic market. Livestock prices were more buoyant than grain – here too, an emphasis on service fitted in with the more evenly spread seasonal labour requirements of an agriculture moving, in the short-term, to a fuller incorporation of animal husbandry.[45]

Alternatively, as Adam Smith pointed out, this rationality behind low prices and the use of servants was reversed by rising returns to the farmer class in an inflationary period (as after 1750). This induced them to pay in wages rather than kind.[46] It also had the effect of forcing labour to buy produce on the market, so intensifying demand and accentuating price, to the greater profitability of the farmer. And later eighteenth-century price movements favoured grain production, with its seasonal labour requirements uncongenial to yearly hiring.

I noted earlier the explanatory terms used by most contemporaries. But a few at any rate were aware of the influence of prices: 'Why do not farmers now *feed* and *lodge* their work-people, as they did formerly? Because they cannot keep them *upon so little* as they give them in wages' (his italics), wrote Cobbett, and we need to note the corollary he drew:

---

[45] On this, see the most interesting discussion in Kussmaul, *Servants in Husbandry*, pp. 107ff, on relative prices and the timing of 'new husbandry' innovations. Some similar points are made by J. V. Beckett, on the regionality of agricultural depression: 'Regional variation and the agricultural depression, 1730–1750', *Econ. Hist. Rev.*, XXXV (1982).

[46] For a similar formulation on the role of prices, see Smith, *Wealth of Nations*, p. 186.

There needs no more to prove that the lot of the working classes has become worse than it formerly was. This fact alone is quite sufficient to settle this point. All the world knows, that a number of people, boarded in the same house, and at the same table, can, with as good food, be boarded much cheaper than those persons divided into twos, threes, or fours, can be boarded. This is a well known truth: therefore, if a farmer shuts his pantry against his labourers, and pays them wholly in money, is it not clear, that he does it because he thereby gives them a living *cheaper* to him; that is to say, a worse living than formerly? ... so much does he gain by pinching them in wages that he lets all these things [facilities for servants in the farmhouse] remain as of no use, rather than feed labourers [sic] in the house. Judge, then, of the *change* that has taken place in the condition of these labourers! [his italics][47]

They would certainly have suffered more from unemployment. In addition, paying labour in cash displaced the burden of inflation onto them. Payment in kind to 'labourers' also was limited, and David Davies complained of this, and the way rising prices induced farmers to deal 'in a wholesale way with the miller; the miller with the mealman; the mealman with the shopkeeper, of which last the poor man buys his flour by the bushel'.[48] The mealman or baker would, added Nathaniel Kent, 'in the ordinary course of their profit, get at least ten per cent of them, upon this principle article of their consumption'.[49] Both Davies and Kent also noted that the growth of larger farms contributed to this, of which more below.

When prices fell after 1813, one might accordingly have expected some resurgence of service, but this does not seem to have occurred in the south-east.[50] A Select Committee was thinking along the lines suggested here when it asked John Ellman: 'Do not you think the low price of agricultural produce would, if rightly understood, induce farmers to keep their servants in their own houses, and in that mode pay them by produce, instead of by money wages?' Ellman replied: 'It is singular that practice should not have been resorted to, but when people get into a habit they cannot easily get out of it.'[51] And he continued to stress the changing social attitudes of farmers and particularly of their wives as having been crucial, as due to their prosperity during the Napoleonic Wars. Similarly, a respondent from Oxfordshire in 1832–4 considered the change 'to be in a great measure owing to the improved condition of the farmers during the high

[47] Cobbett, *Rural Rides*, p. 227.
[48] D. Davies, *The Case of the Labourers in Husbandry* (1795), pp. 44–5.
[49] N. Kent, *Hints to Gentlemen of Landed Property* (1775), p. 264.
[50] It is possible however that there was some movement back to 'living-in' in Lincolnshire. See J. Caird, *English Agriculture in 1850–1* (1851), p. 197.
[51] S.C. on Criminal Commitments and Convictions, VI (1828), p. 53.

prices of agricultural produce. Their families were unwilling to associate with the labourers; and a second table was out of the question.'[52]

I have stressed so far the role of prices, a factor not much discussed at the time, but one strongly implicated by the long-term cycles in marriage seasonality. The profitability brought by high prices also contributed to farmers' social pretensions. But there were many other factors involved. Foremost among these was concern over structural unemployment and rising poor rates, and a desire to limit settlements being gained. This concern was readily apparent in contemporary statements quoted earlier, alongside an appreciation that the labour surplus behind these problems made it less necessary to secure the work force under a yearly contract. Aspects of structural and seasonal unemployment are discussed in other chapters. But it may be helpful here to illustrate changes in unemployment as derived from poor law accounts. This source did, after all, contain information immediately available to contemporaries, from which they judged and acted on rising poor rates and unemployment, of which they complained so persistently in the deluge of pamphlets on pauperism and the poor laws. We may take material on relief expenditure raised by the poor rate as having a direct influence on employment policy.

Many parishes have poor law accounts adequate to this purpose, and surprisingly they have rarely been used. Illustrative material can be given here on the large Essex parishes of Ardleigh and St Osyth; each of which had over 90 per cent of their inhabitants classed as 'chiefly engaged in agriculture' in 1801 and 1831. Both have detailed month by month poor accounts, from which extraneous expenditure and accumulated payments not directly connected with relief can be excluded, to demonstrate long-term trends in absolute annual expenditure, and real per capita expenditure.[53] Changes in the seasonality of payment over time can also be calculated, to supplement settlement data on changes in the seasonal distribution of unemployment. Figure 2.6 accordingly gives the long-term payments for these

---

[52] Poor Law Report, XXXIII (1834), p. 378.

[53] Essex C.R.O., D/P. 263/8/1–3, D/P. 263/12/1–16, D/P. 322/12/2–6. See also D/P. 263/11/1–11. The figures for Ardleigh and St Osyth were calculated by Stephen Davies while at Trinity Hall, Cambridge; and a fuller discussion is available in his most interesting undergraduate dissertation on 'Poor law administration and rural change in the Tendring Hundred of Essex, 1770–1844' – a copy of which is deposited in the Library of the Cambridge Group for the History of Population and Social Structure. I am most grateful to him for permission to use his findings here, and hope that other scholars will apply his innovatory methods to the accounts of other parishes. Such parish accounts remain a largely unexplored source, despite their obvious bearing on the problem of changes in unemployment.

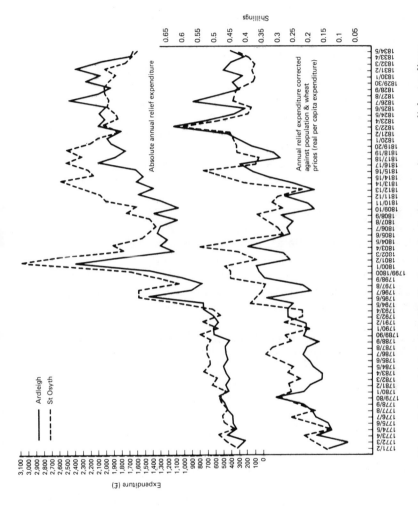

Figure 2.6 *Ardleigh and St Osyth: absolute and real per capita poor relief expenditure*

89

parishes in absolute terms, and then in terms of real per capita expenditure, that is, corrected against population and wheat prices. The movements of poor law expenditure are similar. Both parishes were long-enclosed. But Ardleigh was a strictly agricultural parish (with an integrated four course arable with turnips, and livestock fattening), and St Osyth had a heavier soil, greater pasture, and a rather more mixed economy: being partly agricultural – but also featuring a fishing industry at the mercy of the seasonally instinctive wild herring and sprat.

These findings seem broadly representative, to judge from the few other published poor law accounts, and from contemporary comment. The absolute payment of relief was certainly rising from 1770, and perhaps before, to peaks in the high price years, with a tendency thereafter for the background level to continue rising in uniformity with the general pattern disclosed in official returns.[54] In the few other cases where data from the late eighteenth century is available, the rise was under way in the early 1780s in the hundred of Colneis and Carlford (Suffolk) – and was also manifest to varying degrees in the figures which start around 1790 for Eaton Socon (Bedfordshire), Lidlington (Bedfordshire), Pavenham (Bedfordshire), Roxton (Bedfordshire), or Antingham (Norfolk).[55] There is no doubt that motives governing parochial settlement changed mainly because of concern over increases in absolute expenditure, and the rate per pound rateable value, and when considering the ratepayer one should concentrate on these indicators.[56] But we can supplement this by

[54] See M. Blaug, 'The myth of the old poor law and the making of the new', in M. W. Flinn & T. C. Smout (eds.), *Essays in Social History* (Oxford, 1974), pp. 146–7.

[55] H. Fearn, 'The financing of the poor law incorporations for the hundreds of Colneis and Carlford in the county of Suffolk, 1758–1820', *Proc. Suffolk Inst. Arch.*, XXVII (1958), 104; F. G. Emmison, 'Poor relief accounts of two rural parishes (Northill and Eaton Socon) in Bedfordshire', *Econ. Hist. Rev.*, III (1931); and his 'Relief of the poor at Eaton Socon, Bedfordshire, 1706–1834', *Beds. Hist. Rec. Soc.*, XV (1933), 54 & app.; S.C. of the House of Commons on the Poor Laws, VI (1817), p. 141, app. no. 22. See also D. A. Baugh, 'The cost of poor relief in south-east England, 1790–1834', *Econ. Hist. Rev.*, XXVIII (1975).

[56] Rate per pound rateable value rose by factors between 2.5 and 8 after 1770, in different parishes for which I have evidence. In Ardleigh, for example, it was 5s. in 1796/7, but 13s. in 1820/1. Or in Eaton Socon it was 1s. 4d. in 1775, but had reached 8s. by 1828.

It is clear that real per capita expenditure is not an appropriate way of dealing with this issue from the ratepayer's viewpoint. 'Real expenditure' assumes that an increase of grain prices of given magnitude compensated the parish ratepayer for a proportionately similar rise of total relief expenditure. There are many reasons for this not in fact being the case. For example, it begs questions on the profitability to farmers of different price levels, and it is highly unlikely that profitability (allowing the payment of higher poor rates) was proportionately equivalent to price. And of

noting the trends in real per capita expenditure, shown on the lower half of Figure 2.6. The increase is of course less sharp, but remains essentially the same: upward until about 1804, followed by further increase after the Napoleonic Wars. Real per capita expenditure for these two parishes increased over threefold from the early 1770s to the 1820s; absolute expenditure increased over sixfold. The chronology of these two phases of increased expenditure, in the later eighteenth century, and after 1815, corresponds to the two-phase decline of farm service in Figure 2.3.

The view that the decline of service was significantly caused by growing unemployment and relief expenditure becomes even stronger when we consider changes in the seasonality of payment. For the two parishes, these are contained in Figure 2.7. Extraneous payments not connected with relief have been excluded. In Ardleigh, the patterns will be familiar from my discussion of the agricultural seasonal distributions of unemployment, based on settlement examinations. They are broken down here in chronological sequence, as in chapter 1, with payment seasonalities for five year periods shown as three month moving averages. The rapidly growing acuteness of the seasonal pattern, and the rising absolute levels of expenditure, need little comment. They make clear how unemployment became more seasonally precarious after the 1780s, even in an agriculturally innovative parish like this – complementing the results from settlement records, but producing a more pessimistic picture. Much literary evidence in the parish's poor law records could be added – suffice to say that there were large increases of men stated to be 'out of work'. In St Osyth, change may have begun earlier, although its intensity was similar. The seasonality differed, being influenced by its partly fishing economy. There was little scope for turnip husbandry here, and large areas of pasture. But it is clear that pessimistic arguments on unemployment made for southern agricultural parishes can also be extended to a parish with a mixed economy like St Osyth.

These results support what is known from other expenditure figures, and allow further insight into the changing seasonality of unemployment. We saw earlier how contemporary comment on the

course, many ratepayers as well as the poor suffered directly during high prices (artisans, shopkeepers, publicans, smaller farmers concentrating on livestock, or who were partially or wholly self-subsistent in 'normal' years). In such cases, 'real expenditure' is a quite unrealistic indicator, and greatly minimises the hardship to, or effect on, ratepayers of rising absolute expenditure. 'Per capita' relief more obviously has the same effect. For such reasons, one should concentrate on absolute expenditure in this context.

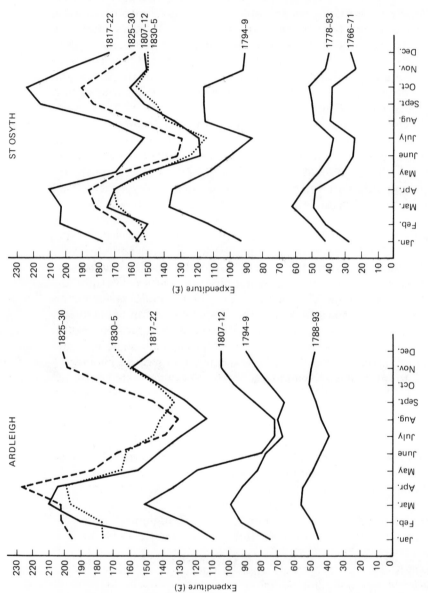

Figure 2.7 *Ardleigh and St Osyth: monthly poor relief expenditure* (3 month moving average: mean for selected 5 year periods, measured April–March)

decline of service stressed concern over settlement, because of rising rates, relief expenditure, and unemployment. Measures were accordingly taken to avoid yearly hiring, as settlement accentuated these problems. This motive most noticeably lay behind fifty-one week hirings, which became more common as relief expenditure rose after the war, compounded by the agricultural depression. Farmers were fined in many parishes for allowing settlements to be gained, and stipulations to this effect were sometimes written into leases. Such fines could be heavy: £50 per settlement, for example. In addition, some parishes paid as much as £2 to their settled farm-servants who were able to settle themselves elsewhere.[57] 'Did not the custom of hiring by the year continue till the Poor-Law Amendment Act?' asked the 1847 Select Committee on Settlement to one witness from Essex. 'No ... I believe it was left off before the passing of the Poor Law Amendment Act, on account of settlement. It would create no settlement now.'[58] Nevertheless it had conferred settlement long before this, which in earlier days had been much less objected to – once again, pointing to the unemployment of the early nineteenth century. And one reason for the 1834 repeal of hiring as a head of settlement was again to prevent settlements.

Because of such unemployment, farmers became less concerned to maintain their labour throughout the winter, ready for the intensive tasks of the summer. This had been one of the motives behind service, to be expected a century earlier, with relatively high real wages, and when high marriage ages had contributed significantly to demographic stabilisation. A range of other factors had obtained then: low prices, and the experience of good harvests demanding a larger work force; a greater degree of regionally autonomous mixed farming; a shift to more emphasis on animal husbandry, and still large livestock numbers in south-eastern unenclosed villages; surplus grain production, itself allowing an expansion of livestock and so more seasonally constant work. These were all factors implying heavier dependence on farm-servants and yearly hired categories of married labour.

This situation contrasted markedly with the early nineteenth century. By then it was still possible for labour availability to fall short of strictly harvest requirement. The Irish harvesters bear witness to this. But the frequent violence against them reported in provincial newspapers – sickle versus scythe – draws us rapidly back to the problem

---

[57] C. R. Oldham, 'Oxfordshire poor law papers', *Econ. Hist. Rev.*, V (1934–5), 88–9.
[58] S.C. on Settlement and Poor Removal, XI (1847), p. 495. Or see S.C. on the Relief of Able-bodied Persons from the Poor Rate, IV (1828), p. 31.

of unemployment, to the new-found vulnerability of the English rural labourer. The scythe itself (so violently used against the Irish near Ely in 1830) contributed to such unemployment by limiting the harvest to smaller bands of skilled scythe-men. 'If a man does his work badly I discharge him' declared a local clergyman-farmer as late as 1847,

and I keep them on in that way; there is no hiring for a year; we never hire in that manner in my county [Essex]. I am not aware of any agricultural labourer being hired by the year, because since we can get plenty of labourers by the week, there is no necessity for us to do so.[59]

Or, as it was put by the Rector of Whatfield, in Suffolk,

If a servant in agriculture leaves his place, it is seldom indeed that he can get another except as an occasional day labourer. Labourers [once again, note the terminology] now seldom live under their employers' roofs for these reasons: the number of unemployed labourers is such, that a Farmer is always sure of hands when he wants them.[60]

And one recalls that the labour shortage during the Napoleonic Wars underlay the halted, or even reversed, decline of service then – further demonstration of the effects of unemployment.[61]

Of course, such unemployment was regionally specific. As Wilson Fox wrote: 'The great difficulty of finding constant employment for a large staff of farm hands all the year round exists chiefly in the great corn-growing districts in the winter months.'[62] Changes in farm size compounded this – the increasingly large cereal farms of the densely proletarian south and east were often thought less compatible with service. With an earlier predominance of family farming, service had been an answer to the labour needs of the family economy before an optimum working unit had been formed with children. Farm-servants had been taken as a life-cycle feature, allowing small tenants, owner-occupiers, or cottagers to maintain an optimum labour force, without significantly altering the size of land farmed. In pastoral regions smaller farms survived longer, with family-based and more seasonally constant labour requirements making farm-servants still a serious option. Table 2.1 (calculated from the 1851 census) shows this. The west and parts of the north had small ratios of labour to farmer (very small in Wales), indicative of smaller farm sizes. In

---

[59] S.C. on Settlement and Poor Removal, XI (1847), p. 495.
[60] Cited in E. J. Hobsbawm & G. Rudé, *Captain Swing* (1969, 1973 edn), p. 25.
[61] There is also a suggestion in the marriage seasonality data of a short-term reversal around 1800. Kussmaul, *Servants in Husbandry*, p. 98.
[62] Cited in Hobsbawm & Rudé, *Captain Swing*, p. 24n. To similar effect, see A. Young, *Political Arithmetic* (1774), p. 295, or his *A Six Months' Tour through the North of England* (1770), vol. 4, p. 253.

association with this, farm-servants in these counties formed a higher proportion of the agricultural labour force. (In almost all cases, wherever farm-servants were over 20 per cent of agricultural labour, the ratio of labour to farmer was 5:1 or lower.) By contrast, the south and east had by 1851 very low proportions of farm-servant labour, and high labour to farmer ratios. For example, Bedfordshire or Essex contrasted markedly with Durham, Cumberland, Lancashire, Westmorland, Yorkshire; and even more so with the Welsh counties.

The census figures for female farm-servants were unreliable, as they encompassed 'in-door' servants and included many more strictly domestic servants. But Table 2.1 also shows the proportions of agricultural 'out-door' labourers which were female. Predictably, the counties where this proportion was high were again usually in the north and west of England: Cumberland, Durham, Northumberland, Wiltshire, or the North Riding – counties with 'high' female wages, high proportions of male labour as farm-servants, and low labour to farmer ratios. (The converse was also true, e.g., Bedfordshire or Essex.) Once again, this suggests that labour shortage (associated with a persistence of female agricultural labour) contributed significantly to the survival of service, and that labour surplus hastened its demise.

While service was clearly congruent with smaller farm pastoral regions, and while such farming contributed to the distribution of survival in 1851, it is still unclear how much importance should be attached to changes in farm size as a cause of decline. On the evidence of marriage seasonality, service appears to have had its heyday in the south-east during a period in the early eighteenth century supposedly notorious for the decline of owner-occupiers and small tenant farmers. Figure 2.3 also suggested that decline set in from 1750. The census evidence on the ratios of labour to farmer, and the survival of service in small farm regions, accordingly leave us with the strong suspicion that the decline of service after 1750 was associated with a continued or even accelerated decline of small farms. Many contemporaries certainly thought so. But current orthodoxy generalised by Mingay from selected land tax assessments has it otherwise.[63] (We will return to this in dealing with the social consequences of enclosure.) At present, then, one should note this logical discrepancy, but stress rather the importance of price determined employment motive; supplemented after 1750 by the accumu-

[63] G. E. Mingay, *Enclosure and the Small Farmer in the Age of the Industrial Revolution* (1968). But see chapter 4 for further discussion.

Table 2.1. *Features of the 1851 agricultural labour force by county*

County	% of total male labour which is farm-servant	Nos. male labour (in-door & out) per farmer	% of total labourers which are female
England			
Beds	3.3	13.0	0.2
Berks	9.2	12.7	0.2
Bucks	6.9	10.5	0.6
Camb	4.3	7.5	7.8
Ches	33.8	3.4	2.2
Corn	31.3	2.9	9.7
Cumb	41.4	2.6	15.0
Derb	30.5	2.3	0.6
Dev	31.5	4.3	3.4
Dors	3.1	8.1	9.2
Dur	27.2	2.7	13.9
Ess	3.3	11.5	1.2
Glos	8.3	7.0	10.4
Hants	7.2	11.3	1.8
Heref	18.7	5.5	5.7
Herts	7.9	14.1	1.4
Hunts	5.6	9.2	1.6
Kent	10.9	9.9	1.2
Lancs	24.2	2.2	2.7
Leics	20.0	5.4	1.2
Lincs	21.7	4.9	1.5
Msx	5.3	11.1	7.4
Mon	32.1	3.3	3.4
Norf	4.7	7.7	4.3
N'hants	6.3	9.6	0.8
N'umb	14.7	4.6	22.3
Notts	24.5	5.0	1.2
Oxon	5.7	9.9	4.5
Rut	14.7	4.9	0.3
Salop	28.7	5.4	1.7
Som	10.3	4.9	6.8
Staffs	23.8	4.1	2.4
Suff	6.3	8.7	0.9
Surr	8.0	11.0	0.9
Suss	7.9	9.5	0.3
Wark	14.4	6.3	4.4
Westm	44.9	1.9	2.3
Wilts	3.1	10.5	15.5
Worcs	11.0	5.5	8.8
York, E. Rid.	39.4	4.4	2.8
York, N. Rid.	37.1	2.8	10.5
York, W. Rid.	25.2	2.2	5.0

County	% of total male labour which is farm-servant	Nos. male labour (in-door & out) per farmer	% of total labourers which are female
Wales			
Ang	42.3	2.2	1.2
Brecons	47.7	1.9	3.0
Caerns	46.9	2.1	1.8
Cards	63.0	1.3	5.4
Cars	51.1	1.5	6.7
Denbs	39.9	2.9	1.4
Flints	41.7	2.6	0.9
Glam	39.9	2.1	3.7
Mer	60.3	1.4	2.2
Mont	53.8	2.1	1.1
Pembs	42.8	2.3	6.9
Radnors	49.1	2.4	1.7

lating effect of unemployment, which was accentuated by the decline of smaller farms after 1813, if not in the sixty years before.[64]

The 1834 abolition of the hiring head of settlement was designed to revive service by removing concern over settlement; but the 1851 census suggests that it had little such effect.[65] T. W. Overman, questioned on the New Poor Law, was asked if service might be revived, and by improving class understanding, could 'entirely remove ... the severity of this new law'. He thought not, believing

[64] A point should be made on the connection of the decline of service and the wage trends of chapter 1. It is unlikely that the extent of the decline of service in each county helps explain the different county movements of farm-servant wages. Were this the case, one would expect correlation between them which was much less marked or did not obtain between county *weekly* wages and the decline of service, between which there is little reason to posit a direct connection. Regression of the percentage changes in nine counties of combined male and female yearly wages (between 1767/70 and 1831/5) on the proportions of agricultural labour which were farm-servant in 1831, gives an r value of .435 (not significant at the .05 level). And a very similar value (r = .454) is obtained by regressing the percentage change in Bowley's *weekly* wage data between these two dates onto the same 1831 county proportions which were farm-servant labour. This similarity suggests that the movements of both weekly and yearly wages were equally determined by other factors initially independent of the decline of service (such as unemployment, or prices), which in themselves undercut service. This is what one would expect.

[65] For contrary views, see: Report of G. Coode to the Poor Law Board on the Law of Settlement and Removal of the Poor, XXVI (1851), p. 275. He believed that there had been a slight recurrence. See also S.C. on Settlement and Poor Removal, XI (1847), pp. 763–4. 'A practice had grown up lately of engaging a labourer for a whole year ... a renewal of the old system that we have not had for years together' (Oxfordshire).

that it had declined because farmers did not approve 'men in the house with the interference of maid servants; the most troublesome thing any man can have, is to have man-servants in the house, to any extent'.[66] As with much contemporary comment, superficial but morally self-confirming observation sufficed as explanation and justification for more deep-rooted change. But he continued, interestingly, by agreeing that the change was 'more the result of an alteration in the state of society than of any calculation as to the advantage or disadvantage of the practice'.[67]

Nevertheless, calculation as to the advantage or disadvantage of the practice had been a cause of the 'alteration in the state of society', and the extent to which such calculation was new should be raised. The change was certainly an economically rational one, given the movement of prices and growing unemployment, and the economic groundswell of decline is clearer to us than it usually was to contemporaries. There was little compromise with the social expectations of the poor, and little the latter could do to restrict the change. Its context was more remote than confrontations over enclosure, food shortage, or market regulation, and it posed less threat to public order. But it is clear that the change in hiring practice *was* resented. It threw unmarried labour onto the parish during the winter, when they had previously been kept by the farmer. For the poor, this became even more serious with the curtailment of out-relief and non-resident relief after 1834. It endangered eligibility for parish assistance, and so threatened them with the settlement laws – with removal at times to a distant and hitherto unvisited parish. Those unprotected by service were also liable to militia service, or to be press-ganged.[68] It was obvious too how examinants felt about refusals to continue hirings for the full year. Thomas Wellstead was working at daily labour in Dorset in the winter of 1825 and 'told his master he did not like to go on in that way and would rather go into service again, and that he should leave him unless he was taken into house'.[69] Or here is a statement from Charles Varley's remarkable autobiography of 1768:

My greatest trouble was that we had no settlement, . . . neither could we gain a settlement, as we were married; therefore . . . we might perish for want.

---

[66] S.C. on the Poor Law Amendment Act, XVIII (1837–8), pt II, p. 535.
[67] *Ibid.*, p. 536.
[68] See for example Wiltshire C.R.O., 533/52. 'The said Henry Adams wished to hire Examinant for a certain term and told him that he should also hire his own son in the same way – as it might prevent their going for soldiers, or being drawn in the Militia' (1825).
[69] Dorset C.R.O., P.11/OV 188B.

Whereupon I was determined to go to be a farmer's servant for one year: in order to gain a settlement, my wife and I were to part for that year, and then to meet as strangers, and to be married in the parish church where I had served my year. Upon our affairs being thus settled, I bought a suit of strong servant-like clothes, and took my way into the country; when I had got about ten miles from London I hired to a farmer, for a year, and served it faithfully, at the end of which we were married in the parish church.[70]

In fact, he had a previous settlement, but in a parish where he owed money, and to which he would not return. But the example clarifies how settlement was seen, and suggests the problems which could follow chargeability in a distant parish, with a settlement geographically and generationally distant. In a later period, no doubt, Varley would have returned to his wife with the disconsolate news that he had been dismissed two days short of his year. But during his life, settlement was still 'a peculiar privilege' of the poor, and their attitude to yearly hiring formed a consistent part of those 'moral economy' values analysed by E. P. Thompson and historians writing on popular protest.[71]

But the term 'moral economy' must be used carefully. Thompson paid particular attention to price fixing 'riots', and popular attitudes to the grain market, to regrating, forestalling, or engrossing. Such attitudes are now taken as the defining ingredients of the 'moral economy', and later research followed Thompson's preoccupations. However, there is no reason to limit discussion to these items – the subject should be pursued to cover the poor law in particular, and Thompson seemed to acknowledge as much when he stopped short at this point.[72] And were one to consider popular consumption, fashion, or leisure activities, the commercial and economic components of 'moral' economy attitudes would become manifest. Similarly, the 'moral' attitudes which came to surround yearly hiring could be described as pertaining to a particular set of employment practices

---

[70] C. Varley, *The Modern Farmer's Guide, by a Real Farmer* (Glasgow, 1768), pp. xxv–xxvi.

[71] Thompson, 'Moral economy of the English crowd'; J. Walter, 'Grain riots and popular attitudes to the law: Maldon and the crisis of 1629', in J. Brewer & J. Styles (eds.), *An Ungovernable People: The English and their Law in the Seventeenth and Eighteenth Centuries* (1980); A. Booth, 'Food riots in the north-west of England, 1790–1801', *Past and Present*, LXXVII (1977); R. A. E. Wells, 'The revolt of the south-west, 1800–1801: a study in English popular protest', *Social History*, VI (1977); J. Stevenson, 'Food riots in England, 1792–1818', in R. Quinault & J. Stevenson (eds.), *Popular Protest and Public Order: Six Studies in British History, 1790–1920* (1974); R. W. Malcolmson, '"A set of ungovernable people": the Kingswood colliers in the eighteenth century', in Brewer & Styles, *Ungovernable People* (1980); R. A. E. Wells, *Dearth and Distress in Yorkshire, 1793–1802* (Univ. of York Borthwick Papers, no. 52, 1977).

[72] Thompson, 'Moral economy of the English crowd', 124: 'The examination of such measures would take us too far into the history of the Poor Laws than we intend to go.'

and social relations (as in the early eighteenth century) when the practice had been an economically appropriate one for employers to pursue. The expectations which grew up to legitimate and presume the practice became 'moral' when economic circumstances outgrew them, or had changed so as to render them less viable. In this sense they were residual, and a token of the poor's conservatism: the once compatible values to economic circumstances and practices which were increasingly disrupted by the changing price, demographic, and employment conditions of the later eighteenth century. Perhaps they are best seen in this way, rather than as having a distant anti-commercial origin, in a form of 'commonweal' ideology disrupted (some might argue) by an emergent eighteenth-century capitalistic 'market economy'. Consideration of popular attitudes over settlement, the poor law, or yearly hiring should also contribute to remedy the amorphous character of Thompson's 'customary' or 'traditional' 'moral economy of the commonweal', and clarify the role and economic intentions of earlier Tudor legislation, which came to legitimate 'moral economy' behaviour in the period he discussed.

This is not to deny an intensified commercial ethic in the eighteenth century. And much earlier yearly employment, of servants or in many trades, had been 'traditional' in the sense that it was bounded by the Statute of Artificers, although one should not overstress this. The Statute was used or laid aside according to circumstance.[73] It is also the case that the disinclination of many farmers to rationalise their activities was lamented by late eighteenth-century agricultural improvers. Nevertheless, one could argue that improvers were condemning an anti-innovative mentality once appropriate to a period when over-production contributed to low prices and consequent depression; and the term 'traditional' is probably best avoided. The likelihood of long-term cycles of service as a feature of price determined employment policy (from at least the mid-sixteenth century), suggests that one should exaggerate neither the novelty of late eighteenth-century market orientation, nor the 'moral', anti-capitalistic elements of previous social attitudes and employment expectations, shared by the poor with the employing classes.

---

[73] Indictments at Quarter Sessions to force unmarried people into service seem to have become much less common after about 1750. In Essex, for example, after thirty-two such cases between 1748 and 1753, there were then three cases between 1754 and 1757, and none subsequently. The figures are only suggestive, but support the chronology argued for here. I am grateful to Peter King for this information. See Burn, *Justice of the Peace* (1797 edn), vol. 4, pp. 38ff, on the categories of occupation which should be yearly hired. I am not of course dealing with yearly hirings of artisans in this chapter.

IV

Be this as it may, the decline of farm service contributed significantly to the deterioration of social relations. Its physical proximity, with farm-servant living with employer, and the shared leisure and mutual toleration fostered by this system gave way to social segregation – to the point where Rev. John Cox could say: 'I do not know how they reason at all.'[74] In the words of the *Morning Chronicle's* Rural Correspondent – 'there is somewhere something very seriously wrong ... one class of society is thus at a loss to account satisfactorily for the mode in which another class manages to exist'.[75] Furthermore,

Another complaint on the part of the labourer is founded on the unfeeling manner in which they consider that they are almost invariably treated by their employers. They feel – to use their own words – that 'they are treated like slaves'. 'It is seldom', they say, 'that the farmer will condescend to speak to them, except in terms of reproach or abuse. There is no display of anything like kindly feeling towards them, nor any desire shown to improve their condition.'[76]

Complaining of reduced wages, the failure to employ men during the winter (as under service), and of the discharging of single men first because of their smaller cost to the rates, one labourer in Buckinghamshire complained: 'You see, sir, it's made a matter of pounds, shillings and pence throughout, and not of rewarding them that faithfully serve them.'[77] From another, near Amesbury – 'They beat the poor people down when things are dear ... they won't pay their poor people because they say they can't; but they ride their nags and keep their greyhounds for all that.'[78] More forcibly, 'They're a screwin', close-fisted, hard set of fellows – that's what the farmers are all about here', added a labourer from the Linton Union;[79] and stronger examples of such language and of class estrangement abound, although rarely found before 1780.

Here is a story told by a young vagrant in 1850, who once probably would have been a yearly servant:

A farmer hired Jack, and instructed him overnight. Jack was to do what he was required, or lose his head. 'Now Jack', said the farmer, 'what's my name?' 'Master, to be sure', says Jack. 'No', said he, 'you must call me Tom per cent.' He showed his bed next and asked, 'What's this Jack?' 'Why, the bed,' said Jack. 'No, you must call that He's of degree ...' (etc.). Jack was to remember these names, or lose his head ...[80].

The story demonstrates resentment at the social pretensions and

---

[74] S.C. on Settlement and Poor Removal, XI (1847), p. 497.
[75] *Morning Chronicle*, 26 Jan. 1850.   [76] *Ibid.*, 22 Jan. 1850.   [77] *Ibid.*, 27 Oct. 1849.
[78] *Ibid.*, 27 Oct. 1849.   [79] *Ibid.*, 18 Oct. 1850.   [80] *Ibid.*, 22 Jan. 1850.

authoritarianism of the farmer, and also implies that it would be unwise to submit to these by being hired. And this came to epitomise the dilemma facing the yearly servant. On the one hand there was the need to gain a settlement, and guard against unemployment; these were sought after and valued ends. But, on the other, there was the view that the prevention of settlements, the hiring for short periods, and the discarding of the obligation of winter employment did not entitle the employer to the deference previously accorded him, which he still insisted on. This ambiguity of response became characteristic of rural social relations. While employers renounced previous economic obligations, they insisted on continued submission, deference, and social prestige – soon to be enforced further by the New Poor Law. 'You must call that He's of degree.' As Hobsbawm and Rudé wrote on agrarian society:

Its rulers wanted it to be both capitalist and stable, traditionalist and hierarchical. In other words they wanted it to be governed by the universal free market of the liberal economist (which was inevitably a market for land and men as well as for goods), but only to the extent that suited nobles, squires and farmers; they advocated an economy which implied mutually antagonistic classes, but did not want it to disrupt a society of ordered ranks.[81]

The labourer now found himself in a situation as remote from the ideals of Cobbett or Oastler as from those of the political economist. He was distanced from his counterpart a century earlier by the new relation to his employer: socially segregated, unprotected against extreme unemployment or price fluctuation – short-term, impersonal, and insecure daily paid labour, with no reward for 'them that faithfully serve them'. As we shall see, the compulsions of the East Anglian 'ticket system', the less eligible workhouse, or the restricted settlement laws came to mock Chadwick's predictions of a free labour market, with 'independent' labour having a choice of employment and finding its own price.

Faced with 'morally' unjustified authority, no longer economically supportive in the old manner, the 'labourer' developed a peculiarly contradictory position. On the one hand he was dependent, if remotely acquiescing in a soured form of the deference once praised by Cobbett. On the other, he moved hesitantly towards principles of self-help, of class isolation and 'independence' – the ambivalent but legitimating cliche of the period. He aspired to a yearly hiring and the social dependence that it involved, as in the early eighteenth century – and for similar reasons. But its discipline and subservience, enforced by a farmer class increasingly unsure of its own wider social

[81] Hobsbawm & Rudé, *Captain Swing*, p. 27.

standing, could now seem unjustified. Service soon jettisoned its role as a protective social obligation. The labourer's contradictory view derived from his experience of changing and indeterminate social obligations, and the ineffectiveness of his inherited attitudes to influence policy. It can be seen as clearly in the attitudes to employment under discussion, as in the dereliction of other components of the 'moral economy' – using that term here simply to denote earlier popular expectations that middlemen and the corn market be regulated; that a 'just' price be fixed; that wages be determined at a fair level; or that the poor be relieved in their 'own' parish.

By the mid-nineteenth century the effect on rural class relations was manifest and being clearly articulated. There had, after all, been three decades of persistent unrest to incite speculation, highlighted by the 'Bread or Blood' riots and by 'Swing'. Farm-servants were, apparently, almost never involved in these events.[82] And the enquiry into later incendiary fires, by *The Times* in 1844, went straight to the point:

Formerly, in the 'good old times', as they are called, it was the custom . . . to hire labourers [sic] by the year . . . There was exhibited much kindliness and good feeling between master and labourer, from the closeness of the tie between them – living in the same house, and sometimes eating at the same board. Now this state of things is entirely changed. Almost all the labourers on the different farms are day-labourers – paid by the day. They no longer go to the farm-house, or near it. The closeness of the tie between master and man is broken; the term of servitude is a more uncertain and changeable one – the vacant days of the year the labourer has no work; and he is compelled to find a home somewhere; often (I may almost say always) without that solid comfort he formerly found at his master's farmhouse.[83]

And it was George Coode's task, in his 1851 Report on Settlement and Removal, to judge the effect of the decline. In part, he argued, it had intensified rural crime, and led to badly overcrowded cottages. But it had done far more than this.

A wide distinction of habits grew up . . . between the two classes . . . It was impossible to restore the old relations, the familiar habits of the master and his servant, their almost equal moral elevation, the personal attachment to the latter, the ancient household accommodation for him, the routine of occupations by which the permanent servant had always a profitable occupation, in-door or out, whatever the season, whatever the weather.[84]

The decline in other words, was very significantly 'an alteration in the state of society':

'I do not know how they reason at all.'

[82] Peacock, *Bread or Blood*, p. 25.   [83] *The Times*, 10 June 1844.
[84] Report on the Law of Settlement and Removal, XXVI (1851), p. 273.

3

Social relations – the poor law

I

According to *The Times*, in its 1844 enquiry into rural incendiarism, there were four causes of the arson which had become so widespread in the southern agricultural counties. These were exceptionally low wages; the decline of farm service; the enclosure of open fields, commons, and wastes; and antagonism to the New Poor Law alongside its detrimental effect on employment.[1] The first three of these causes are dealt with in other chapters, and I want here to discuss the poor law. The subject has an extensive historiography, and it is not my intention to outline relief administration during this period. The wide variety of practice; the nature and effects of Speenhamland and associated policies; the dubious credibility of the Poor Law Report of 1834 – such aspects have been covered by other historians.[2] I want rather to emphasise factors hitherto rather neglected, and consider the effects of the law on the quality of life: on wages and employment, work discipline, the treatment of the elderly, and, primarily, on the quality of social relationships.

The old poor law provides the key to a social understanding of the eighteenth century. Parochial organisation ensured a face to face connection of administrators and the poor; while generous terms of relief and often humble officers facilitated agreement and mutual respect between the ranks and orders of parish society. The old poor

---

[1] *The Times*, 'Inquiry into Incendiary Fires', 7 June 1844.
[2] Perhaps the best bibliography of secondary literature on the old poor law is still that provided by G. W. Oxley, *Poor Relief in England and Wales, 1601–1834* (Plymouth, 1974), pp. 141–52. See also the bibliographies in D. J. Marshall, *The Old Poor Law, 1795–1834* (1968), and M. E. Rose, *The Relief of Poverty, 1834–1914* (1972). For many of the contemporary publications covering the final years of the old poor law, see J. R. Poynter, *Society and Pauperism: Ideas on Poor Relief, 1795–1834* (1969), bibliography.

law constantly intruded in the interchange between views of the ruling and rate-paying classes, and lower-order expectations. It permeated social relationships with its wide-ranging influence over aspects of parish life such as employment and the regulation of wages, price fixing, the grain market, apprenticeship, marriage, settlement, the allocation of relief, or the treatment of the elderly. The parish vestry and poor law officers of overseers, constables, and churchwardens could cut across divides of wealth, and were the means by which the gentry and 'middling' classes secured positions in parish society which would be precarious without the respect received by acting according to certain customary expectations, favourable to the economic interests of the labouring poor.

In looking at the economic benefits to recipients under the old poor law one can be surprised by the generous and widely encompassing nature of relief. Eighteenth-century overseers' accounts contain evidence of payments for numerous items and services needed by the poor, most of which were to be heavily curtailed after 1834. Besides unemployment relief and pensions, parish payments were made for shoes, pattens or boots, clothes of all sorts, furniture (especially bedding), rents, fuel (coals), childbed linen and other lying-in expenses (such as payments to the midwife), flour, meat, marriage costs, burial shrouds, laying-out expenses, grave digging and other burial costs, pensions and cleaning costs for elderly paupers, payment to neighbours for nursing, smallpox inoculation, or even spectacles.[3] The payments of pensions, rent, or for fuel, shoes, lying-in, flour, or burial were especially common. Other payments indicate the generosity of relief: 'To a pint of wine for Susan Ashton'; 'To tobacco for Old Youngs'; 'To cash allow'd Samuel Jones to purchase a cow'; 'Paid Mr. Henry Cook for a bed for Thos. Halls. £2.2s.'; 'paid Mr Bedford filing a saw and shelts [crutches] boy Barker 1/9d.'; 'paid for a wooden leg for the boy Barker 8/6d'; 'to beer for Sterling's wifes burial'; 'the girl Munson at Mrs. Ingrams 5½ yards of clorth, 4 yds grogram, 2 mantles, 1 gown, 4 yds of check, 2 handkerchiefs, 3 caps and 1 pair of shoes'; 'Paid dame Death for nursing dame Hiskey 1/6d.'; and so on.[4]

---

[3] For spectacles being paid for by the parish in the 1730s and 1740s, see F. G. Emmison, 'Relief of the poor at Eaton Socon, Bedfordshire, 1706–1834', *Beds Hist. Rec. Soc.*, XV (1933), 74. For accessible published accounts to illustrate the range of expenditure, see F. H. Erith, *Ardleigh in 1796* (East Bergholt, 1978), pp. 6–22; M. Sheard, *The Records of the Parish of Batley* (Worksop, 1894), pp. 213–19; J. E. Abney (ed.), *The Vestry Book and Churchwardens' Accounts of St. Mary, Leicester* (1912); E. Freshfield (ed.), *Accomptes of the Churchwardens of the Paryshe of St. Christofer's in London* (1885).

[4] These examples are from Erith, *Ardleigh*, pp. 6–22.

Examples of such expenditure can be found in almost all parishes where accounts survive. There were also the costs of boarding out children, or apprenticing them (a full range of clothes usually being provided), the (at times enormous) costs of removal and its associated expenditure, medical expenses (frequently including drink), workhouse and general maintenance costs where a workhouse was partly resorted to, costs of militia substitutes, the bills from constables, churchwardens, or surveyors, or the supplementation of wages from the poor rates – practised at least thirteen years before Speenhamland policy in 1795 brought the matter into prominence.[5] For the poor law was a system of employment as well as relief: regulating paupers on parish work, supplying raw materials for inmates in houses of industry or the poor in their own homes, arranging labour rate and roundsman systems, or 'farming' the poor to local employers. One is struck by the wide terms of relief and extensive use of the law, intruding as it did into most aspects of parish life, in a manner never since replicated on a comparable scale. Inevitably the elderly came to require assistance, and many items of expenditure covered them: nursing and medical care in their own homes, out-door pensions, fuel, rents – even shaving in some cases. Parish workhouses were only occasionally used (in 1802, 8 per cent of relief recipients were workhouse inmates), and if not the supposed 'pauper palaces' of incorporated Norfolk and Suffolk, they were often, Hampson wrote, 'places of refuge or desireable resort'.[6] If the treatment of the elderly is taken as a guide to the humanity of relief policy in general, the old poor law was largely benevolent and sympathetic in operation.

Undoubtedly there was corruption and maladministration, most apparent where a workhouse was contracted, where there could be ill-feeling against a contractor on fixed payments who curtailed expenditure at the expense of elderly inmates, the maimed, or orphan children.[7] The workhouse built after enclosure in John Clare's parish was an example. Similarly, for non-settled inhabitants, vagrants, or bastard bearers, there were cases of inhumanity, and these have to be distinguished from the treatment of *settled* inhabitants. The removal of elderly or sick people to their settlements certainly took place; and

---

[5] For a Speenhamland hiring in 1783, see West Suffolk C.R.O., N2.1.8; E. M. Hampson, 'Settlement and removal in Cambridgeshire, 1662–1834', *Cambridge Hist. Jnl*, II (1926–8), 276; or her *The Treatment of Poverty in Cambridgeshire, 1597–1834* (Cambridge, 1934), pp. 189–92. The principle of Speenhamland can also be found in Gilbert's Act of 1782, 22 Geo III c. 83.

[6] Hampson, *Treatment of Poverty*, pp. 266–8.

[7] The practice of 'farming' workhouses was especially attacked by J. Scott, *Observations on the Present State of the Parochial and Vagrant Poor* (1773), pp. 30ff, 113.

while the poor did indeed see settlement as their 'peculiar privilege',[8] in some cases removal itself could be correctly described as 'that injury to the poor, that wanton or malicious chase of the unhappy from one inhospitable region to another'.[9] Similarly, bastard bearers suffered from the legal stipulation that an illegitimate child be settled in the parish of birth. This led to the removal of mothers before birth (at times by gangs of local men without the warrant of a removal order), sometimes during labour itself, to ensure that birth took place across parish boundaries. And separation of mother from illegitimate child could occur after the child was seven years of age, if the mother found herself chargeable and settled in a different parish from her child's birth place. But in such cases, stigma falls on the settlement laws rather than relief administration, and these practices should be reconciled with otherwise generous terms of relief by insisting on a distinction of practice as applied to the settled and non-settled. Of course, poor law practice differed between 'open' and 'close' parishes (however one assesses the usefulness of that distinction); between town and country, densely or sparsely populated parishes (per capita expenditure was higher in the latter);[10] and could vary according to such factors as regional employment seasonality, provision of cottage industry, or rent levels. But to settled inhabitants rural parishes were indeed 'miniature welfare states', and before about 1780 relief policy was usually generous, flexible, and humane.

It has become fashionable among some historians to deride accounts of parish institutions in the eighteenth century, or in open field villages, which draw attention to their democratic or participatory elements, and certainly one should not exaggerate these. But some further points can be agreed upon, so as to lay groundwork for comparison with a later period. The parish vestry was, in the first case, open, such that any ratepayer (and in many cases, the poor themselves) could attend to hear policy and cases discussed as a matter of right. According to a later Select Committee, they had attended 'continually so'.[11] Parish officers – overseers, constables, and churchwardens – were frequently of humble or low 'middling'

---

[8] R. Pashley, *Pauperism and the Poor Laws* (1852), pp. 267–9.

[9] Scott, *Observations*, p. 73. One should guard against seeing gradual improvement over time. Some of the worst cases were to come after 1846–7, with 9 & 10 Vic c. 66 stipulating that no widow could be removed from the parish of her husband's death for a year after his death. This led to the ejection of men thought likely to die shortly, and leave a widow and children. See, for example, Cambridgeshire C.R.O., G/C/As 9.

[10] M. Blaug, 'The myth of the old poor law and the making of the new', in M. W. Flinn & T. C. Smout (eds.), *Essays in Social History* (Oxford, 1974), p. 152, n. 17.

[11] S.C. on the Poor Law Amendment Act, XVIII (1837–8), pt II, p. 496.

status. Some when later examined claimed their own settlements on the basis of parish offices served. They were, especially before 1818–19, usually unsalaried, and overseers were commonly chosen by parishioners, and then approved by J.P.s.[12] There could be considerable turnover of administrative officers, with labourers and small village artisans serving, even though sometimes almost illiterate, and frequently acting as deputies to the overseer. Women could be overseers (as in Eaton Socon, Pavenham, Ardleigh, Brunting-thorpe, Gnosall or Monkwearmouth), and certainly often served on vestries and in other offices[13] – such a role was curtailed in the early nineteenth century, until the 'can women be poor law guardians?' debate of the later nineteenth century brought the matter more into discussion.[14] In unenclosed villages, participation of 'middling' and lower-status inhabitants was more pronounced, just as in densely populated parishes, such as the 'open' parishes of East Anglia. We can compare these features of office holding and administration in due course with circumstances after 1834. For the moment, it can be stressed that the old poor law allowed much scope for face to face relief between ratepayers and recipients who knew each other well, and who were sometimes of comparable status.

There were, nevertheless, strains after about 1780 which produced re-assessments of earlier relief – the problems for example of structural unemployment, rising poor rates, or of agricultural depression after 1813. One symptom manifest in poor law policy was the alternation between different forms of relief: a roundsman or labour rate system, a contracted workhouse, Speenhamland, in some cases with three to five years before disillusionment with prevailing practice as it failed to halt upward relief costs. Another symptom was a marked tightening up on relief offered. Ardleigh in Essex was an example, from which some earlier citations of generous relief came (and this was a populous parish – relief would commonly be more

---

[12] The Select Vestry Acts authorised the appointment of paid, permanent overseers to assist annually elected overseers (59 Geo III c. 12). In some parishes (for example, Cardington) this had already become the practice.

[13] Emmison, 'Relief of the poor at Eaton Socon', 87; Oxley, *Poor Relief*, p. 43; Erith, *Ardleigh*, p. 7; Leicestershire C.R.O., DE/765/7; S. A. Cutlack, 'The Gnosall records, 1679–1837', in Staffs Record Society (ed.), *Collections for a History of Staffordshire* (Stafford, 1936), p. 7.

[14] For later nineteenth-century discussion, see: Anon., 'The work of women as poor law guardians', *Westminster Rev.*, CXXIII (1885); Anon., 'Women as poor law guardians', *Englishwoman's Review* (1875), 157–9; Ignota, 'Women in Local Administration: England and Wales', *Westminster Rev.*, CL (1898); L. Twining, *Workhouses and Pauperism, and Women's Work in the Administration of the Poor Law* (1898); J. M. E. Brownlow, *Women's Work in Local Government* (1911).

generous where population density was slighter). During the high price years of 1795 and 1800–1 payments for clothes, fuel, nursing, burials, shoes, and the rest were greatly minimised; and after 1815 such payments virtually ceased altogether. There was nothing exceptional about Ardleigh in this regard, although in some parishes change came from the 1790s, and elsewhere there was greater continuity until the 1820s. In 1796 (following hard on the high price year of 1795), expenditure on clothes and shoes in Ardleigh had still amounted to 4.6 per cent of the annual total. But by 1830 this had fallen to only 0.5 per cent. By then in Ardleigh, as for example in Brightlingsea or St Osyth, the large majority of applications for these traditional payments was being rejected.[15] And it was just such items (as shoes or rent), which had proved such a heavy burden for the labourers' families whose budgets were left us by Davies or Eden. Coupled with falling real wages, growing structural unemployment, a curtailment of access to the land and of female work and cottage industry, the implications of savings in this vulnerable area of relief are clear enough, with their detrimental effects on an already deteriorating material standard of life.

The extension of Speenhamland, or the roundsman and labour rate systems, has been widely discussed; and it is clear that they were a reaction to unemployment and pauperism rather than themselves causing such problems, as claimed by the 1834 Report.[16] The administration of Speenhamland, with its sliding price determined bread scale, also changed in a way which adversely affected recipients. The scale was heavily curtailed over time, to become only two-thirds to a half of its 1795 value by the 1820s. The fall in allowances for women was particularly marked. Income accordingly fell far below even the 'minimum' set by the Berkshire magistrates in 1795. Similarly, although the scale theoretically moved with prices, in practice it did not follow them proportionally, and so real income generally fell even further during high prices. As pressure grew to curtail expenditure, especially during the depression after 1813, so other expedients gained ground. One in particular deserves mention – the policy of rating the poor themselves. This developed much further after 1834, but appeared during the final stages of the old poor law, and was widely attacked, as by John Clare in 'The Parish: a Satire':

> Damns all taxes both of church and state
> And on the parish lays a double rate . . .

[15] Essex C.R.O., D/P. 263/12/1–15, D/P. 312/8/1–4, D/P. 322/12/4.
[16] See in particular Blaug, 'Myth of the old poor law'; and his 'The Poor Law Report re-examined', *Jnl of Econ. Hist.*, XXIV (1964).

Or carrying the parish book from door to door,
Claiming fresh taxes from the needy poor . . .
Cheating the poor with levies doubly laid
On their small means, that wealth may be defrayed;
To save his own and others', his compeers,
He robs the poor whom he has robbed for years . . .[17]

Arthur Young by 1801 was strongly deprecating the practice: 'This is abominable', he wrote.[18] An 1818 Select Committee discussed the rating of more lowly priced property than hitherto, with even labourers sometimes having to pay poor rates, and concluded that many of the latter were worse off than those receiving relief.[19] And the 1834 Report actually commended the practice, and advocated its extension, because rating the poor apparently created hostility among them to relief recipients, when such relief was (very) partially being paid by other poor in the parish.[20] This tactic was thereafter widely used, and crucially to influence attitudes to the poor law. (The pittances given as out-relief after 1834 were even taxed towards the poor rates in some areas – a precedent for the proposals of much later governments.)[21] The rating of labourers, it was said, 'makes them exceedingly angry'[22] – and it was widely held to have a damaging effect on class relations.

Such policies were manifestations of the wider deliberation on the poor law after the 1790s. This debate gave rise to a huge crop of pamphlets on pauperism and the poor laws, mostly written by farmers, ratepayers, and clergymen closely concerned with administration, and eager to have their proposals adopted nationally. The

[17] John Clare, *The Parish: A Satire*, in J. W. & A. Tibble (eds.), *John Clare, Selected Poems* (1965), pp. 152–5.

[18] A. Young, *An Inquiry into the Propriety of Applying Wastes to the Better Maintenance and Support of the Poor* (Bury St Edmunds, 1801), p. 113.

[19] S.C. of the House of Lords on the Poor Laws, V (1818), pp. 163ff, 177ff. See also A. Digby, *Pauper Palaces* (1978), p. 86.

[20] S. G. & E. O. A. Checkland (eds.), *The Poor Law Report of 1834* (1974), p. 369.

[21] *The Times*, 'Inquiry into Incendiary Fires', 10 July 1846. (This was the case, for example, in parts of Dorset.)

[22] S.C. on the Poor Law Amendment Act, XVIII (1837–8), pt III, pp. 21, 185ff. Or see the East Suffolk anonymous letter signed by the 'Secret Avenger', which suggested that its recipient imagine: 'an honest man ploding on in the vocation he is placed in earning barely sufficient to maintain his family and cloathing them in prosperous times – what must be the case you think now, when Parish *Rates* rise [?] so high . . . Turn over what Act of Parliament you please and see if it was whether it was ever the intention of the legislative body to *rate* or *tax* a man situated as above, one who is within six days of Pauperism himself . . . What is the consequence think you? Why are they now men fit for the darkest purposes . . . the Evil is to come . . . our numbers are great and are men capable of doing upon the Plan we act upon as wonders without discovery – more *Fires* shall be witnessed.' Cited in M. Rosenthal, *Constable. The Painter and his Landscape* (1983), pp. 208–9.

subject was debated at local level, and proposals which raised fears among the poor must have influenced their social perceptions nearly as much as actual practice did. The peak of poor law expenditure in 1817 saw the most furious pamphleteering, and Committee Reports of 1817 and 1818 came close to advocating entire poor law repeal, to create a situation similar to that in Ireland or France. 'The grand object is to lower the poor rates', reported a witness to the 1817 Select Committee, which was an understandable concern given the threat of agricultural bankruptcy.[23] But many proposals struck the poor as highly unreasonable. The early Arthur Young, for instance, had written that he would prefer the poor to be killed in war than to

be constantly increasing, and remain a dead weight on the industrious; and my humanity [sic] prompts me to the idea, because I apprehend, population would suffer less in the former than in the latter case . . . In a word, when the maxims of a pernicious government have forced a class of the people to be idle, the greatest favour you can do them, is to a range them before a battery of the enemy's canon.[24]

This was not a commonly held proposal, but it was made by a very influential author in perhaps his most widely read publication.

More commonly, there were schemes for forced emigration, or for the banning of relief to those who refused to emigrate. Robert Torrens wanted paupers sent out to America and Australia to produce grain for England, rapidly paying off the cost of the journey, and he advocated forcing certain categories of pauper (the married) to go over. 'The amount of the Poor Rates would afford an infallible political barometer for determining whether emigration to the colonies was going on too slowly or too fast.' Such colonisation would produce 'an instantaneous and almost magical effect . . . want would cease to engender the desire of change; the ideas of relief and of revolution would lose their fatal connexion in the minds of the

---

[23] S.C. of the House of Commons on the Poor Laws, VI (1817), p. 76. But such increases in poor law expenditure, and curtailments of per recipient relief, did not hinder the generosity of parish vestry members towards themselves in the final stages of the old poor law. For example: 'It was unanimously agreed that a Piece of Plate of not more than Twenty Pounds Value shall be presented to Mr. Preston for his excellent Method of Keeping his Accounts and transacting the Parish Business for the past year.' The same vestry meeting 'determined that no Person shall be employed in Labor who has any children belonging to other Parishes until the Child or Children are removed to their respective Parishes'. Oxfordshire C.R.O. (Bodleian) MSS. DD. Par. Eynsham, e. 1 (1834), p. 147. The giving of money (£15–20, raised by the rate) to overseers and constables to buy themselves plate was routine in this parish after 1823, even as allowances for the elderly and unemployment relief were being heavily curtailed (see *ibid.*, p. 122).

[24] A. Young, *Political Arithmetic* (1774), pp. 57–8.

multitude; and the spirit of discontent and disaffection . . . would no longer endanger our establishments'. Colonisation was a

safety valve to the political machine . . . humanity and justice, no less than policy, require that we should avail ourselves of the resources placed in our hands by the vast extent of unappropriated colonial territory . . . The hive contains more than it can support; and if it be not permitted to swarm, the excess must either perish of famine, or be destroyed by internal contests for food.[25]

Here, as elsewhere, we see the pervasive influence of Malthus – whose theories of the interrelation of population and economy sadly lasted long after they had become redundant.[26] Ten years later he was himself before a highly respectful Select Committee. Emigration, he suggested, should be followed by the destruction of cottages; 'those that were born after a certain time should not be allowed to have any parish assistance'.[27] But the poor themselves regarded parish settlement and the right to relief as their birthright. And it was small wonder that they now equated 'emigration' with transportation, as the Rev. Beecher pointed out to the same Committee when Malthus had finished.[28]

Of course, emigration, or the enemy's canon, were only two answers to high rates, although the former was widely advocated. Other authors suggested an encompassing range of alternatives, few of them humane, a couple ludicrous, and almost all obnoxious to the poor. These included the workhouse, frequently with Benthamite and Panopticon-type trappings; badging the poor with labels such as 'infamous Liar', or 'Criminal Poor', so as to instil in them 'nice, and delicate, and virtuous feelings';[29] houses of industry; variants on

---

[25] R. Torrens, *A Paper on the Means of Reducing the Poors Rates, and of affording effectual and Permanent Relief to the Labouring Classes* (1817), p. 521, 524–5. For other emigration schemes to reduce poor rates, see T. P. MacQueen, *Thoughts and Suggestions on the Present Condition of the Country* (1830), or his *The State of the Nation at the close of 1830* (1831; R. F., *Observations on Pauperism* (1832); M. Gore, *Allotments of Land. A letter to Landed Proprietors, on the Advantages of giving the Poor Allotments of Land* (1831); Anon., *Emigration and the Condition of the Labouring Poor* (Colchester, 1832).

[26] E. A. Wrigley & R. S. Schofield, *The Population History of England, 1541–1871* (1981), ch. 10. And see J. P. Huzel, 'Malthus, the poor law and population in early nineteenth-century England', *Econ. Hist. Rev.*, XXII (1969); and his 'The demographic impact of the Old Poor Law: more reflexions on Malthus', *Econ. Hist. Rev.*, XXXIII (1980).

[27] S.C. on Emigration, V (1826–7), p. 537. Or see pp. 622ff for a similar proposal.

[28] *Ibid.*, p. 623. The same point was made by MacQueen, *State of the Nation*, pp. 26–7. See also W. Cobbett, *Rural Rides* (1830, Harmondsworth, 1975 edn), pp. 319–20.

[29] C. D. Brereton, *Inquiry into the Work-House System and the Law of Maintenance in Agricultural Districts* (Norwich, 1822), p. 73. Or see J. Hanway, *Observations on the Causes of the Dissoluteness which reigns among the Lower Classes of the People* (1772), p. 20, for further 'badging' proposals.

roundsman, labour rate, Speenhamland, and ticket systems; interesting proposals to contain working-class sexuality and marriage; schemes of internal migration; proposals for friendly and other societies; changes in the rating system; schools of industry; industrial and agricultural training schemes; agricultural colonies; proposals for a revival of access to the land and the keeping of livestock – pamphleteers enthusiastically espoused these and other less likely proposals. In many pamphlets the dedication had pride of place: pages of sycophantic prose to catch the patronage of some major political figure, with the insinuation that a monetary reward or administrative role would be welcomed should the proposal ever be adopted. And the language and classical terms of reference can strike one today as appallingly ill-equipped to deal with prevailing rural problems. C. D. Brereton, for example, was a pamphleteer more worthy of our attention than most, who produced a number of publications on the problems of agricultural pauperism. The original Elizabethan laws, he was convinced, had been perverted during the eighteenth and early nineteenth centuries. This was a common sentiment. But he continued in a standard manner:

We have seen the black round substance begin to dilate , and after a while the head, the eyes, the tail, to be discernible, and at last become what the ancients called gyrinus, we, a perwigle or tadpole, or to use a figure, less applicable to the puddles through which we have waded, but perhaps less offensive – we have traced the insect from its caterpillar to its aurelia state, and in the next chapter shall see the full-blown moth, that for a while fluttered in our casements, then introduced itself into the wardrobe of our laws, where, undisturbed for years, it has been fretting and corroding the vestments and ornaments of social life.[30]

Other pamphleteers waded through similar puddles, allowing ornately classical language to adorn axiomatic Smithian, Benthamite, and Malthusian dogma – or, in one case, 'Adam Smith's principle of population' – appealing to their audience of 'gentlemen of independent and honourable feelings'; usually seeing the problem as a purely legal one which required a legislatorial and authoritative remedy – to deal with the 'criminal poor', the 'infamous liars', the people who are 'virtually villains, *adscripti glebae* ... degenerate and dishonest', 'terrorless and depraved'.[31] Or as Bicheno put it, by way of opening his curiously entitled *Inquiry into the Nature of Benevolence*, the labouring poor were 'an excrescence on the body politic'; and this 'growing

[30] Brereton, *Inquiry into the Work-house System*, pp. 51–2.
[31] *Ibid.*, pp. 72–3; C. D. Brereton, *A Practical Inquiry into the Number, Means of Employment and Wages of Agricultural Labourers* (Norwich, 1824), pp. 33–4. W. Day, *An Inquiry into the Poor Laws and Surplus Labour* (1833), p. 76.

up in society, with such an augmentation of moral worth in the middle classes, presents a feature unexampled in history . . . One part of society may be refined and improved while the other is degenerating.'[32] The language was typical, although the New Poor Law would soon help to replace this threatening and execrated stereotype with 'Hodge' himself. Almost all such attacks on the poor and proposals for poor law reform shared two elements: an insistence on self-help as the alternative to high rates, and the determination that the poor should remain dependent on and respectful to their social superiors. These contradictory demands were realised in the poor law expedient finally adopted in 1834.

II

A great deal is now known on the making of the New Poor Law and its administration, but there has been surprisingly little assessment of its effect on social relations, or its influence on the labour market, on wages, employment, the family, or the treatment of the aged. At best, the subject was aired in a brief encounter between two scholars asking simply 'how cruel was the Victorian Poor Law?'.[33] The contrast with the heated controversy it aroused among contemporaries is very striking. No doubt the historiographical acquiescence until comparatively recently in the well known views of the 1832–4 Commission led historians to concede that perhaps the 'principles of '34' were necessary; and it took the work most notably of Mark Blaug to confirm the earlier condemnatory verdict of the Webbs on the 1834 Report. Nevertheless, the New Poor Law was enthusiastically held by its supporters to have eased the hostility of class relations, and to have been widely beneficial, and one should assess the terms in which it was praised.

The Commissioners themselves aimed at an 'improved relation of master and man', and contemporaries commenting on their supposed success saw the situation entirely from the employer's viewpoint. H. M. Musgrave (Chairman of the Ampthill Union) declared in a revealing statement that this 'master and man' relation

is increasing very fast indeed ... the men are more willing to work; the farmers have not anything like the same trouble in looking after them; we are getting, generally speaking, more money than we did before; the master can

---

[32] J. E. Bicheno, *Inquiry into the Nature of Benevolence* (1817), pp. 3–4.
[33] D. Roberts, 'How cruel was the Victorian poor law?', *Hist. Jnl*, IV (1963.; U. Henriques, 'How cruel was the Victorian poor law?', *Hist. Jnl*, XI (1968). And the work of A. Digby is exceptional in discussing the poor law's wider social and economic significance.

now leave home with greater comfort than he could before, and when he has
returned he has not to find the same fault; there is a nicer feeling between
master and man; that is increasing very fast indeed.[34]

In the same Union poor 'people now touch their hats to you as they
pass; before they were always sulky ... now they are civil and
polite'.[35] Similarly, Assistant Commissioner James Kay was satisfied
that 'the just and natural relation between the master and the servant'
had been restored.[36] Elsewhere 'An improved state of feeling has
been brought about between the employer and the employed ... men
no longer come before the board in the rudest possible manner, with
their hats on and pipes in their mouths, and insolently demand their
scale allowance.'[37] 'Clericus' praised the 'reform wrought upon the
most hopeless characters in my parish, under the dread of the
workhouse test and the necessity of labour for their subsistence –
labour which brought back with it the religion and contentment of
past happier days'.[38] 'Industry, frugality and good conduct have
been restored to the able-bodied labourer', reported another
pamphleteer.[39] And a witness to the 1838 Select Committee spoke of
'the wonderful change that has taken place in so short a time; a moral
and physical revolution, which is scarcely to be credited'.[40] Nevertheless, in the 'Blood or Money' Ampthill riot of May 1835, which was
directed particularly against the new law, 'one man produced an old
copy of Burn's *Justice*, and quoted a part of some repealed Act, and
also the Bible, as the word of God'.[41] It is unlikely that he was
rejoicing at the newly established 'just and natural relations between
the master and the servant'. And participants in the many other

---

[34] S.C. on the Poor Law Amendment Act, XVIII (1837–8), pt III, p. 208.

[35] *Ibid.*, pt II, p. 69. Compare C. Holdenby, *The Folk of the Furrow* (1913), pp. 26–7:
It is the idea of a legitimate prey, the right to make some folk disgorge, the
suggestion of a just reprisal ... It is often the same spirit, too, which initiates
poaching rather than the actual material gain. There is a satisfaction in carrying
the war right into the enemy's country. I know so well the attitude in which the
villagers touch their hats to the gentry while they are in their employ. The salute is
thrown in with the service, but it ceases with the latter.

[36] S.C. on the Poor Law Amendment Act XVIII (1837–8), pt I, p. 481.

[37] *Morning Chronicle*, 26 Dec. 1849. The notion that the poor had a 'right' to relief was
especially condemned by the 1834 Poor Law Report, and by Malthusian pamphleteers and supporters of the New Poor Law. For Cobbett's arguments to the
contrary, defending this right, see his *Advice to Young Men* (1830, Oxford, 1980 edn),
pp. 314ff, and his *Legacy to Labourers* (1835).

[38] 'Clericus', *Pour et Contre: A Few Humble Observations upon the New Poor Law* (1841), p.
20.

[39] Anon., *Remarks on the Opposition to the Poor Law Amendment Bill, by a Guardian* (1841),
p. 54.

[40] S.C. on the Poor Law Amendment Act, XVIII (1837–8), pt I, p. 481.

[41] *Ibid.*, pt III, p. 197.

incidents which occurred (for example, in Rollesby, Huntingdon, Great Bircham, Heckingham, West Suffolk, or in the agitation led by the Rev. Maberley in Cambridgeshire) certainly did not see the law in the way the above commentators did.[42] As an 1847 Committee commented: 'the farmers were under a delusion; they think there is that tie existing between them and their labourers, but when you come to analyse and investigate it, you find there is no such thing in the present day, though there used to be formerly.'[43]

There were many reasons for this, connected with the poor law. One should mention initially certain administrative changes. The new aspects of centralisation, the formation of the Poor Law Commission, the agglomeration of parishes into Unions catered to by the workhouse, or the creation of boards of guardians had wide reaching significance. They have been discussed elsewhere, albeit primarily from an administrative angle. Alongside these were changes which contributed further to intensify rural class hostility. First, the formation of boards of guardians placed administration more firmly in the hands of the employing and tenant farmer classes. And among such men were those most prone to use the law to their own economic benefit, by compelling acceptance of low wages and precarious employment; and using it in a punitive manner against individuals obnoxious to themselves, who had for instance participated in the 'Swing' unrest.[44] One historian has stressed the landed aristocracy's role in the creation of the law, and also suggested that the provision for property-based plural voting on boards of guardians further enhanced their position.[45] The central board of commissioners, he argued, constructed 'a network of powerful new local boards constituted according to the hierarchical social order of the countryside'.[46] During the deliberation over the Bill, the proposed powers of the central board were apparently curtailed, and the local boards reconstituted from a proposed democratic system to one featuring plural voting. No doubt these measures were indeed to safeguard the

---

[42] More deserves to be written on the opposition to the New Poor Law, which was broadly based and fiercer than often supposed. But see M. E. Rose, 'The anti-poor law agitation', in J. T. Ward (ed.), *Popular Movements, c. 1830–1850* (1970); N. C. Edsall, *The Anti-Poor Law Movement, 1833–4* (1971).

[43] S.C. on Settlement and Poor Removal, XI (1847), p. 406.

[44] See, for example, *The Times*, 'Inquiry into Incendiary Fires', 4 July 1844; Digby, *Pauper Palaces*, p. 118.

[45] A. Brundage, 'The landed interest and the New Poor Law: a reappraisal of the revolution in government', *English Hist. Rev.*, LXXXVII (1972); or see his *The Making of the New Poor Law, 1832–39* (1978).

[46] Brundage, *Making of the New Poor Law*, p. 14.

potential administrative role of the gentry, and it would be surprising
if the latter had not had a major influence on the new legislation.

But Brundage's argument has been questioned by Dunkley, and
implicitly by many others.[47] His work concentrated on Northamptonshire, where the power of greater magnates was almost certainly
more extensive than elsewhere. More commonly, one is struck by
tenant farmer guardians controlling administration; and guardians'
minutes in many Unions suggest that gentry rarely exercised plural
voting, or had agents doing this. Frequently, they were absent from
meetings (there was always a high absentee rate, with only about 10
to 40 per cent of guardians present), and other more interested parties
dealt with the routine matters of relief which, after all, did not directly
concern the gentry. This was also the view of contemporary commentators familiar with administration. One pamphleteer saw the New
Poor Law as depriving 'the rural aristocracy of the chief element of
their power';[48] a change away from the magistracy's power under the
old law which he welcomed and which had been a major recom-
mendation of the 1834 Report. Most people thought, he continued,
that the new law 'was a great blow to the influence of the provincial
aristocracy', and he cited as an example the elections of guardians 'in
which the peer sits and debates at the same board with his tenant and
his tradesman'. Furthermore, 'it gave to a newly created London
authority a right of interference in matters which had hitherto been
reserved for the patriarchal administration of the resident
proprietors'.[49] As Edsall or Digby pointed out, the Union guardians
were large farmers, professional men, middling class shopkeepers –
by now often out of sympathy and understanding with the poor.
Digby stressed the power gained by local farmers as being crucial in
their growing assertiveness.[50] Despite the role attached to the gentry
by Gilbert's Act (1782), or by the Select Vestries Acts (of 1818 and
1819),[51] complaints were being made even before 1834 on the rural
gentry's dereliction of duty; of 'that want of public spirit, and that
aversion to business, which has prevailed of late years amongst our
gentry, who leave the inspection of the poor wholly to the people at

---

[47] P. Dunkley, 'The landed interest and the New Poor Law: a critical note', *Eng. Hist.
Rev.*, LXXXVIII (1973).

[48] Anon., *Remarks on the Opposition to the Poor Law Amendment Bill*, p. 43.

[49] *Ibid.*, p. 63.

[50] Edsall, *The Anti-Poor Law Movement*, ch. 2; Digby, *Pauper Palaces*, pp. 118, 190, 200–2.

[51] 22 Geo III c. 83; 58 Geo III c. 69; 59 Geo III c. 12. The 1818 Act established a plural
voting system, according to the rateable value of property. But the 1819 Act also
made it necessary for there to be two justices (rather than one) to overrule select
vestry decisions. This move against the power of the magistracy was continued in
1834.

large'.[52] And as Sir George Nicholls commented, Gilbert's Act may have increased the power of J.P.s in incorporations against the overseers, but: 'In 1834 there was a reaction in this respect, and the tide of public opinion ran perhaps overstrongly in the opposite direction, attributing an undue share of blame to the magistracy.'[53]

Tenant farmers on short leases, as many contemporaries agreed, were the most likely to use the workhouse as a threat against relief applications; to put families in it during the winter; to curtail sums given as out-door relief and pensions to the elderly; to rate the poor; and use the law to their own immediate self-interest. (Some of the methods by which this was done will be discussed shortly.) The reduced role of the magistracy after 1834 was of associated significance. Previously, paupers had the right of appeal to a magistrate if they felt that inadequate relief had been offered, as increasingly occurred in the early nineteenth century. Out-door relief payment per head and pensions fell still further after 1834, as we shall see, but this right of appeal was virtually ended. The 27th section of the Act seemed to enact that persons of a certain age could be given out-relief on the order of two magistrates. But as A. A. Young commented,

> this, both in theory and operation, is perfectly futile. It is absurd in theory, as a place of appeal; for the two magistrates to whom application is made, being ex-officio guardians of the unions in which the case has transpired, have already had their voice upon it at the board, and probably, from their influence there, have mainly tended to place the complaining party in the position from which he would appeal to them. It is equally absurd in fact; for though the 27th section seems to afford the desired power, it does not state on whom the magistrates shall make their order ... Such justices can go no further than to direct the guardians that the relief to be given shall not be given in the workhouse, leaving the guardians to be the judges of the quantum of relief to be granted, thereby putting the complainant into the position from whence he started, and leaving him exposed to the chance of receiving so small a modicum of relief as shall, after all, against his wishes and in spite of his appeal, oblige him to take refuge in the workhouse.[54]

Similarly, the Act perpetuated the settlement laws

> but authorizes no one to enforce the [removal], in case it should be refused ... the want of an authority to enforce the making of an order being as good as a total exemption from the ... expensive duty of removing the poor to their own parish ... the law had appointed no disinterested third party to secure

---

[52] Rev. J. B. Ferrers, *Observations on the Present Administration of the Poor Laws* (1832), p. 14.

[53] Sir G. Nicholls, *A History of the English Poor Law* (1854, 1898 edn), p. 89. (This was written around 1853.)

[54] A. A. Young, *The Poor Law: Is any Alteration of it Necessary or Tolerably Acceptable?* (1839), pp. 14–15.

to the poor man even the privileges apparently held out to him by the present enactment.[55]

Once again, it placed unprecedented restrictions on the right of appeal. One could find oneself and family stranded in an indifferent London parish, as many did, with the rural parish of settlement ignoring the usual pleading letters for non-resident relief, and so not even be able to return. For many in such situations, this now legitimated abdication of responsibility could raise considerable hardship, throwing a misfortuned family entirely onto its own limited resources.

There was also now considerable confusion and difficulty surrounding an application for relief. The poor had to apply to the Union relieving officer, who would discover the 'facts' of the case, and report to the guardians, to whom the case then went. The relieving officer, dealing with perhaps fifteen to twenty parishes, would commonly visit each parish only once a week, with the poor usually at a considerable distance from the guardians' meeting place. And the law had entailed a large reduction in the number of paid officers: for example, in one county there were 347 before it and 47 after, suggesting a saving in salaries, but an intolerable work-load on the new relieving officers.[56] One of the latter, examined in 1838, took a minute to deal with each case on his circuit through the parishes, and did not usually enter into conversation. 'I find that I can get better information from the neighbouring farmer than from the family itself; I do not expect to hear the truth from any part of the family when I ask them.'[57] Much depended on his individual choice as to whether or how to present the case to guardians from other parishes, who did not know the 'pauper' in question. This was often undergone for short-term relief, for a week, and then the whole protracted procedure had to be repeated. Alternatively, employment might be promised by a farmer guardian at the meeting, and the promise then rescinded, with the man having to wait till the next board day to try again:

I've been at work ... for the last 20 years. My master discharged me, as he said he could not afford to keep me any longer. I've got 5 children, and I was obliged, for the first time in my life, to go to the board. While I was there, one of 'em said to me that, sooner than I should go to the workhouse and be parted from my family, he would find some job for me. I went to him after the board was over. I asked him what I should do, and he told me that he should be glad to employ me, but he had not got the means. I told him how he had

---

[55] *Ibid.*, pp. 19–20.
[56] Anon., *Remarks on the Opposition to the Poor Law Amendment Bill*, p. 96.
[57] S.C. on the Poor Law Amendment Act, XVIII (1837–8), pt II, pp. 378, 458.

promised to give me work, and at last he gave me a day's threshing and discharged me, so I had 1s. 6d. to live on till the next board day; and they've served me so two or three times since that.[58]

The relieving officer would not help in such a case: 'he was told that nothing could be done for him so long as work was offered to him'.

Coupled with this was the unprecedented secrecy of guardians' meetings, with discussion of cases open only to them. Paupers and other parties were sent out of the room. 'The indiscriminate admission of strangers would perhaps be an interruption to the proceedings', commented a circumspect witness to the 1837–8 Committee.[59] For this was in contrast to vestry meetings of the old poor law, where 'the poor could have admission, without being obstructed by overseers or relieving officers'. 'And they did so? – Continually so . . . that has been invaded by the operation of the New Poor Law.'[60] The relieving officer had become the crucial and distancing intermediary, and needless to say, he was usually intensely unpopular with the poor. George Sturt wrote that 'it made Bettesworth miserable to have to sue in the form of a pauper, and he was prepared, as poor folk generally are, to find in the relieving officer a bully if not a brute'.[61] One of the Poor Law Board's own medical inspectors complained of the 'brutality and insolence of relieving officers'.[62] In some Unions they were recruited as a matter of policy from ex-army personnel, especially sergeant-majors, for their ability to intimidate the elderly and other potential 'paupers', and deter applications. The use of such men, or indeed of any salaried 'strangers', was resented by the parish labouring poor, many of them familiar with an earlier more personalised form of relief.[63]

A stated priority of the Poor Law Report had been to instil habits of 'independence' in the labour force – to make them accept market economy conditions and migrate to adjust regional wage imbalance; to escape from the 'habits of indolence' and parish dependency believed to be due to Speenhamland and associated relief methods. It is interesting to pursue this, because far from restricting interference in the labour market, the new law had a remarkably coercive aspect, and could only be operated in a manner distinctly hostile to assertions

---

[58] *Morning Chronicle*, 25 Feb. 1851.
[59] S.C. open the Poor Law Amendment Act, XVIII (1837–8), pt II, p. 496.
[60] *Ibid.* Or see Emmison, 'Relief of the poor at Eaton Socon', 83ff.
[61] G. Sturt, *Memoirs of a Surrey Labourer* (1907), p. 195.
[62] P. Horn, *Labouring Life in the Victorian Countryside* (Bristol, 1976), p. 207. Or see R.C. on the Aged Poor, XV (1895), p. 827.
[63] S.C. on the Poor Law Amendment Act, XVIII (1837–8), pt II, p. 199. And see the evidence of John Marshall, *ibid.*, pp. 443ff.

of 'independence' among the labouring classes. The law, as Poynter
argued, was a disciplinary measure as much as an attempt to remedy
poverty; an extremely significant part (in the countryside), of wider
measures which forced the poor to adopt to new time and work
schedules.[64] The views of William Day in 1833, advocating a workhouse form of relief such as that adopted, were widely held before
1834, and then voiced by many pamphleteers in support of the New
Poor Law. 'The workhouse I propose, joins the discipline of a prison
to the incontamination of a manufactory – it is, in short, a barrack;
and in fact, if strictly acted upon, I am strongly convinced would
ultimately become available *in terrorem* than from being called into
ordinary operation.'[65] As such, he hoped that this system would avoid
the 'degredation' of the labourer, and early marriage, and force
labourers to 'make the utmost exertions of the most enduring
industry'. Another pamphleteer complimented the 'less eligible'
workhouse by claiming that 'its restrictions are intolerable to the
indisciplined minds and vicious habits which generally characterize
paupers'.[66] This unfortunate way of thinking had now become
commonplace.

And it is surprising how close manifestations of these 'indisciplined
and vicious habits' can seem to the 'independence' which Chadwick or
Senior claimed they wanted to instil. One is constantly struck by the
use of the law to increase submissiveness of labour to employers, in a
similar way as we shall see in the language of enclosure advocates.
Some more extreme examples of this were given by Somerville:

Again, there was a point made by one of the speakers, which seemed to be
well understood, about 'pitting potatoes', to keep them until required. On
inquiry I found this to refer to a farmer who had said that he did with his
labourers as he did with his potatoes: he did not keep all the potatoes out for
use every day; and he did not, like some farmers, try to find work for the men
all the year round. When he did not need them he put them in the workhouse
until they were needed.[67]

The use of the workhouse to coerce low wages was, we shall see,
another expedient, as was the forcing of labourers' wives and families
to work at pittance wages for the farmer.[68] 'It has been stated by the

---

[64] Poynter, *Society and Pauperism*, pp. xvff. See also Digby, *Pauper Palaces*, p. 190.
Statements to this effect were widespread in contemporary literature on the poor
law. Just as in rural workhouse schooling, there was apparently need to 'encourage
industrial habits for chanting to the goose step'. Report on the Employment of
Children, Young Persons, and Women in Agriculture, XIII (1868–9), p. 666.

[65] Day, *Inquiry into the Poor Laws*, p. 26.

[66] Anon., *Remarks on the Opposition to the Poor Law Amendment Bill*, pp. 96ff.

[67] A. Somerville, *The Whistler at the Plough* (Manchester, 1852), p. 385.

[68] *Ibid.*, pp. 387–8.

labourers, that the masters cannot wish them well when they want them to be driven into the workhouse, or in fact they have generally termed it prison, when they have no work ... The men now had to be more submissive than they used to be ... and the masters knew it.'[69] The same point was made by parliamentary committees pointing out how the law aided the introduction of machinery (for cutting turnips, drilling, or the reintroduction of threshing machinery). The men's enforced quiescence allowed this, where previously farmers would have encountered opposition.[70] In such cases, greater efficiency was gained at the social cost of worsening class relations.

Among clergymen, farmers, and guardians writing on the poor law after 1834, there were few who valued 'independence' in their labour, except insofar as it would deter relief applications.

You may teach the labourer ... that he is indeed independent of you ... He may then, with some shew of justice, assert his independence, and demand why his richer brother should thrive and fatten on his toils. He may then ask, as the bee would, were Esop alive again, why his honey should be enjoyed by any but by him who gathered it. Heaven avert such independence as this![71]

As is well known, the opposition to allotments stemmed from similar motives, to keep the labour force fully dependent on the farmer class.[72] With the high labour requirements of the harvest in the south-east, and with the Irish harvest gangs shortly to be diverted to the north, there was need not for a 'free labour market', but to hold labour in the parish during the winter, ready for the short arable

---

[69] S.C. on the Poor Law Amendment Act, XVIII (1837–8), pt II, p. 355. Or see the R.C. on the Aged Poor, XV (1895), pp. 826, 838–41, on the equating of the workhouse with prison, and the setting to work of elderly workhouse inmates at picking oakum, much as in an eighteenth-century house of correction. The regular recipient of relief is described as 'the loafer, ne'er-do-weel, the wastrel, and what I may say no better than dirt ... he does not intend to work ... I would have him cast into the union, or prison; in fact it is prisons and unions that these men should be put into' (p. 826).

[70] S.C. on the Poor Law Amendment Act, XVIII (1837–8), pt III, p. 11; Digby, *Pauper Palaces*, p. 119; D. Jones, 'Thomas Campbell Foster and the rural labourer; incendiarism in East Anglia in the 1840's', *Social Hist.*, I (1976), 31; E. J. T. Collins, 'The diffusion of the threshing machine in Britain, 1790–1880', *Tools and Tillage*, II (1972), 19: 'Mechanisation gained real ground only after 1840 ... Innovation was most vigorous in the eastern counties ... At mid-century, threshing machines appear to have been fairly general in the eastern, south-central, south-western, and north and east Midlands counties.'

[71] Rev. H. J. Marshall, *On the Tendency of the New Poor Law* (1842), pp. 31–2.

[72] See for example, Checkland (eds.), *Poor Law Report*, pp. 280ff; D. C. Barnett, 'Allotments and the problem of rural poverty, 1780–1840', in E. L. Jones & G. E. Mingay (eds.), *Land, Labour and Population in the Industrial Revolution* (1967); J. Richardson, *A Letter to Lord Brougham ... on an Alteration in the Poor Laws, the Employment of the People, and a Reduction of the Poor Rate* (Norwich, 1831), pp. 44ff.

season. The New Poor Law was a means of doing this at minimum cost to the ratepayer. Poor rates were held down by 'less eligibility', the initial terror of the workhouse (replaced by long-lasting animosity towards it), the rating of the poor to encourage ill-feeling against relief claimants, or the encouragement of friendly societies; while the perpetuation and use of the settlement laws hindered out-migration. It is significant that the yearly hiring 'head' of settlement was abolished – it had been the legislative support of an institutional framework for high mobility in the past. Similarly, non-resident relief was heavily curtailed after 1834, and it was directed that all in receipt of relief should reside in the parish or Union to which they belonged. This brought labourers back in large numbers to their settlements.[73] And it comes as no surprise that the teaching of geography was forbidden in some workhouses, or that maps were not permitted on their school room walls.[74] We see in all such expedients the complementary means to achieve a submissive (if socially double-faced) proletariat at minimal cost.

In these and many other respects the New Poor Law was the applied culmination of sentiments in favour of submissiveness earlier expressed by men like Arthur Young or Joseph Townsend; without the economically protective measures which had previously made social deference worthwhile to the poor. 'Chuse such [men] as will ... be induced to obey your orders, without that round of murmuring and complaints so often heard from these people.'[75] Or, as Townsend put it:

Hope and fear are the springs of industry ... The poor know nothing of the motives which stimulate the higher ranks to action – pride, honour, and ambition. In general it is only hunger which can spur and goad them on to labour; yet our laws have said that they shall never hunger ... Nothing in nature can be more disgusting than a parish pay-table ... nor in nature can anything be more beautiful ... more pleasing [than] their sparkling eyes, their bursting tears, and their uplifted hands, the artless expressions of unfeigned gratitude for unexpected favours. Such scenes will frequently occur whenever men have the power to dispose of their own property.[76]

By 1840, at any rate, the poor had clearer knowledge of 'the motives

---

[73] See for example, T. Smith, *The Old Poor Law and the New Poor Law Contrasted* (1840), p. 22. This is discussed further in chapter 7.

[74] Digby, *Pauper Palaces*, p. 183. For opposition to education, and suggestions that children be taught to read the Bible in a foreign language, to stop them reading anything else, see S.C. on the Poor Law Amendment Act, XVIII (1837–8), pt I, p. 480.

[75] A. Young, *The Farmer's Kalendar: Containing the Business Necessary to be Performed on Various Kinds of Farms during Every Month of the Year* (1771, 1778 edn), p. 315.

[76] Rev. J. Townsend, *A Dissertation on the Poor Laws* (1786, 1971 edn), pp. 23, 69.

which stimulate the higher ranks to action'. For Chadwick and Senior's New Poor Law, described by the latter as a 'system of police and secondary punishment by which the present semi-Irish system of intimidation may be checked', with a workhouse 'as disagreeable as it can be made', must have left them in little doubt.[77]

It had been a major prediction of the Commissioners and other supporters of the New Poor Law that it would raise wages by creating a 'free labour market', and enhance the value of labour by ending 'demoralisation'. From the start this was unlikely, for to employers and select committees the term 'demoralisation' meant impudence, assertive social action, and free moral behaviour, as for example based on self-reliance partly outside the 'labour market'.[78] (And if this seems to mean 'independence' or 'self-reliance', we again make a semantic misjudgement. Such terms were closer in meaning to 'morally respectable behaviour and dependence on disciplined wage labour'.) These semantic differences help to demonstrate a further way in which the law operated coercively to favour the farmer class. The refusal of out-relief to the able-bodied, coupled with the 'ticket system', in East Anglia, and widespread fear of the workhouse, created conditions of dependence in which precarious employment at low wages had to be accepted. When such employment had been offered and rejected, no relief was forthcoming, for many not even in the workhouse. Indeed, a labourer would come under the vagrancy laws for 'refusing gainful employment' and failing to support his family, giving him one month's hard labour, or placing him on the treadwheel of a house of correction. This was the fate of a growing number of labourers in Cambridgeshire from the 1820s.[79] T. W. Overman (Chairman of the Maulden Board of Guardians) could blurt out to the 1838 Committee: 'He is a blockhead if he takes lower wages than will maintain himself and his family', but in fact a labourer now had few alternatives.[80] There was little incentive to raise wages until out-migration, the attraction of railway employment, or the redirection of Irish harvesters after the famine began to cause labour shortages (as in west Norfolk) in the 1850s. Rising rents after 1834 provided an additional disincentive to raise wages. Even in the 1850s the response of farmers was generally to improve material conditions (cottages, provision of allotments, or village schools) rather than pay

[77] Senior to Brougham, 9 March 1833. Quoted by Brundage, *Making of the New Poor Law*, p. 26.
[78] See chapter 4 for discussion of these semantic problems.
[79] Hampson, *Treatment of Poverty*, p. 196.
[80] S.C. on the Poor Law Amendment Act, XVIII (1837–8), pt III, p. 240.

more.[81] The labourer received no substitute for the loss of parish allowances and wage supplementation, and it was both because of this and a reduction of wages that his income fell, as Cobbett had predicted in Parliament and in his *Legacy to Labourers*.[82]

The 1838 Select Committee discussed the effects on wages. It presented evidence first on some resurgence of work by mothers and children, to try and compensate for the decline of familial income. The gang system was often blamed on the New Poor Law;[83] and elsewhere, in some parts of Huntingdonshire, Cambridgeshire, Bedfordshire, and Hertfordshire, the straw-plait or lace industries could be resorted to. Straw-plait, for the hat industries of Luton and Dunstable, was twice as profitable as lace, but fell in value considerably during the winter when income was most needed. Lace had been depressed since the end of the Napoleonic Wars, but became especially so during the 1840s. The need for child income led children practising these crafts to leave home early, because of parental pressure to make them work, pressure which stemmed from the fall in familial income after 1834.[84] Of course earnings and opportunities for such work in the south were slight – favouring only those families fortunate to live in the appropriate areas – and by now we need to concentrate heavily on male earnings.

James Turner of Ampthill reported to the 1838 Committee:

They have suffered, they do suffer, and they will suffer, if their wages are not advanced in proportion to the relief which has been taken from them, and which formerly would have been given to them; they have suffered in the degree that the wages have not been advanced in the proportion that that relief has been taken away.[85]

[81] E. L. Jones, 'The agricultural labour market in England, 1793–1872', *Econ. Hist. Rev.*, XVII (1964), 334ff.

[82] Cobbett, *Legacy to Labourers*, pp. 30–40. And see G. D. H. & M. Cole (eds.), *The Opinions of William Cobbett* (1944), p. 336; and his speeches in Parliament against the New Poor Law, *Hansard* (1834), XXIII, pp. 1335–7, XXIV, pp. 386–7.

[83] 'One of the prime causes of the increase of the gang-system (I may almost say its origin) was the New Poor Law; for previous to that Act, if an able-bodied man could not maintain his family, the parish assisted him; that assistance being withdrawn, it became necessary that all who could work should support themselves.' Report on the Employment of Women and Children in Agriculture, XII (1843), p. 296.

[84] For discussion of lace and straw-plait see: S.C. on the Poor Law Amendment Act, XVIII (1837–8), pt II, pp. 498ff; P. Horn, 'Child workers in the pillow-lace and straw-plait trades of Victorian Buckinghamshire and Bedfordshire', *Hist. Jnl*, XVII (1974); or her 'The Buckinghamshire straw-plait trade in Victorian England', *Records of Bucks*, XIX (1971); A. J. Tansley, 'On the straw plait trade', *Jnl of the Society of Arts*, IX (21 Dec. 1860); *Morning Chronicle*, 5 April 1850; G. F. R. Spenceley, 'The origins of the English pillow lace industry', *Agric. Hist. Rev.*, XXI (1973); J. C. Dony, *A History of the Straw Hat Industry* (Luton, 1942).

[85] S.C. on the Poor Law Amendment Act, XVIII (1837–8), pt II, p. 311.

Large families suffered most from this decline of allowances. For example, Edward Pullen, a labourer from Kidford with ten children, had an income of 15s. a week under the old poor law. Under the new this fell to 11s. 6d. Richard Ford (with six children) had 15s. 9d. a week before 1834, but only 9s. after 1834. All the other labourers examined by the 1837 Committee had experienced similar losses, with some claiming that they had virtually to starve themselves to feed their children.[86] This committee tried unsuccessfully to force labourers to concede that wages would still rise because of the law.[87] But its successor in 1838 accepted that 'less eligibility' had reduced both wages and income from the old allowances.[88] By now James Kay (never the most cognisant of Assistant Poor Law Commissioners) had decided 'that pauperism among the able-bodied is not dependent upon the state of wages in any district', and felt that this insight vindicated such an effect of the law.[89] The same committee heard how the law had diminished task work rates by about 2d. in every shilling, and how labourers used to earn 2s. more by it every week.[90] It had also reduced winter wages, and this was felt to have increased crime, particularly poaching.[91] The complete vulnerability of labour was very apparent. 'I could have as many men as I wanted, to do all my work at 1s. a day, or 6s. a week', 'if my conscience would let me', commented one of the farmers;[92] and no doubt many did not have such trouble with their consciences.

I say this because such a wage (which would put labourers in sub-Tolpuddle conditions) was now seriously being suggested. Here is a farmer from Clavering, an area notorious for its incendiary fires, speaking to the *Morning Chronicle*'s rural correspondent:

A man with a family of five children will be nearly able with 6s. a week to buy bread enough, if he buys the coarsest flour; his rent he generally gets out of his harvest money; his clothes he gets by some means or other – people sometimes give them to him – and then, when he is unemployed . . . we keep him in the workhouse. So you see, sir, he is amply provided for, even with wages at 6s. a week.[93]

As the correspondent commented: 'Calculations are made with the greatest possible nicety, not so much to ascertain how much he can

[86] S.C. on the Poor Law Amendment Act, XVII (1837), pt I, pp. 142–50, 311–21.
[87] *Ibid.*, pp. 316ff.
[88] S.C. on the Poor Law Amendment Act, XVIII (1837–8), pt I, pp. 20ff., 559ff.
[89] *Ibid.*, pp. 522–8.
[90] *Ibid.*, XVIII (1837–8), pt II, pp. 101, 272–3.
[91] S.C. on the Poor Law Amendment Act, XVIII (1837–8), pt II, pp. 231–2, 269–71; Young, *The New Poor Law*, pp. 7–9.
[92] S.C. on the Poor Law Amendment Act, XVIII (1837–8), pt II, p. 231.
[93] *Morning Chronicle*, 29 Dec. 1849.

live upon, as how much he can live without.' But let us turn to Edwin Chadwick, once Bentham's admiring secretary, now fast on his way to becoming 'the humanitarian reformer of the nineteenth century'; whose noetic dogmatism pervades later reports of the 1830s in the same way as it 'masterminded' that of 1834. He had by 1837 surprisingly forgotten his prediction of rising wages made only three years earlier, and his concerns were now rather different:

It has been proved to me that a single man can live upon 6s. a week, by persons able to form the calculation.

qu. 'Will you have the goodness to state to the Committee what is the average daily expense of yourself living at an inn?' –
   'From 18s. to 20s.'

qu. 'Does that include merely the comforts of living?' –
   'It does.'

qu. 'Do you apply in that estimate of 20s. a day to your own comfort of living your view of 6s. a week being enough for the comfortable subsistence of a labouring single man?' –
   'I hardly know how to answer that question.'[94]

On this occasion at least, Chadwick left the Committee room in a more embarrassed state than was normal for him.

Of course, one reason for this effect of the New Poor Law was fear of the workhouse, as *The Times* showed in its enquiry into incendiary fires. Its remarks bear quoting at length.

The tendency, therefore, both of over-population, and the use of machinery in the hands of small farmers, is as well to reduce the amount of wages on the one hand (through the instrumentality of the New Poor Law), so as to reduce the amount of labour required on the other ... To secure adequate wages to the labourer from his employer, and to ensure employment for him, was, according to its enthusiastic advocates, the professed object, and to be the certain result, of carrying out the principles of the New Poor Law. In theory – on paper – carrying out principles with men as with machines – it seemed feasible: but in practice, men not being machines, or to be dealt with as such, it has wholly failed in effecting these objects. Its advocates said, 'adopt the principle of wholly refusing out-door relief to the able-bodied poor, but offer them and their families the union house, and you will compel the farmers to employ them at sufficient wages to keep them; and as the cost of a family in the union-house will be much more than the man's wages out of it, to save their rates and to get his labour in return for their money, they will be induced to find him employment'. This is a very pretty theory. But it will be seen that it all rests on the foundation of the able-bodied man with his family being willing to go into the union-house, if he be inadequately paid, or out of work. But if he be not so willing? Why, then the theory has a most sandy foundation.[95]

---

[94] S.C. on the Poor Law Amendment Act, XVII (1837), pt I, p. 102. A year earlier, the Rev. F. H. Maberley had attacked Chadwick's 'how cheaply can a man live' approach to the poor. (*To the Poor and their Friends* (1836), pp. 10ff.)

[95] *The Times*, 'Inquiry into Incendiary Fires', 15 June 1844.

As the 1838 Committee was told (and as we shall see with the elderly): they 'suffer the greatest privation before they will go in'.[96] There were other reasons why the law depressed wages. An associated one, particularly in East Anglia, was the use of the 'ticket system'. A labourer out of work would take a 'ticket' round the farmers, which they would sign if unable to employ him. Some would offer exceptionally low wages, which would be rejected by the labourer as too low to maintain his family. The farmer would then refuse to sign the ticket. In turn (farmer) guardians would then refuse relief on the grounds that he had declined to take up 'gainful employment'. If the labourer objected he risked gaol under the 1824 Vagrancy Act for 'refusing wholly or in part' to maintain his family.[97] It is clear how this variant of the old roundsman system operated to force low wages, for example, during the winter rather than incur the costs of workhouse relief. *The Times* gave examples of men who had to accept wages of 5s. a week by it, and had not been offered the workhouse when they found this sum inadequate.[98]

This argument on wages so far has been based on literary evidence. But wage material is available which clearly demonstrates the extent of decline after 1834, and attention should be drawn to it. Bowley published for all counties weekly agricultural wages for 1833, 1837, and 1850.[99] The data for 1833 was taken from the Poor Law Report's detailed appendices. (Only about 10 per cent of parishes returned to the Commission, and we might suppose that they were more highly pauperised and *lowly* paid – being concerned with the question of reform they were more likely to reply.) The 1837 data was supplied by Purdy, from unpublished returns, and was the wage paid in summer. To allow comparison, therefore, I have taken that 1833 data which

---

[96] S.C. on the Poor Law Amendment Act, XVIII (1837–8), pt II, p. 231. Or on the 'terror of the workhouse' see P. A. Graham, *The Rural Exodus* (1892), pp. 188–9; R.C. on the Aged Poor, XV (1895), pp. 825–33, 834ff, 910.

[97] 5 Geo IV c. 83, s. 3.

[98] For discussion of the ticket system, see *The Times*, 'Inquiry into Incendiary Fires', 21 June 1844, and 4 July 1844 – letter from J. Percival; *Morning Chronicle*, 18 Oct. 1850; A. Digby, 'The labour market and the continuity of social policy after 1834: the case of the eastern counties', *Econ. Hist. Rev.*, XXVIII (1975). A more recent variant on the ticket system has been the 'Not Genuinely Seeking Work' clause of the 1927 Unemployed Insurance Act. The onus was put on the unemployed to show that they could not get work, and employers were to sign a paper certifying that an unemployed person had asked for work and that they had none to offer. This was necessary to satisfy local labour exchanges, and many claims for benefit were disallowed because claimants could not give proof of having asked for employment. This clause was much resented, and its abolition was an important aim of subsequent hunger marches.

[99] Bowley, 'Statistics of wages', pt I, 'Agricultural wages' (1898).

Bowley gave as also referring to summer wages. Prices in these two years were very similar (for example, the London bread price series was identical in 1833 and 1837); there was little price fluctuation during this short period to produce an exogenous change in weekly wages.[100] I have also included the data for 1850, derived from Caird's survey. This was of summer wages and so directly comparable with the 1833 and 1837 data. (Prices in and around 1850 were only marginally lower than in the earlier two years.) Accordingly, the comparison before and after the inception of the New Poor Law in the southern counties is shown in Table 3.1. It was being widely operated in the south by 1837. The comparison is striking, and it is surprising that historians have hitherto overlooked it. In *every* county wages were reduced, and in some very heavily. (Between 1833 and 1837 Suffolk was the *only* exception, and the reason is obvious enough: its older parish incorporations were as yet undisturbed by the new law, ensuring relative continuity before and immediately after 1834. Predictably, matters had changed by 1850.) And we recall not only that the 1833 figures were probably atypically *low*, but also that this wage data refers only to weekly wages. That is, it makes no inclusion of the very heavy curtailment of allowances and head money by the New Poor Law. The fall in *familial income*, taking the latter factors into account, would have been very considerably in excess of the changes shown in this table.[101] These figures are the more devastating when we recall the exceptionally precarious budgets of farm labourers' families.

Significantly, in the northern counties, where the law was more intensely opposed and where it took much longer to gain ground, there was on average no change of wage rates between 1833, 1837, and 1850. By contrast, in the twenty-one southern counties where wage rates had fallen most rapidly by 1850 (where they were 65–85 per cent of their 1833 level), fifteen to sixteen of these were in the south-east. Of the south-eastern counties, only Bedfordshire escaped being in this hardest-hit category. Counties to the west (Cornwall,

---

[100] Some series show a price *rise* between 1833 and 1837. Prices for 1850 were 85–92 per cent of their 1833 level, depending on the series used. The (unweighted) average wage in 1850 throughout the south was 79 per cent of its 1833 level; lower in the south-east, and in some counties very much lower. This was despite the accelerating out-migration which was by then producing labour shortages in some regions, and accordingly, some wage increases.

[101] Well documented figures were given for Ampthill, for real net weekly income per head for subsistence, in pints of wheat, covering 46–8 labourers' families. These showed a fall in the order of 24 pints of wheat to 16 between 1834 and 1837. See S.C. on the Poor Law Amendment Act, XVIII (1837–8), pt II, pp. 267–70, for further details.

Table 3.1. *Agricultural weekly wages in 1833, 1837, and 1850*

County	1833	1837	1850	$\frac{1850}{1833} \times 100$
Beds	10/3	9/6	9/–	87.8
Berks	11/–	9/–	7/6	68.2
Bucks	10/9	9/6	8/6	79.1
Camb	11/1	9/6	7/6	67.7
Corn	9/–	8/9	8/8	96.3
Dev	9/–	8/–	8/6	94.4
Dors	8/8	7/6	7/6	86.5
Ess	10/9	10/4	8/–	74.4
Glos	10/–	9/–	7/–	70.0
Hants	10/4	9/6	9/–	87.1
Heref	8/6	8/–	8/5	99.1
Herts	11/4	9/6	9/–	79.4
Hunts	12/6	9/6	8/6	68.0
Kent	13/7	12/–	11/6	84.7
Leics	12/–	10/–	9/6	79.2
Lincs	15/–	12/–	10/–	66.7
Msx	13/8	11/6	11/–	80.5
Mon	11/9	10/6	9/8	82.3
Norf	11/2	10/4	8/6	76.1
N'ants	11/–	9/–	9/–	81.8
Notts	14/–	12/–	10/–	71.4
Oxon	10/7	8/6	9/–	85.1
Rut	12/6	n.f.	n.f.	—
Som	9/–	8/8	8/7	95.3
Suff	10/2	10/4	7/–	68.8
Surr	12/9	10/6	9/6	74.5
Suss	12/6	10/7	10/6	84.0
Wilts	9/5	8/–	7/3	77.0
Worcs	10/–	9/6	7/8	76.7
Wales	8/8	7/6	6/11	79.8
Average for southern England	11/2	9/8	8/9	79.0 ⬎
Average for Lancs, Ches, Yorks, Dur, N'umb, Cumb, & Westm	12/2	12/2	12/2	100

Devon, Hereford, Somerset), escaped with much smaller reductions. The south-east was of course the area where the New Poor Law was applied most rapidly and fully.

A consequence of these falling familial incomes was bankruptcies among local shopkeepers, and further hardship for many rural artisans, already adversely affected by the decline of traditional apprenticeship. Such bankruptcies had been predicted by critics of the New Poor Law, and are well documented. As an Essex linen-draper from a country village complained:

I went on medium well for the first two or three years after 1834, but the alteration of the poor-laws, and the reduction of the agricultural labourers' wages, destroyed my business. My customers were almost all among the working classes ... When the poor laws were altered, the outdoor relief was stopped, and the paupers compelled to go inside the house. Before that, a good part of the money given to the poor used to be expended at my shop ... Besides, the wages of the agricultural labourers being lowered, left them less money to lay out with me ... After their wages came down, they hadn't the means of laying out a sixpence with me; and where I had been taking £65 a-week, my receipts dwindled to £30.[102]

Other examples of bankruptcy among shopkeepers for the same reasons were cited by the 1838 Committee.[103]

Let us turn to a group whose quality of life is increasingly important to us today, as the population's age structure rises. Many contemporaries believed that the elderly suffered most because of the law. From the early attacks of *The Times*, to Alexander Somerville, George Sturt, Richard Jefferies, Thomas Hardy, or Flora Thompson, literature on nineteenth-century rural society is replete with criticism of the New Poor Law's callous treatment of those who were too old to work. We need to tread carefully between the 'Bastilles' literature of horror-struck condemnation, and the casual dismissals of some farmer guardians. Of course, out-relief of sorts continued for some elderly people; although one should be wary of generalising arguments on 'continuity' before and after 1834 which are based on Norfolk and Suffolk.[104] (Continuity was to be expected here, where of course the eighteenth-century Incorporations were left relatively untouched by the new law.) Age-specific figures per recipient for in- and out-door relief were not given – again 'carefully, and perhaps intentionally, hidden from the public'.[105] One has to go to overseers' accounts and union records. Weekly 'pensions' for the elderly shortly before 1834 were generally about 2s. 6d. to 3s. per person, sometimes

---

[102] *Morning Chronicle*, 15 Jan. 1850.
[103] S.C. on the Poor Law Amendment Act, XVIII (1937–8), pt II, pp. 323–4. See also Maberley, *To the Poor and Their Friends*, p. 34; Anon., *Remarks on the Opposition to the Poor Law Amendment Bill*, pp. 19, 80.
[104] Digby, 'The labour market and the continuity of social policy'; or her 'The rural poor law', in D. Fraser (ed.), *The New Poor Law in the Nineteenth Century* (1976); or *Pauper Palaces*, pp. 122ff.
[105] M. Blaug, 'The myth of the old poor law and the making of the new', in M. W. Flinn & T. C. Smout (eds.), *Essays in Social History* (Oxford, 1974), p. 153 n. 34.

more, not including many miscellaneous payments in kind. (Earlier still, one overseer's diary shows them being boarded out with other families at 5s. a week.)[106] After 1834, 'pensions' usually fell to between 1s. and 2s., with curtailment of out-payment in kind (until an 1852 General Order brought this back), and many elderly being forced to go 'inside' because they were refused out-relief altogether. Similarly, elderly widows being examined as to settlement after 1834 claimed that their pensions or allowances from the parish had either ended, or been cut by 9d. or 1s. when the new law came in.[107] The usual figures were from 2s. 6d. before (sometimes rather higher) to 1s. 9d. or 1s. 6d. after. (Overseers' accounts between 1795 and 1834 also suggest a normal sum of 2s. 6d. for widows, which could on occasion rise to 5s.) In the language of poor law commissioners, relief had been 'equalized' – that is, brought down to the lowest levels then given.[108] This change was an immediate effect of the law. In the more long-term, relief became slightly more generous around the 1850s (a sum to those widows allowed out-relief of about 2s., and softer insistence on only in-door relief). But there was then a considerable harshening of administration in the 'return to the principles of 1834', which occurred from the 1870s.[109] The latter period also saw pressure for additional payment from relatives. Throughout, many elderly were refused out-relief altogether, or offered such a small sum as to force them to go 'inside'. And when comparing before and after 1834, one should remember that figures for the New Poor Law based on actual applications merely indicate the tip of the iceberg, suppressing the submerged majority who (by general contemporary opinion) were now too afraid to apply. It is easy to exaggerate 'continuity' by using such figures. They may provide a rough guide to the extent of administrative 'continuity', but not of *experienced* continuity. The new law was aimed at deterring applicants, and in this it was largely successful.

[106] T. Turner, *The Diary of a Georgian Shopkeeper* (1925, Oxford, 1979 edn), p. xxi.

[107] For a typical example: 'I came back to the parish . . . and I received one shilling and sixpence a week till the passing of the new poor law act when they took it off' (Camb C.R.O., G/C/As3).

[108] S.C. on the Poor Law Amendment Act, XVIII (1837–8), pt II, p. 84. Or see pp. 236–7, 265. On widows forfeiting all relief when they turned down the 'offer' of the northern factories, see pp. 227–9, 259ff. For an attack on the curtailment of pensions after 1834, see Young, *The Poor Law*, p. 4. See also Maberley, *To the Poor and Their Friends*, pp. 10ff, condemning the reduced allowances to widows.

[109] On developments affecting the elderly in the later nineteenth century, see in particular the interesting work by David Thomson, 'Provision for the elderly in England, 1830–1908' (unpub. Ph.D. thesis, University of Cambridge, 1980) and his forthcoming book on this important subject. And see the R.C. on the Aged Poor, XV (1895).

Students of early modern England are probably familiar with Peter Laslett asking 'did the peasants really starve'. Whatever their verdict on that period, cases of starvation adduced to the New Poor Law were well documented even in parliamentary reports. They were generally elderly people whose out-door relief was now too small to maintain them (or who were not offered such relief); and who refused the discipline, religionism, uniforms, and 'less eligible' humiliations of the workhouse, which they equated with prison. 'Died from destitution and want of the common necessaries of life' was the consequence for many, complained A. A. Young from Northampton-shire in 1839.[110] He put this down to 'the dreaded alternative of the workhouse', and was one of the less strident critics of the law. The 1837 and 1838 Committees looked with hesitant approval on the fact that elderly people (and others) were selling their furniture to try and avoid the workhouse. It was even proposed that workhouse admit-tance be conditional upon this, and the 1838 Committee suggested this as a policy worth encouraging. After all, 'No law can be too stringent for the agricultural parts of the country, and where the allowance system had prevailed.'[111] The law followed closely on the decline of home spinning and weaving, itself lamented as an end to a traditional employment for elderly people.[112] And the splitting of the family in the workhouse – a case where the Benthamite compartmen-talising habit harmonised nicely with Malthusian policy, to avoid 'scenes of the greatest indecency and disorder' – was as bitterly attacked by some middle-class opponents of the law as it was loathed by the poor. As one elderly man complained: 'They won't give us anything, except we goes into the house, and as long as I can arne a sixpence anyhows, they sharn't part me from my wife.'[113] In their benevolence, Select Committees conceded that 'opportunities should not be refused to members of a family occasionally to converse together'; although one man claimed in 1846 that in ten weeks he had only seen his children when they passed him on the way to chapel.[114]

[110] Young, *The Poor Law*, p. 18.
[111] S.C. on the Poor Law Amendment Act, XVIII (1837–8), pt I, p. 20. And the arrears of rent which commonly accumulated when a family was 'inside' led landlords to take and sell furniture in recompense.
[112] Brereton, *Practical Inquiry*, p. 27: 'I can recollect that there were many aged persons who were distinguished as combers and weavers, even after those employments had ceased in the villages.'
[113] *Morning Chronicle*, 22 Jan. 1850. To the same effect, see R.C. on the Aged Poor, XV (1895), pp. 846–54.
[114] N. Longmate, *The Workhouse* (1974), p. 95. Asked whether it was difficult for a husband and wife to see each other in the workhouse, one witness replied: 'Certainly not, in cases of illness or urgency.' S.C. on the Poor Law Amendment Act, XVIII (1837–8), pt I, p. 568.

And (associated with this), when one reads descriptions of the 'insane' in some workhouses, it is revealing how many were 'raving' about persons 'attempting to burn his children and murder his wife'; or 'says they are murdering his children'; or who were suffering from 'frequently recurring periods of excitement and depression, says she is constantly fearing being hung as well as several other members of her family'; or 'getting out of bed and getting up the chimney because people are about to murder him, taking his child in his arms and running out of the house, because they were about to murder it, not speaking to anyone'.[115] These were just some cases from one workhouse, perhaps best left with historians sympathetic to Szasz, Laing, or Esterson.[116]

Even prisons, a century before, had rarely split up the family, and even married vagrants and beggars had then commonly been imprisoned together.[117] It is probably difficult today for us to comprehend religious sentiments on the inviolability of family life, or the residual values left behind from an age of widespread family production, and the way they were violated by the workhouse's splitting of the family. Certainly such feelings were intense, and contributed to the wider bitterness at the policy of incarcerating the elderly, whose concentration in many workhouses never seems to have disturbed Chadwick, despite his intention to deal with the 'idle' and 'immoral' able-bodied. 'The local government existing at this day in country districts is practically based upon the assumption that every labouring man will one day be a "pauper", will one day come to the workhouse', wrote Richard Jefferies. 'Thither the worn-out cottager is borne away ... to dwindle and die.'[118] As Sir George Crewe put it:

It is but a melancholy sight, to see the aged collected from thirty or forty parishes, like a heap of cast-off, worn out tools, to be buried alive in the solitude of a workhouse ... all ... for what? – to save some paltry sixpence a week, or maybe, a shilling, which the parish grudge to their elderly servant ... in some places it is difficult to ... send a present to an aged pensioner.[119]

---

[115] Camb C.R.O., G/C/As 4–10.

[116] On the social construction and determinants of madness, see: T. Szasz, *The Myth of Mental Illness* (1961); or his *The Manufacture of Madness* (1970); R. D. Laing & A. Esterson, *Sanity, Madness and the Family* (1964); A. Esterson, *The Leaves of Spring* (1970). 'Insanity' imputed to fear of the workhouse is reported in R.C. on the Aged Poor, XV (1895), p. 833.   [117] Scott, *Observations*, pp. 95ff.

[118] R. Jefferies, *The Hills and the Vale* (1909, Oxford, 1980 edn), pp. 238–9.

[119] Sir G. Crewe, *A Word for the Poor, and against the Present Poor Law* (Derby, 1843), pp. 20–1. See also pp. 6–20 of his admirable discussion. Or see R.C. on the Aged Poor, XV (1895), p. 856: 'You have been asked about the reason why the poor are not charmed with the workhouse, and I think you admit that in the workhouse it is possible to provide shelter and also food; well, if you were called upon to provide for an old horse, that would be adequate, would it not?'

Some of the most embittered and depressive writing of the nineteenth century covers this treatment of the elderly, and I have not the space to quote much at length.

They got her stockings on, but no boots; a petticoat or so, but no bodice with sleeves; and for all that they had to struggle, even calling on Bettesworth to come upstairs and help them. Then the fly came, 'and all she kep' sayin' was, "Leave me to die at home. I wants to die at home!"', and she fought and would not be moved.[120]

Or there was Somerville, such a sensitive anomaly in the system-compulsive age residual of Smith, Malthus, and Chadwick: 'To me it has always seemed cruel, terribly cruel, to take the aged and infirm from the cottages they have laboured to keep above their heads, and which they have sanctified with their affections, and shut them up in the workhouses.' And the relentless and damning prose of the subsequent pages of the *Whistler at the Plough* remains a fitting tribute to George Unwin's 'golden age', and the 'extension of freedom to ordinary men and women' which Ashton discovered there.[121] After being carted away to the workhouse like Flora Thompson's old major, and thousands more, Lucy Bettesworth died. And in Bettesworth we glimpse the human sensitivity, of 'ordinary men and women', against which the New Poor Law was such a brutal and superfluous measure:

Nothing sensational happened, nothing extravagantly emotional. But all that he did and said, so simple and unaffected and necessary, was done as if it were an act of worship. No woman could have been tenderer or more delicate than he, when he drew the sheet back from the dead face, to show me . . . The coffin itself (because he is so poor and so lonely) – a decent elm coffin - is a kind of symbol, and so a comfort to him, enabling him to testify to his unspoken feelings towards his dead wife.[122]

The propertied classes had known very well how bitterly the workhouse would be opposed: 'What they expect, is, that the building of the workhouses will be the signal for tumult among the lower orders'[123] – just as the building of the East Anglian Incorporation workhouses had provoked the rioting of 1765.[124] Some commentators rightly pointed out that an (expensive) rural police force would be needed to put the law into effect; and one historian has spoken of the paid watchmen who 'guarded the half finished

---

[120] Sturt, *Memoirs of a Surrey Labourer*, p. 213.
[121] Somerville, *Whistler at the Plough*, pp. 257ff; G. Unwin, *Industrial Organization in the Sixteenth and Seventeenth Centuries* (Oxford, 1904), intro. by T. S. Ashton, p. xiv.
[122] Sturt, *Memoirs of a Surrey Labourer*, p. 219.
[123] Digby, *Pauper Palaces*, p. 209, quoting Sir Edward Parry.
[124] See, for example, E. A. Goodwyn (ed.), *Selections from Norwich Newspapers, 1760–1790* (Ipswich, 1973), pp. 71, 94, 130ff.

workhouses against the guerilla attacks of the poor'.[125] In 1853 a Select
Committee was told: 'My firm persuasion is, that these workhouses
might have been pulled down or nearly destroyed, if we had not had
the assistance of the police. This has occurred in different Suffolk
unions, where the police has afforded the most valuable and prompt
assistance.'[126] They were shortly to become a permanent feature of
the countryside, closely associated – as Senior's letter to Brougham
confirms – with the New Poor Law itself. Hobsbawm and Rudé
invited further research on rural unrest and arson after Swing. One
point entirely clear is that the New Poor Law became a major focus for
discontent. One labourer described his Union as 'the greatest curse
that ever happened to the poor man';[127] and a fire engine operator
reported hearing it said during a fire that 'Unless something be
absolutely done about these unions, the fires will go on.'[128] *The Times*,
in its lengthy enquiry into rural arson, found that in some areas only
guardians' property was being fired, and that they were always
especially vulnerable to this, as well as to cattle maiming or personal
violence.[129] (Predictably, many men refused to serve as guardians for
these reasons.) Of course, other factors contributed to arson – falling
wages, machinery, and unemployment high among them – but we
have seen how these were integrally connected with the New Poor
Law, which produced submissiveness and the fearful atmosphere in
which they had to be tolerated.

Those who mix with the lower classes [wrote George Crewe in 1843], who
obtain their confidence, and hear their opinions freely and unhesitatingly
spoken, know how rapid and great the change is, which has taken place in
their mind towards the higher classes – in the last three or four years
especially: and they must also be fully aware, that of all the various causes
thus operating to promote strife and division, the New Poor Law has been
the most powerful.[130]

[125] Digby, *Pauper Palaces*, p. 75. Maberly, *To the Poor and Their Friends*, correctly predicted that the New Poor Law would require an expensive police force, pp. 34–6.
[126] Second Report of S.C. on Police, XXXVI (1852–3), p. 249. See also Cole (eds.), *The Opinions of William Cobbett*, pp. 330–2: 'I have always said, that the main object of this commission was, to muster up a parcel of stories from people, picked out for the purpose, to justify more severe measures against the working people; and to introduce, under pretence of protecting property, a sort of *Bourbon police* into all the villages and country towns; a police in uniform, carrying daggers and pistols, like those in London . . . I find it that which I expected; abounding with schemes, not to make the poor better off, but to make them receive less money in the way of relief.'   [127] *The Times*, 21 June 1844.   [128] *Ibid.*, 28 June 1844.
[129] *The Times*, 'Inquiry into Incendiary Fires', 4 July 1844.
[130] Crewe, *Word for the Poor*, p. 20. Or see S.C. on the Poor Law Amendment Act, XVIII (1837–8), pt II, p. 108: 'The ill feeling between the labouring people and those above them is very bad; there is a very strong and ill feeling now, much more than is generally imagined, much more than I have witnessed in the north on any occasion.'

Little more need be said – the law had surely the most harmful and socially damaging effect on rural class relations in the south of any nineteenth-century legislation.

4

Enclosure and employment – the social consequences of enclosure

I

I want to open my discussion by citing J. D. Chambers' famous article of 1953, which was reprinted on a number of occasions, and has had a pervasive influence on agrarian historiography.[1] It contributed perhaps above all else to the re-appraisal of the picture presented by the Hammonds, in the *Village Labourer*, of the social consequences of enclosure,[2] and his arguments have now become a virtual orthodoxy, frequently repeated in stronger language than he initially laid down. There was first his stress on the role of 'natural' causes, especially population growth, in the formation of a wage-dependent labour force, rather than 'institutional' causes. 'Sources of growth operated silently and perhaps we may say organically', he wrote, 'they were not the direct or indirect product of compulsion; and for that reason there is a danger that they may be overlooked . . . a proletariat was coming into being by the natural increase of the peasant population.' In his article he was concerned less with 'the institutional origin of the proletariat, but [with] whether enclosure is the relevant institution'.[3] He denied that it could have had such an effect.

One important factor [he argued] which contributed to the stability of the agrarian population during this period was the high level of employment which was maintained both in enclosed and open parishes where the improved agriculture was adopted . . . the spread of turnip cultivation and green fodder crops both in open and enclosed villages called for labour throughout the year in field, barn and stackyard; the maintenance of a milking herd or fat stock involved continuous field work throughout the year

---

[1] J. D. Chambers, 'Enclosure and labour supply in the Industrial Revolution', *Econ. Hist. Rev.*, V (1953), reprinted in D. V. Glass & D. E. C. Eversley (eds.), *Population in History* (1965), to which subsequent reference will be made.

[2] J. L. & B. Hammond, *The Village Labourer* (1911).

[3] Chambers, 'Enclosure and labour supply', 309, 324.

in pasture districts as well as in arable . . . and the hedging and ditching of the new enclosures found winter work for casual labour to a greater extent than the open villages. As for the enclosure of forest, moor and fen, labour was attracted from far and wide . . . there was also the stimulation of rural trades . . . the cottage owning population seems actually to have increased after enclosure. Even the proletarianized labourers continued to remain on the soil in increasing numbers until the 1830's and in many parts to the 1840's.[4]

The article deserves further quotation, but this can suffice as a reminder of it, and of historiographical views which I want to re-assess. The same argument on the benefits to the labour force of enclosure, and the new agricultural methods whose introduction it was held to further, is now widely encountered. At a more trenchant level, it was expressed in Chambers and Mingay's textbook on the agricultural revolution, and in Mingay's summary of recent historiography, *Enclosure and the Small Farmer in the Age of the Industrial Revolution*.[5] The arguments made against that group of agrarian historians represented by the Hammonds, Slater, or Hasbach are well known,[6] and need only be summarised briefly: enclosure brought with it a fuller and more remunerative demand for labour (even in the Midlands where contemporaries noted displacement of arable land by pasture), and a feature of this was more regular and seasonally secure employment; it alleviated the pauperism and miserable standard of living supposedly found in villages before parliamentary enclosure; it did not adversely affect the small landowner and tenant farmer, whose numbers actually grew in many regions during the period of parliamentary enclosure;[7] it did not cause out-migration through an ejection of those rural classes previously dependent on the commons or open field agriculture; and it was on the contrary conducive to further and rapid rural population growth in response to its associated growing labour requirements. Of course, individual authors have laid their emphases differently and concentrated on various aspects of the question, but these are conclusions now taken as virtually established. With the recent exception of a discussion by N. F. R. Crafts, demonstrating that enclosure *did* cause out-

---

[4] *Ibid.*, 319–20, 324.

[5] J. D. Chambers & G. E. Mingay, *The Agricultural Revolution, 1750–1880* (1966); G. E. Mingay, *Enclosure and the Small Farmer in the Age of the Industrial Revolution* (1968). And alongside the various publications of Chambers and Mingay, see in particular the work of Yelling, McCloskey and Armstrong noted below.

[6] J. L. & B. Hammond, *Village Labourer*; G. Slater, *The English Peasantry and the Enclosure of Common Fields* (1907); W. Hasbach, *The History of the English Agricultural Labourer* (1908).

[7] This was the influential view of E. Davies, 'The small landowner, 1780–1832, in the light of the Land Tax Assessments', *Econ. Hist. Rev.*, I (1927).

migration,[8] one is confronted by a historiographical consensus which regards the *Village Labourer* as a remarkable but misguided or badly biased episode in English agrarian historiography.

We should outline the focus of enclosure historiography since the Hammonds. They had concluded that 'enclosure was fatal to three classes: the small farmer, the cottager, and the squatter. To all of these classes their common rights were worth more than anything they received in return.'[9] And yet the re-assessment of the Hammonds has concentrated almost exclusively on the first of these classes, and the question of the social effects of enclosure is now taken as amounting almost solely to the issue of landownership change as it affected the owner-occupier and small tenant farmer. This is of course more easily explained than excused. For the use of the land tax assessments for this problem (and this has since been the major historiographical development covering the scope of documentation) has necessarily narrowed research down to cover only those rural classes assessed. For many historians, the subsequent finding that in some regions (though certainly not in all) the numbers of this class so assessed to the land tax actually seem to rise in the later eighteenth century has proved the final word on this matter. One senses a tone of ultimate satisfaction on this score in much enclosure historiography over the past twenty years. For example, we now find J. A. Yelling asking: 'Does anything remain through which something of the older view of things might be preserved?' – and deciding in reply merely that the 'loophole through which we can continue to see enclosure as a device that severed the labourer from at least some access to land . . . has not yet been entirely closed'.[10]

But as the land tax assessments have supplied the empirical findings for so much enclosure historiography, being almost the sole basis for the re-assessment of the subject, we should briefly discuss their utility as a source, before moving to the effects of enclosure on seasonal distributions of unemployment, on poor relief expenditure, and considering contemporary commentary. Potential users of the land tax assessments are indebted to Mingay for his interesting article 'The Land Tax Assessments and the small landowner',[11] and Mingay has shown himself to be satisfied with the dismissal of the Hammonds on the basis of this source. This dismissal, indeed, led him to

[8] N. F. R. Crafts, 'Enclosure and labour supply revisited', *Explorations in Economic History*, XV (1978).
[9] Hammonds, *Village Labourer* (1978 edn), p. 58.
[10] J. A. Yelling, *Common Field and Enclosure in England, 1450–1850* (1977), p. 216.
[11] G. E. Mingay, 'The Land Tax Assessments and the small landowner', *Econ. Hist. Rev.*, XVII (1964).

describe the Hammonds and their work as 'mistaken', 'exaggerated', 'overdrawn', 'unrealistic', 'unhistorical', 'partial and tendentious', 'seriously astray', 'biased', and 'illiberal'.[12] So it may come as a surprise to find that his article consists of a bewilderingly extensive catalogue of intractable difficulties involved in using the assessments, and that it finally concludes:

the apparent shifts in arbitrary categories of small owners, based only on the acreages of owned land as deduced from the land tax assessments, may not be at all meaningful. And if in addition one allows for the gross inaccuracy of acreage figures deduced from the assessments, and the unreliability of the returns themselves, then it might be concluded that detailed investigation of land tax assessments *is simply not worth while* [my italics].[13]

In fact, as one reads Mingay's discussion of the source's various problems this conclusion seems inescapable, and worthy of special note in being made by this author. These difficulties included the fact that 'owing to the inequitable geographical distribution of the tax at its inception, the county quotas have no relation to acreage';[14] the problem of making comparisons before and after the voluntary redemption of the tax made in 1798 (affecting the completion of the returns from then); the fact that many small owners became not chargeable after 1798; the defective accuracy of the returns before 1780 (and in some counties there was little improvement until a later date) and the inadequate distinction of owners and occupiers before 1786; the careless entry of occupiers' names; the irregular use of titles; the difficulty in distinguishing payments made in respect of houses alone, or houses with land, of tithes, market tolls, local offices, property in the form of canals or mills; the avoidance of the tax by many owner-occupiers, 'so that changes in their numbers may be due to nothing more than variations in the comprehensiveness of the returns';[15] the inability to distinguish properly between lessees for long terms and owners; the risk of double-counting 'the frequent inclusion of names two or three times in the same return'; or the fact that some of the returns were made quarterly rather than half yearly, 'although this was not always noted on the document, again leading to possible confusion and under-estimation of the size of the owners' holdings'.[16]

But, as Mingay continues:

More important than any of these, however, is the question of the validity of Davies' assumption that county quotas of tax were equitably distributed so

---

[12] See in particular his introduction to the 1978 edition of the *Village Labourer*.
[13] Mingay, 'Land Tax Assessments', 388.
[14] *Ibid.*, 382. [15] *Ibid.*, 383. [16] *Ibid.*, 383–4.

that *within* each county a certain amount of tax may be taken as representing fairly accurately a certain acreage of land ... It is precisely here, however, that the meaning of the assessments is most doubtful ... large owners sometimes made use of their local influence to obtain reduced assessments, and in some cases paid no tax at all. There were, indeed, widespread complaints of the venality and partiality of the assessors ... This, and the general failure to make regular and accurate re-assessments, soon brought matters to a chaotic state ... there was, even early in the century, no consistency in the relationship of assessment to acreage. By 1780, the date at which scholars have usually begun their studies of the assessments, the old inequalities had been considerably aggravated ... the small owners ... paid considerably more tax than did the large proprietors ... commutation of tithes at enclosure would reduce the holdings of the owners without affecting the tax they paid. Enclosure thus affected the ratio of tax to acreage (and also to value) of the farms, both within the parish that was newly enclosed and in relation to other parishes still unenclosed. As a consequence, newly enclosed land might bear a lower burden of tax per acre than was the case in the neighbouring parishes which retained their open fields, commons and wastes ... Of course, where enclosure resulted in an intake of much larger areas of waste, or the disappearance of extensive open fields and commons, the changes in the acreage and value equivalents of the assessments must have been very much more drastic.[17]

These problems are technical ones, but quite apart from them

there are yet further problems which arise from the structure of rural society itself ... which ... would still result often enough in a picture of landholding remote from reality. The return referred of course to the parish, but in fact it was not very uncommon for even the smaller owners to have land in more than one parish ... Small owners might therefore be on average somewhat larger proprietors than the figures from the returns would suggest. Furthermore, they might more often be much larger *farmers*. The discussion of the increase or decline of small owners never seems to have taken into account the fact that in this period a significant proportion of small owners rented land; although they were only small *owners* of land, they might still be quite substantial *farmers* of land [his italics].[18]

There were still further difficulties raised initially by Chambers. He wrote of how his figures for a large number of Nottinghamshire parishes were wildly different from those produced by E. Davies, for the same parishes. In fact, Chambers had arrived at almost *three times* the number of owner-occupiers than had Davies. Chambers commented that he 'can offer no explanation of this disparity and ... suspect[s] the same disparity exists in regard to the Lindsey figures but ... [has] no satisfactory basis for a final judgement'.[19] Nothing was ever done to reconcile these figures, which suggest that the source (because of the problems outlined by Mingay) is liable to

[17] *Ibid.*, 384–7.   [18] *Ibid.*, 387.
[19] J. D. Chambers, 'Enclosure and the small landowner', *Econ. Hist. Rev.*, X (1939), 127.

produce results arrived at by different scholars as disparate as this. The thought is hardly reassuring. Nor is Chambers' further statement that 'The large increase in the smallest type of owner following upon enclosure may be explained by the fact that those squatters and cottagers who had not been legally recognised as liable to land tax now came in for the first time.'[20] This is one explanation (to which parallels can easily be found in the levying of the poor rate) which has subsequently been avoided in almost every publication using the assessments, frequently arguing for a rise after enclosure, or during the enclosure movement, of such small owners.

This source is the edifice on which the re-appraisal of the Hammonds has been based – despite its results being 'simply not worth while'. There is in addition simply the opinion of one or two historians defensive of parliamentary enclosure that the commissioners acted 'fairly' in their re-allocations of land to the few who had *legal* rights in the open village ('customary' rights were ignored), or the view (since rebutted) that parliamentarians did not sponsor enclosure acts as personal favours for relatives and clients.[21] It is not my intention to question the long-term chronology of decline affect-

---

[20] *Ibid.*, 123. D. B. Grigg makes the same point in his 'The Land Tax Returns', *Agric. Hist. Rev.*, XI (1963), 83. Similar changes affecting the poor rate, which became more widely assessed after enclosure, will be covered below. For further discussion of the land tax returns as a source, see Grigg, 'Land Tax Returns'; J. M. Martin, 'Landownership and the Land Tax Returns', *Agric. Hist. Rev.*, XIV (1966); J. V. Beckett & D. M. Smith, 'The land tax returns as a source for studying the British economy in the eighteenth century', *Bull. Inst. Hist. Research*, LIV (1981); G. J. Wilson, 'The land tax and West Derby Hundred, 1780–1831', *Trans. Hist. Soc. Lancs and Ches*, CXXIX (1980); G. J. Wilson, 'The land tax problem', *Econ. Hist. Rev.*, XXXV (1982); D. E. Ginter, 'A wealth of problems with the land tax', *Econ. Hist. Rev.*, XXXV (1982). H. G. Hunt is one of the few to stress the very limited coverage of this source:

> Finally, it must be admitted that the statistics derived from the land tax returns tell us little about the fortunes of those exercising cottage common rights in unenclosed parishes. Owners of legal rights, i.e. those owning cottages standing for 40 years or more, were usually allowed an allotment by the commissioners. But such owners (as distinct from tenants) were often large proprietors of land and are thus difficult to identify. Those who lost their common rights, i.e. those who used the commons by custom only, are not mentioned in the land tax returns; thus their number can only be estimated by reference to the few claim books that have survived, or to the qualitative evidence of contemporary observers.

'Landownership and enclosure', *Econ. Hist. Rev.*, XI (1958–9), 505. Squatters, for example, with encroachments of under twenty years, had no rights at all, and forfeited their place. T. H. Swales, 'Parliamentary enclosures of Lindsey', *Lincs Arch. Soc. Reports and Papers*, I, pt I (1936), 106.

[21] W. E. Tate, 'Oxfordshire enclosure commissioners, 1737–1856', *Jnl of Modern History*, XXIII (1951); 'Opposition to parliamentary enclosure in eighteenth-century England', *Agricultural History*, XIX (1945); or his 'Members of Parliament and their personal relations to enclosure, 1757–1843', *Agric. Hist.*, XXIII (1949). But see J. M. Martin, 'Members of parliament and enclosure: a reconsideration', *Agric. Hist. Rev.*, XXVII (1979).

ing the owner-occupying class now widely held. And probably a small proportion of land, perhaps 11–14 per cent (judging from the land tax, and so probably rather more in fact), remained owned by small owners in 1802–4 – although this still entails large numbers of small owners in many regions.[22] But there clearly is need for a fresh approach on the social effects of enclosure. Accounts currently offered from the assessments, merely on those classes rich enough to be assessed, seem inadequate for many reasons. At the least, these accounts – which ignore so much literary evidence on the losses to the poor, on the supposedly contemporaneous decline of owner-occupiers, and engrossing of farms, with its adverse effects on small tenants – should be subjected to the scepticism found in Mingay's article, although less apparent in his other writing. We will find such scepticism further endorsed by the main findings of this chapter.

II

It has not been easy to deal with these issues. As Yelling wrote, 'the great difficulty is to say anything very *definite* as to how contemporaries felt these effects, or to what extent. This may even be impossible ... lacking empirical evidence a point is soon reached beyond which discussion cannot profitably progress.'[23] But this is an unnecessarily pessimistic conclusion. My main source here will be settlement examinations, supplemented by literary evidence and poor relief data, and the earlier introduction to the source covers its use in this context.[24] I am concerned again with changes affecting male and female agricultural seasonal distributions of unemployment. The source can tell us nothing about the numbers unemployed during the year – only about the likelihood of their becoming seasonally unemployed in different places, and about the seasonal regularity or otherwise of their employment. The method has been to plot percentages which fell in each calendar month, correcting to adjust for irregularity in the number of days in each month.[25] This has been

---

[22] D. N. McCloskey, 'The economics of enclosure: a market analysis', in E. L. Jones & W. N. Parker (eds.), *European Peasants and Their Markets* (Princeton, 1975), p. 146; Mingay, *Enclosure and the Small Farmer*, pp. 14–16, who arrives at a figure of 15–20 per cent in his *English Landed Society in the Eighteenth Century* (1963), pp. 23–6. H. J. Habakkuk, 'La Disparition du paysan anglais', *Annales*, XX (1965), 655.

[23] Yelling, *Common Field*, p. 215.

[24] See chapter 1.

[25] The data is calculated in the same manner as in chapter 1, using three month moving averages. Removal orders giving occupations have also been used, and I have supplemented the examinations for some regions with other orders from heavily agricultural parishes, in particular parishes where a reasonable run of examinations

done to provide distributions for those examined *before* the enclosure award of the parish in which they were examined – and similarly for those examined *after* the enclosure award of the parish in which they were examined, upon their declaration of unemployment and application for relief. My aim, of course, is in part to confront the argument made by Chambers, using a source well suited to suggest changes caused by enclosure affecting the *regularity* of employment during the year. If Chambers was correct in associating enclosure with a change to 'more continuous field work throughout the year in pasture districts as well as in arable', partly attributed to the new agricultural methods held to be facilitated by enclosure, and partly to hedging and ditching finding 'winter work for casual labour to a greater extent than the open villages', we would expect this to be clearly manifest in the agricultural seasonal distributions of unemployment.

But prior to this, let us once more be entirely clear which agricultural classes are covered here. I argued in chapter 1 for examinants

demonstrated overwhelming predominance of agricultural occupations, and where independent evidence confirmed this. The addition was helpful in some cases to strengthen numerically the examinations; it confirmed their distributions and did not have any significant effect on them. Every order of course went hand in hand with an examination, and no order for which the examination survives is included.

The same exercise of considering change before and after enclosure was also conducted on a numerically much larger scale using only rural removal orders; and despite some extension of occupational coverage, this produced very similar results to those presented here. This was to be expected: examinations indicate that 80 per cent or more of orders from rural villages would generally cover agricultural occupations (centres of cottage industry aside), and of course other rural occupations were often supplemented by part-time agricultural work, or involved rural craftsmen and their families utilising the benefits of open field and common. Such part-time agricultural work was frequently important to the poorer rural craftsmen who came to be examined as to settlement, and there is evidence in examinations of men who had been apprenticed engaged in both craft production and agricultural work. In the villages and agricultural market towns of the Midlands, south and east, virtually all apprenticed occupations which can be taken separately indicate variants of the 'arable' unemployment distribution, demonstrating the overriding influence of the agricultural economy. In larger urban areas artisan distributions tended to be more diversified. I will discuss this in greater detail elsewhere. See also D. Woodward, 'Wage rates and living standards in pre-industrial England', *Past and Present*, XCI (1981), esp. 39ff: 'For rural craftsmen the involvement in agriculture was more important; all of the 60 rural carpenters in Lincolnshire [from his sample of inventories] and all but one of the 22 rural carpenters in the north-west possessed agricultural goods when they died.' See also D. G. Hey, *An English Rural Community; Myddle under the Tudors and Stuarts* (Leicester, 1974), p. 143; B. A. Holderness, 'Rural tradesmen, 1660–1850: a regional study in Lindsey', *Lincs Hist. and Archaeology*, VII (1972). Further examples of occupational flexibility and versatility, and of agricultural workers engaged in other work, are very numerous. For just one of the less obvious examples, that of fishing, see P. Thompson, with T. Wailey & T. Lummis, *Living the Fishing* (1983), e.g., pp. 13–14.

being representative of the agricultural work force which concerns us. As I pointed out, the marriage ages of men and women found in the examinations were about twenty-six and twenty-four respectively, and on the basis of reconstitution evidence we may take this as typical.[26] Similarly, their illiteracy rates are also what we would expect. The generalised local mobility of those not examined in their parish of settlement (and about a fifth to a half of examinants were examined in their place of settlement, as a preliminary to relief) again cannot be taken as unrepresentative; given the widespread mobility of the rural population in this and earlier periods, it would be more disconcerting if examinants had been geographically stable. Dependence on the parish under the old poor law was both widespread (particularly in the late eighteenth and early nineteenth centuries), and a biographical occurrence closely tied to the family cycle, compounded by the seasonal demand for labour in an agricultural parish. The well documented dependence of southern rural labour on the parish during the period of parliamentary enclosure, and the fact that many examinants claimed settlements on the basis of past rents paid for land or housing, in excess of £10 per annum, or on the basis of property owned, should allay any suspicions that we are dealing with an 'unrepresentative' labour force, either before or after enclosure. On these points I refer the reader back to lengthier discussion in chapter 1.[27]

The range of parishes is extensive. I have formed four groups of counties, to show the changes which occurred in different regions, according to the timing and agricultural changes associated with

---

[26] For summary statistics from parish reconstitutions, see E. A. Wrigley & R. S. Schofield, *The Population History of England, 1541–1871* (1981), pp. 255–6, 423–9; or M. W. Flinn, *The European Demographic System, 1500–1820* (Brighton, 1981), pp. 124–5.

[27] And as was clear in chapter 1, the legislative change of 1795 which laid down that examinants could only be removed when actually chargeable (rather than before 1795 when they were also removable when perceived by the parish officers as likely to become chargeable, as well as actually chargeable), raises no difficulties for comparison before and after that date. As we saw, the male seasonal distributions of unemployment (in open, recently enclosed and long-enclosed parishes) remained remarkably constant over the entire period 1690–1860. For data from the same region applied here to consider male unemployment before and after enclosure, we shall find the most acute changes of all the regions covered. Similarly, male patterns for the south-west are relatively continuous when broken down in strict chronological sequence, but we will see clear changes in the same area before and after enclosure. Figures for all regions were also calculated to give results on changes affecting examinants examined before and after enclosure *before* 1795, and for those so examined *after* 1795. Where the figures were large enough to permit this, there was little change from the clear-cut results presented here, indicating that the 1795 Act had nothing to do with the changes documented, and underlining the emphasis which I shall put on enclosure as bringing about these changes.

various phases of the parliamentary enclosure movement. The method adopted was to take only parishes where enclosure took place by private act, or under the General Acts of 1836 and 1845, of land including open field arable, where the total area awarded by the commissioners exceeded 300 acres.[28] Smaller areas were excluded on the grounds that enclosing them was less likely significantly to alter the seasonal demand for, and supply of, labour. About 65–70 per cent of the parishes used were enclosed to the extent of 1,000 acres or more, which I calculate from the *Doomsday of Enclosure* as to be expected from these counties. There is similarly no reason to suppose that the large number of parishes for which settlement records survive had in any way an experience of parliamentary enclosure which was 'atypical'. Finally, I have included those examined after 1730, but none before that date, and also a relatively smaller number of cases surviving for the initial stages of the New Poor Law, up until 1860.

III

The results are both striking and surprisingly uniform across regions. If Chambers and other authors were correct in arguing for a fuller and more regular demand for labour after enclosure, one would expect this to be reflected in a move to flatter seasonal distributions of unemployment – but quite the opposite of this is the case, for every county or region covered. Figure 4.1 gives the most striking changes, for the southern and eastern counties. The figure hardly requires my commentary: it clearly shows the movement from the relatively flat and seemingly benevolent pattern which I have come to regard (with slight regional variations) as typical of open field agriculture with

---

[28] That is, categories A, C, and E of M. E. Turner (ed.), W. E. Tate, *A Doomsday of English Enclosure Acts and Awards* (Reading, 1978). The figures do not consider enclosed land which did not include any open field arable (categories B, D and F in Tate and Turner). Differing county emphases of enclosure make this necessary in part to facilitate regional comparisons, and in doing this I have also aimed to avoid poorly defined enclosures of marginal and relatively unproductive land. The major categories used here encompass, of course, the great bulk of enclosed acreage, comprising the main significance of the movement; and the category of 'land including open field arable' also includes wastes and common land – perhaps on average to the extent of 20–25 per cent of the whole acreage so enclosed in each parish, although the *Doomsday* is unspecific in this regard at parish level. The method adopted was clearly the most appropriate; but I also calculated figures for *all* enclosures (i.e., including the much fewer cases in categories B, D and F), and the results were much the same as those shown here. Given the detailed information required on enclosure in hundreds of parishes, I am considerably indebted to Tate and Turner's *Doomsday*, without which this fusion of poor law and enclosure data would have taken inordinately longer.

additional access to the commons and waste, to an exceptionally acute grain-growing distribution immediately after enclosure, which was to be only marginally softened and largely perpetuated thereafter. The similarity of the two distributions both before, and then

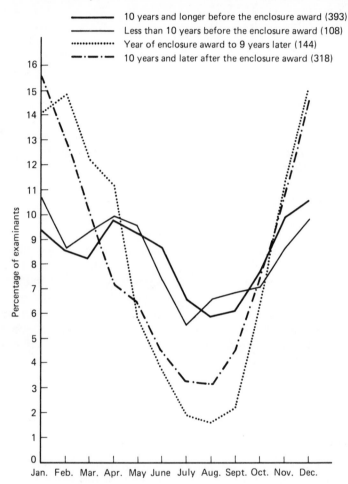

Figure 4.1 *Male seasonal distribution of unemployment – before and after enclosure* Beds, Camb, Ess, Herts, Hunts, Norf & Suff (3 month moving average)

after, enclosure is evident, and makes clear when the break occurred and to what it may be adduced. Material for this region (with many more long-enclosed parishes) produced the reasonably continuous male patterns of chapter 1. We can now add that the tendency towards a more acute distribution of unemployment in the early nineteenth century must have been partly an effect of enclosure.

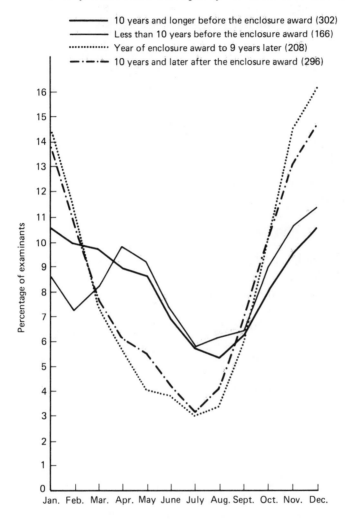

Figure 4.2 *Male seasonal distribution of unemployment – before and after enclosure* Berks, Bucks, Oxon, N'hants & Wark (3 month moving average)

Let us turn to the south Midland counties of Oxfordshire, Berkshire, Buckinghamshire, Northamptonshire, and Warwickshire (Figure 4.2). The figure is similar to that for the east: once more, there is the move to a more acute unemployment distribution during the year, away from the relatively flat pre-enclosure patterns; the graph makes clear the break caused by enclosure in the patterns before and after. The tendency of the very similar patterns after enclosure to fall more sharply during the spring than in Figure 4.1, and then even out more shallowly, is probably due to the spring and early summer labour requirements of livestock – less prominently found in newly enclosed parishes in the east. In both figures the change within the ten year period after the award was sudden, total, and permanent. I have chosen a ten year period before and after enclosure to be certain that we are isolating the effect of enclosure itself, rather than other extraneous factors, and on the basis of how long it generally took to complete the hedging, ditching, and other immediate post-enclosure requirements. It seems that assertions on the benefit of these to the labour force may be overdrawn. The immediate years after enclosure appear to have been less a period of more regular work and slow acclimatisation to new conditions, than a sudden and permanent precipitation into them. In Figure 4.1, the unemployment distribution actually eased after the initial ten years. And while in Figure 4.1 the change is at least in accord with the cropping routines of intensified arable (although far in excess of what might be predicted solely on the basis of such changes), in Figure 4.2 the change runs counter to a cropping shift commonly considered here as a move to pasture. It is clear that there were remarkably similar changes in agriculturally diverse regions. There would seem to be causes behind these changes more fundamental than can be adduced simply to cropping reorientation after enclosure.

Figure 4.3 covers Dorset, Wiltshire, and Somerset, and if the changes it documents are less pronounced than those we have just seen, one can still recognise their basic similarity. Once again, there is movement away from a remarkably flat seasonal distribution of unemployment to a more acute 'arable' one, with its characteristically more insecure winter employment. And, as we shall find to a lesser degree further east when considering long-enclosed parishes, the distribution for such parishes in this south-western region was similar to that promoted by parliamentary enclosure. It seems likely that this area's enclosure brought about an overall intensification of arable, accompanied in some areas by greater dairying – particularly in Somerset. I stress here the similar changes before and after for these south-western counties to those elsewhere.

Finally, let us return to the Midlands, to two counties (Nottinghamshire and Leicestershire) enclosed early by act – almost exclusively in the eighteenth century – where contemporaries widely held that a transition to pasture had occurred, believing that this had frequently produced depopulation (see Figure 4.4). While there is the same more acute post-enclosure distribution, this was much less pronounced,

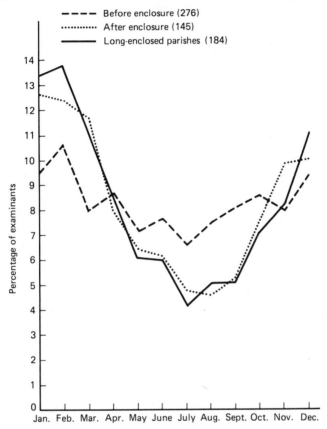

Figure 4.3 *Male seasonal distribution of unemployment – before and after enclosure, and in long-enclosed parishes*
Dors, Wilts & Som (3 month moving average)

and one is struck as much by the continuity before and after enclosure as by the more acute pattern which followed it. It seems probable that the considerable conversion to pasture here, the growth of rural cottage industry, and the proximity of growing urban areas capable of absorbing rural migrants served to counteract the effects of enclosure we have seen elsewhere.

Before developing an explanation for these findings, the series can be completed by comparing seasonal distributions of old-enclosed parishes with those of un-enclosed and recently enclosed parishes. Figure 4.5 allows us to do this for the east. Unlike the south-west, the pattern after enclosure is more extreme than for long-enclosed parishes, with which it nevertheless bears certain resemblances. The

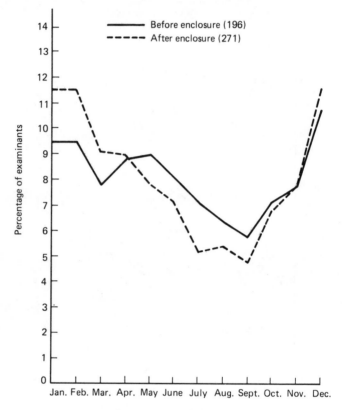

Figure 4.4 *Male seasonal distribution of unemployment – before and after enclosure* Notts & Leics (3 month moving average)

differences between these two around the summer and harvest periods are also of interest. The long-enclosed curve dips in September – the other a little earlier. This may partly be due to the practice (advocated, among others, by Arthur Young) of taking the harvest in earlier than was hitherto customary.[29] And the low point of September in the long-enclosed parishes reminds us that the traditional

[29] A. Young, *The Farmers Kalendar: Containing the Business Necessary to be Performed on Various Kinds of Farms during Every Month of the Year* (1771, 1778 edn), pp. 229–30.

hiring fair for farm-servants took place at Michaelmas (28 September) in this region – perhaps inviting the view that newly enclosed parishes were less reliant on farm-servants than were long-enclosed or un-enclosed parishes. This seems likely for this region, partly

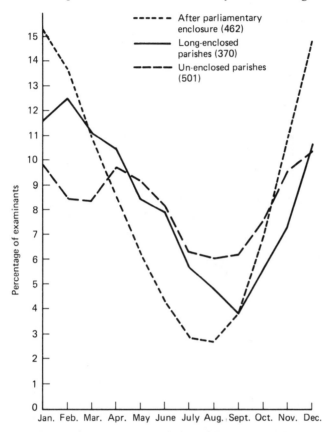

Figure 4.5 *Male seasonal distribution of unemployment – in long-enclosed and un-enclosed parishes, and after parliamentary enclosure*
Beds, Camb, Ess, Herts, Hunts, Norf & Suff (3 month moving average)

because its late parliamentary enclosure occurred when farm service had certainly already begun to decline. And long-enclosed parishes were probably more pasture-based and therefore greater users of farm-servants. Parliamentary enclosure was often associated with a rationalisation of labour usage which hit demand for farm-servants, particularly in areas where it did not bring conversion to the more evenly spread labour requirements of pasture. And farmers intensify-

ing arable production would have preferred day or piece workers. We
shall return to this.

Figure 4.6 gives comparable evidence for the south Midland
counties. Once again, there is some similarity of long-enclosed

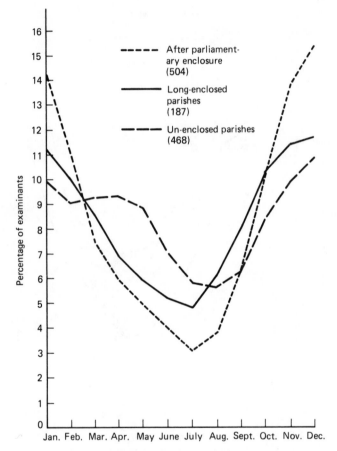

Figure 4.6 *Male seasonal distribution of unemployment – in long-enclosed and
un-enclosed parishes, and after parliamentary enclosure*
Bucks, Berks, Oxon, N'hants & Wark (3 month moving average)

parishes with the distribution of unemployment in parishes lately
enclosed; once again the pattern of the latter is more acute than the
former. And the contrast with the distribution for un-enclosed
parishes is clearly apparent. The reinforcing consistency of these
results is reassuring for the use of the source in this way. The
enclosed, and particularly long-enclosed distributions in Figure 4.6

are closer to what we would expect from a dairying region, with its more regular demand for labour from the early spring through to late summer. This contrasts with the more strictly harvest labour requirements seen in the patterns for the east. It might appear that long-enclosed parishes (Figure 4.6) had frequently been practising forms of pasture or dairying specialisation throughout the period. Parliamentary enclosure in these counties probably changed the more arable open fields to a greater emphasis on dairying, while still maintaining a sufficient arable acreage to manifest the acute pattern of a grain-producing region. As we shall see, there were other effects besides cropping changes produced by enclosure, vital to an explanation of these changes. (The post-enclosure distribution cannot be taken as a literal representation of the farming practices in operation – because of enclosure's disruption to the open field economy of the lower social orders, and the imbalance it could produce between parochial population and resources.) But these suggestions on the extent of pasture and arable in the three categories of parish seem tenable from Figure 4.6, and could be supported by evidence of a more literary nature.[30]

We can now briefly outline the changing female distributions. In chapter 1 I argued for a long-term reduction of female work in south-eastern agriculture, using settlement data, wage material, and literary documentation as evidence. The change had become apparent in the mid- to late eighteenth century, rather than in the late nineteenth century, and was traced in the concentration of women in relatively poorly paid spring and early summer activities: weeding, stone-picking, the calving and dairying season, or haymaking. By the early nineteenth century in the east female security of employment was most apparent in the spring, and they became increasingly liable to unemployment over the rest of the year. This shift occurred from about 1750 to the 1820s. In Figure 4.7 we can see it encapsulated in the transition caused by enclosure. The pattern prior to enclosure (and again, it was one which women shared with men), moved to a more precarious distribution with greatest employment security during the spring, as found in chapter 1, by the early nineteenth century. There is insufficient data to break this down to a pattern immediately before and after enclosure. But it seems certain that the change was hastened by enclosure, and is evident in data from twenty years either side of the award, so as to present us here with the original and final stages of change I earlier contrasted. It would seem that changes occurring more gradually throughout the south-eastern agricultural

[30] See for example Yelling's interesting discussion in *Common Field*, pp. 33–4, 42–3, 58.

sector could be so accelerated by enclosure, which could act as a
catalyst in this regard, rationalising in this way the sexual deployment of labour.

I have not outlined the sexual division of labour in the south

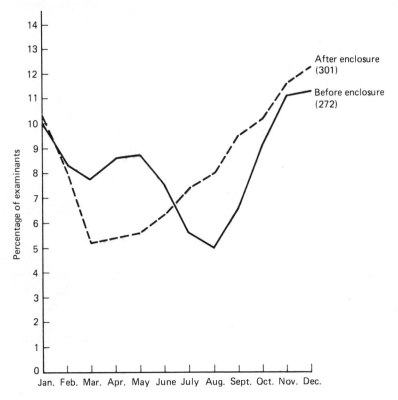

Figure 4.7 *Female seasonal distribution of unemployment – before and after enclosure*
Beds, Camb, Ess, Herts, Hunts, Norf & Suff (3 month moving average)

Midlands. But Figure 4.8 shows changes occurring similar to those
further east. Women once more shared the pre-enclosure male
pattern, but after enclosure they were more securely employed in the
late spring than late summer. This shift became largely established in
the twenty years after the award. Such employment here consisted
particularly of dairying, calving, and haymaking, with the region's
move to such specialisation, and here too an argument might be
made for this sexual division of labour developing in the latter part of
the eighteenth century. We recall that the main enclosure of the
region was between 1760 and 1790, and had been largely completed

by 1800 in Oxfordshire, Buckinghamshire, Warwickshire, and Northamptonshire – the post-enclosure curve certainly dated from before then, reflecting an entrenched situation by about 1820. This could once again be supported by evidence from early nineteenth-century

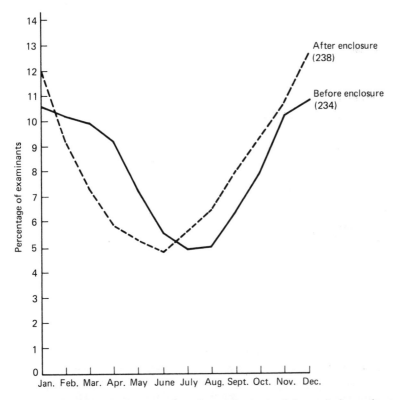

Figure 4.8 *Female seasonal distribution of unemployment – before and after enclosure* Bucks, Berks, Oxon, N'hants & Wark (3 month moving average)

parliamentary reports, although it would detract from my present purpose to enter into that at length here. But we can note how enclosure, as in the east, hastened this sexual division of labour.

Of course, enclosure did not suddenly 'proletarianise' women, in the way sometimes supposed. On the contrary, it tended to curtail their work in a fuller range of agricultural activities alongside men, as well as to hasten their demise as paid farm-servants. But it also altered the terms of employment of those who continued to work for wages. Prior to enclosure (and particularly in the early eighteenth century), most women worked at some point for wages, but in an open field context they had done so on a more part-time basis (just as men), while working for themselves on the commons and open fields as a feature of a more family-based economy. Enclosure, we shall see, markedly curtailed such quasi-independent production, so altering women's position vis-à-vis strictly wage labour. It produced pressures from men, affected in the same way, against female competition in what had become more clearly thought of as the 'labour market'; and enclosure also lessened incentives to employ women where male unemployment and rising real per capita poor relief in the south raised such persistent problems for the local social order. To state the change in terms such as these is rather different to claiming that women had now simply been 'proletarianised'. They had worked for centuries in very large numbers as farm-servants, at a wide range of tasks, saving wages as a life-cycle stage – just as they had worked when married in the open fields or on the commons, or alongside men for wages when these were required.

In Nottinghamshire and Leicestershire, where the least changes occurred after enclosure for men, there was also much continuity in the pattern of female seasonal unemployment (Figure 4.9). The peak in April/May indicates the system of spring hiring fairs affecting women here, as one would find in some areas further west, or in Wales itself. And while men shared the May insecurity of employment prior to enclosure, after enclosure this seems mainly to have persisted for women. It may be that the hiring fair (at least in May) came to deal more strictly with women, who may have survived longer as farm-servants, given these counties' agricultural specialisations. This would be an interesting but tentative variant on the sexual division of labour dealt with more thoroughly elsewhere, to the south and east. Taking a spring hiring fair as one manifestation of pastoral agriculture, the evidence for Nottinghamshire and Leicestershire suggests a growing specialisation of women in pastoral farming, and of men in arable – borne witness to in the move of men after enclosure to a stricter grain-growing pattern. On the basis of changes seen elsewhere, this certainly seems likely.

IV

How then should one explain the most pronounced changes affecting the male seasonal distribution of unemployment, as seen in Figures 4.1 and 4.2? The first step must be to isolate how far these were due to shifts in cropping. This raises difficulties, as there is little systematic and detailed cropping evidence before and after enclosure. But we are fortunate in having the returns to the Board of Agriculture of 1800.[31] And the actual chronology of enclosure in each county is now well known, thanks to the work of Tate and Turner. This can also be a useful guide to the agricultural changes brought about by enclosure

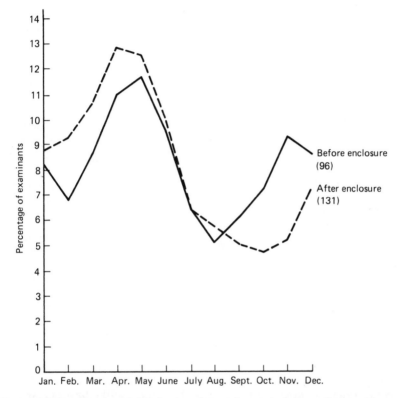

Figure 4.9 *Female seasonal distribution of unemployment – before and after enclosure* Notts & Leics (3 month moving average)

in each county,[32] and confirms the picture provided by the agricultural returns. The first period, from about 1750 to 1780, mainly involved the enclosure of open field arable lands, particularly in the heavier soiled Midlands. Much land here was converted to pasture, although there were also increased acreages of barley and oats. The second phase of the movement saw further enclosure of arable open fields

---

[31] As published in A. Young (Board of Agriculture), *General Report on Enclosures* (1808), pp. 229–54.
[32] See Turner & Tate, *Doomsday of Enclosure,* and most particularly M. E. Turner, *English Parliamentary Enclosure* (Folkestone, Kent, 1980).

Table 4.1. *Acres of wheat increased or decreased by enclosure of open arable fields*

County	Acres of wheat before enclosure	Acres of wheat after enclosure	Acres increased	Acres decreased
Berks	2,900	2,778	–	122
Bucks	9,868	6,571	–	3,297
Oxon	4,882	4,770	–	112
N'hants	19,922	14,135	–	5,787
Wark	8,615	6,435	–	2,180
Total	46,187	34,689	–	11,498
Beds	8,666	7,509	–	1,157
Camb	3,077	2,780	–	297
Ess	80	120	40	–
Herts	652	1,086	434	–
Hunts	5,883	6,361	478	–
Norf	2,602	4,601	1,999	–
Suff	160	370	210	–
Total	21,120	22,827	1,707	–
(Total without Beds & Hunts)	6,571	8,957	2,386	–
Leics	10,173	6,380	–	3,793
Notts	9,219	8,235	–	984
Total	19,392	14,615	–	4,777
Dors	1,321	1,340	19	–
Som	817	2,129	1,312	–
Wilts	7,765	8,362	597	–
Total	9,903	11,831	1,928	–

Source: Young, *General Report*, pp. 229–31 – returns to the Board of Agriculture, by county.

and in particular enclosure of common and waste – this can be dated from about 1790 to 1815. It produced an increase of arable acreage, and was especially pronounced in Norfolk, Cambridgeshire, and other areas in the eastern group of counties. The returns to the Board of Agriculture unfortunately omit some of this phase, but its general character seems well established, and has been discussed at length by Turner and Yelling among many others.[33] Tables 4.1 to 4.4 show in more detail how enclosure affected cropping routines.

There was a clear decline in wheat acreage in Buckinghamshire, Oxfordshire, Northamptonshire, Warwickshire, Bedfordshire,

[33] Turner, *English Parliamentary Enclosure*; Yelling, *Common Field*.

Table 4.2. *Acres of wheat increased or decreased by enclosure of open arable fields*

County	N. of enclosures	Total increase	Total decrease	Average increase in acres per enclosure (i.e. under wheat)	Average decrease in acres per enclosure
Berks	8	312	249	8	–
Bucks	37	161	3,085	–	79
Oxon	19	285	508	–	12
N'hants	86	450	7,044	–	77
Wark	32	93	2,871	–	87
Total	182	1,301	13,757	–	68
Beds	30	668	1,701	–	34
Camb	9	895	184	79	–
Ess	1	40	–	40	–
Herts	4	174	7	42	–
Hunts	16	469	530	–	4
Norf	9	627	10	68	–
Suff	3	150	–	50	–
Total	72	3,023	2,432	8	–
(Total without Beds & Hunts)	26	1,886	201	65	–
Leics	74	453	4,350	–	53
Notts	42	923	1,823	–	21
Total	116	1,376	6,173	–	41
Dors	9	40	177	–	15
Som	2	50	33	8	–
Wilts	23	784	528	11	–
Total	34	874	738	4	–

Source: Young, *General Report*, pp. 232–52 – returns to the Board of Agriculture, by parishes.

Leicestershire, and Nottinghamshire, and for these counties the movement to seasonal distributions more symptomatic of arable goes against the predicted trend from the cropping changes affecting wheat (see Tables 4.1 and 4.2). There was some increase in the south Midland counties of barley and oats, which may have offset the decline of wheat (see Table 4.3). But Table 4.4 clearly shows the

Table 4.3. *Reported statements on cropping change after enclosure*

County	Barley				Oats				Pulse			
	N. enclosures	Increased	Decreased	As before	N. enclosures	Increased	Decreased	As before	N. enclosures	Increased	Decreased	As before
Berks	8	4	2	2	8	6	2	–	8	4	3	1
Bucks	28	18	6	4	28	13	12	3	28	19	5	4
Oxon	29	14	13	2	31	29	2	–	25	11	12	2
N'hants	78	36	29	13	74	50	14	10	70	3	65	2
Wark	35	14	18	3	35	19	11	5	33	4	23	6
Total	178	86	68	24	176	117	41	18	164	41	108	15
Beds	23	8	7	8	21	10	5	6	23	5	11	7
Camb	10	8	–	2	10	6	2	2	7	3	2	2
Ess	2	2	–	–	2	2	–	–	1	1	–	–
Herts	5	3	–	2	6	4	–	2	4	2	–	2
Hunts	16	4	3	9	15	6	6	3	16	2	10	4
Norf	28	23	–	5	27	22	–	5	16	8	3	5
Suff	7	3	–	4	9	5	–	4	7	2	–	5
Total	91	51	10	30	90	55	13	22	74	23	26	25
Leics	72	28	37	7	69	59	8	2	71	13	58	–
Notts	50	33	9	8	46	34	5	7	44	12	24	8
Total	122	61	46	15	115	93	13	9	115	25	82	8
Dors	10	3	6	1	10	5	4	1	3	1	2	–
Som	31	11	2	18	35	14	3	18	32	9	3	20
Wilts	30	12	12	6	30	13	11	6	27	14	9	4
Total	71	26	20	25	75	32	18	25	62	24	14	24

Source: Young, *General Report*, Appendix XII, p. 253.

expansion of cattle, dairy, and sheep in the south Midlands, and on balance it is most unlikely that changes in seasonal distributions upon enclosure here were caused by cropping shifts implying a more arable-based curve. Such changes were on too small a scale (if they took place at all) to have produced this effect. Even in Berkshire, where a rather later chronology of enclosure may imply some intensified grain production (and see Table 4.2), cropping figures do not explain the changes in seasonal unemployment distributions

Table 4.4. *Reported statements on cropping change after enclosure*

County	Cattle				Dairy				Sheep			
	N. enclosures	Increased	Decreased	As before	N. enclosures	Increased	Decreased	As before	N. enclosures	Increased	Decreased	As before
Berks	3	3	–	–	4	3	–	1	7	5	1	1
Bucks	23	17	3	3	30	23	3	4	34	20	13	1
Oxon	13	9	1	3	18	13	1	4	26	20	2	4
N'hants	33	28	4	1	33	16	13	4	43	39	3	1
Wark	23	17	4	2	29	19	7	3	34	30	3	1
Total	95	74	12	9	114	74	24	16	144	114	22	8
Beds	18	6	7	5	22	6	9	7	25	13	6	6
Camb	5	1	2	2	7	1	5	1	9	4	3	2
Ess	–	–	–	–	–	–	–	–	1	–	1	–
Herts	2	1	–	1	4	–	1	3	6	2	2	2
Hunts	13	10	3	–	12	2	9	1	17	14	3	–
Norf	13	4	3	6	17	3	9	5	17	5	5	7
Suff	6	1	–	5	6	1	–	5	6	1	–	5
Total	57	23	15	19	68	13	33	23	81	39	20	22
Leics	57	51	4	2	47	39	7	1	65	59	5	1
Notts	34	19	5	10	26	16	3	7	41	29	8	4
Total	91	70	9	12	73	55	10	8	106	88	13	5
Dors	4	4	–	–	6	2	3	1	7	7	–	–
Som	26	10	–	16	26	9	–	17	28	7	7	14
Wilts	9	1	4	4	17	3	10	4	17	6	7	4
Total	39	15	4	20	49	14	13	22	52	20	14	18

Source: Young, *General Report*, Appendix XII, p. 254.

which occurred. In Nottinghamshire and Leicestershire the same point should be made in stronger terms. Even barley and pulse declined here, and the large increases in cattle, sheep, and dairying (Table 4.4) support contemporary opinion that considerable movement to pasture occurred. If enclosure of open field arable, as an institutional process affecting opportunities for partial self-sufficiency, tended to accentuate 'seasonal unemployment' (and I shall argue that this was the case), then there is reason to suppose that the most pronounced moves to pasture (in Nottinghamshire and Leicestershire) offset the aggravated distributions of unemployment experienced elsewhere. The inherently more regular demand for labour of a pasture district, that is, maintained some continuity in the distribution of unemployment before and after enclosure.

The absolute levels of unemployment may still have increased in Nottinghamshire and Leicestershire after enclosure, producing rising per capita poor relief expenditure, and the out-migration which so struck contemporaries. Chambers himself stressed the latter in Nottinghamshire. It is worth recalling what he initially wrote in *Nottinghamshire in the Eighteenth Century* on the process of enclosure to pasture in the Midlands:

The effect of such a change upon the employment of labour was disastrous, and there is no doubt that many families were displaced . . . there is no doubt . . . that vagabondage increased and that the town of Nottingham had to take drastic steps to keep out families of wanderers . . . The economic gain arising from the differentiation of crop according to the type of soil which enclosure made possible was thus brought at the cost of creating considerable unemployment for which there was no adequate provision. Moreover, such alternative occupation as existed was made difficult of access owing to the apprenticeship regulations and the poor law system based upon the parish . . . Combined with the extension of arable farming in the Forest area . . . innovations must have made heavy demands upon the supply of labour, but whether the demand was sufficient to absorb the redundant labour of the open field village is somewhat doubtful. Moreover, it would be a great mistake to think that enclosure was necessarily followed by improvements in every case. A later investigator came to the conclusion that really intelligent enterprise in the eighteenth century was 'confined to those practices of the few and formed little or no part of' the bulk of Nottinghamshire farmers; and Arthur Young noted that farmers in the Forest district often made no better use of their enclosures than to keep a few sheep on them or take successive crops of corn until they were exhausted and then leave them to turf themselves down. Such agriculture as this, following upon enclosure, could not possibly employ the former population of commoners, squatters, and other semi-independent members of the open field community as well as the regular labourers. In such cases, local unemployment must have resulted.[34]

These are views not commonly associated with Chambers, because he by-passed them in his later article. And Nottinghamshire had greater increases of barley and oats after enclosure than did Leicestershire; in this regard, as in the Forest region discussed by Chambers, it could maintain higher levels of arable employment than Leicestershire. The latter might lay claim to being the most acutely transformed county of all by enclosure, with its movement to pasture. Out-migration was widely reported. But the extension of cottage

[34] J. D. Chambers, *Nottinghamshire in the Eighteenth Century* (1932), pp. 179–82.

industry probably provided alternative employment for those displaced from open field arable. (The seasonal distribution of unemployment for framework knitters in these two counties was almost identical to the male distribution after enclosure.) A movement of labour into such cottage industry may be one clue to the relatively slight change before and after enclosure in the Midland unemployment distributions, alongside the more regular, if absolutely less, labour demand of a pasture district.

What of the other two regions in this regard? The counties of Dorset, Wiltshire, and Somerset were mainly enclosed late, after about 1795 (with the exception of some earlier enclosure in Wiltshire, probably to pasture). If one relates this to the cropping figures it seems likely that they moved to greater emphasis on arable farming. Nevertheless, there was rather slight increase here of barley and oats; seemingly considerable increase of cattle and sheep, and of dairying in Somerset; and the overall increase of wheat acreage indicated in Table 4.2 is very small. The post-enclosure distribution of Figure 4.3 is clearly an arable one, similar to grain-growing areas of East Anglia. It is unlikely that the cropping changes in the south-west, such as they were, would have altered the distribution after enclosure to the extent which occurred; but it is likely that they contributed. Given our current knowledge on cropping changes for this district, it is difficult to be more definite on this.

We can turn finally to the eastern counties, where the most extreme changes occurred affecting seasonal distributions. As shown by Turner, the chronology of enclosure here was late, during the high grain prices.[35] There was an extension of grain growing particularly by bringing into cultivation wastes and commons. This included barley and oats as well as wheat, and contemporaries noted (particularly in Norfolk) an abandonment of dairying.[36] There would be grounds then, for expecting some changes towards an arable pattern upon enclosure. But the changes of Figure 4.1, particularly in the immediate aftermath of enclosure, are drastic beyond all expectations. They are more acute than any distribution found for the region taking parishes regardless of their enclosed state. When we recall that the new husbandry techniques practised here (the introduction of which is held by many to have been facilitated by enclosure) involved also the cultivation of root crops and some maintenance of livestock in the interests of soil fertility – both of which implied seasonalities of labour demand which should at least have softened the purely

---

[35] Turner, *English Parliamentary Enclosure*, apps. 8 and 10.
[36] Young, *General Report*, pp. 259–60; Yelling, *Common Field*, pp. 205–7.

grain-growing distributions which emerged after enclosure – it is clear that these patterns cannot have been brought about merely by the extension of arable cropping which occurred. We have surely to adopt an explanation in wider terms, just as for the south Midlands (where the same effect significantly emerged contrary to cropping changes), and perhaps also for the south-western counties.

V

And, at least in its general form, the explanation comes as readily to mind today as it did to an earlier generation of agrarian historians. Let me shift now to altogether different evidence, of a literary nature. I want to quote at length two of the most clear-sighted writers ever to enquire into English rural life: George Sturt and David Davies. First, here is Sturt, writing his remarkable book *Change in the Village* shortly before the first world war, and I make no apology for the length of this quotation:

The older people talk about things that happened 'before the common was enclosed' much as they might say 'before the flood' ... I question if the benefits experienced here were equal to those which are said to have been realized in similar circumstances elsewhere. In other parishes, where the farmers have been impoverished and the labourers out of work, the latter, at the enclosure of a common, have sometimes found welcome employment in digging out or fencing in the boundaries of the new allotments, and in breaking up the fresh ground. So the landowners say. But here, where there were few men wanting constant labour, the opportunity of work to do was hardly called for, and the making of boundaries was in many cases neglected. In that one way, therefore, not many men can have derived any profit from the enclosure ... the real disadvantages were soon to appear ... the cows – once as numerous as the donkeys – were not given up quite immediately, though in a few years they were all gone, I am told ... [An] ancient mode of life had been cut off at the roots ... that was the effect. To the enclosure of the common more than to any other cause may be traced all the changes which have subsequently passed over the village. It was like knocking the keystone out of an arch. The keystone is not the arch; but, once it is gone, all sorts of forces, previously resisted, begin to operate towards ruin, and gradually the whole structure crumbles down. This fairly illustrates what happened to the village, in consequence of the loss of the common ... The enclosure ... left the people helpless against influences which have sapped away their interests, robbed them of security and peace, rendered their knowledge and skill of small value, and seriously affected their personal pride and their character. Observe it well ... The other causes which have been at work could hardly have operated as they have done if the village life had not been weakened by the changes directly due to the loss of the common.

They consisted – those changes – in a radical alteration of the domestic economy of the cottagers ... For note what it involved. By the peasant system ... people derived the necessaries of life from the materials and soil of their own countryside. Now, so long as they had the common, the inhabitants of the valley were in a large degree able to conform to this system, the common being, as it were, a supplement to the cottage gardens, and furnishing means of extending the scope of the . . . home industries. It encouraged the poorest labourer to practise, for instance, all those time-honoured crafts which Cobbett . . . had advocated as the one hope for labourers. The cow-keeping, the bread-making, the fattening of pigs and curing of bacon, were actually carried on here thirty years after Cobbett's time, besides other things not mentioned by him, such as turf-cutting on the heath and wheat growing in the gardens. But it was the common which made all this possible. It was not only by the spacious 'turn-out' which it afforded that the people were enabled to keep cows and get milk and butter; it was not only with the turf-firing out on the common that they could smoke their bacon . . . and, again, it was only because they could get furze from the common to heat their bread ovens that it was worth their while to grow a little wheat at home and have it ground into flour for making bread. With the common, however, they could, and did, achieve all this. I am not dealing in superstition. I have mentioned nothing here that I have not learnt from men who remember the system still flourishing – men who in their boyhood took part in it, and can tell how . . . it all actually happened . . . But the very heart of it was the open common.

Accordingly, when the enclosure began to be a fact . . . when the cottager was cut off from his resources . . . there was little else that he could do in the old way. It was out of the question to obtain most of his supplies by his own handiwork: they had to be procured, ready-made from some other source. That source, I need hardly say, was a shop. So the once self-supporting cottager turned into a spender of money at the baker's, the coal merchant's, the provision dealer's; and, of course, needing to spend money, he needed first to get it.

The change was momentous . . . To a greater or less extent, most of them were already wage-earners, though not regularly . . . the majority . . . had been obliged to sell their labour itself, when they required money. Wage-earning, therefore, was no new thing in the village; only, the need to earn became more insistent, when so many more things had to be bought with the wages . . . Unemployment, hitherto not much worse than a regrettable inconvenience became a calamity. Every hour's work acquired a market value . . . so that a man was tempted to neglect his own gardening if he could sell his labour in somebody else's garden. Thus undermined, the peasant outlook gave way, perforce, to that of the modern labourer, and the old attachment to the countryside was weakened. In all this change of attitude, however, we see only one of those indirect results of the enclosure of the common which were spoken of above. If the villagers became more mercenary . . . it was . . . because [enclosure] left them helpless to resist becoming so – left them a prey to considerations whose weight they had previously not so much felt. After all, the new order of things did but intensify the need of wage-earning; it made no difference in the procedure of it . . .

But in regard to spending the case was otherwise. Under the old regime . . . in the main the peasant's expenditure was not regular, but intermittent. Getting so much food and firing by his own labour, he might go for weeks without needing more than a few shillings to make up occasional deficiencies . . . the regular expenses were small, the occasional ones not crushing. But today, when the people can no longer produce for themselves ... nearly all the expenses have become regular ... Every week money has to be found ... As a result, the former thrift of the village has been entirely subverted ... the cottagers have been obliged to resort to methods of saving specially adapted to the changed conditions. The point is of extreme importance. Under the old style, a man's chief savings were in the shape of commodities ready for use, or growing into use. They were, too, a genuine capital, inasmuch as they supported him while he replaced and increased them ... Under the new thrift they cannot be so hoarded up ... What the modern labourer chiefly requires ... is not a little hoard of money lying by, but ... a steady income of shillings ... for the first time the importance of a 'demand for labour' came home to them.[37]

I quote Sturt here at length, because this is the clearest statement to be found on the changes to *total* wage dependency after enclosure, and therefore to the precarious existence determined entirely by the fluctuations of agricultural (seasonal) demand. These changes certainly underlie, in large measure, the changing distribution of 'unemployment' after enclosure – and we can now use this word in a more clearly defined manner than it was used by Chambers, or previously in this chapter. The usual implicit narrowing down of discussion on the effects of enclosure to 'employment' (by implication, that is, wage-dependent employment rather than also self-employment), unimaginatively curtails the issue from the start. Just as today, we should use the term unemployment as defined (albeit inadequately) by application for relief. Wage-dependent employment no doubt expanded in some regions after enclosure. We will consider that shortly. But we impose anachronistic criteria to suppose that this provides an adequate judgement on the effects of enclosure on the 'labour force'. David Davies (whose *Case of the Labourers in Husbandry* was published in 1795), can clarify this further, in a discussion similar to that of Sturt's. Note too the changes which he implied affected the sexual allocation of labour upon enclosure:

The depriving the peasantry of all landed property has beggared multitudes ... Instead of giving to labouring people a valuable stake in the soil, the opposite measure has so long prevailed, that but few cottages, comparatively, have now *any* land about them. Formerly many of the lower sort of people occupied tenements of their own, with parcels of land about them, or they rented such of others. On these they raised for themselves a considerable part of their subsistence, without being obliged, as now, to buy all they want at shops. And this kept numbers from coming to the parish. But since those small parcels of ground have been swallowed up in the contiguous farms and inclosures, and the cottages themselves have been pulled down; the families

---

[37] G. Sturt, *Change in the Village* (1912). This quotation is extracted from the classic statement of pp. 77–111, which should be read in its entirety. See also his discussion in *The Bettesworth Book* (Firle, Sussex, 1978), p. 286.

which used to occupy them are crowded together ... with hardly ground enough about them for a cabbage garden: and being thus reduced to be *mere* hirelings, they are of course very liable to come to want. And not only the *men* occupying those tenements, but *their wives and children too*, could formerly, when they wanted work abroad, employ themselves profitably at home, whereas now, few of *these* are constantly employed ... so that almost the whole burden of providing for their families rests upon the *men* ... Thus an amazing number of people have been reduced from a comfortable state of partial independence to the precarious condition of hirelings, who, when out of work, must come immediately to their parish. And the great plenty of working hands always to be had when wanted, having kept down the price of labour below its proper level, the consequence is universally felt in the increased number of the dependent poor [his italics].[38]

The pre-enclosure distributions of unemployment were, to a considerable degree, indicative of the partial independence allowed by access to the commons or open fields. Enclosure ended such access, throwing the work force (and it could now be seen more strictly as such) onto an unprecedentedly complete reliance on wage labour. 'In the open field village', Slater wrote,

the entirely landless labourer was scarcely to be found. The division of holdings into numerous scattered pieces, many of which were of minute size, made it easy for a labourer to obtain what were in effect allotments in the open fields. If he had no holding, he still might have a common right; if no acknowledged common right, he might enjoy the advantage of one in a greater or less degree. From the poorest labourer to the richest farmer, there was, in the typical open field village, a gradation of rank. There was no perceptible social gap between the cottager who worked the greater part of his time for others, and for the smaller part of his time on his own holding, who is therefore termed a labourer, and his neighbour who reversed that distribution of time, and is therefore to be termed a farmer. It was easy for the efficient or fortunate man to rise on such a social ladder; equally easy for the inefficient or unlucky to slip downwards. After enclosure the comparatively few surviving farmers, enriched, elevated intellectually as well as socially by the successful struggle with a new environment, faced, across a deep social gulf, the labourers who now had only their labour to depend upon. In the early part of the nineteenth century, at any rate, it was almost impossible for a labourer to cross that gulf [my italics].[39]

These are the major differences underlying the distributions of unemployment, and they need to be stressed through having so obviously been underplayed in the historiography which reappraised the Hammonds, Slater, or Hasbach. And these changes affecting the labouring poor, from partial independence to wage dependency, can be revealingly illustrated in contemporary com-

[38] D. Davies, *The Case of the Labourers in Husbandry* (1795), pp. 56–7.
[39] Slater, *English Peasantry*, p. 130.

ment, not least in that which was *condemnatory* of the open field village and *favourable* to enclosure.

We need to discuss this so as to emphasise the manner in which contemporary views were permeated with a confusion, to our minds, of moral rectitude with economic well being. To so many advocates of enclosure a change to wage dependency was equated with an improvement in 'moral' standing, in turn presented as tantamount to an improved standard of living. I quote such statements now in part to illustrate this, but essentially to stress how, even in the thinking of these enclosure *advocates*, the fact that enclosure produced a shift to much more (seasonally) precarious wage dependency was taken for granted, and openly acknowledged. 'Many an idler would then be employed' suggested the *General Report on Enclosures* of 1808.[40]

Howlett was more detailed on this, and we should pay close attention to his reasoning:

For even fixt and perpetual benefits to the poor of an [unenclosed] parish, though in themselves clear and certain, yet viewed in their connections and consequences are often highly injurious . . . 'Give the poor', says the sprightly and ingenious Mr. Arthur Young, 'a thousand pounds and do you make them the *less* poor? By no means, but *more* so. Lessen the spur to industry, and you take away what nothing can recompense.' Should we therefore allow . . . that rights of common are . . . a real and certain benefit to the poor; yet would [we] be far from having proved that they render them so easy and comfortable as they might be from that truest source of virtue and happiness, the constant efforts of their own regular industry.[41]

He continued by romanticising the position of a strictly wage-dependent labourer, arguing against the 'trite and common objections' to enclosure that they caused 'a great diminution of the privileges and happiness of the poor'.[42] And there were many other 'sprightly and ingenious' authors who agreed that the commons were 'hurtful to society by holding forth a temptation to idleness, that fell parent to vice and immorality'.[43] The commons produced villagers with 'habits of idleness and dissipation and a dislike to honest labour, which has rendered them the riotous and lawless set of men which they have . . . shown themselves to be'.[44] Enclosure would make the poor take up 'an honest employment, instead of losing time in idleness and waste'.[45] Even Sir Thomas Bernard argued that 'the

---

[40] Young, *General Report*, p. 391.
[41] Rev. J. Howlett, *Enclosures a cause of Improved Agriculture, of Plenty and Cheapness of Provisions* (1787), in A. H. John (ed.), *Enclosure and Population* (Farnborough, 1973), p. 83.   [42] *Ibid.*, pp. 77–9.
[43] J. Clark, 'On commons in Brecknock', *Annals of Agriculture*, XXII (1794), 633. This rampant attack on 'idleness' advocates enclosure 'to put it as much as possible out of their power to live idle', 636.   [44] Cited in Hammonds, *Village Labourer*, p. 50.
[45] *Ibid.*, p. 54.

welfare of the cottager depends more on the improved resources and habits of life, than on any increase or superabundance of wages'.[46] We recognise here the same moralistic habit of thinking, and the displacement of a desire to keep wages depressed (or to lower them) into a self-justifying moral rhetoric.

The 1844 Select Committee on Enclosures is replete with similar examples of this. The comments of a witness from Newbury in Berkshire indicate how such 'moral' concern could harmonise so nicely with employer considerations over labour availability:

> You rarely find cottagers residing on a common who frequent any place of worship; it is with the greatest difficulty in the world you can prevail upon them to send their children to school ... I think the beer-shop is maintained by them. I think that is the place where they meet to concoct their arrangements and habits of plunder; it is their place of constant resort ... they will *not* seek for labour until they are compelled to do it, and they will not be selected for labour where others are to be found ...
> 'Are the committee to understand that you think the poor people are generally *better off* where there are not commons or wastes, than where there are?' – 'Yes; I could point out a strong instance in the parish of East Woodby, where there was an extensive common some few years since; the residents upon that common were of the *loosest description*; hardly a session or an assize passed over, in which there were not prosecutions for sheep-stealing and all other sorts of offences. That common was inclosed against very great opposition, and now it is one of the most *respectable* parishes in our district; it is no longer inhabited by that class of persons, but the parties are *a respectable class looking up to the wealthier classes for labour*' [my italics].[47]

For 'respectable', then, read 'looking up to the wealthier classes for labour', and for 'better off' read 'less likely to steal sheep and commit all other sorts of offences'. As another witness put it: 'I think the population on the verge of these commons are not to be compared, in point of usefulness to society, to labourers who are not on the verge of commons', leaving us to wonder at his implied definition of 'society'.[48]

Similarly, by the term 'demoralised' today we mean a psychological state of apathy or dispiritment, and we might assume that this was being diagnosed as a widespread social condition by parliamentary reports (particularly the 1832–4 Poor Law Commission) in their repetitive use of the term. This would be quite incorrect. Commenting on the 'moral condition of people in the neighbourhood of commons and uninclosed lands' a witness remarked: 'I generally find them demoralized, they are generally of dissolute habits; many of

---

[46] Sir T. Bernard, 'Extract from a further account of the advantages of cottagers keeping cows', *Reports of the Society for Bettering the Condition of the Poor*, II (1800), 257.
[47] S.C. on Enclosure, V (1844), pp. 313–14.   [48] *Ibid.*, p. 77.

them commit depredations, being out of sight of any person of authority.'[49] Here is another witness, in 1844:

I think there is no comparison whatever between the *moral state* of persons who gain their livelihood by day-labour and those who occupy a cottage and garden, and perhaps a small encroachment in the neighbourhood of a common, and who live as cottiers, not as labourers; they get their livelihood merely from the depasturage of the common, or as they can, by any shifting means in their power; *they are never so well off*, and they never educate their children so well; they are much more frequently brought before the magistrates for acts of violence and turbulence than a steady regular day-labourer, who always brings up his family in a better condition than any one of the class to which I allude ... I should say ... it is rather a disinclination on the part of the cottier to be employed. He occupies himself by the care of any stock which he may be able to depasture on the common; it requires, of course, to be looked after; and his little portion of land, whatever it is, demands all his time and attention to cultivate it [my italics].[50]

'In sauntering after his cattle' John Billingsley would have added, 'he acquires a habit of indolence. Quarter, half, and occasionally whole days are imperceptibly lost. Day labour becomes disgusting; the aversion increases by indulgence; and at length the sale of a half-fed calf, or hog, furnishes the means of adding intemperance to idleness.'[51] We should be clear what was meant by terms such as

---

[49] *Ibid.*, p. 372.   [50] *Ibid.*, p. 112.

[51] J. Billingsley, *General View of the Agriculture of the County of Somerset* (1797), p. 52. And see pp. 36–7: 'If he can earn eight or nine shillings in *four* days of the week, the remaining *two* days are devoted to pleasure, or luxury, and the wife and children are in a worse situation than when more moderate wages compelled him to work.' Or see T. Stone, *Suggestions for Rendering the Inclosure of Common Fields and Waste Lands a Source of Population and of Riches* (1787), p. 65: 'The inclosure of a common ... instead of supporting [the cottager] in a degree of idleness, would stimulate his industry ... a situation far more beneficial to him than lounging over two or three thousand acres to hunt up his cow, his ass, or his sheep.' T. Postans, *Letter to Sir Thomas Baring on the Present State of the Agricultural Labouring Poor* (1831), pp. 9ff. 'The poor of this class [with common rights] were not the most moral ... but somewhat independent, and generally idle.' Labour 'ought never to be' independent of the farmer.
  For the contrast epitomised in contemporary painting, see Thomas Gainsborough, *Landscape with a Woodcutter Courting a Milkmaid* – where the life of the open field and common is presented in the leisurely foreground courtship scene, with the woodcutter, milkmaid and cow, and in the more distant couple on the hill with the donkeys. In juxtaposition, the intensified labour of the enclosed environment is seen in the man bent over the plough in the middle distant enclosure. The contrast of the ragged clothes of the man ploughing, with the finery of the milkmaid (with her full pails of milk), and the well dressed woodcutter, is worth noting. In the enclosed section of the painting, the only indication of material well-being is in the horse and plough – both belonging to the farmer. In the distance lies the growing town (Ipswich in this case) for which production is intended. The dead tree on the common suggests that the way of life under it will shortly end. See M. Rosenthal, *British Landscape Painting* (Oxford, 1982), p. 32, and his most interesting book on Constable. *The Painter and his Landscape* (1983), p. 194. For discussion of the pictorial presentation of themes of idleness and work, see in particular John Barrell, *The Dark Side of the Landscape* (Cambridge, 1980).

'demoralised', or 'they are never so well off' – these were 'moral' statements overriding material conditions, and denoted the opposite of what we would understand today.

Such views were found increasingly after the mid-eighteenth century – Arthur Young thought them self-evident to everyone 'but a fool'. Their components were generally the same: the flourishing eulogy to day labour; the complaints of the moral laxity of the commons (oddly, illegitimacy rose most sharply during the period of parliamentary enclosure); the concern for labour cheapness and work discipline constantly lurking behind 'moral' statement; the defence of the large farm. Here is a characteristically pompous statement from Arbuthnot:

Let not the mistaken zeal of well-disposed, but ignorant people, persuade the man of sense that [enclosure] is prejudicial to the Poor ... The benefit which they are supposed to reap from commons, in their present state, I know to be merely nominal; nay, indeed, what is worse, I know that, in many instances, it is an essential injury to them, by being made a plea for their idleness; for, some few excepted, if you offer them work, they will tell you, they must go to look up their sheep, cut furzes, get their cow out of the pound, or perhaps, say they must take their horse to be shod, that he may carry them to a horse-race or cricket-match ... The certain weekly income of the husband's labour, not attended with the anxiety of the little farmer, will procure more real comfort in his little cottage ... if by converting the little farmers into a body of men who must work for others, more labour is produced, it is an advantage which the nation should wish for: the compulsion will be that of honest industry to provide for a family.[52]

And 'men of sense' when reading this will also note that it is to be the *husband's* labour, 'to provide for a family'. A more modern state of affairs was being described, consciously or otherwise, in an increasingly definite manner in this agrarian literature.

It would seem that much contemporary opposition to open fields and commons stemmed not from any belief that these depressed the standard of living and increased parochial dependency and poor rates, but from opposition to the perceived independence and self-reliant resourcefulness which they conferred. (I have deliberately omitted to quote the many other contemporaries whose view that this was a *benefit* led them to condemn enclosure or the way it was conducted.) We find evidence not of 'demoralisation' as understood today (entailed perhaps in an absence of employment or resources), but rather of a scope for independent social and economic action which allowed the poor not to 'seek for labour until they are

[52] J. Arbuthnot, *An Inquiry into the Connection between the Present Price of Provisions and the Size of Farms* (1773), pp. 81, 128.

compelled to it'; not to look up 'to the wealthier classes for labour'; not to be 'useful to society' – in short, to have 'habits of idleness and dissipation and a dislike for honest labour'. Whether one describes this state of affairs in these, or more favourable, terms, we see here, as a feature of open field and common, the economic background to the pre-enclosure seasonal distributions of unemployment – and to the low and seasonally regular pre-enclosure poor relief which I will discuss shortly. And in the sudden change to dependence only on wage labour brought about by enclosure (described, in their various ways, by all these authors and witnesses) we have, supplement it as I shall, the general explanation for the adverse seasonal changes which occurred after the award.[53]

One of the most important factors which contributed to the pre-enclosure distributions, and which was heavily curtailed by enclosure, was the keeping of livestock by the poor. There are many well known statements on this matter, by Arthur Young and others. 'I kept four cows before the parish was enclosed, and now I don't keep so much as a goose; and you ask me what I lose by it!'[54] The matter can be pursued further, to explain how livestock, and especially cows, helped produce the pre-enclosure employment distributions. First, there was almost no disagreement that enclosure virtually ended the long-established practice of cottagers, squatters, labourers, and other poor people keeping their own livestock. The opinions expressed for example from returning parishes in Appendix IV of the 1808 *General Report* were almost unanimous on this. The very large majority complained of the poor's loss of their cows, frequently adding how difficult it had now become to obtain milk for children. Taking various examples from counties covered by Figures 4.1 and 4.2 we learn that:

The poor seem the greatest sufferers; they can no longer keep a cow, which before many of them did, and they are therefore now maintained by the parish.

---

[53] When reading contemporary opposition to open fields and commons, one recalls Cobbett's question: 'But why should men, why should any men, work hard? Why, I ask, should they work incessantly, if working part of the days of the week be sufficient . . . when they now raise food and clothing and fuel and every necessary?' *Rural Rides* (1830, Harmondsworth, 1967 edn), p. 316. Or see G. D. H. & M. Cole (eds.), *The Opinions of William Cobbett* (1944), pp. 139–40, to similar effect. In the contemporary moral discussion surrounding enclosure, we see one of the crucial historical points at which Cobbett's view gave way to the enduring attachment of stigma to 'unemployment', and see why. The importance of the change will be clear in a country faced today with substantial and growing unemployment, whose members still rely to a considerable extent on the work ethic as their standard of self-value.

[54] T. Batchelor, *General View of the Agriculture of the County of Bedfordshire* (1808), p. 235.

The condition of the labouring poor much worse now than before the enclosure, owing to the impossibility of procuring any milk for their young families.

To my knowledge, before the enclosure, the poor inhabitants found no difficulty in procuring milk for their children; since, it is with the utmost difficulty they can procure any milk at all. Cows lessened from 110 to 40.

The poor have not the same means of keeping cows as before.

Cottagers deprived of cows, without compensation.

The poor injured.

Obliged to sell their cows.[55]

And so on – this was the view from virtually all parishes.

The benefit [of enclosure, summarised the *General Report*, using Arthur Young's words of 1801] is by no means unmixed ... in some cases, many cows had been kept without a legal right, and nothing given for the *practice* ... In other cases ... they kept cows by right of hiring their cottages, or common rights, and the land going of course to the proprietor, was added to the farm, and the poor sold their cows. This is a very common case.[56]

This complaint, commonly extending to sheep, geese, donkeys, and hogs as well, was widely made in other sources.

'And what a produce is that of a cow!', wrote Cobbett by way of introducing his enthusiastic eulogy to the creature.[57] But of course a

---

[55] Young, *General Report*, pp. 150ff. On the loss of cows, see also A. Young, *An Inquiry into the Propriety of Applying Wastes to the Better Maintenance and Support of the Poor* (Bury St Edmunds, 1801), pp. 14, 17, 21, 42–3, 88; N. Kent, 'The great advantage of a cow to the family of a labouring man', *Annals of Agriculture*, XXXI (1798), 21–6; Bernard, 'Extract', 263; W. Marshall, *Review and Abstract of the County Reports to the Board of Agriculture. Vol. III: the Eastern Department* (1811, York, 1818 edn), pp. 257, 287: 'An alteration of the ancient practice of commoning, or depasturing stock, on the wastes of the parish of Leverington, has been introduced within these few years, and is continued to the prejudice of the poor cottagers, who are thereby deprived of keeping cows for the succour of their families. If the former custom could be restored, a great benefit to the parish would arise from it. I believe the labourers families would be much more comfortable from the article of milk, as well as more healthy.' G. Sturt, *The Journals of George Sturt, 1890–1927* (Cambridge, 1967), vol. 1, pp. 413, 429. Parson Woodforde considered that a parishioner who had lost a cow had special need for a charitable donation. See Rev. J. Woodforde, *The Diary of a Country Parson, 1758–1802* (Oxford, 1978 edn), pp. 360, 369, 517, 600, 603, 604.

[56] Young, *General Report*, pp. 12–13.

[57] W. Cobbett, *Cottage Economy* (1822, Oxford, 1979 edn), pp. 95ff. See also pp. 91ff, 127, 142–3 on the value of the commons to the poor; and pp. 107–8 on the need to allow land to the poor, so as to relieve parishes 'burdened by men out of work'. Cobbett even claimed that enclosures 'were, for the most part, useless in point of quantity of *production*; and, to the labourers, they were malignantly mischievous. They drove them from the skirts of commons, downs and forests. They took away their cows, pigs, geese, fowls, bees, and gardens ... it was *impossible* to augment the *quantity of produce* by new enclosures.' Cole (eds.), *The Opinions of William Cobbett,*

cow, or even a goat, seems a trivial and disposable commodity to the modern British historian, not commonly featuring highly as a personal priority. We deal with enclosure in terms of 'the landownership debate', with its issues of farm and estate size, and there are certainly important economic reasons for taking such an approach. Nevertheless, priorities stood differently to the writer (in 1816) of an anonymous letter to the gentlemen of Ashill, a parish where 1,986 acres had been enclosed in 1786:

This is to inform you that you have by this time brought us under the heaviest burden and under the harshest yoke we ever knowed; it is too hard for us to bear ... You do as you like, you rob the poor of their commons right, plough the grass up that God sent to grow, that a poor man may feed a cow, Pig, Horse, nor Ass; lay muck and stones on the road to prevent the grass growing ... There is 5 or 6 of you have gotten all the whole of the land in this parish in your own hands and you would wish to be rich and starve all the other part of the poor of the parish ... Gentlemen, these few lines are to inform you that God Almighty have brought our blood to a proper circulation, that we have been in a very bad state a long time, and now without an alteration of the aforesaid, we meant to circulate your blood with the leave of God ... There was 2 cows and an Ass feeding on the road last Saturday, and there was 2 farmers went to the keepers and said they would pound them if they did not drive them away, and one of them ... went home, got a plough and horses, and ploughed up the grass that did growed on the road ... So we shall drive the whole before us ... and set fire to all the houses and stacks as we go along: we shall begin in the Night ... we wish to prepare yourselves

---

pp. 85–6. This view specifically on changes in quantity of production may be doubtful. But it is certainly true that many modern and enthusiastic estimates of the contribution of enclosure to growing agricultural output have ignored the *negative* effects of enclosure's reduction both of livestock owned by the poor, and of output grounded in the poor's partial self-sufficiency – both of which were stressed in contemporary petitions against enclosure. In a curious and value-loaded way, 'agricultural output' or production in most English economic history and historical economics is implicitly defined (before and after enclosure) as the production of tenant farmers and landowners, the 'employers' of 'labour'. The use by Chambers and many others of the term 'employment' reveals a similar way of thinking.

For a useful discussion supporting the argument here, see Deane and Cole's emphasis on the shift from the subsistence sector to the exchange economy: 'In 1688 the cottagers, paupers and vagrants together accounted for 24 per cent of total population' in King's estimates. 'By 1801 when Colquhoun drew up a comparable table the paupers and vagrants were still there ... but the cottagers, swallowed up no doubt by the eighteenth century enclosure movement, were no longer worth mentioning ... the subsistence sector had virtually disappeared from the British economy when the industrial revolution began.' Of course, the 'subsistence sector' went far beyond the cottagers. And on the basis of my experience of the black African countries, I believe them right to suggest that the subsistence sector by the early nineteenth century was already 'far less important than it is currently in some of the modern underdeveloped economies in which an industrial revolution is said to be in progress'. *British Economic Growth, 1688–1959* (Cambridge, 1962, 1969 edn), p. 256.

for action . . . you have had a good long time . . . No: we will fight for it and if you win the day, so be it.[58]

This importance to the poor of their livestock cannot be doubted. Sir Thomas Bernard wrote that cows were

highly conducive to the happiness of my poor neighbours, and advantageous to the occupiers of farms, who have always a set of *industrious labourers* within their respective parishes, *who do not become chargeable in the time of sickness*, or when from age, manual labour cannot any longer be performed by them: at such periods the produce of their cows and gardens affords them the means of a decent maintenance, and of the regular discharge of their rents [his italics].[59]

And Arthur Young estimated the value of a cow to a family at as much as 5–6s. a week – close to the wages of a fully employed labourer.[60]

He believed that livestock helped avoid parish chargeability, and the point was frequently repeated by observers concerned to avoid or lower high poor rates, including Davies, Sinclair, Homer, Marshall, or the Earl of Winchelsea, and many others who generally advocated enclosure.

Whoever travels through the Midland counties [wrote the Earl of Winchelsea], and will take the trouble of inquiring, will generally receive for answer, that formerly there were a great many cottagers who kept cows, but the land is now thrown to the farmers; and if he inquires still further he will find that in those parishes the poor's rates have increased in an amazing degree more than according to the average rise throughout England.[61]

(I will pursue the effects of enclosure on poor relief shortly.) Some parishes paid for cows for their parishioners, as a means of keeping them off the poor rates – such was the perceived effect of livestock.[62] Such was also the thinking behind Pitt's inclusion in his 1797 Poor Law Bill of a clause allowing parishes to make loans for the purchase of a cow, or other animal, so as to release someone from parochial chargeability. The dairy produce from cows was a valuable supple-

---

[58] Anon., 'To the Gentlemen of Ashill' (1816), cited in A. J. Peacock, *Bread or Blood; a Study of the Agrarian Riots in East Anglia in 1816* (1965), pp. 65–6. Or see the anonymous letter against enclosure of 1799 cited in E. P. Thompson, *The Making of the English Working Class* (1963, Harmondsworth, 1975 edn), p. 240.
[59] Bernard, 'Extract', 263.
[60] Young, *Inquiry into . . . Applying Wastes*, pp. 6–9, 14, 102.
[61] *Annals of Agriculture*, XXVI (1796), 243.
[62] See for example Ardleigh Overseers' Accounts 1795–1835, Essex C.R.O., D/P 263/12/1–16; St Osyth Overseers' Accounts 1763–1835, Essex C.R.O., D/P 322/12/2–6: 4 April 1796, 'To cash allow'd Samuel Jones to purchase a cow. £10.' See also Young, *Inquiry into . . . Applying Wastes*, pp. 4–5, 73, on parish loans to the poor to buy livestock, for the same purpose.

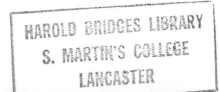

ment to a bread diet, particularly for children.[63] There was the annual sale of animals; the sale of young or fattened geese and fowls; the sale or use of hides; the meat itself; the uses of sheep's wool in a domestic economy.[64] The value of livestock was various and extended beyond our appreciation today. Here is David Davies to stress just one aspect of this:

There are two circumstances which forbid the common people in the richer counties from cultivating potatoes as much as they might otherwise be inclined to do; namely, the want of sufficient garden ground, and the difficulty in procuring milk ... Wheaten bread may be eaten alone with pleasure; but potatoes require either meat or milk to make them go down: you cannot make many hearty meals of them with salt and water only ... Buttermilk is the thing, if they could get it. In Wales and Ireland (and in some parts of England too), potatoes and butter-milk make one meal a day in most families all the year ... But the use of potatoes must be very limited, where milk cannot be cheaply procured.[65]

The same applied for the consumption of oatmeal – the distinction of diets between northern and southern England was significantly determined by milk availability.[66]

Such benefits could be pursued much further. But let us return to the views of the poor, in a petition from Raunds in Northamptonshire, against the enclosure act passed in 1797:

The petitioners beg Leave to represent to the House that ... the Cottagers and other Persons entitled to Right of Commons on the Lands intended to be enclosed, [will be] deprived of an inestimable Privilege, which they now enjoy, of turning a certain Number of their Cows, Calves, and Sheep, on and over the said lands; *a Privilege that enables them not only to maintain themselves and their Families in the Depth of Winter*, when they cannot, even for their Money, obtain from the Occupiers of other Lands the smallest Portion of Milk or Whey for such necessary Purpose, but in addition to this, they can now supply the Grazier with young or lean stock at a reasonable Price, to fatten and bring to Market at a more moderate Rate for general Consumption [my italics].[67]

Other petitions made similar points, arguing also that the loss of these rights would raise parochial dependency and the poor rate:

[63] It would be interesting in this regard to have figures for infant and child mortality shortly before and after enclosure.

[64] For discussion of the uses of open field sheep, see H. S. Homer, *An Essay on the Nature and Method of ascertaining the Specific Shares of Proprietors, upon the Inclosure of Common Fields* (Oxford, 1766), p. 73. For a contemporary estimate of the total value per annum of a cottager's holding formed on the common (£35 15s.), and a breakdown of that, see Slater, *English Peasantry*, pp. 121–2.

[65] Davies, *Case of the Labourers*, pp. 35–7.

[66] See in particular Hammonds, *Village Labourer*, pp. 80ff.

[67] *House of Commons Journal*, 19 June 1797. Cited in Hammonds, *Village Labourer*, pp. 10–11.

That provided the said common be enclosed, many hundreds of poor inhabitants in the said parish will be reduced to distress; as they will be deprived of their present benefit of rearing horned cattle, pigs, etc. *and furnishing themselves with fuel in the winter*, etc., and the consequences will be immediately felt by the parish at large, by the increase of the poors rates, the breaking and carrying away hedges and other petty larcenies, that the distresses of the poor will reduce them to; and which is and must always be experienced where the poor have not commons and wood lands to assist them [my italics].[68]

But the labouring poor (and I use the term as always in the encompassing way of contemporaries)[69] lost more than their livestock through enclosure. They lost also the rights to collect fuel or furze from the commons, wastes, and nearby woods, and gained in the latter for their families the menace of man traps and trip wire operated swivel shot-guns.[70] The loss of fuel in particular must have adversely affected them in the winter. Similarly, they lost during this period (in many regions, though not in all) the right of gleaning after the harvest, through which (from varying accounts) a family might support itself with bread to last from a third to the whole year. The custom of course led to 'idleness', 'demoralisation', 'pilfering', and was 'a legal claim, in its use and exercise . . . nearly approaching to licentiousness'.[71] After a decision in the Court of Common Pleas in

---

[68] Anon., *A Political Enquiry into the Consequences of Enclosing Waste Lands, and the causes of the present high Price of Butcher's Meat* (1785), p. 121. And see the remarkable series of letters and the petition from the labouring poor of Foulmere against enclosure in 1845: 'Your petitioners and their poor Neighbours consisting partly of small Occupiers and Laborers dwelling in the said parish have from time immemorial and from generation to generation without molestation or interruption exercised the rights and privileges of mowing fodder gathering dry manure for fuel and of turning and depasturing Cows thereon . . . farmers being prohibited from turning sheep on that part of the Common about to be inclosed . . . [Your petitioners] have cultivated the same and expended Money in manuring and improving the same Allotments and the occupation thereof has greatly assisted your Petitioners and some of their poor Neighbours being greatly distressed at periods for want of employ and not receiving in too many cases when employed Wages adequate to the support of themselves their Wives and Children and in some cases of their aged relations.' They refer to the adjoining parish of Thriplow, where 'the poor inhabitants . . . having similar rights were utterly and most unjustly deprived of their rights and privileges without any Compensation whatever', and claim that they are 'in great difficulty to provide the means of maintenance for their respective families by Labor and adequate wages and should the Bill pass without protection Clauses will become utterly destitute and . . . must become paupers and inmates of a [town?] workhouse'. (Camb C.R.O., 292/02–36.)

[69] As used for example by Young, *General Report*, p. 14; or Young, *Inquiry into . . . Applying Wastes*, p. 105.

[70] On the bitterness caused by spring guns, see E. G. Wakefield, *Swing Unmasked; or, the Causes of Rural Incendiarism* (1831), pp. 30ff. See also Cobbett, *Rural Rides*, p. 207.

[71] See Hammonds, *Village Labourer*, pp. 67–9, 78n, 83; Hasbach, *English Agricultural Labourer*, pp. 109ff; Postans, *Letter to Sir Thomas Baring*, p. 8.

1788, gleaning was decided upon entirely at the farmer's discretion; discretion which was necessarily all the more crucial and significant on enclosed land. But this custom was peripheral to those mentioned by the *General Report* when it commented that:

> It seems unnecessary to enter much at length into a definition of the different rights of common, at present known to, or acknowledged by the laws of England; *because we trust and hope that* by a division of all the wastes and commons, *every right of that description will be extinguished* [my italics].[72]

These more generally included pasture rights (that is, common appendant, common appurtenant, common in gross, and common because of vicinage); rights to cut turves for fuel (that is, common of turbary); rights to cut wood for fuel, housing, fences, implements, and so on (common of estovers); rights of fishing (common of piscary); as well as rights to kill wild fowl, or the right to cut hay in a common meadow.[73] Needless to say, the hope of the *General Report* was not disappointed, and they were indeed all extinguished, with obvious implications for the security of the poor. Once again, the curtailment of such common rights contributed to produce the more extreme seasonal distributions after enclosure. And such deprivations were self-evident even to most contemporary enclosure enthusiasts. They are surely as fundamental to an appraisal of enclosure's social effects as consideration of 'landownership', based on a source such as the land tax returns.

VI

What can be said on the increase of strictly wage-dependent employment, on which Chambers pinned so much? The crucial question, of course, is not whether there was simply an increase of waged employment after enclosure; but whether such an increase, if it occurred, was such as to compensate the poor for the widespread deprivations on other fronts which enclosure caused. Even this is a restricted formulation of the problem, begging a qualitative assessment from the point of view of the poor between the two forms of existence. (The answer is readily suggested in the poor's conservatism, in the growing rural unrest, arson, cattle maiming, sending of anonymous letters and other class-specific literary evidence.) But ignoring such formulations, Chambers wanted to argue that even in Nottinghamshire – despite conversion of arable to pasture (stressed earlier, alongside its adverse consequences, in his *Nottinghamshire in*

---

[72] Young, *General Report*, p. 56.   [73] *Ibid.*, pp. 56ff.

the Eighteenth Century) – there was sufficient increased demand for hired labour to provide adequate legitimation of enclosure.

The point emerged much more prominently in his article of 1953 than the more thorough and pessimistic book of 1932, and was always a dubious one for this region, where heavy soils were poorly suited to new husbandry techniques, particularly the introduction of root crops important on lighter soils in East Anglia. The importance of such techniques was minimal after enclosure on the Midland clays, and the pre- and post-enclosure methods were frequently almost identical: commonly consisting (where we have evidence) of a three-course rotation and a fallow.[74] Thomas Stone was only one of many contemporaries who were far from enthusiastic about the agricultural benefit of the Midland enclosures:

In some cases poor, thin-stapled clays have been enclosed, which will not admit of any material alteration from the ancient mode of husbandry, or by any means answer the expenses of the business; in other cases, the lands have been laid out in very large farms, and let to persons incompetent to the occupation of them, as well in point of property as in skill to apply the soil to its right use. Want of attention ... has frequently rendered inclosures unprofitable ... small farms, of different sizes ... are now rendered absolutely necessary from the general poverty of farmers.[75]

And there was virtual unanimity that enclosure to pasture here had produced depopulation. When we combine this with the unsuitability of the new husbandry techniques for the region, and the widely reported losses suffered by the poor in this early phase of parliamentary enclosure (long before any parliamentary safeguards for them were laid down, although perhaps these were never to be more than remotely effective), we are drawn towards a final assessment rather different from that eventually advocated by Chambers in 1953. This is not to discard his earlier opinion though, written over twenty years before:

Economic gain ... was necessarily brought at the expense of considerable social dislocation; and owing to the character of the political society within which these changes took place, the social effects received less attention than they deserved ... the gain was great, but the social effects were in proportion to it, and at least as permanent ... The sudden disappearance of the common unaccompanied by an adequate substitute that could be turned to immediate use, was felt not merely by the squatter on the waste, but by the

[74] J. J. Purdum, 'Profitability and timing of parliamentary land enclosures', *Explor. Econ. Hist.*, XV (1978), 320–3.
[75] Stone, *Suggestions for Rendering the Inclosure of Common Fields*, p. 81. On p. 39 he refers to 'the ill success, and I might add the fatal consequences (arising wholly from mismanagement), with which the inclosure of many common fields have been attended of late years'.

day labourer, handicraftsmen and the very small farmers and cottagers who looked to the common to eke out their livelihood ... Compensation for the irregular use of the common by labourers and others was not given, except very occasionally, in the form of allotments for the poor. In any case, the occupant of a cottage would have to stand by and see the common, which might easily be the most important part of his livelihood, exchanged for an allotment which the owner would probably sell rather than go to the expense of enclosing it ... How far [the giving of allotments or annexing of land to cottages] was generally practised it is impossible to say, but it is certain that no such provision is to be found in the Enclosure Acts themselves. In illustration of the effects of loss of common rights it may be noted that the acute distress which the country framework knitters were suffering in the nineteenth century was attributed partly to this cause.[76]

'Local unemployment must have resulted', he wrote.[77] Considering the other losses undeniably suffered by the poor, a pessimistic argument for this region seems inescapable, mitigated in part by the relatively high wages of the Midlands, and the growth of alternative employment much less apparent further south.

But the matter can be pursued elsewhere, dealing with other aspects of Chambers' argument. One view, frequently repeated, was that enclosure led to fuller winter employment in hedging and ditching. But Homer, Cowper, Sturt, and others doubted that this made any difference, claiming that it was very short lived. Much fencing of course had to be completed within a stipulated period – a requirement laid down by the commissioners.[78] Similarly, it was in the farmers' interests (given especially the high rent increases and enclosure costs) to cut their expenses of hedging, ditching, and draining as far as possible. One obvious way to do this was to employ the mobile piece workers who followed the awards, taking work wherever enclosure was occurring. As highly skilled piece workers, they generally completed this work more rapidly and efficiently than local labourers inexperienced in the methods of draining, hedging, and plashing which were needed. John Clare wrote of these men,[79] and one finds evidence of them in settlement examinations. As M. K. Ashby wrote:

The labourers of Tysoe had hopes that at least enclosures would bring incidental opportunities: they would be employed to plant the hedges and drain the fields, but gangs of men accustomed to the new jobs were brought in by the larger owners. There was work for a few men on the roads for which

[76] Chambers, *Nottinghamshire*, pp. 173, 182–4.   [77] *Ibid.*, p. 182.
[78] M. E. Turner, 'The cost of parliamentary enclosure in Buckinghamshire', *Agric. Hist. Rev.*, XVIII (1975), 45.
[79] J. Clare, 'The autobiography, 1793–1824', in J. W. & A. Tibble (eds.), *The Prose of John Clare* (1951), p. 34. I am grateful to John Barrell for this reference.

the Commissioners had provided, enough to prevent any rise in the number of men on the round, but not enough to reduce it. No improvement followed enclosure, even after the lapse of time. The number of relieved persons rose again, and their name was now 'pauper'. The word gathered power to itself and depressed men's spirit and their status.[80]

I will consider the extent of pauperisation after enclosure shortly. But it is worth pointing out here that the argument for greater security during the winter provided by hedging and ditching, so routinely summoned up by historians, is an overdrawn one on which too much emphasis can be placed. John Cowper asked whether hedging and ditching would employ more hands, and continued: 'This is so contrary to constant experience, that it hardly deserves to be taken notice of . . . Raising Hedges and sinking ditches may indeed employ several hands for a year, or hardly so long, but when that is once over, the work is at an end.'[81] Henry Homer commented that the 'Degree of Labour [created through hedging and ditching] is only temporary, and when it is over, there may be less in particular Places than before enclosure.'[82] And Chambers overlooked the fact that the planting of hedges was in any case not usually a winter-time occupation, but one most often done after the harvest, or in April and May. Holly is an example, and the following statement from the *General Report* applies also to the widely used hawthorn quicks: 'The secrecy of the art lies in the time of transplanting: a holly transplanted at Midsummer scarcely receives a check from the removal; a fact this which few planters are aware of. Thousands of hollies are every year destroyed by removing them in the winter months.'[83] Homer dated the planting season for hawthorn during the autumn, and added: 'the Growth of Quicksets depends very much on their being early planted', *before* the winter.[84] If anything, hedging simply accentuated the arable distribution of unemployment, being concentrated, as it was, during periods when employment was least wanted.

There are further reasons to question whether significant increases of wage employment occurred. I want first to extend discussion on the relation of enclosure to the new agricultural techniques. Enclosure advocates used a stereotyped mode for describing the open fields, which, were it true, would indeed incline us to think that

---

[80] M. K. Ashby, *Joseph Ashby of Tysoe, 1859–1919* (Cambridge, 1961, 1974 edn), p. 282. On outside contracting to do the fencing, see Young, *General Report*, p. 309.

[81] J. Cowper, *An Essay proving that inclosing Commons and Commonfield-Lands is contrary to the Interest of the Nation* (1732), cited in Slater, *English Peasantry*, pp. 110–11.

[82] Homer, *Essay*, pp. 28–9, 34–5. See also A Country Gentleman, *The Advantages and Disadvantages of Inclosing Waste Land and Open Fields* (1772), pp. 10–11.

[83] Young, *General Report*, p. 315.   [84] Homer, *Essay*, p. 59.

significant improvements might be immediately effected after enclosure. One thinks not simply of Young's 'Goths and Vandals of open-field farmers'. Here is a specimen description from the *General Report*, ventre à terre:

turnip sands under barren fallows: fertile clays, that under grass would feed the largest oxen, poisoned with water, and the crops choked with weeds: the landlord losing rent, the tenant profit, the poor without employment, and national prosperity at a stop. What system of barbarism can be greater, than that of obliging every farmer of a parish to cultivate in the same rotation! To give ignorance the power to limit knowledge, to render stupidity the measure of talents, to chain down industry to the non-exertions of indolence, and fix an insuperable bar, a perpetual exclusion, to all that energy of improvement which has carried husbandry to perfection by means of enclosure! Yet is all this done by the common-field system ... As to common pastures, the minutes speak but one language ... The best soils, by overstocking are almost reduced to a par with the worst. The value of the food thus gained is so contemptible, that the best farmers despise it too much even to accept it. An utter degradation and ruin of the breed of all the animals thus supported – distempers for ever making a dreadful havock – the poor without industry – the rates enormous – health depraved – and morals destroyed. Such is the uniform picture; and a more wretched or melancholy one is hardly within the compass of the imagination.[85]

Melancholy indeed. But Howlett went one further:

When we hear that commissioners are appointed to enquire into the state of this distinguished territory [the New Forest in Hampshire], as well as others of similar kind, what heart does not glow at the delightful prospect which seems to arise! Who does not see the *wilderness become a fruitful field*; the *heaven directed spires* again to *rise*, and the whole wide extent to people fast, not with beasts of chace, as heretofore, to please a savage tyrant, but with industrious men and women, rational creatures, happy subjects of the best of kings, and candidates for immortality! ... through almost the whole of the northern [part of the forest], our author might see his *happy* commoners very little superior to Hottentots, and crawling out of their huts, with scarcely any thing to cover their nakedness, or to defend them from the inclemency of the weather but a piece of old sacking tied about their middle [his italics].[86]

It is an easy step to assume, reading such descriptions, that enclosure brought with it massive advances in crop or livestock production, large-scale reductions of poor relief expenditure, and permanent moral and economic improvements for the labouring poor. But we have seen that the introduction of new techniques was not especially marked in the Midlands, and should also take account of the significant historical re-appraisal of open field agriculture which has occurred, mainly since Chambers wrote.

That re-appraisal has established that the open fields were far more

[85] Young, *General Report*, pp. 219–20.
[86] Howlett, *Enclosures a Cause of Improved Agriculture*, pp. 72–3.

open to innovative and flexible agriculture than once supposed, that the account of them as seriously backward and by nature inhibitive of new techniques is most certainly incorrect. Havinden, for example, discussing 'agricultural progress in open-field Oxfordshire', suggested that the delay, in a more long-term perspective, of the enclosure of the Midlands, may have been due to the progress which was possible within the open fields, and he demonstrated how a process of agricultural innovation could become self-sustaining without enclosure. The practice of sowing leys in the open fields brought with it a degree of convertible husbandry, increasing the area of grassland, and was widespread by the early seventeenth century. Nitrogen-fixing legumes and artificial grasses such as ryegrass, clover, lucerne, sainfoin, and trefoil had been introduced before, and, in some cases, long before enclosure; the introduction of turnips also certainly predates the enclosure movement in this county. Complex field divisions were entered into which served to reduce the amount of land in fallow, and there could be much flexibility in this regard. The increased provision of fodder, as provided by legumes and new grasses, allowed rising numbers of livestock, particularly of sheep, which apparently increased fourfold in the average size of their flocks between 1580 and 1730; the wheat acreage increased, as did the growth of pulses; and there was a change during the late seventeenth and early eighteenth centuries to the use of four wheeled wagons on farms, away from the old two wheeled long-cart – suggestive of rising output per acre. These practices, taken together, were of course mutually supportive, and a spiralling pattern of innovation was entered into in which growing numbers of livestock permitted by leys, legumes, and artificial grasses could improve soil fertility so as to allow rising yields of wheat. Similar conclusions have been reached by other authors – Kerridge, Hoskins, Thirsk, Grigg, Gray, Overton, or Kussmaul – on this flexibility and compatibility of the open field system with the new husbandry techniques.[87] There has been a historiographical move away from using enclosure as the *sine qua non*

---

[87] M. Havinden, 'Agricultural progress in open-field Oxfordshire', *Agric. Hist. Rev.*, IX (1961); E. Kerridge, *The Agricultural Revolution* (1967), pp. 251–67, 289, 330; B. K. Roberts, 'Field systems of the west Midlands', in A. R. H. Baker & R. A. Butlin (eds.), *Studies of Field Systems in the British Isles* (Cambridge, 1973), p. 205; W. G. Hoskins, *The Midland Peasant: The Economic and Social History of a Leicestershire Village* (1957), p. 164; J. Thirsk, 'Agrarian history, 1540–1950', in *Victoria County History of Leicestershire*, vol. 2 (Oxford, 1954), pp. 221, 212; A. S. Kussmaul, *Servants in Husbandry in Early Modern England* (Cambridge, 1981), pp. 107ff; W. G. Hoskins, 'The Leicestershire farmer in the seventeenth century', *Agric. Hist.*, XXV (1951); D. B. Grigg, *The Agricultural Revolution in South Lincolnshire* (Cambridge, 1966), pp. 54, 190; A. Harris, *Rural Landscape of the East Riding of Yorkshire* (1961), pp. 24–5; R. A. Butlin,

of innovation, as implied by many eighteenth-century commentators. This comparatively recent emphasis in agricultural historiography is well known, and need not be summarised at length. Yelling has commented on the relative lack of change affecting heavier soil districts in the east which continued with arable husbandry after enclosure, citing Vancouver, Arthur Young, and Batchelor on this, and concluded that 'the extent [of innovation after enclosure] must not be exaggerated. Usually common field and enclosed townships and farms on similar soils were much more alike than examples of either type taken from dissimilar soils. Major land-use changes were produced only under certain special conditions.'[88]

Rents are sometimes taken as an indicator of innovation. They could rise considerably upon enclosure, and a doubling was a reasonably average figure. But such increase was not indicative of a proportional increased output.[89] Leases were annulled upon enclosure – this was often a motive to enclose. Insofar as rents had frequently been set long prior to this, given the lengthy leases still generally in operation, the price rises during the parliamentary enclosure period entailed landlords increasing rent to readjust to new price levels obtaining at the time of enclosure. Hence the raising of rent upon enclosure, which tells us little about the extent of increased output through, or expected through, enclosure. It is still unclear how common long leases were; but while some yearly leases can be found in the late eighteenth century, the majority were longer than this.[90] Even in the early nineteenth century, when the three-life lease

'Field systems of Northumberland and Durham', in Baker & Butlin (eds.), *Field Systems*, p. 120; E. Kerridge, 'Agriculture, c. 1500–1793', in *Victoria County History of Wiltshire*, vol. 4 (Oxford, 1959), p. 51; W. G. Hoskins, 'Harvest fluctuations and English economic history, 1620–1759', *Agric. Hist. Rev.*, XVI (1968), 25–8; Yelling, *Common Field*, pp. 146–73: K. J. Allison, 'The sheep-corn husbandry of Norfolk in the sixteenth and seventeenth centuries', *Agric. Hist. Rev.*, V (1957); E. L. Jones, 'Agriculture and economic growth in England, 1660–1750: agricultural change', in his *Agriculture and Economic Growth in England, 1650–1815* (1967), p. 162; M. Overton, 'Estimating crop yields from probate inventories: an example from East Anglia', *Jnl of Econ. Hist.*, XXXIX (1979); H. L. Gray, *English Field Systems* (1959), pp. 130–5. In this connection, one also recalls Lavrovsky's arguments on a growing differentiation in the ranks of the peasantry before parliamentary enclosure: 'Parliamentary enclosure in the county of Suffolk, 1794–1814', *Econ. Hist. Rev.*, VII (1937), 207.

[88] Yelling, *Common Field*, p. 203.

[89] Contrary assumptions notwithstanding: P. K. O'Brien, 'Agriculture and the Industrial Revolution', *Econ. Hist. Rev.*, XXX (1977), 172; McCloskey, 'Economics of enclosure', 156: 'The typical increase in rent is a good estimate of the typical increase in output.'

[90] And the movement to yearly leases after enclosure also adversely affected employment. Farmers under longer leases (for fourteen or twenty-one years) were thought in the nineteenth century to be able to employ more labour, and of course were better placed to undertake improvements. *Morning Chronicle*, 1 Feb. 1850.

was being discontinued, many such leases necessarily lasted for a considerable period in parishes which either remained open, or which had been long enclosed.

We should also refer to Yelling's useful discussion on the relation of rent increases to farmers' profit. 'It might be argued [he wrote], . . . that the profit must have come from increased output, but this is not necessarily the case, for it could have come from a reduction in expenses.' He then produced figures from Appendix XIII of the *General Report* to demonstrate

> that huge rent increases were not necessarily linked with large increases in farmers' profits, and that the latter were not necessarily linked with large increases in the value of farm output. The author of these particular calculations placed very great stress on the savings in labour, horses and general expenses that enclosure brought about.[91]

The implications for our concern with changes affecting demand for labour are evident, although we do not know how typical these figures were. But the *General Report* was strongly pro-enclosure, and not prone to produce evidence unfavourable to a general enclosure act. Given the inadequate evidence available on leases and returns to farmers, and on change in technique and output in particular parishes after enclosure, it is hard to be precise on this matter. But clearly the improvement upon enclosure must have been consider- ably less than claimed by some contemporary enthusiasts. McCloskey has estimated that enclosed land may have been only about 13 per cent more productive than open.[92] And Turner, while suggesting rather higher increases than this for barley and oats, stressed his preference for an interpretation of agricultural innovation which 'places the emphasis firmly on productivity change in the first half of the eighteenth century, *before* the great "improving" parliamentary enclosures [his italics]'. Enclosures, he continued, may have aug- mented total product rather than yields per acre 'by increasing the sown acreage through the extension of arable into wastes, commons, and other margins; by reducing the size of the annual fallow; and by allowing best practice techniques to prevail'. But

> we may rightly place the period of greatest productivity change before 1770 and the onset of rapid population growth . . . productivity, measured by grain yields, stood still from c. 1770 or before, until after 1830, and this at the time of the demographic revolution. Arising from this conclusion, more questions could be raised, not least those concerned with the standard of living.[93]

[91] Yelling, *Common Field*, pp. 212–13.   [92] McCloskey, 'Economics of enclosure', 160.
[93] M. E. Turner, 'Agricultural productivity in England in the eighteenth century: evidence from crop yields', *Econ. Hist. Rev.*, XXXV (1982), 505–6. In view of these conclusions, he suggested that 'diets must have worsened' (505). Similar views on

In short, the introduction of new agricultural techniques in the
seventeenth and eighteenth centuries may well have been largely
independent of enclosure – just as was argued by some authors for
the long-term decline of the small owner-occupier and farmer.

These points should be supplemented by consideration of the very
high costs of parliamentary enclosure, and of how these affected the
ability of farmers to employ labour. We are fortunate in having
detailed information on this, in the work of Turner, Tate, Hunt,
Martin, Swales, and others. The problem here is that of including a
full account of costs incurred; and some authors, as shown by Turner,
or by Martin in his critique of Tate, very badly underestimated
enclosure costs by only including expenses for certain items. Available figures are all probably underestimates of the final cost, through
the availability of partial data in most cases, at times because the final
or total cost had yet to be incurred (e.g., through fencing, roads, and
so on) when returns were made. The frequently used award itself is,
in this regard, an inadequate source for costs. Nevertheless, the more
reliable figures available suggest a rise from about 10s. an acre in the
mid-eighteenth century to over £3 an acre by 1800 – the figures will be
too low, but a sixfold increase may be roughly correct. This is
considerably in excess of the inflation of the period, however we
judge its extent. The increase was owing to such factors as general
inflation affecting cost per acre; the growing time gap between act and
award which occurred, and the factors behind that; the rising fees
charged by commissioners and other professional men; or the rising
parliamentary fees for an enclosure act. The costs were borne by
parishes levying a rate or rates, or by land sales, use of the land
mortgage, or out of current income.

Further costs were incurred in the practice of 'soliciting the act' to
obtain the requisite majority. This majority could be of common right
ownership, rateable value, number and value of acreage owned,
payment to the land tax, to the poor rate, and so on. There was little
standard procedure in what the majority referred to, except that it
covered value rather than heads, leaving considerable scope for local
manipulation. (The general enclosure act of 1773 reduced and stan-

the chronology of changes in agricultural productivity have been expressed by B. A.
Holderness, 'Productivity trends in English agriculture, 1600–1850: observations and
preliminary results' (unpublished paper presented to the 1978 International Economic History Conference at Edinburgh, in the session Factor Productivity in Agriculture in Industrializing Economies). And see E. L. Jones, 'Afterword', in E. L. Jones &
W. N. Parker (eds.) *European Peasants and Their Markets: Essays in Agrarian Economic
History* (Princeton, N.J., 1975), pp. 336–7: 'The role of enclosure in agricultural
change, and hence in economic growth as a whole, is easy to exaggerate.'

dardised the majority required to set in motion parliamentary procedures, from four-fifths to three-quarters.) 'Soliciting the act', Turner
has calculated, could involve 10–30 per cent of total enclosure costs,
and these also would commonly be omitted from those final costs
which have survived to us.[94]

Payments had also to be made for the voidance of leases upon
enclosure – this was usually ordered by the act, and could again be a
heavy burden on owners, to have possible repercussions in due
course on rents charged. Once again, available estimates omit these
payments. There were also more hidden costs, which are difficult to
calculate. In the intermediate period of consternation between act and
award, for example, the practice of overcropping was notorious, with
little regard paid to the future fertility of soil about to change hands.
This cost, usefully termed by McCloskey the 'cost of delay', became
the more significant as the time lag between act and award increased
over time, with land in larger villages being enclosed, farmed by
larger numbers of occupiers, which was the more complex to enclose
because of this.

This and other costs of delay are neglected in studies of the costs of enclosure
[commented McCloskey]. The incentive to overwork land soon to become
another's could be quite expensive. With yields of, say, $2\frac{1}{2}$ quarters of wheat
an acre and a price of £2 a quarter, a loss from this source of as little as, say,
one-fifth of the normal yield for one year after the enclosure would add £1 an
acre to the other costs (which Martin . . . reckons at something over £2 an acre
before the inflation of the Napoleonic Wars).[95]

That cost certainly went far above £2 after the 1780s: the *General
Report*'s thirty-two examples for the 1790s average at about £3 an acre,
if we include many very partial estimates. Homer as early as 1766
estimated the average cost at £3 (a figure over four times higher than
those given for the 1760s by Tate, Martin, Turner, or Hunt).[96] Turner
has stated that parishes would generally allow for costs of £5 an acre,
while more recently agreeing with Holderness that the final bill may
have been as much as £12 per acre.[97]

Contemporaries were unanimous in condemning these high costs
and their consequences, and it is probable that (alongside rising

[94] M. E. Turner, 'The cost of parliamentary enclosure in Buckinghamshire', *Agric. Hist.
Rev.*, XXI (1973), 36.
[95] D. N. McCloskey, 'The enclosure of open-fields: a preface to a study of its impact on
the efficiency of English agriculture in the eighteenth century', *Jnl Econ. Hist.*, XXXII
(1972), 29.   [96] Homer, *Essay*, p. 27.
[97] Turner, 'Cost of enclosure in Buckinghamshire', 44; and his interesting 'Cost,
finance and parliamentary enclosure', *Econ. Hist. Rev.*, XXXIV (1981), 238; B. A.
Holderness, 'Capital formation in agriculture', in S. Pollard & J. P. P. Higgins (eds.),
Aspects of Capital Investment in Great Britain, 1750–1850 (1971), p. 167.

rents) they adversely affected employers of labour, causing a restriction (or insufficient expansion) of labour expenses, so contributing to the changes in the distribution of unemployment. It is also possible (as Turner suggests) that enclosure costs threatened the survival of many small landowners, perhaps bringing some into competition on the labour market.[98] The *General Report* was in little doubt over this – such costs were 'ruinous to small proprietors'. The *Report* continued:

> These expenses have arisen and increased so much, that multitudes set themselves in opposition to the proposal in every part of the kingdom; they dread demands which they are not able to satisfy; and must be deterred from consenting, by seeing so many persons whose means have been exhausted by these expenses, that when the allotments come into their hands, the power of cultivating them was gone. This raises such an opposition, that, if it does not preclude the measure, it adds at least to the expenses, already so great ... it has been a general observation ... that the resources of the small proprietor ... have been for the most part so entirely exhausted by the expense of obtaining the Act, of solicitors, surveyors, commissioners, making new roads, etc., that they have been incapacitated for cultivating their allotments in a proper manner. The mischief has gone farther; for it has rendered them less adequate to cultivate the ancient lands, for which such shares of common were allotted.[99]

The complaint that the poor who were allocated allotments, because of proven *legal* rights to the common, were frequently forced to sell these and turn to day labour shortly after enclosure because of its cost, was very frequently made. 'Where allotments were assigned, the cottagers could not pay the expense of the measure, and were forced to sell their allotments', wrote Arthur Young.[100] Or it was said that 'people of small fortune dread the expense of these applications [for enclosure acts] so much, that they will rather permit their interest in waste lands to lie dormant, than subject themselves to an expense they are unable to bear'.[101] Little had changed by the time of the Select Committee Report in 1844 on enclosure:

[98] Turner, 'Cost, finance and parliamentary enclosure', 237, 239, 247.

[99] Young, *General Report*, pp. 97, 152–3. And see pp. 32–3, 98–9, 122, 154, 170, 276–7, 389; S.C. on Enclosure, V (1844), p. 268.

[100] Young, *General Report*, pp. 12–13. For further complaint of such forced sales, see *ibid.*, pp. 97, 152–3; Young, *Inquiry into ... Applying Wastes*, pp. 17, 21; Chambers, *Nottinghamshire*, pp. 183–4; Hammonds, *Village Labourer*, pp. 68–9; Sturt, *Change in the Village*, p. 3; Stone, *Suggestions for Rendering the Inclosure of Common Fields*, p. 86. Even as late as 1845–75, out of 590,000 acres, less than 0.4 per cent was set aside for allotments – a strong indictment of earlier practice, when the figure was assuredly less. (Slater, *English Peasantry*, p. 118.) L. M. Springall, *Labouring Life in Norfolk Villages, 1834–1914* (1936), p. 40, gave the figure of 2.2 per cent of 6,000 acres enclosed in Norfolk (1845–70) being allocated for allotments. Again, the figure would have been much lower earlier.

[101] Young, *General Report*, p. 389.

The small proprietors are deterred from going into the inclosure, the expense is so great, what with the obtaining of the Bill, and the expense of the Commissioners, which has not been under any control, they cannot bear the expense, which is, in the first instance, laid upon the land, being in many cases almost equal to the fee-simple of the land.[102]

Small proprietors were also charged at a greater proportional rate for general expenses than were larger proprietors, and they were hit harder by the relative costs of fencing a small area being much more than for larger allotments.[103] Such costs would generally hit all employers of labour, but the smallest proprietors were hardest affected. Contemporaries so often saw the decline of small tenants and owner-occupiers as caused by enclosure (and this was true for comment positively favourable to enclosure) that one might take the view that this was indeed a result of enclosure in many regions. These were, at any rate, conclusions arrived at by Hunt in Leicestershire, by Turner in Buckinghamshire (where the decline of original owners between 1780 and 1820 in enclosed parishes was 38 per cent), and by Martin in open parishes in Warwickshire.[104] It is also well known, partly from the work of Hosford, Habakkuk, or Gray, that owner-occupiers were frequently bought out before enclosure as a preparatory move for it.[105] And there was almost no directed dissent to the view of the *General Report*:

There is, however, one class of farmers which have undeniably suffered by enclosures; for they have been greatly lessened in number: these are the *little farmers*; and the diminution of them which have in many cases taken place, caused great complaints by many of the Clergy who made the returns from enclosed parishes. That it is a great hardship, suddenly to turn several,

---

[102] S.C. on Enclosure, V (1844), p. 268.

[103] Young, *General Report*, p. 170; A Country Gentleman, *Advantages and Disadvantages*, pp. 25, 32 (he believed that these relative costs forced the small farmer 'to betake himself to labour'); Swales, 'Enclosures of Lindsey', 89–90; Purdum, 'Profitability and timing', 325.

[104] Hunt, 'Landownership and enclosure', 499–505; M. E. Turner, 'Parliamentary enclosure and landownership change in Buckinghamshire', *Econ. Hist. Rev.*, XXVII (1975); J. M. Martin, 'The parliamentary enclosure movement and rural society in Warwickshire', *Agric. Hist. Rev.*, XV (1967), or his 'The small landowner and parliamentary enclosure in Warwickshire', *Econ. Hist. Rev.*, XXXII (1979). See also Hoskins, *The Midland Peasant*, pp. 164, 249–51, for similar effects on small land-owners.

[105] W. H. Hosford, 'The enclosure of Sleaford', *Lincs Architectural and Archaeol. Soc.*, VII (1957), 88: 'A familiar figure ... of the enclosure movement is the small common-right owner, who, knowing that he cannot meet his share of the costs of enclosure, and the costs of fencing, sells his right for what it will fetch while the commissioners are still at work'; H. J. Habakkuk, 'English landownership, 1680–1740', *Econ. Hist. Rev.*, X (1940), 2–17; H. L. Gray, 'Yeoman farming in Oxfordshire from the sixteenth to the nineteenth century', *Quarterly Jnl of Economics*, XXIV (1910), 321–4; Hunt, 'Landownership and enclosure', 500ff.

perhaps many, of these poor men, out of their business, and reduce them to be day-labourers, would be idle to deny; it is an evil to them, which is to be regretted: but it is doing no more than the rise of the price of labour, tithe, rates, and taxes, would infallibly do, though more gradually, without any enclosure. These little arable occupiers must give way to the progressive improvement of the kingdom, and to the burthens which have accompanied it [original italics].[106]

Such a view allows for the considerable decline of smaller occupiers before the period of parliamentary enclosure, while also questioning whether rising prices were as favourable to this class as some historians have argued. One suspects again that the scepticism raised by the many problems of the land tax is justified, or that the use of this source to cover more extensively the south Midlands and south-eastern counties would produce different results, similar to those obtained by Hunt, Turner, or Martin. The case against enclosure forcing many small tenants and owner-occupiers into open competition for day labour has yet to be made.

Relentless rent increases would have compounded unfavourable effects of enclosure costs on employment. Both were incentives to a greater emphasis on skilled piece workers, to an abandonment of service, reductions in real wages, or the introduction of labour-saving technology (such as that discussed by Collins) to cut labour bills.[107] Further documentary evidence from the farmer class would be welcome here. But a sudden curtailment of long-term leases and a doubling of rents during a sharply inflationary period must surely have led to a re-assessment of labour requirements or wages; especially when, even in the later eighteenth century, there are grounds for supposing that farmers' profit margins were only about 9–14 per cent per annum.[108] It is highly unlikely that agricultural output or profit increased in anything like the same proportion to rents, and rent increases were certainly found very burdensome by farmers. Chambers himself made much of this in *Nottinghamshire in the Eighteenth Century*, quoting contemporaries on oppressive and persistent rent increases after enclosure even in Nottinghamshire, where

---

[106] Young, *General Report*, pp. 32–3. Or see pp. 17, 98, 152–3. And as Lavrovsky wrote, a group certainly adversely affected were the numerous small tenant leaseholders, 'who had no guarantee that after enclosure they would be able to lease their small plots of land'. See his 'Parliamentary enclosure in Suffolk', 208.

[107] E. J. T. Collins, 'Harvest technology and labour supply in Britain, 1790–1870', *Econ. Hist. Rev.*, XXII (1969).

[108] G. Hueckel, 'English farming profits during the Napoleonic wars, 1793–1815', *Explor. Econ. Hist.*, XIII (1976). Edmund Burke arrived at a similar figure of 12 per cent: *Thoughts and Details on Scarcity* (1795), p. 22.

post-enclosure innovation was slight.[109] Or the *General Report* complained that: 'Rents are greatly raised, and too soon; so that if they do not absolutely lose five years, they at least suffer a great check.'[110] We may take a doubling of rents as a further factor accentuating the unemployment distributions after enclosure, to be incorporated among the other considerations outlined.

After the Napoleonic Wars the effects of falling prices and agricultural capital were compounded by a failure of rents to fall commensurate with prices. On newly enclosed land, rents continued to rise despite falling prices. Corn farmers on marginal lands found themselves increasingly uncompetitive. This is well known, and was documented particularly in the 1821 Report on the Causes of Agricultural Distress, among other reports on agriculture, or by Mac-Queen, Richardson, and others writing after 1815.[111] The Select Committee on Criminal Commitments, commenting on the decline of small farmers in Cambridgeshire after the war (when the enclosure movement in that county was still significantly under way),[112] complained that there had been 'very great revolutions in agricultural property ... so that many are reduced from the situation of yeomen to that of labourers', and that farmers were also unable to employ as many labourers as before.[113] This was held partly responsible for increases in winter crime and poaching in Bedfordshire and Cambridgeshire – one of the obvious remedies, alongside Swing or the 'Bread or Blood' riots, for the winter unemployment which, as we

[109] Chambers, *Nottinghamshire*, pp. 175–7. ('Rents have been in many instances raised in a most extraordinary proportion ...', etc.)

[110] Young, *General Report*, p. 31.

[111] Report on the Causes of Agricultural Distress, IX (1821); S.C. on the Poor Laws, V (1818), pp. 163–6, 177–84, 212ff; T. P. MacQueen, *Thoughts and Suggestions on the Present Condition of the Country* (1830); or his *The State of the Nation at the close of 1830* (1831), pp. 16–17. See also J. Richardson, *A Letter to Lord Brougham ... on an Alteration in the Poor Laws, the Employment of the People, and a Reduction of the Poor Rate* (Norwich, 1831); R. Torrens, *A Paper on the Means of Reducing the Poors Rates, and of affording effectual and Permanent Relief to the Labouring Classes* (1817); W. Jacob, 'Inquiry into the causes of agricultural distress', *The Pamphleteer*, X (1817); C. Jerram, *Considerations on the Impolicy and Pernicious Tendency of the Poor Laws* (1818); Rev. G. Glover, 'Observations on the state of pauperism', *The Pamphleteer*, X (1817); Sir C. G. Craufurd, *Observations on the State of the Country since the Peace: with a supplementary Section on the Poor Laws* (1817); J. Davison, *Considerations on the Poor Laws* (Oxford, 1817); R. Torrens, *Address to the Farmers of the United Kingdom, on the low rates of Profit in Agriculture and in Trade* (1831); Rev. C. D. Brereton, *Observations on the Administration of the Poor Laws in Agricultural Districts* (1824). On the failure of rents to fall, especially between 1816 and 1818, and the effects of price reductions on tenants with leases, see H. G. Hunt, 'Agricultural rent in south-east England, 1788–1825', *Agric. Hist. Rev.*, VII (1959); Hasbach, *English Agricultural Labourer*, pp. 232ff.

[112] Turner, *English Parliamentary Enclosure*, pp. 55–8.

[113] S.C. on Criminal Commitments and Convictions, VI (1826–7), p. 26.

have seen, was most acute in recently enclosed parishes. It has also never been disputed that there was after the war a significant and more widespread decline of small farmers and owner-occupiers;[114] while the falling prices can be held partly responsible for this, it seems possible that it was also an effect of the second stage of parliamentary enclosure. Once again, generalisations made on the earlier Midlands' enclosures may be less appropriate with regard to the later enclosed areas of the south and east.

I have now covered the main explanatory points. Prime emphasis must be put on the disruption to the way of life associated with the commons and open fields, and the loss of partial independence suffered by the poor as a consequence of the forced sales of their livestock and curtailment of other open-village benefits. In addition, waged employment cannot have replicated the benefits previously enjoyed by the labouring poor. In itself, an assessment of the problem in terms only of wage employment is an unimaginative one. Such employment may indeed have grown in many regions (indeed, it had to grow, given the changes brought about by enclosure), but there were a range of factors which inhibited this through their operation on farmers' capital: the cost of enclosure itself, so frequently in excess of prediction; the increases of rent immediately after or even before enclosure; the over-cropping between act and award; the tendency of increased output to fall far behind such rises in rent; the rising poor relief costs, which I will discuss next. All were compounded by shallow profit margins and the early nineteenth-century agricultural depression, which particularly affected the more recently enclosed corn-growing parishes; where of course enclosure costs had been higher than anything experienced in the albeit expensive enclosures of the Midland clays. These are all supplementary factors explaining the changes in seasonal unemployment distributions after enclosure, which were clear-cut and uniform across regions in which cropping changes upon enclosure were various and even took opposing directions.

VII

Evidently this discussion invites further comment on a wide range of issues – such as the relation of enclosure to poor relief expenditure, to population growth, labour migration, or rural unrest – and some of these can be covered now. We can begin by drawing attention to the effects of enclosure on poor relief payment, an obvious factor to supplement and support my argument. Gonner has been virtually

[114] Davies, 'Small landowner', 108–13.

the only author seriously to consider this question, and his method and argument were flawed in many respects. Nevertheless, he pointed out (rather reluctantly) that 'considerable enclosure tended to produce some increase in the amount of relief', and that it achieved this result for 'other reasons than because it occasioned . . . conversion from arable to pasture'.[115] The latter is implied in the findings of this chapter. But we can deal with this issue much more conclusively than Gonner. Figure 4.10 presents the results of a regression of per capita poor relief expenditure on the percentage of land enclosed in each of the twenty-four counties most affected by parliamentary enclosure. A mean was used of per capita relief in 1802, 1812, 1821, and 1831.[116] (Correlation results for each of these years separately are very similar.) I have taken first those ten counties where over 35 per cent of land was enclosed by act, as being the counties where parliamentary enclosure was most widespread, and so where I would most expect it to have an effect on poor relief. As can be seen, the correlation coefficient (r) is extremely high (0.911), indicating a very strong relationship between the extent of enclosure and per capita poor relief. The coefficient of determination (r^2) indicates that as much as *83 per cent* of the variation in poor relief in these counties can be explained by the percentage of land enclosed. (And $F_{1,8} = 39.237$, significant at the .001 level.)

Secondly, I have taken all those counties where between 17 and

---

[115] E. C. K. Gonner, *Common Land and Enclosure* (1912), pp. 415ff, 426–7. His discussion was contradictory, badly expressed, and involved two methods. First, at the county level, his findings warranted stronger statement than he gave them, but were based on inaccurate and simplistically presented statistics, which failed even to match consistently the figures from which they were taken in his appendix; and he chose to omit entering figures altogether for some of the counties his tables covered. Secondly, within counties, his basis for comparison between parishes was conceptually meaningless: ignoring the possible effects of out-migration from enclosed parishes; using 'total county' figures to compare with those for enclosed parishes, rather than figures for long-enclosed or un-enclosed parishes; failing to exclude urban parishes from the comparison; misunderstanding the comparability of the 1776 poor relief returns with the early nineteenth-century data; limiting discussion only to five counties which he claimed were 'typical'; allowing the effects of enclosure to be examined for less than maximally six years after, and so on.

[116] Poor relief figures are from M. Blaug, 'The myth of the old poor law and the making of the new', in M. W. Flinn & T. C. Smout (eds.), *Essays in Social History* (Oxford, 1974), p. 145. County enclosure figures are from Turner, *English Parliamentary Enclosure*, app. 3, pp. 180–1.

In regression, the use of percentages can introduce an element of non-linearity, and might be expected to produce a hint of an 'S' tailed distribution. There are statistical methods to deal with this, but insofar as such a distribution is not readily apparent in the figures I have not used them. Their use would be expected to work in favour of my argument, by producing even higher positive correlation coefficients.

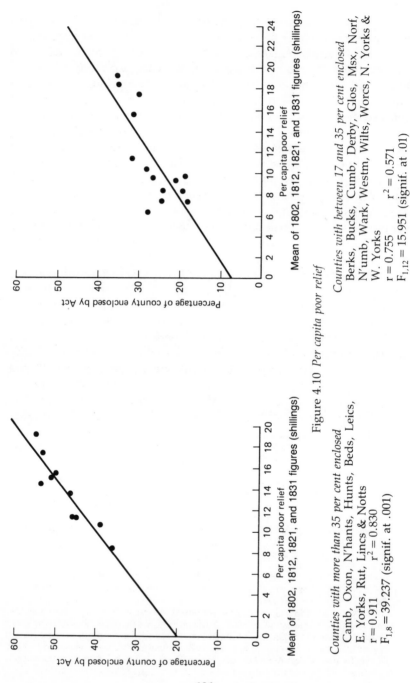

Figure 4.10 *Per capita poor relief*

Counties with more than 35 per cent enclosed
    Camb, Oxon, N'hants, Hunts, Beds, Leics,
    E. Yorks, Rut, Lincs & Notts
    r = 0.911 $r^2 = 0.830$
    $F_{1,8} = 39.237$ (signif. at .001)

Counties with between 17 and 35 per cent enclosed
    Berks, Bucks, Cumb, Derby, Glos, Msx, Norf,
    N'umb, Wark, Westm, Wilts, Worcs, N. Yorks &
    W. Yorks
    r = 0.755 $r^2 = 0.571$
    $F_{1,12} = 15.951$ (signif. at .01)

35 per cent of land was enclosed. (For counties enclosed to a lesser extent little correlation is to be expected.) Here again, the regression reveals a very strong relationship between the extent of enclosure and per capita relief, with a correlation coefficient of 0.755. The coefficient of determination shows that 57 per cent of the variation in per capita relief spending is explained by the percentage of land enclosed. ($F_{1,12} = 15.951$, significant at the .01 level.) And the inclusion of Cumberland in this group significantly affects the results. Were it excluded the correlation would be even higher, with r at 0.832, and r^2 at 0.692. ($F_{1,11}$ would be 24.656, significant at the .001 level.) I argued earlier that enclosure had a similar effect on seasonal distributions of unemployment regardless of whether it involved conversion of arable to pasture or vice versa. The categories chosen here entirely ignore such agricultural distinctions, and the correlations exist regardless of them – strongly corroborating the argument from seasonal distributions.

These results are so clear-cut that it is surprising that they have not been uncovered earlier. One reason for this has been the failure to subdivide counties into adequate categories to consider the question. For on reflection it is only to be expected that the relationship should be studied separately within different categories of my control variable, the percentage of land enclosed. Those counties enclosed to the extent of 17–35 per cent were, of course, those where only 17–35 per cent of land remained open, to be enclosed – hence one would expect dependency upon such open land per acre (were one able realistically to control for parochial demographic density per un-enclosed acre and agricultural specialisation) to be more intense than in those counties where over 35 per cent of land remained open, to be enclosed. Crudely speaking, the enclosure of counties where unenclosed land was *less* prevalent (given the uses of such land to the poor which I have outlined) would have, per acre enclosed, a proportionally greater effect on per capita relief than in those counties where unenclosed land was more extensive. Hence in the second group of counties 16s. per capita poor relief was dependent on 34 per cent of land being enclosed by act; but in the top ten counties the same sum was dependent on 52 per cent of land being so enclosed.[117]

---

[117] The need to divide counties into these two categories, differentiating within the control variable, is clearly apparent from a combined scatter diagram. The only other discussion has been by G. S. L. Tucker, 'The Old Poor Law revisited', *Explor. Econ. Hist.*, XII (1975). His multiple regression was aimed at different problems, and only incidentally included as a variable the percentage of a county enclosed by act. His results on the latter were rendered meaningless by inclusion of *all* counties regardless of whether, or to what extent, they experienced parliamentary enclo-

Contemporary opinion widely held that enclosure increased poor relief expenditure, and we can turn to this to support these findings. But initially, it is necessary to make two methodological points on the use of poor rates and expenditure for this question. Enclosure extended the area over which rates could be spread (just as in relation to the land tax), leading to the rating of smaller units of lower priced land; and so it was possible to lower the actual rate at the same time as the amount collected might rise considerably. This way in which the *rates* could be lowered was an argument used in favour of enclosure, as we find in R. F. Graham's evidence to the 1844 Select Committee: 'While the land remains in common there is little or no assistance given to the poor-rates; you cannot assess the common land itself; you can only assess the property in respect of which it is held for that additional benefit, so that those who are merely enjoying the privilege of common are not in any way chargeable to the poor rates.'[118] The same point was made elsewhere in this report: 'If there be lands which cannot be cultivated at present on account of want of drainage, and they are taken from a state of uselessness and brought into a state of cultivation, they would, of course, be taken into the rate.'[119] And a further consideration which we need to remember, when considering the rise of the poor rate, is that where the rent rose at the same time as the nominal rate, the total sum actually raised for poor relief expenditure would have been increased in a greater ratio than the nominal poor rate. If, for example, the rental of the parish was increased 50 per cent by enclosure, but the poor rate was doubled, the actual yield on that rate would rise threefold.

Now, as Slater pointed out, the association of enclosure even with rising poor *rates* is continually illustrated in Eden's *State of the Poor*, as in Winslow (Buckinghamshire): 'The rise of the Rates is chiefly ascribed to the Enclosure of common fields; which ... has much reduced the demand for labourers ... most of the labourers are on rounds.'[120] In Leicestershire poor rates 'were not one-third of what

sure. It seems quite pointless to measure the effects of parliamentary enclosure on poor relief in long-enclosed counties where such enclosure hardly occurred, or affected only a minute proportion of county acreage (Cheshire, Devon, Kent, Essex, Monmouth, Sussex, Cornwall, etc.) And of course the *absence* of parliamentary enclosure (because a county was long-enclosed) might itself be expected to raise poor relief expenditure – by virtue of the absence of open field and common for the poor. To include all such counties clearly favours the null hypothesis and a meaningless result – a point missed by W. A. Armstrong, 'The influence of demographic factors on the position of the agricultural labourer in England and Wales, c. 1750–1914', *Agric. Hist. Rev.*, XXIX (1981), 79–80, citing Tucker.

[118] S.C. on Enclosure, V (1844), p. 315.
[119] *Ibid.*, p. 366.
[120] Sir F. M. Eden, *The State of the Poor* (1797), vol. 2, pp. 27–33.

they are at present; and the people attribute the rise to the enclosures ... the poor being ... thrown out of employment, must of course be employed by the parish'.[121] There were similar statements by Arthur Young, particularly in his writing after 1800. Here is a well known example which makes clear that *rates* kept rising in many newly enclosed parishes to at least the same extent as in other parishes:

> The rise of poor-rates in many of these parishes that have been enclosed having kept pace with the increase in other parishes, is another proof that there has been something deficient in the principles which have conducted them ... It should therefore seem that notwithstanding the increase of employment, yet there has been some contrary current which has been bearing heavily against the force of such employment. On the contrary, if a right use had been made of a very small portion of these commons, poor-rates might have been done away altogether.[122]

I will not interpret this at the length it deserves. Young and those who have since quoted him omitted the point that if *rates* rose to the same extent in newly enclosed parishes as they did in other parishes, then the relief requirements of newly enclosed parishes must have risen very considerably in excess of the other parishes, whose rent and units of rating remained relatively constant, in comparison with the rating upheavals associated with enclosure. Contemporary comment that rates have risen in newly enclosed parishes to the same extent as in others always indicates relatively excessive relief expenditure in the former. Young was aware of this elsewhere:

> If the act should be framed, like so many others, with a sweeping clause against encroachments, half these people will be thrown at once upon the parish, all of them deeply injured, and the poor rates may reasonably be expected to increase enormously in fact, though not in appearance, by a pound rate; the rental of the parish may and will so increase that the rate will be much less per pound, though the sum raised will be considerably more.[123]

Sir Thomas Bernard's complaints of the loss of cows in the Midlands have already been cited. He continued, if a traveller through the district 'enquires still further he will find that, in those parishes, the poor rates have increased in an amazing degree'.[124] Petitions commonly stated that this would occur as a consequence of enclosure, citing the lessons of nearby parishes. In one case, petitioners complained that they 'would have to sell, become day-labourers, and soon add to the number of paupers, as happened at nearby

---

[121] *Ibid.*, vol. 2, p. 383.
[122] Young, *General Report*, p. 157.
[123] Young, *Inquiry into ... Applying Wastes*, p. 68. He took it as self-evident throughout his discussion that enclosure increased relief expenditure (pp. 32, 68, 109–10).
[124] *Annals of Agriculture*, XXVI (1796), p. 243.

Bledlow'.[125] David Davies emphatically confirmed this, as we have seen.[126] The arguments of the Hammonds, Hasbach, or Slater on this were confirmed by Gonner's rough and ready calculations. More recently, E. L. Jones has cited the case of Broughton, in Hampshire, where 'the expenditure on poor rates was slashed by half for the one year 1791, following the enclosure award of 1790, but thereafter soared away up far into the years after the Napoleonic Wars'.[127] And Hampson similarly, in her book on the treatment of poverty in Cambridgeshire, pointed out that enclosures were accompanied by very large numbers of allowances being granted, and commented that this matter required further investigation.[128]

In the fifty years since her book was published, no one has pursued her statement further at parish level, so let me do so here. The obvious method to supplement the material on seasonal distributions of unemployment, and to check the arguments of Chambers and his followers, is to consider changes in monthly poor relief expenditure immediately before and after enclosure. One requires the survival of parish overseers' accounts, which give monthly breakdowns of expenditure, for the period shortly before and after a parish's enclosure award, and preferably before and after both the act and award. For Cambridgeshire, the survival of parish accounts in the period of enclosure allows this to be done for five parishes: Kirtling, Bassingbourn, Horningsea, Stetchworth, and Toft.[129] All were enclosed during the second parliamentary enclosure movement. And the acreages enclosed were sufficiently large for enclosure to have had an effect on relief expenditure – either by way of alleviating the 'burden' of poverty, unemployment, and high relief expenditure supposed by Chambers and his followers to characterise the unenclosed village, or (in the different terms adopted here) by way of accentuating 'unemployment' and relief expenditure. The results of this method for these parishes are shown in Figures 4.11, 4.12, 4.13, 4.14, and 4.15. I have taken mean monthly expenditure on poor relief for three year periods.[130] The periods chosen were determined by the

[125] See Turner, 'Cost of enclosure in Buckinghamshire', 38. And to the same effect, see n. 68 above.

[126] Davies, *Case of the Labourers*, pp. 56–7.

[127] E. L. Jones, 'Agriculture and economic growth: economic change', in his *Agriculture and the Industrial Revolution* (Oxford, 1974), p. 100.

[128] E. M. Hampson, *Treatment of Poverty in Cambridgeshire, 1597–1834* (Cambridge, 1934), p. 272.

[129] Camb C.R.O., P. 101/12/3–8, P. 11/12/1–6, P. 94/12/1, R. 59/20/4, P. 157/12/1–2.

[130] Miscellaneous expenditure not directly connected with poor relief has been excluded. Such expenditure included quarterage payments, bills, militia substitutes and associated expenses, burial expenses, rents, expenses connected with bastardy,

dates of the enclosure acts and awards, by the survival for sequential months of usable relief accounts, and by the need to avoid the abnormal relief expenditure during the very high price years of 1795–6, 1800–1 and 1811–12. The findings are similar for all five parishes, and strongly corroborate the argument being made. In assessing them, we will be mainly concerned with the date of the award, but need to bear in mind that the act itself was also very significant – for example, raising the anticipation of enclosure, marking the start of legal and enclosure expenses, increasing land sales, reducing agricultural investment or innovation, and probably having negative effects on employment.

Let me start with the most dramatic changes, as found in Kirtling (Figure 4.11). I will not give detailed socio-economic profiles of each parish. But the joint enclosure of Kirtling and Ashley was large-scale (5,351 acres were awarded), and enclosed the clay-soil open fields, suitable for growing wheat, barley, oats, peas, beans, and clover. Kirtling comprised a total of 3,126 acres. Its population in 1801 was 458, and was growing between then and 1821 at a rate of 1.57 per cent per annum. As can be seen, shortly before the act relief expenditure was at a reasonably constant level seasonally – there was no seasonality at all in 1791–3 – and it was low, even during the relatively high prices of 1804–6. The changes after the award are very striking. Mean monthly relief expenditure in the period 1816–21 had increased from the mean monthly levels of 1791–3/1804–6 by a factor of 3.6: from £16.55 in 1791–3/1804–6 (standard deviation of all 72 months (s.) = 11.18), to £59.61 in 1816–21 (s. = 23.81). These figures and their standard deviations assuredly do not support Chambers and his followers, who of course believe that change after enclosure was of an entirely contrary nature.

Similar changes are found for Bassingbourn (Figure 4.12). This parish had a wide variety of soil types (strong clay, loam on gravel, and thin dry soil upon chalk), suitable for a considerably diversified agriculture. There were also 100 acres of common in 1794, on which were depastured cows, sheep, and horses. Bassingbourn's population (excluding that of the hamlet of Kneesworth) was 828 in 1801,

marriage expenses, payments to constables, inoculation of paupers, expenses for journeys, settlement expenses, and so on. I intend to make further use of this source elsewhere. Parish accounts are the major unfathomed source for eighteenth-century social history, and are useful for many other purposes than that to which they are put here: for example, questions of transfer payments and the standard of living, the operation of the poor law, long-term changes in seasonal and yearly unemployment – and all the ways in which such issues can be related to other matters like enclosure, regional agricultural specialisations, cottage industry, and so on.

and was growing at a rate of 1.15 per cent per annum between 1801 and 1821. The enclosure in 1806 awarded 3,216 acres, 73 per cent of the total acreage of Bassingbourn and the hamlet of Kneesworth.

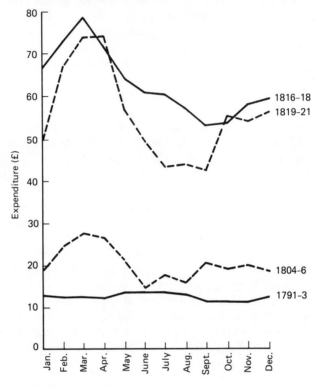

Figure 4.11 *Kirtling – monthly poor relief expenditure, before and after enclosure*
Enclosure Act: 1806. Enclosure Award: 1814 (3 month moving average)

Figure 4.12 shows the changes in relief expenditure before and after the act and award. Even during the very high prices of 1795–7 relief expenditure was seasonally regular, and still low with a mean monthly expenditure of £24.69 (standard deviation of all 36 months (s.) = 8.46). But after enclosure, in 1809–11, this had risen to £44.42 (s. = 13.53), and in 1816–18 to £54.41 (s. = 25.24). The contrast before and after enclosure would be even greater if a pre-enclosure period other than 1795–7 was chosen; but record survival dictates this period, which can suffice insofar as the effect then of very high prices on expenditure works against my argument.

The survival of accounts for Horningsea, Stetchworth, and Toft is more limiting than for Kirtling and Bassingbourn, but demonstrates similar changes. In Horningsea before enclosure wheat, barley, oats, rye, peas, clover, trefoil, and turnips were grown on a thin gravel soil with some loam 'or tender clay'. There were 150 acres of common, with apparently much digging of turf for fuel by the poor. Vancouver

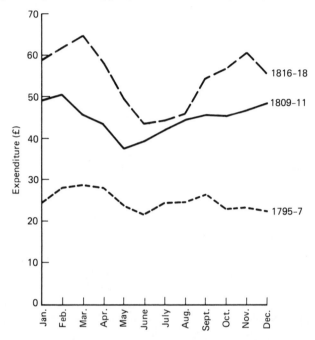

Figure 4.12 *Bassingbourn – monthly poor relief expenditure, before and after enclosure*
Enclosure Act: 1801. Enclosure Award: 1806 (3 month moving average)

commented in 1794 that: 'No enclosing, nor even laying together the intermixed property in the open fields, is desired.'[131] The population in 1801, 1811, 1821, and 1831 respectively was 293, 233, 282, and 272 – unusual in showing no growth over this period. Total parish acreage was 1,647, and 1,570 acres were awarded upon enclosure. The earliest period in Figure 4.13 (1805–7) unfortunately is after the act, so one might expect this to minimise change before and after. But once again there is the same shift to a more acute and expensive seasonality of relief expenditure after the award. Mean monthly relief expenditure

---

[131] C. Vancouver, *General View of the Agriculture in the County of Cambridge* (1794), pp. 44–5.

in 1805–7 was £9.89 (s. = 4.45), but this had risen to £12.68 (s. = 9.40) in 1815–17.

In Stetchworth it is also not possible to provide figures for the period before the act. But it can be seen from Figure 4.14 that relief

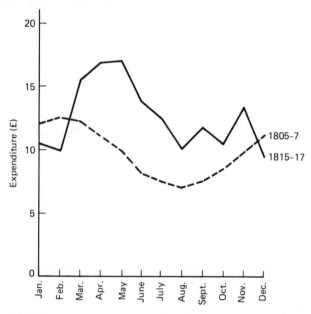

Figure 4.13 *Horningsea – monthly poor relief expenditure, before and after enclosure* Enclosure Act: 1802. Enclosure Award: 1810 (3 month moving average)

expenditure in this parish also became heavier and its seasonality more pronounced after the award. Mean monthly relief expenditure in 1815–17 was £17.48 (s. = 11.63), and this rose to £18.82 (s. = 6.85) in 1824–6. The chalk and clay soil in this parish allowed diversified cultivation of wheat, barley, oats, rye, peas, turnips, and clover. Total parish acreage was 2,891, of which about 850 acres were heath in 1794 (about 1,200 sheep being kept then), and 335 acres were of oak woodland. The population was 342 in 1801, and grew between then and 1821 at a rate of 1.50 per cent per annum. The parish was certainly operating a workhouse system of relief from 1818, and possibly before, and the constraints which could be brought to bear on relief expenditure by this system may provide one clue to the relatively small changes occurring after enclosure. Nevertheless, one recognises in Figure 4.14 comparable changes to those in the other parishes. And it is probable that the use of a pre-enclosure period

(1815–17) already between act and award underrepresents the changes due to enclosure, because the poor rate itself was certainly being levied at a lower level in the mid-1790s than was the case after the act, in 1815–17.

Lastly, there is Toft – growing wheat, barley, oats, and peas, not able to grow either clover or turnips, but engaged in much hollow draining over twenty years prior to enclosure. The population was

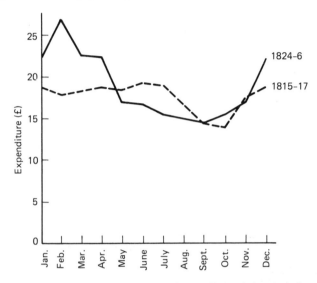

Figure 4.14 *Stetchworth – monthly poor relief expenditure, before and after enclosure* Enclosure Act: 1814. Enclosure Award: 1820 (3 month moving average)

low in 1801 at 208, and between then and 1821 was growing at a rate of 1.10 per cent per annum. Over the entire period 1794–1921 it was never to be higher than in 1851, when it stood at only 380. Virtually the total parish acreage was affected by enclosure, with 1,285 acres awarded. The poor rate in the mid-1790s was very low at 1s. 6d. in the pound. And one can see in Figure 4.15 similar changes to those elsewhere, despite the use of a pre-enclosure period marked by relatively high prices. Mean monthly expenditure moved from £8.88 (s. = 2.74) in 1803–5, to £14.10 (s. = 3.63) in 1817–19.

These five parishes are the only ones in Cambridgeshire for which it is possible adequately to apply this method, and they were not selected to the exclusion of others because their results support the arguments being made. And the use in some cases of the high price period, or the period between act and award, to provide pre-enclosure seasonalities of relief expenditure works against my argument. To judge from the seasonalities of relief expenditure and details in their accounts, these parishes were varied in their agricultural and poor relief practices, and in the specific nature and seasonality of employment they could offer. Despite social and economic particulars

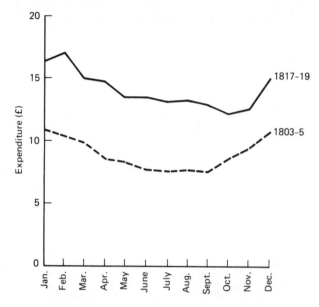

Figure 4.15 *Toft – monthly poor relief expenditure, before and after enclosure* Enclosure Act: 1812. Enclosure Award: 1815 (3 month moving average)

unique to each parish, the changes experienced upon enclosure in all cases took the same direction – one that is quite contrary to that posited by Chambers and his followers.

Finally, in this discussion of change at parochial level, let us consider the effect of enclosure on poor relief and unemployment in Eaton Socon, Bedfordshire.[132] The enclosure act for this parish was in 1795, and of a total parish acreage of 7,602 the large figure of 4,109 acres was awarded in 1800. The changes in poor relief expenditure are revealing. In the long period before enclosure from 1706 to the mid-1780s available figures suggest that poor relief expenditure rarely went above £400 per annum. It was rising in the late 1780s and early 1790s (an average then of about £800 per annum). But in the years

---

[132] Figures are from F. G. Emmison, 'Relief of the poor at Eaton Socon, Bedfordshire, 1706–1834', *Beds Hist. Rec. Soc.*, XV (1933), 54 and app.

between act and award it rose to an average of about £1,290 per annum, and from 1800 to 1819 averaged about £1,835 per annum, rising in the period after 1803. The poor *rate* was 7–8s. in the pound in the 1810s and 1820s – that is, nearly three times its level in the 1780s, despite the rating upheavals associated with enclosure, which would have kept the *rate* low in relation to total expenditure. Figure 4.16 shows the very considerable increases in poor relief expenditure, and in the numbers of parochially settled men in receipt of allowances after enclosure in this parish. While only fifteen men had been in receipt of allowances in 1794, by 1828 the number had risen to *144*, and from 1821 to 1834 there were always over 100 able-bodied men on relief. It is hard not to associate at least partly the enormous increase of men on allowances in 1800 with the fact that this was the year of the award, because the earlier high price years of 1795–6 had seen no such increase. And the rising numbers after 1803 hardly suggest any significant gain in 'employment' due to enclosure, relieving the supposed 'burden' of poverty and unemployment which some historians have suggested as characteristic of unenclosed villages.

These changes in relief expenditure corroborate the argument from settlement records, or the literary evidence cited earlier, and help provide the parochial dimensions of the high county-level correlations between per capita relief expenditure and the percentage of counties enclosed. In all these parishes, the poor rates, numbers relieved, and relief expenditure were at relatively low levels prior to enclosure – in Kirtling they were extremely low. The general rises of relief expenditure after the mid-eighteenth century in long-enclosed parishes – where the labouring poor had no safeguards against unemployment or inflation in the form of access to livestock and land – became manifest in un-enclosed parishes largely after enclosure, when, as Hampson suggested, the overseers' accounts rapidly come to indicate unprecedented and rising numbers 'out of work'. Enclosure immediately put the poor of these parishes into the same precarious situation as those in long-enclosed parishes. It is unnecessary for my argument to make comparisons between recently enclosed and long-enclosed parishes, insofar as the labouring poor of both types of parish were reduced to the same level by parliamentary enclosure. But perhaps it is worth noting that the combined total relief expenditure for the four parliamentarily enclosed parishes of Kirtling, Bassingbourn, Toft, and Eaton Socon indexed from 1803 gives a value of 213 in 1818. For the two long-enclosed parishes of Ardleigh and St Osyth, the 1818 value was lower at 134. Combining these two long-enclosed parishes, total per annum relief expenditure

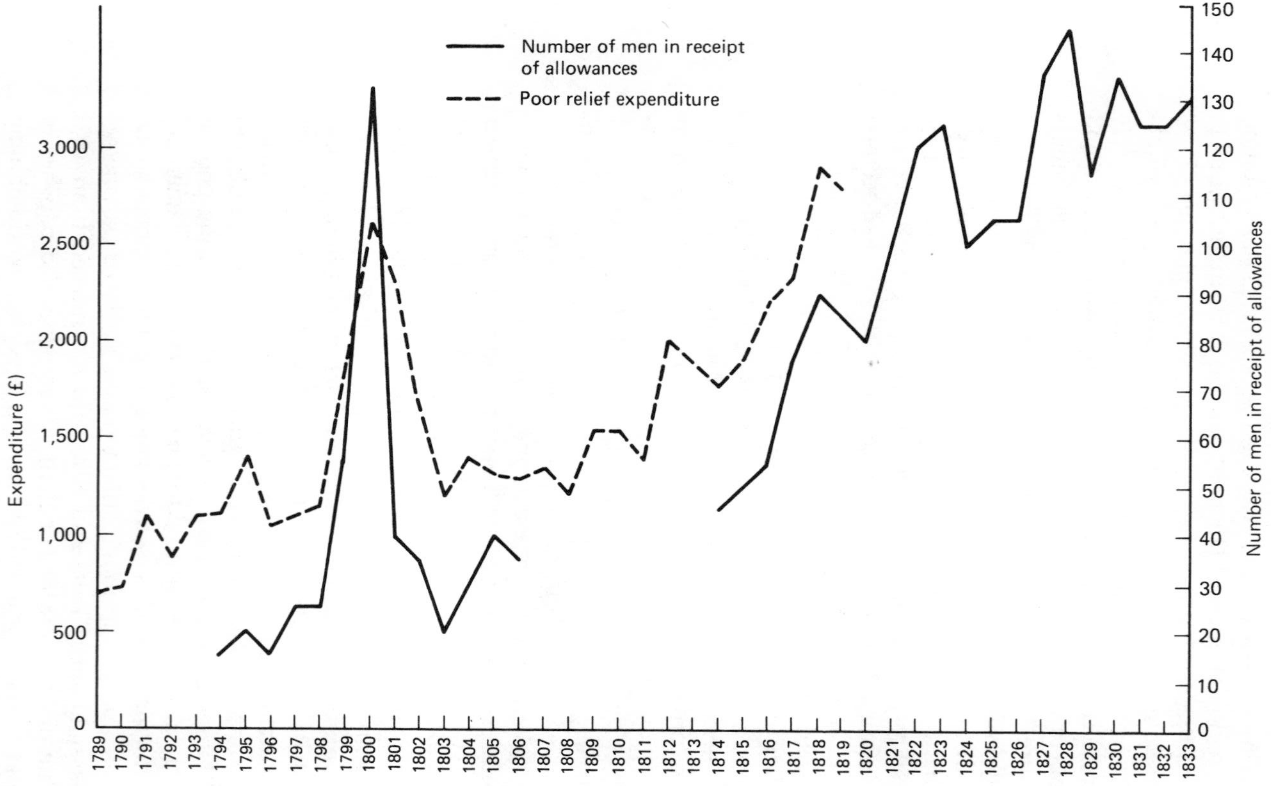

Figure 4.16 *Eaton Socon – poor relief expenditure and numbers of men in receipt of allowances, before and after enclosure*
Enclosure Act: 1795. Enclosure Award: 1800
Source: Emmison, 'Relief of the poor at Eaton Socon'

per inhabitant rose from 1803 to 1818 by a factor of 1.09 – from £1.37 to £1.50. But for the four recently enclosed parishes taken together it rose over the same period by the rather larger factor of 1.67 – from the low, essentially pre-enclosure, figure of £0.64, to £1.07. (The 1801 and 1821 census figures have been used. Population grew (1801–21) by a factor of 1.22 in the two long-enclosed parishes, and by a factor of 1.27 in the four parliamentarily enclosed parishes.) In other words, the four parishes affected by parliamentary enclosure saw more rapid increases of total and per capita expenditure than was occurring in the same period in the two long-enclosed parishes. Of course, any figures on total per annum relief per parish inhabitant raise comparative questions on the generosity of relief per recipient over time, and I do not intend to pursue this in detail here. But it can certainly be shown from parish accounts that the value of relief per recipient was falling during and shortly after the period of enclosure in parliamentarily enclosed parishes – an obvious response of parish authorities to rising total relief expenditure and high enclosure costs, and a response favouring my argument. That is, the growing and seasonally more acute relief expenditure after parliamentary enclosure was assuredly not due to more generous relief being given to each recipient.

VIII

What then do we make of Chambers, and those historians who adopted his arguments on the social effects of enclosure? Or, to re-phrase the question after Yelling, 'do any loopholes remain through which something of their older view of things might be preserved?'.[133] We have seen how Chambers' own writing took on different emphases towards the end of his career, and have frequently quoted his earlier book in support of arguments made here. In itself his article was less objectionable than the palliative edifice since built both upon it and the selected results of some land tax assessments. Many points he made evidently remain valid, and were quite properly directed against extreme interpretations of the relation of enclosure to the supply of industrial labour. The latter came, he thought, 'from the unabsorbed surplus, not from the main body' of the rural population[134] – although (leaving Marx, Dobb, or Levy aside) this point did not really need to be made against the Hammonds, Hasbach, or Slater. Again, 'Enclosure marked only a phase – though an important one – in the ascendancy of the large farm with its lower

[133] Yelling, *Common Field*, p. 216.   [134] Chambers, 'Enclosure and labour supply', 322.

comparative costs; it was not a signal for the extinction of the small farm as an economic unit everywhere.'[135] But then this was surely never being claimed either by most of the authors against whom he wrote – concerned for example, as some of them were, with rural reconstruction schemes, and to extend small landed units by means of land reform. We note also in this last statement, as in his view that 'the curtain which separated the growing army of labourers from utter proletarianization was torn down' (by enclosure),[136] how some historians have since taken his views further than he initially expressed them. We shall see that he may have exaggerated the extent to which 'sources of growth operated silently and perhaps we may say organically, i.e. they were not the direct or indirect product of compulsion'; but these views at any rate remain justifiable.

But there are significant interpretative differences at stake here, and many aspects of his argument now seem dubious. In particular, he exaggerated the benefits of any increase or new found regularity of 'employment' after enclosure. When one reads his arguments carefully it is surprising how far he used evidence from enclosures of waste land. It is particularly unfortunate that he effectively ignored the many areas of deprivation suffered by the poor. But another important argument he made attempted to link up the supposed employment benefits of enclosure with the reasons why the agricultural population grew and persisted until as late as the mid-nineteenth century. Let us reconsider this, not least because developments of demographic sophistication have since produced major advances in statistical knowledge, which currently stand in need of detailed explanation. There is a possibility that the meliorist arguments made by Chambers can be adapted to such a purpose, and the nuptiality changes of the period be seen as a salutary effect of the seasonally more regular and remunerative employment which Chambers thought followed enclosure.

It is particularly hard to interpret the growth of the southern rural population after 1780 as an effect of favourable developments affecting their standard of living. In other regions, notably in parts of the Midlands and the north, falling marriage ages may have owed most to rising real wages, and this was probably widely the case from the late seventeenth century to about 1770.[137] But from then in the south and east (and this area was to have the highest regional demographic

---

[135] *Ibid.*, 312.   [136] *Ibid.*, 322.
[137] Wrigley & Schofield, *Population History of England*, ch. 10, where changes in the gross reproduction rate and the crude marriage rate are explained with reference to real wage change.

growth rate in the early nineteenth century),[138] demographic growth may have been due to rather different factors; and population persistence may well have owed much to a growing dependence on the poor law tying the poor down to their parishes of settlement to a greater extent than in times of fuller employment and higher real wages. As we shall see, in this region after 1780 there is doubtful warrant to the logic which would take a growing rural population as evidence for improved living standards, and then argue that the latter (brought about by supposedly fuller and more remunerative employment after enclosure) was the cause for a rising population. Rising fertility can rather be explained, for example, by the more pessimistic changes of a diminution of female work in agriculture and the trades (and many cottage industries were also badly hit by enclosure, as Sturt was aware),[139] forcing more women to marry earlier as protection against unemployment; or the demographic effects of the decline of service and traditional apprenticeship; and the related absence of incentives to save once the possibilities for partial independence or upward social mobility via the commons and open fields had been curtailed by enclosure.

It is instructive to recall what Hasbach and Slater wrote on this, long before the question of nuptiality change became the important matter for historical debate it now is. Both have been proved correct in their intuitive concentration on fertility, and their arguments were very similar, formulated most precisely by Slater:

Early marriage was particularly encouraged by the change from the open field condition to enclosure. Before enclosure, the conditions of labour made the common field farmers who employed labourers desire young unmarried men and women who could live in the farm house; such farm servants postponed marriage till they had accumulated some savings and could begin their married life with some resources – a cow, for example – over and above their labour. After enclosure, the enriched farming class preferred to pay board wages, and the young labourer with nothing to gain by waiting, with the

---

[138] P. Deane & W. A. Cole, *British Economic Growth* (1967 edn), p. 115. Rural areas in East Anglia and the East Midlands had very low proportions unmarried in the 1861 census. See M. Anderson, 'Marriage patterns in Victorian Britain: an analysis based on registration district data for England and Wales', *Journal of Family History*, I (1976), 59. And the early and mid-nineteenth-century female marriage ages for rural Suffolk provided in the excellent article by D. Jones, 'Thomas Campbell Foster and the rural labourer: incendiarism in East Anglia in the 1840's', *Social History*, I (1976), 7, are among the lowest I have seen for any region in that period.

[139] See also Hasbach, *English Agricultural Labourer*, app. 3; Slater, *English Peasantry*, p. 110, on pre-enclosure woollen industry; Chambers, *Nottinghamshire*, p. 182. For a particularly interesting and wide ranging account of by-employments and the family economy in seventeenth-century villages, before parliamentary enclosure, see J. Thirsk, 'Seventeenth-century agriculture and social change', *Agric. Hist. Rev.*, XVIII (1970), esp. 165ff.

assurance of Poor Law assistance if needed, naturally preferred to marry early.[140]

I have already cited him on the gradation of ranks in the open village and its social mobility. His point on the effect of the commons on marriage ages – the delay before an appropriate accumulation of livestock, or of money to hire a common-right cottage, or to hire or buy strips of land – was repeated by Howlett. The latter thought that a girl would be better advised to hire herself out to service at the age of fifteen, and save perhaps £20–30 before marriage, than to accumulate sheep as a 'shepherdess' while still single. But he spoke of both these options as possibilities which would delay her marriage, while failing perhaps to appreciate how farm service and its potential for saving was declining when he wrote in the late 1780s.[141] But then the option of accumulating livestock was also being abruptly curtailed by enclosure. And both options were in any case closely connected: the small family producers of open field parishes taking farm-servants as a feature of their own family-cycle related labour requirements, the wages paid to the unmarried hired in such conditions being essential for any accumulation of livestock upon marriage.

Here is the author of *A Political Enquiry into the Consequences of Enclosing* (1785), to supplement Slater's view:

> Other classes of people ... besides farmers ... derive very essential advantages from their right of common; namely, the cottager, the mechanic, and inferior shopkeepers ... particularly the cottagers, who in general are labourers to the farmers; this common-right is an incitement to industry ... and of course renders them very valuable members of society. The children ... are sent to yearly service amongst farmers ... the young man can scrape up £20 or £30 and finds a young woman ... possessed with nearly an equal sum, they ... agree to marry ... then stock their cottage with cows, calves, sheep, hogs, poultry etc. During the winter they send their sheep to board with farmers ... at the rate of 2s.–2s. 6d. per score per week ... The wife's management of the live stock, together with the earnings of herself and her children in hay time and harvest, etc, produce nearly as much money in the course of the year, as her husband by all his labour during the same time. How would this class be provided for if the commons were ploughed up?[142]

The answer to that lies in Figures 4.1 and 4.2, or the evidence on poor relief expenditure after enclosure. And when they were ploughed up, there was certainly less motive to save, and the decline of farm service left them little means to do so. Henceforth, their low weekly wages went to the family with whom they boarded, and towards their own

---

[140] Slater, *English Peasantry*, p. 265. See also Hasbach, *English Agricultural Labourer*, p. 390.   [141] Howlett, *Enclosures a Cause of Improved Agriculture*, pp. 75–7.
[142] Anon., *Political Enquiry into ... Enclosing*, pp. 43ff.

subsistence. They moved into the category of strictly wage-dependent day labour described by Homer:

It is likewise an unhappy Circumstance attending the Generality of labouring People, that they are for the most Part upon the same footing at the Year's End, whether their Gains are great or small. If they work for eight Pence a Day, they make a Shift to live; and if they get Eighteen Pence, they do no more than live. When their work is over they consider themselves and their Families as the Victims of Poverty, to be supported by the Parish . . . If they have double Gains this Year, they are not in the least the richer for it in the next. To such Persons as these the extraordinary Profits of one Season are no Counter-ballance to the Defects of another.[143]

The implications of this are also clear enough for any increases of summer paid employment after enclosure, such as hedging, in the absence of means to subsist during the ensuing winter. In this post-enclosure setting, there was hardly motive or means to save or delay marriage in the way Arthur Young described as being typical of open parishes. Here he is, with a statement culminating in a famous passage:

Nothing can be clearer than the vast importance which all these poor people, scattered as they are through so many counties . . . attach to the object of possessing land, though no more than to set a cottage on. Of this there can be no dispute; and as an object does exist, the prospect . . . will induce industry, frugality, patience, and exertion without bounds . . . When we sit by our firesides and ask how a poor labourer can afford to build a comfortable cottage, enclose some land, break up and cultivate a rough waste, acquire some live stock, and get many conveniences about him, we defy calculation; there must be some moving principle at work which figures will not count, for in such an inquiry we see nothing but impossibilities. But we forget a thousand animating principles of human feeling. Such effects could not possibly have been produced without a series of years of great industry and most economical saving – to become independent, to marry a girl and fix her in a spot they can call their own, instigates to a conduct not a trace of which would be seen without the motive ever in view. With this powerful impulse they will exert every nerve to earn, call into life and vigour every principle of industry, and exert all the powers of frugality to save. Nothing less can account for the spectacle, and such animating prospects will account for any thing.

Go to an alehouse kitchen of an old enclosed county, and there you will see the origins of poverty and poor rates. For whom are they to be sober? For whom are they to save? (Such are their questions.) For the parish? If I am diligent, shall I have leave to build a cottage? If I am sober, shall I have land for a cow? If I am frugal, shall I have half an acre of potatoes? You offer no

---

[143] Homer, *Essay*, p. 32. Or see T.A., *A Plan for Relieving the Pressure of the Poor Rates, Affording Employment to the Agricultural Poor and Improving their Condition* (1832), pp. 58–9: 'It has been no uncommon practice with labourers to become burthensome to a parish immediately after harvest, notwithstanding their previous earnings.'

motives; you have nothing but a parish officer and a workhouse! – Bring me another pot –[144]

Young wrote in his autobiography about this pamphlet (which included his valuation of a cow at 5s. or 6s. a week, after repeated interviews with poor families) that

of all the essays and papers I have produced, none I think was so pardonable as this, so convincing by facts, and so satisfactory to any candid reader. Thank God I wrote it, for though it never had the smallest effect except in exciting opposition and ridicule, it will, I trust, remain a proof of what ought to have been done; and had it been executed, would have diffused more comfort among the poor than any proposition that ever was made.[145]

He accurately described one way enclosure affected decisions to marry. The prospects of upward social mobility in the open village, coupled with savings from farm service (and we shall see elsewhere how such savings could be used to apprentice oneself into the trades), acted to delay marriage, and these prudential motives must surely have been destroyed by enclosure.[146]

Such factors are reasonable explanations for the demographic growth which Chambers noticed in parishes enclosed by act, and

---

[144] Young, *Inquiry into . . . Applying Wastes*, pp. 11–13. And see p. 9:

> The motives to industry and frugality are cut up at the roots when every poor man knows that if he does not feed himself, the parish must do it for him; and that he has not the most distant hope of ever attaining independancy, let him be as industrious and frugal as he may. To acquire land enough to build a cottage on is a hopeless aim in 99 parishes out of 100.

Young's arguments might be supplemented by those of Mary Douglas, made with reference to other cultures experiencing rapid demographic growth:

> The argument is that policies of control develop when a smaller family appears to give a relative social advantage. The focus of demographic inquiry should be shifted from subsistence to prestige, and to the relation between the prestige structure and the economic basis of prosperity . . . When social change occurs so rapidly that the prestige structure is no longer consistent, we should expect population explosions to occur.

See her *In the Active Voice* (1982), ch. 6, esp. p. 145. Some contemporaries were aware that small numbers of children might enhance a family's social and material position. See for example, R. Gough, *The History of Myddle* (written in 1701, Harmondsworth, 1981 edn), pp. 132, 197.

[145] A. Young, *Autobiography*, ed. by M. Betham-Edwards (1898), p. 433, and see p. 351.

[146] And see J. M. Martin, 'Marriage and economic stress in the Felden of Warwickshire in the eighteenth century', *Population Studies*, XXXI (1977). See also E. A. Goodwyn (ed.), *Selections from Norwich Newspapers, 1760–1790* (Ipswich, 1973), p. 99, on the decline of small farms and the ending of prudential motives: 'Formerly there were many small farms – an industrious man, by going to service for a few years, was enabled by the money he got to hire a small farm in which he could with good economy bring up his family in a decent manner . . . now there is scarcely a small farm to be met with . . . the money obtained in service is spent in drunkenness and debauchery.' Similar complaints of the decline of small farms and the consequent lack of incentive to save are very common in contemporary literature after about 1770.

there may have been similar results after earlier enclosures. In short, the growth of the southern labour force in the century after 1750, and particularly the very high growth rate of the south-east in the early nineteenth century, could be explained in different terms than those used by Chambers – that is, with at least partial reference to institutional changes which Arthur Young and many others thought had adversely affected the security of livelihood. It now seems inadequate merely to stress 'natural' factors, and plead with Chambers that 'a proletariat was coming into being by the natural increase of the peasant population'. There were a complex range of factors creating this proletariat, some of them 'demographic'; but demographic growth grounded on changes in marriage age and nuptiality is a phenomenon significantly influenced by institutional factors. Enclosure, one such factor, removed a restraint on marriage which had been largely self-imposed, within the adopted limits of certain variable and socially transmitted expectations. Late marriage age (as with other forms of demographic control) would be adopted in the interests of maintaining relatively high living standards, or achieving expectations of social and material advancement – for example, during the high real wage period after 1650, or in un-enclosed villages – and discarded when conditions became adverse and expectations were shaken or came to seem futile. To re-apply one metaphor: the 'invisible hand' of private expectation, in the relatively fluid social structure and partial wage dependency of the open village, could hold population at an 'optimum' level in this way, via a prudential check. Enclosure would be one factor (among others) ending that motive, so contributing to a falling marriage age; but a marriage age the consequences of which were partially 'allowed' or safeguarded by the intensified work discipline and wage dependency of the enclosed village, with its attendant increased output. A balanced demographic system formed once again, perhaps, albeit restructured at a different level – but one now associated with the miserable standard of living of early nineteenth-century southern agriculture, and an unprecedented degree of compulsion to regulate work and production.

There are further reasons for relating enclosure to falling marriage ages and nuptiality change. For the ending of earlier prudential motives was compounded too by the effect of enclosure in hastening the decline of service (an effect complained of, for example, by David Davies), a change to be of major demographic significance. Service had provided savings and security for young people, allowing a late marriage age, and its regional persistence in 1851 was strongly correlated with relatively high proportions of unmarried males and females over the age of twenty. The conditions of the open village had been well suited to its survival. The small family-based open field farms were much more dependent on farm-servants than larger farms, in part because of their family-cycle related labour requirements. Servants allowed such small farmers to maintain or flexibly control their productivity over their family cycle. And the counties in the 1851 and 1861 censuses which had come to have the largest labour to farmer ratios were those where servants formed the smallest proportion of the agricultural labour force, and where (particularly in East Anglia and the east Midlands) there were very low proportions unmarried.[147]

The partial independence allowed to the labouring poor by commons and wastes was also a motive to hire servants, so as to ensure supply of labour throughout the year; supply which was all the more essential in forms of pastoral agriculture often associated with smaller farms. And many of the (part-time) open field crafts and trades, such as alehouse keeping, brickmaking, weaving, nailmaking, basket making, and so on, also involved demands for labour which favoured the hiring of farm-servants. Furthermore, where enclosure brought with it intensification of cereal production, as in the east, so the associated new seasonal labour requirements (on larger farms with very high labour to farmer ratios) also militated against the persistence of service. Enclosure costs and large increases of rent had a similar effect. And of course the seasonally precarious employment provided by such large grain farmers contributed to the structural unemployment, and rising poor rates and per capita relief, which produced motives to avoid yearly hiring, so as to prevent settlements. Some of these points, on the relation of enclosure, service, and farm size, are once again at variance with the generalisations of Mingay and others on enclosure and landownership change (derived from the land tax), and one wishes to be able to discuss that issue with more confidence.[148] Nevertheless, it is quite clear that enclosure had

---

[147] See in particular the excellent discussion by Anderson, 'Marriage patterns in Victorian Britain'. He demonstrates clearly the correlation between the persistence of farm-servants and the proportion unmarried, and stresses the effects on fertility of change in rural areas away from small farms and farm-servants towards larger units employing day labourers. See also Kussmaul, *Servants in Husbandry*, pp. 20–1. And see her supportive comments on the way enclosure hastened the decline of service, pp. 22–3, 76, 82, 84, 117, 193. On the effects on marriage age of the decline of service, *ibid.*, pp. 84, 110–15.

[148] Kussmaul's interesting discussion, because of her close association of service with smaller farms, and the decline of service in the later eighteenth century, constantly implies that the later eighteenth century did indeed see continuing decline of such small owner-occupiers and tenant farmers. (*Servants in Husbandry*, pp. 20–1 and chs.

this effect on service, so producing or accentuating falling marriage ages and a high marriage rate. Both because of this, and its ending of earlier prudential motives, it was highly conducive to rising fertility. I need hardly comment that the usual plea that enclosure allowed the rising population to be fed will lose much of its force if the rising birth rate was significantly promoted by enclosure in these ways. Chambers' 'natural increase' will not seem so 'natural' after all, and the distinction of 'institutional' and 'natural' factors perpetuated by him and Dobb will seem rather simplistic.

The assessment of such demographic changes for the quality of life may have to be subjective. In part, there were the gains or losses of an earlier marriage age (and how should we judge these?), to be assessed against the curtailed opportunities for upward social mobility, and the restrictions on freedom of work and livelihood which became increasingly necessary as population grew. An industrialising economy seen in the terms of modernisation theory had produced features which were 'regressive', and the nuptiality changes of the south were partly a symptom of this. Similarly, one would best abandon the more simple models of community or 'social control' over marriage giving way (before 1870) to a greater autonomy of individual choice. No doubt social pressures influenced marriage in any period, and it has been suggested that their role can be seen in the similar trends of prenuptial pregnancy, the illegitimacy ratio, and age at first marriage. But such social influences can be compatible or confused with private expectation, and perhaps the distinction is a clumsy one which begs questions of epistemology and the social construction of 'private' choice. Positing, for the moment, a balanced compatibility of social pressure and personal expectation in the earlier period (where the personal choice to delay marriage was the personal

6 and 7.) See my chapter 2 for precise dating of the decline of service in the south-east, which tallies closely with Kussmaul's results using a different measure. For the association of service with smaller farms, see also A. Young, *A Six Months' Tour through the North of England*, vol. 4 (1768), p. 253; A. Young, *Political Arithmetic* (1774), p. 295. An associated explanatory issue, relevant if the later eighteenth century saw decline of smaller men, is that of the respective labour requirements per acre of small and large farms. Contemporaries usually held smaller farms to favour fuller employment than large ones. For discussion of this, see: Anon., *An Equitable Property Tax: a financial Speculation and a fair Rate of Wages to the Labouring Poor* (1831); N. Forster, *Enquiry into the Present High Price of Provisions* (1767), pp. 110–14; Rev. J. B. Ferrers, *Observations on the Present Administration of the Poor Laws* (1832), p. 12; S.C. on the Employment of Children, Young Persons, and Women in Agriculture, XIII (1868–9), pp. 581–9; D. R. Mills, 'The poor laws and the distribution of population c. 1600–1860, with special reference to Lincolnshire', *Trans. Inst. of British Geographers*, XXVI (1959), 189–90; Hasbach, *English Agricultural Labourer*, pp. 133–6.

choice to avoid prenuptial pregnancy and illegitimacy), there had occurred by 1820 a collapse of earlier expectations (over partial independence and work, social mobility, marriage), compounded by unrivalled and perceived restrictions on personal choice.

Work discipline after enclosure was one example, and it was closely tied to the rationalisation of labour usage. Enclosure accelerated changes in the sexual division of labour, leaving women more precariously positioned on the labour market, their real wages falling in the south-east. This sexual specialisation (and it occurred also in the south Midlands, and seems likely in Leicestershire and Notting-hamshire) comprised one aspect of rationalisation, just as did the decline of service, and the growing use of day or piece workers after enclosure. Such use was facilitated by the new found vulnerability and availability of wage-dependent labour, as witnessed in its season-al distributions of unemployment. Let me stress this. Moralising comment against the open fields and commons repeatedly reveals underlying motives positing such labour vulnerability after enclo-sure. This was also clear to the Earl of Winchelsea, who complained of the loss of cows and

the dislike ... farmers have to seeing the labourers rent any land ... one of their reasons for disliking this is, that the land, if not occupied by the labourers, would fall to their share; and another ... is that *they rather wish to have the labourers more dependent upon them* ... The moment the farmer obtains his wish, he takes every particle of the land to himself [my italics].[149]

Describing such motives, some historians have spoken strongly of 'class robbery', others of land greed. The *General Report* spoke of 'this uncivilized mode of procedure ... havock! he is the best fellow who gets the most plunder'.[150] There was throughout little doubt as to

[149] Earl of Winchelsea, Communication to Board of Agriculture, 4 Jan. 1796, cited by Slater, *English Peasantry*, pp. 135–6. See also Yelling, *Common Field*, p. 145, citing R. Davis on enclosure allowing 'better superintendence of labourers'. For similar statements see the citations in the Hammonds, *Village Labourer*, pp. 102–7, such as that from the 1834 Poor Law Report: 'We can do little or nothing to prevent pauperism: the farmers will have it: they prefer that the labourers should be slaves; they object to their having gardens, saying "The more they work for themselves, the less they work for us".' See also Anon., *Political Enquiry into ... Enclosing*, p. 48 ('I know many farmers who ... will not employ any cottager who is possessed of any kind of beast'). With similar ends in view, there had been considerable obstruction of the poor on the commons before enclosure: See Young, *Inquiry into ... Applying Wastes*, pp. 10–11: 'their [cottage-building] operations have had enemies everywhere; they have at every place had to fight their way through a host of foes – their fences levelled – their works of all sorts viewed with the most jealous eyes – opposed – in some cases defeated – in all calumniated ... they received little but discouragement when they ought to have been liberally assisted, and they have in some cases been absolutely stopped from all further proceedings of the kind'.
[150] Young, *General Report*, pp. 380–1. And see p. 68.

whose interest was being consulted. As the *General Report* commented: 'On the whole, then, I will venture to assert, that, by the system of enclosing, the landowner will increase the value of his lands; the farmer his profits; *labour will be at least as plentiful . . . we have nothing to fear* from even a General Enclosure Bill [my italics].'[151] It is easy to appreciate why there was less motive to employ farm-servants once the labour subservience described by the Earl of Winchelsea had been reached, as it widely was in the south.

The rural population grew until about 1851, but there was still much out-migration, and we need to consider how enclosure affected this – a subject widely debated at the time. Because Chambers in 1953 thought that enclosure was benevolent in its causes and effects, he believed that it allowed population to expand, and so he dismissed allegations that it caused depopulation. But we have seen that population might grow after enclosure for less congenial reasons, and should now mention arguments made by N.F.R. Crafts on enclosure and out-migration. It seems that enclosure did indeed cause significant out-migration, and that Chambers was misguided in his dismissal of the latter point of view.

Crafts' findings can be summarised in his own words:

The results . . . are in sharp contrast with what one would expect from a reading of Chambers and his followers . . . the figures seem to cast doubt on claims that improvement in parliamentarily enclosed villages was more labor-using than that which occurred in other agricultural villages. Furthermore it may well be that there has been too great a tendency to generalize from Nottinghamshire . . . A positive association between out-migration and enclosure is also observed and this would appear to be in distinct contrast with the conventional wisdom from Chambers . . . This model of migration behaviour is not capable of distinguishing what factors underlay the somewhat greater migration from the enclosed counties or when the greater flows took place . . . It could be that in parliamentarily enclosed villages there was a slightly lower demand for labor; that might reflect the short-term impact of enclosure . . . The population increases which occurred in parliamentarily enclosed villages are not acceptable as evidence of a labor-using bias to improvement in those places . . . Nottinghamshire does not appear to be typical of several other counties.[152]

Such conclusions on migration indicate a compatible and related effect of enclosure to that found on seasonal distributions of unemployment, or on poor relief. Crafts' migration data unfortunately ignores rural–urban movement within the county (perhaps Chambers escapes in Nottinghamshire because of this), and the terms adopted were rather narrow, given limited information, and the need to simplify for his method. But these results are a conclusive advance

[151] *Ibid.*, pp. 288–9. [152] Crafts, 'Enclosure and labour supply revisited', 177, 180, 182.

over those generalised from Chambers. The view that enclosure produced out-migration has, needless to say, been voiced in the past. But we should note with Crafts that there is insufficient evidence to support 'a hypothesis of mass expulsion of labor by parliamentary enclosure'. As he points out, the out-mobility which it caused was on a smaller, if still significant scale.[153]

To contemporaries, this occurred most obviously in the Midlands (although Crafts extends it beyond this), with the conversion there to pasture which is still witnessed today in the undulations on grazing land of open field arable furrows. John Wedge wrote of Warwickshire in 1793 that:

About forty years ago the southern and eastern parts of this county consisted mostly of open fields . . . These lands being now grazed want *much fewer hands* to manage them than they did in the former open state. Upon all enclosures of open fields the farms have generally been made much larger; from these causes the hardy yeomanry of country villages have been driven for employment to Birmingham, Coventry and other manufacturing towns [my italics].[154]

Even Gonner admitted for Leicestershire that: 'there was little doubt among contemporaries that a marked conversion into pasture, resulting in the diminution of the labour on some farms and of population in some rural districts, took place'.[155] One author writing on the Swing riots actually advocated enclosure 'to remove the surplus population of the parishes'.[156] Earlier, Hanway believed that it had produced mobility to London, and he must have met in his work individuals who claimed that this was the case;[157] Howlett admitted depopulation where pasture was increased;[158] and settlement records provide further evidence of this.

In most counties there were more examined as to settlement in the ten years after the award than in the ten years before it, and in cases

---

[153] *Ibid.*, 182.
[154] J. Wedge, *General View of the Agriculture of the County of Warwick* (1794), pp. 20–1.
[155] Gonner, *Common Land*, p. 399. Or see Hoskins, *The Midland Peasant*, p. 212.
[156] Anon., *A Plain Statement of the case of the Labourer* (1830), p. 24, in K. E. Carpenter (advisory ed.), *The Rising of the Agricultural Labourers* (Harvard, 1972).
[157] J. Hanway, *Virtue in Humble Life, containing Reflections on the Reciprocal Duties of the Wealthy and Indigent* (1774), p. xxix.
[158] J. Howlett, *Enquiry into the Influence which Enclosures have had upon the Population of England* (1786), in A. H. John (ed.), *Enclosure and Population* (Farnborough, 1973), p. 28. See also A Country Gentleman, *Advantages and Disadvantages*, p. 8: 'The cottager not only expects to lose his commons, but [also expects] the inevitable consequence of the diminution of labour, the being obliged to quit his native place in search of work'; Young, *General Report*, p. 35; S. Addington, *An Inquiry into the Reasons for and against Inclosing Open Fields* (Coventry, 1772), p. 43; E. P. Brenton, *Letters . . . on Population, Agriculture, Poor Laws and Juvenile Vagrancy* (1832), pp. 10ff.

where they were settled elsewhere they would generally be removed. Entries on settlement cases in overseers' accounts before and after enclosure also suggest this. This is despite the fact that many were also removed in the gap between act and award. In some parishes the year of the act coincides with a noticeable change in the efficiency of poor law practice. Iver, in Buckinghamshire, is an example, a parish which Turner noted as having enclosure costs of 94s. an acre. He added that 'if the minute book or miscellaneous papers were complete, the final cost might well appear as in excess of £5 an acre'.[159] The year of the act coincides with the introduction of a (rare) handsome leather-bound examination and removal book, which bears witness to the unprecedentedly large number of removals which thereafter took place every year. One supposes that the parish officers would have been amused by Chambers' account of the large increased demand for labour upon enclosure, which attracted labour 'from far and wide'. Of course, they could only remove those not actually settled, but many fell through the legal definitions of settlement and found themselves removed from their homes – to place of last yearly hiring, to birth place, father's settlement, place of apprenticeship, or whatever. Their length of residence in the removing parish counted for nothing. The value of their property was usually estimated at under £10; they rarely were able to rent to the value of £10 per annum. In some parishes after enclosure there are pathetic summaries of small rented pieces of land or housing – five or more rents sometimes being paid, and yet still failing to total up to the magical figure of £10.[160] Or we find mention (at Ashby de la Zouch) of 'a House built on the waste in which he has lived ever since' his marriage; a 'house' which, unless he had saved up for it by hiring yearly in that parish before marriage, he would lose if the parish fixed him elsewhere.[161]

Now I am not suggesting that parishes commonly conducted a 'purge' of their chargeable, non-settled inhabitants upon, or preparatory to, enclosure; although some parishes come to mind. And removal was always a risky business because potentially expensive if another parish challenged it. Nevertheless, if Chambers correctly expressed the demand for labour after enclosure, one would expect parishes at least to try and hold resident labourers (whether settled or not) in preparation for the 'great task' ahead. There was, after all, no necessity to remove the non-settled short-term chargeable. But, to judge from the time and number of removals, of men engaging in

[159] Turner, 'Cost of enclosure in Buckinghamshire', 40.
[160] For example, Bucks C.R.O., PR. 115/13/4.   [161] Leics C.R.O., DE. 432/3/1–230.

wage-dependent labour, parishes did not curtail their removing policies. One is struck either by continuity in this regard, or (in fewer parishes) by a very considerable increase of removals at or after the time of enclosure – which could be a way of penalising discontented parties, but which is not indicative of a considerably expanded demand for labour.

Moving to a final issue, Chambers and Mingay wrote that 'there was obviously no connection between the revolt and enclosure', referring to the Swing uprising of 1830, and something must be said on this.[162] Hobsbawn and Rudé denied this, and it seems clear that there was indeed some connection, though not a necessary one, between Swing and recent enclosure. Thus they wrote that close analysis

reveals a distinct connection. In Eynsford four out of the nine parishes enclosed since 1800 rioted; yet only nine out of thirty-one parishes were disturbed. In Erpingham South three out of the five parishes enclosed since 1800 rioted; yet only six out of the thirty-eight parishes were disturbed. In Hartismere half the four parishes recently (since 1800) enclosed were active; yet only a third of all parishes rioted, taking both 1822 and 1830 together.[163]

And they provided a table for different Divisions of parishes taken from Norfolk, Suffolk, Wiltshire, and Hampshire to make this point. Taking ten Divisions (comprising in all 227 parishes), out of forty-eight parishes enclosed after 1800, 50 per cent rioted; whereas for the other parishes, unaffected by parliamentary enclosure during that period, only 25 per cent rioted. In other words, the likelihood of newly enclosed parishes rioting was about twice that of other parishes.

Swing itself occurred mostly in old-enclosed southern counties or in those affected by the second parliamentary enclosure movement, and was diverse in its causes and manifestations. Nevertheless, opposition to threshing machinery was probably its most common feature – opposition because threshing machinery curtailed the winter employment traditionally provided by hand threshing. We have seen how precarious winter employment was in parishes enclosed by parliamentary act, so it would certainly have been in these parishes that one would expect bitter opposition to threshing machinery; compounding, as such machinery did, the winter vulnerability to unemployment which was so much more noticeable there

---

[162] Chambers & Mingay, *The Agricultural Revolution, 1750–1880* (1966), p. 104.

[163] E. J. Hobsbawm & G. Rudé, *Captain Swing* (1969, 1973 edn), pp. 147–8. Their figures clearly refute Chambers and Mingay's statement, and confirm the Hammonds on this.

than in un-enclosed parishes, or to a lesser degree, in long-enclosed parishes. In this regard it seems certain that Hobsbawn and Rudé's insistence on the connection between Swing and enclosure is correct. One would most expect Swing unrest in recently enclosed parishes. But insofar as the seasonal distributions of unemployment in long-enclosed parishes were also acute, it is hardly surprising that long-enclosed counties were also involved. The greater likelihood of 'revolt' in 1830–1 in recently enclosed parishes might be expected from long and recently enclosed unemployment distributions. Of course, I do not wish to reduce this unrest to being a predictable consequence of seasonal unemployment distributions – as my explanations make clear, such patterns were a manifestation of a wider range of problems, all producing the widespread unrest of the period, of which Swing is one of the better known examples.[164] Enclosure, especially after 1790, contributed to Swing by accentuating winter 'unemployment' (so aggravating reactions to the threshing machine in regions probably most likely to introduce it), to a degree less apparent in long-enclosed parishes, and certainly less clearly found in open parishes.

We are finally drawn to conclusions on the social consequences of enclosure which run counter to an appreciation of the gains in productivity and efficiency which it could bring about – gains which, in writing by Chambers and Mingay, Yelling, McCloskey, and others, have been taken not simply as the prime criteria for judgement, but as the only one. Certainly, this chapter lends some support to arguments stressing gains in 'efficiency' after enclosure. One recalls the sexual rationalisation of labour usage, or the growing work-discipline, labour subservience, and wage dependency, with their implications for rising productivity per male worker.[165] And no doubt this raised output for urban areas. But, for all this 'rising output per

---

[164] Armstrong, 'Influence of demographic factors', 71, is surely incorrect in dismissing Swing as an isolated 'colourful episode', explainable by 'short period influences'. Rural unrest persisted throughout the nineteenth century. See for example, Peacock, *Bread or Blood*; Jones, 'Thomas Campbell Foster'; D. J. V. Jones, 'The poacher: a study in Victorian crime and protest', *Historical Journal*, XXII (1979); J. P. D. Dunbabin, *Rural Discontent in Nineteenth-Century Britain* (1974); the *Times* reports of June–August 1844; or the *Morning Chronicle* reports on the Rural Districts of October 1849–February 1851.

[165] On rising productivity per male worker, see N. F. R. Crafts, 'Income elasticities of demand and the release of labour by agriculture during the British Industrial Revolution', *Jnl of European Econ. Hist.*, IX (1980), 154, 167. (I would of course attach a different connotation to his term 'previously underemployed'.) Chambers, Mingay, McCloskey, and others have insisted on considerable gains in efficiency and output after enclosure; but compare the recent and more sceptical arguments on this of Turner, 'Agricultural productivity in England in the eighteenth century'.

worker', or 'greater labour intensity', and (some suppose) 'growing skill composition' of the rural male labour force, it is worth pointing out that real wages *still* fell after about 1780. Their fall is significant when seen in the context of rising productivity. Furthermore, it is clear that many considerations have been ignored in the 'cost-benefit' historiography defensive of parliamentary enclosure, and that it has paid too much attention to benefits to relatively wealthy rural classes, and too little to the costs to the poor. But social emphasis and questions of equity aside, a few of the more 'economic' considerations which have been largely omitted have included the detrimental effects of enclosure on poor relief expenditure; the unfathomed economic costs and long-term effects of increased labour unrest and class tension (nineteenth-century incendiarism, the poaching gangs, the rural constabulary, farmyard pilfering, and so on); the considerably underestimated enclosure costs; the economic and motivational effects of terminating partial self-sufficiency and the keeping of livestock among the poor (comparisons with the different course of events in France would be instructive here); the consequent deterioration in diet, and the economic implications of that; the demise of craft industries and domestic production dependent on raw materials found in the un-enclosed village; the loss of fuel; the contribution to the decline of service; the effects of such changes on prices and aggregate agricultural demand; to say nothing of their effect on out-migration and their wider demographic significance.

Then one should remember the work of Havinden and others on the productive potential of open field agriculture, which was probably never fully realised. And much recent writing on agricultural improvement in under-developed countries has stressed the way in which massive increases of production can occur with only slight institutional adjustments – frequently much more minor than the re-organisation due to parliamentary enclosure in England. Furthermore, yield increases after enclosure seem rarely to have been a requirement of parishes actually enclosed, although they may increasingly have become so. In this respect, village inhabitants suffered from the attractions of landownership and profit to landlord and larger tenant farmer, and this during a period of rising prices when the produce of partial self-sufficiency was increasingly valuable and most needed by the poor. And while productivity increases were creditable, if not necessarily contingent upon enclosure, it is worth recalling that they contributed significantly to the long-term depression of agricultural prices after parliamentary enclosure, which was adversely to affect many sections of the farming community.

Clearly, it is difficult to reduce many of the economic and social costs of enclosure discussed here to a 'quantifiable unit of account', but they should not be side-stepped in the way of current agrarian historiography. In particular, the efforts of some historians to brush aside the social effects of enclosure (in Yelling's case, for example, by insisting in summary fashion that they were beneficial, and then claiming that they are not, in any case, fit matter for research or discussion) seems to ignore important areas of historical understanding, which can be of significance today.[166] There was a time (in 1920) when Curtler, in his charming manner, could write of the squatters that they were 'a class of people ... on whom a vast amount of pity has been wasted'; but that would be an inappropriate judgement to make of historical writing over the past fifty or so years.[167] Of course, we now believe, I hope, that historical study has many more important purposes than that of deciding on specific allocations of pity – but a degree of historiographical humanity shown for the cottager and other labouring classes affected by enclosure is somewhat overdue.

So let me end on a note of empathy. This chapter has shown that the poor were, on their terms, usually justified in what Alexander

---

[166] Yelling, *Common Field*, p. 216. Or see in particular D. N. McCloskey, 'The persistence of English common fields', in E. L. Jones & W. N. Parker (eds.), *European Peasants and Their Markets* (Princeton, N.J., 1975). He insists that earlier emphasis on 'equity' *still* needs redressing with strict emphasis laid on 'efficiency' – as though nothing had been written on enclosure since the only authors he cites in this context: Homans, Maitland, Vinogradoff, the Hammonds, Marx, and Tawney. 'Efficiency' is defined as 'producing the largest attainable satisfaction for given inputs of land, labor, and capital'. His view of the 'inefficiency' of the open village leads him, for example, to explore (with analogies from an 'American middle-western street plan') how much time 'peasants' spent walking every day between plots. His eventual figure of fifteen minutes will not go far to help social historians explain how the high leisure preference of the open village was spent. Nor does he compare it with the long distances walked by day labourers in the post-enclosure environment, particularly between 'open' and 'close' villages. (B. A. Holderness, '"Open" and "close" parishes in England in the eighteenth and nineteenth centuries', *Agric. Hist. Rev.*, XX (1972), discusses the relation of enclosure to the development of open–close dichotomies.)

[167] W. H. R. Curtler, *The Enclosure and Redistribution of Our Land* (Oxford, 1920), p. 142. This book is oddly described by Mingay as 'objective in its approach'. Bibliographical note, Hammonds, *Village Labourer* (1978 edn), p. 280. One is also told here that Slater's *English Peasantry* is 'almost completely outdated and unreliable', but that Yelling's discussion in *Common Field* of the social effects of enclosure 'is highly judicious and well-informed' (pp. 280–1). Mingay comments against the Hammonds that 'The relevance of developments in the poor law to enclosure is by no means obvious to modern scholars' (p. 284). Nevertheless, poor law developments were constantly thought to be relevant by contemporaries, and perhaps this chapter will help to clarify the matter.

Somerville called their 'oppressive horror' of enclosure.[168] Their feelings were never in any doubt, even if, by the late eighteenth century, they commonly found it inadvisable to risk their lives in the ruthless legal recriminations which would follow anti-enclosure riots – just as they followed 'Bread or Blood' in 1816, or Swing.[169] 'Many arguments have been framed, as well as assertions advanced', wrote the *General Report*, 'to prove that enclosing commons has been universally beneficial to the poor . . . this is directly in the teeth of their own feelings and positive assertions, as well as those of many other most respectable eye-witnesses.'[170] One such witness was Arthur Young, transformed from a strident pro-enclosure advocate before 1800 to the man who left us one of the most persuasive and moving defences of the poor against enclosure ever written. The proposals in his *Inquiry into the Propriety of Applying Wastes to the Better Maintenance and Support of the Poor* would have been the most appropriate alternative to the practice of parliamentary enclosure.

> The fact is [he wrote] that by nineteen enclosure bills out of twenty [the poor] are injured, in some grossly injured . . . It must be generally known that they suffer in their own opinions . . . The poor in those parishes may say, and with truth, Parliament may be tender of property; all I know is, I had a cow, and an act of Parliament has taken it from me. And thousands may make this speech with truth . . . To allow [a General Enclosure Act] to be carried into execution in conformity with the practice hitherto, without entering one voice, however feeble, in defence of the interests of the poor, would have been a wound to the feelings of any man, not lost to humanity, who had viewed the scenes which I have visited. May God, of his mercy, grant that the Legislature, whenever they take into consideration the subject of the poor . . . receive their information from those who are best able to give it, from the poor themselves.[171]

Needless to say, God 'in his mercy' was not forthcoming – and historians now usually seem disinclined to follow Young's advice.

---

[168] A. Somerville, *The Whistler at the Plough* (Manchester, 1852), p. 104.

[169] For anti-enclosure rioting during the period of parliamentary enclosure, see Hobsbawm & Rudé, *Captain Swing*, pp. 111–14, 147; Peacock, *Bread or Blood*, p. 17; Dunbabin, *Rural Discontent*, pp. 45ff; *Gentleman's Magazine*, XXXV (1765), 441; Hammonds, *Village Labourer*, p. 42.

[170] Young, *General Report*, p. 12; Batchelor, *General View . . . Bedfordshire*, p. 249 ('the poor have invariably been inimical to enclosures, as they certainly remain to the present day'); S.C. on Enclosure, V (1844), p. 431. *By definition*, parliamentary enclosure implied opposition – hence the need for the Act to override that opposition. The point was well made by Chambers, *Nottinghamshire*, p. 202, although omitted by his successors.

[171] Young, *Inquiry into . . . Applying Wastes*, p. 51. See also his 'General Enclosure', *Annals of Agriculture*, XXXVIII (1801), 214; Hammonds, *Village Labourer*, pp. 21–2, for Lord Lincoln's view of Parliament neglecting 'the rights of the poor'.

But we can allow Somerville, as always one of the most sensitive of commentators, to leave us in little further doubt over these feelings:

In my travels, whenever I find a common . . . I talk to the people living on and around it of the benefit they would derive from its enclosure and careful cultivation: and in all cases they reply with a bitterness expressive of no milder belief than that they think me an agent of some one about to robb them, about to invade their little privileges, and despoil them of an independence which, even if not worth a penny, they would still cherish, merely because it was a soil other than the bare highway, on which they could set the soles of their feet in defiance of the rich man, their landed neighbour.[172]

We are hoping to recreate the lost outlook and priorities of the English agrarian labourer. And family through family, rural out-migration and the path to British industrial relations – where was the groundwork laid in a heritage of distrust? So finally, not as an incitement to incendiarism (there was too much of that), but for the reader simply to ponder, here is the elderly labourer speaking to George Sturt many years after the enclosure of his village:

Pointing to the woods, which could be seen beyond the valley, he said spitefully, while his eyes blazed: 'I can remember when all that was open common, and you could go where you mind to. Now 'tis all fenced in, and if you looks over the fence they'll lock ye up. And they en't got no more *right* to it, Mr. Bourne, than you and me have! I should *like* to see they woods all go up in flames!' [his italics][173]

---

[172] Somerville, *Whistler*, pp. 101–2. To similar effect, see John Clare, *The Parish: a Satire*, in J. W. & A. Tibble (eds.), *John Clare, Selected Poems* (1965), p. 164; *The Village Minstrel*, in *ibid.*, p. 50; *Enclosure* in *ibid.*, pp. 114–15; *Helpstone*, in *ibid.*, p. 6.
[173] Sturt, *Change in the Village*, p. 73.

5

The decline of apprenticeship

The Statute of Artificers had exercised far-reaching control over artisan production for two and a half centuries, and the repeal of its apprenticeship clauses in 1814 was bitterly resisted.[1] It had limited entry into profitable trades in existence in 1563 to the children of masters and the holders of certain property qualifications, in defence of the then status quo. It had codified the compulsion of apprenticeship, fixed quotas of apprentices in many trades, and stipulated the length for apprentices to serve – for 'seven years at the least, so as the term of such apprentice do not expire afore such apprentice shall be of the age of twenty-four years at the least'; for apprenticeships in husbandry 'until his age of twenty-one years at the least'.[2] This had codified the decision of the London guilds in 1556 establishing twenty-four years as the minimum age for completing an apprenticeship, to avoid 'over hastie marriages and over sone [soon] setting up of households of and by the youth and young folkes of the said citie'. The repeal of the Statute was widely condemned by guilds and trade organisations on the grounds that the lack of statutory control would lower standards of production, adversely affect English overseas trade, and depress artisans' living standards.[3] And yet the system had probably been in decline for some decades at least, and (as we shall see) the 1814 repeal was more an acknowledgement of this than conducive to any significant economic changes itself.

Nevertheless, there has been considerable disagreement among historians as to when the older apprenticeship system, and the associated control over trade organisation of the guilds and companies, went into decline. Views on this matter range, at perhaps the extreme chronological limits, from George Unwin's view (shared by

I would like to thank Paul Ryan and Michael Walker for their comments.
[1] 54 Geo III c. 96.   [2] 5 Eliz c. 4.
[3] See for example the S.C. on Apprenticeship, IV (1812–13).

Kramer or Power) that the two institutions of the guild and the trade union were 'separated by centuries of development – and the earlier one was dead before the later one was born'; to E. P. Thompson's occasional assumption that the repeal in 1814 itself brought about decline of the traditional apprenticeship system.[4] The latter view might also be one, for example, which could be arrived at by a reader of the 1812–13 Select Committee's Report on Apprenticeship, where examples were given of workmen intruding into the trades of individual towns without having been fully apprenticed, at times as if this were the exception to the rule, which required immediate remedial action along the lines suggested by the still operative statute.[5] Within these extremes, other historians have assumed a wide range of other chronologies of decline for the apprenticeship system. O. J. Dunlop and R. D. Denman, in their *English Apprenticeship and Child Labour: A History*, published in 1912 (which still remains the most authoritative work on the subject), argued that the system began to collapse from about 1720, and that it had ended around 1780.[6] Dorothy Marshall also saw the decline from 1720, with the diminishing control of the guilds.[7] The Hammonds in their *Town Labourer* appear to have seen the change occurring later, dating it from the petitions of various crafts in the late eighteenth and very early nineteenth centuries insisting that the legislation be upheld.[8] On the other hand, J. R. Kellett or W. F. Kahl, in their various publications concentrating on certain London guilds, dated the decline from the mid- or late seventeenth century.[9] Kellett argued

---

[4] G. Unwin, *The Guilds and Companies of London* (1908); G. Unwin, *Industrial Organization in the Sixteenth and Seventeenth Centuries* (Oxford, 1904), p. 9; S. Kramer, *The English Craft Guilds and the Government* (New York, 1905); E. Power, 'The English craft guilds in the Middle Ages', *History*, IV (1920); E. P. Thompson, *The Making of the English Working Class* (1963), pp. 259–97.

[5] S.C. on Apprenticeship, IV (1812–13).

[6] O. J. Dunlop & R. D. Denman, *English Apprenticeship and Child Labour: A History* (1912), pp. 226–32.

[7] D. Marshall, *The English Poor in the Eighteenth Century* (1926), pp. 183–5.

[8] J. L. & B. Hammond, *The Town Labourer* (1917), pp. 293–4.

[9] J. R. Kellett, 'The breakdown of gild and corporation control over the handicraft and retail trades in London', *Econ. Hist. Rev.*, X (1957–8); W. F. Kahl, 'Apprenticeship and the freedom of the London Livery Companies, 1690–1750', *Guildhall Miscellany*, VII (1956); or his *The Development of the London Livery Companies: an Historical Essay and Select Bibliography* (Boston, 1960). It is also worth stressing that the earlier statutory limit on length had been twenty-four years, or for a *minimum* of seven years. The age of twenty-four was probably being ignored by the mid-seventeenth century in favour of twenty-one. A. J. Willis & A. L. Merson (eds.), *A Calendar of Southampton Apprenticeship Registers, 1609–1740*, Southampton Record Society, XII (1968), draw attention to this, suggesting some earlier downward decline to seven year terms between 1610 and 1682 (p. xviii). But then they argue that there were very few apprenticeships after 1720 (pp. xxxi–xlvi).

that the guilds were being weakened from the late sixteenth century, and saw the seventeenth century as seeing progressively more futile efforts to remedy this. Recruitment of freemen to the city companies he worked on fell heavily in particular between the late 1670s and 1745, paralleled by a similar fall off in the enrolment of apprentices. Kahl largely followed him in this, and saw the first half of the eighteenth century as the crucial period of decline, away from the serving of a full seven year apprenticeship. Taking the grocers', goldsmiths', and fishmongers' companies in London, he demonstrated most rapid decline in apprenticeship enrolments between 1690 and 1720. Many other historians seem to follow this chronology – Peter Clark, for instance, argued recently that the (assumed) decline of apprenticeship in the 1690s renders apprenticeship records from then a dubious source for the study of labour mobility.[10] Then again, to support Unwin's argument for an even earlier decline, we have F. J. Fisher or Margaret James both arguing, in their various ways, for the early or mid-seventeenth century as being the period in which collapse became irreversible.[11]

The debate is indeed in a chaotic state. I am familiar with few other English historiographical issues in which such a wide variety of contradictory views prevails simply over the basic facts of change. With the exception of research limited to the Twelve Great Livery Companies of London, the subject has little quantitative footing, and most historians writing on it or related subjects have confined themselves to impressionistic statements.[12] Hence in part the variety

[10] P. Clark, 'Migration in England during the late seventeenth and early eighteenth centuries', *Past and Present*, LXXXIII (1979), 62.

[11] M. James, *Social Problems and Policy during the Puritan Revolution, 1640–1660* (1930), p. 236; F. J. Fisher, 'The influence and development of the industrial guilds in the larger provincial towns under James I and Charles I' (unpub. M.A. thesis, Univ. of London, 1931); or his 'Some experiments in company organisation in the early seventeenth century', *Econ. Hist. Rev.*, IV (1933). See also H. Hamilton, *The English Brass and Copper Industries to 1800* (1967), p. 322: 'in some cases apprenticeship was still in vogue in the eighteenth century'.

[12] In particular there has been too much concentration of the Twelve Great Livery Companies. As M. J. Walker argued, this: 'has furnished an eccentric view of guild experience. The Twelve were the very Companies deliberately sought out for their social cachet and the political influence of their freedom, and hence their economic role was likely to degenerate earlier and more quickly than that of smaller London Companies or provincial guilds ... The Livery Companies were more numerous (there were over eighty) and controlled a greater range of more specialised trades than the guilds of provincial towns ... the nation's burgeoning trade and expanding population were increasingly channelled through London ... Provincial guilds were exposed to less acute and large-scale pressures.' 'The Guild Control of Trades in England, c. 1660–1820' (paper circulated at Economic History Society Conference, Loughborough, April 1981), p. 4.

of views prevailing, and the consequent futility, at present, in trying to explain the decline in relation to wider economic and demographic changes. We know almost nothing about the regional diversity of decline – limited London evidence is currently generalised to cover the whole country. There is astonishingly little evidence to help us understand the extent to which industrial development grew directly out of, or within, the traditional terms of company control and apprenticeship codified by the Elizabethan Statute (and indeed practised long before then) – or, alternatively, the extent to which the collapse of such monopolistic restrictions was a necessary 'precondition' for the enormously significant changes of the eighteenth and early nineteenth centuries. This is the more surprising in view of the obvious political or pragmatic implications of this matter. Similarly, we know little on the changing nature of apprenticeship, as a system of industrial training, over the period from, say, 1650 to the present day. The later nineteenth-century interest in, and reformulation of, the system in many industries was and is dimly perceived as a revival of aspects of its old form. But the contrasting elements of practical continuity, or complete revival, are usually formulated in merely speculative terms. And, I need hardly add, our knowledge on the related issues of artisan unemployment, changes affecting real wages, artisan discontent and its causes and manifestations, or of changing class relations within the apprenticed trades is, on all these points, severely limited. It is not often the case that English social and economic historiography lags behind comparable developments in the United States, but in this field in particular such a conclusion is increasingly well founded, in view of the excellent recent studies of American artisan life and production since Bridenbaugh by authors such as Nash, Johnson, Rock, Steffen, and others.[13]

My discussion here will hardly go far to remedy this, but it can at least make clearer some of the major chronologies and components of

---

[13] I exclude here of course the recent work of I. T. Prothero, *Artisans and Politics in Early Nineteenth-Century London* (Folkestone, 1979); J. Rule, *The Experience of Labour in Eighteenth-Century Industry* (1981); C. R. Dobson, *Masters and Journeymen* (1980); or the research of M. J. Walker. On America, see: C. Bridenbaugh, *The Colonial Craftsman* (1950); R. F. Seybolt, *Apprenticeship and Apprenticeship Education in Colonial New England and New York* (New York, 1917); M. Jernegan, *Labouring and Dependent Classes in Colonial America, 1607–1783* (New York, 1931); J. L. Axtell, *The School Upon a Hill; Education and Society in Colonial New England* (New Haven, 1974); P. E. Johnson, *A Shopkeeper's Millennium: Society and Revivals in Rochester, New York* (New York, 1978); H. Rock, *The Independent Mechanic, 1800–1820* (New York, 1978); G. B. Nash, *The Urban Crucible* (Cambridge, Mass., 1979); C. G. Steffen, 'Baltimore Artisans, 1790–1820', *William and Mary Quarterly*, XXXVI (1979).

change affecting the apprenticeship system, and allow an explanation for them which can be more specific than has hitherto been possible. I will present quantitative evidence for the period 1700–1840 on the decline of apprenticeship, measured by the declining length of terms actually served, alongside evidence on the age at the start of apprenticeship; the age at completion; the growth of 'illegal' apprenticeships; and some changes in the seasonal distributions of artisan unemployment. My source will be mainly the details given by many hundreds of southern artisans in settlement examinations as to the lengths and conditions of apprenticeships they served. Apprenticeship, we recall, was a means of gaining a settlement under the 1691 Settlement Act, and hence was considered alongside the other 'heads' of settlement in settlement examinations upon chargeability.[14] To judge the legality of an apprenticeship (for an 'illegal' one did not confer settlement) its length, conditions, and other details were subjects of detailed enquiry throughout this period. This 'head' of settlement remained unchanged by the New Poor Law, but for the purposes of my discussion here I will only consider the period up to 1840.

It has been assumed by some historians that artisans rarely came within the terms of the settlement laws in practice, and we need initially to set the record straight on this. Most noticeably, E. J. Hobsbawm has written, largely following the misleading verdict of the Webbs, that

The Settlement Laws hardly incommoded the artisan. The Webbs state categorically that they came across no single case of an eighteenth-century trade unionist removed under them; and a large collection of certificates of settlement from Newark records no single mason, printer or brushmaker (though the latter had a tramp station in the town in the early nineteenth century), and only one hatter and currier over more than a century.[15]

It is not entirely clear whether we are discussing artisans (apprenticed workers) or 'trade unionists' in this regard; and the certificate system was only one (increasingly disused) aspect of the settlement laws. It is possible, for example, that it had a slightly different occupational emphasis than the category of those affected by examination and actual removal. While in some heavily agricultural parishes virtually all settlement cases were of agricultural workers, taking all parishes together one should generally expect about an eighth to a tenth of those examined as to settlement to have been apprenticed artisans,

---

[14] 3 Wm & Mary c. 11.
[15] E. J. Hobsbawm, 'The tramping artisan', in his *Labouring Men* (1964), p. 38.

claiming settlement on the basis of apprenticeship.[16] In rural market towns and urban parishes it could be much higher than this.[17] While artisan examinations in some parishes are sometimes too brief for our purposes, many give the lengths and dates of apprenticeship actually served. There is little reason to suppose that the apprenticeship terms of those so examined were atypical of the general artisan experience of apprenticeship in the south during this period. There was an enormous and surely exhaustive range of trades covered in the settlement records – from high status trades of merchants, jewellers or coachmakers, to the chimney sweeps, gun-flint makers, or fellmongers – more than are contained in Campbell's *London Trades-man* and Collyer's *Parents' Directory* combined.[18] The premiums paid were frequently recorded, and are representative of those in apprenticeship indentures, or of those stated by trade in Collyer's *Directory*.[19] In fact, the latter (commonly £5–15) seem rather low at times by comparison. Taking a sample from Suffolk for example, I calculate a mean premium paid by the family of origin of about £13 for a range of artisans examined as to settlement. While there was in this sample little deviation around the average, the premiums paid for those examined nevertheless could range from a couple of pounds to, in one case, over £400. They usually varied predictably enough by trade, and rose somewhat in the inflation of the Napoleonic Wars to fall thereafter.

Parish or charity apprenticeship premiums were commonly rather lower – £4 or £5 was normal – and in view of the usually earlier age at which these children began their relatively longer apprenticeships they are excluded from the calculations on the decline of apprenticeship terms about to be presented.[20] This is an easy exercise, as the details of such apprenticeships were given, because they raised less

---

[16] Printers, brushmakers, masons, hatters and curriers (the trades mentioned above by Hobsbawm) can all be found in settlement examinations – particularly the latter three trades, for which over a hundred examinations still exist in the south-east. For examples of all five trades see: Camb C.R.O., P 10/13/2–4; G/C/As. 4; G/C/As. 5; G/C/As. 7; Beds C.R.O., P 10/13/2–4; DDP 1/13/4/2; Herts C.R.O. D/P 15/13/1; D/P 15/13/3; West Suffolk C.R.O., N2/1/9; N2/1/8.

[17] I refer the reader, for example, to the readily accessible printed examinations for Mitcham, Surrey. B. Berryman (ed.), *Mitcham Settlement Examinations, 1784–1814* (Surrey Record Society, 1973).

[18] R. Campbell, *The London Tradesman* (1747); and J. Collyer, *The Parents' and Guardians' Directory* (1761).

[19] Collyer, *Parents' Directory*.

[20] I have also excluded female apprentices, and apprentices to agriculture. Girls were bound at the same age as boys, but the legislation allowed for more flexible ages at the end of their apprenticeships than for men. For discussion of female apprenticeship, see chapter 6.

legal problems than did apprenticeships derived from the family paying the premium. The legality of the latter would frequently depend on whether the indentures had been stamped – but pauper indentures did not require this. Hence the examining parish, concerned to discharge responsibility if possible, would enquire and state clearly if the apprenticeship had been a parish or a charity one.

Some artisans included here also came to be examined through illness, of themselves or in the family, or through old age, or as a feature of family-cycle related poverty determined by family size. There is no reason to suppose that their terms were atypical. Even though artisans who came to be chargeable were atypically poor upon examination, it would be difficult and unlikely to argue that this had been determined in some way by their experience of apprenticeship, such that long-term trends in their lengths of terms served were unrepresentative of aggregate changes commonly experienced by all artisans. In addition, we should note that the source has a decided advantage over apprenticeship indentures for the purpose of measuring the terms served. The latter record only the term for which the apprentice was bound – this could vary strikingly from the term actually served, which is recorded in the examination, and is the figure required to look at changes in actual practice.

Figure 5.1 shows how this changed between 1700 and 1840. It covers the south-eastern counties, including London. If one excludes the London artisans there is no change in the overall trend; but we should not take this as indicating that London was typical – its figures are too small for that conclusion. I have also included data for Gloucestershire separately, which I take as reasonably typical of western counties on the Welsh border – illustrative of their rather later, but then comparatively rapid, decline of apprenticeship. I have also plotted on this figure the two available real wage indices for artisans over the whole period: that provided by Tucker for London, and the Phelps-Brown and Hopkins building-craftsmen index for southern England.[21] Both are reworked as five year moving average real wage indices, using the price data provided alongside the wage data by each author. I shall return to these indices in due course to help explain the apprenticeship changes – for the present we need concentrate only on the changing lengths of terms actually served, provided in this figure.

[21] See R. S. Tucker, 'Real wages of artisans in London, 1729–1935', *Jnl of American Statistical Association*, XXXI (1936); E. H. Phelps-Brown & S. V. Hopkins, 'Seven centuries of the prices of consumables compared with builders' wage rates', *Economica*, XXIII (1956), also in E. M. Carus-Wilson (ed.), *Essays in Economic History*, vol. 2 (1955, 1962 edn).

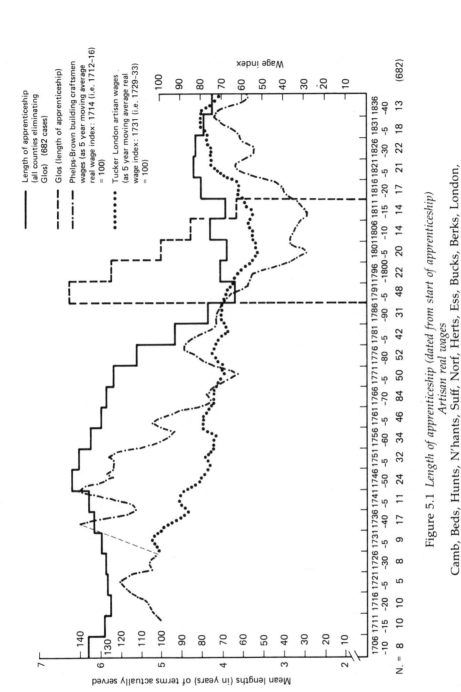

Figure 5.1 *Length of apprenticeship (dated from start of apprenticeship)*
Artisan real wages

Camb, Beds, Hunts, N'hants, Suff, Norf, Herts, Ess, Bucks, Berks, London,
Msx, Surr, Kent, Suss, Hants, Oxon (& Glos) (= 3 point moving average of
5 year means)

235

These are indeed rather striking. Until 1746–50 the older seven years appears still to be the norm – indeed there is some rise between 1716–20 and 1746–50, and we shall turn to other evidence on guild and company membership shortly to indicate that this can be supported from another unrelated source. But from 1750 there was a clear decline, continuing till 1791–5, when it was halted, and there was little change, or even a slight upturn from then until 1840 when the series ends. There was a fall between 1750 and 1795 from a mean length of six and a half years to under four years. In Gloucestershire, the fall came about forty years later, from 1790 to 1815, and was even more rapid and of greater magnitude. As with the decline of service, change in the south-east was most marked in the 1780s.[22] The 1814 repeal had little effect on the length of apprenticeships.[23] Figure 5.2 gives a partial breakdown of Figure 5.1. Data is included from Dorset and Devon here, and changes also shown separately for the counties of Norfolk, Suffolk, Surrey, and Bedfordshire. (Some of these counties have insufficient data to plot for the early nineteenth century.) Norfolk, Surrey, and Bedfordshire indicate considerable falls in the length of apprenticeship in the 1780s, and Suffolk seemingly a more long-term and gradual decline, which it shared with Dorset and Devon. The numbers are small, but there seems to be little regional divergence away from the overall pattern.

Was this shortening of apprenticeship the result of a later age of leaving home and start of apprenticeship, or the result of apprenticeship finishing at a younger age for the apprentice? Figure 5.3 (for those cases where there is exact evidence on this) suggests it was the latter: due to apprentices completing their apprenticeships at just under twenty years of age before 1780, and to their finishing at about seventeen years of age in the 1820s and 1830s. The change set in during the 1780s, and was reasonably continuous, with the 1780s and 1811–20 seeing greatest change.[24] To support these falling completion ages, the mean age of apprenticing stayed reasonably constant over time at fourteen years, although there was a gradual rise discernible between 1700–60 and 1835–60, from 14.0 to 14.7 years.[25]

[22] On the decline of farm service, see chapter 2.

[23] In minimising the economic significance of the 1814 repeal, I do not wish to underrepresent its political importance. Historians have paid most attention to the latter aspect.

[24] The standard deviations for these figures remain reasonably constant over time, with values between 2.2 and 3, and no trend noticeable.

[25] 4.8 per cent of apprentices left home at eleven years of age, 7.8 per cent at twelve, 17.5 per cent at thirteen, 32.2 per cent at fourteen, 12.8 per cent at fifteen, 11.8 per cent at sixteen, and 4.7 per cent at seventeen. (These figures do not include parish apprentices.) For further discussion of this, and change over time, see chapter 7.

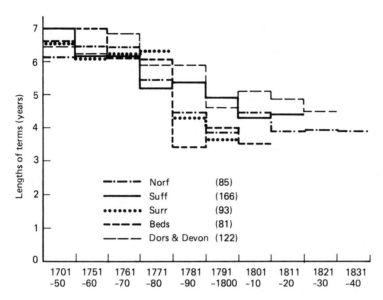

Figure 5.2 *Mean length of apprenticeship*
Norf, Suff, Surr, Beds, Dorset & Devon

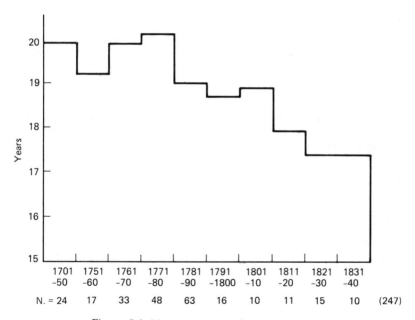

Figure 5.3 *Mean age at end of apprenticeship*
South-eastern counties

Before explaining these changes, it would be convenient to have supplementary support for them from another source. I am fortunate in this regard in having access to the research of Michael Walker, on the decline of guild and company control – measured by fluctuations in annual freeman membership from 1650 to the early nineteenth century.[26] This valuable information is available for major companies in the gildated towns of London, Oxford, Coventry, Exeter, Bristol, and Newcastle. It would be dangerous to generalise to an overall trend for these companies – the decline in Newcastle, for example, was very much later than in the other towns further south – but the general picture in the southern towns was one of expanding membership up to a peak about 1710–30. In outlining the decline thereafter, Walker suggested three chronologies according to the type of trade controlled by the guild. Distributive or 'entrepreneurial' trade guilds (mercers, drapers) went first, starting in 1690–1720. (For the most part, these fall outside the trades I am covering.) In contrast, 'the majority of "manufacturing" trade guilds (such as those of the tailors, cordwainers, smiths, whittawers and cappers) . . . appear to have experienced a much more abrupt loss of membership, and collapse in recruitment . . . notably in the late 1730's and 1740's'. Thirdly:

The guilds controlling 'service' and 'construction' or 'assembly' trades (such as the trades of barber-surgeon, porter, carman, housecarpenter, bricklayer and shipwright) in general declined according to a third pattern characterised by slowly-declining or sustained membership and binding of apprentices until the 1760's or 1770's, and in some cases even later, followed by a period of more rapid decline.

These latter two groupings cover the large majority of trades I am considering here. In some cases decline was halted around 1790, with a few companies even indicating some revival of membership from then, although the major collapse during the second half of the eighteenth century was one, of course, never to be reversed. The changes documented by Walker, using an entirely different method and source, coincide with those presented here. They tend to predate slightly the start of decline in Figure 5.1, and this is mainly owing to my data having rather greater emphasis on rural market-town artisans. Certain differences between the two environments are worth noting. In gildated towns, apprenticeship had given access not only to a trade, but also status within the urban community, which was often social and political to a degree which contrasted with the more purely economic status of the artisan serving a predominantly agri-

[26] Walker, 'Guild control of trades'.

cultural market. The decline in gildated towns, that is, had a political dimension which need not be explored here. Then again, the guild structure of larger towns allowed closer control, but pressures on the trades in terms of numbers, and the structure and determinants of demand, would be quite different. There might for example be closer control until guild breakdown, followed by a more dramatic collapse of apprenticeship regulation in manufacturing trades compared to a more rural context. And in the early eighteenth century it is probable that low prices and agricultural depression limited rural demand for the products of apprenticed labour, compared to the comparatively buoyant demand associated with rising real wages in larger gildated towns. Nevertheless, in the southern counties covered here, Walker's evidence provides almost certain reinforcement for the chronology of change being argued for. It is unlikely that the mutually supportive results on the south of these two methods will be much improved upon, and I believe we may take these as accurately representing the changes which occurred in the eighteenth and early nineteenth centuries, and as resolving the disparity of view hitherto apparent in the subject's historiography.[27]

There may be less agreement as to why decline took place, and I want now to present one general explanation. This will be a tentative exercise, not least because ideally we require further information on the pattern of change affecting individual trades, so as to narrow down explanations more specifically. I have shown the chronology of decline for the frequently encountered trades of shoemaker, carpenter, and tailor in Figure 5.4, which is broadly in agreement with Figure 5.1. But my explanation here necessarily will be generalised to cover the majority of southern manufacturing, service, construction, and assembly trades.

The period of agricultural depression between 1720–45 was one of demographic stagnation and low agricultural, industrial, and pro-

---

[27] Some debate may continue on the century after 1563. As noted above (n. 9), the earlier statutory length had been until the age of twenty-four (or for a minimum period of seven years), and this had changed to twenty-one between 1563 and the mid- or late seventeenth century. Apprenticeships for eight or nine years, for example, were apparently common in the carpenters' company in the sixteenth century. (See B. W. E. Alford & T. C. Barker, *A History of the Carpenters' Company* (1968), p. 30.) These earlier changes do not concern me here, but it may be that there was an earlier stage of decline, and that this has contributed to the muddled historiography. Further research on when a seven year term became the norm will help to pinpoint long-term causes of decline, and enable comparisons to be drawn with the more drastic changes of the eighteenth century. This may entail some emphasis being put on causes which owed much to similar demographic conditions in the two respective periods.

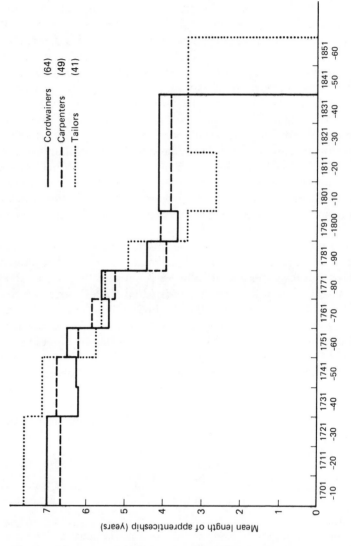

Figure 5.4 *Mean length of apprenticeship: cordwainers, tailors, and carpenters*
South-eastern counties

ducer prices. It saw a significant decline in the level of imports (between 1730–9 and 1740–9, from over £7 million per annum to £6.2 million). There were also falls in most available indices of home production during the period, judging from Deane and Cole's figures.[28] In fact the period has been diagnosed as one of 'deceleration', and on current, if sometimes rather imperfect, statistical evidence it seems unlikely that this period can be associated with a buoyant home market, and a rising demand for non-agricultural goods due to low food prices.[29] One would most expect to find such an effect in larger towns, where indeed it may have occurred. But few of the relevant indicators of the home market (whether of imports, prices, or home production) substantiate the view that this effect of early eighteenth-century low prices produced the emergence of a nationally significant home market. One is drawn to the contrary conclusion that the agricultural sector was the critical component of that market – this was after all still a society with a large predominance of agriculturally related occupations. The agricultural depression brought about by low prices probably caused an overriding depression of the home market itself. Similar arguments have been made by Deane and Cole, or more recently by A. J. Little, and this is not the place to rehearse them at length. When agricultural prices rose after about 1745, alongside rising producer prices, we see the effect of revived agricultural prosperity fuelled by population expansion: a significant home market was then emerging to which the rising real output figures after 1740 were a response.[30]

To meet that demand, still based particularly on the price determined fortunes of the agricultural sector, masters needed to increase output; and, with as yet only minor technological innovations in most of the apprenticed trades covered here, the way to achieve this was to increase their labour force at the cheapest possible rate. Apprentices were an obvious means to do this – a form of cheap and usually rapidly trained labour, held to the master's convenience by the stipulations of apprenticeship; labour which might frequently be expected to stay with the master after the term of training had expired.[31] But there were of course traditional controls in most trades (as laid down in 1563, for example) on the numbers or quotas of

[28] P. Deane & W. A. Cole, *British Economic Growth, 1688–1959* (Cambridge, 1969).
[29] A. J. Little, *Deceleration in the Eighteenth-Century British Economy* (1976).
[30] Deane & Cole, *British Economic Growth*, pp. 51–62, 75–82.
[31] Some newer trades of course took unapprenticed workmen under a foreman, rather than extra apprentices or journeymen. Examples of this include brewers, colour-makers, glue-makers, soap-boilers, vinegar makers, distillers, tobacconists and snuff-makers. My discussion here is concentrated on apprenticeship.

apprentices which could be taken by each master, in relation to the number of journeymen employed.[32] Such restrictions were inhibitive of labour supply, and gave journeymen considerable leeway in wage and other disputes. There was during the eighteenth century growing avoidance of these stipulations by masters, whose deployment of apprenticed labour was complained of by workmen and trade associations. Why, between about 1730 and 1760, did these restrictions first come to be avoided?

One clue to this lies in the slight predating of Figure 5.1 by the decline of guild and company control in gildated towns, which commenced during the low price period. There seems also to have been an expansion of apprenticeship numbers in major provincial towns during that period,[33] efforts to prosecute larger numbers of outsiders or unfree craftsmen, and a number of important court cases allowing an expansion of apprentices in certain trades.[34] Low food prices in the larger provincial towns may have permitted increased spending on other goods, as provided by the artisan sector. While this does not seem to have had an effect on the national market which compensated for the depression of demand from the agricultural sector, it is likely nevertheless that low prices underlay decisions to raise productivity by taking more apprentices in gildated towns. A. H. John's arguments for this effect of low prices on demand always seemed most attractive in such an urban context.[35] The Phelps-Brown and Hopkins building craftsmen's real wages rose between about 1710 and 1745 – perhaps indicating demand for such artisan labour, demand which may even have allowed some artisans themselves initially to be less resistant to the expansion of apprenticeships being undertaken by masters. This seems most consistent with the decline of many companies in such towns from about 1730. Similarly, the decline in lengths served by rural and smaller market-town apprentices after about 1750 (Figure 5.1) suggests an analogous relationship obtaining there: the revival of agricultural prosperity and demand from mid-century producing attempts to increase production, again

---

[32] See for example Alford & Barker, *Carpenters' Company*, pp. 70, 75, 117. And see n. 37, below.   [33] I am grateful to M. J. Walker for this point.

[34] For examples, see M. D. George, *London Life in the Eighteenth Century* (1965), p. 233 (framework knitters), p. 234 (silk-stocking weaving), p. 182 (weavers), p. 197 (shoemakers); Dobson, *Masters and Journeymen*, p. 49 (wheelwrights); D. Levine, *Family Formation in an Age of Nascent Capitalism* (1977), pp. 20–2 (hosiers).

[35] A. H. John, 'Agricultural productivity and economic growth in England, 1700–1760', *Jnl of Econ. Hist.*, XXV (1965), reprinted in E. L. Jones (ed.), *Agriculture and Economic Growth in England, 1650–1815* (1967), pp. 172–89 (see also his postscript there, pp. 189–93); and his 'Aspects of English economic growth in the first half of the eighteenth century', *Economica*, XXVIII (1961).

by taking more apprentices. The slight differences in chronology of decline between gildated towns and a more rural context was in this way a feature of the phases, and rural and urban-specific effects, of movement in agricultural prices – explaining why gildated towns (their demand boosted by low prices) should generally experience decline from a slightly earlier point, with the same expansion of the artisan labour force via the breaking of traditional apprenticeship quotas.[36]

The change away from quota controls over apprentices became more marked after 1750. Rising producer and consumer-good prices underlay this, a witness to the demand caused by resurgent agricultural profitability and rising population. The effect on journeymen became more pronounced. The use of apprentices as cheap labour, conferring on them the right to practise the trade as a journeyman or master in due course, was widely opposed by journeymen and small masters as having the effect of intensifying unemployment and reducing real wages.[37] We can test this against available wage data

[36] An alternative argument would be that low prices were initially responsible for an expansion of apprenticeship numbers, because they led to over-production as an attempt to compensate for the effects of stagnant demand and low producer prices. Such an argument is not consistent with the chronology of decline documented in Figure 5.1. Its role in the decline in gildated towns would depend partly on the extent to which demand for urban artisans' products was indigenous to the town, or rural-based. Similar arguments have been made on the effects of low prices in agriculture. See for example, E. L. Jones, 'Agriculture and economic growth in England, 1660–1750; agricultural change', *Jnl of Econ. Hist.*, XXV (1965); or for the early nineteenth century, D. B. Grigg, *The Agricultural Revolution in South Lincolnshire* (Cambridge, 1966).

[37] For example, see Levine, *Family Formation*, pp. 20–2, on hosiers taking more apprentices after the Fellows and Cartwright case of 1730, and the effect of this in lowering production costs, dispensing with many journeymen, and hitting adult wages. What had once been a journeyman's trade became one in which apprenticeships were not served, or with labour provided by collective indentures of apprenticeship, *ibid.*, pp. 51–2, 76. On the breaking of apprenticeship quotas, see also S.C. on Artisans and Machinery, V (1824), pp. 86, 136, 153; R. A. Leeson, *Travelling Brothers* (1979), pp. 81–5; G. Howell, 'Trades unions, apprentices and technical education', *Contemporary Review*, XXX (1877), 851ff; Dunlop & Denman, *English Apprenticeship*, pp. 226–31; W. J. Shelton, *English Hunger and Industrial Disorders* (1973), pp. 184–7; Unwin, *Industrial Organization*, pp. 117, 197–200; Prothero, *Artisans and Politics*, p. 51; George, *London Life*, chs. 4 and 5. On the London Court of Aldermen's decision to allow masters to engage additional wheelwright apprentices, see Dobson, *Masters and Journeymen*, p. 49. See also E. Howe & H. E. Waite, *The London Society of Compositors* (1948), pp. 20–1, 66–84, 99, 105, 108, 178; S. Thrupp, *A Short History of the Worshipful Company of Bakers of London* (1933), pp. 107–8; H. Stewart, *History of the Worshipful Company of Gold and Silver Wyre-drawers, and of the Origin and Development of the Industry which the Company represents* (1891), pp. 70, 90, 91–2, 97. Such changes are well documented in America. See in particular Steffen, 'Baltimore artisans', 111–16: on the growing numbers of apprentices as a proportion of the work force in separate trades, and accompanying rises in the proportion of propertyless artisans.

and other indications of the artisan's standard of living, so as to make clearer the explanation. For there could be two opposing views here. On the one hand (and let us call this the 'optimist' argument), it could be held that the declining lengths of terms actually served were indicative of expanding demand for journeymen, inducing masters and apprentices to terminate their agreements prematurely, in a context of increasingly regular and well-paid employment among journeymen. One thinks of parallels with early colonial America or Australia.[38] It could be argued to similar effect that economic growth enabled journeymen more readily to set up in the trades as masters – another inducement to curtail their apprenticeships when they became adequately trained, rather than serving their full term. The declining length of terms served would, on the basis of this argument, be taken as indicative of rising living standards in the artisan sector – a benevolent feature of the economic growth of the period.

On the other hand, a contrary and more pessimistic picture could be drawn, stressing precariousness of employment and falling artisan real wages consequent upon the expansion of apprenticeship numbers by masters. The shortening terms could be seen as a manifestation of the awareness of apprentices of their increasingly bleak prospects for setting up in the trades as masters in their own right, and of their poor employment prospects and wages upon completion of their terms. This made the continued drudgery of the apprenticeship, with its multiple restrictions, seem unwarranted when so many journeymen were practising the trade without having served their proper time, ignoring the Elizabethan Statute. Such an argument might stress the growing friction within the apprenticeship system, the growth of 'class' antagonism over any form of 'interest' alignment by occupation, in response to these changes, and in opposition to the policies of masters bent on expanding production through the cheapest possible utilisation of labour.

If the 'optimist' picture of this process were to be substantiated, we would certainly expect it to bear fruit in the form of rising artisan real wages, and indications of fuller employment. Let us first consider wages. The available artisan wage indices were plotted in Figure 5.1. I have not included Gilboy's figures as they stretch no further than the 1790s, but the material supplied by Phelps-Brown and Hopkins, and

---

[38] See for example Axtell, *School Upon a Hill*, p. 120. Scarcity of goods and services led masters not to fear competition from their apprentices, who set up early. For a later period too, see 'Extracts of letters from poor persons who emigrated last year to Canada and the United States', *Quarterly Review*, XLVI (1832), 366–7: on the contrasting position of artisans in Wiltshire and North America or Canada.

Tucker, covers the southern areas dealt with here, and the period for the decline of apprenticeship. I have chosen to present this data as an unweighted five year moving average real wage index, utilising the price data supplied by these authors, and indexing from 1712–16 in the case of the southern building craftsmen, and 1729–33 in the case of the London artisan wages, which is when the series starts. As will be seen from Figure 5.1, this allows us to compare their relative movements, insofar as they are both effectively indexed from 1731. The constancy of the Tucker money wages raises few problems in the choice of an indexing point. The fluctuations of the Phelps-Brown and Hopkins data makes the choice of this more crucial. I have chosen a mid point between extreme possibilities in this regard: one could create an impression of less extensive real wage reductions by indexing from an earlier point, or an impression of even greater real wage falls by indexing from say, 1737, or 1745. Whatever the choice of index point, however, there can be little dissension from the overall picture supplied in Figure 5.1. Artisan real wages, to judge from these indices, were gradually but persistently falling from the 1730s in London, and rapidly from about 1750 for southern building artisans.[39] They continued to fall until about 1802–7, and then there was seemingly some revival as prices fell after the war.[40] The correspondence between these falling real wages and the declining lengths of terms served is notable, particularly for the Phelps-Brown index on southern artisans outside as well as inside London. This wage index is more closely suited to my data, covering as it does artisans in provincial and agricultural market towns, as well as inside London. In both cases real wages fell slightly before the shortening lengths actually served by apprentices. In other words, there is ground here to suggest that it was partly an appreciation of such deteriorating prospects as journeymen which led the apprentices increasingly not to complete their full terms.

If there is evidence from wage data to support an explanation for the decline of apprenticeship in these pessimistic terms, what can be said to supplement this on changes affecting artisan employment? If such employment became increasingly precarious, as seems suggested by the wage data, there could be additional reasons to suppose that the premature ending of apprenticeships was an indication of

---

[39] There were apparently a growing number of wage disputes from the 1760s, as prices rose and real wages fell. 'Claims for wage increases to offset rising prices were almost universal from the 1760's onwards': Dobson, *Masters and Journeymen*, p. 27; Shelton, *English Hunger*, pp. 199–201.

[40] The combination laws were widely held to have further reduced wages. See for example the S.C. on Artisans and Machinery, V (1824), pp. 132, 144, 263.

apprentices' awareness of this, and realisation that there was little point in completing the full seven years to which, *pro forma*, they had been apprenticed. Just as for agriculture, historians have commonly regarded changes in any aspect of artisan unemployment as inaccessible to research. 'The impact of structural unemployment cannot be measured', wrote E. J. Hobsbawm. 'Those who were most affected by it were often precisely those independent small craftsmen, outworkers or part-time workers whose sufferings, short of absolute catastrophe, were reflected in falling piece-prices, in under-employment, rather than cessation of work.'[41] Fortunately, it is possible to supplement the available wage data with material on changes in artisan seasonal distributions of unemployment, to consider this hitherto elusive aspect of the question. The source for this is the settlement examinations used elsewhere for changes in agricultural seasonal distributions of unemployment, and the method the same as used there.[42] As stated when outlining the use of this source to look at the decline of apprenticeship, there is little reason for the seasonal distributions of examined artisans to be atypical in any way. Such distributions closely match what is known from the work of Ashton and others on the specific nature of unemployment in different trades.[43] Figures 5.5, 5.6, and 5.7 give the changing seasonal distributions of unemployment during the year for the building trades (to supplement the Phelps-Brown and Hopkins wage data), for shoemakers, and for tailors. I have split the material up before and after 1790, and not included data from after 1850.[44] In these figures, there is a clear tendency for the distributions to become more acute after 1790 than they had been before. The magnitude of change is

---

[41] E. J. Hobsbawm, 'The British standard of living, 1790–1850', in his *Labouring Men* (1964), p. 73.

[42] See chapter 1. Removal orders also sometimes give occupations. The order was intended to follow the examination by two weeks, but was often drawn up (and even sent) on the same day. Using a three month moving average as here, this difference becomes insignificant, and so some evidence from artisan removals is included here for seasonal distributions of unemployment. Its inclusion does not alter the patterns presented, and usefully supplements them. No cases of removal for which the examination survives are included.

[43] T. S. Ashton, *Economic Fluctuations in England, 1700–1800* (Oxford, 1959). I will discuss elsewhere in greater detail specific artisan and cottage industrial seasonal distributions of unemployment, and their relation to regional agricultural unemployment and demand, or to factors such as the seasonality of prices, marriage, bankruptcy, tramping, vagrancy, wages, and unrest.

[44] 1790 has been chosen as a mid point dividing the available data. Ideally, one would prefer a dividing point from about 1780 or even earlier, as the period before 1790 catches some of the effects of the decline of apprenticeship. The contrasts before and after an earlier point seem more acute, and are slightly lessened by choosing 1790. Nevertheless, in the interests of greater statistical security, 1790 can suffice here.

about the same in all cases. (Taking all trades together, and considering them in the same way, there was a similar intensification of seasonal unemployment distributions, comparable to that affecting the building trades. But the large numbers of trades involved make this a much less useful indicator than can be derived from specific

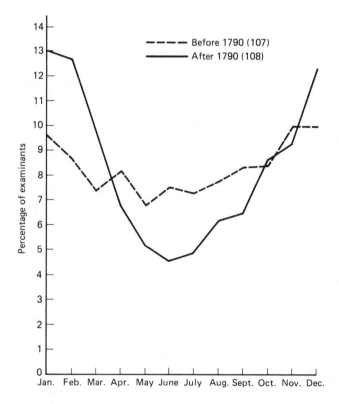

Figure 5.5 *Building trades' seasonal distribution of unemployment, before and after 1790*
Eastern, south-western & Midland counties

trades with adequate documentation, or for certain categories of artisans.) I shall not enter into a detailed trade-specific explanation of these patterns here. While they become more acute after 1790, they all retain their same original character. These changes were surely symptomatic of the increasingly precarious employment facing the artisan during this period, which was both a consequence and further cause of the decline of apprenticeship.[45]

There is indeed much evidence suggesting intensified unemployment in the trades during this period. As Hobsbawm implied in his

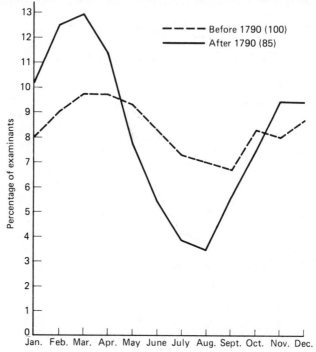

Figure 5.6 *Cordwainers' seasonal distribution of unemployment, before and after 1790*
Eastern, south-western & Midland counties

[45] The 1824 S.C. on Artisans and Machinery is replete with further evidence supporting these figures. Hatters in London retained considerable control over apprenticeship compared with other trades (V, p. 99). Nevertheless, journeymen hatters in London were 'not employed more than about five months in the year ... in the country it is precisely the same'. 'Was the employment of the men formerly more steady than it is now?' – 'Much more so; it was rare to see a man, if he was anything of a workman, out of employ, *and now they are out of employ by scores, in the winter season* ... The masters [were] more anxious twenty years ago, to keep the same man steadily at work ... there are more in the trade than there were at that time' (my italics), p. 154. For growing unemployment among shoemakers and framework knitters, see *ibid.* pp. 147, 263–4. For the seasonal nature of unemployment affecting journeymen tailors, see Campbell, *London Tradesman*, p. 193. Settlement examinations can also be used to explore the interrelation of artisan yearly unemployment with agricultural prices over time, so as to specify more clearly how agricultural demand, as determined by prices, affected artisan employment in different contexts. I will discuss this elsewhere.

article on the tramping artisan, the tramping system expanded considerably in the later eighteenth century because of problems of unemployment, and in its aim to provide employment elsewhere was one attempted remedy for them.[46] More recently, Leeson has written

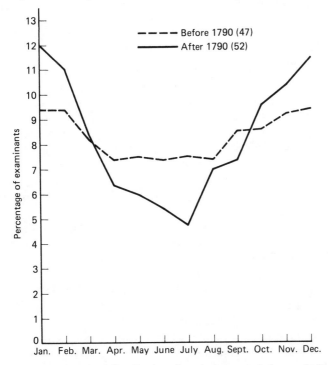

Figure 5.7 *Tailors' seasonal distribution of unemployment, before and after 1790*
Eastern, south-western & Midland counties

in support of this, noting in part the long existence of forms of 'tramping' in an earlier period, but also associating its growth from the late eighteenth century with an intensification of unemployment.[47] 'Tramping' was at its peak in the early nineteenth century, and in the 1840s. The essential reason for the defence by journeymen, trade societies, and by the early unions of the apprenticeship system and associated restrictions lay in this concern to safeguard employment; it was a concern which always lurked behind statements to the 1812–13 Select Committee on Apprenticeship. Another factor held to aggravate the problem of artisan unemployment was

[46] Hobsbawm, 'Tramping artisan'.   [47] Leeson, *Travelling Brothers.*

the practice of 'king's freemen', as established from the late seventeenth century: that is, allowing ex-soldiers and sailors (and their families, after 1784) to set up in trades without having served a legal apprenticeship.[48] There was in any case always considerable, usually short-term, unemployment after demobilisation, as in 1763–4, 1784, or 1814–15, accentuated by the unemployment faced by workers directly connected with the war effort, and dependent on government contracts. Such workers included those involved in munitions, or ship-builders, or those connected with hardware, coal-mining, or textiles and the cloth trade. In many parishes poor families were also allowed to practise trades without having served an apprenticeship, so as to keep relief expenditure down, as for example in Kingston-on-Thames.[49] This was probably common during or immediately after a period of demobilisation. Certainly, it was also true that such a practice became more prevalent in the later eighteenth century, with its rising poor rates, and with growing sentiment among employers and in the courts against the traditional restrictions imposed by apprenticeship.

One can recall too the effect on employment of the slump of trade exports in the twenty years after the late 1760s, due mainly to the American hostilities. It has been suggested by one historian, in view of the widespread artisan unrest at the time, that such trade figures seem a likely if crude indicator of fluctuations in the intensity of unemployment at home during the later eighteenth century, particularly during the later 1760s and thereafter into the 1780s.[50] Little has been written on this period of depression, and we might quote Shelton's useful discussion of artisan unemployment during it:

Unemployment and underemployment were the visible effects of declining trade after 1764 ... Stocks piled up, and manufacturers laid off large numbers of workers, at a time when the prices of provisions were high ... Trade figures do not show conclusively whether there was an internal depression or not in the 1760's, but they do reveal a significant reduction in exports and suggest reasons for the widespread unemployment in certain regions of the country reported in the press. One may reasonably conclude with Professor T. S. Ashton that the years 1765–70 were years of depression, and that they were the beginning of a twenty-year period when overseas trade declined greatly. Ashton has explained the two decades of depression in terms of the economic conflict with America, the economic malaise of Germany, disorders

---

[48] On this practice, see for example Shelton, *English Hunger*, pp. 138, 185. And see 12 Car II c. 16; 22 Geo II c. 44; 24 Geo III c. 6.

[49] A. Daly (ed.), *Kingston Upon Thames Register of Apprentices, 1563–1713* (Guildford, 1974), p. x.

[50] Shelton, *English Hunger*, pp. 145–6. For the effect on framework knitters, see Levine, *Family Formation*, pp. 20–2.

in India, war with France and Spain and a reduction in shipments on the government account. The American difficulties of the 1760's were part of a wider realignment of trade in the eighteenth century, the effect of which was to distress considerable segments of the industrial population and encourage them to riot in times of severely fluctuating prices such as 1766.[51]

Shelton went on to demonstrate how these difficulties affected the artisan and other workers during this period. As George Rudé also argued, rioting among artisans increasingly became directed against employers, with insistence on raising wages, improving conditions, and controlling competition for employment, usually through demands for government intervention.[52] This was true, for example, in the various trade disputes conducted by the tailors, coal-heavers, sawyers, glass-grinders, hatters, or sailors. The trades discussed by Shelton witnessed similar and widespread circumvention of the apprenticeship system, as was the case in the seafaring industry:

Ships carried more apprentices than was customary, as a means of reducing the complement of more expensive, trained seamen, carpenters and other trades. The length of apprenticeships was also reduced by many owners. Men who had not completed a full seven years' apprenticeship frequently served as able seamen or tradesmen at sea ... The practice of carrying an excessive number of apprentices in allied occupations such as lightermen and watermen, because it denied them possible employment, was to the disadvantage of displaced merchant seamen too. The increased use of apprentices during periods of general depression was not solely due to the desire of owners to exploit cheap surplus labour to reduce costs. It also derived from the practice of apprenticing parish dependents, who increased during periods of economic difficulty. Certainly abuses of the apprenticeship system increased during the 1760's, and their correction figured large in the demands of the seamen during their great strike in May 1768.[53]

Parish apprentices could be imposed upon employers under the poor law, who might pay a fine to avoid this, which would be used to enhance the premium offered with the apprentice to the next prospective master or mistress.[54] Such parochially enforced labour supply was not common, but probably grew in the later eighteenth century, judging from complaints against it. The dual practice under Elizabethan statute of apprenticeship restriction and care for parish children had now become worryingly incompatible. Some small masters became more dependent on such parish apprenticed labour,

---

[51] Shelton, *English Hunger*, pp. 141, 145–6.
[52] G. Rudé, 'Wilkes and liberty, 1768–9', in his *Paris and London in the Eighteenth Century* (1974), pp. 263–6.
[53] Shelton, *English Hunger*, pp. 186–7.
[54] See for example, H. Fearn, 'The apprenticeship of pauper children in the incorporated hundreds of Suffolk', *Proc. Suffolk Inst. of Archaeology*, XXVI (1955). Or see 8 and 9 Will III c. 30; 20 Geo III c. 36; 32 Geo III c. 57; 7 & 8 Vic c. 101.

as did many 'masters' working in a putting-out system as outworkers of some sort. We may assume that the trained artisan suffered greater unemployment through such employing motivations of employers, legitimated in this case, as it frequently could be, by 'charity' towards the local pauper children. 'The age-old concern over apprenticeship', wrote Prothero, by way of commencing his discussion of the unsuccessful campaign to enforce apprenticeship in the early nineteenth century, 'had long been heightened by opposition among journeymen and many small masters to the larger employers who were expanding their businesses and labour force and found apprenticeship regulations hampered this, and who cut costs by taking numbers of boys and cheap labour, thereby widening the labour supply.'[55] His own discussion stressed this concern at the threat to employment posed by the introduction of cheap labour and additional apprentices, further supporting the views advanced here that unemployment, of various forms, intensified in the later eighteenth-century skilled trades.

There are reasonable grounds, in short, for believing that the declining lengths of apprenticeship terms owed much to an appreciation among apprentices of the adverse changes described here. We can include among the latter mention of how the terms of trade between the apprenticed and agricultural sectors moved against the artisan after about 1750, and sharply so from the 1770s.[56] This was in contrast to the strong position he had held in the earlier eighteenth century, particularly between 1715 and 1750. But the major factor was the desire of larger masters to increase production via more apprenticed labour, which probably initiated a mutually reinforcing pattern of change: with the consequent effects of over-production and unemployment, falling real wages, hindered social mobility to the status of master, and growing class divergence in the trades informing the attitudes of the swelling numbers of apprentices themselves. The latter were inclined to throw off the discipline of the master or mistress as soon as they felt adequate to the particular skills of the trade, knowing that their employment prospects would suffer little in so doing.

What were the consequences of these changes for the relationship

---

[55] Prothero, *Artisans and Politics*, p. 51. And on the employing of 'foreigners' by masters in London (men from outside the city), rather than freemen (in the trades of painters, carpenters, masons, printers, joiners, plasterers, cabinet makers, blacksmiths, or wheelwrights), see Dobson, *Masters and Journeymen*, pp. 48–56. On the legal easing of apprenticeship restrictions after 1760 in London for master curriers, or gold and silver wire-drawers, see *ibid.*, pp. 56–9.
[56] Deane & Cole, *British Economic Growth*, p. 91.

of apprenticeship, between master and apprentice? As the exclusiveness of the guilds and the value of apprenticeship declined, and as it
became more a contractual and economic relationship strictly to learn
the trade, rather than one of 'subsumption' and familial control, so
there is considerable evidence that apprenticeship relations deteriorated. Any attempt to quantify this is necessarily problematic, if not
rather crude, considering the subjective nature of this aspect of
apprenticeship. But Figure 5.8 will provide initial support for this

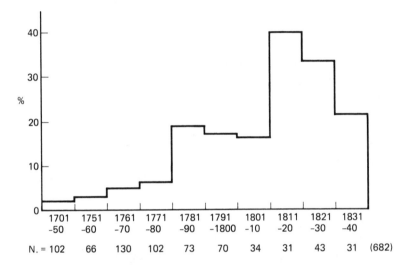

Figure 5.8 *Percentage of apprenticeships which were illegal, or ended by either master
or apprentice running away*
South-eastern counties

contention. It shows the percentage of apprenticeships which were
not legal under the settlement laws (which did not confer a settlement, that is), and those which ended through quarrels, or through
the master or apprentice running away, and which also left the
apprentice without any future claim on the parish. These two features
contained in the figure are almost inseparable. There could for
instance be a failure to gain a settlement through the master's refusal
to give up the indentures, but no account given in the examination of
any quarrel. In such cases it is almost certain that the action of the
master was resented by the apprentice. Or an irregular form of
agreement (and these could take many forms), over which the master
had more control than the apprentice, could nullify the apprenticeship's legality, perhaps to avoid settlements being gained in the

master's parish. Here again, considering the desire of the poor to gain their own settlements, master–apprentice relations may have been very similar to those which we know terminated by quarrels. A few apprenticeships ended with the master running away from the apprentice, contrary to the usual pattern, and while bankruptcy, local debts, or familial desertion could contribute to this, these have also been included in the figure.

It shows a clear rise of illegal or quarrelsome apprenticeships, and once again the 1780s and 1811–20 were the main periods of change. It is also significant that Figure 5.3 (of the age at end of apprenticeship), is in inverse correlation with Figure 5.8, and that this is particularly true for these two periods. The falling percentages of Figure 5.8 after 1820 are also of interest, when related to Figure 5.1, which showed a stabilising of the length of apprenticeship during the same period. It may be that by the 1820s there had been a mutual redefinition of the meaning of an apprenticeship, and agreement by masters that it was now a relatively short-term contractual agreement to learn the trade, and not a period of further socialisation and familial discipline for a particular artisanal elite. This was an agreement or concession which apprentices probably would have preferred forty years earlier. It would after all have been a recognition of the changing economic circumstances facing them between 1780 and 1820, in particular the unemployment and falling real wages contingent upon glutting of the trades.[57]

The key to Figure 5.8, or to the changing relations of apprenticeship, lies in the contradictory and antagonistic views of master and apprentice. Masters maintained perceptions on the nature of apprenticeship felt to be unwarranted by an apprentice faced with problems unique to the period after 1780. The decline of guild regulation, which had previously helped defend the apprentice from ill-treatment, made his situation even more difficult. Consider, for example, the contradictory accounts given by Benjamin Dixon (apprenticed as a tailor in 1804 in South Luffenham, Rutlandshire), and his master, of how his apprenticeship ended.[58] Dixon's account went as follows: sixteen weeks before his time, 'work being very slack ... his master said to him – "if you think you can get work anywhere you are welcome to go and I will give you up your time"'. But his

---

[57] One should stress how these changes render dubious any attempts to assess changes in the 'standard of living' by looking at 'occupational shifts' – i.e., changes in the proportion of the population in certain occupational categories. The economic and status significance of being (for example) a cordwainer, cabinet maker, weaver or whatever in 1840 had become quite different to being one in 1700.

[58] Hunts C.R.O., 136/3/7 (1831–54: Vagrancy).

master claimed 'that in consequence of the misconduct of this pauper he turned him out of the house, and told him to go and shift for himself, as he should not reside in his house'. This 'misconduct' of Dixon's may have been related to his awareness of the unemployment awaiting him. (He became a soldier shortly afterwards.) But we are less concerned to assess the truth of each story, as to see how these accounts illuminate the perception of apprentice and master. For the apprentice lack of work had made his continuing apprenticeship seem futile. He had already served six years. From the master we have no reference to, or denial of, 'work being very slack'. Rather there is the view that 'misconduct', however motivated, is intolerable, and justifies the drastic measure of turning an apprentice who had already served six years out of the house, and so making the apprenticeship illegal. In an earlier period, after all, this would have consigned the apprentice to a life of unskilled day labour.

This example epitomises the problem facing the apprentice: of a master clinging to, and insisting on, old norms of behaviour in a new context where they were felt to be unjustified. The new context was that of a growing precariousness of employment and trades glutted with journeymen, of falling real wages, of the tramping system. We recall also that masters were increasingly producing for a foreign market (in which traditions of craft production were often thought irrelevant); they were making rather different demands on their labour force, were antagonistic to restraints on its expansion, and adopting different commercial ethics.[59] Accordingly, their men became more liable to unemployment determined by fluctuations in foreign trade, and to low wages necessitated by the need for cheap products. The situation deteriorated further after the Napoleonic Wars, and we might cite Prothero's authoritative study of John Gast and the London artisans on this:

There is evidence that in many London trades earnings declined in the post-war period and much of the 1820's ... the fall in prices benefiting the poorer rather than the mechanics experiencing a loss of work ... [An] argument in favour of a rise in real wages after the war does not hold good for the skilled artisans, as it rests on setting a fall in prices against day-rate wages. In many industries piece-work was general, and day-rates take no account of unemployment. We know that after the war the day-rates of shipwrights and tailors remained the same, and those of shoemakers were cut a little; on this line of argument they all became better off. But in all three cases there is unambiguous evidence of a decline in *earnings*, due to unemployment. The calculations of real wages are only valid if the incidence

---

[59] See for example Prothero, *Artisans and Politics*, p. 57; Dunlop & Denman, *English Apprenticeship*, p. 236.

of unemployment stayed constant. But there is evidence that it did worsen, and indeed this is to be expected given the end of the war demand and the demobilisation of 400,000 men (three quarters of them returned to civilian life when the depression was most severe, between mid-1815 and the end of 1816) . . . 'Why should we suppose, in a period of very rapid population-growth, that the proportion of employed and skilled to casual and unemployed workers should move in favour of the former?' In many artisan trades, whatever the situation for the population generally, the development was towards a 'surplus of labour' [his italics].[60]

These remarks were made on London. But Prothero at one point suggested an even worse situation in the country, and in this he was surely correct.[61] For the depression of the agricultural sector after the war, associated in some regions, like Dorset, with the movement into the trades of many declining small farmers, further aggravated the matter.[62] Village and market-town artisans dependent on demand from the poor were especially hit, and the change to the New Poor Law accentuated trends in poor relief policy which undercut a traditional source of artisan income during hard times.[63] The road and railway building boom, and the developments in cottage building after about 1850, were as yet a long way off.

The apprenticeship system changed under these conditions to a more short-term and strictly contractual means to train skilled workers, and something further can be said on how these changes may have affected class relations within the trades, and the role of the family. The nature of the old apprenticeship system is well known, with its elaborate stipulations contained in the indenture, insisting on obedience to the master or mistress, and abstinence from drink, fornication, and other interesting diversions. Apprentices commonly 'lived-in' with the master or mistress (just as did a farm-servant), and in earlier indentures the terms 'apprenticeship' and 'service' were often used together, or interchangeably, indicating the similarity of the two.[64] The apprentice was often bound to the husband and wife – an acknowledgement of the latter's role in family-economy production.[65] The master was commonly expected to provide clothes, food, tools, and so on, for the apprentice, and arrangements were

---

[60] Prothero, *Artisans and Politics*, pp. 66–7.   [61] *Ibid.*, pp. 64–5.

[62] B. Kerr, *Bound to the Soil: A Social History of Dorset, 1750–1918* (1968), pp. 132–3. This can also be documented by occupational histories in settlement examinations.

[63] *Ibid.*, p. 135. For complaints that the 1834 poor law changes adversely affected many artisans dependent on local labouring spending (i.e., of money given as out-relief), see *Morning Chronicle*, 15 Jan 1850; Rev. F. H. Maberley, *To the Poor and Their Friends* (1836), p. 34. On the effect of the New Poor Law in reducing familial income, see chapter 3.

[64] M. K. Dale, 'London silkwomen of the fifteenth century', *Econ. Hist. Rev.*, IV (1932–4), 326.   [65] See chapter 6.

frequently made for the apprentice to receive such items upon the completion of the term to help him set up in the trade independently, at least as a journeyman. Company dues, or entry fines, were often to be paid by the master at the end of the seven year term. But with the erosion of that seven year term, other aspects of apprenticeship changed, and one can see this in details in the examinations, and in the frustrated attempts of poor law authorities to reconcile it with their own outmoded definition of a 'legal' apprenticeship, conferring settlement. The stamping of indentures, for example, had become increasingly neglected from the mid-eighteenth century, with the returns to the Board of Inland Revenue becoming incomplete. R. Garroway Rice argued that most indentures from then were not being sent to the head office for stamping, supporting the chronology of decline documented in Figure 5.1.[66]

Alongside the failure to serve the full seven years stipulated, the other most significant change was the growth in the later eighteenth century of 'clubbing-out' apprenticeships. These would often involve the apprentice living with his family, or boarding, and moving to work or training with the master during the day, much as a journeyman.[67] The arrangement was similar in many respects to the living-out forms of farm service which developed in the same period (and I am speaking here mainly of the years after about 1780). While the term for farm-servants was still usually a yearly one, it could also often be for six or nine months, or for a few days shorter than the full year to avoid settlement. Similarly, for the apprentice the prearranged term was still commonly seven years, but it was increasingly arranged for a shorter time; and in particular there was a growing divorce between the *pro forma* indenture stipulation of seven years and the term eventually served. Just as with farm service, it is possible that one motive behind the changing apprenticeship stipulations embodied in the 'clubbing-out' system was that of avoiding settlement, although for a number of reasons one should not attach excessive importance to this. (It was mainly a consideration in certain parishes where means were found to penalise a master who conferred settlements in this way. And apprenticeship and settlement

[66] R. G. Rice (ed.), 'Sussex apprentices and their masters, 1710–1752', *Sussex Record Society*, XXVIII (1924), xxv. This revenue duty on indentures had given the state a vested interest in preserving apprenticeship. See T. S. Ashton, *An Economic History of England: The Eighteenth Century* (1955), p. 224.

[67] This development can be found in many market-town collections of settlement examinations, covering *c*. 1750–1840. For further examples, see M. B. Rowlands, *Masters and Men in the West Midland Metalware Trades before the Industrial Revolution* (Manchester, 1975), p. 157; George, *London Life*, pp. 234, 262–9, 382–4.

legislation in 1758 tried to ensure that the apprentice would at least be irremovable in parishes where, and however, he was bound, after forty days of the term, although it is my impression that this act was frequently ignored.)[68] Such 'clubbing-out' apprenticeships would be called into doubt in later settlement cases adjudging the legality of settlement so gained. As such training came to be entered into for shorter terms, so also wages were now often to be paid during the actual terms, indicating the use to which the apprentice was being put. Such conditions, agreed to in the indentures, would very rarely have been found in an earlier or purer form of the Elizabethan system. These wages were arranged in advance and gradated with age: one guinea for the first year, two for the second, and so on, for example. Where the apprentice lived with the parents or an uncle (this was the relative most commonly mentioned besides the parents), board wages were not usually paid by the master – in other cases they could frequently be payable, although they were at times patently inadequate given prevailing rents. In some cases apprentices were married during their terms under this form of training, and once again, in the history of the apprenticeship system, this was quite unprecedented, if still rare.

In all these cases (and there could be much variety of practice) one is struck by the unaccustomed importance now being attached to the family of origin, in providing for the apprentice over a longer period than hitherto. Under the Elizabethan system proper, apprentices were bound out most commonly at fourteen years of age. Just as for farm-servants, they would then rarely see their family of origin (and one should speak in these terms – they were now part of another 'family'). The interludes between hirings were the usual occasion for farm-servants to revisit their families – many did not even see parents then. If the apprentice was bound locally, of course, matters would probably stand differently. But he or she was now associated with another family, such that some examinants stated that they had a certain number of children in their 'family', one of whom, it would incidentally be noted, was an apprentice to them.[69] He or she would be removed with the rest of the family to the master's place of settlement. This seems to have been despite the fact that such a place could be remote from the parish in which the apprentice's parents were inhabitants, and in which he had hitherto been residing during the apprenticeship. Such at any rate was the strength of familial transference in an earlier period, say up to about 1780.

By contrast with this, the variants of the 'clubbing-out' system held

[68] 31 Geo II c. 11.   [69] For example, see Beds C.R.O., D.D.P. 1/13/4/2.

the apprentice to his family of origin more closely for longer periods into the apprenticeship. The master became less the trained family craftsman, directing family-based production in which wife, children, and apprentice(s) played a part, and more the employer. The apprentice was no longer seen as a member of the family, but as a boy-worker, taught (increasingly reluctantly) by other journeymen employed. For they had not contracted to do such teaching, and they were acting contrary to their best interests in doing so. In many trades the situation was largely unjustified by precedent, but necessitated in the interests of employment by their own precarious situation in a glutted artisan labour market, increasingly dominated by certain large and more highly capitalised masters.[70] This was a situation conducive neither to satisfactory training nor to mutual good feeling between the parties concerned.

There was much variety of practice. At one extreme, there were wholesale merchant employers and masters, sometimes working a contracting system, taking large numbers of apprentices alongside their journeymen, the latter working in workshops away from the master's home.[71] In other cases, there was greater continuity of small workshop production, frequently at home: one thinks of wood-working, some clothing trades, coopers, chair makers and menders, wheelwrights, cordwainers, cabinet makers, tailors, gun-flint makers, and others. Some trades also had a greater concentration of apprentices as a ratio to master or journeymen than others: tailoring, retail shoemaking, many clothing trades, the London printing trades, metal-working trades, leather trades, parts of the watch making trade, calico printing (particularly in the north), button making, silk weaving, carpet making, and pin making are examples. These trades could on occasion be ones (particularly associated with clothing manufacture, lint-making, and so on) in which women were being relegated and employed to serve a similar function as cheap apprentices, although their roles were also still apparent in home-based crafts such as that of the cordwainer, chair maker, or cabinet maker.

There was, in short, considerable occupational variation behind the generalisations being made on the pattern of change, and it is not my intention here to try and explore in detail the specificities of this. I want to stress, nevertheless, at a more general level, how the

---

[70] Howell, 'Trades unions', 835ff.

[71] One thinks for example of the northern calico printing trades, Coventry silk weaving and watch making, or London printing trades. And in many instances of the putting-out system the 'master' taking apprentices was simply an out-worker or 'journeyman'.

traditional functions of the master and his family were being transferred elsewhere during this period. Such functions stretched back long before the Statute of Artificers – 1261 is the earliest date for which I have noted mention of apprenticeship.[72] But after 1750 the apprentice maintained closer links with his family into late 'teens, frequently looking to it for clothing and board and lodging. Similarly, the more general educative functions of the master's family were being abdicated, and (eventually) transferred elsewhere.[73] The teaching of literacy was one example, less often mentioned in later indentures. The older ways in which the master could care for the apprentice after the term, particularly by paying company entrance fines, by giving tools, clothing, or money (or guaranteeing further employment), were also being discarded. In the short-term, there was little replacement for these obligations. Pressure on children from their families to leave as new children arrived was accompanied by diminishing prospects of a secure alternative until marriage – an alternative which had previously taken the form of living-in apprenticeship or farm service. The displacement by masters of their traditional responsibilities onto the apprentice's family came during a time of rapid increases in the birth rate, a growing dependency ratio, and considerable rural and urban overcrowding.

In this regard these structural changes probably adversely affected the quality of family life, placing an additional burden onto family finances, which had been avoided in less procreative days when living-in apprenticeship and service could be relied upon to take young teenagers away from home. The much later expansion of teenage education which helped to ease the situation was yet to develop. It generally helped the classes whose income and family size meant that they had least need for it. Types of industrial training involving a re-vamped apprenticeship system, which developed more formally in the later nineteenth century in many trades, changed few of the structural and familial conditions arrived at with the 'clubbing-out' system. Broadly speaking, there has never since been a comparable substitute for the pre-industrial, extra-familial provision of teenage apprenticed or serviced education, and longer residence with one's family remains with us today. We can also note here that earlier marriage may have been one response of the young male artisan; and this could also have brought down female marriage ages, given expectations on courting and spouse age differentials.

---

[72] D. Hollis (ed.), *Calendar of the Bristol Apprentice Book (1532–1565)*, Bristol Record Soc. Publications, XIV (1947), vol. 1, p. 6.

[73] For similar changes in America, see Axtell, *School Upon a Hill*, p. 132.

The fall of formal apprenticeship in the Sheffield cutlery districts, for example, was blamed for an increasing number of improvident marriages among cutlers; and this certainly seems likely more generally when one considers the declining age at which apprenticeships were ending.[74] Apprenticeship legislation changed in 1778 to stipulate an earlier age of completion: from twenty-four years to twenty-one, putting into effect what had certainly been common practice since the late seventeenth century, if not earlier.[75] If occupationally specific research can ever establish whether such falling marriage ages took place among artisans, the explanation will be readily apparent.[76]

Associated with these changes was another which can be noticed in settlement examinations. The new found flexibility of the apprenticeship or 'clubbing-out' system allowed teenagers to apprentice *themselves*, sometimes at a later age than had hitherto been customary. In an earlier period one is struck by the passivity of their role in apprenticeship – the language used always illustrates this. 'I (he) was apprenticed by . . . (father, uncle, parish of, etc.) at my (his) age of fourteen' is a common expression. The trade appears to have been almost always chosen for them. But while this frequently continued into the later eighteenth and early nineteenth centuries, one is then often struck by examinants who took the matter into their own hands, usually at a slightly later period in their teens.[77] The flow of labour from agriculture to the trades became less restricted in this regard, as boys would hire themselves out for a couple of years in farm service, save a sum to pay for a premium, and then apprentice themselves. This can be noticed throughout the southern counties, east and west. (Interestingly, at least one intention of the Statute of Artificers had been to prevent the flow of labour out of agriculture.[78] Its property and seven year term qualifications were used particularly

---

[74] D. G. Hey, *The Rural Metalworkers of the Sheffield Region: A Study of Rural Industry before the Industrial Revolution* (Leicester, 1972), p. 58.

[75] 18 Geo III c. 47. This made the provisions of the 1767 London Act (7 Geo III c. 39) universal for England.

[76] 'With the breakdown of the traditional methods of control over the framework knitting trade, apprenticeship became a formality, usually a form of poor relief, rather than a period of initiation into a closed corporate world . . . As a demographic result of this change marriage took place earlier, much earlier.' Levine, *Family Formation*, pp. 142–3. On the demographic importance of changes in nuptiality and falling marriage age during this period, see in particular E. A. Wrigley & R. S. Schofield, *The Population History of England, 1541–1871* (1981).

[77] For two examples, see Dorset C.R.O., P. 34/OV 7.

[78] M. R. Gay, 'Aspects of Elizabethan apprenticeship', *Facts and Factors in Economic History* (Cambridge, Mass., 1932).

in the late sixteenth century against rural labour moving to towns.) An examinant would explain how he had been a farm-servant, and then how he apprenticed himself to the master, usually adding that the apprenticeship was 'a clubbing-out agreement for three or four years, to learn the trade', or something to that effect. In these cases, premiums could be rather lower than normal. A common sum was £4 or £5, although sometimes rather more depending on the trade. Once again, one finds this increasing from the 1780s to be most often encountered in the early nineteenth century, although of course such cases were only a small proportion of total apprenticeships. The trades, in a rural or market-town environment, were usually those of tailors, blacksmiths, carpenters, cordwainers, or retail trades – others such as gun-flint making, brickmaking or laying are also apparent. Once the clubbing-out system developed, with its possibilities for a later, shorter, and more contractual arrangement, the option of moving to a trade was viewed more favourably by a sixteen- or seventeen-year-old 'farm-servant', ploughboy or 'labourer'. (The definitions of such terms were breaking down by now.) Earlier in the eighteenth century, a move to a seven year apprenticeship may have been less acceptable to the master or mistress by that relatively late age, and to the farm-servant might have seemed a loss of independence and wage-earning capacity.

At first glance, these changes might appear conducive to greater upward social mobility. But after these later self-apprenticeships, there is frequent evidence that the examinant returned to agriculture, or engaged in some form of labouring work not involving the skills he had learnt during the apprenticeship. He might be described as a 'labourer' in the opening section of the examination, and then details be given of an apprenticeship, followed by confirmation of his present purely labouring status. More commonly, an initial description of cordwainer or whatever (provided by the examinant) would sit awkwardly on top of an ensuing account of only field or town labour. In practice, one is not often struck by any upward social mobility or advanced status which resulted. These artisans infrequently went on to rent property over £10 per annum, or set up in the trades in their own right – although probably they had had a residual and anachronistic expectation that this would occur. In a glutted and increasingly deskilled labour market, their resulting status was little over that which they had apprenticed themselves out of, and their employment prospects were often little improved, judging from the return to agricultural or town labouring. They could still try and claim a settlement on the basis of the clubbing-out, and may periodically have practised the trade. But then the employment seasonality of many rural trades was broadly similar to that of arable or mixed agriculture. Weavers were one exception, or framework knitters in October and November, or perhaps cordwainers after the harvest. The dual labels of weaver and labourer, or woolcomber and labourer, were sometimes used for the same man.[79] But in the common trades of brickmaking or laying, for example, or the building trades generally, there was little useful complementarity. Those who apprenticed themselves to brickmakers and layers rapidly found that these were trades worked in by agricultural labourers in the nineteenth century as part-time alternatives to agriculture, and that their apprenticeship conferred little special advantage. They had merely forborne unnecessarily during the apprenticeship. The change represented, in short, a tendency to greater homogeneity of both agricultural and artisan labour, with the factors underlying the deskilling or diluted exclusiveness of the latter creating the conditions for greater interflow between the sectors.[80] The 'clubbing-out' system became in the short-term (let us say between 1780 and 1820) a medium for such movement, but was then in turn often ignored altogether in some trades; although for a majority of artisans some form of training or apprenticeship was still undergone, with a very small number of trades successful in holding to the older seven years.[81]

Finally, something can be said on the question of continuity between the old apprenticeship and company system, and the early unions and trade societies. This debate has a long heritage. For the Webbs the trade unions were a new development, which they disassociated from the old craft guilds. In London by the eighteenth century, they argued, 'journeymen had in nearly all cases lost whatever participation they may possibly once have possessed in the companies which had for the most part already ceased to have any connection with the trades of which they bore the name'.[82] When one

---

[79] On the combining of agricultural occupations with weaving, see Dobson, *Masters and Journeymen*, p. 31. I shall discuss elsewhere in much more detail the question of split or dual occupations.

[80] And the payment of yearly wages to 'clubbed-out' apprentices also brought the system closer to the practice of farm service.

[81] Hatters were one trade successful in maintaining intact earlier forms of apprenticeship. Howell, 'Trades unions', 845ff; S.C. on Artisans and Machinery, V (1824), p. 99. Coopers may have been another: E. P. Thompson & E. Yeo (eds.), *The Unknown Mayhew* (1973), p. 511; but compare S.C. on Apprenticeship, IV (1812–13), p. 970. Wood trades were relatively successful in keeping apprenticeship terms intact. E. Hopkins, 'Were the Webbs wrong about apprenticeship in the Black Country?', *West Midland Studies*, VI (1973), 29–31.

[82] S. & B. Webb, *History of Trade Unionism* (1920), pp. 13–14.

held such a view on the early collapse of the craft guilds, it became necessary to argue that the unions were a much later and largely spontaneous response to the conditions created by the Industrial Revolution. The Webbs accordingly took sides against Brentano's view that 'trade unions originated with the non-observance of 5 Eliz. c. 4' (the Statute of Artificers);[83] and, at least in this regard, they allied themselves with views now associated with Unwin, Kramer, Power, and others.

We have seen how the latter authors were largely incorrect in their premature dating of the decline of apprenticeship and guild and company control; and it is worth adding further support to views which stress elements of continuity between the older system and the unionism of the early nineteenth century. The craft guilds were particularly concerned with apprenticeship restrictions, which they tried to enforce, albeit ineffectively, into the very early nineteenth century through the 'right of search'. Leeson has written that:

The first craft company to abandon formally the 'right to search' was the Merchant Taylors Company ... who did so only on the eve of the 18th century ... new craft incorporations ... secured the right of search by Royal Charter and exercised it vigorously into the 18th century. So did the older companies, like the clothworkers, wheelwrights, curriers, blacksmiths, founders, silk weavers and framework knitters. As has been shown, the smaller trades retained, through a licence system, some control right into the 19th century. Craft companies in Bristol were assisted by magistrates to seize and burn goods well into the 18th century.[84]

Machine smashing, after all, began with the destruction of those machines worked by people unauthorised to practice the trade, as in framework knitting in the East Midlands during 1811–12. But such action had many precedents, and it seems probable that the smashers saw their behaviour as partly legitimated by old practices allowing search and the destruction of non-apprenticed workmen's property.

There were prosecutions under the 1563 Statute as late as 1804 and 1809 in London (and apparently nineteen further cases between 1809 and 1813), although trades generally lost financially by conducting these prosecutions, and could gain little by a successful verdict.[85] In the Smithian, anti-Jacobin, and anti-combination climate of the time, many cases went against them, for the old trade regulations seemed to encourage combinations. And masters found themselves vulnerable in times of trade disputes when they could not employ other

---

[83] L. Brentano, *On the History and Development of Gilds, and the Origin of Trade Unions* (1870). 　　[84] Leeson, *Travelling Brothers*, pp. 259–60.
[85] See T. K. Derry, 'The repeal of the apprenticeship clauses of the Statute of Artificers', *Econ. Hist. Rev.*, III (1931), 69–72; Rule, *Experience of Labour*, pp. 116–17.

non-apprenticed workmen. Some trades of course did not come under the original statute, not having existed in 1563, and petitions to bring them under it later were generally unsuccessful – coachmaking, trunk making, periwig making, tobacco pipe making, machine making, patent lockmaking, or paper making were all examples of this.[86] In most of these, however, except machine making, there had since been some control over the numbers of apprentices either informally or through official incorporations. Other trades were excluded from such control after the mid-eighteenth century, such as the hatters or cotton workers. But in the agitation over these cases, and during the campaign for the enforcement of apprenticeship, culminating in the 1812–13 Select Committee, one can see the strength of feeling among journeymen in favour of the earlier restrictions. Similarly, the main concern of the early unions was to limit entry via apprenticeship, and to control the ratio of apprentices and journeymen to masters, as always to maintain their employment and real wages. The same concern (as has been argued by E. P. Thompson, Leeson, and others) can be witnessed right through to later 'new unionism'. 'The early unions', wrote E. P. Thompson, 'were profoundly imbued with the notions of defending the customs, privileges, and standards of "the Trade"'; and indeed many trades did manage to maintain some continuity of practice by insisting on an apprenticeship in some form.[87] The concern during the later nineteenth century over the future of apprenticeship saw frequent mention of elements of continuity in the customs of the trade – 'a veritable survival of the unfittest' wrote S. P. Thompson, in 'The apprenticeship of the future', in the new found language of his time.[88] In these regards, and in view of the late decline of traditional apprenticeship documented here, the essential continuity between craft customs and early trade union concerns seems well supported.

I have been concerned mainly with the broad outline of change in the apprenticeship system, and have chosen not to inundate the argument with details of change affecting specific trades. In view of the historiographical confusion on this issue, it seemed more useful to make clear some general similarities affecting most trades. Perhaps

[86] For paper making, see D. C. Coleman, *The British Paper Industry, 1495–1860: A Study in Industrial Growth* (Oxford, 1958), ch. X.

[87] E. P. Thompson, 'English trade unionism and other labour movements before 1790', *Bulletin Soc. for the Study of Labour History*, XVII (1968), 22. See also S.C. on Artisans and Machinery, V (1824), pp. 86–7, 90, 153; D. J. Lee, 'Craft unions and the force of tradition: the case of apprenticeship', *Brit. Jnl of Industrial Relations*, XVII (1979).

[88] S. P. Thompson, 'The apprenticeship of the future', *Contemporary Review*, XXXVIII (1880).

now, by way of conclusion, attention can be drawn to areas where understanding remains limited. No doubt other historians will make more detailed arguments on how apprenticeship and the company system changed in separate trades; although, to judge from Michael Walker's research into the decline of separate companies, the majority (of those outside the small category of distributive trade guilds) share a similar chronology of collapse. This is supported by the data on the analogous decline of apprenticeship to the trades of cord-wainer, tailor, and carpenter. In addition, it would be helpful to have more data on movements in artisan real wages, and to arrive at a sharper picture of the nature of unemployment in various trades over time. And insofar as rural and small market-town artisans commonly engaged in agricultural work – keeping livestock, and farming allotments or small areas of land – it is clear that they also would frequently have been adversely affected by enclosure, making them more vulnerable, for example, to dependence on poor relief during the winter. Such vulnerability could have inclined them either to turn to alternative *wage* labour at certain seasons, to compensate losses in partial self-sufficiency, or to try and raise their artisanal production once they had become entirely dependent upon it. The corollary of the latter effect would have been increased apprentice numbers, falling piece rates and product prices. Any reduced access to agri-cultural by-employments, in other words would have compounded the factors which produced the pessimistic changes for artisans outlined here.[89]

Most obviously, we need to know more about the structural changes in specific trades which brought craft production from a family-economy basis involving the immediate 'family' of the artisan, to a large workshop unit of production, with a master more distantly involved in the work process itself, employing unprecedented num-bers of journeymen and living-out apprentices on his premises. And in discussing economic causes, no doubt historians will need to pay closer attention to changes in technology and the division of labour than I have done here, particularly in the later eighteenth century; to the possibilities for capital accumulation; to the supply of credit; to the role of foreign and regional trade; and to the interplay of agricultural demand and the expansion of craft production. These

[89] On artisans engaged in agricultural by-employments, see D. Woodward, 'Wage rates and living standards in pre-industrial England', *Past and Present*, XCI (1981), esp. 39ff; B. A. Holderness, 'Rural tradesmen, 1660–1850: a regional study in Lindsey', *Lincs Hist. and Archaeology*, VII (1972); D. G. Hey, *An English Rural Community; Myddle under the Tudors and Stuarts* (Leicester, 1974), p. 143.

factors usually have to be pursued for specific trades, and I have omitted to discuss them here, while remaining aware of their influence on employing motivation. One should stress the way they could contribute to polarisations of wealth and shifting ratios of apprentices and journeymen to masters. In taking such matters into account, other historians may be able to add necessary detail to my general explanation.[90]

There are also indications of a rather different chronology of decline in the western counties than occurred in the south-east, and it is now becoming clearer that the Twelve Great Livery Companies in London had an atypically early collapse. We recall how the evidence provided by Kahl and Kellett led them to argue for a chronology which almost certainly seems too early for other regions. And Walker's research on Newcastle suggests that there the control of the majority of guilds and companies lasted right up to the end of the eighteenth century. It is possible, if paradoxical, that this was common in the north, and it is interesting to recall that farm service also survived throughout this period in many northern regions. The higher wage structure of the north from the late eighteenth century may have helped maintain the old apprenticeship system, avoiding the conditions of structural unemployment and falling real wages which, in the south, contributed to disillusionment with it after 1750. Analogous northern conditions partly underlay the survival there of farm service – presenting us with the paradox that de-industrialising regions (in the south) were areas where traditional controls gave way most rapidly to greater open-market competition; that economic growth in many instances may have perpetuated, and occurred alongside, the survival of these older institutional frameworks.

If the explanatory terms for these regional variations still remain rudimentary and tentative, they would become more so were one to

[90] In considering changes in the artisans' standard of living, historians might pay more attention to the possibilities of poor law sources than has hitherto been the case. Early union and tramping records are the other obvious complementary sources; one should also draw attention to the occupational specificity of many nineteenth-century vagrancy records. (For example, see *Morning Chronicle*, 29 Jan. 1850, for the occupations of vagrants sheltered at the Asylums for the Houseless Poor in the Metropolis, between 1819 and 1849. Toolmakers, weavers, cutlers, smiths and iron-founders, paper makers, shoemakers, tailors, bricklayers, and curriers were especially prominent.) There is also abundant nineteenth-century literary discussion to help answer these questions: most evidently in the work of Mayhew, in Select Committee Reports on apprenticeship and the conditions of artisan trades, in the records of trade societies, and in the late nineteenth-century discussion by various pamphleteers and writers over the future possibilities of the apprenticeship system for 'industrial training'.

try and incorporate aspects of regional population change into the explanation. We await further disclosure from the Cambridge Group on this, and are currently not able to explain the varying regional chronologies of decline in terms which would encompass regional pressure on entry to the trades as a partial symptom of demographic growth. It would, for example, be of considerable interest in relation to Figure 5.1 to have demographic growth rates for the counties near Wales to compare with similar data for the south-east, or Dorset and Devon. Similarly, the demography of gildated towns is virtually non-existent. When we know more about regional variations in the decline of apprenticeship between south and north (we urgently need more research on the latter), and when the decline can be explained with more attention to a fuller range of local economic and demographic factors, we shall be more comfortably placed to posit detailed relationships between it and the industrial growth which became more prominent after 1740, to accelerate after 1780. As I write, the views of Unwin and others who believed that the changes discussed here occurred much earlier – that the decline of such 'restrictions' paved the 'laissez-faire' path to eighteenth-century economic growth – now seem rather dubious, although much will always depend on individual scholars' interpretations of the timing and phases of economic growth. Some historians may prefer to stress the way in which decline occurred simultaneously with many rising output figures; they might see the changes as an economically rational 'modernisation' of the apprenticeship system;[91] they could also quite rightly point out that growth was most rapid in many areas not covered by the old legislation: the Lancashire cotton industry, or the

[91] It would be instructive to compare modern employer calculation on the optimal use and form of 'apprenticeship' with the changing motivations of masters in the past; but discussion of the subject divides itself markedly into two phases, with a curious hiatus in the early to mid-nineteenth century. For an excellent case study of apprenticeship and job training today, see P. Ryan, The costs of job training for a transferable skill', *British Jnl of Industrial Relations*, XVIII (1980). And see his 'Human resources, job training and industrial restructuring in O.E.C.D. countries' (circulated paper for O.E.C.D./C.E.R.I., Sept. 1981), and his 'Job training, employment practices and the large enterprise: the case of costly transferrable skills', in P. Osterman (ed.), *Internal Labor Markets* (1984). See also Report of an Enquiry into Apprenticeship and Training in 1925–6 (H.M.S.O., 1927–8); W. McClaine, *New Views on Apprenticeship* (1948); J. Mincer, 'On-the-job training: costs, returns and some implications', *Jnl of Political Economy*, LXX (1962 supplement); G. Williams, *Apprenticeship in Europe* (1963); K. Liepmann, *Apprenticeship* (1960); R. A. Bray, 'The apprenticeship question', *Econ. Jnl*, XIX (1909); and his *Boy Labour and Apprenticeship* (1911); N.B. Dearle, *Industrial Training* (1914); R. H. Tawney, 'The economics of boy labour', *Econ. Jnl*, XIX (1909); C. More, *Skill and the English Working Class, 1870–1914* (1980); A. P. M. Fleming & J. G. Pearce, *Principles of Apprentice Training* (1916).

manufacturing trades in Birmingham or Wolverhampton come to mind. But there was usually a complicated overlap and proximity of old and new, and one hopes for further scholarly attention to their regionality and inter-connection.

6

The apprenticeship of women

I

To many historians this title may appear curious or even arouse scepticism, and this is both understandable and unfortunate. For, as we have seen, the apprenticeship system itself has been poorly documented, with the decline of its older form in the eighteenth century inadequately understood. Similarly, the involvement of women in the apprenticed trades, whether as apprentices, familial labour, or mistresses, is commonly omitted altogether, or, earlier in the twentieth century, was at times acknowledged only to be understated and devalued, seemingly through its incompatibility with prevailing judgements on the domestic roles of women.[1] A number of factors have contributed to this situation. There has been stress by many authors on the successes of the feminist movement, on the

---

[1] More recent publications which create an impression that the apprenticed trades had always been strictly male preserves include even such authors as E. P. Thompson, *The Making of the English Working Class* (1963, Harmondsworth, 1975 edn), e.g., pp. 368, 455; or I. T. Prothero, *Artisans and Politics in Early Nineteenth-Century London* (Folkestone, 1979). E. J. Hobsbawm may have created a similar impression in his 'The tramping artisan', in his *Labouring Men* (1964), although his general argument in 'Man and woman in socialist iconography', *History Workshop*, VI (1978), while omitting to mention female trades of the nineteenth century and other work which remained for women, was nevertheless essentially correct in its depiction of long-term change affecting the south of England. For an extreme version, see E. Shorter's descriptions of the 'flickering black night of female domestic passivity', and 'watertight division of sex roles and tasks', in *The Making of the Modern Family* (1976), e.g., pp. 6, 66–74, 78. Or see L. Stone, *The Family, Sex and Marriage in England, 1500–1800* (1977), pp. 200–1; R. T. Vann, 'Toward a new lifestyle: women in preindustrial capitalism', in R. Bridenthal & C. Koonz (eds.), *Becoming Visible. Women in European History* (1977), pp. 195, 203; or M. L. McDougall, 'Working-class women during the Industrial Revolution, 1780–1914', in *ibid.*, pp. 268, 275. Among earlier publications, one might mention O. J. Dunlop & R. D. Denman, *English Apprenticeship and Child Labour: A History* (1912); G. Unwin, *The Guilds and Companies of London* (1908, 1938 edn), and his *Industrial Organization in the Sixteenth and Seventeenth Centuries* (Oxford, 1904); P. Mantoux, *The Industrial Revolution in the Eighteenth Century* (1928), e.g., pp. 463–4.

significant advances in the legal position of women over the past century. This, alongside more heroic accounts of the 'long upward struggle against patriarchal dominance towards sexual equality', away from the 'flickering black night of female domestic passivity', has fostered historiographical assumptions of long-held and extreme sexually exploitative attitudes in the past.[2] Such assumptions usually ignore social detail and specificity (often being based on upper-class literary evidence), and presume little discontinuity from preceding centuries of the mid-nineteenth-century status of women. They have provided a static, underrated, and socially undifferentiated picture of the pre-industrial importance of women, which has served to emphasise recent aspects of change. This approach has usually been inimical to a more realistic assessment of pre-industrial female work, which might allow more helpful and perhaps less favourable comparison with the sexual division of labour as we experience it today. A similar effect has been created by the tendency to over-generalise arguments on the supposed benefits to women of industrial employment, only in this case industrialisation takes the credit, rather than later feminist agitation.[3] I intend to help remedy these problems by presenting a general account of the role of women in the apprenticed trades,

---

[2] There is a large 'emancipationist' literature, and one might take as examples: W. L. Blease, *The Emancipation of English Women* (1910); G. W. Johnson, *The Evolution of Women from Subjection to Comradeship* (1926); R. Strachey, *'The Cause'. A Short History of the Women's Movement in Great Britain* (1928); I. B. O'Malley, *Women in Subjection* (1933); V. Klein, 'The emancipation of women: its motives and achievements', in H. Grisewood (ed.), *Ideas and Beliefs of the Victorians* (1949); J. Kamm, *Rapiers and Battleaxes: The Women's Movement and its Aftermath* (1966). The theme is an old one: 'In few respects has mankind made a greater advance than in the position of women – legal, social and educational. From the darkness of ignorance and servitude woman has passed into the open light of equal freedom.' B. Winchester, 'The New Woman', *Arena* (1902).

A wide range of authors, by no means in general agreement with each other, have provided accounts of long-term 'patriarchy' subject to some of the problems briefly outlined above. For examples, see Shorter, *Modern Family*, describing 'the Bad Old Days'; K. Millett, *Sexual Politics* (1971); Simone de Beauvoir, *The Second Sex* (1949); S. Firestone, *The Dialectics of Sex* (1972); Stone, *Family, Sex and Marriage*; P. Laslett, *The World We Have Lost* (1973), pp. 27, 50, 82, 93. For an account which isolates the class context of 'patriarchal' notions, see K. Thomas, 'The double standard', *Jnl of the History of Ideas*, XX (1959).

[3] According to S. B. Kanner, for example, 'the rapid economic and population expansion of the nineteenth century was accompanied by a dramatic increase of employment opportunities for women'. See her very helpful select bibliography, 'The women of England in a century of social change, 1815–1914: a select bibliography', in M. Vicinus (ed.), *Suffer and Be Still* (Bloomington, Indiana, 1972). Similarly another author begins a critical bibliography in the same, rarely questioned manner: 'The emancipation of women is one of the most striking aspects of the industrial phase of development.' See O. R. McGregor, 'The social position of women in England, 1850–1914', *British Jnl of Sociology*, VI (1955).

mainly in the eighteenth and nineteenth centuries, taking notice of the economic and demographic conditions in which such involvement took place; and also to outline and explain changes which contributed to the unprecedentedly acute sexual divisions of the nineteenth century.

The research for this chapter was undertaken partly to see whether the arguments of chapter 1 on long-term changes in the agricultural sexual division of labour could be extended to the artisan trades. The question was an obvious one. For such trades operated in proximity to the south-eastern agricultural sector, experienced comparable structural changes in the form of journeyman unemployment, glutting of labour, and the associated decline of apprenticeship, and were liable to be subject to the same attitudinal changes which had seemingly owed much to economic and demographic pressures. I hope here to pursue this, and consider the nature, timing, and causes of the sexual division of labour in southern apprenticed trades, in the hope that this will clarify further the relation of economic change to attitudes governing the roles of men and women.

It will be argued that in the eighteenth century women participated in trades which later became progressively limited to men. Indeed, women were apprenticed to a wide range of occupations, and this may surprise those familiar with the strict male exclusiveness of so many nineteenth-century trades. I shall not consider the work of middle- or upper-class women, but rather suggest that their very limited economic roles and their experience of marked sexual divisions became less apparent as one progressed down the social scale. It will be argued that lower-class female involvement in the trades declined into the nineteenth century, but that the apprenticeship system certainly cannot be seen as having a strict and long-established application only to men, as so often is assumed. The temporal changes affecting the sexual division of labour in south-eastern agriculture had close parallels in the artisan trades.

Some discussion can be made initially of the treatment of female apprenticeship in the rather sparse and scattered literature on the subject. For interesting historiographical reasons, almost no attention has been drawn to the apprenticeship of girls as a subject of enquiry. Some authors indeed, writing in the early twentieth century, appeared disinclined to discuss it, at times feeling their own sentiments on the proper domesticated roles of women in the family jostled by their knowledge of historical documentation. Even Ivy Pinchbeck, for example, having quoted a despondent comment of 1806 on the fall-off of female employment, continued: 'The attitude revealed in this last statement is somewhat astonishing to the modern mind, but as yet, there was a complete lack of appreciation of the value of women's work in the home and in rearing and caring for children.'[4] That 'lack of appreciation' probably did indeed mark the eighteenth century as different from the mid-nineteenth and after – as a historical statement it was overdrawn but partly valid with regard to the classes considered here. But one should also note the omissions which may occur when evidence is deemed 'astonishing to the modern mind'. Nevertheless, many authors were aware of the extent of female apprenticeship. Dunlop rather reluctantly pointed to both the participation of women in many trades where they had not served an apprenticeship, as the wives and daughters of craftsmen, and in trades to which they were fully apprenticed. Her statement that 'the apprenticeship of girls was an accepted fact', endorses the position taken here.[5] She continued:

In the days of the Elizabethan system [i.e., until 1814], girls were bound to many of the skilled trades in London. In 1675 a girl claimed admittance to the Carpenters' Company by right of apprenticeship ... In the seventeenth century women were not infrequently admitted to the Wheelwrights' Company by right of apprenticeship ... and in the 18th century the records of the Clockmakers' Company show that it was not uncommon for its members to receive girls as apprentices. It was not only in London that girls were apprenticed; from the indentures which are preserved, and from the enrolment and minute books of towns and gilds it is apparent that both in the country and in provincial towns girls were bound to men in all kinds of trades throughout the sixteenth, seventeenth, and eighteenth centuries.[6]

Pinchbeck gave examples for the eighteenth century of a wide range of trades to which women were apprenticed. These included, for example, those of goldsmith, the 'dangerous trade' of gilder, furniture maker, stone-mason and engraver ('bringing up their daughters to assist them in carving, sculpture, drawing and engraving'), clothier, weaver, hairdresser and peruke maker (particularly up to the mid-eighteenth century), linen cloth bleaching, doctor, oculist,

---

[4] I. Pinchbeck, *Women Workers and the Industrial Revolution, 1750–1850* (1930), p. 59. And she wrote that: 'eighteenth century newspapers and accounts ... reveal evidence of women's activities in roles which cause some astonishment at the present day' (p. 286).

[5] Dunlop & Denman, *English Apprenticeship*, p. 150.

[6] *Ibid.*, p. 151. While such female apprenticeship to the elitist London Companies can readily be documented, their involvement was probably more extensive outside these Companies, and in non-gildated towns and elsewhere. Some of the City Companies, and occasional provincial gilds, had at various times rules against female apprenticeship. For female clockmaker apprentices, see C. E. Atkins (ed.), *Register of the Apprentices of the Worshipful Company of Clockmakers, 1631–1931* (1931), e.g., pp. 40, 49, 52, 157, 178.

surgeon (in the earlier eighteenth century), dentist (one female dentist advertised her willingness to transplant 'teeth from the jaws of poor lads into the head of any lady or gentleman'), nailmaker, setmaker, chape filer, screw maker, bit and stirrup maker, black-smith, miner, and, of course, a wide range of cottage industrial and needlework trades.[7] S. R. Smith in his account of the 'adolescent' characteristics of seventeenth-century apprentices gave examples of the mistreatment of female apprentices by their masters.[8] Willis argued that female apprentices were intended to be taught a trade[9] – as the girl apprenticed to a shoemaker 'to be instructed in the making of cutt work',[10] or another 'to be taught the art of spyninge of worsted for serge in the great tourne'.[11] His figures for Southampton showed a fall during the seventeenth century in the percentage of apprentices which were female from 48 to 9 per cent.[12] Plummer discussed female apprentices to weaving; Marshall noted girls apprenticed to framework knitting or mantua making; and Stewart demonstrated female apprenticeship to gold and silver wire-drawers.[13] Levi Fox discussed the Coventry guilds and companies 'with special reference to the position of women', arguing that women 'were admissible during this period into practically every trade or craft guild'. 'A large number of females, some of them married, others obviously single, were engaged in trade in their own right . . . and enjoyed the freedom of the city.' And he also gave examples of female apprentices and of women taking apprentices.[14] Similarly, dealing with the companies,

---

[7] Pinchbeck, *Women Workers*. Speaking of the goldsmiths, she wrote (p. 293)
> that women fairly frequently entered the trade by apprenticeship in the mid eighteenth century, although the number who assisted at home in certain branches of the work without definite technical training was probably far greater. In the last quarter of the century, fewer women took up their freedom by service, and early in the nineteenth century the apprenticeship of women ceased altogether . . . The apprenticeship book shows that the fees paid with girl apprentices in the middle of the century varied from £30 to £63, and that some of them were afterwards working in the craft is shown by their taking apprentices themselves.
> See also the female goldsmiths listed in Sir A. Heal (ed.), *The London Goldsmiths, 1200–1800* (Cambridge, 1935).

[8] S. R. Smith, 'The London apprentices as seventeenth-century adolescents', *Past and Present* LXI (1973), 152.

[9] A. J. Willis & A. L. Merson (eds.), *A Calendar of Southampton Apprenticeship Registers, 1609–1740*, Southampton Records Soc., XII (1968), lii.

[10] *Ibid.*, no. 760.   [11] *Ibid.*, no. 877.   [12] *Ibid.*, li.

[13] A. Plummer, *The London Weavers' Company, 1600–1970* (1972), pp. 72–6; D. Marshall, *The English Poor in the Eighteenth Century* (1926), pp. 198ff; H. Stewart, *History of the Worshipful Company of Gold and Silver Wyre-Drawers, and of the Origin and Development of the Industry which the Company represents* (1891), p. 78.

[14] L. Fox, 'The Coventry guilds and trading companies – with special reference to the position of women', in *Essays in Honour of P. Chatwin*, Birmingham Arch. Soc. and Dugdale Soc. (Oxford, 1962).

Leeson gave examples of 'systeren and bretheren' in an earlier period for masons and carpenters, noted that female blacksmiths paid 'quarterage' to their company, and the coopers' rules included 'sisters' until the sixteenth century, and stressed that women were to be found in many trades, from brewing to leadbeating.[15]

In discussing the fifteenth-century London silkwomen, M. K. Dale noted their full apprenticeship to the trade: 'In this respect the silkwomen kept the same rules and worked under the same conditions as the men.'[16] They could trade in their own right as 'femme sole', and be legally answerable as such (for example, in actions for debt), and as members of the craft were of standing in the city. As Dale concludes with reference to the craft: 'Indeed, perhaps its most important characteristic, considered in the light of the wider question of the economic importance of women at that time, is that it shows them working, not as wives (or widows), but as artisans who were wage-earners, or as traders, supplying a market.'[17] M. D. George gave further examples of girls in eighteenth-century London being apprenticed to trades such as breeches maker, carpenter, weaver, mantua maker, or butcher.[18] When one woman finished her apprenticeship to a butcher in Carnaby Market she 'lived by killing of beasts in which . . . she was very expert'.[19] As George says: 'When we reach the level of the "labouring poor" it can almost be said that there is no work too heavy or disagreeable to be done by women.'[20]

Alice Clark also pointed to the prevalence of women's work in the trades, and to the practice of female apprenticeship; to the acceptability of women working as 'femme sole', responsible for their own debts;[21] to the admittance of women into the guilds, 'such as the Girdlers and Pewterers', where 'they were actively engaged in these crafts and, like men, were subject to and protected by the regulations of their Gild or Company';[22] and she noted their inclusion in lists made of tradesmen working in various boroughs, 'in trades which would seem to modern ideas most unlikely for them',[23] as, for example, the five female blacksmiths of Chester in 1574. It was the case, apparently, that 'many trades which in later times have become

---

[15] R. A. Leeson, *Travelling Brothers* (1979). pp. 27, 50.
[16] M. K. Dale, 'London silkwomen of the fifteenth century', *Econ. Hist. Rev.*, IV (1932–4), 325.   [17] *Ibid.*, 334.
[18] M. D. George, *London Life in the Eighteenth Century* (1925, 1965 edn), pp. 172, 183, 231.
[19] *Ibid.*, p. 172.   [20] *Ibid.*
[21] A. Clark, *Working Life of Women in the Seventeenth Century* (1919), pp. 151–2, 156., 'It was quite usual for a married woman to carry on a separate business from her husband as sole merchant, but it was still more customary for her to share in his enterprise.'   [22] *Ibid.*, p. 155.   [23] *Ibid.*

entirely closed to women were then so dependent on their labour that sisters are mentioned specifically in rules concerning the conditions of manufacture'.[24] Trades in which women worked included the armourers and brasiers, boot and shoemakers, apothecaries, printers, goldsmiths, girdlers, pewterers, merchant tailors, clockmakers, upholsterers, farriers, drapers, embroiderers, glovers, wax-chandlers, chair-bottomers, pin makers, virtually all the retail and provision trades; and Clark provided very extensive evidence to support her view that: 'There can be no doubt that the admission to the world of business and the responsibilities which rested on their shoulders, often developed qualities in seventeenth century women which the narrower opportunities afforded them in modern society have left dormant.'[25] She stressed in particular the family-centred production of the period as laying the basis for these opportunities: 'while the system of family industry lasted, it was so usual in the skilled and semi-skilled trades for women to share in the business life of their husbands that they were regarded as partners'. But with the spread of 'capitalistic organisation' in the seventeenth century:

the numbers of women who could find no outlet for their productive activity in partnership with their husbands were increasing and their opportunities for establishing an independent industry did not keep pace; on the contrary, such industry became ever more difficult ... the wife of the prosperous capitalist tended to become idle, the wife of the skilled journeyman lost her economic independence and became his unpaid domestic servant ... The masters no longer depended upon the assistance of their wives, while the journeyman's position became very similar to that of the modern artisan; he was employed on the premises of his master ... his wife and daughters ... remained at home ... The alternatives before the women of this class were either to withdraw altogether from productive activity, and so become entirely dependent upon their husband's goodwill, or else to enter the labour market independently ... in competition not only with other women, but with men ... At this time the idea that men 'keep' their wives begins to prevail.[26]

While describing the same direction of change for which I will argue (some trades such as brewing, for example, had already changed so as largely to exclude women), she also made it clear that for most trades and crafts the major developments had yet to occur.

II

Before considering detailed evidence on this, some preliminary points should be made. First, I shall treat female artisan activity mainly by using apprenticeship records. This places an immediate

[24] *Ibid.*, p. 183.   [25] *Ibid.*, p. 159.   [26] *Ibid.*, pp. 196–7, 234–5.

limitation on any argument which stresses their economic participation, as most female involvement took place outside of the apprenticeship system. That is, women were massively involved in familial artisan production as the wives or daughters of apprenticed men, and most had never been apprenticed themselves. We have little access to the extent of their involvement in the family, but it was certainly most marked before the intensified capitalisation of skilled trades, and before the split between home and place of production became more apparent after the mid-eighteenth century. As the argument is developed on female artisan activity we should remember that it is being heavily understated, being based on apprenticeship records.

The evidence from these records is also complicated by the decline of seven year apprenticeship. As we have seen, temporal comparisons of female participation cannot be made on the assumption that the apprenticeship system was stable over this period. Its decline after 1750 and consequent restabilisation in the early nineteenth century forms a necessary background to the apprenticeship evidence. I shall return to it in more detail in my concluding explanation for the changes in the apprenticeship of women which occurred.

It can also be noted that the legal background to apprenticeship placed virtually no restrictions on female apprenticeship. The Statute of Artificers spoke of 'persons' when referring to apprentices, and the wording of acts specifically mentioned both boys and girls, and masters and mistresses.[27] The Act of Elizabeth (1601), for example, which laid down the framework for the parish apprenticeship system, stipulated that males were to be bound until they were twenty-four, and girls until they were twenty-one, or until they married. There appears to be little in the apprenticeship legislation which 'discriminated' against female apprentices by excluding them from it. And women practising crafts were able to take apprentices under the law, as we shall see.[28]

[27] See for example 39 Eliz c. 3; 43 Eliz c. 2; 7 Jac I c. 3; 3 Wm & Mary c. 11; 8 Anne c. 5; or 9 Anne c. 21. The most explicit legal discrimination which I have found is in the twentieth clause of the Statute of Artificers, which prohibited those practising the specific trades of overseas merchant, mercer, draper, goldsmith, ironmonger, embroiderer, or clothier to take 'any Apprentice or Servaunte to be enstructed or taughte in any of the artes ... which they ... exercise, except such Servaunt or Apprentice be his Son, orels that the Father or Mother of Suche Apprentice or Servaunte shall have ... landes, tenementes [etc] of the clere yerely value of xl s. of one estate of inheritance or freeholde at the leaste'. It is hard to believe that this can have had much subsequent effect, because these trades (with the exception of merchant and ironmonger) are among those where there is best documentation of female apprenticeship.

[28] See Dunlop & Denman, *English Apprenticeship*, pp. 150–1; R. Ricart, *The Maire of Bristowe is Kalendar*, L. T. Smith (ed.), Camden Soc., V (1872), p. 102.

Two forms of apprenticeship existed: parish or charity apprenticeships, and those where the premium was paid by the apprentice's
family or by the apprentice. Let us first consider the former – that is,
apprentices from the lowest social classes, who were orphans under
parish care, or whose families were too poor to pay the premium.
Because they were bound out by the parish, records for these
apprentices are more abundant than those apprenticed by their
families, and fall into two categories. There are parish apprenticeship
registers, giving details of apprentice, trade, master/mistress, premium paid, and so on. These survive for many parishes. And there
are the parish indentures themselves, giving fuller detail, but their
modest survival probably gives information on fewer apprentices.
Table 6.1 gives such information from better documented parishes in
Suffolk, Norfolk, Cambridgeshire, Essex, Middlesex, Huntingdonshire, Oxfordshire, Northamptonshire, Bedfordshire, Hampshire,
Leicestershire, and Nottinghamshire, and has been subdivided by
century, sex, and trade.[29]

Large numbers were apprenticed to agriculture, particularly in the
eighteenth century; and interest attaches to the fewer numbers of
females apprenticed to cordwainers, curriers, blacksmiths, butchers,
bricklayers, clockmakers or whitesmiths, and to other trades commonly considered strictly male occupations. Over the three centuries
(and the nineteenth-century figures virtually all end by 1834), of the
total apprenticeships as many as 34 per cent were for girls – clearly
indicating that any picture of apprenticeship as an entirely male
institution requires re-examination. The eighteenth-century figures
suggest relatively extensive female participation in the trades. In this
table, males were then apprenticed to a range of forty-six occupations, females to as many as fifty-one. In this regard, the contrast of

---

[29] The figures are from records (in some cases sampled) for the following parishes, in
respective C.R.O.s: *Cambridgeshire*: Cambridge, Trumpington, Royston, Duxford,
Fordham, Wisbech, Chatteris, Elm, Fen Ditton, Hinxton, Ickleton, Manea, Leverington, Great Shelford, Whittlesford, Soham. *Huntingdonshire*: Brampton, Huntingdon,
Great Staughton, Godmanchester, Great Gidding, Whittlesey, Broughton, Rushden, Peterborough. *Essex*: St Osyth, Chelmsford, Ardleigh. *East and West Suffolk*:
Assington, Bramford, Hadleigh, Stowmarket, Bildeston, Bacton, Monksleigh, Weeting, Badwell Ash, Brandon, Hockham, Croxton, Thurston, Finningham, Felsham,
Framlingham, East Bergholt, Polstead, St Peter's and St Clement's Ipswich, Wether-
ingsett, Gislingham, Mendlesham, Debenham, Nacton, Glemham Magna, Rend-
ham, Horham, Hoxne, Benhall, Great Finborough, Little Glemham, Friston, Hales-
worth, Rishangles, Kersey, Pettistree, Wenhaston, Sudbourne. *Oxfordshire*: Oxford,
Witney. *Leicestershire*: Syston. *Norfolk*: Thurston, Thetford, Downham Market, Lynn,
Shimpling. *Middlesex*: St Clement Danes. *Nottinghamshire*: Blyth, Mansfield Wood-
house, Keyworth, Norwell, Ollerton. *Northamptonshire*: Brackley, Cottesbrooke,
Byfield, Dallington, Duston, Pattishall, Wansford, Welford, Bozeat, Weston Favell.
Hampshire: Petersfield, Eling, Rockbourne. *Bedfordshire*: Eaton Socon.

Table 6.1. *Parish apprenticeship – southern counties*

	17th century		18th century		19th century	
Occupations	Male	Female	Male	Female	Male	Female
Agriculture						
'Husbandry'	39	23	237	56	65	31
Food/drink						
Butcher	4	—	2	6	4	2
Baker	—	—	4	3	8	—
Brewer/maltster	3	2	—	1	—	1
Grocer/tallow-chandler/shopkeeper/confectioner/pastry cook	1	1	1	4	1	7
Innholder/publican/victualler	—	1	4	10	—	3
Miller	2	—	6	1	1	—
Clothing						
Button maker	—	1	—	—	2	—
Bead maker	—	—	—	—	—	1
Blanket maker	—	—	—	1	—	—
Breeches maker	—	—	1	—	—	—
Coat maker	—	—	—	2	—	—
Cotton manufacturer	—	—	3	7	44	30
Cloth maker	—	—	—	2	—	—
Childbed linen maker	—	—	—	—	—	2
Cordwainer/cobbler	18	—	33	5	49	1
Draper/hosier/clothier	2	3	5	1	1	—
Dressmaker	—	—	—	—	—	8
Framework knitter	—	—	13	1	12	1
Glover	5	—	8	5	—	—
Gold & Silver orris weaver	—	—	—	—	1	—
Hatter	—	—	—	2	1	—
Hatbox manufacturer	—	—	—	—	—	1
Knitting/spinning	—	4	—	1	—	—
Lacemaker	—	—	1	3	—	1
Leather stay maker	—	—	1	—	—	—
Mantua maker	—	—	—	3	—	5
Ostrich feather maker	—	—	—	—	—	7
Peruke/wig maker/barber	1	—	4	1	5	—
Straw hat maker	—	—	—	2	—	—
Shawl manufacturer	—	—	—	—	—	1

(Continued on next page)

	17th century		18th century		19th century	
Occupations	Male	Female	Male	Female	Male	Female
Sempstress	—	—	—	9	—	3
Shoebinder/closer	—	—	—	2	4	2
Silk stocking grafter/silk woman	—	2	—	—	—	1
Tailor	8	4	25	3	14	2
Tambour worker/ embroiderer/needlework	—	1	—	2	—	2
Umbrella maker	—	—	—	—	2	—
Velvet & figure weaver	—	—	—	—	1	—
Woolcomber	—	1	8	2	—	—
Weaver: linen, say, broad, silk, stocking, shalloon, webster	39	3	12	9	20	2
Worsted spinner/ twisterer	1	—	—	1	—	1
Other occupations						
Armourer	1	—	—	—	—	—
Blacksmith/farrier	6	—	29	1	9	—
Bricklayer/maker	1	—	16	2	—	—
Basket maker	—	—	3	—	2	—
Bookseller	—	—	—	—	1	—
Bookbinder/folder/ sewer	—	—	—	1	1	3
Brazier	—	—	—	—	1	—
Bitmaker	—	—	—	1	—	—
Brush maker	—	—	—	2	1	—
Bill sticker	—	—	—	—	—	1
Butler	—	—	—	—	1	—
Bow Street manufacturer	—	—	—	—	1	—
Carpenter	14	—	12	1	7	—
Currier/tanner	1	—	1	1	—	—
Coach/coach spring maker	—	—	—	—	6	—
Chimney sweeper	—	—	4	—	29	—
Chair/logstool maker	—	—	2	—	—	—
Cooper	4	—	2	—	1	—
Carrier	—	—	—	—	1	—
Coal merchant	—	—	—	—	—	1
Copperplate printer	—	—	—	—	2	—
Cutler & edge tool maker	—	—	—	—	1	—
Coach lamp manufacturer	—	—	—	—	1	—
Clerk/schoolmaster	—	—	—	1	3	—

Occupations	17th century		18th century		19th century	
	Male	Female	Male	Female	Male	Female
Dyer	—	—	—	1	—	—
Enameller	—	—	—	—	1	—
Fisherman/mariner/ waterman/oyster dredger/dredger/ navigating coaster/ wherryman	5	—	55	1	77	—
Filecutter	—	—	—	—	4	—
Flower maker	—	—	—	—	—	2
French horn maker	—	—	—	1	—	—
Footman	—	—	—	—	1	—
Goldsmith/black jeweller	—	—	—	—	2	—
Glass cutter	—	—	—	—	1	—
Gilder/carver & ornament maker	—	—	—	—	2	—
Gold & silver wire drawer/ spangle maker	—	—	—	—	2	—
Gunbarrel maker	—	—	—	—	1	—
Glazier	—	—	1	—	1	—
Gun-flint maker	—	—	2	—	6	—
Gent	7	6	3	—	2	2
Harness/collar maker	1	—	5	1	2	—
Hemp manufacturer	—	—	—	—	1	—
Hickler	—	—	2	—	—	—
Housewifery	—	58	—	103	—	28
Houseservant	—	—	1	2	4	26
Japaner	—	—	—	1	—	1
Lamp lighter	—	—	—	—	1	—
Law writer	—	—	—	—	1	—
Lathriver/cleaver/ turner	—	1	1	—	1	—
Lint manufacturer	—	—	—	—	—	21
Locksmith	1	1	—	—	1	—
Mason	—	—	—	—	2	—
Mercer	—	—	—	—	2	—
Merchant	1	—	—	—	—	—
Painter	—	—	—	—	1	—
Paper maker	—	—	2	1	—	—
Plumber	—	—	—	—	1	—
Pawnbroker	—	—	1	—	1	2
Potash maker	—	—	1	—	—	—
Printer	—	—	—	—	3	—
Projecting letter manufacturer	—	—	—	—	1	—

(Continued on next page)

Occupations	17th century		18th century		19th century	
	Male	Female	Male	Female	Male	Female
Pin sticker	—	—	—	—	—	1
Rope maker	—	—	—	1	1	1
Saddler	2	—	—	—	—	—
Slatner	1	—	—	—	—	—
Smith	—	—	—	—	2	—
Silversmith	—	—	—	1	1	—
Steelworker	—	—	—	—	1	—
Shipwright	—	—	1	—	1	—
Surgeon	—	—	2	—	1	—
Thatcher	—	—	2	—	—	—
Soap boiler	—	—	1	—	—	—
Tobacco pipe maker	—	—	2	1	—	—
Timber hewer/sawyer	2	—	1	—	—	—
Tooth, nail & shaving brush manufacturer	—	—	—	—	1	—
Upholsterer	—	—	—	—	1	—
Vertical jackmaker	—	—	—	—	1	—
Watch glass maker	—	—	—	—	1	—
Watch gilder	—	—	—	1	5	—
Watch hand maker	—	—	—	—	1	—
Watch/clock maker	—	—	1	2	—	—
Wheelwright	—	1	6	—	2	—
Whitesmith	—	—	—	1	2	—
Writing stationer	—	—	—	—	2	—
Workbox & shaving case maker	—	—	—	—	1	—
Widow	—	6	5	1	—	—

Nos. in occupational category

Agriculture	39	23	237	56	65	31
%		19.3		20.4		15.2
Food/drink	10	4	17	25	14	13
%		3.4		9.1		6.4
Clothing	74	19	114	64	156	71
%		16.0		23.4		34.8
Other occupations	47	73	164	129	214	89
%		61.3		47.1		43.6
Total (1748)	170	119	532	274	449	204
%		100		100		100
Percentage female in each century		41.2		34.0		31.2
Nos. of occupations	26	18	46	51	77	35

the seventeenth and eighteenth centuries with the nineteenth was noticeable, for in the latter females were apprenticed to under half the number of male occupations. The percentage of apprentices which was female also fell over time. If one discounts apprentices to husbandry, service (clerk/schoolmaster, widow, gent, houseservant, footman, butler), housewifery, and the collective indentures to lint and cotton manufacture, the percentage female fell from 27 to 17 per cent from the eighteenth to nineteenth centuries. The range of occupations to which females were apprenticed in the eighteenth century was replaced by apprenticeship more strictly to household occupations, cotton and lint manufacture, and (often sweated) needlework occupations, such as dressmaker, sempstress, tambour worker, mantua maker and the like. The breakdown of these figures to occupational category is less useful, given the obvious limitations of such wide categories. But the rise over time in the percentage of females apprenticed to 'clothing' occupations is noticeable. The percentage apprenticed to 'other occupations' declined.[30]

[30] Too much significance should not be attached to the comparative figures for 'husbandry' and the service occupations (especially 'housewifery') before the nineteenth century. Terminological indiscrimination in indentures was common between 'servant', 'servant in husbandry', 'house servant', 'house servant in husbandry', 'house servant in husbandry and housewifery', 'husbandry', 'husbandry and housewifery', 'good housewife or servant in husbandry', and 'housewifery'. These terms could be used interchangeably, as was clear from some indentures and accompanying documents, and cases where indentures overlapped with parish apprenticeship registers. I have taken husbandry as the occupational category wherever it was stated. The point was also made in nineteenth-century government reports that apprenticeship to 'housewifery' often involved 'husbandry'. See for example Report of the Poor Law Commissioners, XXIX (1836), pp. 491ff. The notion of 'housewifery' would indeed repay historical investigation and comparison with modern usage, for it had a much broader meaning than in western Europe today, and was also sometimes used in conjunction with trades to be taught – it was itself an occupation covering many different skilled crafts. This reflected a latitude of female roles in agriculture and the home similar to that found in many 'underdeveloped' countries today. (I refer here to countries where I have lived in east and west Africa, such as Tanganyika, Uganda, Kenya, or Nigeria.)

I will not dwell on regional terminology, but something further can be said on apprenticeship to husbandry. This was common throughout the southern counties, but most apparent in south-western counties not included in Table 6.1. In particular, some collections of settlement examinations in that region (notably Devon, Dorset, Somerset, and Wiltshire) show extensive female apprenticeship having taken place to agriculture, as well as to the trades. In some agricultural parishes there, one has the impression that apprenticeship to agriculture was almost a life-cycle phase, with perhaps a third or more of female examinants having gone through this (e.g., the records of Bovey Tracey in Devon, or North Bradley in Wiltshire). This was also the case for male examinants. The region had a slower rate of population increase, and a later decline of yearly hiring and apprenticeship than the south-east, with more seasonally regular employment in pastoral agriculture. It may have been able to sustain a steadier demand for artisan goods during the year than could the rural

It is worth stressing that those apprenticed by the parish or charity were generally taught the trade, and later practised it. This was clear from biographical information in settlement examinations, giving accounts of work as journeymen/women, as masters and mistresses. Certainly, there was occasional mistreatment of parish apprentices, just as of other apprentices, and the exploitation of those unfortunate enough to be 'apprenticed' to manufacturing mills appears evident. Ill-treatment could occur in other cases – as for chimney sweeps. But it is less possible to extend such cases to the family-based trades mainly dealt with here; and the evidence condemning the treatment of pauper and other children in factories does not apply to apprentices bound out under the localised administration of the old poor law, in or from the parishes to which they 'belonged'. In the latter regard, the old poor law seems favourably humane. There was obvious care taken by parish authorities over the future of their charges. Prospective masters and mistresses, for example, were enquired into to check their suitability to have an apprentice bound to them:

We the said Justices having particularly enquired and considered whether the said Charles Jackson resides and has his business within a reasonable distance from the said Parish of Kettleburgh to which the said Sarah Holmes belongs, having had regard to the means of communication between the said Parishes, and having also particularly enquired into the circumstances and character of the said Chas. Jackson, do think it proper that the said Sarah Holmes should be bound out an Apprentice.[31]

One should stress this wide scope of the old poor law, against misleading views on the supposedly novel growth and functions of the 'welfare state' in the nineteenth and twentieth centuries. Parish officers frequently made decisions in the interests of 'parentally deprived' children, and acted on them – whether in support or defiance of parents and guardians – and such practice formed only a small aspect of their activities. There was extensive legislation covering parish apprentices, which provided legal protection for them, at

south-east, and unemployment in the trades was probably less acute, although the region (particularly Dorset and Wiltshire) was to suffer considerable pauperism in a later period. We shall see that the percentage female of Wiltshire apprentices whose families paid their premiums was higher than counties to the east (Table 6.4). Literary evidence indicating the wide range of work that female apprenticeship to agriculture entailed in this region is provided in chapter 8.

[31] East Suffolk C.R.O., FC 101/G11/2–1. The unfavourable distinctiveness of factory apprenticeship compared to normal practice is demonstrated by popular opposition to factory apprenticing by parishes. See the rioting against the apprenticeship of six girls to a factory cited in J. Lane, 'Apprenticeship in Warwickshire cotton mills, 1790–1830', *Textile History*, X (1979), 171.

times exceeding that to which other apprentices had access.[32] And details of prematurely ended apprenticeships in settlement examinations provide no evidence of more common mistreatment of parish or charity apprentices than of other apprentices. The common nineteenth-century misrepresentation of the old poor law, notably in the 1834 Report, should not lead one to assume long-term development of humane interventionist administration. Such an assumption corresponds interestingly to that on the supposedly modern movement to sexual equality of work, although it is not always clear why either should be held.

Another point should be made. Given prevailing forms of family production, distinctions between 'domestic drudgery' and 'learning the trade' are not altogether realistic for any class of apprentice, and this is not a consideration which only affects those bound by the parish or charity. In the concept and practice of apprenticeship in this period, the integration into another productive household for the purposes of education (literacy was often to be taught) and general upbringing was inextricably combined with the associated training in the artisan skills of that family. The 1811–31 censuses, for example, significantly gave occupations only of *families* – a practice which ended in 1841. It is anachronistic to separate these aspects of apprenticeship, on the assumption that the more formalised and almost exclusively male industrial training away from the home, to which the apprenticeship system lent itself later in the nineteenth century, was true for earlier periods.

Table 6.2, drawn from the Poor Child Register of Southampton (1609–1708), also covers children apprenticed by the parish or by charities.[33] Many would be orphans, others would have parents deemed by parish authorities to be too irresponsible for their upbring-

---

[32] In particular the compulsory binding of them by formal indenture (3 Wm & Mary c. 11); the various enactments allowing the fining of masters and mistresses found guilty of mistreatment, and *raising* the upper limit of premiums under which this legislation applied (8 & 9 Will III c. 30; 20 Geo III c. 36; 32 Geo III c. 57; 33 Geo III c. 55 (which also allowed the fining of parish officers); 4 Geo IV c. 29 and 34); the right of apprentices to appeal to justices against masters or mistresses (20 Geo II c. 19); the securing of settlement by apprenticeship even when indentures were absent (31 Geo II c. 11); the setting of minimum premiums, conditionally payable in instalments, and the creation of 'Guardians of the Parish Poor Children' in each parish to check on them regularly (7 Geo III c. 39, and 18 Geo III c. 47); the control by two justices of the transferral of apprentices between masters (32 Geo III c. 57); the keeping of apprenticeship registers (42 Geo III c. 46); the limitation on binding of apprentices to distances of over forty miles – mainly applying to apprenticeship to the factory districts (56 Geo III c. 139). For the main post-1834 legislation, see the New Poor Law itself (section 61); 7 and 8 Vict c. 101; and 14 and 15 Vict c. 11.

[33] Willis & Merson, *Southampton Apprenticeship Registers.*

Table 6.2. *Southampton apprenticeship, 1609–1708*

Occupations	Male	Female
Agricultural		
Husbandry	2	5
Gardener	1	—
Food/drink		
Butcher	5	1
Baker	3	1
Brewer	2	—
Innholder	2	—
Victualler	3	3
Fisherman	7	—
Vintner	2	—
Clothing		
Tailor	26	4
Glover	5	2
Weaver	8	2
Woolcomber	14	3
Sergeweaver/ sayweaver	31	9
Cordwainer	32	4
Feltmaker	2	1
Clothier	18	1
Cloth worker	5	1
Cobbler/ translator	9	1
Kersiweaver	1	—
Button maker	1	2
Silk weaver	9	—
Sempstress	—	1
Other occupations		
Joyner	5	3
Blacksmith	7	—
Turner	1	—
Cooper	8	2
Goldsmith	—	1
Mariner	5	—
Freemason	5	—
Barber	1	2
Musician	3	1
Basket maker	3	2
Shipwright	5	2
Hellyer/ plumber	12	—
Shearman	—	1

Occupations	Male	Female
Other occupations (cont'd)		
Carpenter	7	2
Painter	2	—
Bricklayer	2	1
Sailor	1	4
Fuller	2	—
Currier	2	—
Ropemaker	8	—
Chapman	—	1
Tobacco pipe maker	4	—
Wine cooper	2	—
Blockmaker	4	—
Tanner	2	—
Farrier	—	1
Pointmaker	1	—
Castermaker	1	—
Sawyer	1	—
Ironmonger	—	1
Labourer	1	4
Widow	—	10
Housewifery	—	5
Total (367)	283	84
% of total	77.1	22.9

Mean	Male	Female
Length of apprenticeship	10.1 (s = 2.40)	9.4 (s = 2.42)
Sample no.	42	43
Age at end of term	22.0 (s = 1.99)	19.4 (s = 2.22)
Sample no.	56	39
Premium	£1.78 (s = 1.29)	£1.96 (s = 1.63)
Sample no. (1609–37)	63	41

ing, or who were given parish or charity money to help apprentice their children. This is a group of boys and girls from a very low social background. And there is a surprisingly wide female involvement, as found in Table 6.1. Agriculture, as one would expect, was relatively insignificant in Southampton, but again there were girls apprenticed to masters and mistresses in heavy or skilled trades. Entries in the Register provide less detail than indentures, making it more difficult to tell how far apprentices were taught the trades. But again there were the cases where the girl was to learn 'housewifery'. As with the indentures in Table 6.1, where this was the case it was stated as such – the term 'housewifery' being clearly specified.

Table 6.2 provides further information on the length the apprentice was to serve, and the premiums paid. The latter were about half to a quarter of those paid for parish apprentices in the eighteenth century, and were much lower than for non-parish apprentices, as we shall see. It is noticeable that the mean female premium was actually slightly higher than the male, although small samples allow little statistical significance to be attached to the difference. The lengths of terms are similar, and were longer than the usual seven years because the circumstances leading to a parish apprenticeship produced younger children being apprenticed than was the case under other apprenticeships. The standard deviations for these figures show little sexual difference, and might suggest that neither the experiences of male nor female parish apprentices were more variable than the other. And once more a significant percentage (nearly a quarter) of the total apprenticed were girls.

Clearly, this evidence from the seventeenth and eighteenth centuries goes against preconceptions formed from the well-documented nineteenth century, when female apprenticeship had become rarer, and when labour in most trades was much more exclusively male. The unprecedented acuteness of the early nineteenth-century sexual specialisations of apprentices by trade can readily be demonstrated. For example, let us take the parish apprenticeship register of St Clement Danes, in Middlesex, surviving for 1803 to 1822.[34] The occupational split by sex is summarised in Table 6.3. It was remarkably the case that the sexual segregation of occupations was almost total, with only 5 trades out of 74 indicating both male and female apprenticeship. As can be seen from Tables 6.1 and 6.2, such a marked occupational division earlier would have been unlikely for parish apprentices.

[34] City of Westminster Archives Dept, B. 1268.

Table 6.3. *St Clement Danes (Middlesex) apprenticeship, 1803–22*

Occupations	Male	Female
Black jeweller	1	—
Bootcloser	4	2
Bookbinder	1	2
Button maker	2	—
Butler	1	—
Bow Street manufacturer	1	—
Coach lamp manufacturer	1	—
Cutler & edge tool maker	1	—
Cordwainer	17	—
Cotton manufacturer	44	30
Carver, ornament maker, pattern cutter, gilder	2	—
Chimney sweeper	25	—
Copper plate printer	2	—
Enameller	1	—
Farrier	1	—
Fisherman	1	—
File cutter	4	—
Glass cutter	1	—
Gunbarrel maker	1	—
Gold and silver wire drawer	1	—
Gold and silver orris weaver	1	—
Hair dresser	2	—
Ivory and bone brush maker	1	—
Lamp lighter	1	—
Law writer	1	—
Newsman and stationer	1	—
Painter and glazier	1	—
Printers	3	—
Projecting letter manufacturer	1	—
Smith	2	—
Silversmith	1	—
Silk weaver/warper	7	3
Steelworker	1	—
Spangle maker and wire drawer	1	—
Tooth, nail, and shaving brush manufacturer	1	—
Taylor	9	—
Umbrella maker	2	—
Velvet and figure weaver	1	—
Vertical jackmaker	1	—
Watch glass maker	1	—
Watch band maker	1	—
Watch gilder	5	—
Weaver	4	3
Writing stationer	1	—

Occupations	Male	Female
Wig maker	3	—
Workbox and shaving case maker	1	—
Water gilder	1	—
Working goldsmith and jeweller	1	—
Baker	—	1
Bill sticker	—	1
Bed maker	—	1
Bitmaker	—	1
Childbed linen maker	—	2
Coal merchant	—	1
Dressmaker	—	2
Flower maker	—	2
Fancy brush maker	—	1
Gentleman	—	2
Housewifery	—	4
Japaner	—	1
Labourer	—	1
Lint-maker	—	21
Mantua maker and milliner	—	2
Ostrich feather maker	—	7
Pin sticker	—	1
Pocket book maker	—	1
Shoe binder	—	3
Silk stocking grafter	—	1
Tacker	—	1
Tambour maker	—	2
Tailoress	—	1
Victualler	—	1
Watch house keeper	—	1
Wine dealer	—	1
Total (271)	168	103
% of total	62	38

Total occupations 74
Shared occupations 5

This nineteenth-century development can easily be demonstrated in other areas. In Cambridgeshire in the eighteenth century, there is much evidence of female parish apprenticeship. But between 1827 to 1907, out of ninety-seven parish indentures for Cambridge, only one was for a girl, to the trade of milliner.[35] None of the boys were bound

[35] Camb C.R.O., G/C/AW 15–17.

to a woman, which, as we shall see, would certainly not have been the case in the eighteenth century. Whereas in the eighteenth century printed parish indenture forms for rural and urban Cambridgeshire were almost universally left blank for the insertion of 'he' or 'she', 'his' or 'her', referring to apprentice and master/mistress – in the nineteenth century they were usually printed with 'he' and 'his', and almost always so after about 1820. This generalisation applies to the various and different indenture forms being used in Cambridge, Chatteris, Elm, Fen Ditton, Hinxton, Ickleton, Great Shelford, Whittlesford, and Wisbech. In Soham, of the 1,297 poor children bound out by Bishop Laney's charity between 1818 and 1914, none were girls, and of the masters and mistresses taking them, four were mistresses in the 1810s, three in the 1820s, two in the 1830s, and 1840s, one in the 1850s, and none thereafter.[36] The four female mistresses of the 1810s were a tailor, carpenter, plumber, and blacksmith. The last female mistress of the 1850s was a basket-maker.

The 1841 census (the first to record occupations of individuals) is too late to track usefully the changes being argued for, and bears witness to the extreme sexual specialisation of work which had evolved by then. However, one can see clearly the tail-end of this process in the 1841, 1851, and 1861 Census Occupational Tables, with virtually all 'male' trades becoming proportionately even more male dominated during these twenty years (e.g., blacksmith, carpenter/joiner, cooper, tanner, bricklayer, brewer, clockmaker, wheelwright, miller, sawyer, millwright, plumber/glazier/painter, patten and clog maker, maltster, or mason and pavior). The 'female' trades progressively moved to even heavier proportional emphasis on female labour (e.g., dressmaker/milliner, lace manufacture, lint manufacture, stay and corset maker, fan and screen maker, glover, confectioner, fringe and tassel maker, ribbon maker, button maker, or bead maker). The overwhelming majority of these trades were 90 per cent or more either male or female dominated, and in very few were numbers more equally balanced by sex (e.g., button maker, confectioner, or ribbon maker). The 'male' trades moved to become by 1861 commonly 99 per cent or more male dominated.

We have concentrated so far on the better documented parish apprenticeships. This has allowed discussion of long-term change, and helped ensure that apprentices' class backgrounds remain reasonably constant, so as not to interfere with temporal comparisons. In the eighteenth century, female apprentices figured notice-

[36] Camb C.R.O., P. 142/25/1–3, 26. These declining numbers of mistresses are not due to any decline in the numbers of children being apprenticed by the charity over time.

ably in these parish indentures, and were put out to trades on terms of apprenticeship similar to those for boys. How did the situation of girls apprenticed through *familial* payment of premium, who were therefore of slightly higher social status, compare with them? To consider this, material from the Board of Inland Revenue was consulted. Under an Act of 1709 payment of duties on apprenticeship indentures was demanded, to the Board of Inland Revenue.[37] This tax was payable by the master or mistress in all cases except those of pauper, parish or charity apprenticeships, and the indentures were to be stamped at the head office in London. Pauper indentures were not taxed and did not require stamping. In other words, the records of the Board of Inland Revenue allow us easily to differentiate between the two forms of apprenticeship, in a way that takes account of the social background of the apprentice. In using them, we can be sure that we are not dealing with the somewhat lower status parish apprentices.

Table 6.4 gives evidence on female apprenticeship from this source for the counties of Surrey, Wiltshire, Warwickshire, Sussex, and Bedfordshire, for the first half of the eighteenth century.[38] Once again a wide range of occupations was involved, but with more emphasis on those of mantua maker, tailor, and milliner. Indeed, 'mantua maker' heads the list for all these counties, and the trades to which girls were apprenticed in large numbers were more obviously ones which required skill with a needle: mantua maker, milliner, draper, child's coat maker, sempstress, tailor, coat maker, stay maker, or glover. But many other trades were in evidence – as pin maker, gardener, weaver, cordwainer, ironmonger, carpenter, bricklayer, butcher, goldsmith, gun maker, blacksmith, or watch maker – pointing to the possibilities of a wider involvement in supposedly 'male' trades than in only those associated with needlework. This source ends after the mid-eighteenth century, because the decline of seven year apprenticeships entailed increasing numbers of indentures not being stamped, with no duties paid to the Board of Inland Revenue. However, indentures for the same category of apprentice in parish collections indicate almost no female apprenticeship whatever after

---

[37] See 8 Anne c. 5 and 9 Anne c. 21 – to be repealed by 44 Geo III c. 98.

[38] See H. Jenkinson (ed.), 'Surrey apprenticeship, 1711–1731', Surrey Record Society, X (1929); C. Dale (ed.), 'Wiltshire apprentices and their masters, 1710–1760', *Wilts Arch. and Natural History Soc.*, XVII (1961); R. G. Rice (ed.), 'Sussex apprentices and their masters, 1710–1752', *Sussex Record Soc.*, XXVIII (1924); H. Jenkinson (ed.), 'Bedfordshire apprentices, 1711–20', *Beds Historical Record Society*, IX (1925); K. J. Smith (ed.), 'Warwickshire apprentices and their masters, 1710–1760', *Dugdale Soc.*, XXIX (1975).

Table 6.4. *Female apprenticeship in Surr, Suss, Beds, Wark & Wilts*

Occupations	Surr (1710–31)	Suss (1710–52)	Beds (1711–20)	Wark (1710–60)	Wilts (1710–60)	Total
Mantua maker	36	37	5	30	66	174
Tailor/merchant tailor	8	4	—	4	36	52
Milliner	15	9	3	4	15	46
Weaver (broad, silk, narrow, Kersey, ribbon, worsted)	3	1	—	14	21	39
Farmer/husbandman/ yeoman/dairyman	4	5	1	9	3	22
Sempstress	9	4	1	1	6	21
Glover	3	3	—	1	11	18
Coat maker/child's coat maker/seller	15	2	—	—	—	17
Stay maker	4	1	—	3	6	14
Spinster	6	3	1	1	3	14
Widow	5	2	1	1	1	10
Carpenter	2	4	—	2	—	8
Cordwainer	2	1	—	1	4	8
Lacemaker/joyner	1	1	2	—	3	7
Pin/needle maker	6	1	—	—	—	7
Housewifery	—	3	—	1	3	7
Mercer/linen draper/ clothier	—	1	1	1	4	7
Fan maker	4	1	—	—	—	5
Blacksmith	1	2	1	—	—	4
Bricklayer	—	3	—	1	—	4
Miller/fuller	2	—	—	—	2	4
Victualler	—	—	—	2	2	4
Labourer	—	—	1	1	2	4
Mariner/waterman/ fisherman	2	1	—	—	—	3
Clear starcher	2	—	—	1	—	3
Ironmonger	1	—	—	2	—	3
Goldsmith	2	1	—	—	—	3
Gardener	3	—	—	—	—	3
Clothworker/burler	—	—	—	—	3	3
Stationer/bookbinder/ folder	1	—	1	—	1	3
Embroiderer/fringe maker	2	—	—	1	—	3
Bodice maker	—	—	—	—	3	3
Pistol/gun maker	—	—	—	2	—	2
Watch maker	—	2	—	—	—	2
Butcher	2	—	—	—	—	2
Upholsterer	1	—	—	—	1	2
Mealman	1	—	—	—	1	2
Hatmaker	1	—	—	—	1	2
Grocer/confectioner	1	—	1	—	—	2
Beaver cutter/puller	2	—	—	—	—	2
Schoolmaster/mistress	1	—	—	—	1	2
Wool spinner/spinner	1	—	—	—	1	2
Gent	—	1	1	—	—	2
Sawyer	—	1	—	—	—	1
Barber	1	—	—	—	—	1
Barber surgeon	1	—	—	—	—	1
Apothecary	—	1	—	—	—	1
Toy maker	—	—	—	1	—	1
Spectacle maker	1	—	—	—	—	1

Occupations	Surr (1710–31)	Suss (1710–52)	Beds (1711–20)	Wark (1710–60)	Wilts (1710–60)	Total
Packer	1	—	—	—	—	1
Candlestick maker	—	—	—	1	—	1
Skinner	—	—	—	1	—	1
Pipe maker	—	—	—	1	—	1
Painter	—	—	—	1	—	1
Baker	—	—	—	—	1	1
Haberdasher	—	—	—	—	1	1
Clerk	1	—	—	—	—	1
Quilter	—	—	—	1	—	1
Collar maker	—	—	—	—	1	1
Wheeler	—	—	—	—	1	1
Total women	154	95	20	89	204	562
Total men & women	2,952	2,989	401	2,454	2,759	11,555
Women as % of total	5.2	3.2	5.0	3.6	7.4	4.9
Premiums						
Men (sample)	£23.2	£11.0	£14.1	£9.4	£15.1	£14.5
	(s = 41.08)	(s = 9.74)	(s = 11.78)	(s = 10.33)	(s = 20.56)	(s = 22.94)
Women	£11.0	£13.1	£10.6	£7.6	£7.7	£9.6
	(s = 7.54)	(s = 9.32)	(s = 7.13)	(s = 5.31)	(s = 5.54)	(s = 7.20)
Length of apprenticeship (years)						
Men (sample)	6.9	6.5	7.0	6.9	6.9	6.8
	(s = 0.44)	(s = 1.32)	(s = 0.30)	(s = 1.09)	(s = 0.79)	(s = 0.95)
Women	5.7	5.0	4.7	6.0	6.7	6.0
	(s = 2.63)	(s = 2.21)	(s = 1.87)	(s = 2.60)	(s = 2.23)	(s = 2.47)

1800 – no cases were found in over 300 scattered indentures in the south-east. The wide range of trades seeing female apprenticeship in the early eighteenth century had disappeared.

The main feature which distinguished the early eighteenth-century female apprentices of Table 6.4 from their parish counterparts was the relative dominance of needlework occupations, which was less noticeable for eighteenth-century parish apprentices. The difference was essentially one of class background, with families able to pay a premium favouring the 'genteel' occupations, and the female parish apprentices having less choice, often being apprenticed to more lowly occupations. As Pinchbeck wrote: 'In an age when it was desired above all things to be considered "genteel", millinery and mantua-making were the favoured occupations for those [girls] in the class "a little above the vulgar".'[39] And Joseph Collyer, whose *Parents' Directory* of 1761 catered to such a class, used the same phrase in relation to the trade of child's coat maker – 'for those a little above the vulgar it is a very proper one'.[40] The other trades to which he recommended female apprenticeship accord well with Table 6.4, and included those of glover, petticoat maker, milliner, quilter, ribbon weaver, silver and

[39] Pinchbeck, *Women Workers*, p. 289.
[40] J. Collyer, *The Parents' and Guardians Directory* (1761), p. 101.

gold thread spinner, tassel maker, upholsterer, embroiderer, basket maker, bodice maker, button maker, or fan painter. 'I know of none fitter', he wrote of the trade of millinery, 'for the daughters of numerous families, where the parents live handsomely, yet have no fortunes to leave their children.'[41]

If the occupations to which girls were apprenticed in Table 6.4 shows more concentration on 'genteel' occupations, attention can also be drawn to the smaller percentage females were of the total apprenticed. For eighteenth-century parish apprentices, between 23 and 35 per cent were female, but for those apprenticed by their family it seems generally to have been under 10 per cent. As the social status of family of origin rose, so women participated in a more 'genteel' range of occupations, and so also their likelihood of participating in *any* occupation fell relative to boys. The social significance attached to not having a working wife (or daughter), alongside the difficulty of poorer families to survive only on low and precarious male earnings, help explain these class differences. Clearly, it is important to control carefully for social background when treating the economic roles of women in this period; and this should qualify discussion of sexual inequality, and point to the social location of 'patriarchal' ideologies. These most obviously belonged to the elite culture, from which they filtered downwards in the sense that they were grasped by classes with upward aspirations. It seems probable that rather different and historically less accessible attitudes both governed and reflected the position of women from lower social classes, particularly before the late eighteenth century.

The premiums paid for male and female apprentices (Table 6.4) were much higher than for the (earlier) Southampton parish apprentices of Table 6.2, and emphasise that female apprenticeship was nearly as costly as for boys. Indeed, in Sussex the mean figure was higher (£13.1 as against £11). The generally higher male averages were because more boys than girls were apprenticed with very large premiums indeed, and if one discounts high premiums (over £30) the average sums were almost identical between the sexes, with both Sussex and Surrey having higher average female premiums than male. The higher Southampton poor child female premiums provide an additional indication that female apprentices were apprenticed in much the same way as boys – to learn a trade or craft, with which they could later earn a livelihood, or contribute towards the familial income if married. Indeed the greater flexibility in length of terms for female apprentices (see the standard deviations, Table 6.4) probably

[41] *Ibid.*, p. 195.

acknowledged the likelihood of their earlier marriage, but also took more realistic account of the time needed to learn separate trades. In the latter respect this presaged changes which increasingly came to affect the seven year term for males after 1750. (Seven years was still the modal term for girls, however.)

It is most unlikely that women were always apprenticed to be taught and employed in 'housewifery' (skilled though that could be) rather than to learn a craft. Such a view anachronistically applies Victorian middle- and upper-class assumptions on the roles of women to an earlier lower-class environment, featuring very different female work. In any case, 'housewifery' was the term used in the eighteenth century where the employment of the girl was to take this form. Female apprentices were sometimes apprenticed to the same trade as their fathers (just as boys),[42] and were frequently daughters of apprenticed men; their premiums were comparable to those for boys; duties were paid by the master or mistress, and the lengths of their apprenticeship terms similar to those for boys. When girls were promised money at the end of their apprenticeships the sum was much the same as that sometimes allowed boys – to whom, of course, it was by no means always the case that such sums were promised.[43] And the premiums given where 'housewifery' was stated were very low indeed – usually around £1–£2 for non-parish female apprentices, whose mean premium was between £7–£14 when apprenticed to all other trades. Where the age of the apprentice is known it is clear that those apprenticed to 'housewifery' were atypically young.[44] More-over, women examined as to their settlements often mentioned apprenticeships, making it clear that they had continued to practise the trade either as a 'journeywoman' or mistress, and successfully claimed settlements on the basis of apprenticeship – just as did men.[45]

[42] Willis & Merson, *Southampton Apprenticeship Registers*, p. xxx.　　[43] *Ibid.*, p. lxiii.
[44] The same point is also made in J. Lane, 'Apprenticeship in Warwickshire, 1700–1834' (unpub. Ph.D. thesis, University of Birmingham, 1977), pp. 484–6.
[45] This was true throughout the southern counties. For examples from just one parish, see Westminster Archive Dept, B. 1173, nos. 152, 226, 242; or see B. 1194, p. 47. The wording is the same as for male apprenticed examinants: 'Ann Hart aged upwards of 22 years upon Oath saith that she served seven years apprenticeship with Mr Nowland a Peice [sic] Broker ... and has been out of her time about one year.' 'Susanna Stears aged about 21 years upon Oath saith that she never was married and that she was bound Apprentice for five years to Mr Sam Randal Clogmaker and lived with the sd. Mr Randal as an Apprentice for four years and 9 months ... and then her sd. Master gave up her Indres' (Indentures). Similar cases can be extensively documented for other parishes. See for example Dorset C.R.O., P. 34/OV 7; Surrey C.R.O., LA 5/5/54; Wilts C.R.O., 533/52/4–5, 59/1; Camb C.R.O. G/C/As 7; G/C/As 9; Beds C.R.O., DDP 1/13/4/1–3; Hunts C.R.O., Q/S Vagrancy Box, 1782 and 1824, 136/3/5–7; Herts C.R.O., D/P 24A 13/2; D/P 15/13/3; West Suffolk C.R.O., EL 159/7/11 (1–34), 28; N2/1/8–10; EL25/7/18; Devon C.R.O., 2160 Al. P.O.

'Journeywoman' was a term in use in the seventeenth and eighteenth centuries, to describe skilled apprenticed women, although it died out thereafter.[46] The evidence (and that to be presented on women actually practising the trade after apprenticeship) strongly suggests that when a girl was apprenticed to the trade of goldsmith, or cordwainer, she was apprenticed just as a boy, to learn the trade, and not to seven years of 'housewifery' – to which she could have been cheaply apprenticed, or most obviously put even more cheaply via the normal yearly hirings of servants.[47]

To confirm this argument for the reality of female apprenticeship we can turn briefly to some literary evidence. Perhaps it is felt that it is unnecessary to argue the point at length. And yet one so frequently encounters the historiographical assumption that the acute sexual division of labour which had developed by 1850 existed long before then, in all classes, that it is still a point worth emphasising. So let us take perhaps the most extreme case of female labour in forges, for which eighteenth-century evidence exists in the form of a few women apprenticed to blacksmiths and farriers. Here is William Hutton:

When I first approached Birmingham, from Walsall, in 1741, I was surprised at the prodigious number of blacksmith's shops upon the road; and could not

[46] See for example Collyer, *Parents' Directory*, pp. 90, 248; R. Campbell, *The London Tradesman* (1747), pp. 208, 228; H. Fielding, *The Miser. A Comedy* (1733), I, ii; C. E. Tonna, *The Wrongs of Woman* (1843–4), pt I, p. 99; Pinchbeck, *Women Workers*, p. 293; Berks C.R.O., D/P 34/13/1.

[47] See also the S.C. on Parish Apprentices, V (1814–15). About 35 per cent of those who had been apprenticed from London were female. There was no occupational breakdown by sex provided, but it is clear from the classification that even if one assumes that only girls were apprenticed to 'Household employments' (which would not be the case), then the large majority of girls were still apprenticed to 'Various trades and professions'. In America, much higher sex ratios, lower female marriage ages, higher fertility, and an associated greater value being placed on women as potential wives with a more strictly 'domestic' function, probably led to a greater tendency for girls to be apprenticed to 'housewifery' than was the case in England. On this, see M. Jernegan, *Labouring and Dependent Classes in Colonial America, 1607–1783* (New York, 1931); R. Seybolt, *Apprenticeship and Apprenticeship Education in Colonial New England and New York* (New York, 1917); J. Axtell, *The School Upon a Hill; Education and Society in Colonial New England* (New Haven, 1974); C. Bridenbaugh, *The Colonial Craftsman* (1950); E. S. Morgan, *The Puritan Family* (New York, 1944), pp. 68, 75–6. In America, the terms servant and apprentice were often used interchangeably. This was also true of the Statute of Artificers, but a stronger distinction developed over time in England; and it may be that the joint use of the two terms in the 1563 Statute was partly because the Bill was initially intended to cover all categories of servant, and only later was extended to encompass the industrial and trade sectors. (See S. T. Bindoff, 'The making of the Statute of Artificers', in S. T. Bindoff, J. Hurstfield & C. H. Williams (eds.), *Elizabethan Government and Society* (1961), pp. 68, 88–93.) American apprenticeship was also more erratic than in England, without the constraints of the 1563 Act, with the movement out of the trades into farming, and with the scarcity of services and goods. See Axtell, *School Upon a Hill*, pp. 116ff.

conceive how a county, though populous, could support so many people of the same occupation. In some of these shops I observed one or more females, stripped of their upper garments, and not overcharged with the lower, wielding the hammer with all the grace of the sex. The beauties of their faces were rather eclipsed by the smut of the anvil.[48]

Or as late as 1842, it was said of Sedgeley (in relation to the manufacture of nails in forges there) that it 'might appropriately be termed the district of female blacksmiths. They are its most prominent characteristic.'[49] In the region which concerns us it would be

[48] W. Hutton, *History of Birmingham* (Birmingham, 1781, 1835 edn), p. 192.
[49] S.C. on the Employment of Women and Children in Agriculture, XV (1843), p. 683: 'The physical condition of the girls is better than that of the boys ... they bear the heat of the forges better, and often become strong by the work.' For further details of female nail makers, see C. Tomlinson (ed.), *Cyclopaedia of Useful Arts* (1854), vol. 2, p. 307; A. Rees, *Cyclopaedia: or, an Universal Dictionary of Arts and Sciences* (1819–20, Trowbridge, 1972 edn), vol. 4, p. 18. See also Anon., 'Autobiography of a Navvy', *Macmillan's Magazine* (Dec. 1861), 143: 'I used to call this girl "my little mouse", because she worked hard all the summer, and laid up a store for the winter. She used to work in her father's brickfield, for he was a brickmaker ... She was the only woman ever I knew killed herself by hard work. She used to do just the same as a man, and she was nearly as strong. She had a sister who was stronger than a man ... She is so strong, that she can lift a blacksmith's anvil up by her hair. She also lies down and has the anvil placed on her chest.' For illustrations of female brickmakers, see W. H. Pyne, *Microcosm: or, a Picturesque Delineation of the Arts, Agriculture, Manufactures etc of Great Britain* (1808, Luton, 1974 and 1977 edns), pt I, Plate IV. (For illustrations of women working in the trades of rope maker, cable maker, brewer, cyder maker, gravel-digger or potter, see *ibid.*, Plates X, XI, XIII, and XVII. For a female chairmender, see *ibid.*, pt II, Plate IX.)
For an example of a girl working in the trade of a blacksmith, see J. Lodey's letter to *Local Population Studies*, XXV (1980), 58, recalling a conversation with 'the octogenarian daughter of a blacksmith, who told me that when her father's health was beginning to fail she used to have to help him shoe the ponies. He'd say "come on girl, you can do that job", and she would take the shoes off and clean the feet out and he would fit the new shoes.' The same volume contains an account of female chain makers in the Black Country (pp. 58–9). For an account of a female blacksmith taking apprentices, see Oxfordshire C.R.O., Witney apprenticeship indentures (uncatalogued), 1816: 'William Jackson son of Mary Jackson of Witney ... doth put himself Apprentice to his said Mother ... to learn her art and with her [to dwell] after the Manner of An Apprentice ... And the said Mary Jackson for and in consideration of the natural love and affection she hath and beareth for and towards her said son, and also in consideration of the sum of six pounds to her in hand paid by the ffeoffees of certain Charity lands given to the town of Witney for that purpose the receipt wherof is hereby acknowledged [!] [will teach] her said Apprentice in the Art of a Blacksmith which she useth.'
Servants would often be employed in trades, even in that of a blacksmith, and such work was not limited only to master/mistress, journeymen, and apprentices. The distinction between servants and apprentices was often a loose one in workplace practice. For example, E. Chambers wrote that: 'If a smith's servant lames a horse while he is shoeing him, an action lies against the master, and not against the servant' (E. Chambers, *Cyclopaedia: or an Universal Dictionary of the Arts and Sciences* (1741–3, 1786 edn), see under 'servant'). If even a smith's servant would work in this way, it seems likely that a female apprenticed to a blacksmith would also be involved in aspects of smithy work.

unusual to find female work or apprenticeship in such an environment as late as this. Just as in the agricultural labour force, it seems likely that changes in the south and east occurred rather later elsewhere. But it was clearly the case that women could, and did, participate in heavy occupations, and there seems little reason to question the fact of their apprenticeship even to this trade. There were 512 female blacksmiths in Great Britain in 1841, although by then they were only a very small proportion of the total numbers practising the trade.[50] To quote again from the 1843 Report on the Birmingham region: 'The effects of early work, particularly in forges ... render these girls perfectly independent. They often enter the beer-shops, call for their pints, and smoke their pipes, like men; indeed there seems little difference in their circumstances from those of men.'[51] And, of course, even heavier female labour as, for example, in coal mines, or as coal-heavers, could be easily documented, as it was by early photographers.[52] As E. P. Thompson wrote on the very active role of women in popular unrest: 'These women appear ... to have been unaware that they should have waited for some two hundred years for their Liberation.'[53]

III

If women in the eighteenth century were apprenticed to a wide range of trades, what evidence is there that they went on to practise the trade, or to become 'mistresses' in their own right? Dunlop wrote that 'those girls who were bound and who served seven years could attain the position of independent mistresses and rank with master craftsmen ... There are instances ... of women working on their own account; and though this seems never to have been very general, it was not so unusual as to arouse comment or surprise.'[54] Widows took up the freedom of their husbands' companies and carried on the trade as a matter of course, and there is abundant evidence of their taking

---

[50] 1841 Occupational Census.

[51] Report on the Employment of Women and Children in Agriculture, XV (1843), p. 622.

[52] There were for example 2,966 women working as coal miners/heavers/porters/labourers in 1841 (1841 Occupational Census, pp. 45, 50). See also M. Hiley, *Victorian Working Women: Portraits from Life* (1979), pp. 83–98; or Thompson, *Working Class*, pp. 369–70, 377.

[53] E. P. Thompson, 'The moral economy of the English crowd in the eighteenth century', *Past and Present*, L (1971), 116. And see 116 quoting Southey: 'Women are more disposed to be mutinous ... in all public tumults they are foremost in violence and ferocity.'

[54] Dunlop & Denman, *English Apprenticeship*, pp. 150, 154.

apprentices in apprenticeship material.[55] Such a woman did not have to serve an apprenticeship to be eligible to practise the trade, and the assumption was that as the wife of a craftsman she would have learnt the trade, and worked with her husband at it, to a degree which allowed her the status of an independent mistress after his death.[56]

But such participation was certainly not only limited to unapprenticed widows of craftsmen, and, as Dunlop pointed out, it was often found among single women recently apprenticed. There is much evidence of women entering guilds, practising their trade, and becoming 'free', after apprenticeship.[57] This frequently seems to have been assumed at the time of binding. In February 1541/2 for example, Elenor Morgan was apprenticed to Robert Jeoffreys, mercer, and Johanna his wife, shepster, to learn the trade of mercer, and her master covenanted to pay the fee of 4s. 6d. for her freedom of the city of Bristol.[58] Kahl mentioned women becoming members of London Livery Companies;[59] Levi Fox gave many more examples of this in Coventry;[60] and Seybolt's view on this issue fully confirms the position taken here. Speaking of the English situation, he observed:

It may be pertinent, at this point, to mention the fact that girls were admitted into the crafts under the same conditions that regulated the practice for boys. It is not an uncommon thing to find women and girls enrolled as members of crafts where one would least expect them, such as the founders, barbersurgeons, brewers, carpenters, wheelwrights, and clockmakers.[61]

---

[55] There are, for example, 120 independent mistresses in the Wiltshire apprentice material. Dale, 'Wiltshire apprentices', xiv.

[56] See A. Daly (ed.), *Kingston Upon Thames Register of Apprentices, 1563–1713* (Guildford, 1974), p. x; Jenkinson, 'Bedfordshire apprentices', xvi.

[57] For example see: J. C. L. Stahlschmidt, *Surrey Bells and London Bell-Founders* (1884), pp. 51–4; S. Young, *The Annals of the Barber-Surgeons of London* (1890), p. 260; W. H. Overall & S. E. Atkins, *Some Account of the Worshipful Company of Clockmakers of the City of London* (1881), p. 155; E. B. Jupp & W. W. Pocock, *An Historical Account of the Worshipful Company of Carpenters of the City of London* (1848, 1887 edn), pp. 161–2; Fox, 'Coventry guilds'; C. A. Markham & J. C. Cox (eds.), *Records of the Borough of Northampton* (1898), vol. 2, pp. 311, 316; Heal, *London Goldsmiths* (1972 edn); H. H. Bobart (ed.), *Records of the Basketmakers' Company* (1911), p. 108: 'Indentures with "free sisters" are recorded as late as the end of the eighteenth century, when the practice of admitting women to the freedom had almost ceased'; C. Welch, *History of the Pewterers' Company* (1902), vol. 1, p. 18: 'It is clear also from the receipt of quarterage from "Sustren" as well as "Bretheren" that women were admitted, not only to the religious fellowship connected with the guild, but also to the craft, which included their contributions in its accounts.' Atkins, *Register of the Apprentices of the Company of Clockmakers*, e.g., pp. 40, 49, 52, 157, 178.

[58] D. Hollis (ed.), *Calendar of the Bristol Apprentice Book (1532–1565)*, Bristol Record Soc. Publications, XIV (1949), vol. 1, p. 7.

[59] W. F. Kahl, 'Apprenticeship and the freedom of the London Livery Companies, 1690–1750', *Guildhall Miscellany*, VII (1956), 19.

[60] Fox, 'Coventry guilds'.   [61] Seybolt, *Apprenticeship*, p. 15.

And Melville, making a similar argument for the frequent apprenticeship of girls in the eighteenth century, continued by stating that
the girl was 'able to continue her trade and support herself should she
not marry'.[62] Material from settlement examinations, covering as it
does past rents paid by the examinant,[63] provided further evidence of
single apprenticed women in the eighteenth century who had never
been married, renting properties with a value in excess of £10 per
annum, from which to practise trades.

The range of trades practised by women in the eighteenth century
on their own account was very large, as their apprenticeship to them
might lead us to expect. The trades where there is firm evidence of a
mistress taking apprentices in her own right include, for example,
those of: blacksmith, carpenter, tin plate worker, founder, mason,
cooper, shipwright, vintner, glazier, tallow-chandler, weaver,
breeches maker, baker, clothworker, barber, collar maker, butcher,
soap maker, apothecary, miller, gloveress, mercer, cordwainer, vic-
tualler, bell-founder, barber-surgeon, wheelwright, clockmaker, and
of course all the trades (as mantua maker, milliner, tailor) which I
earlier characterised as having a more 'genteel' aspect. And additional information could be presented on the wide range of occupations of
women debtors petitioning for release under the Relief Act of 1742; on
women mistresses in the building trades, contracting for repairs to
eighteenth-century houses of correction;[64] or of apprenticed women
in the London Company of Carmen, working along the docks and
warehouses of the Thames, owning carts in their own right, and
having them registered in their own names by the Company, even
when married.[65]

---

[62] R. Melville, 'Records of apprenticeship and settlement in a Berkshire village in the
eighteenth century', *Trans. Newbury and District Field Club*, X (1954), 34. In this
context, it is also worth noting Richard Wall's findings on the position of women. He
wrote that there is 'little difference in the frequency with which never married and
widowed women head households in Great Britain in the late twentieth century
compared with the situation in pre-industrial England'. For the pre-industrial period
he also found that 'single and widowed men are at almost every age less likely to be
heading their own household than women of the same marital status', and that 'in
the past, as now, women rather than men are likely to be solitary'. See his
interesting discussion in 'Women alone in English society', *Annales de démographie
historique* (1981), esp. 307–15.

[63] Renting to the value of £10 or more per annum conferred a settlement, and
consequently there is much information on past rents paid by examinants.

[64] As encountered by Joanna Innes in her research on eighteenth-century houses of
correction, to whom I am grateful for this point. She also finds that women often
came up before Sessions as disorderly apprentices.

[65] Michael Walker's research on the decline of guild and company control in the
eighteenth century has produced abundant evidence of apprenticed women entering the guilds, and practising their trades in their own right. He supports this

Clearly, there were in the eighteenth century many trades open to women, and it would be mistaken to see such involvement as limited only to widows. The participation of married women in trades (and not necessarily those practised by their husbands) is even better documented. This can now be discussed, to formulate more clearly the reasons for female apprenticeship, and to stress how such an economic partnership formed an important aspect of the marital relationship among the poorer classes. As Alice Clark wrote on the seventeenth century: 'the idea is seldom encountered that a man supports his wife: husband and wife were then mutually dependent and together supported their children.'[66] We should recall a point made earlier. The actual involvement of women is heavily under-represented by the use only of apprenticeship records, which fail adequately to encompass their work as non-apprenticed members of an artisan family, and as widows. Such work should not be underestimated on the basis of the fairly small percentages of apprentices which were female, and a brief outline of the scope of women's work within marriage may help us realise the full significance of the later decline of familial forms of production. My subsequent comments will be made not only on the basis of changes in female apprenticeship *per se*, but also in the belief that these represented the surface manifestations of changes which had a far deeper effect on the vast majority of women in artisan families, who were never actually apprenticed.

In Bristol in the sixteenth century it had apparently been very common for apprentices, whether male or female, to be bound to both the husband and wife, and this practice continued there into the seventeenth and eighteenth centuries.[67] It is difficult to know how common this practice was in the later period, because the marital status of a master is clear only when a wife was named in the indentures. But it can be suggested that when a wife was so named a particular significance attached to this, and the trade practised by the man was also participated in by his wife. The expectation was that her participation in the trade with her husband entailed her responsi-

argument that female participation was most apparent, and very common, in the lower classes, and provides the point made above regarding the Carmen Company. Where the husband and wife both practised this trade together carts were registered in the names of each, *separately*, and it was clearly indicated that the wife owned her carts, and the husband his. Women were fined for offences against company regulations to the same extent and sum as were men, and their offences leave no doubt that they were engaged in the heavy dockside work on the carts, alongside men. I am grateful to him for these points.

[66] Clark, *Working Life of Women*, p. 12.   [67] Hollis, *Bristol Apprentice Book*, p. 7.

bility, alongside his, for the training of an apprentice. An alternative explanation for the naming of the wife in the indentures, but one which is entirely acceptable for this argument, is that the apprentice was actually bound to the wife rather than the husband – the latter in fact being tradeless, or practising a different trade from that to be taught to the apprentice. Ricart acknowledged the right of married women to take apprentices when they were practising a craft on their own account.[68] But in a case like this the apprentice usually had to be indentured to both husband and wife, even when the husband did not practise the trade. As the Customs of London made clear in the seventeenth century:

> Married women who practise certain crafts in the city alone and without their husbands, may take girls as apprentices to serve them and learn their trade, and these apprentices shall be bound by their indentures of apprenticeship to both husband and wife, to learn the wife's trade as is aforesaid, and such indentures shall be enrolled as well for women as for men.[69]

It will be apparent that the major documentary source available to us to study the involvement of female artisans may heavily underrepresent the *de facto* female participation, because of this stipulation that the husband also be mentioned in the indentures. Historians may all too readily assume that he was the master, in cases where his name may have been added to that of the person intended to teach the trade – namely his wife.

The naming of the wife in the indentures, then, can be seen as indicating either that both wife and husband practised, and were to teach, the trade, or (perhaps less commonly) that the apprentice was to be taught the trade by the wife alone. When husband and wife practised different trades, and where both trades were stated after each name, it is usually clear who was mainly responsible to teach the apprentice. Much more often this is not clear. But the assumption can be made that where the wife was named in the indentures she was heavily involved in the trade, either entirely in her own right, or more probably alongside her husband.

As the evidence on female apprenticeship suggests, the range of trades where the wife was involved in either of these ways was very wide. Indeed, it would be quite impossible to limit these eighteenth-century trades to certain occupational categories, and proceed to

[68] Ricart, *Maire of Bristowe*, p. 102.
[69] Cited in Clark, *Working Life of Women*, pp. 194–5. See also Ricart, *Maire of Bristowe*, p. 102.

define such categories as 'women's work'.[70] They included, among many others, those of shearman, cloth presser and dresser, merchant, beer brewer, clothworker, serge weaver, joyner, husbandman, tailor, mariner, musician, basket maker, clothier, cobbler, currier, grocer, dyer, hatmaker, mercer, baker, dornex-weaver, worsted weaver, upholsterer, hosier, fishmonger, cordwainer, cooper, woolcomber, skinner, carpenter, collar maker, haberdasher, glover, tobacco pipe maker, barber and periwig maker, joiner, plumber, and blacksmith. The list could be considerably extended. There was perhaps more emphasis on shopkeeper categories (grocer, mercer, haberdasher, baker), on trades such as tailor, mantua maker, milliner, glover, and on the wide range of weaving occupations. But one is most struck by the enormous range of trades indicating such involvement by the wife.

Clearly, marriage was not characterised by a husband working to keep his wife (as was the case for about 58 per cent of marriages in 1971). Rather, for the classes considered here (especially the lowest before the nineteenth century) it was very much an economic partnership, with the wife's work contributing to the production of a surplus for the market.[71] Her labour was certainly not limited to non-surplus producing, purely domestic labour, in the way, arguably, the work of women of higher social status increasingly was in

---

[70] Only the indentures of male apprentices are used for this list, because if the earlier argument for female apprentices being taught the trade was not accepted, it could then be argued that women would be mentioned in the indentures only of girls, to whom they might be intending to teach 'housewifery'. So no female indentures are included in this discussion of the role of married women as mistresses, teaching the trade by themselves, or with their husbands.

[71] In illustration of this, see for example the descriptions of the old family economy among the handloom weavers of Middleton in S. Bamford, *Early Days* (1849), and his *Passages in the Life of a Radical* (1842, 1967 edn). See also P. Laslett, 'Les Rôles des femmes dans l'histoire de la famille occidentale', in E. Sullerot (ed.), *Le Fait feminin* (Paris, 1977); A. Yarbrough, 'Apprentices as adolescents in sixteenth-century Bristol', *Jnl of Social History*, XIII (1979), 69, and n. 16. For a similar situation in France, with references to female apprentices there, see O. Hufton, *The Poor of Eighteenth-Century France, 1750–1789* (Oxford, 1974), pp. 25–33; or her 'Women and the family economy in eighteenth-century France', *French Hist. Studies*, IX (1975). For further evidence on the economic roles of women within marriage, see in particular app. VI in George, *London Life*, p. 425. This gives occupations of the witnesses, prosecutors, and prisoners appearing at the Old Bailey. It is apparent from this that while the wife frequently followed the same trade as her husband, she often pursued one quite independently of him. Some of them were practising trades normally associated with an apprenticeship, as a plumber, cloakmaker, milliner, stay maker, tailor, hatmaker, weaver, mantua maker, glover, or quilter. They were all working for wages, or producing a product for purchase, and it is clear that they made significant contributions to the familial income, rather than being supported by their husbands.

the seventeenth and eighteenth centuries.[72] For artisan and handicraft classes the sexual division of labour along lines of male surplus
production away from the home place, and female non-surplus
production (i.e., purely domestic work), had generally not developed
before 1750, and in some trades and regions was delayed until a much
later period. Such a division of labour became more pronounced
higher in the social scale. Plummer's description of the weavers
before the nineteenth century supports these statements: 'The weavers, like other craft gilds, regarded a wife as a trade partner having
the right to succeed to and carry on the business after her husband's
death. Widows in fact, took over all the rights, privileges and
liabilities of their deceased husbands, for example as to the proper
number of looms, journeymen and apprentices.'[73] Or the compositor
J. B. Leno wrote of his wife 'who laboured at the press and assisted
me in the work of my printing office, with a child in her arms'.[74]
Similarly, in the families of London silkworkers women 'were expected to share in the necessary financial obligations, a position fairly
common in the fifteenth century, when husbands and wives, for
varied reasons, were frequently named jointly in pleas of debt
brought either by them or against them'.[75]

The economic involvement of the wife implied a more shared
domestic division of labour, parallel to the shared division of surplus-
producing labour. One recalls Alice Clark's statement that

men were much more occupied with domestic affairs then than they are now.
Men in all classes gave time and care to the education of their children, and
the young unmarried men who generally occupied positions as apprentices
and servants were partly employed over domestic work . . . a considerable
proportion of [which] in former days fell to the share of men.[76]

Such male involvement in the affairs of the household had probably
been strongest among the lowest classes of domestic craftsmen,
whose wives participated most significantly in forms of craft production similar or identical to those practised by their husbands. For

[72] See R. Hamilton, *The Liberation of Women* (1978); C. Middleton, 'The sexual division
of labour in feudal England', *New Left Rev.* (1979), 113–14, and his 'Sexual inequality
and stratification theory', in F. Parkin (ed.), *The Social Analysis of Class Structure*
(1974); Pinchbeck, *Women Workers*, pp. 283–4; Clark, *Working Life of Women*, ch. 2.
[73] Plummer, *London Weavers' Company*, p. 63.
[74] Cited in D. Vincent, 'Love and death and the nineteenth-century working class',
Social History, V (1980), 239.
[75] Dale, 'London silkwomen', 328. A similar situation, with the wife as 'trade partner',
may occasionally be found today, for example with couples selling market-garden
produce or second-hand goods on a market stall, but it is now very rare.
[76] Clark, *Working Life of Women*, p. 5. For an example of a male 'housekeeper' in 1712
see Bucks C.R.O., PR. 159/13/121–160.

these families marriage was a natural economic partnership determined largely by the persisting possibility of mutual work within the family at home, and by the alternation between prolonged leisure and intense periods of work which had always affected or (if you prefer) been the inclination of the pre-industrial artisan.[77]

This characteristic of marriage was much less apparent by the mid-nineteenth century, but certainly continued for some trades. The 1851 Occupational Census, for example, listed as a separate occupation that of 'shoemaker's wife', of which there were as many as 79,649 in Great Britain, for a total of 199,798 male 'shoe and boot makers' aged twenty or over – a wider category than just the 'shoemaker' one should note, and many of these men would be unmarried. The logic of this categorisation lay in the participation of these women in their husbands' still essentially family-based trade. Here, at least, there had been significant continuity of female familial involvement in the trade, although not in the possibility of their being apprenticed to it in their own right. Such familial involvement in shoemaking broke down after the mid-nineteenth century, with the introduction of factory- and warehouse-based machinery, which was bitterly resented for its disruption of the family economy. The trade was one of the last to see such changes, and in this sense the 1851 census was particularly significant in indicating the nature of familial engagement in it which would earlier have been the case for a much wider range of trades. This trade was also one of the few in the late eighteenth and early nineteenth centuries in which wives tramped with their husbands, alongside the tanners, curriers, tin-plate workers, and masons.[78] The census also recorded the existence of 6,002 'shopkeepers' wives', 17,447 'innkeepers' wives', 26,584 'beershop keepers' wives', 201,736 'farmers'/graziers' wives' and 26,015 'butchers' wives' – but no other trades were deemed by this late stage to be still

---

[77] See D. C. Coleman, 'Labour in the English economy of the seventeenth century', *Econ. Hist. Rev.*, VIII (1956); E. P. Thompson, 'Time, work discipline and industrial capitalism', *Past and Present*, XXXVIII (1967).

[78] Prothero, *Artisans and Politics*, p. 30; R. A. Church, 'Labour supply and innovation, 1800–1860: the boot and shoe industry', *Business History*, XII (1970), 36. (Out of about 600 striking Northampton shoemakers on tramp in 1858–9, 133 were women.) Leeson, *Travelling Brothers*, pp. 130, 243. I suspect (from settlement evidence) that tradesmen from a much wider range of trades actually tramped with their wives. Trades listed above are the ones cited by these authors. For women shoemakers, see also T. Wright, *The Romance of the Shoe: Being the History of Shoemaking* (1922), pp. 171ff; D. Bythell, *The Sweated Trades* (1978), pp. 106–13; S.C. on Artisans and Machinery, V (1824), p. 140; Prothero, *Artisans and Politics*, p. 44; E. Suffolk C.R.O., FC 101, G11/13/3: 'And the said Susanna Freeman shall teach the said apprentice during the said term in the art, trade and mystery of a Cordwainer which she now useth in the best way and manner that she can.'

based sufficiently on family cooperative production to justify such a categorisation for the wife. Of course, some other trades in the mid-nineteenth century remained partly based on this system, and these included brush making, straw-plaiting, tailoring, dressmaking and other needlework trades, silk weaving, cabinet making, chain and nailmaking, lacemaking and hosiery, glove making, toy making, some small-ware trades, or felt making in the north. Others could be added. But they were comparatively few by this date.[79]

It should be evident that this stress on the economic aspects of marriage implies nothing detrimental about the 'quality' of familial relationships within the seventeenth- and eighteenth-century family economy, or domestic form of artisan production. Were there any credibility in the supposed eighteenth-century rise of 'Romantic Love', as discordantly celebrated in familial histories of the mid-1970s, it could as well be seen as a developing artefact of infrequent association than as a qualitative improvement over the supposedly 'instrumental' relationships of earlier periods.[80] It might describe a deterioration in the experienced quality of family life brought about by the decline of the family economy; and by consequent changes in the place of work of the husband (now increasingly an agricultural proletarian, or, given the decline of apprenticeship and its consequences, a partially employed journeyman), and by changes in the nature and significance of his wife's work. But there is surely overwhelming literary evidence to suggest most affectionate courting and familial relations in earlier periods.[81] And with regard to class differences, one might recall Keith Thomas' account of the relative absence of the 'double standard' among the working class, compared

[79] For female labour in the cabinet-making trade in 1850, see E. P. Thompson & E. Yeo (eds.), *The Unknown Mayhew* (1971, Harmondsworth, 1973 edn), pp. 477–8.

[80] *Pace* Shorter, *Modern Family*; Stone, *Family, Sex and Marriage*. On the use of arbitrary barriers to intensify love, see S. Freud's discussion of 'obstacle love' in his 'The most prevalent form of degradation in erotic life', in *Collected Papers*, ed. by J. Strachey, vol. 4 (1950), p. 213. The decline of the family economy would of course have contributed towards the setting up of such obstacles or barriers. See also the discussion in T. Tanner, *Adultery and the Novel. Contract and Transgression* (1979), pp. 88–9.

[81] For example, see R. Gough, *The History of Myddle* (Harmondsworth, 1981 edn), pp. 152, 169, 183. William Cobbett pointed out that marriages of love were found least among the upper classes, and became much more common further down the social scale, among those living by manual labour. See his *Advice to Young Men* (1830, Oxford, 1980 edn), p. 93. And see A. Macfarlane, review of Stone, *Family, Sex and Marriage*, in *History and Theory*, XVIII (1979); his *The Family Life of Ralph Josselin* (Cambridge, 1970), and his *Origins of English Individualism* (Oxford, 1978), pp. 24, 28, 59–60, 197–8. (I am also sympathetic to the argument made in the latter work for a relatively high degree of female independence in pre-industrial England, pp. 78, 80–2, 91, 131–5.)

to the middle or upper, and his statement that: 'The double standard, therefore, was but an aspect of a whole code of social conduct for women which was in turn based entirely upon their place in society in relation to men. The value set on female chastity varied directly according to the extent to which it was considered that women's function was a purely sexual one.'[82] If this was so, one might expect that the crucial economic importance of women in the labouring and artisan classes was associated with rather different sexual attitudes than those typical of the 'double standard', found higher in the social order. If one accepts these terms, and bearing in mind the trends affecting female work analysed here, a possible explanation emerges for the sexual and familial attitudes which became most pervasive in the nineteenth century, and which persist to a lesser degree 'even today'.

One should also note that the character of familial relations probably changed more irreversibly in the late eighteenth century, particularly if one considers the range of shared experience. The antipathy to the decline of family production brought about by factory-based machinery could, of course, be extensively demonstrated with reference to many late eighteenth- and early nineteenth-century social movements,[83] and the attitudes to the family revealed in these movements awaits discussion. But perhaps it was the later Thomas Hardy who most forcefully articulated the sense of loss and personal estrangement associated with the decline of the shared labour and cooperation of the family economy – without, one suspects, fully appreciating the historical relativity and significance of that loss for his own lifetime and concerns. Indeed, a central theme of his novels was a search for the conditions in which loving relationships could develop, and the consequent stress on the 'falsity' of marriage where such cooperation in work was absent. His thinking on the basis for emotional understanding came back repeatedly to this, as for example at the end of *Far From the Madding Crowd*:

Their's was that substantial affection which arises (if any arises at all) when the two who are thrown together begin first by knowing the rougher sides of

---

[82] Thomas, 'The double standard', 213. And see B. Harrison, 'Underneath the Victorians', *Victorian Studies*, X (1967), 261. See also de Beauvoir, *The Second Sex* (1976 edn), pp. 120, 133: 'The oppression of women has its cause in the will to perpetuate the family and keep the patrimony intact . . . The richer the husband, the greater the dependence of the wife . . . On the contrary, a common poverty makes the conjugal tie a reciprocal tie . . . in free labour woman found real autonomy because she played an economic and social part of real importance . . . the rich woman paid with her subjection for her idleness.'

[83] See, for example, Thompson, *English Working Class*, pp. 339–40, 367–74; or Church, 'Labour supply and innovation', 40.

each other's characters, and not the best till further on, the romance growing up in the interstices of a mass of hard prosaic reality. This good fellowship – camaraderie – usually occurring through similarity of pursuits, is unfortunately seldom superadded to love between the sexes, because men and women associate, not in their labours, but in their pleasures merely. Where, however, happy circumstance permits its development, the compounded feeling proves itself to be the only love which is strong as death.[84]

Or in *The Woodlanders*:

They had planted together, and together they had felled; together they had, with the run of the years, mentally collected those remoter signs and symbols which seen in few were of runic obscurity, but all together made an alphabet . . .' He ought to have married *you*, Marty, and nobody else in the world!' said Grace with conviction, after thinking in the above strain.[85]

This interpretation of Hardy will be developed elsewhere, against the late decline of agricultural and craft family economies in Dorset.[86] But it serves usefully to highlight qualitative changes which occurred in the family during this period, and may encourage the morally problematic attempt to place the value of the 'modern family', with its unprecedentedly acute sexual division of labour and high separation rates, in historical perspective. In Hardy's terms, late eighteenth- and nineteenth-century 'romantic love' might be seen as pleasure sharing stripped of economic sharing and mutual cooperation in work. This is not to deny the continued and important contribution of women to the familial standard of living, whether through housework and the direction of consumption, or wage-earning outside the home place. But the range of shared experience had diminished considerably from that of the earlier family economy, and the high separation rates which mark the twentieth-century family from those of the past may derive more from this than from its lower fertility, and reduced role vis-à-vis children – from the relative ease with which household units may be reformed where association has become less work and more pleasure orientated.

IV

Some of the main points of this chapter can now be brought together, and an explanation developed for them. The argument complements

---

[84] *Far From the Madding Crowd* (1874, 1971 edn), p. 439. See also M. Young & P. Wilmott, *The Symmetrical Family: A Study of Work and Leisure in the London Region* (1973, Harmondsworth, 1980 edn), pp. 98–9: 'A partnership in leisure has therefore succeeded a partnership in work.'

[85] *The Woodlanders* (1887, 1971 edn), pp. 340–1.   [86] See chapter 8.

the description of changing female involvement in agriculture. The chronological precision of the latter cannot be duplicated here, but the general picture of relatively more equal and sexually shared labour before the nineteenth century is supported by evidence on female apprenticeship and artisan activity. Women, particularly in the eighteenth century, could be apprenticed to many trades, and supposedly 'male' trades were open to them, with female participation either via apprenticeship or more often in the family economy. Such participation was most apparent among the lowest social classes, becoming less common as one moved higher in the social scale. And this involvement has frequently been missed by historians because it was experienced by those women who left least behind them in the form of literary documentation. The wide class divergence of female work can once again be stressed. Even in the labour force itself minor differences of social origin and familial wealth (determining the type of apprenticeship) produced different emphases in the trades to which girls might be apprenticed.

The late eighteenth and early nineteenth centuries saw a narrowing of the possibilities for female artisan activity, and the trades to which they were apprenticed became more limited to needlework occupations. As in south-eastern agriculture, women again became relegated to economically less significant labour, which was sexually segregated to an unprecedented extent, and at times heavily exploited. Eric Richards' statement that 'in the pre-industrial framework, women were absorbed in a broad range of activity which was subsequently narrowed by the structural changes associated with the Industrial Revolution', quoted in chapter 1 for its applicability to the south-eastern agricultural sector, seems also borne out for the apprenticed trades.[87]

---

[87] E. Richards, 'Women in the British economy since about 1700: an interpretation', *History*, LIX (1974). For similar arguments see most notably Pinchbeck, *Women Workers*; Clark, *Working Life of Women*; and E. Boserup, *Women's Role in Economic Development* (1970). For the associated 'surplus female problem' of the nineteenth century, see: J. Boucherett, 'How to provide for surplus women', in J. Butler (ed.), *Woman's Work and Woman's Culture* (1869); A. Kenealy, 'New view of the surplus of women', *Westminster Review*, CXXXVI (1891); W. R. Greg, 'Why are women redundant?', in *Literary and Social Judgements* (Boston, 1869).

It is worth suggesting also that this broader female involvement in the earlier period may have contributed to the home market between 1700 and 1780, just as high female participation rates probably did in the southern agricultural sector before the 1770s. But as in the agricultural sector, the diminution of female work, coupled with falling male real wages in many trades, meant that benefits to familial income probably dwindled after the 1780s. When one considers the rising male real wages in south-eastern agriculture from the 1740s or earlier, but then their decline after about 1780 through to the late 1840s, and the falling female real wages from the

While I have stressed that women were indeed apprenticed to many trades, and certainly worked in them to a significant degree, one should not exaggerate the extent of their participation via apprenticeship. The percentage female of apprentices could be quite small, ranging from 3 to 41 per cent. In making an argument of this nature, it is always possible to overdraw it, to direct attention forcibly to common omissions of historiography and interesting aspects of change. The eighteenth century assuredly was not a 'golden age' for women; they were usually not involved in trades to the same extent as men, nor were they as economically independent. The 'male' trades of the period were unquestionably male dominated, just as they were in the nineteenth century. Similarly, there were significant and marked sexual divisions between many trades, as can be seen from the apprenticeship evidence, and I have not discussed these in any detail. Sex ratios by trade – between male and female apprentices, journeymen and journeywomen, masters and mistresses – will remain unknown for the period before the occupational census, depending on assessment of elusive factors such as the ratios of parish or charity to other apprentices. And inadequate sources make it difficult to discuss female participation after apprenticeship, as single or married women, although biographical evidence in settlement examinations can be helpful here.[88] I have drawn attention to

mid-eighteenth century, it seems that a hitherto buoyant section of the home market – the agricultural and artisan labour force of the south and east – became much less significant after about 1780. The continued course of industrialisation may have entailed a precarious transition: from reliance on a broadly based southern male and female market before 1780, to dependence on trade exports, and a middle-class and northern market thereafter. For the possible significance of female demand in the north, see N. McKendrick, 'Home demand and economic growth: a new view of the role of women and children in the Industrial Revolution', in his (ed.) *Historical Perspectives. Studies in English Thought and Society in Honour of J. H. Plumb* (1974). It is unlikely that such arguments could be made for southern England after the late eighteenth century.

[88] Insurance records can also be useful in this regard. See, for example, the extensive evidence of female dyers, pressers, clothiers, shopkeepers, sergemakers, stuffmakers, and fullers in S. D. Chapman (ed.), *The Devon Cloth Industry in the Eighteenth Century*, Devon and Cornwall Record Soc. (1978), e.g., pp. 4, 7, 8, 12, 13, 24, 38, 58, 72, 81, 87, 89, 105, 108, 117, 135, 140, 149. These are from the Sun Fire Office inventories of merchants' and manufacturers' property. Trade directories and newspapers are other obvious sources. The latter are used in Pinchbeck's interesting and supportive account of 'Craftswomen and business women', *Women Workers*, ch. XII. Quarter Session Registers of persons who have had weights and balances checked also provide evidence on the wide range of female retailers. In a period when most shops were little more than open shanties, there were many women working in this way. See A. W. Tuer, *Old London Street Cries* (1885, 1978 edn). On the reduced role of women as mercers and haberdashers after the seventeenth century, see S. M. Thompson, 'The London 'prentices', *New Monthly Magazine* (1822), 172.

the way apprenticeship records underrepresent the roles of women in the trades. And it is often hard to decide whether female involvement after apprenticeship was in a managerial or skilled capacity. These are all questions on which it is difficult to reach reliable answers. To avoid misinterpretation, I re-emphasise that the 'male' trades were indeed male dominated, but were not exclusively male as so often is supposed; that there did indeed exist opportunities for women to be apprenticed to these trades; and, in particular, that such opportunities were more noticeable before the nineteenth century.

What were the conditions conducive to this wider female involvement, and why did it change? I can outline here some of the major considerations, although the task of allocating precise importance to them is difficult in a period for which our knowledge still remains limited, and the interaction of factors is potentially complex. First, the apprenticeship of women might appear partly as a corollary of certain demographic characteristics, particularly of the period before the mid-eighteenth century. Wrigley and Schofield have argued that England was demographically a 'low pressure' society, in which fertility and mortality rates were relatively low by comparison with many economically underdeveloped societies, with growth significantly determined by fluctuations in fertility, which in turn reflected changes in nuptiality. They have made clearer the variability within western Europe of demographic determinants, and in particular the importance of changes in the age at marriage and the proportion never marrying in England.[89] Two very significant demographic changes occurred which may have affected female apprenticeship. Female marriage ages fell from about twenty-seven to twenty-four between the late seventeenth century and the 1820s, and the proportion of women never marrying fell from about 25 per cent in the late seventeenth century to about 6 per cent in the late eighteenth and early nineteenth centuries. It seems possible that some allowance for female apprenticeship was especially important, in a period of family artisan production, when women were marrying late and many would not marry at all. It was an essential aspect of training for the independence and autonomy interwoven with prevailing demographic circumstances, and in this regard it seems significant that the extent of female apprenticeship declined alongside the fall of female marriage ages and the proportion never marrying, to their low points in the early nineteenth century. Allowance for female apprenticeship was necessitated by prevailing family production (their skills would be important to their family after marriage), but also by expectations

[89] E. A. Wrigley & R. S. Schofield, *The Population History of England, 1541–1871* (1981).

of female independence probably associated with these demographic conditions, and perhaps by demographically linked labour shortages. As yet one is unable to determine how far female artisan involvement had fluctuated in earlier centuries according to demographic influences. It is likely that the earlier predominance of the 'family economy' dictated a relatively constant level of female participation, and some evidence has been used for earlier periods which suggests this. Nevertheless, the late sixteenth century may have seen some limited but similar changes to those of the late eighteenth century, because of comparable demographic effects on the labour market. Evidence is as yet inadequate to determine this.

In explaining the changes which seem to have occurred during and after the late eighteenth century, let us first recall the demographic situation in the preceding century. Population growth had been negligible, or less than 0.5 per cent per annum, with late marriage ages, a high proportion celibate, and low fertility. A 'balanced' labour supply and falling food prices produced rising real wages and demand for non-agricultural products, made by the apprenticed sector. In contrast to this, population growth accelerated after 1750. An inadequate expansion of agricultural employment to compensate for this demographic growth allowed it to contribute to a glutted rural labour market, raising prices and poor rates. Male real wages were shortly to fall, and female labour was curtailed, their real wages heavily cut, and so their marriage ages fell further as a protection against unemployment. As argued in chapter 1, the immediate causes of the diminution of female agricultural work were increasing male unemployment after about 1760, with a more economically rational use, by employers, of male harvest labour coupled with growing use of the scythe, to take advantage of rising prices.

Similarly, falling agricultural real wages in the south after about 1770–80 probably reduced demand for the apprenticed sector's goods, and a problem of labour surplus in the trades became more apparent. Here, too, more sexually selective employment of labour may have been a reaction to employment problems. With the decline of apprenticeship after 1750, the stepping up of the tramping system, the depression of many trades faced with factory production, the labour glutting attendant on falling apprenticeship restrictions, the move to more acute seasonal distributions of unemployment in trades for which there is adequate evidence, and the effects of demobilisation, it seems probable that male unemployment was also a major factor behind reduced female artisan involvement. One recalls from the last chapter that masters waived apprenticeship entry quotas to increase production; that this resulted in a glutting of the trades, and growing prospects of unemployment facing journeymen after 1750. The serving of a full seven years became increasingly seen by the apprentice as an unjustified imposition, which only delayed the inevitable partial employment, and bleak prospects for setting up as a master. Most trades could be learnt in well under seven years. While masters continued to act in a conservative manner by attempting to enforce the seven year term (which provided labour in the form of trained and productive apprentices), the desire of the apprentices in this context for earlier participation in the trade in their own right was a main cause of the declining lengths of terms actually served. The consequent 'debasement' of the system (into a less obligatory, short-term contractual, 'clubbing-out' system of training), with increasingly impotent attempts to enforce its earlier form, opened the trades to those technically ineligible to practise, in turn providing further motive for a reduction of the terms served.

These conditions of a glutted artisan labour force produced recurrent measures to exclude women from trades.[90] Ribbon weavers, for example, faced with price cutting and unemployment, and expressing their discontent in riotous activity, took steps to try and exclude women from their trade in all periods except those of war. Conditions stipulating this, and agreed to by masters and men in 1769, went as follows:

No woman or girl to be employed in making any kind of work except such works as are herein fixed and settled at 5½d. per ell or . . . per yard or under for the making and those not to exceed half an ell in width . . . And no woman or girl is to be employed in making any sort of handkerchief of above the usual or settled price of 4s. 6d. per dozen for the making thereof PROVIDED always . . . that in case it shall hereafter happen that the Kingdom of Great Britain shall engage in war . . . that then every manufacturer shall be at liberty to employ women or girls in the making of any sort of works as they shall think most fit and convenient without any restraint whatsoever.[91]

Female ribbon weavers continued of course into the nineteenth century, but in many other trades feminine exclusion may have owed much to similar measures as these, originating from male artisans facing unemployment.[92]

---

[90] For more detailed accounts of the conditions facing the trades after 1815, see Thompson, *English Working Class*, ch. 8; Prothero, *Artisans and Politics*, ch. 4.

[91] George, *London Life*, p. 183.

[92] Or see S.C. on the State of the Woollen Manufacture, III (1806), pp. 261–3. One recalls E. J. Hobsbawm's argument that 'the normal attitude of male trade unionists towards women seeking to enter their occupation was, in the words of S. & B. Webb, "resentment and abhorrence" . . . they represented a threat to the rates and conditions of men. They were – to quote the Webbs again – "as a class, the most

Certainly the glutting of trades brought a conservative reaction, most noticeable in the early nineteenth century, which aimed to re-establish the elitism and control of the guilds, and the older terms of apprenticeship, and a probable effect of this was pressure brought to bear against the training of female apprentices. Their exclusion may have been seen as one possible remedy for the problems of those (often recently formed) groups defending the apprenticeship system. It is also probable that most women working in the trades had never been apprenticed, and that efforts to enforce apprenticeship restrictions in the late eighteenth century were directed particularly at them. Arguments that the success of English trade depended on control over company membership (in the interests of quality production), and the enforcement of the Statute of Artificers, failed to halt the repealing legislation of 1814.[93] But this frame of mind helped reduce the possibility of female cordwainers, goldsmiths, or hatters. The legislation itself merely acknowledged the *de facto* decline of apprenticeship, and it seems likely that pressure against women working was an attempt to remedy the unemployment which was part cause and effect of that decline. And such pressure was, of course, part of a wider refutation of women's rights during the

dangerous enemies of the artisan's Standard of Life" ... the policy of all unions capable of doing so was to exclude them from their work, and the policy even of those unions incapable of doing so (e.g. the cotton weavers) was to segregate the sexes or at least avoid women and girls in conjunction with men.' As he said: 'It is a paradox of nineteenth-century industrialization that it tended to increase and sharpen the sexual division of labour between (unpaid) household work and (paid) work outside.' See his 'Man and woman in socialist iconography', 130–2. Particularly in relation to southern England, this argument for the long-term pattern of change was unobjectionable. It met with a critical response, mainly on the grounds that it minimised women's work outside the home in the nineteenth century. The argument which countered this provided a helpful corrective in drawing attention to many (regionally very diverse) examples of nineteenth-century women's work, but stopped short of assessing questions of frequency and the numbers of women involved, the long-term changes affecting such work, and the form and extent of this in earlier periods. See S. Alexander, A. Davin & E. Hostettler, 'Labouring women. A reply to Eric Hobsbawm', *Hist. Workshop*, VIII (1979). Statements in this chapter on nineteenth-century women's work are all made by way of comparison with earlier centuries. The contribution of women to the nineteenth-century economy or working-class household was of course an important one, if regionally very various. But without minimising that contribution, it is my intention here to deal with it in chronological perspective. On the role of male opposition to women working, see also J. Humphries, 'Class struggle and the working-class family', *Cambridge Jnl of Economics* (1977), 252–3. See Pinchbeck, *Women Workers*, p. 294, on the particular use of the Statute of Artificers against non-apprenticed women.

[93] 54 Geo III c. 96 – which repealed the apprenticeship clauses of the Statute of Artificers. See also S.C. on Apprenticeship, IV (1812–13).

Napoleonic Wars (by Paley, Gisborne, and others), when such rights were associated with 'Jacobinism'.[94]

Unemployment was aggravated by the effects of demobilisation in 1784 and 1815. When dealing with the agricultural sector it became clear that these dates were followed by rising unemployment, contributing to the declines of yearly hiring, falling real wages, rising poor rates, increased difficulty in gaining settlements, and shifts in the sexual division of labour. There is good reason to suspect that the artisan sexual division of labour was also much affected in the 1780s, and after the Napoleonic Wars. For these had been significant periods of change within the apprenticeship system, as we saw with the falling age at which apprenticeships ended, and the percentage of illegal apprenticeships. The decline of apprenticeship was also most rapid in the 1780s. It is now customary, perhaps in reaction to an earlier historiographical emphasis on military history, for historians to minimise the social significance of eighteenth-century warfare, although they have little doubt about the consequences of that in the twentieth century. But with an eighth of the male work force in the forces during the Napoleonic Wars, with the disruptive consequences of the practice of 'King's Freemen' – that is, of allowing ex-servicemen to set up in any trade regardless of their apprenticed eligibility[95] – and with the noticeable consequences of demobilisation for the agricultural sector, one should stress the effects of war, against a background of demographic growth, the decline of apprenticeship, and alternative factory production, in creating considerable fluctuations of male artisan unemployment, and thus in raising opposition to women in the trades. Interestingly, this is a rather different argument than that usually made for the effects of war in the twentieth century on women's work.

One should also stress that this explanation needs more accurate location to specific trades than it will receive here, and I do not wish to minimise the occupational diversity of the period. Many trades had narrower optimal, or working, numbers of employees or artisans than others. Such trades (one thinks for example of the building trades) could very quickly experience pressure on employment, and a reduction of female work could occur much more rapidly than in

---

[94] W. Paley, *Concise Admonitions for Youth* (1809), pp. 67–8; T. Gisborne, *An Enquiry into the Duties of the Female Sex* (1797), pp. 226–30.

[95] For the legislation which permitted this, see: 12 Charles II c. 16; 22 Geo II c. 44; and 24 Geo III c. 6. The latter also allowed wives and children of ex-servicemen to set up and practise trades to which they had not been apprenticed, and this may have contributed to opposition against female involvement.

others. I am pointing here only to the *general* effect of male unemployment, in those trades which became more completely male dominated, in bringing about female exclusion, rather than presenting a
more detailed analysis of the structural nature (and vulnerability to
unemployment) of specific trades. It is the case (perhaps paradoxically)
that the decline of apprenticeship did not generally allow intrusions
of female labour into the trades, and was more commonly followed
by successful pressure against this. Within the protective structure of
the 1563 Act, female work in the trades had been little threat to
employment or the position of male artisans. But without that
Elizabethan structure (i.e., increasingly after 1750), and with the
adverse consequences for journeymen of its decline, female work
rapidly came to be seen in a different light – with 'resentment and
abhorrence', as the Webbs put it. There were then two possible
outcomes for women of the growing class divisiveness in the trades.
They could be successfully ousted from the labour market – as
occurred in many trades where the majority of the work force had
always been male. Or, as in trades where earlier I noted greater
female concentration in the nineteenth century (which had once seen
significant male participation), the decline of apprenticeship and the
associated vulnerability of employees would allow growing deployment of cheap female labour. This occurred, for example, in London
'slop-shop' tailoring, Spitalfields silk, lace manufacture, stay or corset
making, glove making, fringe and tassel making, ribbon making, or
button making.[96] In such trades (often arranged on an out-work basis)
the work force was too vulnerable to prevent recourse to, and
exploitation of, female labour. And of course for some such trades in
a domestic environment vulnerability to unemployment coupled with
falling piece rates led to the need to increase production, and female
work here might persist as long as such conditions lasted – often well
into the nineteenth century.

In arguing for a reduction of female work in the trades it is not my
intention to deny their continuing roles throughout the nineteenth

---

[96] In the later nineteenth century, there is also evidence of three year female
'apprenticeships' to bookbinding and printing in London and Edinburgh with
women sometimes working as compositors. They were trained as cheap labour, the
apprenticeship did not compare with that for males, and the unions insisted
throughout on their exclusion. It is not my intention to deny later cases such as this,
although women had certainly worked in printing in earlier centuries. On the later
nineteenth century, see G. Howell, 'Trade unions, apprentices and technical
education', *Contemporary Rev.*, XXX (1877), 845; J. Zeitlin, 'Craft regulation and the
division of labour: engineers and compositors in Britain, 1890–1914' (unpub. Ph.D.
thesis, Univ. of Warwick, 1981), pp. 157–62, 321–7.

century in many significant, but usually increasingly sexually segregated, areas of production: particularly in the textile industry, the potteries, or in small industries like lace, straw-plaiting, embroidery, button making, or needlework occupations. The continuity and similarity of this 'women's work' to the occupations their apprenticeship became limited to is readily apparent.[97] However, in the south and east employment opportunities for women were much fewer than elsewhere, with their dwindling agricultural role, and the decline of many cottage industries – such as hand lacemaking, button making, hand-knitting, or glove making. Expanding (if sometimes exploitative) sectors requiring female labour in the south existed – for example, domestic service, the silk mills in a couple of Essex parishes, the straw-plait industry, the Northampton, London, or Norwich boot and shoe industry, dressmaking, millinery or 'tailoring', Spitalfields silk, or bonnet making. But more remunerative alternatives to agriculture or familial crafts were much more common in areas of the north. The complaint of the 1804 Ladies Committee for Promoting the Education and Employment of the Female Poor,[98] that women were being reduced to 'profligacy and misery', excluded from many occupations and 'grievously and unjustly intruded upon by the other sex ... confined, most frequently, to a few scanty and unproductive kinds of labour', seems a generally accurate description of the apprenticeship changes and of alternative female work in the south.

So far, changing demographic conditions, and male artisan unemployment, have been discussed as explanations for the reduced scope of female apprenticeship. These should now be supplemented by a crucial consideration which was closely related to male unemployment, but to which we have as yet less access – that is, the increasing capitalisation of the trades and its relation to the decline of artisan family economies. Pinchbeck's arguments on the reduced role of women have been supported here, and her discussion of the rather earlier sexual division of labour in the woollen industry is worth citing at length:

Women's work was most varied where the influence of capital in the trade was negligible, as among the small Yorkshire clothiers. When every process from the fleece to the woven piece of cloth was undertaken in the home, the women of the family commonly assisted in all operations. Big capitalistic production, on the other hand, meant a division of labour in which women

---

[97] For their main mid-nineteenth-century work, see the 1841 and 1851 Occupational Censuses, or C. Mackeson, 'Occupations and vital statistics of England and Wales', *The British Almanac and Companion* (1875), 89–110.

[98] Cited in Pinchbeck, *Women Workers*, p. 304.

were relegated to certain occupations, the number of which tended to be reduced as capitalistic organisation developed. In the early days in the 14th and 15th centuries, women had been employed in every branch of the woollen industry, as wool sorters, wrappers, carders, spinners, dyers and weavers, and had been enrolled as apprentices and admitted to the membership of the crafts. As the industry became more highly organized their employment was attacked as competing with that of men, and on these grounds they were excluded from certain branches of the trade. Later . . . the tendency to employ an increasing number of journeymen on the premises of their employer still further limited women's work . . . the wives of journeymen who worked entirely away from home either lost any share they had had in the industry, or were restricted to carding and spinning. They could no longer warp the yarn or take a turn in the loom as they so often did when the journeyman was employed at home.[99]

These remarks could be extended to a wide range of trades beyond the woollen industry. Most of the trades discussed here moved away from home-based family production to forms of economic organisation characterised by greater investment of capital, and the employment of journeymen in a larger context away from their homes. This transition was facilitated by the decline of apprenticeship and the increased vulnerability of journeymen to unemployment. While one can point to such non-familial production in an earlier period for some trades, the major changes certainly occurred after 1750. Beyond the presumed corollaries of technological change in specific trades or industries, and impressions gleaned from the growth of clubbing-out apprenticeship, we know little about temporal changes affecting the sexual *location* of work place, and class and economic divides within the trades. Until these can be specified in greater detail, preferably for individual occupations, the explanation will remain in its present form – that is, stressing the high female participation found in earlier family-economy trades before their decline, alongside both the demographic changes affecting women in the eighteenth century, and the effects of male unemployment; but omitting to articulate with greater precision the diverse relations of these factors to capital intensification and the decline of home-based artisan production.

The most pressing problem remains that of the interrelation of demographic change, the decline of the family economy, unemployment, and shifts in the familial standard of living – focussed here on

---

[99] *Ibid.*, p. 121. And see K. Stadin, 'Den gomda och glomda arbetskraften. Stadskvinnor i produktionen under 1600-och 1700-talen', *Historisk tidskrift* (1980), 319. ('The changes that took place in Swedish society during the 17th and 18th centuries had the effect, among others, that women living in towns . . . obtained a changed role in production: from having worked in traditional "male" labour fields they increasingly worked in textile manufactures or as maids and suchlike in home or household.')

the question of how social attitudes change, and on how it affected the economic relations, cooperation, and emotional ties of the sexes. Perhaps the arguments made will advance understanding of these matters. Faced today with economic recession, and the unemployment prospects for women of the evolving micro-industrial revolution, one is tempted to end by way of prediction. (In just the two years after January 1976 male unemployment rose by 9 per cent – female unemployment by 53 per cent.) But I will simply conclude by stressing how important a satisfactory formulation of these issues is to an understanding of the markedly divided sex roles which we experience today, and, more specifically, of the diminution of women's work in the apprenticed trades.

7

The family

A number of familial changes emerged in earlier chapters. These included the reduction of agricultural 'live-in' servants in husbandry and of 'live-in' apprenticeships, the possible effects of enclosure on marriage age, and the agricultural and artisan sexual division of labour. I want now to look specifically at the familial effects of such changes, and to discuss other aspects of family life. These will include the idea of the family; ages at which children left home; the notion of 'adulthood' in the past; generational and occupational settlement patterns and their influence on the meaning of 'community'; family formation by occupation; factors influencing the age of marriage; attitudes to marriage and sex; the domestic division of labour; the family poverty cycle; family break-up and desertion; kin connections and the effect of the poor law on these; and the changing quality of family life. These issues help to place some of our current priorities in historical perspective, and are of major importance to family history. But they also enter (sometimes problematically) into an assessment of the standard of living. I hope to place them more closely within their social and economic context than has been possible in much family historiography.

What is meant by the 'idea of the family'? Ann Smith, married to a publican who had deserted her, found herself examined as to settlement in Bedford, in 1777. She had five children – four were her own, and the other, an apprentice aged fifteen, had been 'bound to her husband two years since, being also part of her family'. She also had a girl aged sixteen with her, the daughter by another marriage of her husband's, who was not included among her five children. The

I am grateful to Michael Anderson, Peter Laslett and Richard Wall for their comments.

320

apprentice was removed with the family to the husband's settlement at Eveshott, and he was considered an integral part of the family – perhaps more so than Ann Smith's stepdaughter.[1] Similarly, servants were considered part of their family of service. Here, for example, was Arbuthnot in 1773, speaking of a farm of 800 acres: 'If the tract is in the hands of one man, his family will consist of himself, a wife, three children, twelve servants, and ten labourers, each with a wife and three children; in all fifty. Thus the farmer's family — 17.'[2] Or as Thomas Turner wrote in his diary: 'My whole family at church – myself, wife, maid, and the two boys.'[3]

Service, or apprenticeship, when accompanied by traditional 'living-in', brought a transference of familial ties from one's family of origin to the family of service or apprenticeship. The degree of transferred attachment could vary. It certainly lessened over time. It had been common for a yearly hiring to end with a few days' visit back to one's family of origin, the members of which were frequently referred to simply as the servant's 'friends'. As the later practice grew of preventing the gaining of settlements by yearly hiring, this visit was sometimes 'benevolently' extended for longer. In fact, so concerned were employers that servants should see their families that they often insisted on the visit starting one or two days before the service was due to end. This was one manifestation of the decline of service, increasingly apparent from the 1780s, which, alongside the decline of 'live-in' apprenticeship, was of considerable significance for the families of both employers and employees. As Wrigley has written, the most important change in the composition of the family between Tudor and Victorian times 'was probably the decline in the importance of live-in servants in husbandry'.[4] The effect of this was a more solid isolation of families within firmly entrenched 'class' confines, with unmarried people less commonly living with higher status households before marriage and belonging to their family of service, as during the eighteenth century.

We have seen how this affected the quality of social relationships. The growth of 'class' antagonisms was accelerated by these familial

---

[1] Beds C.R.O., DDP. 1/13/4/2.
[2] J. Arbuthnot, *An Inquiry into the Connection between the Present Price of Provisions and the Size of Farms* (1773), p. 26.
[3] T. Turner, *The Diary of a Georgian Shopkeeper* (1925, Oxford, 1979 edn), p. 14.
[4] E. A. Wrigley, 'Reflections on the history of the family', *Daedalus*, CVI (1977), 78. Nevertheless, I do not wish to exaggerate the decline of service for the young unmarried, and it may be noted that in 1851 25 per cent of nineteen-year-old girls and 17 per cent of nineteen-year-old boys were living-in servants or living-in apprentices in Britain. I am grateful to Michael Anderson for this information, taken from his National Sample data.

changes derived particularly from the employing rationality associated with price levels, and the pressures of structural unemployment and rising rates within an outmoded settlement legal structure. The apprenticeship system underwent parallel changes: the emerging practice of 'clubbing out', the residence of the apprentice with his parents, rather than master, and the shortening of the term. These similarly reduced social communication and accentuated class isolation. Once again, there were significant alterations of family structure. But the social consequences were equally clear. These changes illustrate an approach taken here, in which the family will be studied less for its own sake, as an isolated phenomenon of historical social structure – a statistical mean household size – but rather as an important and still poorly fathomed intermediary between economic change and its qualitatively experienced effects, as for example on social relations.

II

We should consider first the age at which children left home – a subject closely connected with such factors as demographic change, the decline of 'living-in', the family poverty-cycle, the growth of cottage industry, and questions of parental 'responsibility' and influence over their children. This subject is relevant in many respects to us today. For example, in Britain in the 1930s unemployment was at about 5 per cent for fourteen- to twenty-year-olds, and 15 per cent for all males; but today about 25 per cent of eighteen- to nineteen-year-olds are unemployed, and about 8 per cent of thirty-five- to forty-five-year-old males. (In O.E.C.D. countries today those under twenty-five years of age comprise 48 per cent of total unemployment.) In other words, there has been a striking change in the age-specific incidence of unemployment. Our modern problems of large-scale unemployment among the young, and the related inner-city unrest – alongside remedial proposals such as 'opportunity' schemes, or attempts to make the family more accountable – have made it important to be more aware of youth life-cycle practices in the past, most particularly in the period when the decline of service and apprenticeship contributed to youth unemployment, and to what early nineteenth-century commentators described as a 'juvenile vagrancy problem'.

We have as yet the most rudimentary historical knowledge of life-cycle practices affecting the young, and it is fortunate in this regard that a small minority (usually between a tenth and a thirtieth) of settlement examinations give the age of leaving home, commonly for service or apprenticeship. For a few parishes the age of leaving home is regularly obtained, but in others rarely so. This matter depended largely on the efficiency of the parish clerk. There is no reason to suppose that the examinants for whom it was given were atypical, and these details were entirely peripheral to any purpose of the examination in establishing settlement. The information has some decided advantages. The precision with which the leaving age can be established (frequently down to half years, and always by precise year of age), and the way in which this can be related to sex or intended occupation of the person leaving, the precise date of departure, and other information in the examinations, make the latter a more detailed source than literary evidence, and a useful supplement to the community listings of inhabitants hitherto used for a similar purpose – which only provide information on the percentage of children within certain age groups remaining at home.[5] The examinations also hint at changes over time, and the age at which people were apprenticed to various occupations.

Table 7.1 gives the mean age of leaving home for some of the better documented counties, broken down by sex for agricultural and apprenticed sectors. Some of the numbers involved are small, particularly for women, for whom such information is infrequently given. But even the smaller figures are an advance over our current knowledge, which has usually been generalised from a couple of literary examples. A number of interesting points emerge. The ages are in the first place not so young as some writing suggests, and may jolt historiographical preconceptions. For males in the agricultural category (mainly farm-servants) the mean age was 14.8 years in the east, and for apprenticed males, 14.2 years. We should therefore be wary of contemporaries who over-generalised the experience of factory recruitment or apprenticeship, to give an impression of very early ages of leaving home. Secondly, in the eastern counties the agricultural leaving age for males was almost always younger than for girls, and overall nearly a year and a half younger. In the west, the contrast was much less marked, and the two sexes left home at almost exactly the same age. Thirdly, there is a strong impression that

---

[5] For discussion of this subject, see: R. Wall, 'The age at leaving home', *Jnl. of Family Hist.*, III (1978); M. Anderson, *Family Structure in Nineteenth-Century Lancashire* (Cambridge, 1971), pp. 124–32; P. Laslett, *Family Life and Illicit Love in Earlier Generations* (Cambridge, 1977), p. 34. A. Macfarlane uses literary evidence for the seventeenth century, covering middling and upper classes, in *The Family Life of Ralph Josselin* (Cambridge, 1970), pp. 92, 114, 208–9. The ages are lower than those documented here.

Table 7.1. *Age of leaving home by county and occupational category,*
1700–1860

County	Male				Female			
	Agricultural Mean	N.	Apprentices Mean	N.	Agricultural Mean	N.	Apprentices Mean	N.
Eastern & Midland counties								
Camb	15.8	40	14.6	45	16.1	22	12.7	3
Beds	15.4	19	14.3	27	18.7	3	—	—
Hunts	15.2	32	14.5	13	17.2	8	12.0	1
Herts	13.8	10	12.7	12	16.0	5	—	—
Ess	16.5	12	12.8	13	15.3	3	—	—
Norf	13.9	15	14.0	5	14.6	5	—	—
Suff	14.7	78	14.0	103	16.8	9	—	—
Surr	15.3	19	15.3	36	16.7	15	14.0	2
Oxon	15.7	10	14.6	10	14.7	3	14.0	1
Berks	14.7	20	14.4	19	16.0	2	—	—
Bucks	14.0	21	14.6	17	15.0	6	—	—
Leics	13.4	26	13.6	54	14.2	2	—	—
Total	14.8	302	14.2	354	16.2	83	13.2	7
Western & south-western counties								
Devon	13.3	28	13.4	7	12.9	8	—	—
Dor	14.1	68	15.5	18	14.1	13	—	—
Wilts	14.0	38	14.7	10	17.2	6	—	—
Som	13.9	7	14.1	5	14.6	5	14.5	1
Glos	15.0	22	14.5	21	13.9	8	14.0	1
Mon/Heref/ Worcs	14.1	18	13.9	5	13.2	7	14.0	1
Total	14.1	181	14.6	66	14.2	47	14.2	3
Overall total	14.5	483	14.3	420	15.5	130	13.5	10

western pastoral areas had an earlier agricultural leaving age (for both sexes) than the more arable eastern counties.[6]

Throughout most of the period farm service was still the major factor influencing the age of leaving home, and it persisted longer in the west. In that respect, these regional contrasts are best explained by employers' demand for labour, and this was probably a dominant

---

[6] See Table 7.2 for total category standard deviations. Difference of means tests on the comparison of east and west give z values of 7.915, 5.590, and 5.941 for the male agricultural, male apprentices and female agricultural categories respectively. The z value for the male and female contrast in the east is 8.288. All values are significant at .001. (See also and compare J. Thirsk, 'Industries in the countryside', in F. J. Fisher (ed.), *Essays in the Economic and Social History of Tudor and Stuart England* (Cambridge, 1961), p. 84.)

factor over the need for resident wage labour from the family itself. The explanation for the regional difference by sex probably lies in the demand for female farm-servants and dairymaids in the west, and their diminishing usefulness in the east. Of course, in both regions the eldest daughter often stayed with the family to help with other children (a custom surviving well into the twentieth century in parts of Wales),[7] and it would be helpful to know more about completed family size in the two regions, which may have influenced the regional female leaving ages. For apprentices, whether male or female, the prevalence of apprenticeships at the age of fourteen clearly suggests a customary expectation to that effect.[8]

With farm service on the decline, and the early nineteenth-century incidence of rural unemployment, the family itself may have exercised increasing control over the age of leaving home, with wages of teenagers living with parents becoming a more significant consideration. The importance of male labour in the east by the nineteenth century would incline families to hold their sons at home longer, and more eagerly place out their daughters as domestic servants. We shall see that much contemporary literature suggests this. Table 7.2 lends tentative support to these remarks, although some of the numbers are small. The better documented male agricultural ages rise over time, particularly after 1834, and in contrast there is a suggestion that the female leaving ages fell. This seems true of both the eastern and western counties. Male apprentices' ages stayed more constant over time, with only a slight rise occurring, compatible with the features of the decline of apprenticeship discussed elsewhere.[9] The standard deviations for male apprentices are also smaller than the agricultural figures: boys leaving home to work in agriculture, that is, left more gradually than did their apprenticed counterparts. For neither is there any suggestion of greater variability of leaving ages over time (to judge from the standard deviations), and for apprentices there is simply a hint of greater uniformity.[10]

The divergent changes for boys and girls reflect the declining scope

---

[7] This was quite clear from the ages of children with the family in settlement examinations, and the ages given of other children who had left home. On Wales, oral evidence of Mrs L. Hoskins and Mrs D. M. Snell.

[8] 4.8 per cent of apprentices left home at eleven years of age, 7.8 per cent at twelve, 17.5 per cent at thirteen, 32.2 per cent at fourteen, 12.8 per cent at fifteen, 11.8 per cent at sixteen, and 4.7 per cent at seventeen. (These figures do not include parish apprentices.)

[9] See chapter 5.

[10] The figures are too small to suggest anything reliable on the uniformity of leaving age over time. And for apprenticed occupations, one would require a more detailed analysis of conditions affecting the trades being averaged.

Table 7.2. *Mean age of leaving home by occupational category*

	Male agricultural			Male apprentices			Female agricultural		
	Mean	N.	s.	Mean	N.	s.	Mean	N.	s.
Eastern & Midland counties									
1700–60	15.1	38	3.5	14.0	71	2.4	17.8	8	2.4
1761–80	14.0	88	2.7	14.1	131	2.2	16.2	11	3.1
1781–1815	15.0	122	2.6	14.2	117	2.4	16.8	30	4.4
1816–34	14.9	41	3.0	14.1	23	1.8	15.4	20	2.2
1835–60	17.3	13	2.2	15.0	12	2.2	15.2	14	2.8
Total	14.8	302	2.9	14.1	354	2.3	16.2	83	3.4
Western & south-western counties									
1700–60	13.0	13	2.0	13.8	3	0.3	14.0	2	0.0
1761–80	13.0	24	3.0	14.3	3	0.3	16.4	5	3.2
1781–1815	14.7	35	3.6	15.4	6	3.1	15.0	5	2.1
1816–34	14.2	96	3.4	14.6	50	2.3	13.8	31	3.2
1835–60	14.6	13	2.4	14.1	4	0.2	13.7	4	1.4
Total	14.1	181	3.3	14.6	66	2.2	14.2	47	3.0
All counties									
1700–60	14.6	51	3.3	14.0	74	2.3	17.0	10	2.6
1761–80	13.9	112	2.8	14.1	134	2.1	16.2	16	3.0
1781–1815	14.9	157	2.8	14.3	123	2.4	16.6	35	4.1
1816–34	14.3	137	3.3	14.4	73	2.1	14.4	51	2.9
1835–60	15.9	26	2.6	14.7	16	1.9	14.9	18	2.6
Total	14.5	483	3.0	14.2	420	2.4	15.5	130	3.3

of female agricultural labour from the later eighteenth century, with their work becoming less significant to the family, particularly in the east. The decline in many regions of domestic industry, alongside falling female real wages, also diminished the value to the family of female work.[11] Especially after the New Poor Law, literary evidence supports the suggestion that boys were leaving home later than girls, indicating that this was to be the case for the rest of the nineteenth century. Flora Thompson, describing rural Oxfordshire in the 1880s, wrote:

The parents did not want the boys to leave home. Later on, if they wished to strike out for themselves, they might even meet with opposition, for their money, though barely sufficient to keep them in food, made a little more in the family purse, and every shilling was precious. The girls, while at home,

[11] See also R. S. Schofield, 'Age-specific mobility in an eighteenth-century rural English parish', *Annales de démographie historique* (1970).

could earn nothing ... If there was any inconvenience it must not fall on the boys; if there was a limited quantity of anything, the boys must still have their full share.[12]

The sentiment was a very common one by then, found also in Richard Jefferies:

If a thoughtful English peasant-woman rejoiced that in her house a son was born, it would be, not because 'she had gotten a man from the Lord', but a thanksgiving that it was not a girl ... An aged agricultural woman said she would rather have seven boys than one girl; for the former, when they became lads, went out and earned their own living, but the girls you never knew when they were got rid of – they were always coming back ... the girl is made day by day to feel her fault in being a girl.[13]

Or as George Sturt wrote: 'At an earlier age than the boys, the girls are taken off their parents' hands and become self-supporting' (in domestic service), and he added that parents had more to gain from the earnings of the boys.[14] *The Times* confirmed this: 'A lad of course lives at home ... till he grows to be 16 or 17 years of age.'[15]

Government Reports support this nineteenth-century picture. In one case the lack of female employment led local ladies to take girls from agricultural families 'out of charity'.[16] Elsewhere, in 1843, complaints were made of cottage overcrowding because the youths now stayed at home longer.[17] Or it was even being complained that mothers tried to get their daughters seduced, to make them marry and so leave the family.[18] George Crewe (in 1843) thought the New Poor Law intensified these circumstances, as the reduction of familial income which it entailed forced families to send their girls away from home earlier. 'With the female sex,' he wrote in his interesting discussion,

still worse has been the result ... of late, numbers of young women are coming home, unable from ill health, to continue their servitude, to an extent not formerly known ... Masters and mistresses, finding that they can get a stout girl of 14 or 15, at any low wages, say £3 or £4 per ann., and that when they have hired such girls, they can, to use a common expression, get more work out of such children, than they could get out of a grown-up person, hire

[12] F. Thompson, *Lark Rise to Candleford* (1939, Harmondsworth, 1976 edn), pp. 155, 166.
[13] R. Jefferies, *The Toilers of the Field* (1892, 1981 edn), pp. 82–3, 93.
[14] G. Sturt, *Change in the Village* (1912), pp. 58–63.
[15] *The Times*, 10 June 1844. Or see H. J. Little, 'The agricultural labourer', *Jnl of Royal Agric. Soc.*, XIV (1878), 800. (He claimed that girls left home at thirteen to fourteen and boys at seventeen to eighteen years of age.)
[16] S.C. on Poor Law Amendment Act, XVII (1837), pt. I, pp. 121ff.
[17] Report on the Employment of Women and Children in Agriculture, XII (1843), p. 163. (On overcrowding, see n. 129 below.)
[18] Poor Law Report, XXXVII (1834), p. 127.

them in preference to a woman, at £7 or £8 per annum. They can give children musty bread and scraps of victuals to feed upon, which a woman would not submit to; they can put them to sleep in holes and corners, where a woman would not consent to be stowed away at night ... the poor child, half clothed, half fed, and over worked ... becomes ill; goes home, and too often, dies, or becomes an incurable invalid ... I say that the increase of such lamentable facts since the Poor Law was passed has been great, and is an evil chargeable to the cruel rigours of that law, upon the working people.[19]

Perhaps this seems exaggerated today, but we recall the precarious health resulting from an upbringing badly lacking in protein, essential vitamins and minerals (particularly for mothers and girls) – descriptions of dizziness were common – and the high incidence of T.B. and other infective illnesses.[20]

I suggested elsewhere that the abolition of family allowances by the New Poor Law forced a greater dependence on child labour, to supplement family income. This was also a factor raising the male leaving age. Under the old poor law, 'when boys of 13, 14, or 15 years of age, begin to earn more than their allowance, the allowance of the parent is diminished by that excess; and to avoid that diminution, parents turn their children adrift upon the world', wrote Rev. C. D. Brereton.[21] Any such motive, for better or worse, was largely ended after 1834, and indeed was reversed by the decline of weekly wages and the widespread termination of allowances brought about by the New Poor Law. There was now stronger motive to keep boys at home, despite overcrowding and employment preference for married men; the lack of cottage accommodation also left many unmarried youths little alternative other than more drastic and risky migration from the region. In this way, the new law contributed to the later male leaving ages of the mid-nineteenth century.

Some broad contrasts emerge from these tables between the agricultural and apprenticed sectors, but it is possible to be more detailed. Table 7.3 gives a breakdown of average leaving ages for some of the better documented occupations.[22] Predictably, the chim-

[19] Sir G. Crewe, *A Word for the Poor, and against the Present Poor Law* (Derby, 1843), pp. 33–4.

[20] See S. R. Johannson, 'Age-specific mortality patterns of Victorian women', in M. Vicinus (ed.), *A Widening Sphere: Women in the Victorian Age* (Bloomington, Indiana, 1977); R. Wall, 'Inferring differential neglect of females from mortality data', *Annales de démographie historique* (1981).

[21] Rev. C. D. Brereton, *Observations on the Administration of the Poor Laws in Agricultural Districts* (1824), p. 49.

[22] All are male, except the prostitutes, and the citations of leaving ages are included regardless of whether an apprenticeship was served or not. Again, some occupations are poorly documented, and these have been included on the principle of some evidence being better than none. As for Tables 7.1 and 7.2, I have excluded those apprenticed to their fathers.

Table 7.3. *Mean age of leaving home by occupation (all counties), 1700–1860*

Occupation	Mean	N.	s.
Calico printer	17.9	18	4.2
Soldier	17.0	17	3.4
Millwright	17.0	5	2.3
Stonemason	16.7	8	1.3
Whitesmith	16.4	5	1.5
Painter	16.4	5	2.7
Sawyer	16.2	4	4.9
Stay maker	16.0	6	4.4
Gun-flint maker	16.0	4	2.8
Prostitute	16.0	3	0.0
Cooper	15.7	6	2.7
Bricklayer	15.6	12	2.2
Gardener	15.3	6	1.7
Carpenter/cabinet maker/joiner	15.2	46	2.8
Paper maker/stainer	15.2	4	1.5
Blacksmith	15.2	28	2.5
Whitster	15.0	3	2.0
Flax dresser	15.0	3	0.0
Wheelwright	14.9	13	1.4
Shoemaker	14.6	71	3.0
Farm-servant/labourer	14.5	483	3.0
Baker	14.4	11	1.8
Peruke maker/barber	14.4	10	1.9
Butcher	14.3	10	3.0
Tin plate worker	14.3	3	1.1
Gunstock maker	14.3	7	2.6
Saddlemaker	14.2	4	2.1
Framesmith	14.0	4	0.0
Tailor	14.0	37	2.3
Currier/tanner	13.9	11	2.4
Weaver	13.8	12	3.4
Woolstapler	13.7	7	0.5
Hatmaker	13.6	9	1.2
Brickmaker	13.5	5	0.5
Shearman	13.5	4	2.9
Watch maker	13.3	3	1.1
Sailor/mariner	13.3	20	2.8
Woolcomber	13.2	18	1.8
Breeches maker	12.8	7	1.6
Glazier/plumber	12.7	6	2.6
Felmonger	12.7	5	2.3
Framework knitter	12.5	10	2.9
Chimney sweeper	10.7	4	2.8

ney sweeper is bottom of the league, but still with a surprisingly high leaving age of nearly eleven years. But then, should the reader be comparing age-specific girth with chimney diameter, we remember that this was still a society in which an agricultural labourer over five foot six inches was considered exceptional.[23] Also low on the list are occupations which some historians might describe as 'proto-industrial': the framework knitter and framesmith, woolcomber, woolstapler, or weaver. These were becoming heavily depressed and exploited trades. They were also, as we shall see, occupations with an early marriage age, which had a high proportion of members failing to gain a settlement in their own right, and who therefore took that of their father. We shall return to these features shortly. It is noticeable that of the trades with a higher age of leaving, only the calico printers are to be included among the usual categories of the most depressed early nineteenth-century trades. The leaving ages in this trade were abnormally high, partly because many boys stayed longer at home to help their parents, and then eventually left to continue it themselves, sometimes without an apprenticeship. Others left earlier, apprenticed at the usual age – hence the high standard deviation. (There was a high incidence of sons following parental occupation in this trade.) It is also possible that the decline of hand calico printing in the early nineteenth century (when most cases for this trade were obtained) may have contributed to the late ages.

Then there were those in more traditional trades, at about fourteen: the blacksmiths, whitsters, wheelwrights, shoemakers, bakers, peruke makers/barbers, butchers, gunstock makers, saddlemakers, tailors, or curriers. Including some of these, it is notable how those entering trades requiring physical strength (blacksmith, bricklayer, cooper, sawyer, mason, millwright, wheelwright) left home rather later than average. Apprenticeships were often planned and arranged long in advance, with parental trust placed in a prospective master or mistress, and entry into heavy trades could then be delayed. By contrast, watch makers, breeches makers, tailors, or hatmakers left home earlier. Then, with a very high age, there were the soldiers – those for whom the opportunity of apprenticeship had largely passed, and whose despondency over the inadequate local employment which had kept them at home so long probably contributed to the decision to enlist. In many agricultural communities the choice of 'soldiery' was heavily despised, particularly in the eighteenth cen-

---

[23] For example, see Report on the Employment of Children, Young Persons, and Women in Agriculture, XIII (1868–9), p. 602. 'There is scarcely one young man in the village reaching the height of 5'6"' (Berkshire).

tury. The association of the army and militia with the scourings of parochial society, the fear of the press-gang, the experience of recruitment tactics, or of migrant, impoverished, and wounded ex-soldiery contributed to make this occupation a last resort. Auto-biographers have left us with the sense of despair, even of horror, which their parents felt when they enlisted, and similar sentiments abound in folksong. The decline of service was much regretted insofar as it now became more likely that the young would enlist, or be press-ganged, or have no legal safeguard against being drawn for the militia. Efforts in the early nineteenth century to improve army conditions and the calibre of recruits eventually softened such feel-ings, and the forces were one escape from rural unemployment – but much antagonism persisted.[24]

The three prostitutes all left home at sixteen. An absence of domestic work, or the failure to enter another occupation earlier may have forced them into prostitution. This may also have been consi-dered a suitable age. One of them was apprenticed as 'a pupil', 'to learn the trade' in a house in Soho 'carried on as a place of ill fame', rented by her mother. Unfortunately, occupational hazard stepped in, as she was soon to contract 'a scrofulous disease of the toe', which brought her to the parish clerk's table. Her apprenticeship indentures were then found to be neither sealed nor stamped.[25] However, for all her difficulties, the age of leaving home for these eighteenth- and early nineteenth-century prostitutes at least is the current age of consent. As we know from other sources, the later 'Cult of the Little Child', when the sexual exploitation of very young girls has been described as 'frightening. . . the most repellent aspect of Victorian sex', lay with the Victorian values of the incipient 'new age'.[26]

It would be helpful to supplement this discussion with evidence on social expectations as to when children should leave, and when they were considered 'adult'. The examinations provide information on this. Thomas Bell, for example, examined in 1772 in Bedford, 'went out young to service, being about twelve years of age'.[27] Fourteen or fifteen would indeed have been a more usual age. The Select Committee on Parish Apprentices (1814–15) gave ages of children bound from parishes within the Bills of Mortality, and attacked 'the

---

[24] On parental opposition to sons enlisting as soldiers, see A. Smith, *The Wealth of Nations* (1776, 1904 edn), p. 97; W. Surtees, *Twenty-five Years in the Rifle Brigade* (Edinburgh, 1833), p. 64; P. Horn, *The Rural World* (1980), pp. 61–2.

[25] Camb C.R.O., G/C/As 7.

[26] R. Pearsall, *The Worm in the Bud: The World of Victorian Sexuality* (1969, Harmonds-worth, 1972 edn), pp. 358–67, 430–7.   [27] Beds C.R.O., DDP. 1/13/4/1.

very early age at which these children are bound Apprentices'.[28] The numbers apprenticed for different age groups were as follows:

under 8	:	73
8–11	:	1,501
11–12	:	799
12–14	:	2,091
14–18	:	1,309

The high numbers apprenticed between 8–11 years were certainly unusual compared with the earlier tables, although it is worth noting how many were apprenticed between 14 and 18. (Parish apprentices, of course, always left comparatively early: at 13.4 years for a group of eighty male Essex apprentices for example.) Rather earlier, in 1766, Hanway wrote on the need to put young people to service at ten and eleven, because: 'where young people are not early in servitude, under the eye of a good master, in the world, they had better be dead than in idleness or vice'.[29] But such ages were exceptionally young. Similar literary evidence led Lawrence Stone, among others, to the erroneous view that the labouring poor 'left home at between seven and fourteen to begin work as domestic servants, labourers (sic) or apprentices ... in all cases living in their masters' houses'.[30] But as can be seen from the tables, such literary evidence is nearly as misleading as Shakespeare on Juliet's marriage age.

What can be said about the age of 'adulthood', or 'manhood'? First, it was not usually synonymous with marriage. Laslett's disclaimer 'that children are rather uncomfortably defined by taking them ... to be all unmarried persons' was quite correct.[31] But there remains

[28] S.C. on Parish Apprentices, V (1814–15), pp. 3–4. It is not possible to eliminate the lack of exclusivity of the categories in this table.

[29] J. Hanway, *An Earnest Appeal for Mercy to the Children of the Poor* (1766), p. 96.

[30] L. Stone, *The Family, Sex and Marriage in England, 1500–1800* (1977), pp. 107–8. See also p. 375. While it is important not to exaggerate the youthfulness at which children left home, it is also important to note that (with a mean age of leaving of about fourteen) most children left home considerably earlier than they do today, when the average age of leaving home in Britain is twenty-one, with less variance around the mean than was the case in previous centuries. Notwithstanding the views of those who believe that there was much stricter parental control over teenage children in the past, and who advocate a return to greater familial responsibility and restraint over teenage sexuality, 'rebelliousness', and so on, it is clear from these figures that parents today exercise a far more prolonged influence over their children than in the past. And insofar as an earlier home-leaving age in previous centuries helped to avoid child–parent conflict, the implications of the nineteenth-century social changes documented here are interesting in many respects – for example, in their bearing on inter-generational conflict, or on the reception in England to Freudian Oedipal theory.

[31] Laslett, *Family Life and Illicit Love*, p. 163.

disagreement over whether eighteen, nineteen or twenty-one was the age of adulthood. Thomas Rogers (examined Bury St Edmunds, 1792), 'lived with his father and worked with him about eight years after he was grown up' – eighteen being the age at which he was thought 'grown up'.[32] Oliver Blower, examined in Hockwold cum Wilton in 1820,

resided with his father about seven years as part of his family. He then left his Father's house without his Father's consent being then about nineteen years of age. He has been wandering about the country and working as a Laborer until he returned to his Father a short time before Christmas twelvemonth . . . He staid with his Father . . . about two months as part of his Father's family, not being then twenty one years of age. He left his father again without his consent and returned again to the Father at Hockwold aforesaid about a Fortnight before new Christmas last and has been with him until the present time.[33]

In his case, twenty-one was the age of adulthood, with parental consent expected before that age. This did not always apply to women, and, as regarding the completion of apprenticeship, their ages could be lower. Mary Ann Pittam (examined Cambridge, 1856)

resided and lived with my said father as a part of his family in or upon or at the said Messuage or Tenement at Wootton aforesaid for a period of three years or thereabouts, when I left my said father's house and became emancipated [aged nineteen], and thenceforth discharged the duties of School Mistress at and in the Workhouse of Pottersbury Union in the said county of N'Hants.[34]

In her case the age of, or for, emancipation was nineteen.

More generally, age-specific material showed adult farm-servant wages being reached by nineteen in most counties.[35] There was also a rather higher proportion of examinants stating that they left home at nineteen than at eighteen or twenty-one. In an economic sense, in agriculture, nineteen seems usually to have been the age of *effective* adulthood. Nevertheless, many examinants still talked of activities 'at my/his/her age of twenty-one', suggesting the social significance of this age. Certainly apprenticeships were intended to end then. John Challis (examined Bury St Edmunds, 1788) was apprenticed a carpenter at sixteen, but the indentures were backdated two years, on the assumption that he should finish at twenty-one.[36] This assumption lay behind the high proportion of boys being apprenticed at fourteen, which stayed constant throughout this period. Given its social

[32] West Suffolk C.R.O., N2.1.11.   [33] *Ibid.*, EL. 25/7/18.1–18.146.
[34] Camb C.R.O., G/C/Ac 5, pt 1.
[35] I will discuss age-specific wages in greater detail elsewhere.
[36] West Suffolk C.R.O., N2.1.8.

significance, we should take twenty-one as the age of adulthood, while appreciating that it had often effectively arrived before then, particularly for those without a trade. Twenty-one can also be supported by much folk-lore evidence. And Hanway's flourishing statement was probably sufficiently reliable on this: 'Common apprenticeships are for seven years; the indentures of girls generally run to the age of twenty one . . . Is not the male a man also at twenty one? . . . This is the age of manhood, for the possession of the largest fortunes, in the widest empires.'[37]

III

In an earlier chapter on the decline of service, I showed the growing proportion of examinants over time who had failed to gain a settlement in their own right, and who therefore took that of their father. (The reader should refer to Figure 2.5.) We recall how the decline of yearly hiring, coupled with its repeal as a head of settlement in 1834, underlay a change from a mere (and still young) 10 per cent who had failed to gain their own settlement in the early eighteenth century, to over 70 per cent by the later nineteenth century. The changes came after 1780, and during the early protraction of the New Poor Law. They implied greater local persistence through the generations as a consequence, as settlement and the right to relief in a parish became passed down from father to son in a way never hitherto experienced. There were many other factors influencing mobility, but by the mid-nineteenth century this was an inducement for families to stay in the same place, and the change probably hindered local mobility within the agricultural sector itself compared to the earlier high levels in the heyday of service. Early nineteenth-century mobility ran the risk of sharp return when non-resident relief was refused, as Chadwick urged it to be after 1834.[38] These settlement changes can be examined here, for the agricultural sector and in occupationally specific detail.

The implications of changes in generational settlement for mobility can readily be demonstrated, by reference to the distances of examinants from their places of birth and settlement. Table 7.4 shows this, for parochially comparable samples of examinants from Hertfordshire, Bedfordshire, Cambridgeshire, Huntingdonshire, Norfolk, and

---

[37] Hanway, *Earnest Appeal*, p. 108.

[38] See for example Chadwick's clarificatory circular 'To the Overseers of the Poor', 8 Nov. 1834, section 5. (Office of the Poor Law Commissioners, London.) See also the circular of 4 Sept, 1834, and n. 45, below.

Table 7.4. *Distances upon examination from birth and settlement place, by category of settlement (samples of 175), 1700–1860 (Camb, Beds, Norf, Suff, Herts, Hunts)*

			Mean (miles)	N.
Own settlement gained				
Villages only	–	birth	18.8	137
Total	–	birth	21.2	175
Villages only	–	settlement	19.3	137
Total	–	settlement	21.2	175
Father's settlement taken				
Villages only	–	birth	9.9	131
Total	–	birth	10.4	175
Villages only	–	settlement	9.4	131
Total	–	settlement	10.1	175

Suffolk, for whom all such information was given. Mean distances are presented (of male agricultural labourers), first for those who had gained their own settlements, and secondly for those who took their fathers' settlements, having failed to gain their own. These categories have been subdivided to give distances for those whose places of examination, birth, and settlement were all villages; and a total category which includes those for whom one of the places of examination, birth, or settlement was a market town – that is, towns such as Bury St Edmunds, Royston, Cambridge, Huntingdon, or Bedford. The distance at examination from settlement or birth place of those who had gained their own settlement was twice that of those who had failed to do this, and so took their father's settlement.[39] Furthermore, the place of birth was the same as settlement place for 31 per cent of those who had gained their own settlement; but the figure was much higher for those who took their father's settlement, at 76 per cent. Similarly, 14 per cent of those who had gained their own settlement were examined in their place of settlement *and* birth, compared to 31 per cent of those who took their father's settlement. More long distance mobility, to different and securer employment, leaving the region's agricultural sector altogether, usually escapes us

[39] For these samples, the z statistic was as follows: 'Villages only – birth' = 3.230; 'Total – birth' = 3.649; 'Villages only – settlement' = 4.030; 'Total – settlement' = 4.653. All are significant at the .001 level. It is, in other words, highly unlikely that the difference of sample means was the result of the chances of sampling.

with this source. Such employment allowed a person also to escape the settlement laws. But for those who remained in these or similar southern counties, it seems very likely that the changes in generational settlement reduced both the prevalence and distances of local mobility.[40]

The family was integrally connected with these developments, for the economic changes which undermined settlement as gained by yearly hiring and traditional apprenticeship produced an anachronistic legal system of settlement – one which altered the family in a way conducive to further social change. The late seventeenth-century settlement laws had laid down that parental settlement be taken if a settlement was not gained in one's own right. This was rightly presumed at the time to be an unlikely eventuality. But the failure to reform substantially the legislation in the changed conditions after 1780 brought this residual legal stipulation into play on a massive scale, and its effects were felt particularly in the south.[41] Elsewhere (in the north, in parts of the west) a greater continuity of statute fairs and yearly hiring still kept labour highly mobile, even during periods of depression. The legislative changes of 1834 (aimed at southern problems) produced similar effects on generational settlement in the north or west, but their influence on the labour market was counterbalanced by institutional continuity, and fuller employment lessening the relative impact of settlement. In an area like Northumber-

---

[40] Contrasts of the same order exist in the distances of those examined in separate market towns from birth and settlement places. Mean distances of those taking their fathers' settlements were usually about 12 miles from birth and settlement. Equivalent distances of those who had gained their own settlements were about 24 miles. And similar contrasts exist for artisan occupations between these two settlement categories. My comments here of course apply mainly to the period before the 1846 and 1861 Settlement Acts; although obstacles were placed against the gaining of irremovability under these acts, and 'irremovability' was a different concept from settlement, and did not confer the latter. Space is lacking here to enter into a wider discussion of labour mobility and the effects of the settlement laws on the labour market, computing the enormous body of information provided by the settlement records. This can await future publication.

[41] 'More and more will the question of settlement resolve itself, as it has already begun to resolve itself, into one of pedigree, and into determining the locality of a father's or grandfather's birth.' R. Pashley, *Pauperism and the Poor Laws* (1852), p. 261. 'The marriages among the peasantry are now very much confined to their respective villages, or villages immediately adjoining each other. The close intermarriage of near relatives ... is of course more frequent. We have in this parish four old men, none of whom are natives of this village ... This is the case of the oldest inhabitants in the adjoining villages ... they migrated in early life, in quest of employment and improvement. Whereas now ... where they have been born, there they usually (to use the common phrase) belong; and there they seem to think they are to ... exist and die.' Rev. C. D. Brereton, *A Practical Inquiry into the Number, Means of Employment and Wages of Agricultural Labourers* (Norwich, 1824), pp. 33–4.

land, even 'labourers' (to use southern terminology) still worked within a similar institutional framework for local mobility once experienced by unmarried labour in the south and east. Such a system had produced (in the later seventeenth century) the high population turnovers every decade of villages like Clayworth and Cogenhoe, once so surprising to historians.[42] These labour conditions persisted in the north into the later nineteenth century, both in the agricultural sector, and, by extension, to provide labour for developing industry. Northern demographic and agricultural conditions, that is, with the relatively constant seasonal demands for labour of pastoral farming, had contributed to keep intact a hiring system associated with extensive migration, eminently suited to the supply of young labour demanded by new forms of industrial production.

In these northern conditions, rural out-migration and the persistence of annual hiring were perpetually disruptive of agrarian 'community'. When historians speak of northern working-class 'consciousness' they rightly look to the urban proletariat – hardly to the northern migratory rural labourer. The latter came relatively innocent to the urban scene until at least the unionism of the 1860s. By contrast, the south had developed by 1850 a stronger village 'community' (the word is not used nostalgically) than in the past two centuries, with greater familial stability in the same place. The nature of southern labour mobility had changed from the late seventeenth or early eighteenth centuries. As always, the young remained the most mobile; but by 1850 this mobility was more transient, more exploratory of the possibilities of a total break from 'their village' than in 1700. The earlier flexible use by employers of annual hiring to accommodate their labour requirements – the regional shuffling of labour annually at the statutes – had given way to the nineteenth-century short-term migratory task gangs. Whether they followed the south-eastern harvest like Bettesworth, or migrated to the hop districts or to the maltings, to the Fens between May and November, to brickmaking areas, or to the closed parishes of north and west Norfolk, they usually shared one thing in common before 1851 – the return to their family's settlement parish at the end of the season. Overseers might give young men 5s. at the start of the hay season to go and 'seek their fortunes' – but they almost invariably returned by the winter. So complained the 1826–7 Committee on Criminal Convictions.[43]

This temporal comparison need be sketched only broadly. 'The

---

[42] See P. Laslett, 'Clayworth and Cogenhoe', in his *Family Life and Illicit Love*.
[43] S.C. on Criminal Commitments and Convictions, VI (1826–7), p. 31.

labourers scarcely ever remove', complained the 1834 Poor Law Report, 'and those who found labour out of the parish formerly, have been sent home to their respective parishes.'[44] Nevertheless, this was accentuated yet further by the New Poor Law's heavy curtailment of non-resident relief, and by Chadwick's circulars against this – 'By Order of the Board'. For all the 1834 dogma of a 'free labour market', this restriction on non-resident relief brought labourers back to their parishes of settlement, at times in large numbers.[45] In an age so heavily influenced by Adam Smith and by political economy, it may seem a paradox that writers on rural society were soon lamenting the narrow geographical horizons of rural labour, in a way we do not find in the eighteenth-century picaresque novel. 'The Vale of Blackmoor was to [Tess] the world, and its inhabitants the races thereof . . . Every contour of the surrounding hills was as personal to her as that of her relatives' faces; but for what lay beyond her judgment was dependent on the teaching of the village school.'[46] 'Like so many of his friends', wrote Holdenby of a young labourer, 'he had never been out of a ten-mile radius; he had never even climbed to the top of yonder great round hill.'[47] P. A. Graham adopted the same theme: 'A ten mile journey was an event that kept him in talk for a life-time. Even at this day I know rustics who live within that distance of the sea and yet have never beheld it . . . This stay-at-home tendency was largely due to lack of money.'[48] 'Low wages and ignorance of a wider field of competition make his labour something akin to real serfdom', added Holdenby.[49] The complaint was a very common one, recognisable in most nineteenth-century writers on southern rural society. The growing use of tied cottages also inhibited mobility;[50] as did threats

---

[44] Poor Law Report, XXXIII (1834), p. 319.

[45] As Thomas Smith wrote, the commissioners directed that 'all paupers, between the ages of 16 and 60, whilst in the receipt of Relief, should reside in the Parish or Union to which they belong . . . A long list might be made of cases removed into the Union in consequence of the rule of the Commissioners being adhered to, but . . . it would occupy considerable space.' T. Smith, *The Old Poor Law and the New Poor Law Contrasted* (1840), p. 22. The payment of non-resident relief had by contrast been expanding in the late eighteenth century. See for example, E. M. Hampson, *The Treatment of Poverty in Cambridgeshire, 1597–1834* (Cambridge, 1934), p. 149.

[46] T. Hardy, *Tess of the D'Urbervilles* (1891, 1970 edn), p. 46.

[47] C. Holdenby, *Folk of the Furrow* (1913), p. 35.

[48] P. A. Graham, *The Rural Exodus* (1892), p. 24.

[49] Holdenby, *Folk of the Furrow*, p. 267.

[50] For discussion of tied cottages, see the evidence of Joseph Arch to the Royal Commission on Agriculture, XIV (1882); R.C. on the Housing of the Working Classes, XXX (1884–5); B. Kerr, *Bound to the Soil: A Social History of Dorset, 1750–1918* (1968), pp. 23–4; Report on the Employment of Women and Children in Agriculture, XVII (1867–8), p. 677; J. Burnett, *A Social History of Housing, 1815–1970* (1978).

from farmers that elderly parents would be ejected from such cottages unless young labourers stayed to work the same farm as their fathers had done.[51] Early marriage and large families; resistance to 'furriners' from other parishes; the conditions of structural or periodic unemployment which often accompanied this, compounded by the settlement laws; acute shortages of accommodation – there were many reasons for the 'stay-at-home tendency'.

Without discounting these, one should also stress how the changes of generational settlement operated to the same end. And we have seen how male ages of leaving home rose in agriculture. There must have been closer generational contact as a result; nearer familiarity with one's parents and grandparents as they grew old (poor law authorities were eager to exploit this, as we shall see); consciousness of parish history, and of the local religious and political concerns of one's parents, over, for example, enclosure or (for the Ashby's) the use of parish lands. It is hard to imagine this occurring to the same degree when 60 per cent of village populations might disappear every twelve years (both through migration and a relatively low life expectancy), as in the late seventeenth century. Rural population grew until about 1851, and while out-migration then accelerated, rural immigration rates throughout the nineteenth century remained considerably lower than those of the late seventeenth century. Rising life expectancy also contributed to develop the community consciousness of a relatively immobile core of village populations. Conditions were now conducive to a festering of long-term resentments, for class bitterness to animate the unionism of the 1870s.

And so we should turn to Raymond Williams:

Community must not always be seen in retrospect. In Tysoe there was a revival of community, as the village came together in the nineteenth century, to fight for its rights of allotment in the Town Lands. In many parts of rural Britain, a new kind of community developed as an aspect of struggle, against the dominant landowners or, as in the labourers' revolts in the time of the Swing machine-smashing and rick-burning or in the labourers' unions from Tolpuddle to Joseph Arch, against the whole class-system of rural capitalism. In many villages, community only became a reality when economic and political rights were fought for and partially gained ... In many thousands of cases, there is more community in the modern village, as a result of this process of new legal and democratic rights, than at any point in the recorded or imagined past.[52]

The generational continuity of many families was an important

---

[51] See for example B. Kerr, 'The Dorset agricultural labourer, 1750–1850', *Proc. Dorset Nat. Hist. and Arch. Soc.*, LXXXIV (1962), 176.

[52] R. Williams, *The Country and the City* (St Albans, 1973), p. 104.

structural consideration to complement this – a key to understanding some dominant features of southern rural communities. The settlement laws most obviously enhanced those features when they became anachronistic to economic circumstances. They then had an effect, mediated through the family, which contributed to the conditions of 'community' in which labouring-class political feeling was expressed.

The figure for the proportion over time failing to settle themselves encompassed all male occupations, and it is certain that all experienced similar long-term changes. It is possible to break this down further by occupation, to provide a profile of inter-generational settlement patterns by trade. Table 7.5 supplies this, covering 1700–1834. As we should expect, the yearly hiring system allowed agricultural workers to gain their own settlements much more readily than artisans. The latter were mainly dependent on a legal apprenticeship outside their father's parish of settlement, or on renting £10 per annum. Apprenticeship to their father, legal troubles surrounding apprenticeship, or the waiving of apprenticeship altogether led to failure to settle themselves in their own right. Hence, for artisans the decline of apprenticeship which commenced from 1750 began the change away from an earlier greater ease of self-settlement, and this accelerated after 1780. Members of poorer trades, for which that decline was more pronounced, were especially liable to take their paternal settlement. They were also least able to hire for £10 per annum. One thinks of the framework knitters, weavers, cordwainers, bricklayers, woolcombers, and so on. And among occupations high on the table, those which did not involve an apprenticeship at all predictably stand out: militiaman, soldier, some bricklayers, some publicans. Framework knitting rapidly became another such occupation, as did weaving and perhaps woolcombing. Other trades further down the table were ones for which the renting of premises for business was crucial, and this could confer settlement if it had not been gained by a legal apprenticeship. One thinks of publicans (although many beer shops were small), butchers, bakers, barbers, grocers, or millers. Most shopkeeper occupations would have fallen into this category, with between 10 and 25 per cent taking their father's settlement.

But the two salient features of this table are first the contrast of the agricultural with the artisan, and secondly, the high proportions in 'proto-industrial' trades who had failed to gain their own settlements. The abolition of yearly hiring as a head of settlement produced a rapid rise in the proportion of servants and labourers taking their

Table 7.5. *Male occupational settlement, 1700–1834 (Camb, Beds, Norf,*
Suff, Ess, Herts, Hunts & Surr)

Occupation (county)	% taking father's settlement	% gaining their own settlement	N.
Framework knitter (Leics)	40.7	59.3	81
Weaver	40.0	60.0	39
Militiaman	36.2	63.8	94
Cordwainer	30.4	69.6	148
Soldier	30.2	69.8	149
Bricklayer	28.6	71.4	35
Woolcomber	27.5	72.5	51
Carpenter	26.6	73.4	94
Brewer	26.1	73.9	23
Tailor	25.8	74.2	62
Cooper	25.0	75.0	24
Publican	25.0	75.0	24
Currier/tanner	23.5	76.5	34
Mason	19.2	80.8	26
Hatmaker	19.1	80.9	21
Butcher	18.2	81.8	22
Whitesmith	17.4	82.6	23
Calico printer	16.3	83.7	43
Baker	16.2	83.8	37
Blacksmith	15.8	84.2	76
Wheelwright	14.7	85.3	34
Barber	14.3	85.7	21
Grocer	14.3	85.7	21
Miller	13.8	86.2	29
Male servants & labourers (samples)			
Suff	10.6	89.4	254
Camb	9.1	90.9	117
Beds	8.1	91.9	131
Herts	6.6	93.4	107

father's settlement after 1834, but less change then for artisan
occupations. The long-term changes discussed earlier alongside the
decline of service would, in other words, be even steeper if artisans
were excluded. The main points of change would be little affected.[53]

Secondly, in view of the above discussion of settlement, community, and political sentiment, it is revealing that framework knitters,

[53] The higher proportion of servants and labourers in Suffolk unable to gain their own
settlements may be related to more extreme seasonal distributions of unemployment
found there, and its low wages. This measure helps indicate regional contrasts in
unemployment and the decline of service – or for comparable groups of artisans, in
the decline of apprenticeship and its consequences.

weavers, cordwainers, and woolcombers head this table. Once again, such a settlement pattern for these trades implies relative stability of their communities over the generations. The traditional settlement legal structure was redundant to them (most notably, to the framework knitters), by virtue of their intensified cottage production, increasingly outside the apprenticeship system, and by their poverty not enabling them to settle themselves elsewhere by renting. The political and community consciousness of such groups was notorious. We remember the political activity of the northern weaving communities described by Samuel Bamford.[54] Or we have Levine's account of the endogamously fertile but depressed and embittered framework knitting community of Shepshed.[55] Cordwainers, too, in the more long-term, were perhaps the most politicised of all trades.[56] They were particularly prone to be apprenticed to their fathers, were frequently too poor to rent over £10 per annum; and the political implications of these features were compounded by the high entry rate into this trade of ex-soldiers, benefiting from the practice of 'King's Freemen'.[57] Similarly, ex-soldiers were notoriously active in local political affairs, although no doubt for them there were other factors more important than a close residential familiarity with, and harboured resentment at, parochial issues stretching back into their family history, bequeathed them by their parents. Their experience in the army had brought them home to their parents' settlement with a new and often radical perspective on local issues. There was significance in the term 'Captain Swing'.

The decline of traditional apprenticeship and service led the generational settlement patterns for all occupations in a direction inviting concern at such issues. The table also provides one reason why artisans were more politicised than labourers. It suggests too that the later eighteenth-century framework knitters, weavers, cordwainers, soldiers, or woolcombers in this respect may have presaged or embodied elements of the nineteenth-century 'working class community' – to be contrasted with the mobile agricultural workers, who, for much of this period, rapidly dispersed their families by their ease of gaining settlements. It is unnecessary to introduce further evidence on these trades to develop such points. Historians familiar with weavers or framework knitters will recognise aspects of their

---

[54] S. Bamford, *Passages in the Life of a Radical* (1842, 1967 edn); or his *Early Days* (1849).
[55] D. Levine, *Family Formation in an Age of Nascent Capitalism* (1977).
[56] See E. J. Hobsbawm & J. W. Scott, 'Political shoemakers', *Past and Present*, LXXXIX (1980).
[57] See chapter 5.

community structure being pointed to here.[58] But once again, it is worth stressing how the settlement and poor law structure became divorced from economic circumstances; and, by ending an earlier ease of gaining settlements, became a factor which could perpetuate families practising certain trades in the same place over the generations, accentuating aggrieved political and class feelings already aroused by unfavourable terms of production and glutted labour supply.[59]

IV

Something can briefly be said on occupational family formation. This varied partly because of the work roles of children in different trades, and Table 7.6 indicates this, taking family formation as the combined product of marriage age and marital fertility. Only a sample of examinations from some counties have been used, but fuller investigation would not alter these clear findings. Families were divided by

Table 7.6. *Occupational family formation, 1700–1860*

County	'Familial occupations'			'Non-familial occupations'		
	Mean no. of children	N.	Mean age of family head	Mean no. of children	N.	Mean age of family head
Surr	3.8	285	37.5	2.7	468	40.4
Beds	2.0	51	27.3	1.5	118	35.6
Herts	1.8	40	27.5	1.6	192	28.2
W. Suff	1.6	209	32.3	1.4	244	32.6
Camb	2.1	27	37.6	0.9	50	30.7
Total	2.2	612	33.7	1.6	1,072	34.0

[58] See Bamford, *Early Days*, or his *Passages in the Life of a Radical*; Levine, *Family Formation*; D. Bythell, *The Handloom Weavers* (Cambridge, 1969); P. Richards, The state and early industrial capitalism: the case of the handloom weavers', *Past and Present*, LXXXIII (1979); E. P. Thompson, *The Making of the English Working Class* (1963), chs. 8 and 9.

[59] Such labour over-abundance was aggravated by the 'proto-industrial' trades' young ages of leaving home – perhaps suggestive also of resentment at work pressures within the family, which had led such trades to form an 'optimum' family labour unit relatively early. These issues also raise questions on generational conflict and changing socialisation. For some interesting possibilities, see: F. Weinstein & G. M. Platt, *The Wish to be Free* (Berkeley, Calif., 1969); and their *Psychoanalytic Sociology* (1973); W. E. Bridges, 'Family patterns and social values in America, 1825–1875', *American Quarterly*, XVII (1965); T. K. Hareven, 'The history of the family as an interdisciplinary field', *Jnl of Interdisciplinary Hist.*, II (1971).

occupation, first into those where children would frequently follow the occupation of the father, or be helpful by cooperating in the father's occupation (that is, mainly home-based or family-economy trades); and secondly, into those where this was not the case. The former category has been termed 'familial occupations', and the latter 'non-familial'. For some occupations this division is easy to make, for others more problematical, and some details of categorisation might be questioned. But similar problems would arise in making alternative distinctions, as for example 'proto-industrial' occupations and 'pre-industrial' ones, and these divisions can suffice.[60] The male head of family's age was thirty-four for both groups (usually the age at which the family poverty-cycle bit deepest). But by that age men in the 'familial' category had 2.2 children, while those in the 'non-familial' had only 1.6 – strongly suggesting a tendency for the 'familial' occupations either to marry earlier, or form families more rapidly, or both. This had probably been a long-standing tendency for this category of occupations in England. It is not always clear in historiography on what is currently termed 'proto-industry' which occupations are so classified, although they would be a subset of my 'familial' category. But 110 families of weavers, framesmiths,

---

[60] In part, these divisions were made on the basis of information given in examinations, for many hundreds of artisan families, and from my reading of apprenticeship records (i.e., trades where apprenticeship to one's father was common). The two-fold division here covers occupations only for this sample, excluding some which are difficult to categorise. The total range of occupations covered by examinations (for other counties) is of course much wider than this. For '*familial*' occupations the following have been included: tailor, weaver, blacksmith, shoemaker, hatmaker, glover, tallow-chandler, cooper, baker, chairmender, shaguin case maker, breeches maker, clockmaker, chairbottomer, tin plate worker, harness and saddlemaker, malter, pattern maker, currier, gun-flint maker, whitesmith, woolcomber, stay maker, fellmonger, dyer and woolcomber, clogmaker, broad cloth maker, basket maker, potash maker, collar maker, cloth presser, gunsmith, peruke maker, watch maker, worsted twisterer, silk dyer, hemp manufacturer/dresser, calico printer, skinner, copperplate printer, coppersmith, pewterer, blockcutter, copperforger, paper/parchment maker, coachmaker, gunstock maker, brazier, hosier, silversmith, whipmaker, tanner, maltmaker, ring turner, tammy weaver, thatcher, carpenter, mason, wheelwright, millwright, cabinet maker, stonemason, woolsorter, tinker, calico printer's pinciller, worsted manufacturer, carpet maker, flax dresser, steel toy maker, stocking maker, ribbing weaver, framesmith, framework knitter, woolstapler. And for the '*non-familial*' occupational category: servant, farm-servant, labourer, soldier, publican, militiaman, gardener, yearly servant, ostler, schoolmaster, turnpike keeper, painter, hairdresser, yeoman, farmer, woolman, plasterer, auctioneer, coal dealer, excise officer, sawyer, bricklayer, husbandman, sailor, builder, glazier, coachman, shopkeeper, fishmonger, footman, toll gate keeper, slatner, plasterer, woodcutter, stable boy, Caius bedmaker, under-hostler, highway surveyor, gamekeeper, ploughman, under-ploughman, horse keeper, poulterer, tapster, post chaise driver, rabbit warrener, shearman, hopfactor, miller, butcher, brewer, seedsman, navvy, and cook.

framework knitters, woolcombers and woolsorters (presumably archetypical) also had a mean family size of 2.2 at a mean age of family head of 34. Such a tendency for 'proto-industrial' occupations, just as for 'familial' occupations, was probably a long-established practice, rather than being unique to a particular 'phase' of 'proto-industrial' production. The demographic significance of 'proto-industry' thus partly depends on the as yet unmeasured extent to which membership of such trades expanded in relation to all other occupations – particularly those in the 'non-familial' category. And it would seem worth examining this and related issues by using not simply 'proto-industrial' occupations, but a broader category such as that of the 'familial' occupations taken here.[61]

V

The demographic importance of changes in marriage age and nuptiality in England has now been established by Wrigley and Schofield, although further reconstitution studies will help pinpoint with greater precision regional and perhaps occupational differences. From the reconstitution evidence which currently exists, it seems that southern parishes shared in a more widespread reduction of female mean age at first marriage between 1650/99 and 1800/49: from about 26.5 to 23.4. (In some areas it had fallen further: to 22.8 years for a group of Suffolk villages in 1837–51, for example.) For men there was also a fall, of less magnitude: from about 27.8 to 25.3. (Again, in the latter Suffolk villages it had fallen to 24.8.)[62] In earlier chapters some main determinants of this besides real wage trends were discussed: the diminution of female work in agriculture and the trades, the decline of apprenticeship, the effect of enclosure in ending prudential motives to delay marriage, and the decline of farm service. Without re-covering that ground, I want here to pursue the matter further by discussing the institution of marriage and labouring attitudes to it; the

[61] For discussion of 'proto-industry' and demographic change, see P. Kriedte, H. Medick & J. Schlumbohm, *Industrialization before Industrialization* (Cambridge, 1981); F. Mendels, 'Proto-industrialization: the first phase of the process of industrialization', *Jnl of Econ. Hist.*, XXXII (1972), and his 'Industrialization and population pressure in eighteenth-century Flanders', *Jnl of Econ. Hist.*, XXXI (1971). For an extended critical discussion of the literature on 'proto-industry', see R. Houston & K. D. M. Snell, 'Proto-industrialization? Cottage industry, social change and the Industrial Revolution', *Historical Journal*, XXVII (1984).

[62] For the reconstitution evidence, see E. A. Wrigley & R. S. Schofield, *The Population History of England, 1541–1871* (1981), p. 255. The Suffolk data is from D. Jones, 'Thomas Campbell Foster and the rural labourer; incendiarism in East Anglia in the 1840's', *Social History*, I (1976), 7.

arrangements surrounding service and saving for marriage; and to draw out further points which contemporaries stressed as influencing marriage decisions. The question of marriage determinants will remain with demographers, and it is for them finally to assess the importance of factors which social and economic historians, working from different sources of a more literary nature, may be able to suggest as serious possibilities.

It would be helpful first to establish the sums saved in service preparatory to marriage, and to assess the effect of the decline of service – a matter which is also important insofar as the life-cycle spending upon marriage of such a numerically significant group as servants must have made an important contribution to the home market.[63] I have cited Howlett on the choice for a female servant between accumulating livestock (in an open village as a 'shepherdess'), or saving perhaps £30.[64] Another source (for Hertfordshire in 1817) gave the figure of £40 as the combined sum considered a normal precondition for marriage, and furniture was cited as the major item of expense. Farm service (which this source stated to be almost universal in Hertfordshire and Middlesex for the agricultural poor before marriage) was the means to save such a sum.[65]

Now, wages could range from £2 to £12 per annum for 'adult' farm-servants. Female money wages in the south-eastern counties were about £3.3 to a male wage of £4.6 around 1750 – about three-quarters of the male wage (but in some districts nearly the same). The differential grew somewhat to about £5.1 to a male wage of about £8.3 in 1800–15 – rather under two-thirds the male wage. In Glynd, near Lewes (in 1828), about two to three women saved to every man; and the reliable John Clare left us with the impression of spending at fairs being more indulged in by male servants than their female counterparts.[66] In the 1820s, servants were thought more likely to use savings banks than labourers. This was partly because of the different forms of payment to the two groups, but also because labourers felt that such saving would come to the notice of overseers, and so would disqualify them for relief.[67] (In a later period, with a

---

[63] I shall discuss the significance for the home market of farm-servant saving and life-cycle spending elsewhere.   [64] See chapter 4.

[65] S.C. of the House of Commons on the Poor Laws, VI (1817), pp. 72, 133. For supportive evidence see H. White, *The Record of my Life: an Autobiography* (Cheltenham, 1889), p. 116; Anon, *A Political Enquiry into the Consequences of Enclosing Waste Lands, and the causes of the present high Price of Butchers' Meat* (1785), pp. 43–4; W. Pitt, *General View of the Agriculture of the County of Stafford* (1794, 1813 edn), p. 219.

[66] S.C. on Criminal Commitments and Convictions, VI (1828), p. 56. John Clare, *The Village Minstrel*, in J. W. and A. Tibble (eds.), *John Clare, Selected Poems* (1965), p. 48.

[67] S.C. on Criminal Commitments and Convictions, VI (1826–7), p. 22.

more reliable postal service, labourers used distant savings banks for this reason.)[68] More commonly of course, savings banks were not available, especially before the nineteenth century. (No rural parishes in Bedfordshire in 1818 had savings banks, and there was only one in Bedford.)[69] Savings had to be carried with the servant, or deposited with a trusted employer or local clergyman. David Davies complained that the poor were antipathetic to saving with employers, fearing that by doing so they would lose their money.[70] For many, safeguarding savings must have been a major worry. Settlement examinations sometimes mention complaints that a master had both refused to pay proper wages at the end of the year, and had also pocketed savings deposited with him. The possibility that a service would end in bad feeling, or with the servant being sent away before time, must have raised doubts as to whether the employer could be trusted. The spending of wages on drink which so annoyed Defoe may often have reflected a sense that there was no other feasible option.[71]

However, there is no doubt that money *was* saved. And the potential was certainly there. Allowing for gradations of age-specific earnings, a thrifty female servant marrying (let us say) at the age of twenty-five could potentially save £30–£50, depending on the period and place; and a male servant might at best be able to save around £80, if he left home at the start of the Napoleonic Wars. An important consideration, which could interfere with this, was how much of farm-servants' wages were sent home to parents. Examinations indicate that the wages of a minority of servants were even paid direct to the father in their first year of service, and sometimes examinants did not know how much they had been paid because of this. John Hyde (examined Fordington, Dorset, in 1817) was unusual in having such an arrangement stretch even longer:

His late Father made an agreement with her for the examinant (he being present) to serve her for a year at so much per week wages, but how much he can't say with certainty as his said late Father or Mother always received the wages to their own use, and that under such yearly hiring this Examinant continued in the said Mrs. Cull's Service for some years, and that he believes his wages were advanced towards the latter part thereof, but to what amount he does not at this time recollect.[72]

[68] Report on the Employment of Women and Children in Agriculture, XVII (1867–8), p. 169.
[69] S.C. of the House of Lords on the Poor Laws, V (1818), pp. 163–6.
[70] D. Davies, *The Case of the Labourers in Husbandry* (1795), p. 130. Parson Woodforde safeguarded the savings of his mother's maid, allowing her 5 per cent interest per annum: 'I do it purely to encourage her to be careful, and to make her saving.' See Rev. J. Woodforde, *The Diary of a Country Parson, 1758–1802* (Oxford, 1978 edn), pp. 30, 37. [71] D. Defoe, *Giving Alms no Charity* (1704), p. 27.
[72] Dorset C.R.O., P11/OV 188B.

The hiring was anomalous in other respects, as he lodged at home during it. More commonly, wages were soon paid direct to the live-in servant, particularly before the nineteenth century, and farm-servants would at most only expect a year's wages to go to parents, if that. They would often volunteer this, sending it themselves. In the nineteenth century, pressure from their families for contributions seems to have intensified, with money sometimes being sent home for longer into the 'teens – but still usually not for more than the first couple of years at service.[73] The wages of young female servants, most noticeably in the nineteenth century, were sometimes sent home to provide clothes for younger children to be put to service in, or even to apprentice a younger brother. But by a certain age (usually sixteen), the girl would expect to keep her own wages, preparatory to marriage.[74] Her wages would then be used to provide linen (considered her particular duty to provide), and perhaps a bed and household utensils. Sometimes an employer's wife might help out, with old items from her own household. And the help from the servant to family was not always one way – parents might send food or clothes to the person in service, and then contribute some items (usually furniture) upon marriage.[75] Taking pre-marital spending and such connections with the family into account, the average sum saved in the late eighteenth century between the two marrieds was probably about £50–60, with the woman saving more assiduously than the man, and providing at least £30.

The decline of farm service and the effects of enclosure permanently curtailed the ability and motive of single people to save for marriage. As David Davies pointed out, both these changes made for poverty-stricken marriages.[76] And other considerations rapidly stepped in. In the first place, as female employment became more precarious and lowly paid, there were obvious motives to marry younger as defence against the unemployment which was increasingly the lot of women. Hampson was quite correct when she pointed out that female wages were so low that marriage must have seemed the only way to live

---

[73] However, Fred Kitchen paid his mother part of his yearly wages right up to marriage. See his *Brother to the Ox: the Autobiography of a Farm Labourer* (1940, 1963 edn), pp. 194ff.

[74] Kerr, *Bound to the Soil*, p. 137; Graham, *Rural Exodus*, pp. 183–4. On apprentices in agriculture infrequently returning home, see Report on the Employment of Women and Children in Agriculture, XII (1843), p. 127.

[75] For mothers sending food to children in service, see Clare, *Selected Poems*, p. 45. For other connections with their parents of those in service, see Woodforde, *Diary of a County Parson*, pp. 209, 313, 405, 597.   [76] Davies, *Case of the Labourers*, pp. 75ff.

adequately.[77] In the absence of traditional savings, pre-marital pregnancy was an answer to ensuring oneself a husband, and illegitimacy the consequence when such a tactic misfired. Both of course rose sharply over this period. But there was, within the terms of the old poor law at any rate, considerable parish support and aid for marriage in such cases – women must have been aware of this. And the growing numbers receiving parish assistance during the later eighteenth century altered the perceptions of single people over traditional saving requirements for marriage, contributing to keep marriage ages low once the potential and motive for saving had collapsed. Marriage was expected for the majority, and, for all the features of the European or perhaps English 'marriage pattern', most women certainly looked to the future expecting it. The rising southern male agricultural real wages before about 1770 were probably important initial reasons for marriage age to have fallen. And elsewhere, in the west for women, or in parts of the north, a continued rise of real wages (or at any rate an absence of considerable reductions) may help explain further reductions of marriage age. But in the rural south the causation was to become rather different after the 1760s, albeit conducive to the same end. The subsequent decline of service, the reduced scope for female work in agriculture and the trades, the ending of older incentives to delay marriage when the common fields had still been intact, or the large numbers assisted under the old poor law were all factors which stepped in to lower further, and hold down, female marriage age.[78] And there were now good reasons for men to marry earlier too, with the decline of service and apprenticeship. A fall in male marriage age could well bring about a corresponding fall in that for women (given assumptions on courting

---

[77] Hampson, *Treatment of Poverty*, p. 218: 'It is hardly surprising that marriage at any price, or even illegitimate relations, seemed to women the only solution.'

[78] For supportive discussion on how absence of female employment was associated with low marriage age and high fertility, see M. Hewitt, *Wives and Mothers in Victorian Industry* (1958), pp. 35-46. Of mining districts, for example, Durham had the highest proportion of young people married, but mining there hardly offered any employment to women. In 1840 female employment as textile operatives was commended because 'it is to the interest of the community that every young woman should have this in her power. *She is not then driven into an early marriage by the necessity of seeking a home*' (p. 46, my italics). See also the interesting discussion of M. Haines, *Fertility and Occupation. Population Patterns in Industrialization* (1979), demonstrating the strong occupational correlation of scarce female employment with early marriage age, high nuptiality, and high marital fertility (e.g., pp. 23–5, 46, 55, 156, 177–8, 235–7). For further supportive discussion on this, see his bibliography and items he includes in n. 31, p. 55; M. Anderson, 'Marriage patterns in Victorian Britain: an analysis based on registration district data for England and Wales', *Jnl of Family History*, I (1976), 64.

and spouse age differentials), so let us pursue a further factor acting on male marriage ages.

By the early nineteenth century, partly because of problems of structural unemployment and the decline of service, unemployment among single men (as well as women) was widely cited as a reason for early marriages. The married and their families were more expensive to maintain on the rates, and so were given priority in employment. This was a problem raised by the 1834 Poor Law Report – in part against the scale systems of the old poor law, which favoured married men over single, and (incidentally) often cut single working women out of consideration altogether. But it is improbable that the New Poor Law remedied it, and there was little improvement before the mid-nineteenth century. Earlier, an 1826–7 Committee spoke of how it was married men with families who were mainly employed in Bedfordshire, where even during the harvest some young men were unemployed. Poaching among them was adduced to this, and the 1828 Committee on Criminal Commitments made similar complaints.[79] Discussion of the 'early Victorian juvenile vagrancy problem' repeatedly came back to this issue.[80] Independent accommodation in many regions was almost unobtainable for the young unless they were married, just as with council housing today. And this was the context against which modern demographers have noted rises in mean household size in the early nineteenth century, and young marrieds living with parents, also commented on by contemporaries. In Norfolk complaints were made as late as 1847 of farmer guardians' preference to employ married men over single. And the latter had little hope of out-migrating locally: 'the farmers there would hardly dare to employ a stranger'.[81] Out-migration increasingly had to be more long distance, to another sector of the economy. We are reminded of George Coode in 1851, who wrote of young unmarried people that they had become, 'in rural places, mere outcasts, the last to be employed and the first to be pauperized, as they still remain, whenever and wherever work is scarce for the heads of large families'. He felt that the influence of the New Poor

---

[79] S.C. on the Poor Rates, V (1822), p. 544; S.C. on Criminal Commitments and Convictions, VI (1826–7), pp. 22, 31–7, 43–54; S.C. on Criminal Commitments and Convictions, VI (1828), pp. 50–70; S.C. on the Relief of Able-Bodied Persons from the Poor Rates, IV (1828), pp. 6–10; S. G. & E. O. A. Checkland (eds.), *The Poor Law Report of 1834* (1974), p. 219; West Suffolk C.R.O., El. 110/7/168 (Circular: 'Situation of Labourers', 26 Nov. 1830); A. Digby, 'The labour market and the continuity of social policy after 1834: the case of the eastern counties', *Econ. Hist. Rev.*, XXVIII (1975), 78–80.

[80] For example, see *Morning Chronicle*, 18, 22, 25, 29, 31 Jan. 1850.

[81] S.C. on Settlement and Poor Removal, XI (1847), p. 372.

Law had 'been but little' in this regard.[82] Single people in particular suffered by being put into the workhouse, because the main loophole by which the married might escape it was by pleading sickness in the family – hardly an option for the unmarried person. Married men were also more commonly offered piece work than single. It is hardly surprising that unmarried men were so widely blamed for starting incendiary fires: the average age of those acquitted before the assizes of 1844 on charges of arson was 22.3, and the age for those convicted was 24.3.[83] This group had of course traditionally been farm-servants, the most securely employed of any occupation.

In much the same way that economic recession and large-scale unemployment since 1978 have been associated with a rising number of marriages, so these aspects of rural unemployment compounded other factors which reduced the marriage age, particularly the decline of service.[84] A demographer has written of how 'In mid-nineteenth century England late marriage was correlated with the persistence of servants in agriculture whereas early marriage was linked with day labour.'[85] And as MacQueen wrote in 1830: 'The labourer [sic], driven from the comforts of his master's fireside, and no longer held under the domestic restraint which had formerly regulated his conduct, married prematurely *in his own defence*, to obtain the comforts of a home' (my italics).[86] The vulnerable position of an unmarried man on

---

[82] Report of G. Coode to the Poor Law Board on the Law of Settlement and Removal of the Poor, XXVI (1851), pp. 273–9. See also S.C. on Settlement and Poor Removal, XI (1847), p. 561.

[83] D. Jones, 'Thomas Campbell Foster', 20. See also E. J. Hobsbawm & G. Rudé, *Captain Swing* (1973 edn), p. 248; J. P. D. Dunbabin, *Rural Discontent in Nineteenth-Century Britain* (1974), p. 69; *Morning Chronicle*, 22 Jan. 1850, p. 40.

[84] In the 1960s and early 1970s the causation was different and optimistic developments then had an effect similar to the rising real wages and probably fuller employment of the early eighteenth century. But such demographic results need not only be produced by optimistic changes.

[85] Levine, *Family Formation*, p. 110. See also A. Kussmaul, *Servants in Husbandry in Early Modern England* (Cambridge, 1981), pp. 84, 110–15; J. P. Huzel, 'Malthus, the poor law and population in early nineteenth-century England', *Econ. Hist. Rev.*, XXII (1969), 436; Anderson, 'Marriage patterns in Victorian Britain'. Or see S.C. on Emigration, V (1826–7), p. 603:
> There is another change that has taken place ... the labourers [sic] no longer live in farmhouses, as they used to do, when they were better fed and had more comforts than they now get in a cottage, in consequence there was not the same inducement to early marriage, because if a man up to the age of twenty-five or thirty had been accustomed to live in a better way of life, he would consider twice before he married and went to live in a wretched cottage upon potatoes and tea.

[86] T. P. MacQueen, *Thoughts and Suggestions on the Present Condition of the Country* (1830), p. 9. The preconditions to marriage advocated by many contemporaries would have excluded virtually all southern agricultural labourers. See for example, C. Maclaren, *The Scotsman's Advice to the Labouring Classes, on the best means of raising their Wages and securing themselves and their Families against want* (Edinburgh, 1830), pp. 4ff.

the labour market by the early nineteenth century would indeed have inclined him to marry early, 'in his own defence' – and potential wives were there, in doleful abundance.

VI

Contradictory evidence abounds on the attitudes of agricultural labouring people to sexuality and marriage itself. As Eileen Yeo pointed out, the early statisticians (and we should add, many other commentators) 'assumed any divergence from middle-class behaviour to equal bestiality'.[87] This was certainly true of commentators on rural affairs. Around the hiring fairs, for example, there grew up middle-class notions which must have caused many a sleepless night for the country parsons' wives. Arthur Young's suspicion that farm-servants 'sleep where and with whom they please' was one which spread rapidly in the age of Harriet Martineau, and by the mid-nineteenth century the vexatious 'truth' about hiring fairs had finally transpired:

There are certain inevitable evils arising from the indiscriminate mixture of several hundreds of young people in the same town, on the same day, for the same purpose, which no precaution can prevent, or even do much to mitigate. The grossness of the scene does not unveil itself till the shades of night have fallen. Then the orgies begin.

The strains of agricultural songs wafting over the hedgerow ('which are frequently obscene and disgusting'), were felt by many to be merely an everyday expression of working-class instincts periodically liable to erupt in such bestial bacchanalia.[88]

It was an uncomfortable and perturbing thought, often expressed. Of course remedies were prescribed; foremost among them the splitting of families in the New Poor Law workhouses: to prevent 'scenes of the greatest indecency and disorder'.[89] Even this arrangement was not always entirely watertight, for a dismayed Parliamentary Committee was presented with yet another horror – surreptitious copulation between a married couple in the workhouse toilets.

[87] E. P. Thompson & E. Yeo (eds.), *The Unknown Mayhew* (1971, Harmondsworth, 1973) p. 100.

[88] Report on the Employment of Women and Children in Agriculture, XVII (1867–8), p. 101.

[89] S.C. on the Poor Law Amendment Act, XVIII (1837–8), pt I, p. 33. Or see pp. 481–2, where rather than simply taking into the workhouse some of the children of large families, it is recommended that the whole family be taken in earlier, and split up there. This guardians 'believed afforded a larger amount of protection to the labourer having a large family' (i.e., it stopped further breeding). Even before 1834. Cobbett complained of attempts 'forcibly to separate a labourer from his wife to prevent their having children' – see his *Advice to Young Men* (1830, Oxford, 1980 edn), p. 326.

Pamphleteers suggested other preventive measures, lacking the medical expertise of more modern schemes put into effect in China or India, but comparable in other respects. The concern of 'R. F.' over the matter led him to suggest the formation of corps of workmen for public work, on a national scale, consisting only of unmarried men, boarded and lodged in complete isolation from the other sex.[90] (There were to be alternative corps on the same principle for single women.) The term of service would be fifteen years, and the government would determine the amount of 'pocket money' (his phrase) received by those engaged in this early youth 'opportunity' programme. 'Promiscuity' and early marriage were to be effectively controlled by this method. Rowland Hill's equivalent plan featured 'home colonies', to which morally suspect individuals would be sent to mend their ways, and so 'render it possible soon to restore them to society'.[91] There was, he constantly stressed, need for very strict moral behaviour to counter early marriages. More generally, proposals accepted the institutional opportunities which already existed, and pleaded for closer supervision from employers and the clergy. Thomas Smith's thoughts on the matter were typical enough:

It might be remarked, that the restraints between the sexes which exist in other ranks of society, do not obtain among the poor . . . The serious attention of farmers and others, who employ men and women servants, should be directed to the importance of using every means to prevent an undue freedom between them, and of discouraging the loose conversation that is so painful to a well-regulated mind; it is possible that masters and mistresses, in country situations especially, might, by exercising a proper care, prevent much that is evil.[92]

But, for all this concern, agricultural labouring people were largely free of the exploitative sexual perversions practised by many Victorian middle- and upper-class men. The well documented tastes of the latter for adulterous literature, pornography, flagellation, garment fetishism, young virgins, and child prostitutes ('probably eight per cent of *all women* in London were prostitutes'),[93] coupled with their syphilophobia and fear of 'masturbatory insanity', do not appear among the rural poor.[94] Perhaps a paucity of historical sources has

---

[90] R. F., *Observations on Pauperism* (1832).
[91] R. Hill, *Home Colonies. Sketch of a Plan for the Gradual Extinction of Pauperism and for the Diminution of Crime* (1832), pp. 22ff.
[92] Smith, *Old Poor Law and New Poor Law*, pp. 32–3.
[93] Pearsall, *Worm in the Bud* (1972 edn), p. 328.
[94] There is a large literature on this. See in particular *ibid.*, and S. Marcus, *The Other Victorians* (1966). Also, W. Acton, *Prostitution, Considered in its Mental, Social and Sanitary Aspects* (1857); K. Chesney, *The Victorian Underworld* (1970); F. Harrison, *The Dark Angel* (Glasgow, 1977); B. Harrison, 'Underneath the Victorians', *Victorian Studies*, X (1967), 239–62.

exonerated the latter. Perhaps, in a rare quarter session case, featuring the eye-witness account of how one luckless labourer expressed affection for his employer's brown mare, we glimpse only the tip of a class-specific perversity as unique and pervasive as that of their more leisured male employers.[95] I think it unlikely. Less dogmatically adherent to the principle of marriage, they were less likely to infringe it, and their attitudes currently seem refreshing in class perspective. Regarding marriage, the statement by this clergyman is probably most apt, and Anglican clergy, after all, were usually prone to stress immoral aspects of working-class life: 'Two-thirds or three-fourths of the women when married are in the family way [a figure of about 45 per cent was more general in the early nineteenth century] but there is no prostitution, and no infidelity ever heard of after marriage, they simply don't care much about the marriage ceremony.'[96]

The large majority would marry, of course, especially by the early nineteenth century, but potential children were a higher concern than the fact of marriage itself. The large proportion of premarital pregnancies was explained by one woman as follows: 'the first child never counts for nothing: my husband acted on the old saying about here, "No child, no wife", and I had one afore I was married'.[97] (The bastardy enactment of the New Poor Law was aimed against this sort of practice.) And the incidence of unmarried people living together, sometimes with an expectation that they would eventually get married, seems to have been more common than is often supposed. One woman for example, 'being then with child by Richard Jones, Bricklayer, went to live with him upon a promise of marriage which he never performed'. But still she stayed, and had a total of four children by him.[98] Or Elizabeth Pilsworth, examined in Cambridgeshire in 1835, declared: 'I am a single woman ... rather more than nine years ago I became acquainted with John Hutchinson. We agreed ... to live together as Man and Wife but we were never

---

[95] West Suffolk C.R.O., N2/1/8–12.

[96] Report on Employment of Women and Children in Agriculture, XVII (1867–8), p. 765. The figure of 45 per cent is a mean of figures for Terling and Great Oakley, kindly supplied by Roger Schofield.

[97] *Morning Chronicle*, 29 Jan. 1850, p. 46. To similar effect, see J. Hanway, *The Defects of the Police the Cause of Immorality* (1775), p. 163; or his *A Candid Historical Account of the Hospital for the Reception of Exposed and Deserted Young Children* (1759), pp. 42–3. 'The male and female often come together before marriage; and if the woman *proves*, as they term becoming pregnant, then the parties marry by a kind of honour and decency.' See also Thompson, *Lark Rise*, p. 138 – speaking of 'the children of couples who had married after the birth of their first child, a common happening at that time and little thought of'; T. Hardy, *The Well-Beloved* (1897, 1975 edn), pp. 40, 64, 91, 208.

[98] Berks C.R.O., D/P/132. 13/4A.

Married . . . he took my name and we always went by the name of Pilsworth.' They had five children together under this arrangement.[99] (Today, of course, the 'liberated' couple assert their values merely by having the wife keep her maiden name.) Or Ann Fuller (examined 1776) was deserted when 'great with child' soon after her first marriage to William Fuller, and later married William Holder 'upon a supposition that the said William Fuller was dead'. 'That during her Cohabitation with [the second husband] she has seen William Fuller her first husband who peaceably acquiesced with such her cohabitation with William Holder.'[100] Or to take another case:

the said Emma Cole absented herself from her said husband and cohabited with a man named Jonas Bendall. She left him (the husband) on the 13 July 1872 . . . He [the husband] drove her over and she took her things. Saw no more of her until the 26th September, when she came over and asked whether he was going to find her a home. Told her she could come and live here, she then went away and I have not seen her since.[101]

For most, just as today, there were obvious reasons of expedience to marry: one's children would not be shunted off to their respective places of birth under the terms of bastardy settlement; the settlement of man and wife would become as one (the wife took the man's settlement); terms of poor relief became more favourable; it was easier to gain aid for children under the poor law; employment and charity were offered more readily, and so on. None of these motives necessarily implied unqualified enthusiasm for the institution as such, and in many regions bastardy was not considered much of a stigma among the working classes. One consequence of this was an element of flexibility within marriage: of agreed annulments of an informal nature; of family break-up and remarriage regardless of the law; or of many men and women living together without being married, often for long periods, and bringing up children.[102] The disdain for the letter of the law is well illustrated in the following passage from *The Bettesworth Book*. Edmund, says Bettesworth,

[99] Camb C.R.O., G/C/As. 2.   [100] Camb C.R.O., P. 76/13/7.
[101] Camb C.R.O., G/C/As. 9.
[102] I have never encountered wife selling in examinations, although one might expect to find it there. Common law marriages were usually sufficient for the wife to take the husband's settlement, although there are almost no explicit references to them either, not even in the west. See S. P. Menefee, *Wives for Sale* (Oxford, 1981), pp. 55–6, 66, on settlement considerations affecting common law marriage and wife sales. This book (paradoxically) provides much evidence of female independence within marriage. See for example pp. 61–4, 72, 74, 76–7, 97, 279–80. The small number of documented sales over many centuries, the large crowds turning out and their frequent hostility to sale, the associated broadsheets and so on do not suggest that this practice was common.

'never got married not afore he was – what now? – fifty, I reckon. An' then he married two sisters.'

Before I could vent my astonishment at this, Bettesworth explained, 'One of 'em first; an' when she died then he took t'other. The vicar, he was down on 'n for that; but Edmund says, "Well, if I didn't marry her, somebody else would".'

'You see', I began, 'it's —'

'Illegal, en't it, sir? . . . Well Edmund didn't care.'

'Well, but the vicar didn't marry 'em?'

'No, *he* wouldn't have no hand in 't. But Edmund never cared. He wanted her, an' he had her.'[103]

Another feature was resentment among labourers over parish interference in their marriages, which sometimes surfaced to suggest tension between their own attitudes and the self-imposed responsibilities of parish officials. One example can serve to illustrate this. Its full background details are now lost; although in the temporary absence of the husband, the overseers had decided to step in and send his wife away from her parish of residence to his settlement parish. The husband found out and replied in revealingly chaotic fashion:

To the Overseers of the parish of Thatcham, nr. Newbury, Berks.

Sedworth December 1st 1770

Sir,

this is to let you know unsettled for it is my Desier you littil Buggeirs that I have inquierd from five tustlers and three of Decourerum and it is my Desier you will send my wife to me on Demande as for your carrying of my wife to my parish without me will be of no Signification if you send or come to me it will oblige you to pay me two shillings per Day from my marriage if you take the thing in your one minds it will be the best to send her to me for it is me that must find her parish and not you. I Desier you to send me answer by the return of the post what you purpose to Do. Drecket for me at John Dippo in Worton Lane Sedworth from your humbell servant

Thomas Clevraly

p.s. please to give the inclose to my wife and if you please you may read it if I have not answer by the return of the post you may expete a Lawers Letter.[104]

Similar letters of a later period found it wise to omit the 'littil Buggeirs', although the feelings were usually much the same. After all, labouring people faced considerable interference with their families: the parish taking their children into custody, apprenticing them in circumstances of 'parental irresponsibility', putting pressure on families to send their children into service, imposing conditions of

---

[103] G. Sturt, *The Bettesworth Book* (Firle, Sussex, 1978), p. 285. Or see *The Journals of George Sturt, 1890–1927* (Cambridge, 1967), vol. 1, pp. 324–5.

[104] Berks C.R.O., P. 130/13/1/1.

moral and religious eligibility to parish benefits, and so on. Just as sometimes with Anglican doctrine, these were worth enduring when the relief and benefits offered could be generous, as under the old poor law.

VII

A further aspect of family history on which light can be thrown is the domestic division of labour. One should draw attention in particular to the wife's important role in managing household finances, a role which was to be further augmented by her withdrawal from many economic activities in the early nineteenth century. There is little to support the view that 'working women ... were more like servants than partners ... the money they earned was controlled by the husband, who anyway was in legal theory entitled to it'.[105] In fact, the money the husband earned was usually controlled by his wife, to whom the budgeting of the household almost always fell, and marital legal theory was for the most part quite irrelevant to actual practice. The men, wrote Flora Thompson, handed their wages 'straight over to their wives, who gave them back a shilling for the next week's pocket-money. That was the custom of the countryside. The men worked for the money and the women had the spending of it.'[106] M. K. Ashby confirmed this: 'only a few men ever touched the money at all; mostly the wives took it at the door and spent it too'.[107] 'I had a great inclination to travel', wrote Charles Varley, 'but as my mother carried the purse, it was impossible for my father to do much for me.'[108] Or a migrant harvester spoke of how 'I've still remained taking my money home ever since, and she [his wife] always buys just what she likes with it, and lays it out to the best advantage.'[109] The morally affirmed role of the 'housewife', seen by Galbraith today as an important agent to 'administer consumption', to spend household

[105] Stone, *Family, Sex and Marriage*, p. 200.   [106] Thompson, *Lark Rise*, p. 62.
[107] M. K. Ashby, *Joseph Ashby of Tysoe, 1859–1919* (Cambridge, 1961), p. 48. Or see Sturt, *Bettesworth Book*, p. 163. Thomas Turner spoke of his wife as 'the only friend, I believe, I have now in this world', and some time after her death wrote of how there was now 'no one person to whom I may entrust the management of my affairs, it almost drives me to distraction'. Turner, *Diary of a Georgian Shopkeeper*, pp. 46, 63–4. See also Cobbett, *Advice to Young Men* (Oxford, 1980 edn), pp. 119, 203, 308, on the wife taking care of financial affairs.
[108] C. Varley, *The Modern Farmer's Guide, by a Real Farmer* (Glasgow, 1768), p. xx.
[109] Anon., 'Autobiography of a navvy', *Macmillan's Magazine* (Dec. 1861), 150. Or see D. Vincent, 'Love and death and the nineteenth-century working class', *Social History*, V (1980), 239. For a similar situation in France, see, for example, O. Hufton, 'Women and the family economy in eighteenth-century France', *French Hist. Studies*, IX (1975), 16.

income and so perpetuate the home market, was highly developed by the nineteenth century, even among this lowly class.[110]

VIII

Something can now be said on the family poverty-cycle. We have already seen how men aged about thirty-four were most liable to become chargeable. They had by that age a number of young children who were still economically unproductive, and such a family was especially prone to chargeability.[111] Table 7.7 accordingly gives the numbers of children over time which it took to bring a family onto the poor rates, as taken from a large sample of examinations. Only families comprising man, wife, and children have been used, and I have included all occupations. In the hypothetical case of all other considerations remaining equal, one would expect a rise in the number of children accompanying chargeability to indicate an improvement in the standard of living – that is, an ability of families to survive unaided to higher than previous family sizes. There was little change in this under the old poor law, with the figures for the three districts usually varying between 2.1 and 2.6.[112] (This is, incidentally, well under the three, four, or five children needed before parishes would pay family allowances.) It would be hard to make any argument on the basis of these slight differences, given that poor law administration changed during this period, affecting in small details the framework within which applications for relief were made. The major changes of the table come after 1834 for all three regions, when there was an immediate rise in the number of children producing chargeability. This almost certainly says more about the fear of the New Poor Law workhouse in deterring families from poor relief than it does about a mitigation of the family poverty-cycle. If this is accepted, it still remains of interest as an indication of how effective this law was in making relief more inaccessible – a consideration of

---

[110] J. K. Galbraith, *Annals of an Abiding Liberal* (1980), pp. 36–47.

[111] For similar accounts of the family poverty-cycle, see Graham, *Rural Exodus*, pp. 182–3; B. S. Rowntree, *Poverty: A Study of Town Life* (1901); H. Medick, 'The proto-industrial family economy', *Social History*, I (1976), 305–6. See also T. K. Hareven, 'The family as process: the historical study of the family cycle', *Jnl of Social Hist.*, VII (1974).

[112] See also Hampson, *Treatment of Poverty*, pp. 139ff. She found 2.4 to be the average number of children upon chargeability. The comparison of these figures with the larger number of children usually needed before parishes would pay family allowances contributes to question the charge that such allowances were an incentive to procreate. This supports the view of M. Blaug, 'The myth of the old poor law and the making of the new', *Jnl of Econ. Hist.*, XXIII (1963).

Table 7.7. *Family poverty-cycle: numbers of children per family*
(man and wife)

	Eastern counties (Camb, Beds, Hunts, Herts, Norf, Suff, N'hants, Ess)			South Midland counties (Leics, Bucks, Berks, Oxon)			Western counties (Mon, Heref, Worcs, Wilts, Glos, Dors, Dev, Som)		
	Mean	N.	s.	Mean	N.	s.	Mean	N.	s.
1700–50	2.21	65	1.23	2.60	65	1.53	2.53	30	1.38
1751–60	2.31	29	1.65	2.32	44	1.65	2.58	31	1.59
1761–70	2.11	56	1.23	2.40	62	1.63	2.29	31	1.37
1771–80	2.09	103	1.34	1.89	97	1.20	2.33	39	1.59
1781–90	2.36	235	1.51	2.01	92	1.32	2.58	48	1.48
1791–1800	2.39	180	1.83	2.49	96	1.38	2.95	41	1.76
1801–10	2.15	81	1.36	2.27	70	1.60	2.76	59	1.72
1811–20	2.56	124	1.64	2.68	161	1.97	2.64	95	1.43
1821–30	2.30	110	1.55	2.32	122	1.46	2.78	119	1.83
1831–34	2.67	30	1.81	2.37	35	1.31	2.64	48	1.66
1835–40	3.19	42	1.84	3.36	14	2.02	3.45	20	1.85
1841–50	3.05	65	2.12	3.27	11	2.10	3.22	23	2.00
1851–60	2.37	41	1.16	2.89	9	1.83	3.30	10	1.49
1861–70	2.44	52	1.74	—	—	—	—	—	—
1871–80	2.60	40	1.58	—	—	—	—	—	—
Total	2.40	1,253	1.60	2.38	878	1.59	2.71	594	1.65

obvious significance in assessing changes in the quality and security of life.[113] Similarly, the decline after 1840 till 1870 probably reflects some relaxation of the law, and the suggestion of a rise again in the 1870s may be a reflection of the return to 'the principles of 1834'. The figures were also calculated using only the numbers of children under the age of eight (those most obviously making little contribution to the family's income), and by separating artisan from agricultural families. The results indicated a similar constancy under the old poor law, with the same rise after 1834 the only notable change over time.

IX

Let us turn to family break-up, a subject of great interest because of the rising modern divorce rate, but one on which there has been little

[113] For example, only about a quarter of those offered in-door relief in Norfolk (1835–6) accepted it. A. Digby, *Pauper Palaces* (1978), p. 108. And of course there was later to be an enormous disparity between the large proportion of the population found by Rowntree and Booth to be living below the poverty line and the much smaller percentage of the population officially receiving poor relief.

historical discussion in Britain. E. M. Hampson argued that the later eighteenth century saw growing numbers of men coming under the vagrancy laws for abandoning their families, and that this indicated a weakening of family ties.[114] David Davies, too, noted that families were breaking up because of the man's inability to support a large family, and the inadequacy of parish relief during the high prices of the late eighteenth century.[115] And Arthur Young also complained of an increase of familial desertion, and blamed it on enclosure:

Is it not a common crime at present in almost every parish in the kingdom? And why do they do it? Because under the present laws they have not the motive to abstain from it, which they would have if they were in a better situation. The system of land [i.e., allowing labourers renewed access to land as before enclosure] would probably be found the best prevention of this crime.

He blamed the loss of cows and other assets after enclosure for why a man 'enlists for a soldier, and leaves the wife and children to the parish'.[116]

It is possible to complement such statements with quantitative data. Table 7.8 gives details of 289 cases of family desertion, taken from 4,961 examinations for south-eastern counties. Information provided by the deserted spouse (almost always the wife) is presented under different heads, wherever it was available, broken down over time, and all occupations are included. In the two final columns this information for break-up families is summarised, and compared with similar data from examinations for other families headed by a man and wife. If we concentrate first on that comparison, some interesting characteristics emerge. Families which broke up had larger family sizes than other families: 2.55 children with those deserted partners who had children, as compared with 2.28 children for other families with children. Similarly, the proportion of break-up families with children was higher than for other families: 61 per cent as compared with 54. They had also been married longer, by about four years. Additionally, their marriage ages (for both men and women) were younger than normal, by about two years. Their illiteracy was normal. Finally, they were much more mobile than other families, being considerably further afield from the parishes where the partners were perhaps best known locally, that is from the parishes of settlement and marriage. The seasonality of desertion by

---

[114] Hampson, *Treatment of Poverty*, p. 141.   [115] Davies, *Case of the Labourers*, pp. 25ff.
[116] A. Young, *An Inquiry into the Propriety of Applying Wastes to the Better Maintenance and Support of the Poor* (Bury St Edmunds, 1801), pp. 35, 42.

Table 7.8. *Family break-up (sample of 289 cases from south-eastern counties)*

1700–50 N.	1751–80 N.	1781–1800 N.	1801–34 N.	1835–80 N.	Total for break-up families	Total for comparable sample of 300 other families
Abandoned wives as % of examinations						
4.4 (18)	4.0 (38)	6.5 (112)	5.1 (72)	10.5 (49)	5.8	—
Mean N. of children with wife						
2.52 (23)	2.10 (34)	2.30 (164)	2.58 (109)	3.20 (121)	2.55	2.28
% abandoned wives with children						
50.7	42.6	63.7	58.7	77.2	61.2	54.3 (N. = 1,350)
Years since marriage						
3.8 (4)	3.7 (5)	7.2 (58)	12.0 (17)	14.5 (41)	10.0	6.4
Mean age of wife when examined						
40.3 (3)	37.0 (4)	30.5 (22)	33.1 (9)	41.3 (27)	36.2	(30.8)
Years since husband left						
2.0 (2)	2.7 (3)	4.5 (32)	2.7 (14)	2.2 (29)	3.2	—
Deserted wife's mean marriage age						
21.2 (3)	24.0 (3)	21.7 (19)	22.9 (5)	22.1 (10)	22.1	24.4
Departed husband's mean marriage age						
— —	26.0 (2)	24.2 (4)	25.0 (2)	24.7 (14)	24.7	26.4
Illiteracy of abandoned wife						
79.0% (100)			66.7% (39)		75.5%	76.8%
Distance of wife from settlement (miles)						
47.3 (10)	34.0 (24)	30.7 (91)	28.2 (50)	27.9 (36)	30.8	16.0
Distance of wife from place of marriage (miles)						
21.0 (2)	33.3 (3)	44.3 (37)	17.8 (13)	38.2 (30)	37.2	8.8

Nos. of abandonments by month: Jan., 1; Feb., 1; Mar., 2; Apr., 2; May, 5; June, 3; July, 5; Aug., 7; Sept., 10; Oct., 6; Nov., 2; Dec., 5.

the man is also interesting, for this was most prevalent in September and around the period of the harvest. We are rarely dealing here with cases of short-term abandonment during harvesting – the wives had almost all been deserted for a longer period, usually much longer. Such seasonality owed more to favourable weather and the high wages of summer and harvest (the latter paid in September) which helped allow the man to desert. In other seasons he had less means to do so.

What can be said about change over time? As a percentage of the numbers actually examined, deserted wives remained reasonably constant. The slight rise after 1781 is mainly attributable to soldiers during the wars. These have been included because of the troublesome task of separating those soldiers whose patriotism came before a genuine attachment to their wives, from those whose dislike for their wives underlay their patriotism. And even in the former case, male patriotism hardly brought much joy to the wife and children who suffered in consequence. Enlistment was the institutionally acceptable form of familial desertion. The rising proportion of abandoned wives under the New Poor Law may be significant, but points also to a growing reluctance to apply for relief from other poor people better placed to maintain themselves. For such a reason one might expect the mean number of children with the wife to grow under the New Poor Law, and this was notably the case. (Because of these considerations affecting application for relief, the proportion of examinations before and after 1834 which covered broken families is an unreliable indication as to whether break-up became more or less common.) The distance of the wife from place of settlement (she took her husband's) fell, from 47 to 28 miles, and perhaps this was a feature of the changes outlined earlier affecting generational settlement. The most notable change was the length of time for which the break-up family had been married: from four years to fourteen. Such a finding is numerically very tentative, but a rising adult life expectancy may have contributed slightly to such an effect over this period.

If we were to advise an eighteenth-century English-woman on the choice of her husband – assuming that she wanted the marriage to last – some suggestions could be made on the basis of the examinations. Irishmen were particularly prone to desert. However, such desertion may have been seen as an altruistic act by a man who could no longer support his family, and hoped, by leaving them, that someone else would. Irishmen commonly lacked settlements in England, and so their deserted wives would revert to their premarital settlements. And Irish labourers were actively, even very violently, opposed by the English in many regions (such as the Fens); contemporary accounts of their diet, state of health, and conditions of work in England often make for shocking reading. Cases of desertion by them may derive more from the despair of failure than from casual indifference to their wives. Soldiers, as one might expect, head an occupational list of deserting husbands, followed by labourers. Then publicans (also notoriously fathers of bastards) were highly unreliable, particularly those with a history of paying their rent irregularly. Militiamen were little better, and Scottish ex-soldiers from the American war who married and settled in England were also prone soon to head for the Highlands. A handful of carpenters who served an apprenticeship with their fathers and left home late in consequence were curiously unreliable, as were a few ex-prisoners, alongside gentry and aristocratic servants who stayed on in service after marriage. But as yet more detailed advice cannot be given.

To summarise, youthful marriages were especially prone to break-up. This has also been shown for revolutionary France, and of course remains true today.[117] A married man might feel he could desert his wife more easily were he some distance from his parishes of settlement and marriage, away from the more concerned eyes of parish authorities and relatives. He would leave with his harvest wages, allowing him to get well away and maintain himself until he found other employment. For he was now an outcast from the poor law system. Chargeability had to be avoided, for it would bring him back to his parish of settlement to face not only the proverbial rolling-pin, but also the charge of having deserted his family – which paradoxically would take him away from them again, this time to a house of correction. He would, just as David Davies suggested, be more prone to abandon his family if it was large, for such a family was more difficult to maintain. Predictably, he would leave when the family poverty-cycle, related to his children's ages, was most acute – in his mid-thirties. The rising fertility and dependency ratio of the period must have accentuated this cause, to produce families which were more likely to break-up through reasons related to their structure than had been the case earlier. This would imply a rising rate of family break-up until the dependency ratio peaked in the mid-1820s, which also seems probable insofar as other major causes (e.g., enlistment, falling marriage age) also moved in a direction in the later eighteenth century which would have accentuated the prevalence of break-up.

Unfortunately, it is not possible to show whether an urban environment was more conducive to break-up than a rural one, although one might suspect this. Most cases dealt with here were of course rural and small market-town. Nor is it possible adequately to locate break-up against the family economy, although the argument made from the excellent French evidence by Phillips – that the decline of the family economy (the separation of home and work place) loosened economically associative ties of marriage – is a suggestive one. In England, the comparative scarcity of sources will continue to restrict our knowledge; but we recognise in this data major structural factors

---

[117] See in particular, R. Phillips, *Family Breakdown in Late Eighteenth-Century France, 1792–1803* (Oxford, 1980), pp. 61–70. And O. R. McGregor, *Divorce in England – A Centenary Study* (1957); J. Dominian, *Marital Breakdown* (Harmondsworth, 1971), pp. 130–1. Richard Gough also stressed that youthful marriages were very likely to break up in his *The History of Myddle* (written in 1701, Harmondsworth, 1981 edn), pp. 124–5.

since used to help explain the much greater rates of marital separation in modern society: early marriage, high mobility, the length of marriages, large families, or a cultural difference between spouses. Prime importance should also be attached to these before the twentieth century; alongside considerations such as real wages which determined how a family could cope with them, and the still unfathomed effect (stressed by Arthur Young) of the decline of family economies. Other causes, such as changing lower-class religious attitudes towards marriage (perhaps entailed in the growth of non-conformity), probably had only a slight effect in this period, and did not alter fundamentally the reasons for break-up.

X

The use of kin for support by agricultural families was not widespread, although there was frequent mention of uncles by examinants, and sometimes of grandparents, who had occasionally brought them up.[118] Migration, especially to London, often involved kin who had drawn attention to vacancies in the city, and helped provide accommodation for the new arrival. One examinant from Berkshire spoke in 1831 of how

His sister, nearly 3 years ago, then living in London, wrote down to his Father and told him of a Place where she was then living at Mr. Moore's, Ivy Cottage, Shepherd's Bush, in the Parish of Hammersmith, which she thought would suit him. That in consequence he went up to Hammersmith and saw his sister and brother there and also met there Mrs. Moore who took him to her House and set him to work ... he continued there about two years and three quarters.

(Brothers might also serve out services for each other if one of them was taken sick, although there was no legal compulsion on them to do this.)[119] Further afield, an apprentice cordwainer in Gloucestershire was abandoned by his master when the latter became insolvent, and so he was

left without any master. He then wrote to his uncle who was a shoemaker in London, and his uncle wrote to him to come to him. On going to his house, his uncle said: 'If you will be a good boy I will be friend to you and you may stay here'. He staid with his uncle upwards of a twelvemonth, working as a

---

[118] On kinship behaviour, see in particular M. Anderson, *Family Structure*; and his 'Household structure and the Industrial Revolution; mid nineteenth-century Preston in comparative perspective', in P. Laslett & R. Wall (eds.), *Household and Family in Past Time* (Cambridge, 1972).

[119] Berks C.R.O., D/P. 71/13/6. For brothers completing services for each other, see e.g., Berks C.R.O., D/P. 20/13.27.

shoemaker, during which time his uncle found him board, lodging, and clothes, and gave him money whenever he asked for it and sometimes when he did not.[120]

But beyond many such cases involving brothers, sisters, and uncles, there is little evidence of other kin contributing in this way. Grand-parents would sometimes be looked after, or female cousins might occasionally rent premises together for business. But kin did not feature prominently, and the nuclear family was usually isolated and insular, buttressed only by charity and the poor law.

However, attempts were made to change this, particularly after 1834. The matter is worth outlining, as policy changes were enforced to make kin more accountable, which had an immediately de-trimental effect on the quality of family relationships, and contributed to create 'moral' attitudes concerning the care of family members which today are widely held. It is useful to understand how these originated; and, as so often, parallels with more recent government policies can be striking. The re-appraisal gained ground during the debate on pauperism after 1815. As we might expect, Arthur Young had been among early exponents of a policy aimed at increasing the financial responsibility of kin, to reduce poor rates and the scope of the old poor law. He wanted to

revive a spirit of humanity in poor families, for aged and helpless relations, which is so strikingly manifest in Ireland, where there is not the vestige of a poor rate . . . a spirit of care and foresight would be kindled among the poor, industry would flourish in consequence, and the only visible change in the economy of the poor families, would probably be a less liberal consumption of tea, sugar and spirits.[121]

Predictably, too, Harriet Martineau complained (in 1838) of old people becoming chargeable because children 'refused' to support them. She ignored the long tradition of support for such people under the old poor law (partly because of the widespread settlement of children in other parishes), or the fact that wages were by then commonly too low for children to support adequately their own families, let alone their elderly parents.[122] Nor were such points troublesome to Chadwick or Senior, as they strode on their way to grand anthropological comparison:

---

[120] I. Gray (ed.), *Cheltenham Settlement Examinations, 1815–1826* (Bristol and Glos. Arch. Soc., 1968), no. 77, p. 11.

[121] A Young, *Political Arithmetic* (1774), p. 20.

[122] H. Martineau, *Poor Laws and Paupers Illustrated* (1833), p. 17. Or see Rev. C. D. Brereton, *Inquiry into the Workhouse System and the Laws of Maintenance in Agricultural Districts* (Norwich, 1822), p. 102.

The duty of supporting parents and children, in old age or infirmity, is so strongly enforced by our natural feelings that it is often well performed even among savages, and almost always so in a nation deserving the name of civilized. We believe that England is the only European country in which it is neglected . . .

Those whose minds have been moulded by the operation of the Poor Laws appear not to have the slightest scruple in asking to be paid for the performance of those domestic duties which the most brutal savages are in general willing to render gratuitously to their own kindred.[123]

Parish officers, still paying neighbours weekly sums to look after elderly people, would snatch any opportunity to reduce their expenditure. The enforcement of such a moral imperative – one now discovered to be an archetypical ethic – was an obvious tactic to justify this abdication of responsibility. But to the labouring classes, it was another indirect expedient to lower effective familial income. For employment and wages had (by the early nineteenth century) become controlled by parish poor law officials; and a sudden reluctance of parishes to pay for elderly people was experienced as equivalent to a large reduction of parish payment in lieu of wages, or relief per head, to those families who were made to care for them. And 'contributions' from relatives were of course obtainable by legal means, enforced at the sessions.

This insistence on greater aid from relatives began before 1834, but the New Poor Law marked the sharpest change in policy. There was further intensification during and after the 1870s, although this was partly a return to the measures enforced during the late 1830s and 1840s, after a relaxation in the mid-nineteenth century.[124] It became customary after 1834 to place orders on sons or daughters, making them remit part of the cost of relief to the elderly – 1s. to 2s. a week. This was enforced at petty sessions. George Edwards in the late nineteenth century described a situation which had rarely occurred a century before, when he spoke of how he looked after his mother

for six years out of my 15s. a week, without receiving a penny from anyone, the Board of Guardians refusing to allow her anything in the nature of poor relief. My wife's mother also lived with us for sixteen years, and died at our

---

[123] Checkland, *Poor Law Report*, pp. 115, 178.

[124] See in particular D. Thomson, 'Provision for the elderly in England, 1830–1908' (unpub. Ph.D. thesis, Univ. of Cambridge, 1980); S. & B. Webb, *English Poor Law History* (1929), pt II, p. 351. Also see M. E. Rose, 'The allowance system under the New Poor Law', *Econ. Hist. Rev.*, XIX (1966); S.C. on the Poor Law Amendment Act XVIII, pt II (1837–8), p. 430; C. Booth, 'Poor law statistics as used in connection with the Old Age Question', *Economic Jnl*, IX (1899); P. Horn, *Labouring Life in the Victorian Countryside* (Bristol, 1976), pp. 204–18.

house, and for twenty-two years of my married life I maintained these two old people.

His own evidence to the 1895 Royal Commission on the Aged Poor stressed how many labourers were forced to contribute towards elderly parents, while unable to do so. And in his work on the Parish Council he tried to liberalise poor relief payments which today seem almost incredible in their meanness: weekly sums of between 6d. and 2s. 6d. being given as late as the 1890s, sometimes with very bad flour.[125]

The pressure on relatives to pay (and this extended beyond children, even, informally, to neighbours) placed a heavy strain on the family, and must frequently have raised ill-feeling between spouses and animosity against the elderly. It was reported that: 'Many sons contribute to support of aged parents only when forced by law'; that children might move away from the area 'to evade claim'; that 'Quarrels frequently arise between children as regards giving the help'; or that the 'aged prefer a pittance from the parish (regarded as their due) to compulsory maintenance by children; compulsion makes such aid very bitter'.[126] And these were also circumstances in which parents were constrained to think of their children as insurance for old age, as Rowntree pointed out.[127] The threat of the workhouse, the 'pittances' granted as out-door relief, the dismissal of those too old to be profitable to employers, rising life expectancy, and the factors which perpetuated agricultural labourers in the same settlement place as their parents, were all conducive to this. The old saying 'No child, no wife' gained a harder compulsion with the policy changes of 1834; ironically made all the more bitter for women by the moral enactments against illegitimacy of the same act. Robert Spurr must have been representative of many when he wrote of how the death of his son 'filled all our harts [sic] with sorrow . . . a strong boy, a Child of hope. We was looking to him to ade us in old age.'[128]

---

[125] G. Edwards, *From Crow-Scaring to Westminster* (1922), pp. 23, 43, 69–80.
[126] C. Booth, *The Aged Poor in England and Wales* (1894), p. 226. See also R.C. on the Aged Poor, XV (1895), pp. 586, 779–83, 843, on the forcing of assistance for the elderly from children, the opposition to this, and the way in which it was held to embitter family life when children were hardly able to support their own families.
[127] B. S. Rowntree & M. Kendal, *How the Labourer Lives: A Study of the Rural Labour Problem* (1913), p. 330.
[128] R. Spurr, 'The autobiography of Robert Spurr', in R. J. Owen (ed.), *Baptist Quarterly*, XXVI (1976), 286. The R.C. on the Aged Poor, XV (1895), pp. 785–6, was told that parents were insuring their children in case they died, because of the need for support. And as Anderson argued, the contrast of the old and new poor laws,

XI

These poor law measures adversely affected the quality of family life, alongside the overcrowding of cottages (produced by the decline of service, 'open' and 'close' parish divides, lack of housing, and high birth rates), the 'problem' of female children, or the fall of real familial income (accentuated by the rising dependency ratio) until a more favourable trend in real wages set in after about 1850.[129] They also further isolated the family from outside agencies; as did the decline of service and apprenticeship, rising male ages of leaving home, or the continuity of generational settlement. Paradoxically, such isolation occurred when mean household size was growing (partly with greater in-kin residency),[130] when the earlier prevalence of the nuclear family household was if anything declining, and when impediments were being placed on previously widespread local mobility within the agricultural sector. The paradox of course is a residual symptom of

and the removal of earlier parish supports after 1834, would have contributed to enhance short-term calculative use of kin. *Family Structure*, pp. 177–9. One structural change which possibly underlay these new policies was the lowered age structure, about which Wrigley and Schofield wrote: 'the relative burden of the care for the elderly ... was substantially greater in the seventeenth than in the nineteenth century' (*Population History of England*, pp. 449–50). Perhaps this helps explain why the needs of the elderly were so obviously set aside in the early nineteenth century and particularly after 1834, compared to the earlier more favourable treatment of them, although it does little to exonerate the change of policy.

[129] On the shortage of cottage accommodation and consequent overcrowding, see S.C. on Agricultural Labourers' Wages, VI (1824), p. 47; T.A., *A Plan for Relieving the Pressure of the Poor Rates and Affording Employment to the Agricultural Poor and Improving their Condition* (1832), p. 54; J. Scott, *Observations on the Present State of the Parochial and Vagrant Poor* (1773), p. 119. One response to overcrowded cottages was to have the children sleep elsewhere. For example, William Hunter 'hired also at Michaelmas 1818 another house ... in Brandon at the Rent of £5 and 5 shillings. He furnished this house, his three children slept in it, and he put things off hand in it, the other house not being large enough for his family he wanted them both.' His eldest child at the time would have been under fourteen years old (West Suffolk C.R.O., EL 25/7/18.1–18.146). Of course, most were not able to afford this. Children might also sleep at the houses of neighbours or relatives – for example, see R. Heath, *The English Peasant* (1893, Wakefield, 1978 edn), p. 126.

[130] 'When a young man does marry, he and his wife not uncommonly live for a length of time with his parents, occupying a part of the cottage' – see R. Jefferies, *Hodge and his Masters* (1880), vol. 2, p. 147. This would have been uncommon earlier. See also R. Wall, 'Mean household size in England from printed sources', in P. Laslett & R. Wall (eds.), *Household and Family in Past Time* (Cambridge, 1972), p. 191; Anderson, 'Household structure'; and his *Family Structure*, pp. 44, 82–4; P. Laslett, 'Mean household size in England since the sixteenth century', in Laslett & Wall, *Household and Family*.

sociological theories once applied to the 'development' of the family, particularly before 1965.[131]

Some issues discussed here invite moral judgement, and could be absorbed unproblematically into an assessment of the standard of living – the family poverty-cycle, for example, or effects on the family of the decline of service. But other aspects will remain outside such discussion until much greater historical awareness exists on generational attitudes towards them amongst the poor. Judgements on some familial changes depend so often merely on historians' own familial values. For example, the implications for the quality of life of family break-up (if it became more prevalent) should depend on an assessment of the attitudes and control the poor themselves had over this – rather than a historian's view on the sanctity or dispensability of married life. More broadly, the question of living standards usually has been tacitly defined as covering areas of current moral concern, which permits easy value judgement. Its confines simply ended where moral insensibility began. Perhaps in retrospect it will seem historically insensitive to have defined a subject for discussion only to the extent that it invited value judgement. Undeniably, there is a place for projecting historically our current concerns with real wages, health, diet, housing, and the like. But one hopes that the tension between such an approach and the purist effort to enter empathetically into attitudes of people long dead will continue, for they properly complement each other. Most evidently, the latter method can illuminate blinkered perspectives of the present, and draw attention to qualitative aspects of past social life we have unwittingly lost. In that regard, there is still a long way to go for the family history of the poor.

Alongside the unfortunate results of social policies to increase kin responsibility – and particularly as the family's economic and domestic divisions of labour hardened – there were qualitative changes of dubious benefit. Today we have virtually lost sight of these, although they are worth considering when we stage ourselves against our past. First, there is evidence throughout this period of a widely various

---

[131] I refer to P. Laslett, *The World We Have Lost* (1965), or see his *Family Life and Illicit Love*, ch. 1, and his introduction to Laslett & Wall, *Household and Family*. See also and compare S. M. Greenfield, 'Industrialization and the family in sociological theory', *American Jnl of Sociology*, LXVII (1961); T. K. Hareven, 'Modernization and family history: perspectives on social change', *Signs*, II (1976); N. Smelser, 'The modernization of social relations', in M. Weiner (ed.), *Modernization. The Dynamics of Growth* (New York, 1966); T. Parsons, 'The social structure of the family', in R. N. Anshen (ed.), *The Family: Its Functions and Destiny* (New York, 1959); and particularly M. J. Levy, Jr, *Modernization and the Structure of Societies* (Princeton, N.J., 1966).

quality of marital relations, and the historiographical trend towards self-assured and simplistic statement on this is one usefully avoided.[132] Experience of family affection ranged from some cases of wife beating: 'I have been compelled to leave him this time owing to his ill treatment. I will never live with him any more';[133] to a great many declarations of affection, which make generalisations about working men brutally treating their wives seem as irrelevant as Victorian paranoia over working-class sexuality. One husband refused, for example, to allow his wife to go alone into the workhouse, and so he went in too. As she said: 'Where I was he would be.'[134] Letters from agricultural emigrants to their relatives were phrased in the most affectionate of terms. And readers of working-class autobiographies, such as those by Varley, Kitchen, Edwards, Somerville, Arch, or of George Sturt's accounts of Bettesworth, will not require further demonstration of the affectionate and close ties of many rural marriages.

Nevertheless, when some historians congratulate the nineteenth century on its supposedly novel 'companionate marriage', or on being a high point of 'romantic love', 'affective individualism', or whatever other quintessential concept they may wish to explore, they might listen to this woman (around 1900) on her loneliness in marriage:

D'you know, sir, as they always used to say in the village as how I was the happiest girl about, afore I got married. I knows I used to be in the fields all day a-picking flowers and a-listening to the birds singing and watching the lambs jumping. They all used to call me 'Merry Kate'. But Bill – well, 'e's my 'usband and the bes' man I knows – but 'e jus' didn't understand, and so 'e laughed me out on it all. An' then came this time as 'e got into trouble and thought as I didn't know. Of course I knowed, which only made it worse, for w'en 'e came back that there drunk with despair I 'ad to preten' to be angry, and all the time I was sorry. Well, all the natural life was kind o' gone out o' me, and if I hadn't had God and His pries' to talk to, I think I'd 'a died.[135]

'Country-women . . . have not even a human being to whom they can

---

[132] I refer in particular to E. Shorter, *The Making of the Modern Family* (1976). See also Stone, *Family, Sex and Marriage*. [133] Camb C.R.O., G/C/As. 8.

[134] Camb C.R.O., G/C/As. 8. Or see *Morning Chronicle*, 22 Jan. 1850: They won't give us anything except we goes into the house, and as long as I can arne a sixpence anyhows, they sharn't part me from my wife.'

[135] Holdenby, *Folk of the Furrow*, p. 154. And see his discussion of how agricultural labourers talk of their wives, pp. 133–4, 141, 149–52. 'Harris was mystified at the relationship which he saw existing between men and women around him . . . "They talks of their womenfolk just as they would of a glass o' beer, or rather they reckons them a bit lower . . . these chaps looks on their women just as animals, by the way they talks".'

lay open their hearts', added Holdenby to this. Women had largely withdrawn from field work, and their occupation by 1850 had become more strictly that of 'housewife' – yet the men had a contempt for effeminacy, for the role which their wives had been forced to adopt. 'Among labourers there is such peril in effeminacy that to yield to it is a kind of treason. Bettesworth had nothing but contempt for it. I more than once heard his scorn of "tip-toeing".'[136] His own wife, of course, had been increasingly unusual in accompanying him as a migrant harvester. Similarly, leisure activities were becoming more sexually divisive, seemingly in step with changes in the sexual division of labour. The beerhouse, Flora Thompson tells us in a rather pathetic passage, was

exclusively a men's gathering. Their wives never accompanied them; though sometimes a woman who had got her family off hand, and so had a few halfpence to spend on herself, would knock at the back door with a bottle or jug and perhaps linger a little, herself, unseen, to listen to what was going on within.[137]

The male gathering inside would, apparently, 'discuss local events, wrangle over politics or farming methods, or sing a few songs "to oblige"'. And this mini-precursor of the modern T.U.C. agreed in one regard: wives were to blame for the failure of union:

To this day [1913] it is held as a firm belief in many parts of the country that 'Twas the women as put an end to our Union. They used to go at me and ask us why we wanted to keep ol' Joey Arch a gennelman. S'pose they wanted the money. So we stopped a-paying to get a bit o' peace'.[138]

The accusation was hardly a fair one, but was significant in showing a restrainedly contemptuous view of the wife's role – 'S'pose they wanted the money.'

Holdenby stressed how divisive the domestic division of labour had become:

Even in [the men's] ordinary attitude to family life they show an utter lack of being conscious of any companionship. The family is the woman's affair. When I inquired of one labourer about his family, which was a large one, he told me of Bill, Ned, Liza, and Jess. Then he got held up. 'But those aren't all, are they?' I asked with a smile. 'Lor', I can't tell 'e', he replied, scratching his

---

[136] G. Sturt, *Memoirs of a Surrey Labourer* (1907), p. 68.

[137] F. Thompson, *Lark Rise to Candleford* (Harmondsworth, 1976 edn), pp. 64–5. Compare for example the S.C. on the Poor Law Amendment Act, XVIII (1837–8), pt III, p. 228, where (rather earlier) the complaint was of men and wives going out drinking *together*. Comparison of changes in the sexual division of leisure activities would repay further research.

[138] Holdenby, *Folk of the Furrow*, p. 153.

head; 'I never can tell 'ow many there be or where they be – but Nance'll know'.[139]

Some male examinants under the New Poor Law had exactly the same difficulty. And (in contrast to the earlier period) men without their wives in the nineteenth century (widowers, family break-up cases, temporary absences, and so on) almost never had the children with them when examined. By 1900 we were a far remove from Alice Clark's description of the seventeenth century, when

> men were much more occupied with domestic affairs . . . than they are now. Men in all classes gave time and care to the education of their children, and the young unmarried men who generally occupied positions as apprentices and servants were partly employed over domestic work . . . a considerable proportion of which in former days fell to the share of men.[140]

By contrast, the advice given to late nineteenth-century agricultural emigrants was that they should try occasionally to help with the children en voyage, and not leave it all to the wife as they did at home.[141] Hannah, wrote M. K. Ashby,

[139] *Ibid.*, pp. 149–50. On the effects of the growing sexual division of labour and the decline of the family economy (by which term I mean the identity of home-place and place of work for man and wife), it is worth noting that modern studies have demonstrated clearly the correlation of highly segregated divisions of labour between husband and wife with marital break-up and sexual frustration. See in particular L. Rainwater, 'Some aspects of lower-class sexual behaviour', *Jnl of Social Issues*, XXII (1966), esp. 100–1, 106. His empirical findings indicate that: 'the lower value placed on sexual relations by lower class wives, and to a lesser extent by lower class husbands, can be seen as an extension of the high degree of segregation in their conjugal role relationship generally . . . Since the wife's interest in sex tends to be more heavily dependent upon a sense of interpersonal closeness and gratification in her total relationship with her husband, it is very difficult for her to find gratification in sex in the context of a highly segregated role relationship . . . Among those couples who have a lesser degree of conjugal role segregation there is a much greater probability of an emphasis on sexual relations as an extension of the socio-emotional closeness that is valued in husband–wife relationships.' See also Dominian, *Marital Breakdown*, pp. 81ff.

[140] A. Clark, *Working Life of Women in the Seventeenth Century* (1919), p. 5. Or, for a middling class, see Macfarlane's account of Josselin's close involvement in family and child affairs, such as weaning: *Family Life*, p. 88. For details of William Cobbett looking after his babies, and his deep interest in matters such as childbirth, midwives or breast-feeding (and his antagonism to wet-nursing), see his *Advice to Young Men* (Oxford, 1980 edn), pp. 162, 167ff, 175–6, 216ff, 221ff, 234–9, 243. He wrote of how such domestic work by men was 'much more duly performed by the poor than by the rich. The fashion of the labouring people is this: the husband, when free from his toil in the fields, takes his share in the nursing . . . This used to be the way of life amongst the labouring people.' His advice to young men was of course that they should be similarly interested: 'Much more necessary is it to inculcate these principles in the minds of young men in the middle rank of life.' It is doubtful whether the detailed advice which he gave on intimate domestic matters would have been given in similar manuals for young men later in the nineteenth century.   [141] Dunbabin, *Rural Discontent*, p. 170.

would never greatly develop her literary taste or any other intellectual quality, for it seemed her duty to be perpetually poised for swift service to husband, child, animal, neighbour and the chapel. Her delicate senses and vivid emotions were under the severest control – no job too hard or dirty once its necessity was seen; the most innocent tastes permitted no indulgence ["'e laughed me out on it all']; no strong feeling was allowed to break through her resignation to heaven, husband, and fate. And so, naturally, she passes into the background of her husband's and her children's lives, not often to emerge.

Mothers 'might be all to their children in the uncorrupted years before the patterns of the time affected them: but from that point mothers were the source of comparatively little in their children's minds'.[142] Above all, the contrast of these late nineteenth-century 'patterns of the time' with an earlier period, when women working alongside men in a family economy context would even: 'often enter the beer shops, call for their pints and smoke their pipes like men', was a sharp and disappointing one. Disappointing in the early 1980s, that is, although perhaps the effects of unemployment and the micro-revolution on female work and marriage already re-produces a society which thinks differently, one which may agree with Ivy Pinchbeck (in 1930) that 'the attitude revealed [in an earlier period when the wife contributed "her share towards the weekly expenses"] is somewhat astonishing to the modern mind, but as yet, there was a complete lack of appreciation of the value of women's work in the home and in rearing and caring for children'. It remains to be seen whether the movements of the 1960s and 1970s were an unrepresentative aberration of 'the modern mind', the temporary diversion of a more long-term pattern of change.

[142] Ashby, *Joseph Ashby*, pp. 98, 108–9.

8

Thomas Hardy, rural Dorset, and the family

I

This chapter aims to contribute an historical and social interpretation of Hardy's novels in the light of changes outlined earlier, setting his work against its social and economic context in Dorset. I will outline the conditions faced by the Dorsetshire labourer, and the nature of rural class relations, relating these issues closely to the novels – to assess and largely reject the accounts which stress Hardy's originality as lying in his 'realism' and social verisimilitude, and to suggest what historical changes in nineteenth-century Dorset underlay his major preoccupations. The matter is important not only because Hardy's writing encompassed so many of the features of rural life discussed in this book. For it aids first an understanding of questions raised earlier on the reliability and interpretation of literary evidence, whether by social and economic historians or literary critics. The cross-verification of quantitative and empirical evidence with literary statement has been a method of earlier chapters, which aimed to escape the dangers of reliance only on one type of evidence. Social historians traditionally have been dependent on various forms of literary evidence, but have made virtually no attempts to set the bounds to what a writer may know and be able to express of his society and its social structure: to understand in what areas his knowledge is likely to be limited, occluded, or distorted, and for what reasons. Nor is it always appreciated that some literary texts cannot be forced to yield information or 'evidence' that they do not intend, and are unable of themselves to give. In practice, nothing approaching a literary sociology or precautionary schema exists, and the potential links of social history to the divided but usually ahistorical discipline of

I am grateful to John Barrell, James Hazen, and Adrian Poole for their comments.

literary criticism are still largely undrawn. Historical methods dependent only upon literary sources have frequently lacked caution, independent confirmation from other sources, and a defined or properly limited social focus. And secondly, social historians have often not been concerned either to realise the specific 'questions' to which a literary work was both addressed and an attempted solution – the senses in which the work formed a dialogue with its own history – or to understand those shifts or moments in social history which suggest new potential and meanings in a text, new interpretations of an author in later situations, and the contextual links from present to past which underlie interpretation. One way forward can be with case studies of individual authors, making allowance for the different genres in which they wrote. I want here to draw attention to such problems in Hardy's work, and to outline how the major novelist of English rural society depicted and interpreted the needs and priorities of the poor, and the main themes and social changes outlined earlier.

First, let me briefly sketch the local social and economic context. Dorset by the mid-nineteenth century had achieved an unenviable position which it retained throughout Hardy's life, as having the lowest agricultural wages of any county in England. Only Norfolk in the later nineteenth century, parts of Suffolk, and south Wiltshire could rival it in this regard. In 1850 its average agricultural weekly wage was 7s. 6d., and in some areas it was as low as 6s. – much the same sum as had been paid in the mid-eighteenth century, and one which was about 2s. 6d. below the cost of keeping a man in the calculatedly 'less eligible' New Poor Law workhouses. Table 8.1 gives the trends in Dorset and 'national' weekly real wages (for the years when there is data), indexed from 1767–70.[1] It is clear that Dorset real wages fell very markedly in the fifty years after 1770, and, astonishingly, it was as late as 1880 before they rose back to their 1767–70 level or higher. Weekly wage data for this county does not currently exist between 1795 and 1824, but other series for farm-servant wages suggest that male wages failed badly to keep up with prices during that period.[2] Without pursuing other supportive and broader indicators of living standards, it can certainly be said that the standard of

---

[1] Weekly wages are from A. L. Bowley, 'The statistics of wages in the United Kingdom during the last hundred years', pts I and IV, 'Agricultural wages', *Jnl Roy. Stat. Soc.*, LXI (1898), LXII (1899). The Phelps-Brown & Hopkins price index for a composite unit of consumables has been used, taking a three year mean of prices centred on the year or years for which wage data is available, to help avoid erratic fluctuations of real wages for these isolated years.

[2] See chapter 1, Figure 1.12.

Table 8.1. *Dorset & national weekly agricultural real wages*
(1767–70 = 100)

	Dorset	National
1767–70	100	100
1795	82	86
1824	62	81
1833	83	103
1837	72	92
1850	84	100
1860	87	95
1861	81	93
1867–9	78	101
1869–70	84	103
1872	83	112
1880	99	118
1892	115	145

Sources: Bowley, 'Statistics of wages', pt I, 'Agricultural wages' (1898). Prices: Phelps-Brown & Hopkins price of composite unit of consumables. 3 year average centred on the year or years in question.

living of the Dorsetshire labourer fell significantly after about 1770. It is also clear from Table 8.1 that Dorset real wages fell relative to the 'national' trend. Their rise after about 1872 was mainly due to large-scale out-migration and agricultural trade unionism, and occurred despite the late nineteenth-century depression. The fact that during the depression farmers were still able to increase money wages points to considerable exploitation of wage labour earlier. Hardy himself commented on this:

The reflection is forced upon everyone who thinks of the matter, that if a farmer can afford to pay thirty per cent more wages in times of agricultural depression than he paid in times of agricultural prosperity, and yet live, and keep a carriage, while the landlord still thrives on the reduced rent which has resulted, the labourer must have been greatly wronged in those prosperous times.[3]

Dorset labourers remained very badly paid compared to those of other counties, undernourished and usually poorly housed – but conditions at least in real wage terms, for those in employment, improved from 1872 onward.

[3] T. Hardy, 'The Dorsetshire labourer', *Longman's Magazine* (July 1883), reprinted in J. Moynahan (ed.), *The Portable Thomas Hardy* (1977), p. 731. This article was Hardy's socio-economic account of conditions in Dorset, and makes explicit many of the assumptions found in the novels.

Dorset had long been noted for sheep and corn farming (sheep being folded on land soon to be put to corn), and for dairying. Arable farming in 1850 still generally proved more profitable than pastoral, although there were agricultural variations within the county, and sheep were particularly significant in chalkland areas. However, falling grain prices after 1870 intensified a shift to livestock and dairy production. (In the 1870s alone, the proportion of wheat supplies home grown in the United Kingdom fell from 61 per cent to 27 per cent.)[4] This transition in Dorset became marked after 1879, and was permitted by the development of railway systems (from 1857 for Dorset), and the growing urban demand for dairy produce, consequent upon rising urban living standards.[5] Specialisation in dairy produce was associated with a declining demand for labour (dairy farming being less labour intensive than grain), and so accentuated the rural unemployment which lay behind out-migration. But for those actually in employment it must have brought more seasonally regular work than was available in more heavily grain-producing counties. Pastoral farming, as we have seen, had a more constant labour requirement during the year than arable. The rising money wages after 1870, then, probably conceal an aggravation of total unemployment, which was a feature of the relatively low demand of pastoral farming for labour.

Another feature of that specialisation was some resurgence of low paid female labour in dairying. In eastern areas, opportunities for female labour had been diminishing from as early as the mid-eighteenth century.[6] But in Dorset in the nineteenth century, as grain

[4] G. McCrone, *The Economics of Subsidising Agriculture. A Study of British Policy* (1962), p. 34.

[5] On these agricultural changes affecting Dorset, see: D. B. Grigg, 'An index of regional change in English farming', *Trans. Inst. Brit. Geographers*, XXXVI (1965), 64–5; J. D. Chambers & G. E. Mingay, *The Agricultural Revolution, 1750–1880* (1966, 1978 edn), p. 182; T. W. Fletcher, 'The Great Depression of English agriculture, 1873–1896', *Econ. Hist. Rev.*, XIII (1960); E. L. Jones, *The Development of English Agriculture, 1815–1873* (1968), pp. 19–20; E. H. Whetham, 'Livestock prices in Britain, 1851–1893', *Agric. Hist. Rev.*, XI (1963), 27–35; G. E. Fussell, *The English Dairy Farmer* (1966); L. E. Taverne, 'Whither sheep? A review of the decline in sheep farming in Dorset', *Somerset and Dorset Notes and Queries*, XXVI (1953); Lord Ernle, *English Farming Past and Present* (1912); C. S. Orwin & E. H. Whetham, *History of British Agriculture, 1846–1914* (1964); J. T. Coppock, 'The changing face of England: 1850–c. 1900', in H. C. Darby (ed.), *A New Historical Geography of England after 1600* (Cambridge, 1973); J. Darby, 'The farming in Dorset', *Jnl of the Bath and West of England Society*, 3rd ser., IV (1872); and on the earlier period see W. E. Minchington, 'Agriculture in Dorset during the Napoleonic Wars', *Proc. Dorset Nat. Hist. and Arch. Society*, LXXVII (1955); L. H. Ruegg, 'The farming of Dorsetshire', *Jnl Royal Agric. Society*, XV (1854); W. Stevenson, *General View of the Agriculture of the County of Dorset* (1812).

[6] See chapter 1.

prices fell while livestock and dairy prices rose, such a reduction of female work came later. Growing pastoral specialisation accentuated a division of labour in which women may traditionally have been more associated with dairying, and so permitted a longer continuation of women in the labour force than occurred in the south-east. Nevertheless, even in Dorset, it would have been very unusual, if not unheard of, to find women attending threshing machinery in the late 1870s or 1880s (as in *Tess*), and their work in the fields had been declining long before then – partly in favour of dairy work, but more significantly in favour of a role as housewife, domestic servant, or of migration from the land altogether. I shall return to aspects of the sexual division of labour in connection with Hardy.

Dairy specialisation did not allow Dorset entirely to escape depression, and its agriculture suffered from the mid 1870s, with falling arable prices producing bankruptcy, particularly among small farmers. Indeed, this class declined numerically throughout the nineteenth century, particularly in Dorset. The county came to have an average farm size which was 50 per cent larger than Devon, or Britain as a whole, by the 1880s,[7] and the point that this small-farmer class had characteristically relied upon the family as its unit of production will be developed later. The severity of the agricultural depression in Dorset, as in pasture districts generally, is still debated, and it seems probable that the adverse effects of cereal imports and falling prices were felt most in arable areas in the south-east of England. Rising urban living standards and demand for pastoral products which were less easily imported, and the move in Dorset to a form of mixed farming with greater pastoral emphasis, helped to offset the depression. But while Dorset may have partially escaped in this way, there was no cause for optimism there, and its gross farm output fell after the 1870s.[8] The county moved from a general use of three-life leases to one-year leases, which had become almost universal by the later nineteenth century; given the precarious state of farming, tenant farmers refused to bind themselves to anything longer. Commenting on this, and the county's economy, the 1895 Royal Commission on Agriculture reported that: 'with every desire to avoid pessimism, it is impossible to view the situation in Dorset as a whole without gloomy forebodings of the immediate future of agriculture'.[9]

The growing unemployment which accompanied the depression,

[7] R.C. on Agriculture, XV (1882), pp. 28ff.
[8] Information supplied by F. M. L. Thompson, unpublished seminar paper, delivered 5 Nov. 1981.   [9] R.C. on Agriculture, XVII (1895), p. 274.

and relatively low wages, produced widespread depopulation. Hardy showed himself to be aware of the latter in his article on 'The Dorsetshire Labourer', or in his letter on Dorset to Rider Haggard,[10] and expressed his concern at its 'curious and unexpected' consequences – for example, the 'sinking . . . into eternal oblivion of village traditions and folk-lore'. In 1871 there were 18,000 agricultural labourers in Dorset; in 1881, 15,700, and in 1891, 12,500 – a decrease of over 30 per cent in only twenty years. The whole county's population also fell in this period, and the Royal Commission on Agriculture commented on how: 'Some of the rural parishes show a startling decrease.'[11] And within the agricultural sector itself, Hardy claimed that labour turnover became more rapid, suggesting that movement after each year became more common for yearly hired labour.

We have seen how this yearly hiring system had provided an institutional nexus for mobility via the statute fairs, and how it declined after 1750 in the south and east.[12] In Dorset it survived slightly longer because of greater emphasis on pastoral farming, and this was more generally the case in the west and north of England and Wales. Service of course had been associated with extensive mobility. In early or mid-eighteenth-century Dorset, there had been considerable annual turnover at the time of the hiring fair at Candlemas, producing a situation similar to that documented for Clayworth and Cogenhoe.[13] In this respect, Hardy's account in the 1874 Preface to *Far From the Madding Crowd*, which was persistently affirmed in his novels, of an historically immobile population, 'attached to the soil of one particular spot by generation after generation', allowing continuity of local history, 'the preservation of legend, folk-lore, close inter-social relations, and eccentric individualities', was largely his own imaginary one. The historical alienation from a 'primal', local sense of place which Hardy depicted as occurring in his own lifetime, supposedly affecting 'the old fashioned stationary sort' of rural labourer, was, as John Barrell has suggested, based on a nostalgic fiction of the past: on the notion of an original unity and its subsequent break-up.[14] Certainly there was growing emigration and

[10] This letter can be found in R. Haggard, *Rural England* (1902), pp. 282–5.

[11] R.C. on Agriculture, XVII (1895), pp. 259–60.   [12] See chapter 2.

[13] P. Laslett, 'Clayworth and Cogenhoe', in his *Family Life and Illicit Love in Earlier Generations* (Cambridge, 1977).

[14] See John Barrell's very perceptive and interesting analysis of subjective senses of geography in *Tess* and the *Return of the Native*, in his 'Geographies of Hardy's Wessex', *Jnl of Historical Geography*, VIII (1982). The same view of an immobile past with intense local and social attachments can also be found among the gentry and middle classes in Dorset. See for example the evidence of Rev. Huxtable to the S.C. on Settlement and Poor Removal, XI (1847), pp. 554ff.

out-migration to the towns in the late nineteenth century, and it was late in this region compared to other areas of England and Wales, where it generally gathered momentum from mid-century.[15] But for the period between about 1780 and the 1870s, it is questionable whether interparochial agricultural mobility in Dorset was as extensive as during an earlier period, like the early eighteenth century, when service had been more common.

Hardy's explanation of rural out-migration was suspiciously narrow. He was essentially correct when he wrote to Rider Haggard that 'migrations to cities [from Dorset] did not largely take place till within the last forty years or so ... the labourers have become more and more migratory, the younger families in especial'.[16] But he stressed as causes broadened education, insecurity of tenure, the influence of the agricultural unionist leader Joseph Arch after 1872, and the removal of stabilising classes of artisans and small freeholders ('the backbone of village life') – curiously omitting to mention in this connection the generally acknowledged fundamental and more pessimistic causes of extreme poverty, unemployment, and low wages.[17] One should include another cause (which contemporaries noted particularly in Dorset), and which Hardy again drew virtually no attention to. Cottage building was far behind by the 1830s, and remained so until very late in the nineteenth century. In many parishes cottages remained the squalid mud huts they had been in 1843, when it was reported to a parliamentary commission that: 'In nine villages out of ten the cottage is still nothing but a slightly improved hovel.' One labourer spoke of his bedroom to Rowntree in the early 1900s: 'You fit into it as you will one day into your coffin.'[18] And Lord Shaftesbury, the factory reformer, complained of his property in Wimborne St Giles as follows:

Inspected a few cottages ... filthy, close, indecent, unwholesome ... Shocking state of cottages; stuffed like figs in a drum. Were not the people as cleanly as they can be, we should have an epidemic ... I have passed my life in rating others for allowing rotten houses and immoral, unhealthy dwellings; and now I come into an estate rife with abominations! Why, there

---

[15] See P. J. Perry, 'Working class isolation and mobility in rural Dorset, 1837–1936', *Inst. of Brit. Geographers*, XLVI (1969); A. K. Cairncross, 'Internal migration in Victorian England', *Manchester School*, XVII (1949), also in his *Home and Foreign Investment, 1870–1913* (Cambridge, 1953).

[16] Haggard, *Rural England*, p. 283. Or see Hardy, 'The Dorsetshire labourer'.

[17] J. Saville, *Rural Depopulation in England and Wales, 1851–1951* (1957).

[18] B. S. Rowntree & M. Kendal, *How the Labourer Lives: A Study of the Rural Labour Problem* (1913), pp. 330ff. Or see the descriptions of Wiltshire cottages in 1909 by R. Jefferies, *The Hills and the Vale* (1909, Oxford, 1980 edn), p. 148: 'mere sheds, in fact'.

are things here to make one's flesh creep; and I have not a farthing to set them right.[19]

The agents of various factory owners, berated by Shaftesbury, were delighted to ratify this account when they quietly arrived to inspect his estate. And to Shaftesbury's further embarrassment, Edward Stanhope agreed with this verdict when reporting to a Select Committee in 1868, and noted that 'the cottages of this county are more ruinous and contain worse accommodation than those of any county I have visited except Shropshire'.[20]

The causes of this, according to Shaftesbury, lay with the non-migratory small-holders – the class which Hardy saw fit to label 'the backbone of village life'. As Shaftesbury continued:

What a domicile for men and Christians I found in that village (Hinton Martell). Yet, what can I do? and the management of the estate, too, has in great measure passed from me by the grants of these small lifeholds . . . what griping, grasping, avaricious cruelty. These petty proprietors exact a five-fold rent for a thing in five-fold inferior position. It is always so with these small holders. Everything – even the misery of their fellows – must be turned to profit.[21]

Or as another Select Committee reported in 1869 with respect to Lord Rivers' estate: 'having long been held by life tenants [it] is notorious for its bad cottages'.[22]

II

The hostile character of class relations in rural Dorset emerging here can be documented more strongly. 'However much you worked and scrambled, the farmers just wiped their boots on you', recalled one elderly labourer.[23] Even Hardy wrote that it had been

common enough on inferior farms to hear a farmer, as he sat on horse-back amid a field of workers, address them with a contemptuousness which could not have been greatly exceeded in the days when the thralls of Cedric wore their collars of brass. Usually no answer was returned to these tirades; they were received as an accident of the land on which the listeners had happened to be born, calling for no more resentment than the blows of the wind and rain.[24]

But he implied reassuringly that this attitude to labour was long since passed, and one should question this, as well as the Hodge-like animal indifference of response which Hardy ascribed to the labourer.

[19] Cited in J. L. & B. Hammond, *Lord Shaftesbury* (1923, Harmondsworth, 1939 edn), p. 162.   [20] *Ibid.*, p. 172.   [21] *Ibid.*, p. 162.
[22] Cited in B. Kerr, *Bound to the Soil: A Social History of Dorset, 1750–1918* (1968), p. 222.
[23] Cited in Kerr, *Bound to the Soil*, p. 111.
[24] Hardy, 'The Dorsetshire labourer', in Moynahan, *The Portable Thomas Hardy*, p. 729.

For influential arguments have been made that Hardy's originality lay in his social and economic verisimilitude – suggesting that he is a dependable witness to the social history of Dorset. To Merryn Williams for example he was 'the first writer to achieve the necessary range and realism of the novel of English country life'.[25] And Raymond Williams has written strongly in support of this view. According to him, 'the fiction is not only about Wessex peasants, it is by one of them'.[26] Similarly, Norman Page has argued that Hardy 'demonstrates a strikingly well-informed acquaintance with the circumstances of [agricultural labourers'] lives' in *Tess* and 'The Dorsetshire labourer', indicating his 'intimate knowledge of the life and customs of the rural labourer, and his understanding of the forces that were making for change'.[27] And Carl Weber believed that Hardy 'surveyed the entire nineteenth century with a view to making his historical study as accurate as were his topographical observations'.[28] To W. J. Hyde, 'Hardy's accuracy in depicting the rural labourer must be credited to his proximity to and intimacy with peasant life, as well as to a power of keen observation';[29] and G. M. Young in his *Victorian England* described Hardy as an 'observer of unquestioned competence'.[30] Other authors have made similar arguments in designating to Hardy a particular and accurate understanding of the social history of the period. In *The Great Web*, Ian Gregor suggested that 'Hardy introduces in a sustained and explicit way the agricultural and economic crisis that has overtaken Wessex, and turned families like the Durbeyfields, into migratory 'labour'.'[31] Or Arnold Kettle opened his discussion of *Tess* in the following way:

The subject . . . is stated clearly by Hardy to be the fate of a 'pure woman'; in fact it is the destruction of the English peasantry . . . It is a novel with a thesis . . . that in the latter half of the last century the disintegration of the peasantry – a process which had its roots deep in the past – had reached its final and tragic stage.[32]

---

[25] M. Williams, *Thomas Hardy and Rural England* (1972), p. 193. And see her *A Preface to Hardy* (1976), e.g., pp. 61ff.

[26] R. Williams, *The Country and the City* (St Albans, 1975), p. 199, or his *The English Novel. From Dickens to Lawrence* (St Albans, 1974), p. 100.

[27] N. Page, *Thomas Hardy* (1977), pp. 62–3, 136ff.

[28] C. J. Weber, 'Chronology in Hardy's novels', *Publications of the Modern Languages Association*, LIII (1938), 320.

[29] W. J. Hyde, 'Hardy's view of realism: a key to the rustic characters', *Victorian Studies*, II (1958), 50.

[30] G. M. Young, *Victorian England. Portrait of an Age* (1936, 1960 edn), p. 166.

[31] I. C. S. Gregor, *The Great Web; the Form of Hardy's Major Fiction* (1974), p. 192.

[32] A. Kettle, *An Introduction to the English Novel* (1953), vol. 2, p. 49. And see also A. Fleishman, *The English Historical Novel* (Baltimore, 1971), p. 190.

Another version of this approach can be found in Sherman's *The Pessimism of Thomas Hardy*:

The main reason for the pessimism of the Wessex novels is the farmworkers' loss of their freeholds that they had enjoyed as yeomen, and their plight of not having any voice in Parliament ... In *Tess* and *Jude*, Hardy most fully depicts the effect of the Industrial Revolution in Wessex and London, and both bear out the historical change.[33]

And the argument for Hardy's verisimilitude was also made by some contemporaries. Charles Kegan Paul, for example, argued for Hardy's realism on the question of social conditions, and preferred Hardy's presentation of the 'rustic' to that provided by George Eliot: 'Only a few [writers] have attained to know the labourer as he is, and fewer still have written, or can write about him with truth and insight, yet without false condescension.'[34] Hardy himself made similar claims for the accuracy of his representation of rural life, in the General Preface to the Wessex edition of 1912:

At the dates represented in the various narratives things were like that in Wessex: the inhabitants lived in certain ways, engaged in certain occupations, kept alive certain customs, just as they are shown doing in these pages. And in particularizing such I have often been reminded of Boswell's remarks on the trouble to which he was put and the pilgrimages he was obliged to make to authenticate some detail, though the labour was one which would bring him no praise. Unlike his achievement, however, on which an error would as he says have brought discredit, if these country customs and vocations, obsolete and obsolescent, had been detailed wrongly, nobody would have discovered such errors to the end of Time. Yet I have instituted inquiries to correct tricks of memory, and striven against temptations to exaggerate, in order to preserve for my own satisfaction a fairly true record of a vanishing life.[35]

To assess this, it will be instructive first to quote at length the views of Dorset agricultural workers interviewed by Alexander Somerville (himself a Scottish farm labourer by origin). Their responses may indicate at times the ignorance of their class, which the common stereotype of 'Hodge' celebrated – but they demonstrate also an intense bitterness and class animosity, which that stereotype (as used by so many of Hardy's contemporaries) served conveniently both to

[33] G. W. Sherman, *The Pessimism of Thomas Hardy* (New Jersey, 1976), pp. 227, 230.
[34] C. Kegan Paul, 'Mr Hardy's novels', *British Quarterly Review*, LXXIII (1881), 349–50: 'there is not in all Mr Hardy's works one exaggerated or untrue word in his descriptions of those whom he knows so well'; 'The rustic of George Eliot and Thomas Hardy', *Merry England*, I (1883), 40–51; 'The Wessex labourers', *Examiner*, 15 July 1876. Or see E. Gosse, 'Thomas Hardy', *The Speaker*, 13 Sept. 1980.
[35] General Preface to the Wessex edition of 1912. This is reprinted in *The Hand of Ethelberta* (1876, 1975 edn), p. 426.

conceal and discount. And so for a sense of social realism and class feeling – to be measured against Hardy's supposed verisimilitude – one can turn to the interviews in Somerville's *Whistler at the Plough*:[36]

A labourer; wife and two children; wages 8s. weekly.

– 'It be not much, be it?'

'No, it is not much. How do you manage to live?'

'Not well; and there be three more – wife and two children. We had another boy, but he died two weeks aback; as fine a boy as you could wish to see he wur, and as much thought on by his mother and I; but we ben't sorry he be gone. I hopes he be happy in heaven. He ate a smart deal; and many a times, like all on us, went with a hungry belly. Ah! we may love our children never so much, but they be better gone; one hungry belly makes a difference where there ben't enough to eat . . .'

' – you must have a very hard struggle to keep yourselves alive?'

'Ees, hard enough. It makes one think on doing what one would never do, but for hunger . . .'

'He, the late Lord I mean, was a clergyman – was he not?'

'I've heard he wur once, but I don't know much of what he wur, 'cept that he transported me'.

'Transported you! What for?'

'For poaching. I got seven year; and wur killed near almost. And they killed my brother at once – knocked his skull to pieces'.

'Who – the gamekeepers I suppose? Did you make much resistance?'

'No; I heard them fall on my brother, and I wur fifty yards from him. And when I wur hiding, they came and took hold on me, and beat in my skull. Here, you can feel with your hand; out of that part, and this, and this, eleven pieces of bone were taken. I never wur expected to live for a long time. No, I never made no resistance; for they had broken my head and killed my brother afore I knew they saw me . . .'

He wishes, he says, and prays to God, that he could now for himself and family at home have such an allowance of food as he had in the West Indies when a convict.

'We had a terrible good living', this was his expression, 'by as ever I had for working in England. Fresh beef three times a-week, pork and peas four times a-week . . . father died soon as I wur gone – one son killed, and me a'most, and then transported, wur too much for him to stand. Ah! he wur broken hearted . . .'

A labourer putting flints on the highway. He says he has eight shillings a week, and has received notice that after next week he will only have seven. Says he saw me talking to old-un, and would like to know what *he* said about wages. I told him that we talked of many things, but I forgot to mention wages . . .

'And what did old-un say to thee then?'

'He said he never forgot anything'.

'Never forgot anything!' exclaimed the labourer, as if highly amused with his examination and my replies; 'Never forgot nothing!' he again repeated, 'no, old-un be not likely to forget nothing as will put a penny in his pocket and

[36] A. Somerville, *The Whistler at the Plough* (Manchester, 1852), pp. 37–43.

keep it out of another man's. Old-un won't forget that he told his men last week he would take them down a shilling; but he be's a long as a journey from here to London on a pig's back afore his memory be's good enough to raise wages, at the time he promises when he takes them down!'
And having thus spoken, he applied himself with great vigour to his work . . .
'I ben't no farmer myself; wish I wur'.
'Why do you wish you were?'
'What do thee think I work for?'
'For wages'.
'And how much do thee think I get?'
'You told me you had only eight shilling, that you are to be reduced to seven'.
'And how much do thee think I eat over a whole week out of that?'
'I cannot say; I should like to know; perhaps you will tell me?'
'Suppose, rather than I tell thee, that thou tries. Take thee to breaking flints and making roads at eight shillings a week for a year, do thee think thou could tell what thee lived on? . . . Well, an I wur a farmer I would always have as much to eat as to be able to know what it wur; I don't be able to tell it now at times, 'cause how I go with an empty belly so often that my grub ha'n't no name. Ah! you be a precious lot o' hard screws on a poor man, the whole lot of you be . . . I see you ha' got a good coat on your back, and a face that don't look like an empty belly; there be no hunger looking out atween your ribs I'll swear. You be either a farmer or somebody else that lives on somebody else. May be you be a lord for aught I know on; or a squire; or a parson, dang it – you be a parson perhaps! One thing I see, you ben't one of them as works fourteen hours a day, to feed lords, and squires, and parsons, and farmers; dang the farmers, they be the worst of the lot of ye'.
'Why do you think the farmers are the worst?'
'Why! What need of me to tell you why? You wouldn't believe me wur I to tell why; but I dare say you know without telling. I dare say you be one of them as has your daughter, an you ha' a daughter, playing the piano on a Saturday night to drown the noise of them brutes of labouring men what come to get their wages through a hole in the wall; what cannot be allowed to set foot within a farmer's house now-a-days; what must be paid through an opening in the partition, lest they defile the house of a master what gets rich as they get poor; a master what must get his daughter to play music lest the voice of a hard-working man be heard through the hole in the wall! Ah! it be enough to drive men mad; it ha' made men think on things they never would ha' thought on'.
'But', said I, 'you are wrong in supposing every person to be your enemy who is not one of yourselves. Do you speak of a farmer in particular who pays his men through a hole in the wall while his daughter plays the piano inside, or do you say all the farmers do so?'
'Oh, you know, master, what I mean; you be not such a stranger here as you would make me believe . . . I dare say you be about to go and tell all you heard me say now. I dare say you be one of 'em as come from London to kill game, that a poor man, like I, must not look at. Ah! I don't care; we must just go on. We be all like to have justice sometime; there ben't no noblemen in heaven, they say . . .'
'Will there by any poor men there?'
'Not an the rich can help it; not an the rich can keep the poor out, I should

think. But I be told no rich be to get there neither ... Ah! I ben't like to be much longer here; I be like to try my hand in another part of the country. Seven shillings won't do; eight wur bad enough, but seven won't do'.

These statements are worth quoting at length as they make clear the subjective feelings and experience of farm labourers in a way never found in Hardy, and provide a good indication of the range of discontents: for example, the game laws, low wages, pretentious living standards of the farmers, or the bad diet and difficulty in keeping their families alive. One could add in particular labourers' concern with the precariousness of employment; with the widespread payment of wages in kind – or rather, in 'grist' (that is, substandard corn too bad to be sold on the market);[37] or their hostility to the New Poor Law, being enforced in an increasingly rigid fashion from the 1870s by farmer guardians, particularly with regard to the aged – whose predominance in the countryside was growing because of youthful out-migration. There had been much unrest in Dorset earlier – for example, the 'Swing' rioting of 1830–1, particularly acute in the Blackmoor Vale[38] – and this continued throughout the nineteenth century, falling off during the briefly profitable mid-century years, but very evident again from about 1870. One recalls also the nonconformist and trade union organisations (the early case of the Tolpuddle Martyrs in 1834 comes readily to mind), and evidence of political radicalism. A reporter for the *Morning Chronicle* wrote as early as 1850 of his being

astonished at the extent to which I have found Socialist doctrines prevailing among the rural poor [in Dorset] ... its principles have made their way amongst them to a considerable extent – their progress being promoted, if it was not originated, by the daily contemplation of their own wretched lot ... They contend that they have 'a right to live, and to live comfortably, as well as the best of them', and they ... reason with themselves that they cannot do this until land is treated not as a property, but as a trust ... They are becoming more and more imbued with these sentiments, and many of them will tell you so.[39]

And the rising money wages after 1872 bear witness to the effects of rural Unionism, which significantly came as a surprise to many contemporaries who held to the bovine and Hodge-like stereotypes of the labourer. From Tolpuddle on throughout the nineteenth century,

---

[37] On the payment in 'grist', see for example *The Times*, 25 June 1846; R. Heath, *The English Peasant* (1893, Wakefield, 1978 edn), p. 126.

[38] On 'Swing' unrest in Dorset, see W. H. Parry Okeden, 'The agricultural riots in Dorset in 1830', *Proc. Dorset Nat. Hist. and Archaeol. Soc.*, LII (1930), 75–95; and more generally, E. J. Hobsbawm & G. Rudé, *Captain Swing* (1969, 1973 edn).

[39] *Morning Chronicle*, 7 Nov. 1849, reprinted on 1 Jan. 1850.

in literary and blue book reportage, the Dorset agricultural labourer was associated with about the most squalid and depressed living standards to be found in England, and the most embittered class relations. As late as the 1880s and 1890s there was so much arson in some areas of Dorset that it was reported, and later recalled by elderly labourers, that many young men dared not go out in the evenings for fear of being accused as arsonists.[40]

III

This then was the economic environment and class context of Hardy's Dorset. Parts of it may be familiar from his novels. But we should now consider the extent and limitations of his 'realism', in view of the arguments that it was in this that he was original. Hardy's father was a builder, and employed six or more men, and Hardy himself trained as an architect in London.[41] He attended an expensive school in Dorchester where he learnt classics, literature, and mathematics; he moved socially among the London literati for much of his life; he insisted on his family having an old Dorset lineage; he carefully cultivated his connections with the landed and professional classes; and when in 'Wessex' he lived comfortably in Sturminster Newton and Wimborne. So he was hardly a 'peasant'. Agricultural labourers feature remotely in his novels, and very rarely as developed characters. Jude's early crow-scaring gives way to his scholastic aims and work as a stone-mason. Henchard's work as a rather incompetent hay-trusser rapidly ends as Hardy scoops him up to become Mayor of Casterbridge (an incredible feat of upward social mobility, surely far beyond the reach of a nineteenth-century rural labourer in Dorset). Tess' work in the fields is described to epitomise her degradation and humiliation, rather than to portray the experience and sentiments of agricultural labour as a class – distinctly separable from the employing class to which her fortunes were more closely associated. Gabriel Oak's dependable and responsible values are clearly thought to pertain more to the farm bailiff or small owner-occupier class, than to labourers dependent on short-term hired labour. And other developed Hardy characters bear even less proximity to 'Wessex peasants' – by now, of course, not a 'peasantry' in any sense of the

[40] Kerr, *Bound to the Soil*, p. 61. On the depressed state of Dorset agriculture, and the large number of strikes there, see Haggard, *Rural England*, p. 265.
[41] R. Gittings, *Young Thomas Hardy* (1975, Harmondsworth, 1980 edn), p. 23, indicates that Hardy's father employed six or more men as a master mason. However, Hardy claimed that his father employed twenty-five. See A. Eustice, *Thomas Hardy. Landscapes of the Mind* (1979), p. 2.

word, but an agrarian proletariat with almost no opportunities for upward social mobility in rural society. Hardy's interest in the theme of social mobility in itself underlines the point that he was concerned with the agricultural labourer in only a very marginal fashion.

Certainly there is little evidence that he had successfully by-passed the stereotype of 'Hodge' which he discussed in 'The Dorsetshire labourer'. Even that article of 1883, as we have seen, perpetuated an image of animal indifference to farmer contemptuousness while it sought to question it: 'an accident of the land . . . calling for no more resentment than the blows of the wind or the rain'.[42] We learn, for example, that: 'ploughmen as a rule do not give sufficient thought to the morrow to be miserable when not in physical pain . . . drudgery in the fields results at worst in a mood of painless passivity'.[43] Indeed, throughout this article – which was commissioned by Longman as one of a series on the rural 'quality of life' – Hardy ignored the disagreeable conditions of Dorset, romanticised or remained silent on the issues highlighted in government and other reports, and presented a similar picture to that wishfully imagined by his contemporary Richard Jefferies, writing of nearby Wiltshire:

the farm labourer is the most peaceful of all men, the least given to agitation . . . Permit him to live and he is satisfied. He has no class ill-feeling, either against farmer or landowner, and he resists all attempts to introduce ill-feeling. He maintains a steady and manly attitude, calm, and considering, without a trace of hasty revolutionary sentiments.[44]

And yet this was a period when fire insurance companies refused to insure farmers against arson in many areas of Dorset; when cattle-maiming could take on ugly proportions; when the agricultural unionist George Edwards wrote of how 'the whole countryside was seething with discontent';[45] when attacks on poor law guardians and relieving officers were regularly reported in county newspapers, insisting on an intensification of the rural police force.

If Hardy's discussion in 'The Dorsetshire labourer' fell into the usual dismissive stereotypes, how did he present the rural worker in his novels? Repeatedly, one finds an image of comic and derisory Hodge, with an occasional touch of ludicrous magniloquence. Consider the behaviour of Tess' father (a huckster and carter) when made aware of his ancient lineage:

Boy, take up that basket! I want 'ee to go on an errand for me . . . Now obey my orders, and take the message I'm going to charge 'ee wi' . . . Well, Fred, I

---

[42] 'The Dorsetshire labourer', in Moynahan, *The Portable Thomas Hardy*, p. 729.
[43] *Ibid.*, p. 718.   [44] Jefferies, *Hills and the Vale* (Oxford, 1980 edn), p. 268.
[45] G. Edwards, *From Crow-Scaring to Westminster* (1922), p. 37.

don't mind telling you that the secret is that I'm one of a noble race – it has just been found out by me this present afternoon. P.M.

Sir John d'Urberville – that's who I am; . . . That is if knights were baronets – which they be. 'Tis recorded in history all about me. Dost know of such a place, lad, as Kingsbere-sub-Greenhill? . . .
Well, under the church of that city there lie –
'Tisn't a city, the place I mean; leastwise 'twaddn' when I was there – 'twas a little one-eyed, blinking sort o' place.
Never you mind the place, boy, that's not the question before us. Under the church of that there parish lie my ancestors – hundreds of 'em – in coats of mail and jewels, in gr't lead coffins weighing tons and tons. There's not a man in the County o' South-Wessex that's got grander and nobler skillentons in his family than I.[46]

Tess' mother is presented in similar fashion: 'We've been found to be the greatest gentlefolk in the whole county – reaching all back long before Oliver Grumble's time – to the days of the Pagan Turks – with monuments, and vaults, and crests, and 'scutcheons, and the Lord knows what all.'[47]

The image can readily be found in the other novels, as for example Joseph Poorgrass and his drinking companions after Fanny Robin's death in *Far From the Madding Crowd*.[48] Hardy's 'rustics' in *The Mayor of Casterbridge* giggle 'I do, hee-hee, I do', 'Ay – that I do – hee-hee'; and in depicting Abel Whittle, Christopher Coney, Buzzford, 'and the rest of that fraternity' he clearly had his readers' amusement in mind:

'There is sommit wrong in my make, your worshipful!' said Abel, 'especially in the inside, whereas my poor dumb brain gets as dead as a clot afore I've said my few scrags of prayers. Yes – it came on as a stripling, just afore I'd got man's wages, whereas I never enjoy my bed at all, for no sooner do I lie down than I be asleep, and afore I be awake I be up. I've fretted my gizzard green about it, maister, but what can I do?'

What indeed? Here is another example: 'It was fear made my few poor hairs so thin! No busting out, no slamming of doors, no meddling with yer eternal soul and all that; and though 'tis a shilling a week less I'm the richer man; for what's all the world if yer mind is always in a larry, Miss Henchet?' After all, wrote Hardy, these were 'farm-labourers and other peasants, who combined a little poaching with their farming and a little brawling and bibbling with their poaching' – a 'mixed assemblage of idlers'. As for their wives, their seeming industry and cleanliness was 'belied by the postures and gaits of the women . . . their knuckles being mostly on their hips (an

---

[46] *Tess of the D'Urbervilles* (1891, 1970 edn), pp. 16–17.   [47] *Ibid.*, p. 29.
[48] *Far From the Madding Crowd* (1874, 1971 edn), ch. XLII.

attitude which gave them the aspect of two-handled mugs), and their shoulders against doorposts'. Even the language of movement implies animalistic comparison: 'Whittle then trotted on down Back Street.' And Hardy makes clear that Whittle was, of course, illiterate.[49]

In *A Pair of Blue Eyes* Hardy even names two lower-class villagers 'Lickpan' and 'Worm', and their names are matched by their stupid and derisory behaviour throughout. Or in *The Hand of Ethelberta* the hostler refers to himself and the milkman as 'you or I or any other poor fool'. The conversation continues: '"I think to myself, more know Tom Fool than Tom Fool knows".'"

'Ah! That's the very feeling I've feeled over and over again, hostler, but not in such gifted language. 'Tis a thought I've had in me for years, and never could lick into shape! – O-ho-ho-ho! Splendid! Say it again, hostler, say it again! To hear my own poor notion that had no name brought into form like that – I wouldn't ha' lost it for the world! More know Tom Fool than – than – h-ho-ho-ho-ho!'

And the 'ho-ho-hoing' continues for the next two paragraphs.[50] In a similar passage in *A Pair of Blue Eyes* each rustic is given his own onomatopoeic guffaw, like so many donkeys:

'Ha, ha, ha! . . .'
'Haw, haw, haw! . . .'
'Huh, huh, huh! . . .'
'Hee, hee, hee! . . .'

Each laughs in turn to the same silly joke, told for the 'thousandth' time by 'Lickpan' himself.[51] The descriptions could be multiplied endlessly – all approximate closely to the usual reassuringly comic and bovine stereotypes, and have nothing whatever in common with the deeply felt statements recorded in Dorset by Somerville. Reading Hardy's descriptions, landowning and tenant farmer classes could readily ignore their guilt over the condition of the labourer. Hardy's own 'rustic' in the novels came close to the one he outlined at the start of 'The Dorsetshire labourer': 'a degraded being of uncouth manner and aspect, stolid understanding, and snail-like movement . . . Hodge hangs his head or looks sheepish when spoken to, and thinks Lunnon a place paved with gold' – a comic, lazy, and very marginally more intelligent 'creature' than that depicted by William Howitt:

as simple, as ignorant, and as laborious a creature as one of the wagon-horses that he drives . . . the clodhopper, the chopstick, the Rawbuck, the hind, the

---

[49] *The Mayor of Casterbridge* (1886, 1968 edn), pp. 88, 100–2, 222, 254, 256, 264, 267–8, 332.   [50] *The Hand of Ethelberta*, pp. 36–7.
[51] *A Pair of Blue Eyes* (1873, 1975 edn), p. 257.

Johnny-raw, or by whatever name, in whatever district, he may be called, is everywhere the same . . . he sees no newspaper, and if he could, he could not read it . . . He knows there is such a place as the next town . . . and that is all he knows of the globe and its concerns, beyond his own fields . . . He is as much of an animal as air and exercise, strong living and sound sleeping can make him, and he is nothing more.[52]

Even when Hardy consciously engages the stereotype of 'Hodge', in a passage from 'The Dorsetshire labourer' – repeated almost word for word in a similar part of *Tess* describing Clare's first close encounter with 'farm-folk' – his stress is on generic types, and reveals a way of thinking which led readily to the casting of lower-class characters into separate stereotyped and predictably comic moulds: 'A number of dissimilar fellow-creatures, men of many minds, infinite in difference; some happy, many serene, a few depressed; some clever, even to genius, some stupid, some wanton, some austere; some mutely Miltonic, some Cromwellian.'[53] This description fulfils much the same function, in a different manner, as did that of 'Hodge' itself – taking, as it does, any threat out of divergent lower-class moral and social values. It can be found in another form in Hardy's frequent reduction of men to their occupation, as with the drinking group of 'Billy Wills the glazier, Smart the shoemaker, Buzzford the general dealer, and others of a secondary set of worthies', 'the members of the philosophic party', he added else-where, pushing the irony further.[54] If the presentation of 'Hodge' had acknowledged class separateness, but shown its harmlessness be-cause Hodge had only a comic animal, contented, and unthinking character, Hardy, at least in 'The Dorsetshire labourer', capped his list of generic types by implicitly denying class antagonism in his emphasis on the 'more numerous features common to all humanity'. 'Men', he added in the same passage in *Tess*, 'every one of whom walked in his own individual way the road to dusty death' – ignoring the fact, notorious in nineteenth-century Dorset, that the individual way of some led them to walk over others.

So the argument that Hardy was a 'peasant', immersed in the values of the labouring poor, writing about them in an unpre-cedentedly realistic fashion, seems misplaced. Certainly one finds in Hardy (and perhaps this is more common in his earlier writing)

---

[52] W. Howitt, *The Rural Life of England* (1838), vol. 1, pp. 157–8. For further criticism of Hardy's artificial presentation and humouring of the rural worker, see Henry James, review of *Far From the Madding Crowd*, in the *Nation*, 24 Dec. 1874. This is reprinted in his *The House of Fiction* (1957, 1962 edn).

[53] 'The Dorsetshire labourer', in Moynahan, *The Portable Thomas Hardy*, p. 717. See also *Tess*, pp. 139–40.   [54] *Mayor of Casterbridge*, pp. 45, 307.

occasional mention of overcrowded cottages (although they persistently contain a reassuring abundance of hanging hams and bacon);[55] or accounts of agricultural work (where intermittent realism is usually subsidiary or coincidental to a metaphorical purpose, as with sheepfarming processes in *Far From the Madding Crowd*, or perhaps of dairying in *Tess*); occasionally perceptive descriptions of the experience of landscape and geographical horizon; or accounts of village superstitions, and I do not wish to discount these. But the novels rarely enter seriously and sympathetically into the area of labourers' values, priorities, and subjective experience, and are revealingly reticent on the actual conditions of life in Dorset: on the low wages and unemployment; on the prevalence of and reasons for religious nonconformity; on the reality and character of political belief; on the agricultural unionism and bitterness of class antagonism; on labourers' attitudes to work and the use of the land; on working-class sexuality; on familial relationships and the treatment of the elderly; on the notorious hostility to the New Poor Law and its administrators. For Dorset, these and other matters bearing on social relations and the standard of living were being brought constantly to the attention of contemporaries by parliamentary blue books and newspaper reportage. But one finds them ignored in Hardy, and replaced by a romanticising and pastoral gloss which, from the viewpoint of the social historian, is simplistically misrepresentative in suggesting an amiable docility of labourers seen largely as bucolic clowns; a misrepresentation which held reassurance for the agricultural employing class and Hardy's readership, and which reveals its political partiality in all that it deliberately omits and discounts.[56]

The arguments against Hardy's verisimilitude should be developed on other fronts. Take his account of female field work for example, most notably in *Tess*. Such work for women was almost unheard of by the 1880s in this region, as would have been women working with threshing machines. The 1843 parliamentary report on women's work had suggested that a relatively wide range of female work in

---

[55] See for example, *Under the Greenwood Tree* (1872, 1971 edn), pp. 51, 99, 190; or *The Woodlanders* (1887, 1971 edn), p. 10.

[56] I do not wish to discount the problems Hardy had with his readership, particularly in his presentation of sexuality. 'Remember the country parson's daughters. I have always to remember them', Leslie Stephen wrote to him. See P. Collins, review of D. Kramer (ed.), *The Woodlanders* (Oxford, 1981 edn), in *The Times Higher Education Supplement*, 14 Aug. 1981, p. 15. The remarkable sheep-shearing scene in *Far From the Madding Crowd* (1971 edn), pp. 165–9, was one way around this problem. And on sexuality, see also R. Gittings, *Young Thomas Hardy* (1975, Harmondsworth 1980 edn), pp. 277, 287; and his *The Older Hardy* (1978, Harmondsworth, 1980 edn), pp. 113, 184.

agriculture still existed then in Dorset, providing evidence of women ploughing, for example. Similarly, poor law settlement material for the region can be used to indicate that in the late eighteenth and early nineteenth centuries, at any rate, the seasonal distribution of unemployment for men and women in agriculture was still very similar.

Figure 8.1 *Male and female seasonal distribution of unemployment, 1780–1834* Devon & Dorset (3 month moving average)

This can be seen in Figure 8.1.[57] But by the time of the reports on women's work of the late 1860s the situation had changed markedly, with the reduction of female work clearly apparent. Where they continued to work it was mainly in a dairying capacity, and the general diminution of female labour had now occurred in Dorset. Rider Haggard was struck merely by two women helping a shepherd to pick swedes, which he described as 'a very curious sight'.[58] The accounts of Flintcomb Ash, or of Tess on the threshing machine, were

[57] The method here is the same as in chapter 1.
[58] Haggard, *Rural England*, p. 262.

assuredly not realistic portrayals of female work in the 1880s.[59] They may of course have a literary and artistic purpose: symbolising the degree to which Tess had fallen; though the success even of such a purpose would have relied on the reader's immediate appreciation that both morally and in practice such tasks were no longer women's work. I shall return to these matters and their relation to Hardy's thinking on marriage.

Similarly, a reader of 'The Dorsetshire labourer' (1883) would imagine that the massive yearly turnover of population described there, at the time of the yearly hiring fair, was a near universal experience of labour in late nineteenth-century Dorset. But this would be quite misplaced. Even in the hey-day of the yearly hiring system, in the early eighteenth century, it had been the unmarried farm-servants who were generally hired by the year. Married men (in eighteenth-century terms, 'labourers') settled for the more precarious employment of a day or weekly hiring, although remaining far more immobile than unmarried labour. Certain classes of married farm labour (e.g., shepherds or carters) might still be yearly hired – but they were the exception. The decline of service occurred even in Dorset. Service had created settlements, so raising poor rates; its accompanying 'living-in' arrangements were increasingly distasteful to a farmer class made affluent and socially conscious during the Napoleonic Wars; it was unsuited to a situation of labour surplus partly consequent upon a high birth rate. This labour surplus in Dorset was so great that even the migrant Irish harvesters avoided the county, knowing they had more favourable employment prospects elsewhere, in almost any other region.[60] The New Poor Law of 1834 did little to alleviate this structural unemployment – indeed, it may have aggravated it in a number of ways. And so in Hardy's time the yearly hiring system he described in *Far From the Madding Crowd* or 'The Dorsetshire labourer' had become a very minor aspect of the labour market, and was notably uncommon in north and west Dorset. Such hiring was carried on mainly in east Dorset, and even there it only affected some of the unmarried, and certain bailiff,

[59] See chapter 1. The same point was made by Gittings, *Young Hardy*, p. 304. See also M. R. Bouquet, 'The sexual division of labour: the farm household in a Devon parish' (unpub. Ph.D. thesis, University of Cambridge, 1981). Most Hardy novels were set in a period after the mid-1870s, usually in the 1880s. But a few were set in earlier periods – notably *The Trumpet Major* (set in 1800–10), and *The Mayor of Casterbridge* (probably set in 1846, although claims have also been made for 1843, and 'about 1850'). My remarks here do not refer to these, and are directed mainly at *Tess*, set in the late 1880s.

[60] See the *Morning Chronicle*, 15 Jan. 1850, p. 81.

shepherd, or carter occupations. Probably less than 15 per cent of the labour force was so involved in east Dorset (in 1851), and certainly less than 9 per cent then in Dorset generally. The figure would have fallen even lower by 1883. Most were hired by the day, or less commonly by the week.[61] Here again, Hardy certainly did not present a realistic picture of rural Dorset. We saw earlier that he created an imaginary picture of an immobile past, which he depicted as breaking up during his own lifetime. Now, with regard to the mobility of the yearly-hired, he was exaggerating considerably and with nostalgia a situation largely ended, having been in decline for over a century.

IV

As yet this discussion has been negative – but where does Hardy's failure to deal adequately with class attitudes, and his unrealistic and evasive presentation of conditions in Dorset take us? It is possible to suggest first why he adopted this literary position. He would of course have been a far less successful writer had he not done so, for the attitudes of the labouring poor were a worrying matter to his country readership, who preferred reassurance. Those who did attempt a realistic portrayal of the labouring poor – one thinks, for example, of George Morland or Alexander Somerville – usually paid the penalty, and lived and died in penury. Hardy's first novel, *The Poor Man and the Lady*, was rejected by Macmillan explicitly because of its attack on the middle classes, and Hardy rapidly learnt the lesson;[62] indeed he had to in order to be published in *Longman's*, *Blackwood's*, *Cornhill* and the other magazines where much of his work first appeared. And as he rose socially there were even stronger reasons to eschew realistic portrayal. Autobiographical elements abound in his novels, and in Ethelberta's attempt to escape 'the ironical cheers which would greet a slip back into the mire' (back to her humble social origins), it is hard not to detect a major concern of Hardy

---

[61] A. Kussmaul, *Servants in Husbandry in Early Modern England* (Cambridge, 1981), p. 20.

[62] The letter of rejection from Macmillan is printed in the Introduction by T. Coleman to Hardy's *An Indiscretion in the Life of an Heiress*, pp. 7–9. (First written, under the title of *The Poor Man and the Lady*, in 1867. Adapted and published under its present title in *New Quarterly Magazine*, July 1878. First published (private edition of 100 copies) as a book in 1934. Reference is made here to the 1976 edition, edited by T. Coleman.) There is no surviving copy of the initial version of *The Poor Man and the Lady*, and *An Indiscretion in the Life of an Heiress* probably comprises only about a third of the original. Some lengthy passages of the original version were probably integrated into other novels, such as *Under the Greenwood Tree*, but much of the original manuscript was destroyed by Hardy in old age.

himself.[63] As Robert Gittings has persuasively argued, Hardy studiously distanced himself from working-class relatives. In his memoirs:

He omits almost totally all his other close relatives, uncles, aunts, and very numerous cousins. The touchstone throughout seems to have been social class. Labourers, cobblers, bricklayers, carpenters, farm servants, journeymen, joiners, butlers have no place in Hardy's memoirs, though he was related to all of these; nor, among women, do cooks, house-servants, ladies' maids, or certificated teachers, regarded in the 19th century as little better than servants . . . Hardy himself did not want to record the lives of his lower class relatives.[64]

Similarly, in his 'Hardy Pedigree' (a genealogical table drawn up in old age), he gave

elaborate attention to a branch only very remotely related to his mother, called Childs . . . This . . . family eventually came to contain a certain number of professional men, particularly surgeons, and, as a culminating triumph, an Assistant Commissioner of Metropolitan Police. All this . . . is meticulously noted by Hardy . . . To shut the door on a social past from which he had escaped became a compulsion in his later life . . . The gulf between someone with whom he could talk freely in an educated way, and one of his own background, who . . . could literally not speak the language which Hardy had acquired, haunted his mind.[65]

And he felt he had much to hide. His mother had received poor law assistance, as a pauper child; relatives in Puddletown and Stinsford were servants and labourers; his cousin Ellen Hand had a bastard child; his mother and both grandmothers were pregnant prior to marriage (common among the working classes); he himself had been unable to go to university (but preferred to think that his father could have afforded it); and he entered in *Who's Who* the information that his wife was the niece of an archdeacon. In cycling through Puddletown: 'the Hardys would bicycle stiffly through the main street, looking neither to right nor to left. Cottage doors were full of his close relatives . . . but Hardy neither gave nor acknowledged greetings as he pedalled resolutely on with Emma.'[66]

---

[63] *The Hand of Ethelberta*, p. 221. As Gittings points out, in this novel Hardy wrote himself out of the class of his relatives. 'From now onward, he surveyed such people as one who had escaped from their world', remaining nevertheless 'a writer of humble origins acclaimed by a society which might, if knowing, have found them contemptible': Gittings, *Young Hardy*, ch. 19, esp. pp. 289–99 on the autobiographical aspects of this novel.   [64] Gittings, *Young Hardy*, p. 18.

[65] *Ibid.*, p. 18. See also pp. 19, 31, 273, 281, 289, 300. And Gittings, *Older Hardy*, pp. 238–9, 245.   [66] Gittings, *Young Hardy*, p. 300.

Hardy could write perceptively on quite minor social differences and rivalries in the middle or upper classes, but evidently he was rarely concerned with or sympathetic to the realities of lower-class attitudes and rural poverty as an author. These were to be forgotten as one advanced socially – an embarrassment to a popular author striving for eligibility in unfamiliar literary and class circles, where a capacity for empathetic verisimilitude in depicting the rural poor might prove socially uncongenial and threaten his newly acquired connections. His patronising presentation of the 'rural vulgar' as comic – the approach used on occasion by Scott, George Eliot, Thomas Hood, Tennyson, even Mrs Gaskell – was a way of avoiding connections with this class and isolating himself from it – stressing his social distance by blunting possible comparison with his position in the London literary world. Once more there is autobiographical suggestion in Hardy's *An Indiscretion in the Life of an Heiress*. Egbert moves upward socially in London, and as he does so 'several habits which he had at one time condemned in the ambitious classes now became his own'.[67] The same theme of social advancement and removal from the countryside is of course constantly present in the novels: Clym, Grace, Tess, Jude, Henchard, Farfrae, and others come readily to mind. And Hardy's own aspirant class mobility is apparent in his descriptive prose: with its juxtaposition of differing and socially specific vocabularies – of pretentious classical or artistic reference alongside more rural or practical turns of phrase. These social aspirations – Hardy's move into what he called 'the ambitious classes' – are central to an understanding of his depiction or negation of the rural worker.

Another, perhaps related, factor was his fatalism and gloom – 'as if enveloped in a leaden cloud', as he described it – his view that 'the universe is totally indifferent to men and women', which may have made detailed literary exposure of social and material realities seem superfluous. Certainly they seemed superfluous to his sense and purpose as an artist. Despite his own claim to verisimilitude cited earlier, he wrote in his memoirs:

I don't want to see the original realities ... I want to see the deeper reality underlying the scenic, the expression of what are sometimes called abstract imaginings. The 'simply natural' is interesting no longer. The much decried, mad, late-Turner rendering is now necessary to create my interest. *The exact truth as to material fact ceases to be of importance in art* ... it does not bring anything to the object that coalesces with and translates the qualities that are

---

[67] *An Indiscretion in the Life of an Heiress*, p. 82.

already there – half hidden, it may be – and the two united are depicted as the All [my italics].[68]

There is a similar passage in the 1912 Preface to *Under the Greenwood Tree*. Accordingly we find in Hardy the *principle* of detail, used simply to create a feeling of social realism, and detail used as metaphor, symbol or omen (underestimated by many critics), rather than the detail itself, of social and economic life as lived in Dorset – a romantic, stylised, frequently anachronistic and antiquarian depiction of 'Wessex' interpreted with fatalism and pessimism. Perhaps his contemporary George Sturt was rather critical. But his verdict on Hardy as a '"subjective" student of labour' is worth recalling, for it came from an author with far more convincing claims to 'realism' or verisimilitude:

For an example [Sturt wrote], 'Far from the Madding Crowd' does not appear typical of any life known to me. The story does not; nor yet (do) the individual characters so appear. And as for showing how delightfully Fate might work out, or how attractive real people might be . . . well, really! To me it exhibits an irritating lunacy in Fate, and a depressing idiocy in a population mostly fools [i.e., as depicted by Hardy].[69]

And a device which could help express his fatalism was the depiction of the countryside as unchanging, and its working population as individual stereotypes with predictable natures, as for example, in *Far From the Madding Crowd*. It has of course been argued that Hardy's novels do not depict a timeless rural social order, that they show an awareness of the changing fluctuations of agricultural fortune.[70] There is an element of truth in this. But the image of timelessness in rural life as we find it in Jefferies and others (which could be both reassuring or fatalistic) *is* unquestionably and forcefully espoused by Hardy. One thinks for example of the descriptions of Egdon Heath, or classically 'In Time of "The Breaking of Nations"':

> Yet this will go onward the same
> Though Dynasties pass.

– a statement which was patently untrue in its economic context, for all its ambiguous appeal.

---

[68] Florence Hardy, *The Life of Thomas Hardy, 1840–1928* (1928, 1962 edn), p. 185. This *Life* was written by Hardy himself. Elsewhere he wrote to similar effect: 'Like former productions of this pen, *Jude the Obscure* is simply an endeavour to give shape and coherence to a series of seemings, or personal impressions, the question of their consistency or their discordance, of their permanence or their transitoriness, being regarded as not of the first moment' (1895 Preface to *Jude the Obscure*).

[69] G. Sturt, *The Journals of George Sturt, 1890–1904* (Cambridge, 1967), vol. 1, pp. 364–5. See also my Introduction, p. 6, citing Sturt on Hardy.

[70] Williams, *English Novel*, pp. 113–15; or his *Country and City*, pp. 200–3.

V

Hardy's social perspective, then, was that of a detached and educated member of the Dorset market-town middle or professional class, with close literary connections in London; and perhaps all that is required is an account of why the stereotyping of the labourer occurred (earlier in the nineteenth century) among this class, and in the literary traditions which influenced him, drawing attention to the obvious political functions which it served. It may be excessive to blame Hardy for adopting such a stereotype (and this is not my purpose), in the sense that his artistic method was not one of realism, and his literary preoccupations were more related to his experience of up-ward mobility, and his unfortunate first marriage. An appreciation of the social nexus and attitudes of nineteenth-century Dorset is certain-ly helpful when assessing his 'realism', and might further clarify the repeated theme of class mobility in the novels – unrealistic though that mobility sometimes seems. Comparisons suggest themselves with the responses of other authors moving upwards from a lowly background, such as Lawrence, although there is not space to develop them here. But this avowedly historical explanation can be taken further in a more positive direction, and I want to end this chapter and book by outlining what Hardy's primary concerns were, and why, in mid- and late nineteenth-century Dorset, it was under-standable that he should have developed these in his novels.

Throughout his major novels – *Tess, Jude, The Woodlanders, Return of the Native, The Mayor of Casterbridge, Far From the Madding Crowd*, or even *Under the Greenwood Tree* – Hardy attempted to formulate the conditions in which affectionate and lasting relationships could take place. This is a constant theme and arguably his major focus. *Jude the Obscure* was, as he put it in his preface to the first edition,

a novel addressed by a man to men and women of full age; which attempts to deal unaffectedly with the fret and fever, derision and disaster, that may press in the wake of the strongest passion known to humanity; to tell, without a mincing of words, of a deadly war waged between flesh and spirit; and to point to the tragedy of unfulfilled aims . . . an endeavour to give shape and coherence to a series of seemings, or personal impressions, the question of their consistency or their discordance, of their permanence or their transitoriness, being regarded as not of the first moment.

And, as he wrote in the 1895 Preface to *The Woodlanders*, his concern lay with 'the immortal puzzle – given the man and woman, how to find a basis for their sexual relation'. He clearly needed an answer, for his work persistently gives an embittered and bleak account of marriage and marital relations in its descriptions of what he termed the 'false marriage'. The cases are numerous and are found in virtually every novel: one thinks for example of Jude and Arabella, Sue Bridehead and Richard Phillotson, Troy and Bathsheba, Fitzpiers and Grace. Let us take examples just from *Jude the Obscure*. Jude and Arabella's lives, he wrote, were 'ruined by the fundamental error of their matrimonial union: that of having based a permanent contract on a temporary feeling which had no necessary connection with affinities that alone render a life-long comradeship tolerable'. Marriage was

a social ritual which made necessary a cancelling of well-formed schemes involving years of thought and labour . . . a gin which would cripple him, if not her also, for the rest of a life-time . . . a sordid contract, based on material convenience in householding, rating and taxing, and the inheritance of land and money by children, making it necessary that the male parent should be known . . . an artificial system . . . under which the normal sex-impulses are turned into devilish domestic gins and springes to noose and hold back those who want to progress.

Wifehood, Jude tells Sue, 'has not yet squashed up and digested you in its vast maw as an atom which has no further individuality'. 'I think I should begin to be afraid of you, Jude [says Sue], the moment you had contracted to cherish me under a Government stamp, and I was licensed to be loved on the premises by you – Ugh, how horrible and sordid!'[71] The theme is stressed strongly in *Jude the Obscure*, but is a relentless and persistent one throughout Hardy's work. The reasons he gave for the 'false marriage' included the difficulties surrounding class pretence or emulation with partners from unequal social backgrounds, or ambitions to escape from their present position. But he stressed one lesson in addition to this, which was indeed closely associated with it historically, and was best formulated at the end of *Far From the Madding Crowd*, in the union of Bathsheba and Gabriel Oak:

He accompanied her up the hill, explaining to her the details of his forthcoming tenure of the other farm. They spoke very little of their mutual feelings; pretty phrases and warm expressions being probably unnecessary between such tried friends. Theirs was that substantial affection which arises (if any arises at all) when the two who are thrown together begin first by knowing the rougher sides of each other's character, and not the best till further on, the romance growing up in the interstices of a mass of hard

[71] *Jude the Obscure* (1896, 1969 edn), pp. 68, 76, 198, 218, 226, 267–8. In a lesser known example, that of the short story *Fellow Townsmen*, in *Wessex Tales* (1888, 1979 edn), Hardy provides a picture of marriage in which Mr Barnet calls his wife 'Mrs. Barnet' when addressing her in private (something also found in Jane Austen or George Eliot), and in which Barnet is prepared to think Mrs Downe 'a too demonstrative woman' because she expresses concern that her husband has fallen into the gutter.

prosaic reality. This good-fellowship – camaraderie – usually occurring through similarity of pursuits, is unfortunately seldom superadded to love between the sexes, because men and women associate, not in their labours, but in their pleasures merely. Where, however, happy circumstance permits its development, the compounded feeling proves itself to be the only love which is strong as death.[72]

None of Hardy's 'false' relationships are grounded in shared work, and they lack any single-mindedness of conjugal affection – they are fouled by superficial romance, by a separation of interests and aspirations, by emotional detachment because of education away from the country, by the connected complications of social emulation, and by the personal distancing of a marked sexual division of labour. In *The Woodlanders*, great stress is laid on the fact that:

Marty South alone, of all the women in Hintock and the world, had approximated to Winterborne's level of intelligent intercourse with Nature. In that respect she had formed his true complement in the other sex, had lived as his counterpart, had subjoined her thoughts to his as a corollary . . . They had planted together, and together they had felled; together they had, with the run of the years, mentally collected those remoter signs and symbols which seen in few were of runic obscurity, but all together made an alphabet . . . 'He ought to have married *you*, Marty, and nobody else in the world!' said Grace with conviction, after thinking in the above strain.[73]

And the affection bred by such shared work was demonstrated in Marty's final speech over his grave.

Let us take a further example. In *The Distracted Preacher* (a short story written in 1879, and set in the 1830s), Mr Stockdale, a visiting Wesleyan preacher to the coastal parish of Nether-Moynton, becomes infatuated with Lizzy Newberry, only to discover her late-night smuggling activities and associates. One feature of the smuggling is that Lizzy dresses as a man while engaged in it, and some of the male smugglers she works with dress as women. Stockdale is 'dreadfully depressed' and 'ashamed' by her enthusiasm for smuggling, and by finding her one night 'in man's clothes', and he prevails upon her to abandon these practices. His moral exhortations finally succeed. In a story which reads as an allegory of the triumph of nineteenth-century morality over that of the eighteenth, they eventually marry; Lizzy

---

[72] *Far From the Madding Crowd*, p. 439. Or see his stress in *Jude* on those 'affinities that alone render a life-long comradeship tolerable', p. 76. As Sue explains to Jude, the views of the people around them 'of the relation of man and woman are limited . . . Their philosophy only recognizes relations based on animal desire. The wide field of attachment where desire plays, at least, only a secondary part, is ignored by them' (pp. 175–6).

[73] *The Woodlanders*, pp. 340–1. See also the superficial relationships and incompatible interests of *Under the Greenwood Tree*, e.g., pp. 143–7, 175.

leaves 'her old haunts' and goes back with him to his home, 'where she studied her duties as a minister's wife with praiseworthy assiduity', in due course writing an 'excellent' anti-smuggling tract 'called *Render unto Caesar; or, The Repentant Villagers,* in which her own experience was anonymously used'.[74] So much for the ostensible moral of the story. And yet, in describing the feelings of the couple, Hardy suggests lessons which are not consistent with it. This is evident for example in the passage where Lizzy tells the minister details of her smuggling business:

Stockdale sighed as she enumerated each particular, for it proved how far involved in the business a woman must be who was so well acquainted with its conditions and needs. And yet he felt more tenderly towards her at this moment than he had felt all the foregoing day. Perhaps it was that her experienced manner and bold indifference stirred his admiration in spite of himself.

'Take my arm, Lizzy,' he murmured.[75]

Despite it being Lizzy's role to 'take his arm', one recognises here a similar thought to that expressed in *The Woodlanders* or *Far From the Madding Crowd*. *The Distracted Preacher* was published in 1879; but in 1912 Hardy added a note at the end which is significant as an acknowledgement of the ambivalent exhortation of the story, and as an indication of his real predilection:

The ending of this story with the marriage of Lizzy and the minister was almost *de rigueur* in an English magazine at the time of writing. But at this late date, thirty years after, it may not be amiss to give the ending that would have been preferred by the writer to the convention used above . . . Lizzy did not, in fact, marry the minister, but – much to her credit in the author's opinion – stuck to Jim the smuggler, and emigrated with him after their marriage.[76]

The tension here between the morality of late nineteenth-century convention and Hardy's contrary preference is evident: the story's outcome was dictated by convention, but Jim the smuggler was, by virtue of his shared smuggling experiences with Lizzy, her 'true complement in the other sex'.

A similar moral is illustrated in Hardy's propitious account of the short period of Jude and Sue's relationship when their children were born; particularly in the language of comradeship describing Sue's

---

[74] *The Distracted Preacher,* in *Wessex Tales* (1888, 1979 edn), p. 242.
[75] *Ibid.,* p. 215. Of course, Victorian admiration for an 'experienced manner and bold indifference' in women extended beyond Hardy's depiction of Lizzy Newberry or Bathsheba Everdene, although it was often necessarily covert. See for example, D. Hudson, *Munby. Man of Two Worlds* (1972). I hope to explore this subject further elsewhere.   [76] *Distracted Preacher,* pp. 242–3.

assistance at Jude's work. But Hardy also makes clear that the attitude of onlookers to this was initially one of surprise that a woman was assisting in such work, and that this was so critically regarded by them as to compound a subsequent suspicion of immorality:

Sue was assisting Jude very materially now: he had latterly occupied himself on his own account in working and lettering head-stones, which he kept in a little yard at the back of his little house, where in the intervals of domestic duties she marked out the letters full size for him, and blacked them in after he had cut them . . .

'There you see,' he said cheerfully. 'One more job yet, at any rate, and you can help in it' . . . Sue came to see what assistance she could render, and also because they liked to be together . . . Standing on a safe low platform erected by Jude . . . she began painting in the letters of the first Table while he set about mending a portion of the second. She was quite pleased at her powers . . . They were not, however, to be left thus snug and peaceful for long. About half-past twelve there came footsteps on the gravel without. The old vicar and his churchwarden entered, and, coming up to see what was being done, seemed surprised to discover that a young woman was assisting . . . Meanwhile the door had opened again, and there shuffled in with a business-like air the white-aproned woman who cleaned the church . . . The church-cleaner looked at Sue, gaped, and lifted her hands . . . Next came two ladies, and after talking to the char-woman they also moved forward, and as Sue stood reaching upward, watched her hand tracing the letters, and critically regarded her person in relief against the white wall, till she grew so nervous that she trembled visibly.

They went back to where the others were standing, talking in undertones . . . 'I wonder Biles and Willis could think of such a thing as hiring those!' . . . Jude . . . looking at her . . . found she had been crying silently. 'Never mind, comrade!' he said . . . 'How could we be so simple as to suppose we might do this!' said she, dropping to her tragic note. 'Of course we ought not – I ought not – to have come!'[77]

As Raymond Williams writes, Hardy

created continually the strength and the warmth of people living together: in work and in love; in the physical reality of a place. What is defeated but not destroyed at the end of *The Woodlanders*, or the end of *Tess* or the end of *Jude* is a warmth, a seriousness, an endurance in love and work that are the necessary definition of what Hardy knows and mourns as loss . . . Hardy does not celebrate isolation and separation.[78]

Such literary concern during this period with the quality of family life, with the distanced relationships of sexually segregated work, was to be expected in view of changes in women's work and the family; and perhaps it was in the qualitative nature of the change that it should have been expressed in the literary form of the novel rather than in documentary reportage. We have seen how more sexually equal, 'pre-industrial', wage-dependent labour and family economies

[77] *Jude the Obscure*, pp. 270, 310–14.   [78] Williams, *Country and City*, p. 213.

declined, how the nineteenth century witnessed growing sexual divisions of labour and a reduction of female economic roles, particularly among the working classes. These changes partly emulated those affecting higher social groups long before (in the seventeenth century or earlier), which had become strongly entrenched there both morally and in practice; but the nineteenth-century changes were determined largely by economic compulsions accentuating and hardening earlier sexual roles which had been much more relaxed and flexible. Men came more to dominate economic production, now based on capital-intensive technology sited increasingly outside the family and home place, independent of family-based labour; and women, particularly in the south, became relegated to more strictly domestic functions. These changes began before Hardy was born, but certainly they continued into the period of his literary career. As another historian has written: 'Female participation as a whole fell markedly. If age and marital status are taken into account, and the 1911 census categories used, the proportion of women employed was 8 per cent smaller in 1911 than in 1881, whereas the male proportion was about the same ... the evidence suggests that female participation was even higher in 1861.'[79] A large pamphlet literature bears witness to what contemporaries widely perceived as a 'surplus female problem'; the vulnerable economic position of women is manifest in the size of the Victorian servant class (by far the largest contemporary employment category for women), or in the 80,000–120,000 'prostitutes' of Victorian London. In Dorset, women in many parishes worked very long hours at domestic button making for a weekly wage of between 3d. and 8½d., and it is no surprise that they were the first to out-migrate, with young men following them from the 1870s.[80]

By the mid-nineteenth century the working classes were adopting the values which followed and justified these changes. Aspects of this changing sexual division of labour were dealt with earlier. But its characteristics in Dorset can be mentioned here, to suggest how it produced social and familial problems which surfaced most intrusively after the mid-nineteenth century, arguably to stay with us ever

[79] D. E. Baines, 'The labour supply and the labour market, 1860–1914', in R. Floud & D. McCloskey (eds.), *The Economic History of Britain since 1700* (Cambridge, 1981), vol. 2, p. 152.

[80] On the so-called 'surplus women' problem of the period, see W. R. Greg, 'Why are women redundant?', in *Literary and Social Judgements* (Boston, 1869); J. Boucherett, 'How to provide for superfluous women', in J. Butler (ed.), *Woman's Work and Woman's Culture* (1869); or her 'On the obstacles to the employment of women', *English Women's Journal*, IV (1860), 361–75; A. Kenealy, 'New view of the surplus of women', *Westminster Review*, CXXXVI (1891), 465–75. And on female out-migration from Dorset, see Kerr, *Bound to the Soil*, p. 117.

since – for later social movements have achieved (statistically speaking) surprisingly little return to the fuller economic participation of women in the pre-industrial period.[81] It seems likely that Hardy, in his 'endeavour to give shape and coherence to a series of seemings, or personal impressions', expressed these problems more than most contemporary authors, without fully realising or articulating their historical relativity: 'the question of their consistency or their discordance, of their permanence or their transitoriness, being regarded as not of the first moment'. Certainly his proposed remedy – his formulation of the conditions in which lasting relationships could occur – found appropriateness in historical experience before sexual

---

[81] In some respects this trend against female employment has continued since 1900. And the effects of the micro-revolution, particularly on female secretarial work, employment in textiles, clothing and footwear manufacture, will aggravate it much further, especially during the 1990s. The percentage of women working in Britain has risen from 40 per cent in 1911 to 45 per cent in 1971; and the percentage of the work force which is female has risen from 29.2 to 36.7 between 1901 and 1971. But in many respects the type of work has undergone a qualitative deterioration. The last seventy years has seen a trend towards women being concentrated in the lowest grades of white collar and blue collar work (in service sector employment and in unskilled and semi-skilled manufacturing jobs), and very much underrepresented in the higher grades. (There has also been a move to much greater frequency of part-time employment among women than men.) For example, 19.8 per cent of women who worked in 1911 were in management and administrative posts – the level was 13 per cent in 1931, and little higher in 1961. There were more women in the higher ranks of the Civil Service in 1919 than there are today. In 1919, 63 per cent of employed women were in the 'lower professions', in white collar jobs but below 'management and executive' levels. There were only 52 per cent in 1971. Of the female work force 24 per cent was skilled in 1911 – 13.5 per cent in 1971. The percentage of women in unskilled 'married women's jobs – no prospects' has risen over the same period from 15.5 to 37. In 1979, 61 per cent of *all* employed women worked in only ten occupations.

Female employment gains during the two world wars were of course very rapidly reversed after 1918 and 1945; and the role of women as a 'reserve labour force' has been particularly apparent during periods of unemployment. Rising unemployment since the mid-1970s has disproportionately affected women: in just the two years after January 1976 female unemployment rose by 53 per cent – male unemployment by 9 per cent, and the disparity may have widened since – a disparity which is, of course, understated by the under-registration of female unemployment. (The E.O.C. estimated that total female unemployment, officially at 460,000 in 1980, was actually over 700,000.) On the concentration of women's work today into very few employment categories (and those most likely to be affected by micro-technology), see C. Hakim, 'Sexual divisions within the labour force: occupational segregation', *Employment Gazette* (November 1978). And for further analysis of this, and for an interesting but very pessimistic outline of the effects of the new technology on women's work, see in particular U. Huws (Equal Opportunities Commission), *New Technology and Women's Employment. Case Studies from West Yorkshire* (E.O.C., 1982). To similar effect, see also J. Rada, *The Impact of Microelectronics* (International Labour Office, 1980), esp. pp. 60ff; and J. Sleigh, B. Boatwright, P. Irwin & R. Stanyon, *The Manpower Implications of Microelectronic Technology* (Dept. of Employment, H.M.S.O., 1979), p. 68.

divisions of labour hardened, and before the decline of the family economy.

In this earlier period, and as late as the early nineteenth century in Dorset and Devon, male and female seasonal distributions of unemployment had been very similar, and female wages high in relation to male wages. There had been relatively equal sexual work in the major events of the agricultural year. In Dorset before the 1840s family members had commonly been hired *together*, and worked for daily wages as a unit, much as they would previously have done in less vulnerable forms of partially subsistent or surplus-producing family production on small farms.[82] Parliamentary enclosure, which adversely affected such agricultural and rural-craft family economies, occurred relatively late in Dorset: only 12,000–14,000 acres were so enclosed before 1800, but 53,000 acres in the nineteenth century. Of the county's parliamentary enclosure, 79 per cent occurred after 1793, relatively speaking a very high figure.[83] And the county came to have an above average farm size by the 1880s, with a decline in the nineteenth century of small farmers and owner-occupiers, who were unable to cope with falling grain prices by using the capitalised methods of 'high farming'. The earlier changes in the eastern arable sexual division of labour were very noticeable in Dorset after the mid-nineteenth century. Here, for example, is literary evidence from a farm labourer's wife, indicating the broad range of women's work in the early nineteenth century in this district, and we may take this as typical of earlier family production characteristic of small-farm pastoral agriculture:

I used to be employed when I was apprenticed [women had very frequently been apprenticed to agriculture in this area] in driving bullocks to field, and fetching them in again; cleaning out their houses, and bedding them up; washing potatoes and boiling them for pigs; milking; in the fields leading horses or bullocks to plough: maidens would not like that work now. Then I was employed in mixing lime and earth to spread; digging potatoes, digging and pulling turnips, and anything that came to hand, *like a boy* [my italics].[84]

This quote, itself reminiscent of a changed state of affairs, is from the

[82] See for example, W. Hasbach, *The History of the English Agricultural Labourer* (1908), p. 411.

[83] Ruegg, 'The farming of Dorsetshire', 440; M. E. Turner, *English Parliamentary Enclosure* (Folkestone, Kent, 1980), p. 194.

[84] Report on the Employment of Women and Children in Agriculture, XII (1843), p. 125. Or here is a farmer: 'I remember formerly when girls turned out regularly with the boys to plough etc., and were up to their knees in dirt, in the middle of winter, in all kinds of employments. Now you never see a girl about the fields', *ibid.*, p. 122. See also C. Vancouver, *General View of the Agriculture of the County of Devon* (1808, 1969 edn), pp. 360–1, on the very extensive scope of female agricultural work.

1843 Report. By the time of the reports in the 1860s, women's work had been limited much more strictly to dairying, and even in this employment their work continued to decline. By 1900 Baring Gould was writing of this region that:

No maids now go a-milking; that is why there are now no true milkmaids. The old order changeth. Nowadays . . . men milk. Women cannot be found to do it. They object to the trudge through the dirt and the planting of the three legged peggy stool and their feet in the ooze substance that forms the cushion enveloping the floor of the cowstall. I do not blame them. It is a dirty place.[85]

Similar developments can be traced in the apprenticed trades. We have seen that women in the early eighteenth century had been apprenticed to trades which later became more strictly male pre- serves, and that they had participated in them alongside their husbands at home.[86] Greater male vulnerability to unemployment associated with the decline of apprenticeship, and the removal of production from the family to larger workshops, were the main factors behind this reduced female role. It is significant in this connection that Puddletown, where Hardy had been closely con- nected by residence, and where many of his relatives lived, remained heavily dependent on family economies well into the nineteenth century. As Gittings remarks:

This small town, for it was considerably more than a village, was still practically medieval in its way of life, neglected by absentee landlords and untouched by eighteenth-century enclosure. It remained so throughout Hardy's youth, until a new reforming squire in the 1860's and 1870's literally cleaned up and rebuilt the place . . . Puddletown was always a town of artisans and small craftsmen, serving the agricultural community, but skilled and independent of the fluctuations of agriculture . . . an unreformed, partly unenclosed rural community of the old sort.[87]

As such it was the model for Weatherbury in *Far From the Madding Crowd*, the scene against which Hardy spoke of the need for men and women to associate in labour, and not in their pleasures merely.

For artisans, the erosion of seven year apprenticeships allowed less qualified men to enter the trades and so depress wages, overproduce, and threaten employment. In Dorset, many such newcomers had been small tenant farmers or owner-occupiers, forced to abandon small farms during the depression after 1813, who turned to jobbing shoemaking, carpentry, tailoring, and other trades as alternatives.[88] Their competition contributed to glut the labour market, to open the labour supply for larger employers, to raise sentiments against female

[85] S. Baring Gould, *In a Quiet Village* (1900), p. 149.   [86] See chapter 6.
[87] Gittings, *Young Hardy*, p. 32.   [88] Kerr, *Bound to the Soil*, pp. 132–3.

work, and to undercut hitherto more secure family economies – forcing the man to leave home and seek employment as a journey-man in a larger master's workshop, and his wife to remain at home to endure the very high Victorian birth rate. There were also growing pressures faced by artisans from the competition of factory goods, with the railway and developments in internal marketing facilitating their introduction into rural Dorset. Hardy repeatedly complained of the decline of this more stable artisan element, whose production (like that of the small life-holders) had been dependent on the family unit.[89] The decline of these classes hastened the end of a sexual division of labour which he thought beneficial. Without fully realising the historical extent of the change and its culmination in his own lifetime, Hardy nevertheless regretted an emotional distance which had resulted from the severance of male work place and home place, from the detachment of women from economically productive labour to a more exclusively domestic, child-rearing role – from the trans-formation of the family from a family-based economy to a unit of primary socialisation and recreative convenience. And he moved further away from the labouring class where these changes were occurring, to a class where they had taken place long before; in other words, the change was accentuated by his own upward social mobility.

It seems significant that he particularly noted one 'experienced reviewer', who claimed that he had created in the figure of Sue Bridehead: 'the first delineation in fiction of the woman who was coming into notice in her thousands every year – the woman of the feminist movement – the slight, pale "bachelor" girl – the intellectual-ised, emancipated bundle of nerves that modern conditions were producing'.[90] That is, the 'discarnate' woman with little experience of productive labour, the 'New Woman', or the 'girl of the period' – found also in *A Laodicean*, *Far From the Madding Crowd*, and in the characters of Ethelberta Chickerell, Paula Power, and others. Sue Bridehead was 'a mere cluster of nerves', 'so ethereal a creature', 'that aerial being' – described by Jude as:

you spirit, you disembodied creature . . . hardly flesh at all; so that when I put my arms round you I almost expect them to pass through you as through air! Forgive me for being so gross, as you call it! . . . But you, Sue, are such a phantasmal, bodiless creature, one who – if you'll allow me to say it – has so

---

[89] See for example 'The Dorsetshire labourer', p. 734, or the 1874 Preface to *Far From the Madding Crowd*, where he discusses the decline of 'the class of stationary cottagers'.
[90] In the Postscript to the 1912 edition of *Jude the Obscure*, in Moynahan (ed.), *Portable Hardy*, p. 689.

little animal passion in you ... You are absolutely the most ethereal, least sensual woman I ever knew to exist without human sexlessness.[91]

One recalls what D. H. Lawrence wrote of her:

One of the supremest products of our civilization is Sue ... the female was atrophied in her ... she could only *live* in the mind ... She knew well enough that she was not alive in the ordinary human sense. She did not, like an ordinary woman, receive all she knew through her senses, her instincts, but through her consciousness ... For the senses, the body, did not exist in her; she existed as a consciousness ... She was unhappy every moment of her life, poor Sue, with the knowledge of her own nonexistence within life ... she was a void unto herself.[92]

'How modern you are!' Jude was to exclaim. As Hardy remarked on this: 'And no doubt there can be more in a book than the author consciously puts there.'[93]

Even Tess, in her way, shared much with these women, with her 'primitive instincts and modern nerves'. She appeared to Angel Clare as 'a visionary essence of woman ... merely a soul at large'. 'Tess had spiritually ceased to recognise [her body] as hers – allowing it to drift, like a corpse upon the current, in a direction dissociated from its living will'. Her movement is described by phrases such as a 'quiescent glide'; 'the least irregularity of motion startled her'. As Tanner has pointed out, she lacks a wholeness of being, is split between the soul and the body – as epitomised by the contrasted interests in her of Angel and Alec.[94]

Angel's instinct towards stillness is countered by Alec's instinct for sexual motion ... it is both men who drive Tess to her death: Angel by his spiritualised rejection, Alec by his sexual attacks. It is notable that both these men are also cut off from any fixed community; they have both broken away from traditional attitudes and dwellings.[95]

Tess and Angel at Talbothays are a poor resonance of earlier family-economy work in agriculture – Angel with his harp, his ethereal remoteness, suppressed spontaneity, and inhibited personal feeling, and of course his lack of genuine economic incentive and involvement. The approved impending relation of Gabriel Oak and Bathsheba

[91] *Jude the Obscure*, pp. 255, 268, 356. See also pp. 115, 118, 141, 195, 226, 233, 235, 365, 372.
[92] D. H. Lawrence, *Phoenix: The Posthumous Papers of D. H. Lawrence* (1936, 1961 edn), pp. 501–2. Also in A. L. Guerard (ed.), *Hardy – A Collection of Critical Essays* (Englewood Cliffs, 1963), pp. 71–6.
[93] Postscript, *Jude the Obscure* (1912 edn), in Moynahan, *Portable Hardy*, p. 689.
[94] I am indebted here to the fascinating discussion by Tony Tanner, 'Colour and movement in *Tess of the D'Urbervilles*', *Critical Quarterly*, X (1968), reprinted in R. P. Draper (ed.), *Hardy. The Tragic Novels* (1975), pp. 182–208.
[95] Tanner, 'Colour and movement', in Draper, p. 196.

had been different. And one recalls too Angel's fetish of chastity, his double standard, so characteristic of the Victorian period: 'a brutal caricature of human justice in that what was damned in the woman was condoned in the man'.[96] Such a double standard applied to women, suggested Keith Thomas, was 'based entirely upon their place in society in relation to men. The value set on female chastity varied directly according to the extent to which it was considered that women's function was a purely sexual one.'[97]

Hardy isolated developments which underlay marital estrangement, or the 'false marriage': the problem of class aspirations and the acquisitive possibilities of total male wage dependency, of rural out-migration and associated intellectual distance, the cynicism of commercial wealth, and, most explicitly, the absence or rareness of shared and cooperative labour between the sexes. All were closely associated historically with the decline of the family unit of production and its values. We should doubt whether Hardy described in adequately realistic prose many features of rural Dorset. But then this was not an important consideration for him as artist. 'Realism', he wrote, 'is not art.' 'Art is a changing of the actual proportions and order of things, so as to bring out more forcibly than might otherwise be done that feature in them which appeals most strongly . . . to show more clearly the features that matter in those realities, which, if merely copied or reported inventorially, might possibly be observed, but would more probably be overlooked.'[98] To this end, Hardy by-passed many of the important but transient rural issues of his day. But in his choice of signification, in his artistic emphasis on problems of personal alienation and marital estrangement, he was firmly embedded in and responsive to the social history of the period.

[96] *Ibid.*, p. 204.
[97] K. Thomas, 'The double standard', *Jnl of the History of Ideas*, XX (1959), 213.
[98] Hardy, *Life*, pp. 228–9.

Appendix: yearly wages

This appendix gives the yearly wage material used in chapter 1. Mean ($\bar{x}$) wages (in £ per annum) are given for five year periods, with the number of wage citings (N.) in each period. The data graphically presented in chapter 1 is a three point moving average of these five year means, with the moving average indexed from 1741 to 1745. The aggregates in chapter 1 of south-eastern and western yearly wages were unweighted. Other details can be found in chapter 1. I intend to provide comparable wage material for the northern counties in a later publication.

	Norfolk				Cambridgeshire, Bedfordshire, Huntingdonshire & Northamptonshire			
	Male		Female		Male		Female	
	$\bar{x}$	N.	$\bar{x}$	N.	$\bar{x}$	N.	$\bar{x}$	N.
1736–40	3.98	10	2.56	4	3.67	3	2.60	3
1741–5	3.99	9	3.75	3	3.45	5	2.66	4
1746–50	4.06	7	2.37	6	3.75	3	2.62	2
1751–5	5.31	11	3.13	5	3.73	11	2.42	3
1756–60	5.89	8	3.17	6	3.71	15	2.68	6
1761–5	5.31	11	2.81	7	5.03	13	2.49	10
1766–70	6.18	7	4.62	4	6.84	18	1.99	9
1771–5	5.94	18	2.91	5	4.38	12	2.31	5
1776–80	5.54	10	3.31	10	5.12	30	2.84	11
1781–5	6.29	19	3.14	13	5.03	17	2.79	4
1786–90	6.32	15	3.21	11	6.32	10	3.44	6
1791–5	6.48	18	3.56	12	6.04	15	4.19	5
1796–1800	8.16	18	3.15	12	8.54	17	3.71	7
1801–5	7.59	22	4.33	6	8.59	10	4.79	9
1806–10	7.08	9	4.46	7	7.80	12	4.59	17
1811–15	5.57	13	4.06	6	7.75	20	4.75	4
1816–20	4.95	10	3.36	7	5.32	15	4.03	7
1821–5	5.00	10	3.80	7	6.88	17	3.89	9
1826–30	5.25	5	3.40	3	6.30	12	3.68	11
1831–5	6.13	8	2.98	4	4.77	6	4.09	9
1836–40	4.67	3	2.90	2	4.06	6	3.72	3
1841–5					5.56	6		
		241		140		273		144

	London & Middlesex				Surrey, Kent, Essex & Hertfordshire			
	Male		Female		Male		Female	
	x̄	N.	x̄	N.	x̄	N.	x̄	N.
1736–40	6.00	2	4.25	1	4.39	5	3.98	3
1741–5	6.00	3	4.30	3	4.81	10	3.92	5
1746–50	6.23	2	4.25	2	5.38	12	4.26	5
1751–5	6.50	4	3.97	4	4.93	8	4.25	5
1756–60	7.15	7	4.43	5	5.94	14	4.46	7
1761–5	6.00	11	3.68	5	6.93	22	4.77	5
1766–70	7.25	15	4.22	5	6.62	30	4.28	7
1771–5	8.00	7	2.84	10	7.34	38	4.02	10
1776–80	9.87	19	2.12	4	8.62	50	3.90	9
1781–5	10.70	9	4.73	9	8.48	48	4.25	15
1786–90	6.13	8	4.62	3	8.00	43	3.12	12
1791–5	7.80	8	6.69	7	6.09	25	3.64	9
1796–1800	14.73	15	7.70	8	8.33	17	4.69	9
1801–5	9.87	5	6.88	6	8.62	9	5.20	9
1806–10	9.34	7	5.62	5	10.83	10	6.87	7
1811–15	11.96	7	7.08	3	12.57	12	7.87	8
1816–20	15.01	7	11.22	6	14.54	10	5.94	8
1821–5	15.69	4	12.39	4	9.90	11	5.37	6
1826–30	16.31	4	11.10	2	8.13	10	5.75	5
1831–5	17.02	3	10.25	3	6.62	7	5.21	5
1836–40			9.92	2	5.95	4	4.95	5
1841–5								
		147		97		395		154

	Devon & Dorset				Wiltshire & Somerset			
	Male		Female		Male		Female	
	x̄	N.	x̄	N.	x̄	N.	x̄	N.
1731–5	5.09	9	2.30	5				
1736–40	4.49	14	2.50	9	4.47	3	2.75	2
1741–5	4.18	15	2.50	4	4.47	6	2.60	4
1746–50	4.71	16	2.50	4	4.52	5	2.60	5
1751–5	5.00	7	2.20	5	5.67	6	2.75	4
1756–60	5.13	20	2.64	4	5.00	7	2.85	2
1761–5	4.11	19	2.62	4	5.61	6	2.75	3
1766–70	5.02	26	3.33	6	4.39	7	3.15	3
1771–5	5.90	26	3.43	5	4.70	13	3.50	6
1776–80	6.24	19	4.00	4	5.65	18	3.29	5
1781–5	5.32	22	4.13	5	5.75	12	3.35	5
1786–90	6.31	16	3.33	5	5.64	13	4.10	5
1791–5	6.29	15	3.64	9	6.83	10	4.01	7
1796–1800	7.27	25	5.11	11	6.68	12	4.03	6
1801–5	7.27	28	5.25	9	6.82	7	4.08	3
1806–10	7.35	26	6.19	14	6.37	9	3.56	4
1811–15	6.76	29	5.63	16	7.07	7	3.43	4
1816–20	5.86	16	6.57	17	5.82	10	3.99	7
1821–5	6.74	14	6.71	15	5.81	8	5.00	3
1826–30	6.79	17	6.34	8	5.88	6	5.53	14
1831–5	6.26	10	5.86	7	5.68	6	5.86	7
1836–40	6.50	6	6.37	5	5.81	4	5.78	3
		395		171		175		102

	Buckinghamshire, Berkshire, Oxfordshire & Hampshire				Suffolk			
	Male		Female		Male		Female	
	x̄	N.	x̄	N.	x̄	N.	x̄	N.
1701–5	4.00	2						
1706–10	4.05	4	2.58	3				
1711–15	4.25	6	2.75	3				
1716–20	4.37	21	2.60	4				
1721–5	4.48	21	2.71	4				
1726–30	4.61	13	2.83	4				
1731–5	5.09	13	2.93	5				
1736–40	4.56	8	2.91	7	3.44	5	2.75	3
1741–5	4.66	10	3.00	6	2.95	6	2.72	5
1746–50	4.70	16	3.35	5	3.71	11	2.80	2
1751–5	4.89	19	3.41	12	2.42	11	2.62	3
1756–60	4.99	30	3.06	12	4.68	14	3.00	4
1761–5	5.71	39	3.90	11	3.98	12	2.84	5
1766–70	6.25	32	3.43	13	4.67	14	3.69	4
1771–5	6.38	50	3.28	15	4.81	27	3.35	10
1776–80	6.63	46	3.02	16	5.26	42	4.85	11
1781–5	6.58	46	3.22	18	5.14	36	2.83	22
1786–90	5.98	44	3.83	8	6.17	59	3.64	18
1791–5	6.73	27	3.77	11	6.49	40	3.29	16
1796–1800	6.93	22	3.41	12	7.48	35	2.67	11
1801–5	7.41	17	4.18	5	5.88	28	4.44	10
1806–10	6.80	25	4.09	14	7.51	30	4.60	6
1811–15	6.32	20	3.92	3	8.50	27	4.00	12
1816–20	6.61	11	4.11	8	5.67	17	5.31	8
1821–5	7.26	6	5.28	8	5.92	10	3.37	9
1826–30	6.01	5	3.03	6	3.51	7	3.53	6
1831–5	7.17	6	4.64	8	4.73	7	2.55	6
1836–40	5.64	7	4.00	2	4.16	8	2.40	2
1841–5					4.17	3	2.50	3
		566		223		449		176

	St Clement Danes (Middlesex)				Leicestershire, Nottinghamshire & Rutland			
	Male		Female		Male		Female	
	x̄	N.	x̄	N.	x̄	N.	x̄	N.
1721–5	6.00	4	3.60	5				
1726–30	6.00	1	3.30	5				
1731–5	6.08	2	4.33	3				
1736–40	5.33	3	3.88	20	4.40	3	2.51	5
1741–5	6.06	9	3.75	26	5.08	5	2.50	2
1746–50	6.17	9	4.06	16	5.56	4	2.75	1
1751–5	6.12	4	4.93	3	6.28	4	2.50	1
1756–60	6.62	2	4.97	3	5.29	7	2.62	3
1761–5	6.92	3	5.13	4	4.67	15	2.50	1
1766–70	7.06	4	5.55	13	6.84	18	2.19	4
1771–5	7.63	8	5.45	20	7.04	18	2.92	5
1776–80	7.88	4	5.50	22	6.58	20	3.00	2
1781–5	7.35	3	5.83	30	7.11	15	2.81	4
1786–90	10.87	3	6.13	32	7.85	7	3.14	6
1791–5	10.15	5	7.99	14	7.97	13	3.56	4
1796–1800	10.25	5	7.35	11	8.46	12	4.56	4
1801–5	11.08	3	7.72	25	9.52	7	5.32	3
1806–10	10.83	3	7.87	36	12.15	14	5.20	5
1811–15	10.25	2	8.07	46	8.45	8	4.90	5
1816–20	10.32	3	7.97	17	9.38	12	4.15	3
1821–5	11.44	4	9.80	5	7.96	6	3.67	3
1826–30	11.25	3	9.93	3	8.44	5	3.75	2
1831–5	11.00	2	7.97	7	6.88	4	3.60	1
1836–40	11.42	3	9.75	4	8.00	1		
		92		370		198		64

| | Monmouthshire, Herefordshire, Worcestershire, Shropshire, Glamorganshire, Breconshire & Gloucestershire | | | |
| | Male | | Female | |
	x̄	N.	x̄	N.
1735–40	3.72	3	2.40	4
1741–5	3.75	5	2.25	4
1746–50	3.81	6	2.18	7
1751–5	4.61	7	2.21	5
1756–60	5.22	8	2.57	6
1761–5	5.75	4	2.15	1
1766–70	5.37	5	3.00	1
1771–5	5.26	8	2.91	6
1776–80	4.99	5	3.58	5
1781–5	5.53	4	3.37	5
1786–90	5.74	5	3.00	6
1791–5	6.45	12	2.97	6
1796–1800	6.40	10	5.88	6
1801–5	8.22	14	5.02	6
1806–10	8.25	19	5.74	10
1811–15	9.64	28	7.01	25
1816–20	8.28	20	6.08	74
1821–5	4.56	9	7.27	32
1826–30	5.18	8	5.19	8
1831–5	4.92	6	5.29	12
1836–40	4.91	7	5.74	5
		193		234

Bibliography

Bibliographical note on sources, methodology, and secondary material

This bibliography is divided into sections which cover the parishes providing settlement documentation, government reports and pre- and post-1900 publications footnoted in the text. The footnotes of each chapter are treated as self-contained, and after an initial full reference to a publication subsequent references are abbreviated. Place of publication is London unless otherwise stated. Full details of abbreviated publications can be obtained either by back-referral in the notes of specific chapters, or by reference to the bibliography here. The latter covers all government reports which were read for the book, and pre- and post-1900 publications which were actually footnoted in the text. Inevitably, a far wider range of items were read for this book, but unfortunately there is not the space to include in this limited bibliography many influential publications which were not footnoted.

One source has been settlement examinations, and in a large number of southern counties their availability was virtually exhausted. These documents, with the associated removal orders, correspondence, and other records, can be found in parish collections (of parishes conducting examinations, and in the collections of parishes where they were sent pending removal), in petty and quarter sessions records, in records of the New Poor Law, and in some estate records. Initially, my approach was to compile all the information available in the documents, such as: names of examinant and family; ages; family size and marital status; mention of kin; age of leaving home; marriage age; details of family break-up; places of birth, examination, marriage, past employment, or residence; wages; length and terms of hiring; unemployment; rents paid; parish offices served; length and terms of apprenticeship; literacy, and so on. This was done for most southern counties, in a first phase of research lasting a few years, but not exhausting the availability of records, and concentrating mainly on those in parish collections. This provided the material used in this book on such matters as family formation and size, the age of leaving home, apprenticeship, literacy, or the decline of service.

Because of the wide range of information being gathered, the method was extremely time consuming. And so, when sufficient data had been collected on these aspects of examinants' lives, attention was focussed more narrowly on subjects, areas, and periods where it was felt helpful to have more extensive documentation. This second phase of research gathered in particular further data on wages, unemployment, family break-up, apprenticeship, and aspects of geographical mobility. The latter, incorporating more extensive material from removal orders and settlement certificates, will be published as a separate study. The same counties were dealt with, only more completely and comprehensively. At the end of the day, my approach to the records has been in effect to work through parish catalogues for each record office and in particular to consult all examinations and settlement correspondence, alongside very large numbers of removal orders. Parish collections were largely exhausted (Kent, Surrey, Warwickshire, or Devon are exceptions), uncatalogued material used, and intrusions made into the settlement documents found in sessions' records. Differences in quantitative coverage of various topics in each chapter are due to this progressive narrowing over time of fieldwork focus, to my pursuit of different questions during the years of research, and to the sampling of collected data for different issues. Some aspects of family life in particular (for example, the age of leaving home, or family formation) are based on smaller numbers of cases than are wages or unemployment. To have gathered full information on all issues dealt with in all the records consulted would have taken a prohibitively longer period of time, and often would have been quantitatively superflous.

Because of the nature of the source, it is not feasible to give a full list of all parishes and record-office call numbers used in particular figures and tabulations based on settlement records – in some cases there are very large numbers of parishes used. The practical difficulties are obvious enough. For example, data from a wider region is often being focussed on a smaller area, and data (unemployment, apprenticeship, hiring, wages, etc.) is constantly being used with reference to different parishes than those in which it has survived. It is in the character of the source that some parishes are documented in various ways in the records of record-holding parishes, but lack any settlement records of their own. The quality of data surviving for them is sometimes as good as or better than for parishes with records in their own collections. Records in a record-holding parish may even provide no usable information on that parish (i.e., on what happened to certain individuals when they lived there), but something on or from other parishes. Such matters are intrinsic to the use of settlement records, which after all are biographical statements on a periodically mobile labour force sent through the post between parishes.

And because of the enormous number of records used, it is also impracticable to give a complete list of all the record-office call numbers consulted. In some record offices even single documents are frequently call-numbered, and the final list would be very extensive indeed. In effect it would comprise nearly a complete catalogue of three types of surviving parish settlement records in the south of England and Wales, and that might virtually amount to another book. In preference, I have chosen to list the parishes in each county providing documentation (including the small number of other settlement administrative units, such as townships, extra-parochial places, and the like); and I have given also the record offices concerned, and the total number of administrative units of settlement (including urban parishes) in each county around 1800, as a rough guide to the density of coverage by county. The parish lists which follow indicate which records were used and which parishes are covered by the data. Surviving collections specifically of examinations and settlement correspondence for all the parishes, hamlets, and towns listed below were consulted, alongside most of their removal orders. And further parishes which lack their own collections are also included if I used data which was available for them in the records of other parishes or in sessions, or data on yearly wages which was available in independent material such as farm accounts, diaries, pamphlets on pauperism, and the like.

Parishes providing settlement documentation

Bedfordshire
Bedfordshire County Record Office. Total settlement administrative units: 143.

Ampthill, Arlesey, Biddenham, Biggleswade, Blunham, Bedford (St Cuthbert, St Mary, St Paul, St Peter, St John), Great Barford, Bromham, Bushmead, Bletsoe, Chawson, Campton, Caldecote, Clapham, Cople, Cranfield, Caddington, Carlton, Cardington, Dunstable, Nether Dean, Over Dean, Eaton Socon, Elstow, Everton, Eaton Ford, Flitton, Felmersham, Flitwick, Goldington, Henlow, Harrold, Houghton Conquest, Haynes, Hatley Cockayne, Keysoe, Kempston, Leighton Buzzard, Lidlington, Luton, Maulden, Milton Ernest, Moggerhanger, Northill, Newbury, Old Warden, Oakley, Pertenhall, Potton, Renhold, Roxton, Ravensden, Ridgmont, Risely, Sandy, Southill, Studham, Sharnbrook, Swineshead, Shillington, Stagsden, Thurleigh, Turvey, Toddington, Wilshamstead, Wotton, Woburn, Westoning, Wyboston, Willington, Wilstead, Wymington, Yelden.

Berkshire
Berkshire County Record Office. Total settlement administrative units: 219.

Ashbury, Ashampstead, Aldworth, Aldermaston, Abingdon, Appleton, Aston Upthorpe, Basildon, Bray, Bradfield, Blewbury, Binfield, Boxford, Brightwalton, Benham, Beedon, Brightwell, Bucklebury, Burghfield, Beenham, Brimpton, Chipping Lambourn, Chaddleworth, Challow, Clewer, Compton, Cookham, Cumnor, Chieveley, Drayton, Easthampstead, Englefield, Early, Froxfield, Faringdon, Grove, Hurst, Harwell, Hagbourne, Hungerford, Hampstead Norris, Hanney, Inkpen, Ilsley, Kingston Lisle, Kintbury, Lambourn, Up Lambourn, Longworth, Milton, Maidenhead, Moulsford, New Windsor, Newbury, Old Windsor, Pangbourne, Peasemore, Purley, Reading, Sparsholt, Shinfield, Great Shefford, Speen, Sutton Courtenay, Shellingford, Sunninghill, West Shefford, Sulhampstead Abbots, Sonning, Shalbourne, Stanford, Shaw, Shottesbrooke, Thatcham, Tilehurst, Uffington, Wantage, Wallingford, Walcot, Winterbourne, Waltham St Lawrence, Welford, Woodley and Sandford, West Hanney, White Waltham, Wootton, Woolhampton, Winkfield, Warfield, Yattendon.

Buckinghamshire
Buckinghamshire County Record Office. Total settlement administrative units: 241.

Aylesbury, Ashendon, Amersham, Buckingham, Burnham, Bledlow, Boveney, Great Brickhill, Little Brickhill, Bletchley, Brill, Bradwell, Bow Brickhill, Cuddington, North Crawley, Chalvey, Chalfont St. Peter, Chesham, Coleshill, Cublington, Chepping Wycombe, Clifton Reynes, Cuddington, Claydon, Dorney, Denham, Drayton Parslow, Emberton, Ellesborough, Eddlesborough, Farnham Royal, Fulmer, Grendon Underwood, Granborough, Hitcham, Hardmead, Horton, Hitchendon, Hardwicke, Hartwell, Hulcott, Ickford, Iver, Great Kimble, Ludgershall, Loughton, Langley, Lavendon, Lathbury, Long Crendon, Maids Moreton, Great Marlow, Mursley, Newport Pagnell, Olney, Oakley, Pitstone, Pightlestone, Quainton, Ravenstone, Stoke Mandeville, Stoke Poges, Swanbourne, Stantonbury, Taplow, Turville, Upton, Warrington, Waddesdon, Westbury, Winslow, Wing, Lower Winchendon, Little Woolstone.

Cambridgeshire
Cambridgeshire County Record Office. Total settlement administrative units: 178.

Great Abington, Little Abington, Barton, Bassingbourn, Balsham, Bourne, Bottisham, Burrough Green, Burwell, Barrington, Burrough Fen, Cambridge (All Saints, St Benedict, St Botolph, St Clements, St Edwards, St Giles, St Mary the Great, St Mary the Less, St Michael, St Peter, Holy Trinity, St Andrew the Great, St Andrew the Less, St Sepulchre), Chippenham, Conington, Chatteris, Chesterton, Caxton, Cottenham, Castle Camps, Coveney, Comberton, Cherry Hinton, Caldecote, Drayton, Dullingham, Elm, Ely (St Mary), Elsworth, Eltisley, Fordham, Fenstanton, Fen Ditton, Fen Drayton, Fulbourn, Foulmire, Little Gransden, Guilden Morden, Gamlingay, Grantchester, Hinxton, Horningsea, Harston, Haddenham, Histon, Haslingfield, Isleham, Ickleton, Kirtling, Kingston, Knapwell, Littleport, Linton, Long Stanton, Landbeach, Melbourn, March, Madingley, Meldreth, Manea, Milton, Newton, Oakington, Over, Redmere, Rampton, Reach, Royston, Swaffham Bulbeck, Swaffham Prior, Great Shelford, Sawston, Sutton, Soham, Steeple Morden, Stow-cum-Quy, Swavesey, Shudy Camps, Teversham, Thorney, Tadlow, Trumpington, Upwell, Whaddon, Wood Ditton, Witchford, Wimblington, West Wratting, Wisbech (St Peter), Whittlesford, Whittlesey, Wicken, West Wickham, Waterbeach, Weston Colville, Witcham, Wilburton, Willingham.

Devon
Devon County Record Office. Total settlement administrative units: 471.

Ascombe, West Alvington, Bere Ferrers, Bovey Tracey, Blackadon, East Budleigh, Blackawton, Cadeleigh, Crediton, Colebrooke, Drake, Dodbrooke, Diptford, Exeter, Farrington, Highweek, Hartland, Harford, Honiton, South Huish, Ilfracombe, Kenton, Kingsbridge, Lustleigh, Merton, Modbury, South Milton, Northleigh, Northam, Peter Tavy, Sidmouth, Sandford, Stoke Fleming, Stonehouse, Sowton, Topsham, Totnes, Teignmouth, Thurlstone, Withycombe Raleigh, Warkleigh, Woolborough.

Dorset
Dorset County Record Office. Total settlement administrative units: 285.

Arne, Affpuddle, Blandford Forum, Bishops Caundle, Bradford Abbas, Beaminster, Broadway, Bloxworth, Buckland Newton, Bere Regis, Canford Magna, Corfe Castle, Chickerell, Charlton Marshall, Church Knowle, Castleton, Cerne Abbas, Corscombe, Dewlish, Dorchester, Fifehead Magdalen, Fordington, Farnham, Folke, Fontmell Magna, Hammoon, Hilton, Hayes, Hooke, Hamworthy, Holwell, Kington Magna, Leigh, Langton Maltravers, Litton Cheney, Lillington, Mosterton, Motcombe, Melcombe Regis, Milton Abbas, Newton, Poole, Puddletown, Powerstock, Pimperne, Sherborne, Studland, Swanage, East Stoke, Sydling, Stoke Abbott, Shipton Gorge, Sturminster Marshall, Shaftesbury, Sturminster Newton, Tindleton, Tolpuddle, Thornford, Walcot, Wareham (St Martin), Wimborne Minster, Weymouth, Winfrith Newburgh, Whitchurch, Winterbourne Whitchurch, Winterbourne Kingston, Wootton Glanville, Wyke Regis, Winterbourne Monkston, West Orchard.

Essex
Essex County Record Office. Total settlement administrative units: 420.

Ashdon, Aveley, Ashen, Bradwell, Braintree, Bradfield, Brentwood, Great Burstead, Bocking, Great Bromley, Bradwell juxta Mare, Beaumont with Moze, Barking, Little Baddow, Barling, Boreham, Benfleet, Great Bardfield, Colchester (St Botolph, St Giles, St Runwold), Great Clacton, Little Clacton, Chelmsford, Chipping Ongar, Great Chesterford, Coggeshall, Chrishall, Chigwell, Canewdon, Castle Hedingham, Chingford, Dedham, East Danyland, Great Dunmow, Dovercourt, Eastwood, Earls Colne, Elmstead, Epping, Fryerning, Felstead, Helion Bumpstead, Great Holland, Hallingbury, Heybridge, Harwich (St Nicholas), Hadleigh, Hockley, Halstead, Harlow, West Hanningfield, Kirby le Soken, Kelvedon, Leyton, St Lawrence, Langham, Lexden, Linford, Great Leighs, Manningtree, West Mersea, East Mersea, Maldon, Margaretting, Mucking, South Ockendon, Great Oakley, St Osyth, Prittlewell, Rayleigh, Rawreth, Ramsden Bell House, Rochford, Romford, Ramsey, Rainham, Raydon, Saffron Walden, Southweald, Southchurch, Southminster, Sandon, Sible Hedingham, Stanford Rivers, Sturmer, Great Stambridge, Steeple Bumstead, Sutton, Stanway, Stifford, Terling, Tolleshunt Major, Thorpe le Soken, Tillingham, Thundersley, Tolleshunt D'Arcy, Tendring, Upminster, Waltham Abbey, Waltham Holy Cross, Wickham, Wormingfield, Weathersfield, Wix, White Colne, Walton, Weeley, Great Wakering, Walthamstow, Little Wakering, Little Waltham, Woodford, Witham, Writtle, Great Yeldham.

Gloucestershire
Gloucestershire County Record Office. Total settlement administrative units: 431.

Arlingham, Awre, Alstone, Arle, Alderton, Aston-upon-Carvant, Ashchurch, Avening, Aston, Bishop's Cleve, Badgeworth, Bisley, Bristol (St Peter), Great Barrington, Bibury, Blockley, Great Badminton, Barnwood, Boddington, Brockworth, Bourton on the Water, Brockhampton, Boulsdon, Brimpsfield, Charfield, Charlton, Chedworth, South Cerney, Chipping Campden, Coln St Dennis, Cheltenham, Coln Rogers, Cirencester, Coberley,

Cold Aston, Clifton, Cam, Cowley, Cerney Wick, Deerhurst, Duntisborne Abbots, Dymock, Dixton, Dowdeswell, Dumbleton, Eastington, Elmstone Hardwicke, Eastleach Martin, Foxcote, Fiddington, Gloucester (St John the Baptist, St Michael), Gotherington, Hawkesbury, Huntley, Up Hatherley, Highnam Over, Haresfield, Down Hatherley, Kings Stanley, Kempsford, Kingswood, Leonard Stanley, Lydney, Leigh, Leckhampton, Lassington, Mickleton, Matson, Mitcheldean, Moreton Valence, Minchinhampton, Newland, Newnham, North Nibley, Newent, Norton, Painswick, Prestbury, Preston, Rodborough, Redmarley, Saintbury, Upper Slaughter, Slimbridge, Stinchcombe, St Briavels, Shurdington, Sudeley Tenements, Upper Swell, Stroud, Staverton, Southam, Sevenhampton, Standish, Sandhurst, Sherborne, Shipton Oliffe, Salperton, Swindon, Tetbury, Tirley, Twigworth, Tredington, Tewkesbury, Thornbury, Todenham, Upton, Uckington, Wickwar, Woolaston, Westbury-on-Severn, Whaddon, Whittington, Winchcomb, Yanworth.

Hampshire
Hampshire County Record Office, City of Portsmouth Record Office, and City of Southampton Record Office. Total settlement administrative units: 304.

Andover, Appleshaw, West Aston, Amport, Alverstoke, Alton, Bramshaw, Bramley, Basing, Barton Stacey, Baughurst, Burghclere, Broughton, Bishop's Waltham, Basingstoke, Christchurch, Chilbolton, Lower Clatford, Eling, Ellingham, Ecchinswell, Fordingbridge, Farnborough, Fareham, Gosport, Heckfield, Hambledon, Holdenhurst, Highclere, Hound, Kingsclere, Kimpton, Langley, Longparish, Mattingley with Hazeley, Mortimer West End, Nataly Scures, Nether Wallop, Ovington, Petersfield, Portsmouth (St Thomas), Privett, Preston Candover, Portchester, Rockbourne, Romsey Extra, St Mary Bourne, Soberton, Southampton (St Mary, St Michael, All Saints), Stockbridge, South Stoneham, West Sherborne, South Town, Shipton, Timsbury, Titchfield, Tufton, Twyford, Up Nataly, Vernham's Dean, Wickham, Widley, Wymering, Winton, Winchester (St John, St Mary Kalendar, St Maurice, St Michael, St Peter Chesil, St Swithin-upon-Kingsgate, St Thomas), Woodcott.

Herefordshire
Hereford and Worcester County Record Office. Total settlement administrative units: 280.

Aston Ingham, Abbey Dore, Aymestrey, Barton, Bridstow, Bromyard, Bodenham, Clifford, Clifton, Callow, Colwall, Clodock, Eye, Frome, Hereford (St Peter, St John the Baptist, All Saints), Kington, Kingsland, Kilpeck, Ledbury, Linton, Longtown, Lyonshall, Moccas, Mathon, Great Malvern, Newton, Ocle, Orcop, Pitchard, Peterstow, Ross, Sellack, Stoke Edith, Stanway, Titley, Upton Bishop, Wellington, Whitchurch, Whitbourne, Yarpole.

Hertfordshire
Hertfordshire County Record Office. Total settlement administrative units: 149.

Ayot St Peter, Albury, Ashwell, Aldenham, Aspenden, Great Amwell, Barkway, Broxbourne, Berkhamstead, Baldock, Barnet, Brickendon, Bishops Hatfield, Bushey, Codicote, Chipping Barnet, Cheshunt, Caldecote, Essendon, Great Gaddesden, Little Gaddesden, Hertingfordbury, Great Hormead, Hoddesdon, Hemel Hempstead, Hemingford Grey, Hertford (All Saints, St Andrews, St John), Hitchin, Little Hadham, Hunsdon, Hadley, Hexton, Hudnall, Ickleford, North Mimms, South Mimms, Monken Hadley, Norton, Pelham, Pirton, Ridge, Radwell, Royston, Southweald, St Albans, Shenley, Stevenage, Stapleford, Standstead Abbotts, Sandon, Therfield, Totteridge, Watton, Wallington, Wheathampstead, Ware, Welwyn, Wormely, Wilstone.

Huntingdonshire
Cambridge County Record Office (Huntingdon branch). Total settlement administrative units: 107.

Alconbury, Abbotsley, Alwalton, Bythorn, Buckworth, Buckden, Brampton, Bluntisham, Bury, Broughton, Conington, Great Catworth, Colne, Diddington, Easton, Ellington, Eynesbury, Elton, Fletton, Farcet, Fenstanton, Folksworth, Great Gransden, Great Gidding, Little Gidding, Godmanchester, Grafham, Hemingford Grey, Hemingford Abbots, Hail Weston, Hilton, Huntingdon (St John and All Saints, St Mary), Holywell-cum-Needingworth, Holme, Houghton, Haddon, Hartford, Kimbolton, Kings Ripton, Keyston, Leighton, Molesworth, Offord Cluney, Offord Darcy, Orton Waterville, Great Paxton, Low Papworth, Ramsey, Sawtry, Spaldwick, Stanground, St Ives, St Neots, Great Stukeley, Little Stukeley, Great Staughton, Sibson cum Stibbington, Stonely, Stow, Steeple Gidding, Stibbington, Stilton, Tetworth, Upwood, Upton, Woodhurst, Wistow, Wennington, Wandesford, Old Weston, Water Newton, Warboys, Wood Walton, Yaxley, Yelling.

Kent
Kent County Archives Office. Total settlement administrative units: 420.

Beckenham, Boxley, Canterbury, Chatham, Capel, Chislehurst, Cranbrook, Crayford, Chatham, Cudham, Deptford (St Paul), Dartford, Dover (St James the Apostle), Eynsford, West Farleigh, Gillingham, Harrietsham, Hothfield, Langley, Loose, Lewisham, Maidstone, Stone, Sittingbourne.

Leicestershire and Rutland
Leicestershire County Record Office. Total settlement administrative units: 387.

Ashby de la Zouch, Aylstone, Barrow upon Soar, Belton, Breedon, Belgrave, Billesdon, Bisbrooke, Bottesford, Bitteswell, Burton on the Wolds, Burton Overy, Carlton, Castle Donington, Coleorton, Congerstone, South Croxton, Cossington, Countesthorpe, Claybrooke, Desford, Evington, Eastwell, Exton, Earl Shilton, Empingham, Frisby, Glen Magna, Gumley, Hambleton, Hugglescote, Humberstone, Houghton on the Hill, Heather, Hoby, Hallaton, Harby, Hinckley, Hathern, Ibstock, Knaptoft, Kilby, Kirby Bellars, Kirkby Mallory, South Kilworth, Leicester, Lubenham, Loughborough, Lutterworth, Lyddington, East Langton, Melton Mowbray, Measham, Mountsorrel, Markfield, Norton juxta Twycross, Newton Burgoland, Nether Broughton, Oadby, Osbaston, Peckleton, Pickworth, Plungar, Quorndon, Ratcliffe Culey, Redmile, Shepshed, Sapcote, Sibstone, Sheepy, Sibson, Stoke Dry, Stoke Golding, Swannington, Syston, Sproxton, Stony Stanton, Tur Langton, Thurcaston, Thornton, Thurmaston, Uppingham, Ullesthorpe, Whitwick, Wigstone Magna, Worthington.

London and Middlesex
Greater London Record Office, Westminster City Library (Archives Department), Lambeth Archives Department. Total settlement administrative units: 223.

Acton, Aldgate (St Botolph), Aldersgate (St Ann), Balham, Brentford, Bow (St Mary), Bermondsey (St Mary Magdalen), Bloomsbury (St James), Bethnal Green (St Matthew), Bromely (St Leonard), Cheshunt, St Clement Danes, Camberwell, Clerkenwell (St James), Covent Garden, Clapham, Chelsea (St Luke), Chiswick, Cripplegate, Clapton, Deptford (St Nicholas, St Paul), Ealing, Eltham, Enfield, Enfield Chase, Euston, Edmonton, Friern Barnet, Finchley, Fenchurch, Greenford, St Giles without Cripplegate, St Giles-in-the-Fields, St George Hanover Square, St George the Martyr, Greenwich, Harmondsworth, Harrow-on-the-Hill, Hayes, Hillingdon, Hampstead (St John), Hackney (St John), Hendon, Hatton, Hornsey, Hammersmith, Heston, Holborn (St Andrew), Highgate, Isleworth, Islington (St Mary), Kensington, Kentish Town, St Luke, Lambeth, London Bridge, Ludgate, St Lawrence Jewry, Mile End, St Martin-in-the-Fields, St Marylebone, Norwood, Newington, Paddington, St Pancras, Poplar (All Saints), Piccadilly, Rotherhithe, Ruislip, Strand, Stanmore, Shoreditch (St Leonard), Stepney (St Dunstan), Stanwell, Southwark (St Saviour), Staines, Stoke Newington (St Mary), Streatham, Tottenham, Tooting Graveney, Uxbridge, Walworth, Wandsworth, Whitechapel (St Mary), Westminster (St James, St Margaret), West Ham, Woolwich (St Mary), Wimbledon, West Wretham.

Monmouthshire
Gwent County Record Office. Total settlement administrative units: 151.

Abergavenny, Aberystruth, Bedwelty, Caerleon, Chepstow, Clytha, Caerwent, Chapell Hill, Caldicot, Clawrplwyf, Grosmont, Gwehelog, Graig, Itton, Llanellen, Llandenny, Llanbadock, Llangattock, Llanarth, Llangoven, Llangstone, Llanhilleth, Llanllowell, Llansoy, Llanishen, Llanover, Llanthony, Mathern, Monkswood, Monmouth, Machen, Mynyddyslwyn, Nash, Newport, Penmaen, Panteague, Raglan, Risca, St Woollos, St Briavels, Shirenewton, Trelleck, Trevethin, Usk, Wolves Newton.

Norfolk
Norfolk County Record Office. Total settlement administrative units: 745.

Anmer, Bressingham, Old Buckenham, Beeston, East Bilney, West Bilney, Bacton, West Beckham, Brampton, Carbrooke, Cockley Cley, Crimplesham, Caston, Croxton, Dickleburgh, Dunston, Diss, Downham Market, Denton, Denver, Edingthorpe, Emneth, Foulden, Feltwell, Foulsham, Gooderston,

Gillingham, Garboldisham, Holkham, Hilgay, Honingham, Hockwold-cum-Wilton, Hillington, Hitcham, Harpley, Heacham, Ickburgh, Kings Lynn (St Margaret), Kirby Bedon, Kirby Cane, Kenninghall, Langham, Limpenhoe, Lexham, Lynford, South Lynn, North Lopham, Mundford, Mattishall, Great Melton, Northwold, Norwich (St Andrew, St George, St Gregory, St Michael, St Peter), Palgrave, Poringland, Roydon, Rockland All Saints, Reymerston, Scottow, Santon, Snetterton, Shingham, Stanford, Stradsett, Stoke Holy Cross, Sturston, Stoke Ferry, Sedgeford, Shelfanger, Starston, Sparham, Swaffham, Stratton, Scole, Saxlingham, Swannington, Thwaite, Thornham, Thetford (St Mary, St Peter), Tottington, Trowse with Newton, Walcott, Watlington, Winfarthing, Wilton, Winston, Witton, North Walsham, Wretham, Weeting, Walsoken, Great Yarmouth.

Northamptonshire
Northamptonshire County Record Office. Total settlement administrative units: 333.

Aynhoe, Ashton, Addington, Ashley, Abington, Ashby St Ledgers, Benefield, Bainton, Bugbrooke, Blisworth, Braunston, Upper Boddington, Bozeat, Bamwell All Saints, Braybrooke, Bradfield on Green, Brigstock, Great Brington, Brixworth, Brackley, Brafield, Brampton Ash, Broughton, Byfield, Clopton, Catworth Magna, Corby (St John), Cogenhoe, Castle Ashby, Corby, Cotterstock, Chelston, Chelveston cum Caldecott, Cottingham, Chacombe, Carlton, Daventry, Desborough, Denford, Earl's Barton, Finedon, Glinton, Guilsborough, Harlestone, East Haddon, West Haddon, Little Houghton, Hardingstone, Helpstone, Islip, Kettering, Kings Sutton, Lowick, Longthorpe, Laxton, Middleton Cheney, Moulton, Northampton, Oundle, Great Oxendon, Pattishall, Peterborough (St John the Baptist), Passenham, Pottersbury, Ringstead, Rushton, Rothwell, Roade, Rushden, Sudborough, Sibson, Stanion, Thrapston, Thurning, Wilby, Weldon, Wicken, Wellingborough, Warmington, Wootton, Welford, Wollaston, Wakerley, Whilton, Wansford, Winwick, Walgrave, Wappenham, Whitfield, Whiston, Woodford, Werrington, Little Weldon, Yardley Hastings, Yardley Gobion.

Nottinghamshire
Nottinghamshire County Record Office. Total settlement administrative units: 260.

Arnold, Barton, Beeston, Bleasby, Blyth, Upper Broughton, Bothamsall, Cromwell, Costock, Cotgrave, East Drayton, Elkesley, Granby, Harworth, Hodstock, Keyworth, Laxton, South Leverton, East Leake, Mansfield, West Markham, Misson, Mansfield Woodhouse, Morton, Newark, Nottingham (St Mary), Norwell, Normanton, Ollerton, Rempstone, Ranskill, Ruddington, Shelford, Selston, Southwell, Strelley, Scrooby, Syerston, Sutton, Upton, Wysal, Walkeringham, Willoughby on the Wolds.

Oxfordshire
Bodleian Library (Department of Western Manuscripts), Oxfordshire County Record Office. Total settlement administrative units: 297.

Aston, Adderbury West, Adderbury East, Alvescot, Brightwell Baldwin, Benson, Bensington, Burford, Bloxham, Bampton, Bicester, Banbury, Brize Norton, Blackbourton, Charlbury, Charlton, Cogges, Claydon, Chalgrove, Chinnor, Chipping Norton, Culham, Chadlington, Chislehampton, Dorchester, Dunstice, Eynsham, Fringford, Fulbrook, Garsington, Henley on Thames, Hanborough, Hook Norton, Harpsden, Headington, Haseley, Kinston Blount, Kidlington, Kingham, Lewknor, Milton, Marsh Baldon, Minster Lovell, Northmoor, Northleigh, Oxford (St Clement, St Ebbe, St Giles, St Mary, St Peter, St Aldate), Rotherfield Greys, South Stoke, Souldern, Stoke Lyne, Stratton Audley, Stanton Harcourt, Swinbrook, Sarsden, Stokenchurch, Shipton-on-Cherwell, Swalcliffe, Swinbrooke, Stanton St John, Shiplake, Taynton, Tetsworth, Thame, Towersey, Watlington, Warborough, Wolvercote, Woodstock, Witney, Wootton, Wheatley.

Shropshire
Shropshire County Record Office. Total settlement administrative units: 236.

Acton Burnell, Bucknell, Burlington, Bridgnorth (St Leonard), Bromfield, Cardington, Cheswardine, Claverley, Chetwynd, Condover, Cleobury Mortimer, Drayton-in-Hales, Eaton Under Heywood, Grindle, Hanmer, High Ercall, Hodnet, Kinnerley, Loppington, Mainstone, Marbury, Melverley, Madeley, Moreton Corbet, Great Ness, Prees, Pontesbury, Ryton, Shawbury, Smethcott, Stokesay, Stanton Lacy, Stoke on Tern, Stapleton, Stanton, Great Wollaston, Wellington, Wrockwardyne, Wem, Whixall.

Somerset
Somerset County Record Office. Total settlement administrative units: 487.

Ashcott, Axbridge, Bath, Babcary, Baltonsborough, Broadway, Batcombe, Beckington, Bridgwater, Bishop's Hull, Broomfield, West Buckland, Carhampton, Charlton Mackrell, Chew Magna, Clapton, Croscombe, Congresbury, Chiselborough, Chilton, Ditcheat, Enmore, Fitzhead, Fiddington, Frome Selwood, Grenton, Huish Episcopi, Hemington, Halse, Hutton, Kewstoke, Locking, Mark, Misterton, Norton St Philip, Othery, Penselwood, Pitney, Queen Camel, St George, St Michael Church, Somerton, Shepton Mallet, Staple Fitzpaine, Weare, Winscombe, Wootton, Winsford, Worle, Yeovil.

Suffolk
East and West Suffolk County Record Offices. Total settlement administrative units: 509.

Acton, Great Ashfield, Alderton, Aspall, Bradfield, Bardwell, Burgh, Brettenham, Boxford, Barrow, Bradfield Combust, Beyton, Great Barton, Brent Eleigh, Bramfield, Baylham, Great Bradley, Little Bradley, Belstead, Barking, Barton Mills, Brandon, Brockford, Little Barton, Bradwell, Beccles, Blundeston, Brantham, Burgate, Bury St Edmunds (St James, St Mary), Barningham, Bacton, Badwell Ash, Belton, Brome, Bungay, Badingham, Combs, Clare, Cosford, Cockfield, Cotton, Coldham Hall, Coddenham, Cavendish, Culford, Cowlinge, Cavenham, Capel, Crowfield, Creeting St Mary, Debenham,

Depden, Denston, Drinkstone, Denham, Eriswell, Elden, Elmswell, Exning, Elmsett, Edwardstone, Eye, East Bergholt, Finningham, Framlingham, Framsden, Great Finborough, Felsham, Farnham, Fakenham, Fornham All Saints, Freckenham, Great Glenham, Groton, Gislingham, Gazeley, Gipping, Gosbeck, Grundisburgh, Hadleigh, Hawstead, Harleston, Haverhill, Higham, Horham, Hilton, Hintlesham, Hundon, Hardwick, Horningsheath, Henley, Hasketon, Helmingham, Hemingstone, Haughley, Ipswich (St Clement, St Margaret, St Mary, St Matthew, St Nicholas, St Peter), Ixworth, Ingham, Icklingham, Kettleburgh, Kenton, Kersey, Lakenheath, Lidgate, Lavenham, Lawshall, Long Melford, Mettingham, Metfield, Mickfield, Moulton, Mildenhall, Mendlesham, Monks Eleigh, Milden, Mellis, Newmarket, Needham Market, Norton, Nayland, Newton, Oakley, Occold, Onehouse, Pakenham, Polstead, Peasenhall, Palgrave, Preston, Redgrave, Risbridge, Rishangles, Rickinghall Superior, Risby, Redlingfield, Rattlesden, Sudbury, Snape, Stonham Aspall, Stowmarket, Earl Stonham, Stratford, Little Stonham, Stuston, Stowupland, Stanningfield, Saxmundham, Stansfield, Stanton, Santon Downham, Great Saxham, Little Saxham, Stradbrooke, Thetford (St Cuthbert), Thorndon, Thwaite, Great Thurlow, Thorpe, Thurston, Little Thurlow, Thorpe Morieux, Thornham Parva, Thornham Magna, Wingfield, Wyverstone, Worlingworth, Wetheringsett-cum-Brockford, Wickham Skeith, Wickham Market, Wortham, Wattisfield, Wickhambrook, Worlington, Walsham-le-Willows, Little Waldingfield, Great Waldingfield, Woolpit, Wangford, Westley, Westhall, Great Wratting, Whepstead, Walpole, Great Welnetham, Wetherden.

Surrey

Surrey County Record Office (Kingston upon Thames), and Guildford Muniment Room. Total settlement administrative units: 158.

Albury, Ashstead, Battersey, Betchworth, Bishopsgate, Camberwell, Cheam, Croydon, Caterham, Clapham, Carshalton, Cranley, Cobham, Christchurch, Ewell, Epsom, Godalming, Godstone, Guildford, Hook, Horsley, Kingston-on-Thames, Mitcham, Morden, Merton, Newington, Peckham, Richmond, Reigate, Sutton, Tooting, Thorpe, Wandsworth, Wallington, Walton-on-Thames, Warlingham, Walworth.

Warwickshire

Warwick County Record Office. Total settlement administrative units: 263.

Alcester, Aston Cantlow, Astley, Ansley, Austrey, Bedworth, Barston, Berkswell, Butler's Marston, Bulkington, Claverdon, Corley, Cubbington, Little Compton, Dunchurch, Exhall, Foleshill, Fenny Compton, Fulbrook, Hampton-in-Arden, Hatton, Hillmorton, Hartshill, Kenilworth, Kingsbury, Kineton, Kinwarton, Langley, Leamington Hastings, Monk's Kirby, Newbold-on-Avon, Nether Whitacre, Newbold Pacey, Nuneaton, Newton Regis, Great Packington, Little Packington, Quinton, Radford, Rugby, Rowington, Southam, Tanworth, Tredington, Ufton, Wellesbourne Hastings, Welford-on-Avon, Weston-under-Weatherley, Willington.

Wiltshire
Wiltshire County Record Office. Total settlement administrative units: 335.

Alderbury, Alvediston, West Ashton, Bradford-on-Avon, Beckington, Baydon, North Bradley, Bashwill, Bromham, Corsley, Calne, Chippenham, Cricklade, Castle Eaton, Great Cheverell, Devizes, Dauntsey, Downton, Ebbesbourne, Enford Pewsey, Eastrop, Enford, Froxfield, Fifield Bavant, Fyfield, Little Hinton, Hilmarton, Heywood, Highworth, Hilperton, Horningsham, Hankerton, Lacock, Longbridge Deverill, Lydiard Millicent, Malmesbury, Minety, Marlborough, Manton, Nettleton, Nunton, Norton Bavant, Norton, Ogbourne, Pinkney, Potterne, Poulton, Patney, Pewsey, Ramsbury, Stratford sub Castle, Staunton, Salisbury (St Edmund), Swindon, Shaw, Seend, Steeple Aston, Great Somerford, Little Somerford, Sherston Magna, Tytherton Lucas, Trowbridge, Wokingham, Wilton, Westbury, Wroughton, Winkfield, Westport St Mary, Walcott.

Worcestershire
Hereford and Worcester County Record Office. Total settlement administrative units: 225.

Astley, Bengeworth, Bishampton, Bredon, Bromsgrove, Bredons Hardwicks, Bedwardine, Beckford, Cow Honeybourne, Church Lench, Claines, Castlemorton, Droitwich, Evesham, Hallow, Hanley Child, Hanley Castle, Hanbury, Kemerton, Kidderminster, Knightwick, Kempley, Lye, Leigh, Great Malvern, Ombersley, Pendock, Pershore, Powick, Redmarley, Ripple, Sandford, Strensham, Upton, Welland, Worcester.

Government reports
S.C. to Consider the Laws of Poor Relief and Settlement, IX, 1775.
S.C. on the Returns made by the Overseers of the Poor, IX, 1777.
Abstract of Returns made by the Overseers of the Poor, IX, 1787.
Abstract of Answers and Returns . . . Relative to the Expense and Maintenance of the Poor, VIII, 1803–4.
S.C. on the State of the Woollen Manufacture, III, 1806.
S.C. on Apprenticeship, IV, 1812–13.
Report from the Committee on Poor Houses and Poor Rates, III, 1813.
S.C. on Parish Apprentices, V, 1814–15.
Report from the Committee on the Nature and Effect of the Game Laws, IV, 1816.
S.C. of the House of Commons on the Poor Laws, VI, 1817.
S.C. of the House of Lords on the Poor Laws, V, 1818.
S.C. on the Poor Laws, V, 1818.
S.C. on the Poor Laws, II, 1819.
S.C. on Apprenticeship, II, 1820.
Report on the Causes of Agricultural Distress, IX, 1821.
S.C. on the Vagrancy Laws, IV, 1821.
S.C. on the Poor Rates, IV, 1821.

S.C. on the Poor Rates, V, 1822.
S.C. on Vagrancy, XXII, 1822.
S.C. on the Poor Rates, V, 1823.
S.C. on Vagrancy, XV, 1823.
S.C. on Agricultural Labourers' Wages, and the Condition and Morals of Labourers in that Employment, VI, 1824.
S.C. on Artisans and Machinery, V, 1824.
S.C. on Vagrancy, XIX, 1824.
Abstract of Return on Labourers' Wages, XIX, 1825.
S.C. on Vagrancy, XXI, 1825.
S.C. on Emigration, IV, 1826.
S.C. on Criminal Commitments and Convictions, VI, 1826–7.
S.C. on Emigration, V, 1826–7.
S.C. on the Law of Parochial Settlements, IV, 1828.
S.C. on Irish and Scottish Vagrants, IV, 1828.
S.C. on the Relief of Able-Bodied Persons for the Poor Rates, IV, 1828.
S.C. on Criminal Commitments and Convictions, VI, 1828.
S.C. of the House of Lords on the Poor Laws, VIII, 1830–1.
S.C. on Vagrancy, XLIV, 1831–2.
S.C. on Vagrancy, XVI, 1833.
S.C. on Irish Vagrants, XXXII, 1833.
S.C. on Agriculture, V, 1833.
Extracts from Information Received by Poor Law Commissioners, 1833.
Poor Law Report, XXVII–XXXVIII, 1834.
S.C. on the Handloom Weavers, X, 1834.
S.C. on Vagrancy, XLVII, 1835.
S.C. on the Causes and Extent of Agricultural Distress, VIII, 1836.
Report of the Poor Law Commissioners, XXIX, 1836.
S.C. of the House of Lords on the State of Agriculture, VIII, 1836.
S.C. of the House of Lords on Agriculture, V, 1837.
S.C. on the Poor Law Amendment Act, XVII, 1837, pt I.
S.C. on the Poor Law Amendment Act, XVIII, 1837–8, pts I, II, and III.
S.C. of the House of Lords on the Poor Law Amendment Act, XIX, 1837–8.
Report on Means to Establish a Constabulary Force, XIX, 1839.
Report on the Handloom Weavers, XXIII, 1840.
S.C. on Vagrancy, XXI, 1841.
Return of Persons who were Removed from Agricultural Districts to Manufacturing Districts, XLV, 1843.
Report on the Employment of Women and Children in Agriculture, XII, XV, 1843.
Return on Insane Paupers, XXI, 1843.
S.C. on the Labouring Poor, XLV, 1843.
S.C. on the Allotment System, VII, 1843.
Ages and Descriptions of Persons Committed for Trial for Incendiary Offences in Norfolk and Suffolk, 1844.
S.C. on Enclosure, V, 1844.
S.C. on Vagrancy, VII, XXXVI, 1846.
S.C. on Settlement and Poor Removal, VIII, XI, 1847.
S.C. on Vagrancy, LIII, 1847–8.
S.C. on Agricultural Customs, VII, 1848.

Reports to the Poor Law Board on the Laws of Settlement and Removal, XXVII, 1850.

Report of George Coode to the Poor Law Board on the Law of Settlement and Removal of the Poor, XXVI, 1851.

S.C. on Vagrancy, XLVI, 1851.

Return of Medical Officers under the Poor Law, LXXXIV, 1852–3.

S.C. on Police, XXXVI, 1852–3.

S.C. on Irremovable Poor, VII, 1859.

S.C. on Children's Employment, XVIII, 1863.

Return on Aged Married Couples in Workhouses, LII, 1863.

S.C. on Vagrancy, XXXV, 1866.

Fifth Report of the Children's Employment Commission, XXIX, 1866.

Sixth Report of the Children's Employment Commission, XVI, 1867.

Report on the Employment of Women and Children in Agriculture, XVII, 1867–8.

Report on the Employment of Children, Young Persons, and Women in Agriculture, XIII, 1868–9.

R.C. on Agriculture, XIV, XV, 1882.

R.C. on the Housing of the Working Classes, XXX, 1884–5.

R.C. on Agriculture, XVII, 1895.

R.C. on the Aged Poor, XIV, XV, 1895.

Report of an Enquiry into Apprenticeship and Training in 1925–6 (H.M.S.O., 1927–8).

Pre-1900 publications and published documents

Place of publication is London unless otherwise stated.

Abney, J. E. (ed.), *The Vestry Book and Churchwardens' Accounts of St. Mary, Leicester* (1912).

Acton, W., *Prostitution, considered in its Moral, Social and Sanitary Aspects, in London and other Large Cities* (1857).

Addington, S., *An Inquiry into the Reasons for and against Inclosing Open Fields* (Coventry, 1772).

Anon., *A Political Enquiry into the Consequences of Enclosing Waste Lands, and the causes of the present high Price of Butchers' Meat* (1785).

'The impolicy of emigrating to America', *Annals of Agriculture*, XXVI (1796).

A Plain Statement of the case of the Labourer (1830), in K. E. Carpenter (advisory ed.), *The Rising of the Agricultural Labourers* (Harvard, 1972).

An Equitable Property Tax: a financial Speculation and a fair Rate of Wages to the Labouring Poor (1831).

Emigration and the Condition of the Labouring Poor (Colchester, 1832).

'Wiltshire emigrants', *Quarterly Review*, XLVI (1832).

Remarks on the Opposition to the Poor Law Amendment Bill, by a Guardian (1841).

'Autobiography of a Navvy', *Macmillan's Magazine* (Dec. 1861).

'Women as poor law guardians', *Englishwoman's Review* (1875).

'The work of women as poor law guardians', *Westminster Review*, CXXIII (1885).

Arbuthnot, J., *An Inquiry into the Connection between the Present Price of Provisions and the Size of Farms* (1773).

Atkins, C. E. (ed.), *Register of the Apprentices of the Worshipful Company of Clockmakers, 1631–1931* (1931).

Bamford, S., *Early Days* (1849).
  Passages in the Life of a Radical (1842, 1967 edn).

Barclay, C. (ed.), *Letters from the Dorking Emigrants who went to Upper Canada in the Spring of 1832* (1833).

Baring Gould, S., *In a Quiet Village* (1900).

Batchelor, T., *General View of the Agriculture of the County of Bedfordshire* (1808).

Bernard, Sir T., 'Extract from a further account of the advantages of cottagers keeping cows', *Reports of the Society for Bettering the Condition of the Poor*, II (1800).

Berryman, B. (ed.), *Mitcham Settlement Examinations, 1784–1814* (Surrey Record Society, 1973).

Bicheno, J. E., *Inquiry into the Nature of Benevolence* (1817).

Billingsley, J., *General View of the Agriculture of the County of Somerset* (1797).

Bloomfield, R., *The Farmer's Boy* (1800, Lavenham, 1971 edn).

Bobart, H. H. (ed.), *Records of the Basketmakers' Company* (1911).

Booth, C., *The Aged Poor in England and Wales* (1894).
  'Poor law statistics as used in connection with the Old Age Question', *Economic Journal*, IX (1899).

Boucherett, J., 'On the obstacles to the employment of women', *English Women's Journal*, IV (1860).
  'How to provide for surplus women', in J. Butler (ed.), *Woman's Work and Woman's Culture* (1869).

Bowley, A. L., 'The statistics of wages in the United Kingdom during the last hundred years', pt I, 'Agricultural wages', *Journal of the Royal Statistical Society*, LXI (1898).
  'The statistics of wages in the United Kingdom during the last hundred years', pt IV, 'Agricultural wages – concluded. Earnings and general averages', *Journal of the Royal Statistical Society*, LXII (1899).

Brentano, L., *On the History and Development of Gilds and the Origin of Trade Unions* (1870).

Brenton, E. P., *Letters . . . on Population, Agriculture, Poor Laws and Juvenile Vagrancy* (1832).

Brereton, Rev. C. D., *Inquiry into the Work-House System and the Laws of Maintenance in Agricultural Districts* (Norwich, 1822).
  Observations on the Administration of the Poor Laws in Agricultural Districts (1824).
  A Practical Inquiry into the Number, Means of Employment and Wages of Agricultural Labourers (Norwich, 1824).

Burke, E. *Thoughts and Details on Scarcity* (1795, 1800 edn).

Burn, R., *The Justice of the Peace and Parish Officer* (1755, 1797 edn) (4 vols.).

Caird, Sir James, *English Agriculture in 1850–1* (1851).

Campbell, R., *The London Tradesman* (1747).

Chambers, E., *Cyclopaedia: or an Universal Dictionary of the Arts and Sciences* (1741–3, 1786 edn).

Chapman, S. D. (ed.), *The Devon Cloth Industry in the Eighteenth Century* (Devon and Cornwall Record Society, 1978).

Checkland, S. G. & E. O. A. (eds.), *The Poor Law Report of 1834* (1974).

Clare, John, 'The autobiography, 1793–1824', in J. W. & A. Tibble (eds.), *The Prose of John Clare* (1951).
  Enclosure, in J. W. & A. Tibble (eds.), *John Clare, Selected Poems* (1965).
  Helpstone, in J. W. & A. Tibble (eds.), *John Clare, Selected Poems* (1965).
  The Parish: a Satire, in J. W. & A. Tibble (eds.), *John Clare, Selected Poems* (1965).
  The Village Minstrel, in J. W. & A. Tibble (eds.), *John Clare, Selected Poems* (1965).
  John Clare, Selected Poems, ed. by J. W. & A. Tibble (1965, 1979 edn).
Clark, J., 'On commons in Brecknock', *Annals of Agriculture*, XXII (1794).
'Clericus', *Pour et Contre. A Few Humble Observations upon the New Poor Law* (1841).
Cobbett, W., *Cottage Economy* (1822, Oxford, 1979 edn).
  Advice to Young Men (1830, Oxford, 1980 edn).
  Rural Rides (1830, Harmondsworth, 1967 & 1975 edns).
  (speeches in Parliament against the New Poor Law), *Hansard*, XXIII (1834), pp. 1335–7; *Hansard*, XXIV (1834), pp. 386–7.
  Legacy to Labourers (1835).
Cole, G. D. H. & M. (eds.), *The Opinions of William Cobbett* (1944).
Collyer, J., *The Parents' and Guardians' Directory* (1761).
A Country Gentleman, *The Advantages and Disadvantages of Inclosing Waste Lands and Open Fields* (1772).
Cowper, J., *An Essay proving that inclosing Commons and Commonfield-Lands is contrary to the Interest of the Nation* (1732).
Craufurd, Sir C. G., *Observations on the State of the Country since the Peace: with a supplementary Section on the Poor Laws* (1817).
Crewe, Sir G., *A Word for the Poor, and against the Present Poor Law* (Derby, 1843).
Cutlack, S. A., 'The Gnosall records, 1679–1837', in Staffordshire Record Society (ed.), *Collections for a History of Staffordshire* (Stafford, 1936).
Dale, C. (ed.), 'Wiltshire apprentices and their masters, 1710–1760', *Wiltshire Archaeological and Natural History Society*, XVII (1961).
Daly, A. (ed.), *Kingston Upon Thames Register of Apprentices, 1563–1713* (Guildford, 1974).
Darby, J., 'The farming in Dorset', *Journal of the Bath and West of England Society*, 3rd series, IV (1872).
Davies, D., *The Case of the Labourers in Husbandry* (1795).
Davison, J., *Considerations on the Poor Laws* (Oxford, 1817).
Day, W., *An Inquiry into the Poor Laws and Surplus Labour* (1833).
Defoe, D., *Giving Alms no Charity* (1704).
Dickens, C. & Chisholm, C. (eds.), 'A bundle of emigrant letters', *Household Words*, I (1850).
Dyer, G., *The Complaints of the Poor People of England* (1792).
Eden, Sir F. M., *The State of the Poor*, 3 vols. (1797).
Eliot, G., *Felix Holt* (1866, Harmondsworth, 1795 edn).
Erith, F. H., *Ardleigh in 1796* (East Bergholt, 1978).
Ferrers, Rev. J. B., *Observations on the Present Administration of the Poor Laws* (1832).
Fielding, H., *The Miser. A Comedy* (1733).
Fitzherbert, Sir A., *Book of Husbandry* (1534), ed. by W. W. Skeat (1882).

Forster, N., *Enquiry into the Present High Price of Provisions* (1767).

Frend, W., *Peace and Union recommended to the associated Bodies of Republicans and Anti-Republicans* (Cambridge, 1793).

Freshfield, E. (ed.), *Accomptes of the Churchwardens of the Paryshe of St. Christofer's in London* (1885).

Gisborne, T., *An Enquiry into the Duties of the Female Sex* (1797).

Glover, Rev. G., 'Observations on the state of pauperism', *The Pamphleteer*, X (1817).

Goodwyn, E. A. (ed.), *Selections from Norwich Newspapers, 1760–1790* (Ipswich, 1973).

Gore, M., *Allotments of Land. A letter to Landed Proprietors, on the Advantages of giving the Poor Allotments of Land* (1831).

Gosse, E., 'Thomas Hardy', *The Speaker*, 13 Sept. 1890.

Gough, R., *The History of Myddle* (written in 1701, Harmondsworth, 1981 edn).

Graham, P. A., *The Rural Exodus* (1892).

Gray, I. (ed.), *Cheltenham Settlement Examinations, 1815–1826* (Bristol and Gloucester Archaeological Society, 1968).

Greg, W. R., 'Why are women redundant?', in *Literary and Social Judgements* (Boston, 1869).

Hanway, J., *A Candid Historical Account of the Hospital for the Reception of Exposed and Deserted Young Children* (1759).

An Earnest Appeal for Mercy to the Children of the Poor (1766).

Observations on the Causes of the Dissoluteness which reigns among the Lower Classes of the People (1772).

Virtue in Humble Life, containing Reflections on the Reciprocal Duties of the Wealthy and Indigent (1774).

The Defects of the Police the Cause of Immorality (1775).

Hardy, T., *Under the Greenwood Tree* (1872, 1971 edn).

A Pair of Blue Eyes (1873, 1975 edn).

Far From the Madding Crowd (1874, 1971 edn).

The Hand of Ethelberta (1876, 1975 edn).

The Trumpet-Major (1880).

'The Dorsetshire labourer', *Longman's Magazine* (July 1883), reprinted in J. Moynahan (ed.), *The Portable Thomas Hardy* (1977).

The Mayor of Casterbridge (1886, 1968 edn).

The Woodlanders (1887, 1971 edn).

The Distracted Preacher, in *Wessex Tales* (1888, 1979 edn).

Fellow Townsmen, in *Wessex Tales* (1888, 1979 edn).

Tess of the D'Urbervilles (1891, 1970 edn).

Jude the Obscure (1896, 1969 edn).

The Well-Beloved (1897, 1975 edn).

An Indiscretion in the Life of an Heiress (first written, under the title of *The Poor Man and the Lady*, in 1867; adapted and published under its present title in *New Quarterly Magazine*, July 1878; first published (private edition of 100 copies) as a book in 1934; 1976 edn ed. by T. Coleman).

Heal, Sir A. (ed.), *The London Goldsmiths, 1200–1800* (Cambridge, 1935, 1972 edn).

Heath, F. G., *The English Peasantry* (1874).

Heath, R., *The English Peasant* (1893, Wakefield, 1978 edn).

Henslow, J. S., *Suggestions towards an Enquiry into the Present Condition of the Labouring Population of Suffolk* (Hadleigh, 1844).

Hill, R., *Home Colonies. Sketch of a Plan for the Gradual Extinction of Pauperism and For the Diminution of Crime* (1832).

Hollis, D. (ed.), *Calendar of the Bristol Apprentice Book (1532–1565)*, 2 vols., Bristol Record Society Publications, XIV (1947).

Homer, H. S., *An Essay on the Nature and Method of ascertaining the Specific Shares of Proprietors, upon the Inclosure of Common Fields* (Oxford, 1766).

Horne, R. H., 'Pictures of life in Australia', *Household Words*, I (1850).

Howell, G., 'Trades unions, apprentices and technical education', *Contemporary Review*, XXX (1877).

Howitt, W., *The Rural Life of England*, 2 vols. (1838).

Howlett, Rev. J., *Enquiry into the Influence which Enclosures have had upon the Population of England* (1786), in A. H. John (ed.), *Enclosure and Population* (Farnborough, 1973).

Enclosures a Cause of Improved Agriculture, of Plenty and Cheapness of Provisions (1787), in A. H. John (ed.), *Enclosure and Population* (Farnborough, 1973).

letter to *Annals of Agriculture*, XXV (1795), p. 609.

An Examination of Mr. Pitt's Speech in the House of Commons, Feb. 12, 1796 (1796).

Hutton, W., *History of Birmingham* (Birmingham, 1781, 1835 edn).

Ignota, 'Women in Local Administration: England and Wales', *Westminster Review*, CL (1898).

Jacob, W., 'Inquiry into the causes of agricultural distress', *The Pamphleteer*, X (1817).

James, Henry, review of Thomas Hardy, *Far From the Madding Crowd*, in *The Nation*, 24 Dec. 1874, reprinted in his *The House of Fiction* (1957, 1962 edn).

Jefferies, R., *Hodge and His Masters*, 2 vols. (1880, 1949 edn).

The Toilers of the Field (1892, 1981, edn).

Jenkinson, H. (ed.), 'Bedfordshire apprentices, 1711–1720', *Bedfordshire Historical Record Society*, IX (1925).

'Surrey apprenticeship, 1711–1731', *Surrey Record Society*, 10 (1929).

Jerram, C., *Considerations on the Impolicy and Pernicious Tendency of the Poor Laws* (1818).

John, A. H. (ed.), *Enclosure and Population* (Farnborough, 1973).

Jupp, E. B. & Pocock, W. W., *An Historical Account of the Worshipful Company of Carpenters of the City of London* (1848, 1887 edn).

Kegan Paul, C., 'The Wessex labourers', *Examiner*, 15 July 1876.

'Mr. Hardy's novels', *British Quarterly Review*, LXXIII (1881).

'The rustic of George Eliot and Thomas Hardy', *Merry England*, I (1883).

Kenealy, A., 'New view of the surplus of women', *Westminster Review*, CXXXVI (1891).

Kent, N., *Hints to Gentlemen of Landed Property* (1775).

'The great advantage of a cow to the family of a labouring man', *Annals of Agriculture*, XXXI (1798).

Kitchen, F., *Brother to the Ox: the Autobiography of a Farm Labourer* (1940, 1963 edn).

Letters from Sussex Emigrants (1833, 1837 edn).

Little, H. J., 'The agricultural labourer', *Journal of the Royal Agricultural Society*, XIV (1878).

Logan, W., *An Exposure, from Personal Observation, of Female Prostitution in London, Leeds and Rochdale, and especially in the City of Glasgow* (Glasgow, 1843).

The Great Social Evil (1871).

Maberley, Rev. F. H., *To the Poor and Their Friends* (1836).

Mackeson, C., 'Occupations and vital statistics of England and Wales', *The British Almanac and Companion* (1875).

Maclaren, C., *The Scotsman's Advice to the Labouring Classes, on the best means of raising their Wages and securing themselves and their Families against want* (Edinburgh, 1830).

MacQueen, T. P., *Thoughts and Suggestions on the Present Condition of the Country* (1830).

The State of the Nation at the close of 1830 (1831).

Markham, C. A. & Cox, J. C. (eds.), *Records of the Borough of Northampton*, 2 vols. (1898).

Marshall, Rev. H. J., *On the Tendency of the New Poor Law seriously to impair the Morals and Condition of the Working Classes* (1842).

Marshall, W., *Review and Abstract of the County Reports to the Board of Agriculture. Vol. III: The Eastern Department* (1811, York, 1818 edn).

Review of the Reports to the Board of Agriculture from the Southern and Peninsular Departments of England (York, 1817).

Martineau, H., *Poor Laws and Paupers Illustrated* (1833).

Mathieson, J. (ed.), *Counsel for Emigrants and Interesting Information from Numerous Sources with Original Letters from Canada and the United States* (Aberdeen, 1835).

Melville, R., 'Records of apprenticeship and settlement in a Berkshire village in the eighteenth century', *Transactions of the Newbury and District Field Club*, X (1954).

Moynahan, J. (ed.), *The Portable Thomas Hardy* (1977).

Newby, T. C., *Our Plague Spot* (1859).

Nicholls, Sir G., *A History of the English Poor Law, in Connection with the Legislation and other Circumstances affecting the Condition of the People* (1854, 1898 edn).

Overall, W. H. & Atkins, S. E., *Some Account of the Worshipful Company of Clockmakers of the City of London* (1881).

Paley, W., *Concise Admonitions for Youth* (1809).

Pashley, R., *Pauperism and the Poor Laws* (1852).

Pitt, W., *General View of the Agriculture of the County of Stafford* (1794, 1813 edn).

Postans, T., *Letter to Sir Thomas Baring on Causes which have produced the Present State of the Agricultural Labouring Poor* (1831).

Pyne, W. H., *Microcosm: or, a Picturesque Delineation of the Arts, Agriculture, Manufactures etc of Great Britain*, parts I and II (1808, Luton, 1974 and 1977 edns).

Radcliffe, Rev. T. (ed.), *T. W. Magrath, Authentic Letters from Upper Canada* (Dublin, 1833).

Rees, A., *Cyclopaedia: or, an Universal Dictionary of Arts and Sciences*, 4 vols. (1819–20, Trowbridge, 1972 edn).

R. F., *Observations on Pauperism* (1832).

Ricart, R., *The Maire of Bristowe is Kalendar*, ed. by L. T. Smith, Camden Society, V (1872).

Rice, R. G. (ed.), 'Sussex apprentices and their masters, 1710–1752', *Sussex Record Society*, XXVIII (1924).

Richardson, J., *A Letter to Lord Brougham . . . on an Alteration in the Poor Laws, the Employment of the People, and a Reduction of the Poor Rate* (Norwich, 1831).

Ruegg, L. H., 'The farming of Dorsetshire', *Journal of the Royal Agricultural Society*, XV (1854).

Ryan, M., *Prostitution in London, with a Comparative View of that of Paris and New York* (1839).

Scott, J., *Observations on the Present State of the Parochial and Vagrant Poor* (1773).

Sheard, M., *The Records of the Parish of Batley* (Worksop, 1894).

Smith, A., *The Wealth of Nations* (1776, 1904 edn, and Harmondsworth, 1977 edn).

Smith, K. J. (ed.), 'Warwickshire apprentices and their masters, 1710–1760', *Dugdale Society*, XXIX (1975).

Smith, T., *The Old Poor Law and the New Poor Law Contrasted* (1840).

Somerville, A., *The Whistler at the Plough* (Manchester, 1852).

Spurr, R., 'The autobiography of Robert Spurr', in R. J. Owen (ed.), *Baptist Quarterly*, XXVI (1976).

Stahlschmidt, J. C. L., *Surrey Bells and London Bell-Founders* (1884).

Stephen, G., *A Letter to the Right Hon. Lord John Russell on the Probable Increase of Rural Crime in Consequence of the Introduction of the New Poor Law and Railroad Systems* (1836).

Stevenson, W., *General View of the Agriculture of the County of Dorset* (1812).

Stewart, H., *History of the Worshipful Company of Gold and Silver Wyre-drawers, and of the Origin and Development of the Industry which the Company represents* (1891).

Stone, T., *Suggestions for Rendering the Inclosure of Common Fields and Waste Lands a Source of Population and of Riches* (1787).

Surtees, S. F. (ed.), *Emigrants' Letters from Settlers in Canada and South Australia, collected in the Parish of Banham, Norfolk* (1852).

Surtees, W., *Twenty-five Years in the Rifle Brigade* (Edinburgh, 1833).

T. A., *A Plan for Relieving the Pressure of the Poor Rates and Affording Employment to the Agricultural Poor and Improving their Condition* (1832).

Tait, W., *Magdalenism. An Enquiry into the Extent, Causes, and Consequences of Prostitution in Edinburgh* (Edinburgh, 1840).

Talbot, J. B., *The Miseries of Prostitution* (1844).

Tansley, A. J., 'On the straw-plait trade', *Journal of the Society of Arts*, IX (21 Dec. 1860).

Thompson, S. M., 'The London 'prentices', *New Monthly Magazine* (1822).

Thompson, S. P., 'The apprenticeship of the future', *Contemporary Review*, XXXVIII (1880).

Thomson, J., *The Seasons* (1744).

Tomlinson, C. (ed.), *Cyclopaedia of Useful Arts*, 2 vols. (1854).

Tonna, C. E., *The Wrongs of Woman* (1843–4).

Torrens, R., *A Paper on the Means of Reducing the Poors Rates, and of affording effectual and Permanent Relief to the Labouring Classes* (1817).

Address to the Farmers of the United Kingdom, on the low rates of Profit in Agriculture and in Trade (1831).

Townsend, Rev. J., *A Dissertation on the Poor Laws* (1786, 1971 edn).

Tuer, A. W., *Old London Street Cries* (1885, 1978 edn).
Turner, T., *The Diary of a Georgian Shopkeeper* (1925, Oxford, 1979 edn). First published in 1925 as *The Diary of Thomas Turner of East Hoathly (1754–1765)*.
Twining, L., *Workhouses and Pauperism, and Women's Work in the Administration of the Poor Law* (1898).
Vancouver, C., *General View of the Agriculture in the County of Cambridge* (1794). *General View of the Agriculture of the County of Devon* (1808, 1969 edn).
Varley, C., *The Modern Farmer's Guide, by a Real Farmer* (Glasgow, 1768).
Wakefield, E. G., *Swing Unmasked; or, the Causes of Rural Incendiarism* (1831).
Wardlaw, R., *Lectures on Female Prostitution: its nature, extent, effects, guilt, causes, and remedy* (Glasgow, 1842).
Wedge, J., *General View of the Agriculture of the County of Warwick* (1794).
White, H., *The Record of my Life: an Autobiography* (Cheltenham, 1889).
Willis, A. J. & Merson, A. L. (eds.), *A Calendar of Southampton Apprenticeship Registers, 1609–1740*, Southampton Record Society, XII (1968).
Woodforde, Rev. J., *The Diary of a Country Parson, 1758–1802* (1924–31 (5 vols.), 1935, Oxford, 1978 edn).
Young, A., *A Farmer's Letters to the People of England* (1767).
A Six Months' Tour through the North of England, 4 vols. (1770).
The Farmer's Kalendar: Containing the Business Necessary to be Performed on Various Kinds of Farms during Every Month of the Year (1771, 1778 edn).
Political Arithmetic (1774).
'General enclosure', *Annals of Agriculture*, XXXVIII (1801).
An Inquiry into the Propriety of Applying Wastes to the Better Maintenance and Support of the Poor (Bury St Edmunds, 1801).
General View of the Agriculture of the County of Norfolk (1804).
(Board of Agriculture), *General Report on Enclosures* (1808).
Autobiography, ed. by M. Betham-Edwards (1898).
Young, A. A., *The Poor Law. Is any Alteration of it Necessary or Tolerably Acceptable?* (1839).
Young, S., *The Annals of the Barber-Surgeons of London* (1890).

Post-1900 publications

Place of publication is London unless otherwise stated.
Alexander, S., Davin, A. & Hostettler, E., 'Labouring women. A reply to Eric Hobsbawm', *History Workshop*, VIII (1979).
Alford, B. W. E. & Barker, T. C., *A History of the Carpenters' Company* (1968).
Allison, K. J., 'The sheep-corn husbandry of Norfolk in the sixteenth and seventeenth centuries', *Agricultural History Review*, V (1957).
Anderson, M., *Family Structure in Nineteenth-Century Lancashire* (Cambridge, 1971).
'Household structure and the Industrial Revolution; mid nineteenth-century Preston in comparative perspective', in P. Laslett & R. Wall (eds.), *Household and Family in Past Time* (Cambridge, 1972).
'Marriage patterns in Victorian Britain: an analysis based on registration district data for England and Wales', *Journal of Family History*, I (1976).
Approaches to the History of the Western Family, 1500–1914 (1980).

Ankarloo, B., 'Agriculture and women's work: direction of change in the west, 1700–1900', *Journal of Family History*, IV (1979).

Armstrong, W. A., 'The influence of demographic factors on the position of the agricultural labourer in England and Wales, c. 1750–1914', *Agricultural History Review*, XXIX (1981).

Ashby, M. K., *Joseph Ashby of Tysoe, 1859–1919* (Cambridge, 1961, 1974 edn).

Ashton, T. S., *An Economic History of England: The Eighteenth Century* (1955). *Economic Fluctuations in England, 1700–1800* (Oxford, 1959).

Axtell, J. L., *The School Upon a Hill; Education and Society in Colonial New England* (New Haven, 1974).

Baack, B. D. & Thomas, R. P., 'The enclosure movement and the supply of labour during the Industrial Revolution', *Journal of European Economic History*, III (1974).

Baines, D. E., 'The labour supply and the labour market, 1860–1914', in R. Floud & D. McCloskey (eds.), *The Economic History of Britain since 1700*, vol. 2 (Cambridge, 1981).

Barnett, D. C., 'Allotments and the problem of rural poverty, 1780–1840', in E. L. Jones & G. E. Mingay (eds.), *Land, Labour and Population in the Industrial Revolution* (1967).

Barrell, J., *The Idea of Landscape and the Sense of Place, 1730–1840. An Approach to the Poetry of John Clare* (Cambridge, 1972).
The Dark Side of the Landscape (Cambridge, 1980).
'Geographies of Hardy's Wessex', *Journal of Historical Geography*, VIII (1982).
English Literature in History, 1730–1780. An Equal Wide Survey (1983).

Baugh, D. A., 'The cost of poor relief in south-east England, 1790–1834', *Economic History Review*, XXVIII (1975).

de Beauvoir, S., *The Second Sex* (1949, Harmondsworth, 1976 edn).

Beckett, J. V., 'Regional variation and the agricultural depression, 1730–1750', *Economic History Review*, XXXV (1982).

Beckett, J. V. & Smith, D. M., 'The land tax returns as a source for studying the English economy in the eighteenth century', *Bulletin of the Institute of Historical Research*, LIV (1981).

Bindoff, S. T., 'The making of the Statute of Artificers', in S. T. Bindoff, J. Hurstfield & C. H. Williams (eds.), *Elizabethan Government and Society* (1961).

Blaug, M., 'The myth of the old poor law and the making of the new', *Journal of Economic History*, XXIII (1963), reprinted in M. W. Flinn & T. C. Smout (eds.), *Essays in Social History* (Oxford, 1974).
'The Poor Law Report re-examined', *Journal of Economic History*, XXIV (1964).

Blease, W. L., *The Emancipation of English Women* (1910).

Booth, A., 'Food riots in the north-west of England, 1790–1801', *Past and Present*, LXXVII (1977).

Boserup, E., *Women's Role in Economic Development* (1970).

Bouquet, M. R., 'The sexual division of labour: the farm household in a Devon parish' (unpublished Ph.D. thesis, University of Cambridge, 1981).

Bray, R. A., 'The apprenticeship question', *Economic Journal*, XIX (1909).
Boy Labour and Apprenticeship (1911).

Bridenbaugh, C., *The Colonial Craftsman* (1950).

Bridges, W. E., 'Family patterns and social values in America, 1825–1875', *American Quarterly*, XVII (1965).

Brownlow, J. M. E., *Women's Work in Local Government* (1911).

Brundage, A., 'The landed interest and the New Poor Law: a reappraisal of the revolution in government', *English History Review*, LXXXVII (1972).
The Making of the New Poor Law, 1832–39 (1978).

Burnett, J., *A Social History of Housing, 1815–1970* (1978).

Butlin, R. A., 'Field systems of Northumberland and Durham', in A. R. H. Baker & R. A. Butlin (eds.), *Studies of the Field Systems in the British Isles* (Cambridge, 1973).

Bythell, D., *The Handloom Weavers* (Cambridge, 1969).
The Sweated Trades (1978).

Cairncross, A. K., 'Internal migration in Victorian England', *Manchester School*, XVII (1949).
Home and Foreign Investment, 1870–1913 (Cambridge, 1953).

Chambers, J. D., *Nottinghamshire in the Eighteenth Century* (1932).
'Enclosure and the small landowner', *Economic History Review*, X (1939).
'Enclosure and labour supply in the Industrial Revolution', *Economic History Review*, V (1953), reprinted in D. V. Glass & D. E. C. Eversley (eds.), *Population in History* (1965).

Chambers, J. D. & Mingay, G. E., *The Agricultural Revolution, 1750–1880* (1966, 1978 edn).

Chesney, K., *The Victorian Underworld* (1970, Harmondsworth, 1974 edn).

Church, R. A., 'Labour supply and innovation, 1800–1860: the boot and shoe industry', *Business History*, XII (1970).

Clark, A., *Working Life of Women in the Seventeenth Century* (1919).

Clark, P., 'Migration in England during the late seventeenth and early eighteenth century', *Past and Present*, LXXXIII (1979).

Coleman, D. C., 'Labour in the English economy of the seventeenth century', *Economic History Review*, VIII (1956).
'Growth and decay during the Industrial Revolution: the case of East Anglia', *Scandinavian Economic History Review*, X (1962).
The British Paper Industry, 1495–1860; A study in Industrial Growth (Oxford, 1958).
Courtaulds, an Economic and Social History, vol. 1 (Oxford, 1969).

Collins, E. J. T., 'Harvest technology and labour supply in Britain, 1790–1870', *Economic History Review*, XXII (1969).
'The diffusion of the threshing machine in Britain, 1790–1880', *Tools and Tillage*, II (1972).
'Migrant labour in British agriculture in the nineteenth century', *Economic History Review*, XXIX (1976).

Collins, P., review of D. Kramer (ed.), Thomas Hardy, *The Woodlanders* (Oxford, 1981 edn), in *The Times Higher Education Supplement*, 14 Aug. 1981.

Coppock, J. T., 'The changing face of England: 1850–c.1900', in H. C. Darby (ed.), *A New Historical Geography of England after 1600* (Cambridge, 1973).

Crafts, N. F. R., 'Enclosure and labour supply revisited', *Explorations in Economic History*, XV (1978).
'Income elasticities of demand and the release of labour by agriculture

during the British Industrial Revolution', *Journal of European Economic History*, IX (1980).

'National income estimates and the British standard of living debate: a reappraisal of 1801–1831', *Explorations in Economic History*, XVII (1980).

Curtler, W. H. R., *The Enclosure and Redistribution of Our Land* (Oxford, 1920).

Dale, M. K., 'London silkwomen of the fifteenth century', *Economic History Review*, IV (1932–4).

Darby, H. C. (ed.), *A New Historical Geography of England after 1600* (Cambridge, 1973, 1976 edn).

Davies, E., 'The small landowner, 1780–1832, in the light of the Land Tax Assessments', *Economic History Review*, I (1927).

Davies, S., 'Poor law administration and rural change in the Tendring Hundred of Essex, 1770–1844' (unpublished dissertation, deposited in the Library of the Cambridge Group for the History of Population and Social Structure).

Deane, P. & Cole, W. A., *British Economic Growth, 1688–1959* (Cambridge, 1962, 1967, 1969, and 1976 edns).

Dearle, N. B., *Industrial Training* (1914).

Derry, T. K., 'The repeal of the apprenticeship clauses of the Statute of Artificers', *Economic History Review*, III (1931).

Devine, T. M., 'Social stability and agrarian change in the eastern lowlands of Scotland, 1810–1840', *Social History*, III (1978).

Digby, A., 'The labour market and the continuity of social policy after 1834: the case of the eastern counties', *Economic History Review*, XXVIII (1975).

'The rural poor law', in D. Fraser (ed.), *The New Poor Law in the Nineteenth Century* (1976).

Pauper Palaces (1978).

Dobson, C. R., *Masters and Journeymen* (1980).

Dominian, J., *Marital Breakdown* (Harmondsworth, 1971).

Dony, J. C., *A History of the Straw Hat Industry* (Luton, 1942).

Douglas, M., *In the Active Voice* (1982).

Dunbabin, J. P. D., *Rural Discontent in Nineteenth-Century Britain* (1974).

Dunkley, P., 'The landed interest and the New Poor Law: a critical note', *English Historical Review*, LXXXVIII (1973).

Dunlop, O. J. & Denman, R. D., *English Apprenticeship and Child Labour: A History* (1912).

Edsall, N. C., *The Anti-Poor Law Movement, 1833–4* (1971).

Edwards, G., *From Crow-Scaring to Westminster* (1922).

Emmison, F. G., 'Poor relief accounts of two rural parishes (Northill and Eaton Socon) in Bedfordshire, *Economic History Review*, III (1931).

'Relief of the poor at Eaton Socon, Bedfordshire, 1706–1834', *Bedfordshire Historical Record Society*, XV (1933).

Ernle, Lord, *English Farming Past and Present* (1912).

Esterson, A., *The Leaves of Spring* (1970).

Eustice, A., *Thomas Hardy. Landscapes of the Mind* (1979).

Evans, G. E., *The Farm and the Village* (1969).

Fearn, H., 'The apprenticeship of pauper children in the incorporated hundreds of Suffolk', *Proceedings of the Suffolk Institute of Archaeology*, XXVI (1955).

'The financing of the poor law incorporation for the hundreds of Colneis and Carlford in the county of Suffolk, 1758–1820', *Proceedings of the Suffolk Institute of Archaeology,* XXVII (1958).

Finnegan, F., *Poverty and Prostitution: A Study of Victorian Prostitution in York* (Cambridge, 1979).

Firestone, S., *The Dialectics of Sex* (1972).

Fisher, F. J., 'The influence and development of the industrial guilds in the larger provincial towns under James I and Charles I' (unpublished M.A. thesis, University of London, 1931).

'Some experiments in company organisation in the early seventeenth century', *Economic History Review,* IV (1933).

Fleishman, A., *The English Historical Novel* (Baltimore, 1971).

Fleming, A. P. M. & Pearce, J. G., *Principles of Apprentice Training* (1916).

Fletcher, T. W., 'The Great Depression of English agriculture, 1873–1896', *Economic History Review,* XIII (1960).

Flinn, M. W., 'The Poor Employment Act of 1817', *Economic History Review,* XIV (1961).

'Trends in real wages, 1750–1850', *Economic History Review,* XXVII (1974).

'Real wage trends in Britain, 1750–1850: a reply', *Economic History Review,* XXIX (1976).

The European Demographic System, 1500–1820 (Brighton, 1981).

Fox, L., 'The Coventry guilds and trading companies – with special reference to the position of women', in *Essays in Honour of P. Chatwin,* Birmingham Archaeological Society and Dugdale Society (Oxford, 1962).

Fox, N. E., 'The spread of the threshing machine in central southern England', *Agricultural History Review,* XXVI (1978).

Fraser, D. (ed.), *The New Poor Law in the Nineteenth Century* (1976).

Freud, S., 'The most prevalent form of degradation in erotic life', in his *Collected Papers,* ed. by J. Strachey, vol. 4 (1950).

Fussell, G. E., *The English Dairy Farmer* (1966).

Fussell, G. C. & Compton, M., 'Agricultural adjustments after the Napoleonic Wars', *Economic History,* IV (1939).

Galbraith, J. K., *Annals of an Abiding Liberal* (1980).

Gash, N., 'Rural unemployment, 1815–1834', *Economic History Review,* VI (1935).

Gay, M. R., 'Aspects of Elizabethan apprenticeship', *Facts and Factors in Economic History* (Cambridge, Mass., 1932).

George, M. D., *London Life in the Eighteenth Century* (1925, 1965 edn).

England in Transition (1931, Harmondsworth, 1965 edn).

Gilboy, E. W., *Wages in Eighteenth-Century England* (Cambridge, Mass., 1934).

Ginter, D. E., 'A wealth of problems with the land tax', *Economic History Review,* XXXV (1982).

Gittings, R., *Young Thomas Hardy* (1975, Harmondsworth, 1980 edn).

The Older Hardy (1978, Harmondsworth, 1980 edn).

Gonner, E. C. K., *Common Land and Enclosure* (1912).

Gourvish, T. R., 'Flinn and real wage trends in Britain, 1750–1850: a comment', *Economic History Review,* XXIX (1976).

Granger, C. W. J. & Elliott, C. M., 'Wheat prices and markets in the eighteenth century', *Economic History Review,* XX (1967).

Gray, H. L., 'Yeoman farming in Oxfordshire from the sixteenth to the nineteenth century', *Quarterly Journal of Economics*, XXIV (1910).

English Field Systems (Cambridge, Mass., 1915, 1959 edn).

Greenfield, S. M., 'Industrialization and the family in sociological theory', *American Journal of Sociology*, LXVII (1961).

Gregor, I. C. S., *The Great Web; the Form of Hardy's Major Fiction* (1974).

Grigg, D. B., 'The Land Tax Returns', *Agricultural History Review*, XI (1963).

'An index of regional change in English farming', *Transactions of the Institute of British Geographers*, XXXVI (1965).

The Agricultural Revolution in South Lincolnshire (Cambridge, 1966).

Guerard, A. L. (ed.), *Hardy – A Collection of Critical Essays* (Englewood Cliffs, 1963).

Habakkuk, H. J., 'English landownership, 1680–1740', *Economic History Review*, X (1940).

'La Disparition du paysan anglais', *Annales*, XX (1965).

Haggard, R., *Rural England* (1902).

Haines, M., *Fertility and Occupation. Population Patterns in Industrialization* (1979).

Hajnal, J., 'European marriage patterns in perspective', in D. V. Glass & D. E. C. Eversley (eds.), *Population in History* (1965).

Hakim, C., 'Sexual divisions within the labour force: occupational segregation', *Employment Gazette* (November 1978).

Hamilton, H., *The English Brass and Copper Industries to 1800* (1967).

Hamilton, R., *The Liberation of Women* (1978).

Hammond, J. L. & B., *The Village Labourer* (1911, 1978 edn).

The Town Labourer (1917).

Lord Shaftesbury (1923, Harmondsworth, 1939 edn).

Hampson, E. M., 'Settlement and removal in Cambridgeshire, 1662–1834', *Cambridge Historical Journal*, II (1926–8).

The Treatment of Poverty in Cambridgeshire, 1597–1834 (Cambridge, 1934).

Hardy, F., *The Life and Times of Thomas Hardy, 1840–1928* (1928, 1962 edn).

Hareven, T. K., 'The history of the family as an interdisciplinary field', *Journal of Interdisciplinary History*, II (1971).

'The family as process: the historical study of the family cycle', *Journal of Social History*, VII (1974).

'Modernization and family history: perspectives on social change', *Signs*, II (1976).

Harris, A., *The Rural Landscape of the East Riding of Yorkshire* (1961).

Harrison, B., 'Underneath the Victorians', *Victorian Studies*, X (1967).

Harrison, F., *The Dark Angel* (Glasgow, 1977).

Hasbach, W., *The History of the English Agricultural Labourer* (1908).

Havinden, M., 'Agricultural progress in open-field Oxfordshire', *Agricultural History Review*, IX (1961).

Henriques, F., *The Immoral Tradition: Prostitution and Society* (1965).

Henriques, U., 'How cruel was the Victorian poor law?', *Historical Journal*, XI (1968).

Hewitt, M., *Wives and Mothers in Victorian Industry* (1958).

Hey, D. G., *The Rural Metalworkers of the Sheffield Region: A study of Rural Industry before the Industrial Revolution* (Leicester, 1972).

An English Rural Community; Myddle under the Tudors and Stuarts (Leicester, 1974).

Hiley, M., *Victorian Working Women: Portraits from Life* (1979).

Hobsbawn, E. J., 'The British standard of living, 1790–1850', *Economic History Review*, X (1957), reprinted in his *Labouring Men* (1964).

'The nineteenth-century London labour market', in R. Glass (ed.), *London: Aspects of Change*, ed. by the Centre of Urban Studies (1964).

'The standard of living debate: a postscript', in his *Labouring Men* (1964).

'The tramping artisan', in his *Labouring Men* (1964).

'Man and woman in socialist iconography', *History Workshop*, VI (1978).

Hobsbawm, E. J. & Rudé, G., *Captain Swing* (1969, 1973 edn).

Hobsbawm, E. J. & Scott, J. W., 'Political shoemakers', *Past and Present*, LXXXIX (1980).

Holdenby, C., *The Folk of the Furrow* (1913).

Holderness, B. A., 'Capital formation in agriculture', in S. Pollard & J. P. P. Higgins (eds.), *Aspects of Capital Investment in Great Britain, 1750–1850: a Preliminary Survey* (1971).

'"Open" and "Close" parishes in England in the eighteenth and nineteenth centuries', *Agricultural History Review*, XX (1972).

'Rural tradesmen, 1660–1850: a regional study in Lindsey', *Lincolnshire History and Archaeology*, VII (1972).

'Productivity trends in English agriculture, 1600–1850: observations and preliminary results' (unpublished paper presented to the 1978 International Economic History Conference at Edinburgh, in the session Factor Productivity in Agriculture in Industrializing Economies).

Hopkins, E., 'Were the Webbs wrong about apprenticeship in the Black Country?', *West Midland Studies*, VI (1973).

Horn, P., 'The Buckinghamshire straw-plait trade in Victorian England', *Records of Buckinghamshire*, XIX (1971).

'Pillow lacemaking in Victorian England: the experience of Oxfordshire', *Textile History*, 3 (1972).

'Child workers in the pillow-lace and straw-plait trades of Victorian Buckinghamshire and Bedfordshire', *Historical Journal*, XVII (1974).

Labouring Life in the Victorian Countryside (Bristol, 1976).

The Rural World (1980).

Hosford, W. H., 'The enclosure of Sleaford', *Lincolnshire Architectural and Archaeological Society*, VII (1957).

Hoskins, W. G., 'The Leicestershire farmer in the seventeenth century', *Agricultural History*, XXV (1951).

The Midland Peasant: The Economic and Social History of a Leicestershire Village (1957).

'Harvest fluctuations and English economic history, 1620–1759', *Agricultural History Review*, XVI (1968).

Hostettler, E., 'Gourley Steell and the sexual division of labour', *History Workshop*, IV (1977).

Houston, R. & Snell, K. D. M., 'Proto-industrialization? Cottage industry, social change and the Industrial Revolution', *Historical Journal*, XXVII (1984).

Howe, E. & Waite, H. E., *The London Society of Compositors* (1948).

Hudson, D., *Munby. Man of Two Worlds* (1972, 1974 edn).

Hueckel, G., 'English farming profits during the Napoleonic Wars, 1793–1815', *Explorations in Economic History*, XIII (1976).

Hufton, O., *The Poor of Eighteenth-Century France, 1750–1789* (Oxford, 1974).
'Women and the family economy in eighteenth-century France', *French Historical Studies*, IX (1975).

Humphries, J., 'Class struggle and the working-class family', *Cambridge Journal of Economics*, I (1977).

Hunt, E. H., *Regional Wage Variations in Britain, 1850–1914* (Oxford, 1973).

Hunt, H. G., 'Landownership and enclosure, 1750–1830', *Economic History Review*, XI (1958–9).
'Agricultural rent in south-east England, 1788–1825', *Agricultural History Review*, VII (1959).

Huws, U. (Equal Opportunities Commission), *New Technology and Women's Employment. Case Studies from West Yorkshire* (E.O.C., 1982).

Huzel, J. P., 'Malthus, the poor law and population in early nineteenth-century England', *Economic History Review*, XXII (1969).
'The demographic impact of the Old Poor Law: more reflexions on Malthus', *Economic History Review*, XXXIII (1980).

Hyde, W. J., 'Hardy's view of realism: a key to the rustic characters', *Victorian Studies*, II (1958).

Inglis, B., *Poverty and the Industrial Revolution* (1971, 1972 edn).

James, H., *The House of Fiction* (1957, 1962 edn).

James, M., *Social Problems and Policy during the Puritan Revolution, 1640–1660* (1930).

Jefferies, R., *The Hills and the Vale* (1909, Oxford, 1980 edn).

Jernegan, M., *Labouring and Dependent Classes in Colonial America, 1607–1783* (New York, 1931).

Johannson, S. R., 'Age-specific mortality patterns of Victorian women', in M. Vicinus (ed.), *A Widening Sphere: Women in the Victorian Age* (Bloomington, Indiana, 1977).

John, A. H., 'The course of agricultural change, 1660–1760', in L. S. Pressnell (ed.), *Studies in the Industrial Revolution* (1960).
'Aspects of English economic growth in the first half of the eighteenth century', *Economica*, XXVIII (1961).
'Agricultural productivity and economic growth in England, 1700–1760', *Journal of Economic History*, XXV (1965), also in E. L. Jones (ed.), *Agriculture and Economic Growth in England, 1650–1815* (1967).

Johnson, G. W., *The Evolution of Women from Subjection to Comradeship* (1926).

Johnson, P. E., *A Shopkeeper's Millennium: Society and Revivals in Rochester, New York* (New York, 1978).

Jones, D., 'Thomas Campbell Foster and the rural labourer: incendiarism in East Anglia in the 1840's', *Social History*, I (1976).

Jones, D. J. V., 'The poacher: a study in Victorian crime and protest', *Historical Journal*, XXII (1979).

Jones, E. L., 'The agricultural labour market in England, 1793–1872', *Economic History Review*, XVII (1964).
'Afterword', in E. L. Jones & W. N. Parker (eds.), *European Peasants and Their Markets: Essays in Agrarian Economic History* (Princeton, N.J., 1975).
'Agriculture and economic growth in England, 1660–1750; agricultural

change', *Journal of Economic History*, XXV (1965), also in his *Agriculture and Economic Growth in England, 1650–1815* (1967).

Agriculture and Economic Growth in England, 1650–1815 (1967).

The Development of English Agriculture, 1815–1873 (1968).

'Agriculture and economic growth: economic change', in his *Agriculture and the Industrial Revolution* (Oxford, 1974).

Kahl, W. F., 'Apprenticeship and the freedom of the London Livery Companies, 1690–1750', *Guildhall Miscellany*, VII (1956).

The Development of the London Livery Companies: An Historical Essay and Select Bibliography (Boston, 1960).

Kamm, J., *Rapiers and Battleaxes: The Women's Movement and its Aftermath* (1966).

Kanner, S. B., 'The women of England in a century of social change, 1815–1914: a select bibliography', in M. Vicinus (ed.), *Suffer and Be Still* (Bloomington, Indiana, 1972).

Kellett, J. R., 'The breakdown of gild and corporation control over the handicraft and retail trade in London', *Economic History Review*, X (1957–8).

Kerr, B., 'The Dorset agricultural labourer, 1750–1850', *Proceedings of the Dorset Natural History and Archaeological Society*, LXXXIV (1962).

Bound to the Soil: A Social History of Dorset, 1750–1918 (1968).

Kerridge, E., 'Agriculture, c. 1500–1793', in *Victoria County History of Wiltshire*, vol. 4 (Oxford, 1959).

The Agricultural Revolution (1967).

Kettle, A., *An Introduction to the English Novel*, 2 vols. (1951–3, 1967 edn).

Kitteringham, J., 'Country work girls in nineteenth-century England', in R. Samuel (ed.), *Village Life and Labour* (1975).

Klein, V., 'The emancipation of women: its motives and achievements', in H. Grisewood (ed.), *Ideas and Beliefs of the Victorians* (1949).

Kramer, S., *The English Craft Guilds and the Government* (New York, 1905).

Kriedte, P., Medick, H. & Schlumbohm, J., *Industrialization before Industrialization* (Cambridge, 1981).

Kussmaul, A. S., 'Servants in husbandry in early-modern England' (unpublished Ph.D. thesis, University of Toronto, 1978).

Servants in Husbandry in Early Modern England (Cambridge, 1981).

Laing, R. D. & Esterson, A., *Sanity, Madness and the Family* (1964)

Lane, J., 'Apprenticeship in Warwickshire, 1700–1834' (unpublished Ph.D. thesis, University of Birmingham, 1977).

'Apprenticeship in Warwickshire cotton mills, 1790–1830', *Textile History*, X (1979).

Laslett, P., *The World We Have Lost* (1965, 1973 edn).

'Mean household size in England since the sixteenth century', in P. Laslett & R. Wall (eds.), *Household and Family in Past Time* (Cambridge, 1972).

'Clayworth and Cogenhoe', in his *Family Life and Illicit Love in Earlier Generations* (Cambridge, 1977).

Family Life and Illicit Love in Earlier Generations (Cambridge, 1977).

'Les Rôles des femmes dans l'histoire de la famille occidentale', in E. Sullerot (ed.), *Le Fait feminin* (Paris, 1977).

Laslett, P. & Wall, R. (eds.), *Household and Family in Past Time* (Cambridge, 1972).

Lavrovsky, V. M., 'Parliamentary enclosure in the county of Suffolk, 1794–1814', *Economic History Review*, VII (1937).

Lawrence, D. H., *Phoenix: The Posthumous Papers of D. H. Lawrence* (1936, 1961 edn).

Lee, D. J., 'Craft unions and the force of tradition: the case of apprenticeship', *British Journal of Industrial Relations*, XVII (1979).

Leeson, R. A., *Travelling Brothers* (1979).

Levine, D., *Family Formation in an Age of Nascent Capitalism* (1977).

Levy, M. J., Jr, *Modernization and the Structure of Societies* (Princeton, N.J., 1966).

Liepmann, K., *Apprenticeship* (1960).

Lindert, P. H. & Williamson, J. G., 'English workers' living standards during the Industrial Revolution: a new look', *Economic History Review*, XXXVI (1983).

Little, A. J., *Deceleration in the Eighteenth-Century British Economy* (1976).

Lodey, J., Letter to *Local Population Studies*, XV (1980).

Longmate, N., *The Workhouse* (1974).

MacClaine, W., *New Views on Apprenticeship* (1948).

McCloskey, D. N., 'The enclosure of open-fields: a preface to a study of its impact on the efficiency of English agriculture in the eighteenth century', *Journal of Economic History*, XXXII (1972).

'New perspectives on the Old Poor Law', *Explorations in Economic History*, X (1972–3).

'The persistence of English common fields', in E. L. Jones & W. N. Parker (eds.), *European Peasants and Their Markets: Essays in Agrarian Economic History* (Princeton, N.J., 1975).

'The economics of enclosure: a market analysis', in E. L. Jones & W. N. Parker (eds.), *European Peasants and Their Markets: Essays in Agrarian Economic History* (Princeton, N.J., 1975).

McCrone, G., *The Economics of Subsidising Agriculture. A Study of British Policy* (1962).

MacDonagh, O. (ed.), *Emigration in the Victorian Age; Debates on the Issue from Nineteenth-Century Critical Journals* (Farnborough, 1973).

Macdonald, S., 'The progress of the early threshing machine', *Agricultural History Review*, XXIII (1975).

'Further progress with the early threshing machine: a rejoinder', *Agricultural History Review*, XXVI (1978).

McDougall, M. L., 'Working-class women during the Industrial Revolution, 1780–1914', in R. Bridenthal & C. Koonz (eds.), *Becoming Visible, Women in European History* (1977).

Macfarlane, A., *The Family Life of Ralph Josselin* (Cambridge, 1970).

The Origins of English Individualism (Oxford, 1978).

review of L. Stone, *The Family, Sex and Marriage in England, 1500–1800* (1977), in *History and Theory*, XVIII (1979).

McGregor, O. R., 'The social position of women in England, 1850–1914', *British Journal of Sociology*, VI (1955).

Divorce in England – A Centenary Study (1957).

McKendrick, N., 'Home demand and economic growth: a new view of the role of women and children in the Industrial Revolution', in his (ed.) *Historical Perspectives; Studies in English Thought and Society in Honour of J. H. Plumb* (1974).

Malcolmson, R. W., '"A set of ungovernable people": the Kingswood colliers in the eighteenth century', in J. Brewer & J. Styles (eds.), *An Ungovernable People: The English and their Law in the Seventeenth and Eighteenth Centuries* (1980).

Mantoux, P., *The Industrial Revolution in the Eighteenth Century* (1928).

Marcus, S., *The Other Victorians* (1966).

Marshall, D., *The English Poor in the Eighteenth Century* (1926).

Marshall, D. J., *The Old Poor Law, 1795–1834* (1968, 1973 edn).

Martin, E. W., *The Secret People: English Village Life after 1750* (1954).

Martin, J. M., 'Landownership and the Land Tax Returns', *Agricultural History Review*, XIV (1966).

'The parliamentary enclosure movement and rural society in Warwickshire', *Agricultural History Review*, XV (1967).

'Marriage and economic stress in the Felden of Warwickshire in the eighteenth century', *Population Studies*, XXXI (1977).

'Members of parliament and enclosure: a reconsideration', *Agricultural History Review*, XXVII (1979).

'The small landowner and parliamentary enclosure in Warwickshire', *Economic History Review*, XXXII (1979).

Medick, H., 'The proto-industrial family economy', *Social History*, I (1976).

Mendels, F., 'Industrialization and population pressure in eighteenth-century Flanders', *Journal of Economic History*, XXXI (1971).

'Proto-industrialization: the first phase of the process of industrialization', *Journal of Economic History*, XXXII (1972).

Menefee, S. P., *Wives For Sale* (Oxford, 1981).

Middleton, C., 'Sexual inequality and stratification theory', in F. Parkin (ed.), *The Social Analysis of Class Structure* (1974).

'The sexual division of labour in feudal England', *New Left Review*, CXIII–CXIV (1979).

Millett, K., *Sexual Politics* (1971).

Mills, D. R., 'The poor laws and the distribution of population, c. 1600–1860, with special reference to Lincolnshire', *Transactions of the Institute of British Geographers*, XXVI (1959).

'The quality of life in Melbourn, Cambridgeshire, in the period 1800–1850', *International Review of Social History*, XXIII (1978).

Mincer, J., 'On-the-job training: costs, returns and some implications', *Journal of Political Economy*, LXX (1962 supplement).

Minchington, W. E., 'Agriculture in Dorset during the Napoleonic Wars', *Proceedings of the Dorset Natural History and Archaeological Society*, LXXVII (1955).

Mingay, G. E., *English Landed Society in the Eighteenth Century* (1963).

'The Land Tax Assessments and the small landowner', *Economic History Review*, XVII (1964).

Enclosure and the Small Farmer in the Age of the Industrial Revolution (1968, 1976 edn).

Rural Life in Victorian England (1977, Glasgow, 1979 edn).

More, C., *Skill and the English Working Class, 1870–1914* (1980).

Morgan, E. S., *The Puritan Family* (New York, 1944, 1966 edn).

Nash, G. B., *The Urban Crucible* (Cambridge, Mass., 1979).

O'Brien, P. K., 'Agriculture and the Industrial Revolution', *Economic History Review*, XXX (1977).

Oldham, C. R., 'Oxfordshire poor law papers', *Economic History Review*, V (1934–5).

O'Malley, I. B., *Women in Subjection* (1933).

'Orme Agnus' (Higginbotham, J. C.), *Jan Oxber* (Boston, 1902).

Orwin, C. S. & Felton, B. I., 'A century of wages and earnings in agriculture', *Journal of the Royal Agricultural Society*, XCII (1931).

Orwin, C. S. & Whetham, E. H., *History of British Agriculture, 1846–1914* (1964).

Overton, M., 'Estimating crop yields from probate inventories: an example from East Anglia', *Journal of Economic History*, XXXIX (1979).

Oxley, G. W., *Poor Relief in England and Wales, 1601–1834* (Plymouth, 1974).

Page, N., *Thomas Hardy* (1977).

Parry Okeden, W. H., 'The agricultural riots in Dorset in 1830', *Proceedings of the Dorset Natural History and Archaeological Society*, LII (1930).

Parsons, T., 'The social structure of the family', in R. N. Anshen (ed.), *The Family: Its Functions and Destiny* (New York, 1959).

Peacock, A. J., *Bread or Blood; a Study of the Agrarian Riots in East Anglia in 1816* (1965).

Pearsall, R., *The Worm in the Bud: The World of Victorian Sexuality* (1969, Harmondsworth, 1972 edn).

Perry, P. J., 'Working class isolation and mobility in rural Dorset, 1837–1936', *Institute of British Geographers*, XLVI (1969).

Phelps-Brown, E. H. & Hopkins, S. V., 'Seven centuries of the prices of consumables compared with builders' wage rates', *Economica*, XXIII (1956), also in E. M. Carus-Wilson (ed.), *Essays in Economic History*, vol. 2 (1955, 1962 edn).

'Builders' wage-rates, prices and population: some further evidence', *Economica*, XXVI (1959).

A Perspective of Wages and Prices (1981).

Phillips, R., *Family Breakdown in Late Eighteenth-Century France, 1792–1803* (Oxford, 1980).

Pinchbeck, I., *Women Workers and the Industrial Revolution, 1750–1850* (1930, 1981 edn).

Plummer, A., *The London Weavers' Company, 1600–1970* (1972).

Pollard, S., 'Investment, consumption and the Industrial Revolution', *Economic History Review*, XI (1958).

Power, E., 'The English craft guilds in the Middle Ages', *History*, IV (1920).

Poynter, J. R., *Society and Pauperism: Ideas on Poor Relief, 1795–1834* (1969).

Prothero, I. T., *Artisans and Politics in Early Nineteenth-Century London* (Folkestone, 1979).

Purdum, J. J., 'Profitability and timing of parliamentary land enclosures', *Explorations in Economic History*, XV (1978).

Putnam, B. H., 'Northamptonshire wage assessments of 1560 and 1667', *Economic History Review*, I (1927).

Rada, J., *The Impact of Microelectronics* (International Labour Office, 1980).

Rainwater, L., 'Some aspects of lower-class sexual behaviour', *Journal of Social Issues*, XXII (1966).

Raj, K. N., 'Towards the eradication of poverty – an European precedent', in K. S. Krishnaswamy *et al.* (eds.), *Society and Change. Essays in Honour of S. Chaudhuri* (Oxford, 1977).

Richards, E., 'Women in the British economy since about 1700: an interpretation', *History*, LIX (1974).

Richards, P., 'The state and early industrial capitalism: the case of the handloom weavers', *Past and Present*, LXXXIII (1979).

Richardson, T. L., 'Agricultural labourers' standard of living in Kent, 1790–1840', in D. J. Oddy & D. Miller (eds.), *The Making of the British Diet* (1976).

Roberts, B. K., 'Field systems of the west Midlands', in A. R. H. Baker & R. A. Butlin (eds.), *Studies of Field Systems in the British Isles* (Cambridge, 1973).

Roberts, D., 'How cruel was the Victorian poor law?', *Historical Journal*, IV (1963).

Roberts, M., 'Sickles and scythes: women's work and men's work at harvest time', *History Workshop*, VII (1979).

Rock, H., *The Independent Mechanic, 1800–1820* (New York, 1978).

Rose, M. E., 'The allowance system under the New Poor Law', *Economic History Review*, XIX (1966).

'The anti-poor law agitation', in J. T. Ward (ed.), *Popular Movements, c. 1830–1850* (1970).

The Relief of Poverty, 1834–1914 (1972, 1974 edn).

Rosenthal, M., *British Landscape Painting* (Oxford, 1982).

Constable. The Painter and his Landscape (1983).

Rowlands, M. B., *Masters and Men in the West Midland Metalware Trades before the Industrial Revolution* (Manchester, 1975).

Rowntree, B. S., *Poverty: A Study of Town Life* (1901).

Rowntree, B. S. & Kendal, M., *How the Labourer Lives: A Study of the Rural Labour Problem* (1913).

Rudé, G., 'Wilkes and liberty, 1768–9', in his *Paris and London in the Eighteenth Century* (1974).

Rule, J., *The Experience of Labour in Eighteenth-Century Industry* (1981).

Ryan, P., 'The costs of training for a transferable skill', *British Journal of Industrial Relations*, XVIII (1980).

'Human resources, job training and industrial restructuring in O.E.C.D. countries' (circulated paper for O.E.C.D./C.E.R.I., Sept. 1981).

'Job training, employment practices, and the large enterprise: the case of costly transferrable skills', in P. Osterman (ed.), *Internal Labor Markets* (1984).

Salaman, R. N., *The History and Social Influence of the Potato* (Cambridge, 1949).

Sales, R., *English Literature in History, 1780–1830. Pastoral and Politics* (1983).

Samuel, R. (ed.), *Village Life and Labour* (1975).

Saville, J., *Rural Depopulation in England and Wales, 1851–1951* (1957).

Schofield, R. S., 'Age-specific mobility in an eighteenth-century rural English parish', *Annales de démographie historique* (1970).

'Dimensions of illiteracy, 1750–1850', *Explorations in Economic History*, X (1973).

Scott, J. W. & Tilly, L. A., 'Women's work and the family in nineteenth-century Europe', *Comparative Studies in Society and History*, XVII (1975).

Seybolt, R. F., *Apprenticeship and Apprenticeship Education in Colonial New England and New York* (New York, 1917).

Shelton, W. J., *English Hunger and Industrial Disorders* (1973).

Sherman, G. W., *The Pessimism of Thomas Hardy* (New Jersey, 1976).

Shorter, E., *The Making of the Modern Family* (1976).

Slater, G., *The English Peasantry and the Enclosure of the Common Fields* (1907).

Sleigh, J., Boatwright, B., Irwin, P. & Stanyon, R., *The Manpower Implications of Microelectronic Technology* (Department of Employment, H.M.S.O., 1979).

Smelser, N., 'The modernization of social relations', in M. Weiner (ed.), *Modernization. The Dynamics of Growth* (New York, 1966).

Smith, S. R., 'The London apprentices as seventeenth-century adolescents', *Past and Present*, LXI (1973).

Spenceley, G. F. R., 'The origins of the English pillow lace industry', *Agricultural History Review*, XXI (1973).

Springall, L. M., *Labouring Life in Norfolk Villages, 1834–1914* (1936).

Stadin, K., 'Den gomda och glomda arbetskraften. Stadskvinnor i produktionen under 1600-och 1700-talen', *Historisk tidskrift* (1980).

Steffen, C. G., 'Baltimore artisans, 1790–1820', *William and Mary Quarterly*, XXXVI (1979).

Stevenson, J., 'Food riots in England, 1792–1818', in R. Quinault & J. Stevenson (eds.), *Popular Protest and Public Order: Six Studies in British History, 1790–1920* (1974).

Stone, L., *The Family, Sex and Marriage in England, 1500–1800* (1977).

Strachey, R., *'The Cause'. A Short History of the Women's Movement in Great Britain* (1928).

Sturt, G., *Memoirs of a Surrey Labourer* (1907).

  Change in the Village (1912).

  The Journals of George Sturt, 1890–1927, 2 vols. (Cambridge, 1967).

  The Bettesworth Book (Firle, Sussex, 1978 edn).

Swales, T. H., 'Parliamentary enclosures of Lindsey', *Lincolnshire Archaeological Society Reports and Papers*, I (1936).

Szasz, T., *The Myth of Mental Illness* (1961).

  The Manufacture of Madness (1970).

Tanner, T., 'Colour and movement in *Tess of the D'Urbervilles*', *Critical Quarterly*, X (1968), reprinted in R. P. Draper (ed.), *Hardy. The Tragic Novels* (1975).

  Adultery and the Novel. Contract and Transgression (1979).

Tate, W. E., 'Opposition to parliamentary enclosure in eighteenth-century England', *Agricultural History*, XIX (1945).

  The Parish Chest (Cambridge, 1946).

  'Members of Parliament and their personal relations to enclosure, 1757–1843', *Agricultural History*, XXIII (1949).

  'Oxfordshire enclosure commissioners, 1737–1856', *Journal of Modern History*, XXIII (1951).

Taverne, L. E., 'Whither sheep? A review of the decline in sheep farming in Dorset', *Somerset and Dorset Notes and Queries*, XXVI (1953).

Tawney, R. H., 'The economics of boy labour', *Economic Journal*, XIX (1909).

Taylor, A. J. (ed.), *The Standard of Living in Britain in the Industrial Revolution* (1975).

Thirsk, J., 'Agrarian history, 1540–1950', in *Victoria County History of Leicestershire*, vol. 2 (Oxford, 1954).

  'Industries in the countryside', in F. J. Fisher (ed.), *Essays in the Economic and Social History of Tudor and Stuart England* (Cambridge, 1961).

'Seventeenth-century agriculture and social change', *Agricultural History Review*, XVIII (1970).

Thomas, K., 'The double standard', *Journal of the History of Ideas*, XX (1959).

'Work and leisure in pre-industrial society', *Past and Present*, XXIX (1964).

Thompson, E. P., *The Making of the English Working Class* (1963, Harmondsworth, 1975 edn).

'Time, work discipline and industrial capitalism', *Past and Present*, XXXVIII (1967).

'English trade unionism and other labour movements before 1790', *Bulletin of the Society for the Study of Labour History*, XVII (1968).

'The moral economy of the English crowd in the eighteenth century', *Past and Present*, L (1971).

Thompson, E. P. & Yeo, E. (eds.), *The Unknown Mayhew* (1971, Harmondsworth, 1973 edn).

Thompson, F., *Lark Rise to Candleford* (1939, Harmondsworth, 1976 edn).

Thompson, P. with Wailey, T. & Lummis, T., *Living the Fishing* (1983).

Thomson, D., 'Provision for the elderly in England, 1830–1908' (unpublished Ph.D. thesis, University of Cambridge, 1980).

Thrupp, S., *A Short History of the Worshipful Company of Bakers of London* (1933).

Tucker, G. S. L., 'The Old Poor Law revisited', *Explorations in Economic History*, XII (1975).

Tucker, R. S., 'Real wages of artisans in London, 1792–1935', *Journal of the American Statistical Association*, XXXI (1936), also in A. J. Taylor (ed.), *The Standard of Living in Britain in the Industrial Revolution* (1975).

von Tunzelmann, G. N., 'Trends in real wages, 1750–1850, revisited', *Economic History Review*, XXXII (1979).

Turner, J., *The Politics of Landscape* (Oxford, 1979).

Turner, M. E., 'The cost of parliamentary enclosure in Buckinghamshire', *Agricultural History Review*, XXI (1973).

'Parliamentary enclosure and landownership change in Buckinghamshire', *Economic History Review*, XXVII (1975).

English Parliamentary Enclosure (Folkestone, Kent, 1980).

'Cost, finance and parliamentary enclosure', *Economic History Review*, XXXIV (1981).

'Agricultural productivity in England in the eighteenth century: evidence from crop yields', *Economic History Review*, XXXV (1982).

(ed.), W. E. Tate, *A Doomsday of English Enclosure Acts and Awards* (Reading, 1978).

Unwin, G., *Industrial Organization in the Sixteenth and Seventeenth Centuries* (Oxford, 1904).

The Guilds and Companies of London (1908, 1938 edn).

Vann, R. T., 'Toward a new lifestyle: women in preindustrial capitalism', in R. Bridenthal & C. Koonz (eds.), *Becoming Visible. Women in European History* (1977).

Vincent, D., 'Love and death and the nineteenth-century working class', *Social History*, V (1980).

Walker, M. J., 'The guild control of trades in England, c. 1660–1820' (paper circulated at Economic History Conference, Loughborough, April 1981).

Walkowitz, J. R. & D. J., '"We are not beasts of the field": prostitution and the poor in Plymouth and Southampton under the Contagious Diseases

Act', in M. Hartman & L. W. Banner (eds.), *Clio's Consciousness Raised* (New York, 1974).

Wall, R., 'Mean household size in England from printed sources', in P. Laslett & R. Wall (eds.), *Household and Family in Past Time* (Cambridge, 1972).

'The age of leaving home', *Journal of Family History*, III (1978).

'Inferring differential neglect of females from mortality data', *Annales de démographie historique* (1981).

'Women alone in English society', *Annales de démographie historique* (1981).

Walter, J., 'Grain riots and popular attitudes to the law: Maldon and the crisis of 1629', in J. Brewer & J. Styles (eds.), *An Ungovernable People: The English and their Law in the Seventeenth and Eighteenth Centuries* (1980).

Webb, S. & B., *History of Trade Unionism* (1894, 1920 edn).

English Poor Law History (1929).

Weber, C. J., 'Chronology in Hardy's novels', *Publications of the Modern Languages Association*, LIII (1938).

Weinstein, F. & Platt, G. M., *The Wish to Be Free* (Berkeley, California, 1969).

Psychoanalytic Sociology (1973).

Welch, C., *History of the Pewterers' Company*, 2 vols. (1902).

Wells, R. A. E., *Dearth and Distress in Yorkshire, 1793–1802* (University of York Borthwick Papers, no. 52, 1977).

'The revolt of the south-west, 1800–1801: a study in English popular protest', *Social History*, VI (1977).

Whetham, E. H., 'Livestock prices in Britain, 1851–1893', *Agricultural History Review*, XI (1963).

Wilkes, A. R., 'Adjustments in arable farming after the Napoleonic Wars', *Agricultural History Review*, XXVIII (1980).

Williams, G., *Apprenticeship in Europe* (1963).

Williams, M., *Thomas Hardy and Rural England* (1972).

A Preface to Hardy (1976).

Williams, R., *The Country and the City* (St Albans, 1973).

The English Novel. From Dickens to Lawrence (St Albans, 1974).

Wilson, G. J., 'The land tax and West Derby Hundred, 1780–1831', *Transactions of the Historical Society of Lancashire and Cheshire*, CXXIX (1980).

'The land tax problem', *Economic History Review*, XXXV (1982).

Winchester, B., 'The New Woman', *Arena* (1902).

Woodward, D., 'Wage rates and living standards in pre-industrial England', *Past and Present*, XCI (1981).

Wright, T., *The Romance of the Shoe: Being the History of Shoemaking* (1922).

Wrigley, E. A., 'Reflections on the history of the family', *Daedalus*, CVI (1977).

Wrigley, E. A. & Schofield, R. S., *The Population History of England, 1541–1871* (1981).

Yarbrough, A., 'Apprentices as adolescents in sixteenth-century Bristol', *Journal of Social History*, XIII (1979).

Yelling, J. A., *Common Field and Enclosure in England, 1450–1850* (1977).

Young, G. M., *Victorian England. Portrait of an Age* (1936, 1960 edn).

Young, M. & Wilmot, P., *The Symmetrical Family: A Study of Work and Leisure in the London Region* (1973, Harmondsworth, 1980 edn).

Zeitlin, J., 'Craft regulation and the division of labour: engineers and compositors in Britain, 1890–1914' (unpublished Ph.D. thesis, University of Warwick, 1981).

Index